*The Cassell
Book of
English Poetry*

The Cassell
Book of
English Poetry

SELECTED AND INTRODUCED BY JAMES REEVES

HARPER & ROW, PUBLISHERS, NEW YORK

ACKNOWLEDGEMENTS *

ateful thanks are due to the following for permission to reproduce copyright
ems in this anthology:

orge Allen & Unwin Ltd., for 'Jason and Medea' by Alun Lewis.
aatto & Windus Ltd., for 'Hospital barge at Cérisy', 'Futility' and 'Dulce et decorum
est' by Wilfred Owen.
nstable & Co. Ltd., for 'Madly singing in the mountains' by Arthur Waley.
rs. H. M. Davies, for 'The hospital waiting-room', 'I am the poet Davies, William'
and 'The inquest' by W. H. Davies.
ber & Faber Ltd., for 'The love song of J. Alfred Prufrock' by T S. Eliot; 'Tea at
the Palaz of Hoon' by Wallace Stevens; 'Merlin' by Edwin Muir; and 'Tears' and
'Tall nettles' by Edward Thomas.
rcourt, Brace & World Inc., for 'The Cambridge ladies' by E. E. Cummings.
pert Hart-Davis Ltd., for 'Field-glasses' and 'A prehistoric camp' by Andrew Young.
an Hodge, for 'The winter house' and 'The compassionate fool' by Norman
Cameron.
ternational Authors N.Y., for 'Despite and still', 'The Devil's advice to story-tellers'
and 'On dwelling' by Robert Graves.
e Literary Trustees of Walter de la Mare and the Society of Authors, for 'The
railway junction', 'The quartette' and 'The bead mat' by Walter de la Mare.
e Liveright Publishing Corporation, New York, for 'Black tambourine' by Hart
Crane.
e Macmillan Co., New York, for 'The Daniel jazz' by Vachel Lindsay.
thur V. Moore, for 'A pact' by Ezra Pound.
D. Peters, for 'The recovery', 'Report on experience' and 'The sunlit vale' by
Edmund Blunden.
urence Pollinger Ltd., for 'Piazza piece' and 'Winter remembered' by John Crowe
Ransom.
urence Pollinger Ltd. and Holt, Rinehart & Winston, Inc., for 'The tuft of flowers,'
'Too anxious for rivers' and 'The bearer of evil tidings' by Robert Frost.
urence Pollinger Ltd. and the Estate of the late Mrs. Frieda Lawrence for 'Piano'
and 'Discord in childhood' by D. H. Lawrence.
egfried Sassoon, C.B.E., for his 'Concert interpretation'.
narles Scribner's Sons, for 'Miniver Cheevy' by E. A. Robinson.
e Society of Authors as literary representative of the Estate of the late A. E.
Housman, for 'Oh who is that young sinner?', 'Tell me not here, it needs not saying'
and 'Her strong enchantments failing' from A. E. Housman's Collected Poems.
e Trustees of the Dylan Thomas Estate and J. M. Dent and Sons Ltd., for 'The
force that through the green fuse drives the flower' by Dylan Thomas.
e Trustees of the Hardy Estate and Macmillan & Co. Ltd., for 'Heredity', 'I look
into my glass', 'A broken appointment' and 'Afterwards' from Thomas Hardy's
Collected Poems.
rs. Iris Wise and Macmillan & Co. Ltd., for 'A glass of beer' and 'Egan O Rahilly'
from James Stephen's Collected Poems.
rs. Yeats and Macmillan & Co. Ltd., for 'Sailing to Byzantium' by W. B. Yeats.

Permissions from American publishers will be found on next page.

AMERICAN PERMISSIONS

CONTENTS

CONTENTS

FOREWORD

In this book you will find a thousand of the best short poems in English. In my choice I have had to draw some arbitrary lines, or the book would have been too big to be manageable. No poet has been included unless he was born not later than 1900 or, if born in the present century, has already died. Some of the best living poets, therefore, are not included; nor are any young poets. Taste and fashion change, especially in contemporary literature, and it is not easy to be certain of choosing the most significant in the poetry of our own day.

This book is confined, for obvious reasons, to comparatively short poems. Most of them are what are called lyrics, apart from certain narrative poems, especially ballads. Thus, much important poetry is left out: epic, dramatic, and longer narrative verse. Each of these poems is complete in itself; there are no extracts from longer works. Even with these limitations, it may be claimed that this book gives a liberal representation of the wealth and variety of English poetry during the past six centuries.

A chronological arrangement has been adopted as being, on balance, the best. This does not mean that there is any special virtue in a historical approach, nor is such an approach imposed. Few people read an anthology straight through, yet most readers have a historical sense strong enough to be helped by this arrangement to find most easily a poem or poet they are looking for. Nor is this introduction the place for historical considerations. Instead, I prefer to suggest some ideas as to the nature, quality and value of poetry.

Many have tried to define poetry, but no one has yet succeeded in evolving a definition which has proved widely acceptable or even useful. One reason for this is that, by its nature, poetry seeks to evade definition. A poem is a living thing: to define it precisely and fully would kill it. We can agree that a poem is some sort of utterance in words: even when it is written down, it has the quality of living speech. We can agree that it is an utterance of some significance or importance. A good poem conveys a feeling of inner compulsion: it is not only something the poet wanted to say, it is something he had to say: something he had to get off his chest, in the familiar phrase. Here we meet the first of the many paradoxes by which alone we can understand the nature of poetry in all its wealth and variety. A poet is, in Wordsworth's phrase, 'a man speaking to men'. He wants to tell them something; he wants to give pleasure, to enlarge the experience of others, he wants to earn applause or gratitude for having said something memorable. But this is not enough: not all the desire in the world to please others can make a poet. A poet must also feel an inner compulsion to say something unique and new: a true poet will do this even if there is no one to read his poems. This double need—to express and to communicate—makes poetry akin to one of the most basic of human activities. An infant will express pleasure or pain, alarm or surprise, whether there is anyone listening or not. As soon as he realizes that others are interested in what he expresses, he will wish to gain their attention by further communication. A poem is an advanced form of expression and communication; it develops and refines a basic human urge.

Another paradox of the human situation is that each of us is alone, yet, in Donne's phrase, 'no man is an island'. Each is unique, separate, and alone. Yet each is the centre of a series of concentric circles—family, neighbourhood, profession, religion, nation, species. We cannot escape from this twofold relation. We are divided from our kind both in space and in time: an Englishman may feel a kinship with Americans he has never seen, or with Englishmen who have been dead for centuries. It is one of the functions of poetry, as significant utterance, to help bridge the spaces between man and man. Through reading Chaucer we can feel our kinship with our fourteenth-century ancestors; through reading Emily Dickinson or Robert Frost, an Englishman can feel his kinship with unseen cousins in America.

There is thus about every good poem something universal, something which makes it available to anyone else who speaks or understands the language in which it is written. A man 'surprised by joy' at the coming of Spring feels kinship with the Elizabethan who wrote, 'Spring, the sweet Spring, is the year's pleasant king'; the man who is saddened by the coming of winter, or stricken with grief at the death of a friend, or overcome with anxiety at the behaviour of a woman he loves, will feel less isolated in his emotion if he knows that these things have been experienced and communicated by poets in other places and at other times.

Its universality, then, is one side of the coin: the other side, without which it is not current, is its particularity. This paradox, again, is easier to enunciate than to comprehend. A good poem is an expression of something you have felt: it is at the same time quite new, the expression of something you never precisely felt—or did not feel until you read the poem. Every good poem has a life of its own, yet partakes of the life of all men. It is unique, as every human being is unique, yet it has significance by virtue of its availability, through our common language, to every reader who cares to understand it. If it were not unique, we should not value it; but if it were not at the same time of wide appeal, how should we recognize it as true? We know that Shakespeare in love was a solitary and unique individual. Yet anyone who has been in love can at once apprehend something of the feeling in his sonnet, 'Shall I compare thee to a summer's day?' The sonnet derives its particularity from having been inspired by Shakespeare's unique and personal emotion: it derives its universality from its capacity to awaken a response in the mind of any reader who, in his own unique way, has experienced a feeling akin to Shakespeare's. What a love poem does for the reader is to particularize the emotions which he has felt in a more general and more inarticulate way. We do not derive our emotions from poetry, but we are helped to discover their wealth, their depth and their variety.

Of course we could live without poetry, as presumably we could live without speech. But life would be immeasurably the poorer and the more limited, narrow and dull. Poetry is simply significant speech —speech of wider and more permanent application than the casual utterances of everyday communication, speech which can give pleasure as well as relief from the isolation of the human condition. Where does its significance lie? Where does its power to delight come from? Some would say that the unique quality of poetry derives from the skill of the poet in choosing and arranging words. A poet, they affirm, is an artist in words, as a painter is an artist in shapes, lines and colours, or a composer in musical sounds. But this account does not explain why some skilfully constructed verse fails to come alive, why many poems apparently composed with the utmost artistry fail to move us. Indeed, it really explains nothing at all. It does not explain why some lines of poetry, apparently written casually and without effort, can move more people and move them more deeply, than the most carefully and skilfully contrived verse ever written. In the one case, you must admit, the poet was 'inspired', in the other he was not. Now the idea of inspiration is not at present thought very creditable. We live in a scientific and sceptical age, and anything as difficult to measure and define as 'inspiration' is frowned on. Yet I believe that we have to accept some such idea if we want to account for the existence of true poetry. I believe that, however hard a poet tries, the poetry is what comes when he is not, for the moment, trying. You may say, if you wish to sound more scientific, that 'inspiration' is the action of the poet's subconscious at work, without his volition, on material stored in his memory, beneath the surface of his conscious thought. Nobody knows how this works, and until we do, we might as well call it inspiration. Many pages have been written enumerating the hundreds of details that became transferred, when Coleridge wrote his Ancient Mariner, from books he had read to the poem he wrote. But of the process by which this transference took place, with all the complicated procedure of its selection and arrangement until it resulted in the poem, nothing at all is known. Now a process by which, through some unexplained force, a significant event takes place (such as the creation of a poem) may truly be called 'magical'. This, again, is not an acceptable notion in a scientific and sceptical age; but I see no cause why we should shudder at the word 'magic'. A poem is felt to be true and significant by virtue of its magic. In the best of Shakespeare's sonnets, the best of the traditional ballads, the best lyrics of Emily Dickinson or Thomas Hardy, we are aware of an abundance of magical energy; we feel that its magic is transferred to us directly and powerfully from whatever source, internal or external, the poet drew on. With other poems we feel less aware of magic: it is feebler, more diluted with non-significant material. Yet any poem which can give lasting pleasure has, if only in a very few of its lines, some trace of that unexplainable power we call magic.

One of the sources on which a poet draws—and perhaps the most important—is the strength of the emotion behind his experience. I do not believe, though some would maintain it, that it is possible to write a good poem without being deeply moved, either before or during composition. There must at least be some deeply felt mental disturbance. In the case of Emily Dickinson it was often fear, caused by a profound sense of insecurity. With Hardy the emotion is often nostalgia for the past, or a sense of the tragic discrepancy between the actual and the ideal. With Hopkins the emotion is often a conviction of the terrible demands of his religious vocation. With all of these, as with all true poets, the emotion is mixed with a sense of the need or desire to communicate the mental excitement, perhaps also to understand and alleviate, through communication, the distress or disturbance occasioned by the emotional experience.

We can go no further in exploring the nature of poetry without considering its language. For however strong a poet's emotion, however profound his mental disturbance, however overpowering the excitement, however compelling the need to communicate, without a command of language he will achieve nothing. But even as I use the word 'command', I realize its inadequacy—indeed, its fundamental untruth. For in a sense a poet is not so much one with a command over language as one under the power of language. Words command the poet, not the other way round. If we fail to find in such a marvellously accomplished technician in words as Tennyson the power, the magic, the spontaneous felicity we find in the greatest poetry, it is just because he is too much in control. His poems rarely, if ever, take hold of him and, as we might say, 'write themselves'. Yet without skill in the use of language a poet may achieve much less than he otherwise would. Most good poets, perhaps, are ceaselessly learning their trade, pondering and comparing words, experimenting with rhymes and rhythms; then in the act of composition they forget all they have taught themselves—or, if you like, relegate it to the subconscious. As a matter of fact, the best poets have rarely, if ever, been the best technicians, if we think of technique as the conscious manipulation of language to get the effects they aim at. Good verse, in a sense, is the enemy of true poetry. However, we cannot ignore a poet's technique—if by that we mean, more or less, his effectiveness in handling words, in achieving the appearance of spontaneity and naturalness, in securing interest through rhythmic and other means. Nowhere is a poet's 'technical' skill more evident than in his achievement of vitality in rhythm. The rhythmic quality of poetry is one of the most striking evidences of poetic magic. Once a poet's inspiration fails, his rhythm goes dead and mechanical. You will find in this book infinite variety of rhythm, often with very slight differences. The best poems are differentiated from one another by their extremely personal rhythms, each variety seeming to correspond to a tone of voice, a quality of speech and accent. You could not read many lines of Donne without recognizing his extremely personal and vigorous rhythm. A poet's distinctive rhythm is, in essence, the expression of his particular relation to the speech of his day—the ordinary everyday speech of the man in the street. We have here yet another paradox: for the rhythm of poetry, like its vocabulary, is the rhythm of common speech heightened or modified according to the temperament of the poet. Donne sounds like a man having an impassioned argument with intelligent and sophisticated friends; the rhythm of Hardy is that of a man brooding on human fate and ruminating half-aloud; the rhythm of Byron is that of a man making an impressive formal oration: there is always an element of the theatrical. The rhythm of Clare is the very opposite: he is never declamatory, but always recollecting the rhythm and language of the traditional songs he had heard as a child brought up in the country.

I have come back almost to the point at which I started. I began by writing of the variety and wealth of poetry, of the uniqueness and universality of all true poems. Every poem has its peculiar life and character; this is because it is an expression of the life and character of a man or woman. The life of poetry is its difference, its uniqueness. Of the members of any profession, if poetry can be called a profession, poets are perhaps the hardest to recognize and define. This is because in poets human differences are most strongly marked and most obstinately preserved. One of the elements in poetry which gives most pleasure is the element of surprise. Men who are inwardly the same as everyone else are not likely to achieve surprise in what they create. It is sometimes said that poets are different from other men: it would be truer to say they are the same only more so. They share the same passions and appetites, but they are aware of these, inwardly, with greater self-consciousness and a more articulate understanding of what is going on. Every human being is articulate: speech is, essentially, the distinguishing mark of the human kind. I do not mean that animals cannot communicate through sound. But the faculty of speech, and especially the communication of ideas, whether through concrete or abstract language, is the mark of a man. Poets are the same as other men—and most, I believe, passionately resent being regarded as a race apart—but they are, as it were, over-developed in one direction: the faculty of speech. They are more continuously aware of words than non-poets; they undertake continual self-training in the use of words; they have an instinct for the effectiveness of words as the agents of magical power; so strongly developed is their power of speech that they can tell others what they are thinking and feeling more clearly than others can tell themselves. A poet transmutes his most significant experience into permanent form: in doing so, he makes it comprehensible and tolerable for himself. In doing this for himself, he does it also for others, if they care to read his poems.

Lewes   J. R.
1964

BOOK ONE

Chaucer to the Early Tudors

INTRODUCTION

The poems in this first part were written or composed during
the two centuries which followed the birth of Chaucer in
1340. The expression 'written or composed' is used deliber-
ately; for while all the poems by Chaucer and other named
poets were undoubtedly *written* in the usual sense of the word,
many of the anonymous poems were probably *composed*, or
made up, for oral communication long before they were
written down.

The anonymous lyrics of the Middle Ages are among the
most beautiful in our literature. It is tantalizing that we know
so little of them. The ballads just referred to, such as *Clerk
Saunders* and *The Dæmon Lover*, must have been composed by
singing men or minstrels, probably in the households of rich
lords. It was the invention of printing in the late fifteenth
century which put an end to the employment of minstrels in
great houses. But they left us a legacy of fine, vigorous,
narrative poems, profoundly moving and dramatic even
without the melodies to which they were originally sung.

Another class of lyric was the religious song, such as the
beautiful *I Sing of a Maiden* and *Suddenly Afraid*. We may
surmise that the authors of these were pious men, 'clerks' as
they were called, humble priests or scholars in monasteries
and other places of learning. What strikes us about many of
these short, simple poems is their everlasting freshness, their
wit and clarity, and above all their sincere feeling, unsophis-
ticated but by no means crude or clumsy.

It should never be forgotten that much of the best of
English poetry, especially the poetry of songs, is the work of
forgotten men and women. But of course the poets we most

value and esteem are those who had this anonymous work behind them, but who rose out of the general run of humble and nameless singing men, monks or minstrels. Of these the first was Chaucer, whose greatness it is difficult to measure. He is not the first English poet, but he remains one of the greatest, creating almost alone a body of national poetry in the last years of the fourteenth century which has even now scarcely been equalled by a single poet. Most of Chaucer's poems are long, and so cannot be included here. Indeed, the half dozen short lyrics by which he is represented are quite insufficient to give more than an inkling of his large and universal genius. To savour that fully, you must go to his great collection of *Canterbury Tales*.

For the next name in this book we have to wait for more than a century, for after Chaucer's death the decline in lyric poetry was almost complete. John Skelton, the Norfolk priest, was one of the most original poets in our language and the first of the early Tudors. His Scottish contemporary, William Dunbar, is not easy to read, on account of the medieval Scots in which his poems were written. But they are worth the effort, on account of their vigour, their irony, and their sombre and powerful feeling.

Of the remaining poets in these pages, the most important are Henry VIII's two courtiers, Sir Thomas Wyatt and Henry Howard, Earl of Surrey. Surrey is credited with the invention of blank verse, a form which played an ever-increasing part in English poetry from the time of Shakespeare till well on in the nineteenth century. Wyatt introduced the Italian sonnet form into English; but, far more important than this, he was the first great lyricist of personal love. Once you have mastered Wyatt's occasionally awkward rhythm and peculiar turn of phrase, you will realize how modern—that is, how universal—is his expression of the emotions of a man in love.

It is this 'modernity' to be found in medieval and early Tudor poetry which gives it its appeal to the contemporary reader; once the reader has familiarized himself with the language of this poetry, he will understand how it can help the modern mind, more perhaps than any other work of man, to traverse the centuries between us and the people who lived when England was emerging as a distinct and unique nation.

CONTENTS

ANONYMOUS

GEOFFREY CHAUCER 1340–1400

1 *Summer is icumen in*

Summer is icumen in,
   Loudë sing cuckoo!
Groweth seed, and bloweth mead,
   And springs the woodë new—
                Sing cuckoo!

Ewë bleateth after lamb,
   Loweth after calvë cow;
Bullock starteth, buckë farteth,
   Merry sing cuckoo!

Cuckoo, cuckoo, well singës thou, cuckoo:
   Nay swikë[1] thou never now;
Sing cuckoo, now, sing cuckoo,
   Sing cuckoo, sing cuckoo now!

Anonymous

1 cease

2 *Alone walking*

Alone walking,
In thought plaining,
And sore sighing,
   All desolate,
Me remembring
Of my living,
My death wishing,
   Both early and late,

Unfortunate
Is so my fate,
That—wot ye what?—

Out of measure
My life I hate.
Thus desperate
In poor estate
    Do endure.

Of other cure
Am I not sure;
Thus to endure
    Is hard, certain.
Such is my ure,[1]
I you ensure.
What creature
    May have more pain?

My troth so plain
Is take in vain,
And great disdain
    In remembrance;
Yet I full fain
Would me complain,
Me to abstain
    From this penance.

But in substance
No allegiance[2]
Of my grievance
    Can I not find.
Right so my chance
With displeasance
Doth me advance.
    And thus an end.

Anonymous

1 fate   2 alleviation

3   *My ghostly father*

My ghostly father, I me confess
First to God and then to you

That at a window—wot ye how?—
I stole a kiss of great sweetness,
Which done was out advisedness;[1]
But it is done, not undone now.
My ghostly father, I me confess
First to God and then to you.

But I restore it shall doubtless
Again, if so be that I mo;
And that to God I make a vow
And else I ask for forgiveness.
My ghostly father, I me confess
First to God and then to you.

                                        Anonymous

1 on an impulse

4   *Let not us*

Let not us that young men be
From Venus' ways banished be.
Though that age with great disdain
Would have youth from love refrain,
In their minds consider you must
How they did in their most lust.

For if they were in like case,
And would then have gotten grace,
They may not now then gainsay
That which then was most their joy.
Wherefore indeed the truth to say,
It is for youth the meetest play.

                                        Anonymous

5   *Western wind*

Western wind, when will thou blow,
    The small rain down can rain?
Christ, if my love were in my arms
    And I in my bed again!

                                        Anonymous

6 Who shall have my fair lady?

Who shall have my fair lady?
  Who shall have my fair lady?
Who but I, who but I, who but I?
  Under the leavès green!

The fairest man
That best love can,
Dandirly, dandirly, dandirly dan,
  Under the leavès green!

Anonymous

7 That ever I saw

She is gentle and also wise;
Of all other she beareth the prize,
    That ever I saw.

To hear her sing, to see her dance!
She will the best herself advance,
    That ever I saw.

To see her fingers that be so small!
In my conceit she passeth all
    That ever I saw.

Nature in her hath wonderly wrought.
Christ, never such another bought
    That ever I saw.

I have seen many that have beauty
Yet is there none like to my lady
    That ever I saw.

Therefore I dare this boldly say,
I shall have the best and fairest may
    That ever I saw.

Anonymous

8   Is it not sure?

Is it not sure a deadly pain,
To you I say that lovers be,
When faithful hearts must need refrain
The one the other for to see?
I you assure, ye may trust me,
Of all the pains that ever I knew
It is a pain that most I rue.

Anonymous

9   Adam lay ibounden

Adam lay ibounden,
  Bounden in a bond;
Four thousand winter
  Thought he not too long;
And all was for an apple,
  An apple that he took,
As clerkës finden
  Written in their book.
Ne had the apple taken been,
  The apple taken been,
Ne had never our lady
  A-been Heavenë queen.
Blessed be the time
  That apple taken was.
Therefore we mun singen
  Deo gracias.

Anonymous

10   I sing of a maiden

I sing of a maiden that is makeless;[1]
King of all kingës to her son she ches.[2]
He came all so still there his mother was,

As dew in April that falleth on the grass.
He came all so still to his mother's bower
As dew in April that falleth on the flower.
He came all so still there his mother lay
As dew in April that falleth on the spray.
Mother and maiden was never none but she;
Well may such a lady Goddës mother be.

Anonymous

1 without a mate   2 chose

11   *The shepherd upon a hill*

The shepherd upon a hill he sat;
He had on him his tabard and his hat,
His tarbox, his pipe and his flagat;[1]
His name was called Jolly, Jolly Wat,
   For he was a good herdës boy.
      Ut hoy!
   For in his pipe he made so much joy.

The shepherd upon a hill was laid;
His dog to his girdle was tied;
He had not slept but a little braid,[2]
But *Gloria in excelsis* was to him said.
      Ut hoy!
   For in his pipe he made so much joy.

The shepherd on a hill he strode;
Round about him his sheep they yode;[3]
He put his hand under his hood,
He saw a star as red as blood.
      Ut hoy!
   For in his pipe he made so much joy.

The shepherd said anon right,
'I will go see yon farly[4] sight,
Where as the angel singeth on height,
And the star that shineth so bright.'
      Ut hoy!
   For in his pipe he made so much joy.

'Now farewell, Mall and also Will!
For my love go ye all still
Until I come again you till,
And ever more, Will, ring well thy bell.'
          Ut hoy!
   For in his pipe he made so much joy.

'Now must I go there Christ was born;
Farewell! I come again to-morn.[5]
Dog, keep well my sheep from the corn,
And warn well "Warrock" when I blow my horn!'
          Ut hoy!
   For in his pipe he made so much joy.

When Wat to Bedlem come was,
He sweat, he had gone faster than a pace;
He found Jesu in a simple place,
Between an ox and an ass.
          Ut hoy!
   For in his pipe he made so much joy.

'Jesu, I offer to thee here my pipe,
My skirt, my tarbox and my scrip;
Home to my fellows now will I skip,
And also look unto my sheep.'
          Ut hoy!
   For in his pipe he made so much joy.

'Now farewell, mine own herdës man Wat!'
'Yea, for God, lady, even so I hat;[6]
Lull well Jesu in thy lap,
And farewell Joseph with thy round cape!'
          Ut hoy!
   For in his pipe he made so much joy.

'Now may I well both hope and sing,
For I have been at Christës bearing;
Home to my fellows now will I fling.

Christ of Heaven to his bliss us bring!'
Ut hoy!
For in his pipe he made so much joy.

Anonymous

1 flagon   2 time   3 roamed   4 marvellous
5 to-morrow   6 am called

12   *Suddenly afraid*

Suddenly afraid,
Half waking, half sleeping,
And greatly dismayed,
A woman sat weeping,
With favour in her face far passing my reason
And of her sore weeping this was the encheson.[1]
Her son in her lap laid, she said, slain by treason,
If weeping might ripe be, it seemed then in season.
Jesus, so she sobbed,
So her son was bobbed[2]
And of his life robbed;
Seeing these words I say thee,
'Who can not weep, come learn of me.'

I said I could not weep, I was so hard-hearted.
She answered me shortly with words that smarted,
'Lo, nature shall move thee, thou must be converted,
Thine own father this night is dead.'
This she thwarted.[3]
'Jesus, so my son is bobbed,
And of his life robbed,'
For sooth then I sobbed
Verifying these words, saying to thee,
'Who can not weep come learn of me.'

'Now break heart, I thee pray! This corpse lieth so
   rewly,[4]
So beaten, so wounded, entreated so foully.

What wight may behold, and weep not? None truly,
To see my dead dear son bleeding, lo, thus newly.'
Ever still she sobbed,
So her son was bobbed
And of his life robbed.
Newing⁵ these words, as I say thee,
'Who can not weep, come learn of me.'

On me she cast her eye, and said 'See, man, thy
　　brother!'
She kissed him and said 'Sweet, am I not thy mother?'
And swooning she fell; there it would be no other.
I know not which is more deadly, the one or the
　　other.
Yet she revived and sobbed
How her son was bobbed
And of his life robbed.
'Who can not weep,' this is the lay,
And with that word she vanished away.

Anonymous

1 cause　2 mocked　3 retorted　4 pitifully　5 renewing

13　Lully lullay

Lully lullay, lully lullay,
The falcon hath borne my make¹ away.

He bare him up, he bare him down,
He bare him into an orchard brown.

In that orchard there was an hall,
That was hangèd with purple and pall.

And in that hall there was a bed,
It was hangèd with gold so red.

And in that bed there lieth a knight,
His woundès bleeding day and night.

By that bed side kneeleth a may,[2]
And she weepeth both night and day.

And by that bed side there standeth a stone,
Corpus Christi written there on.

Anonymous

1 sweetheart   2 maid

14   *Quia amore langueo*

In a valley of this restless mind
I sought in mountain and in mead,
Trusting a true love for to find.
Upon an hill then took I heed;
A voice I heard, and near I yede,[1]
In huge dolour complaining tho,
'See, dear soul, how my sides bleed,
     Quia amore langueo.'

Upon this hill I found a tree,
Under the tree a man sitting;
From head to foot wounded was he;
His heartë blood I saw bleeding;
A seemly man to be a king,
A gracious face to look unto.
I askèd why he had paining;
     '*Quia amore langueo.*'

'I am true love that false was never;
My sister, man's soul, I loved her thus;
Because we would in no wise dissever
I left my kingdom glorious.
I purveyed her a palace full precious;
She fled, I followed, I loved her so
That I suffered this pain piteous,
     Quia amore langueo.

'My fair love and my spousë bright,
I saved her from beating and she hath me beat;
I clothed her in grace and heavenly light;
This bloody shirt she hath on me set;
For longing of love yet would I not let;
Sweet strokes are these: lo!
I have loved her ever as I her het[2]
    Quia amore langueo.

'I crowned her with bliss and she me with thorn;
I led her to chamber and she me to die;
I brought her to worship and she me to scorn;
I did her reverence and she me villainy.
To love that loveth is no mastery;
Her hate made never my love her foe:
Ask me then no question why—
    Quia amore langueo.

'Look unto mine handës, man!
These gloves were given me when I her sought;
They be not white, but red and wan;
Embroidered with blood my spouse them brought.
They will not off; I loose them not;
I woo her with them wherever she go.
These hands for her so friendly fought
    Quia amore langueo.

'Marvel not, man, though I sit still.
See, love hath shod me wonder strait:
Buckled my feet, as was her will,
With sharp nails (well thou mayest wait!)
In my love was never deceit;
All my members I have opened her to;
My body I made her heartës bait[3]
    Quia amore langueo.

'In my side I have made her nest;
Look in, how wide a wound is here!
This is her chamber, here shall she rest,
That she and I may sleep in fere.[4]

Here may she wash, if any filth were;
Here is seat for all her woe;
Come when she will, she shall have cheer
    Quia amore langueo.

'I will abide till she be ready,
I will her sue if she say nay;
If she be reckless I will be greedy,
If she be dangerous⁵ I will her pray;
If she weep, then bide I ne may:
Mine arms be spread to slip her me to.
Cry once, I come: now, soul, assay
    Quia amore langueo.

'I sit on this hill for to see far;
I look into the valley my spouse to see;
Now runneth she awayward, yet comes she me near,
For out of my sight may she not flee.
Some wait her pray to make her to flee;
I run before, and fleme⁶ her foe.
Return, my spouse, again to me,
    Quia amore langueo.

'Fair love, let us go play!
Apples are ripe in my garden.
I shall thee clothe in a new array;
Thy meat shall be milk, honey and wine.
Fair love, let us go dine!
Thy sustenance is in my crippë,⁷ lo!
Tarry thou not, my fair spouse mine,
    Quia amore langueo.'

Anonymous

1 went   2 promised   3 resting place   4 together
5 haughty   6 put to flight   7 scrip, wallet

15   *Earth out of earth*

Earth out of earth is wonderly wrought,
Earth has gotten on earth a dignity of nought,

Earth upon earth has set all his thought,
How that earth upon earth may be higher brought.

Earth upon earth would be a king;
But how earth to earth shall, thinks he no thing.
When earth breeds earth, and his rents home bring,
Then shall earth of earth have full hard parting.

Now why that earth loves earth, wonder me think,
Or why that earth for earth should either sweat or
    swink;[1]
For when that earth upon earth is brought within brink,
Then shall earth of earth have a foul stink.

Anonymous

1 toil

16   *Pride is out*

Man be ware ere thou be woe;
Think on pride, and let him go.

Pride is out and pride is in,
And pride is root of every sin,
And pride will never blin[1]
Till he hath brought a man in woe.

Lucifer was angel bright
And conqueror of much might;
Through his pride he lost his light
And fell down to endless woe.

Weenest thou for thy gay clothing,
And for thy great oaths swearing,
To be a lord or a king;
Little it shall avail thee to.

When thou shalt to churchë glide,
Worms shall eat through thy side,
And little shall avail thy pride,
Or any sins that thou hast do.

Pray to Christ with bloody side,
And other woundës grile² and wide,
That he forgive thee thy pride
And thy sins that thou hast do.

Anonymous

1 cease   2 painful

17   *Service is no heritage*

Be ware, squire, yeoman and page,
For service is no heritage.

If thou serve a lord of prize,
Be not too boistous in thy service,
Damn not thy soul in no wise,
For service is no heritage.

Winter's weather and woman's thought
And lord's love changeth oft.
This is the sooth, if it be sought,
For service is no heritage.

Now thou art great, to-morrow shall I
As lordës changen here bailey;
In thy wealth work sikerly,¹
For service is no heritage.

Then serve we God in allë wise;
He shall us quiten our service
And give us giftës most of prize,
Heaven to be our heritage.

Anonymous

1 securely

18   *Discretion*

I hold him wise and well y-taught,
Can bear a horn and blow it not.

Blowing was made for greater game;
Of thy blowing comes mickle grame;[1]
Therefore I hold it for no shame
To bear a horn and blow it not.

Horns are made both loud and shrill;
When time is, blow thou thy fill,
And when need is, hold thee still,
And bear a horn and blow it not.

Whatsoever be in thy thought,
Hear and see and say right nought;
Then shall men say thou art well taught
To bear a horn and blow it not.

Whatsoever be in thy breast,
Stop thy mouth with thy fist,
And look thou think well of had-I-wist,
And bear a horn and blow it not.

And when thou sittest at the ale,
And criest like a nightingale,
Beware to whom thou tellest thy tale,
But bear a horn and blow it not.

Anonymous

1 much evil

19 *Lord, how shall I me complain*

Lord, how shall I me complain
    Unto my own lady dear,
For to tell her of my pain
    That I feel this time of year?
    My love, if that ye will hear,
Though I can no songës make,
    So your love changeth my cheer
That when I sleep I may not wake.

Though love do me so mickle woe,
  I love you best, I make a vow,
That my shoe bindeth my little toe
  And all my smart it is for you.
    Forsooth, methinketh it will me slay,
  But ye somewhat my sorrow slake,
    That barefoot to my bed I go
And when I sleep I may not wake.

Whoever wist what life I lead,
  In mine observance in divers wise;
From time that I go to my bed
  I eat no meat till that I rise.
    Ye might tell it for a great emprise
  That men thus mourneth for your sake;
    So mickle I think on your service
That when I sleep I may not wake.

I may scarce button up my sleeves
  So mine armës waxen more;
Under my heel is that me grieves
  For at my heart I feel no sore;
    Every day my girdle goeth out a bore;[1]
  I cling[2] as doth a wheaten cake;
    And for your life I sigh so sore
That when I sleep I may not wake.

Therefore, but you quit me my hire,
  Forsooth I know not what to do,
And for your love, lady, by this fire,
  Old glovës will I wearë none.
    I laugh and sing and make no moan,
  I wax not lean as any rake,
    Thus in languor I live alone,
And when I sleep I may not wake.

Thus in languor I am lent.[3]
  Long ere you do so for me
Take good heed to mine intent,
  For this shall my conclusion be.

Methinketh I love as well as ye,
Never so coy though ye it make;
  By this example you may see
That when I sleep I may not wake.

1 hole   2 shrink   3 become lean

20   *As I went out on Christmas Day*

As I went out on Christmas Day
In our procession
Knew I jolly Jenkin
By his merry tone.
Jenkin began the office
Upon Christmas Day;
And yet methinketh it does me good
So merry gan he say
    Kyrie eleison.

Jenkin read the epistle
Full fair and full well
And yet methinketh it does me good
As ever have I sel.[1]
Jenkin at the *sanctus*
Cracketh a merry note
And yet methinketh it does me good,
I payëd for his cote.
Jenkin cracketh notës
An hundred to a note,
And yet he hacketh them smaller
Than wortës[2] to the pot.
    Kyrie eleison.

Jenkin at the *agnus*
Beareth the *pax* bread;
He twinkled but said nought
And on my foot he trod.
Benedicamus Domino,

Christ from shame me shield!
Deo gracias thereto,
Alas, I go with child.
    Kyrie eleison.

Anonymous

1 joy   2 cabbages

21   *Holly and ivy*

Holly and Ivy made a great party,
Who should have the mastery
In lands where they go.

Then spake Holly, 'I am fresh and jolly;
I will have the mastery,
In lands where we go.'

Then spake Ivy, 'I am loud and proud;
And I will have the mastery
In lands where we go.'

Then spake Holly, and set him down on his knee,
'I pray thee, gentle Ivy,
Say me no villainy
In lands where we go.'

Anonymous

22   *I have been a forester*

I have been a forester long and many day;
    My locks are hoar.
I shall hang up my horn by the greenwood spray;
    Forester will I be no more.

All the whiles that I may my bow bend
    Shall I wed no wife.
I shall build me a bower at the woodës end
    There to lead my life.

Anonymous

23 *I have a gentle cock*

I have a gentle cock
   Croweth me day;
He doth me risen early
   My matins for to say.

I have a gentle cock;
   Comen he is of great;[1]
His comb is of red coral,
   His tail is of jet.

I have a gentle cock;
   Comen he is of kind;
His comb is of red coral,
   His tail is of ind.[2]

His leggës are of azure,
   So gentle and so small;
His spurs are of silver white
   Into the wortëwale.[3]

His eyes are of crystal
   Locked all in amber;
And every night he percheth him
   In my lady's chamber.

Anonymous

1 come from a noble line   2 indigo   3 skin of the claws

24 *The maidens came*

The maidens came
When I was in my mother's bower;
I had all that I would.
The bailey beareth the bell away;
The lily, the rose, the rose I lay.

The silver is white, red is the gold;
The robes they lay in fold.
The bailey beareth the bell away;
The lily, the rose, the rose I lay.
And through the glass window shines the sun.
How shall I love, and I so young?
The bailey beareth the bell away;
The lily, the rose, the rose I lay.

Anonymous

The exact meaning of this deeply evocative poem has been
the subject of controversy. 'The bailey beareth the bell
away' may mean 'The bailiff (i.e. some estate official) wins
the prize', meaning the hand of the girl who is being married
too young. On the other hand, this line may simply mean
'The boundaries of my home are what I like best'—i.e. the
girl does not want to go away and be married to a stranger.
The line 'Through the glass window shines the sun' is a
symbolic reference to the loss of virginity.

25   *Fowls in the frith*

Fowls in the frith,[1]
      The fishes in the flood,
   And I must go mad;
Much sorrow I walk with
      For the best of bone and blood.

Anonymous

1 wood

26   *Now goeth sun under wood*

Now goeth sun under wood—
Me rueth,[1] Mary, thy fair rood.
Now goeth sun under tree—
Me rueth, Mary, thy son and thee.

Anonymous

1 I grieve for

When the nightingale sings, the woods wax green,
Leaf and grass and blossom spring in April, I ween,
And love is to my heart gone with a spear so keen,
Night and day my blood it drinks, my heart doth me
    teen.[1]
I have loved all this year, that I may love no more,
I have dug many ditches, leman, for thine ore;
Love is no nearer me, and that me rueth sore.
Sweet leman, think on me, I have loved thee yore.
Sweet leman, I pray thee of love one speech;
While I live in world so wide, no other will I seek.
With thy love, my sweet love, my bliss thou mightèst
    eke;[2]
A sweet kiss of thy mouth might be my leech.[3]
Sweet leman, I pray thee, if thou hast loving been,
If thou me lovest as men say, leman, as I ween,
And if it thy will be, then look that it be seen.
So much I think upon thee, that I wax all green.

                                        Anonymous

1 grieve   2 increase   3 cure

28   *All night by the rose*

All night by the rose, rose—
    All night by the rose I lay;
Dared I not the rose steal,
    And yet I bore the flower away.

                                        Anonymous

29   *Go little ring*

Go little ring to that same sweet
That hath my heart in her domain
And look thou kneel down at her feet

Beseeching her she would not disdain
On her small fingers thee to strain;
Then will I that you say boldly:
'My master would that he were I.'

Anonymous

30 *I must go walk the woods*

I must go walk the woods so wild
And wander here and there
In dread and deadly fear;
For where I trusted I am beguiled,
    And all for one.

Thus am I banished from my bliss
By craft and false pretence,
Faultless without offence,
As of return no certain is,
    And all for far-off one.

My bed shall be under the greenwood tree,
A tuft of brakes under my head,
As one from joy were fled;
Thus from my life day by day I flee,
    And all for one.

The running streams shall be my drink,
Acorns shall be my food;
Nothing may do me good,
But when of your beauty I do think
    And all for love of one.

Anonymous

31 *The key of the Kingdom*

This is the key of the Kingdom:
In that Kingdom is a city;

In that city is a town;
In that town is a street;
In that street there winds a lane;
In that lane there is a yard;
In that yard there is a house;
In that house there waits a room;
In that room an empty bed,
And on that bed a basket—
A basket of sweet flowers
    Of flowers, of flowers;
    A basket of sweet flowers.

Flowers in a basket;
Basket on the bed;
Bed in the room;
Room in the house;
House in the yard;
Yard in the winding lane;
Lane in the street;
Street in the town;
Town in the city;
City in the Kingdom—
This is the key of the Kingdom.
    Of the Kingdom this is the key.

Anonymous

32 *Nay, Ivy, nay*

Holly standeth in the hall fair to behold,
Ivy stands without the door; she is full sore a-cold.
    Nay, Ivy, nay, it shall not be, I wis,
    Let Holly have the mastery as the manner is.

Holly and his merry men, they dance now and they sing;
Ivy and her maidens, they weep and their hands wring.
    Nay, Ivy, nay . . .

Holly he has berries as red as any rose,
The foresters, the hunters, keep them from the does.
Nay, Ivy, nay . . .

Ivy she hath berries as black as any sloe,
There come the owls and eat them as they go.
Nay, Ivy, nay . . .

Holly he hath birds a full fair flock,
The nightingale, the popinjay, the gentle laverock.
Nay, Ivy, nay . . .

Good Ivy, say to us, what birds hast thou,
None but the owlet that cried How! How!
*Nay, Ivy, nay, it shall not be, I wis,
Let Holly have the mastery as the manner is.*

Anonymous

33 The oak-tree

Says the old man to the oak-tree,
'Young and lusty was I, when I kenned thee;
I was young and lusty, I was fair and clear,
Young and lusty was I mony a lang year;
But sair failed am I, sair failed now,
Sair failed am I, sin I kenned thou.'

Anonymous

34 Clerk Saunders

Clerk Saunders and may Margaret
　　Walked o'er yon garden green;
And deep and heavy was the love
　　That fell they two between.

'A bed, a bed,' Clerk Saunders said,
　　'A bed for you and me!'
'Fie na, fie na,' said may Margaret,
　　'Till once we married be.'

'Then I'll take the sword from my scabbard
    And slowly lift the pin;
And you may swear and save your aith,
    Ye ne'er let Clerk Saunders in.

'Take you a napkin in your hand,
    And tie up both your bonny e'en,
And you may swear, and save your aith,
    Ye saw me na since late yestreen.'

It was about the midnight hour,
    When they asleep were laid,
When in and came her seven brothers,
    Wi' torches burning red:

When in and came her seven brothers,
    Wi' torches burning bright;
They said, 'We hae but one sister,
    And behold her lying with a knight.'

Then out and spake the first of them,
    'I bear the sword shall gar him die.'
And out and spake the second of them,
    'His father has nae mair but he.'

And out and spake the third of them,
    'I wot that they are lovers dear.'
And out and spake the fourth of them,
    'They hae been in love this mony a year.'

Then out and spake the fifth of them,
    'It were great sin true love to twain.'
And out and spake the sixth of them,
    'It were shame to slay a sleeping man.'

The up and gat the seventh of them
    And never a word spake he;
But he has striped[1] his bright long brand
    Out through Clerk Saunders' fair body.

Clerk Saunders he started, and Margaret she turned
    Into his arms as asleep she lay;
And sad and silent was the night
    That was atween them twae.

And they lay still and sleepit sound
    Until the day began to daw;
And kindly she to him did say,
    'It is time, true love, you were away.

But he lay still and sleepit sound,
    Albeit the sun began to sheen;
She looked atween her and the wa',
    And dull and drowsy were his e'en.

'O Saunders I'll do for your sake
    What other ladies would na thole;[2]
Till seven years is come and gone,
    There's ne'er a shoe go on my sole.

'O Saunders, I'll do for your sake
    What other ladies would think mair;
Till seven years is come and gone
    There's ne'er a comb go in my hair.

'O Saunders I'll do for your sake
    What other ladies would think lack;
Till seven long years is come and gone,
    I'll wear nought but dowie[3] black.'

Then in and came her father dear;
    Said, 'Let a' your mourning be;
I'll carry the dead corse to the clay,
    And I'll come back and comfort thee.'

'Comfort weel your seven sons,
    For comforted I will never be:
I ween 'twas neither knave nor loon
    Was in the bower last night wi' me.'

Anonymous

1 thrust   2 endure   3 gloomy

Ye highlands and ye lowlands,
  O where hae ye been?
They hae slain the Earl of Murray,
  And hae laid him on the green.

Now woe be to thee, Huntley!
  And wherefore did ye sae?
I bade you bring him wi' you,
  But forbade you him to slay.

He was a braw gallant,
  And he rode at the ring;
And the bonny Earl of Murray,
  O he might hae been a king!

He was a braw gallant,
  And he played at the ba';
And the bonny Earl of Murray
  Was the flower among them a'!

He was a braw gallant,
  And he played at the glove;
And the bonny Earl of Murray,
  O he was the Queen's love.

O lang will his lady
  Look o'er the castle down,
Ere she see the Earl of Murray
  Come sounding through the town.

Anonymous

36   *The wife of Usher's well*

There lived a wife at Usher's well,
  And a wealthy wife was she;
She had three stout and stalwart sons,
  And sent them o'er the sea.

They hadna been a week from her,
   A week but barely ane,
When word came to the carlin[1] wife,
   That her three sons were gane.

They hadna been a week from her,
   A week but barely three,
When word came to the carlin wife,
   That her sons she'd never see.

'I wish the wind may never cease,
   Nor fashes[2] in the flood,
Till my three sons come hame to me,
   In earthly flesh and blood!'

It fell about the Martinmas,
   When nights are lang and mirk,
The carlin wife's three sons came hame,
   And their hats were o' the birk.[3]

It neither grew in dyke nor ditch,
   Nor yet in ony sheugh;[4]
But at the gates o' Paradise,
   That birk grew fair eneugh.

'Blow up the fire, my maidens,
   Bring water from the well!
For a' my house shall feast this night,
   Since my three sons are well.'

And she has made to them a bed,
   She's made it large and wide;
And she's ta'en her mantle her about,
   Sat down at the bedside.

Up then crew the red red cock,
   And up and crew the grey;
The eldest to the youngest said,
   "Tis time we were away.'

The cock he hadna crowed but once,
  And clapped his wings at a',
When the youngest to the eldest said,
  'Brother, we must awa.'

'The cock doth craw, the day doth daw,
  The channerin'⁵ worm doth chide;
Gin we be mist out o' our place,
  A sair pain we must bide.'

'Fare ye weel, my mother dear!
  Farewell to barn and byre!
And fare ye weel, the bonny lass,
  That kindles my mother's fire.'

Anonymous

1 old 2 troubles 3 birch 4 trench 5 fretting

37   Lord Randal

'O where hae ye been, Lord Randal, my son?
O where hae ye been, my handsome young man?'
'I hae been to the wild wood; mother make my bed
  soon,
For I'm weary wi' hunting, and fain wad lie down.'

'Where gat ye your dinner, Lord Randal, my son?
Where gat ye your dinner, my handsome young man?'
'I dined with my true-love; mother make my bed soon,
For I'm weary wi' hunting, and fain wad lie down.'

'What gat ye to your dinner, Lord Randal, my son?
What gat ye to your dinner, my handsome young
  man?'
'I gat eels boiled in broth; mother make my bed soon,
For I'm weary wi' hunting, and fain wad lie down.'

'And wha gat your leavings, Lord Randal, my son?
And wha gat your leavings, my handsome young man?'
'My hawks and my hounds; mother make my bed soon,
For I'm weary wi' hunting and fain wad lie down.'

'What became of your bloodhounds, Lord Randal, my
    son?
What became of your bloodhounds, my handsome
    young man?'
'O they swelled and they died; mother make my bed
    soon,
For I'm weary wi' hunting, and fain wad lie down.'

'O I fear ye are poisoned, Lord Randal, my son!
O I fear ye are poisoned, my handsome young man!'
'O yes! I am poisoned; mother make my bed soon,
For I'm sick at the heart and I fain wad lie down.'

Anonymous

38   *Sir Patrick Spens*

The king sits in Dumfermline town
    Drinking the blude-red wine,
'O whare will I get a skeely[1] skipper
    To sail this new ship o' mine?'

O up and spak an eldern knight,
    Sat at the king's right knee;
'Sir Patrick Spens is the best sailor
    That ever sailed the sea.'

Our king has written a braid[2] letter,
    And sealed it with his hand,
And sent it to Sir Patrick Spens,
    Was walking on the strand.

The first word that Sir Patrick read
    So loud, loud laughed he;
The next word that Sir Patrick read
    The tear blinded his e'e.

'O wha is this has done this deed
    And told the king of me,
To send us out, at this time of year,
    To sail upon the sea?'

'Be it wind, be it weet, be it hail, be it sleet,
    Our ship must sail the faem;
The king's daughter o' Noroway,
    'Tis we must fetch her hame.'

They hadna been a week, a week,
    In Noroway but twae,
When that the lords o' Noroway
    Began aloud to say:

'Ye Scottish men spend a' our king's gowd,
    And a' our queenis fee.'
'Ye lee, ye lee, ye leears loud,
    Fu' loud I hear ye lee!

'For I brought as much o' the white monie
    As gane[3] my men and me,
And a half-four[4] o' the gude red gowd,
    Out ower the sea with me.

'Mak' ready, mak' ready, my merry men a'!
    Our gude ship sails the morn.'
'Now ever alack, my master dear,
    I fear a deadly storm.

'I saw the new moon late yestreen
    Wi' the old moon in her arm;
And if we gang to sea, master,
    I fear we'll come to harm.'

They hadna sailed a league, a league,
    A league but barely three,
When the lift[5] grew dark, and the wind blew loud,
    And gurly[6] grew the sea.

The ankers brak, and the topmast lap[7]
    It was sic a deadly storm:
And the waves cam owre the broken ship
    Till a' her sides were torn.

They fetched a web o' the silken claith,[8]
    Another o' the twine,[9]
And they wapped[10] them round that gude ship's side,
    But still the sea came in.

O laith,[11] laith were our gude Scots lords
    To wat their cork-heeled shoon;
But lang or a' that play was played
    They wat their hats aboon.[12]

And mony was the feather bed
    That flattered[13] on the faem;
And mony was the gude lord's son
    That never mair cam hame.

O lang, lang may the ladies sit
    Wi' their gowd kames[14] in their hair,
A-waiting for their ain dear loves!
    For them they'll never see mair.

Half-owre,[15] half-owre to Aberdour,
    'Tis fifty fathoms deep;
And there lies gude Sir Patrick Spens,
    Wi' the Scots lords at his feet!

Anonymous

1 skilful   2 broad, plain   3 suffices   4 half-bushel   5 sky
6 rough   7 cracked   8 cloth   9 sacking   10 packed   11
loath   12 above   13 floated   14 golden combs   15 half-
way over

39   Edward

'Why does your brand sae drop wi' blude,
    Edward, Edward?
Why does your brand sae drop wi' blude,
    And why sae sad gang ye, O?'—
'O I hae killed my hawk sae gude,
    Mither, Mither;
O I hae killed my hawk sae gude,
    And I had nae mair but he, O.'

'Your hawk's blude was never sae red,
    Edward, Edward;
Your hawk's blude was never sae red,
    My dear son, I tell thee, O.'—
'O I hae killed my red-roan steed,
    Mither, Mither;
O I hae killed my red-roan steed,
    That erst was sae fair and free, O.'

'Your steed was auld, and ye hae got mair,
    Edward, Edward;
Your steed was old, and ye hae got mair;
    Some other dule ye dree[1], O.'
'O I hae killed my father dear,
    Mither, Mither;
O I hae killed my father dear,
    Alas, and wae is me, O!'

'And whatten penance will ye dree[1] for that,
    Edward, Edward?
Whatten penance will ye dree for that?
    My son, now tell me, O.'—
'I'll set my feet on yonder boat,
    Mither, Mither;
I'll set my feet on yonder boat,
    And I'll fare over the sea, O.'

'And what will ye do wi' your tow'rs and your ha',
    Edward, Edward?
And what will ye do wi' your tow'rs and your ha',
    That were sae fair to see, O?'—
'I'll let them stand till they doun fa',
    Mither, Mither;
I'll let them stand till they doun fa',
    For here never mair maun I be, O.'

'And what will ye leave to your bairns and your wife,
    Edward, Edward?
And what will ye leave to your bairns and your wife,
    When ye gang owre the sea, O?'—

'The warld's room: let them beg through life,
    Mither, Mither;
The warld's room: let them beg through life;
    For them never mair will I see, O.'

'And what will ye leave to your ain mither dear
    Edward, Edward?
And what will ye leave to your ain mither adear,
    My dear son, now tell me, O?'—
'The curse of hell frae me shall ye bear,
    Mither, Mither;
The curse of hell frae me shall ye bear:
    Sic counsels ye gave me, O!'

Anonymous

undergo

40   *Thomas Rhymer*

True Thomas lay on Huntlie Bank;
    A ferlie[1] he spied wi' his e'e;
And there he saw a lady bright
    Come riding down by the Eildon Tree.

Her skirt was of the grass-green silk,
    Her mantle of the velvet fine,
At ilka tett[2] of her horse's mane
    Hung fifty silver bells and nine.

True Thomas he took off his hat,
    And bowed him low down till his knee;
'All hail, thou mighty Queen of Heaven!
    For your peer on earth I never did see.'

'O no, O no, True Thomas,' she says,
    'That name does not belong to me:
I am but the queen of fair Elfland,
    And I'm come here for to visit thee.

'Harp and carp, Thomas,' she said;
  'Harp and carp along wi' me;
And if ye dare to kiss my lips,
  Sure of your body I will be.'

'Betide me weel, betide me woe,
  That weird[3] shall never daunten me.'
Syne he has kissed her rosy lips,
  All underneath the Eildon Tree.

'But ye maun go wi' me now, Thomas,
  True Thomas, ye maun go wi' me,
For ye maun serve me seven years,
  Thro' weel or wae, as may chance to be.'

She's mounted on her milk-white steed,
  She's ta'en true Thomas up behind;
And aye whene'er her bridle rang,
  The steed gaed swifter than the wind.

O they rade on, and farther on,
  The steed gaed swifter than the wind;
Until they reached a desert wide,
  And living land was left behind.

''Light down, light down now, true Thomas,
  And lean your head upon my knee;
Abide ye there a little space,
  And I will show you ferlies three.

'O see not ye yon narrow road,
  So thick beset wi' thorns and briers?
That is the path of righteousness,
  Tho' after it but few enquires.

'And see not ye that braid braid road,
  That lies across yon lillie leven[4]?
That is the path of wickedness,
  Tho' some call it the road to heaven.

'And see not ye that bonny road,
    Which winds about the fernie brae?
That is the road to fair Elfland,
    Where you and I this night maun gae.

'But, Thomas, ye maun hold your tongue,
    Whatever you may hear or see,
For gin ae word you should chance to speak,
    You will ne'er get back to your ain country.'

O they rade on, and farther on,
    And they waded rivers abune the knee;
And they saw neither sun nor moon,
    But they heard the roaring of the sea.

It was mirk, mirk night, there was nae starlight,
    They waded thro' red blude to the knee;
For all the blude that's shed on earth
    Runs through the springs o' that country.

Syne they came to a garden green,
    And she pulled an apple frae a tree:
'Take this for thy wages, true Thomas;
    It will give thee the tongue that can never lee.'

'My tongue is my ain,' true Thomas he said;
    'A gudely gift ye wad gie to me!
I neither dought to buy or sell
    At fair or tryst where I might be.

'I dought neither speak to prince or peer,
    Nor ask of grace from fair lady!'
'Now hold thy peace, Thomas,' she said,
    'For as I say, so must it be.'

He has gotten a coat of the even cloth,
    And a pair of shoes of the velvet green,
And till seven years were past and gone
    True Thomas on earth was never seen.

Anonymous

1 marvel   2 lock of hair   3 fate   4 smooth lawn set with lilies

41 *Down in the meadows*

Down in the meadows the other day,
Gathering flowers both fine and gay,
Gathering flowers both red and blue,
I little thought what love could do.

I leaned my back against an oak,
Thinking it was a trusty tree.
First it bended and then it broke,
And so did my false love to me.

There is a ship that sails the sea;
It's loaded deep as deep can be,
But not so deep as the love I'm in;
I care not if I sink or swim.

Love is handsome and love is fine,
Love is charming when it is new.
As it grows older, it grows colder
And fades away like morning dew.

Anonymous

42 *The twa sisters*

There was twa sisters in a bow'r,
   Edinburgh, Edinburgh,
There was twa sisters in a bow'r,
   Stirling for aye,
There was twa sisters in a bow'r,
There came a knight to be their wooer,
   Bonny Saint Johnston stands upon Tay.

He courted the eldest wi' glove an' ring,
But he loved the youngest above a' thing.

He courted the eldest wi' brooch an' knife,
But loved the youngest as his life;

The eldest she was vexed sair,
An' much envied her sister fair;

Into her bower she could not rest,
Wi' grief an' spite she almost brast.

Upon a morning fair an' clear
She cried upon her sister dear:

O sister come to yon sea-stran',
And see our father's ships come to lan'.

She's ta'en her by the milk-white han',
And led her down to yon sea-stran'.

The youngest stood upon a stane,
The eldest came an' threw her in;

She took her by the middle sma',
An' dash'd her bonny back to the jaw;[1]

O sister, sister, take my han',
And I'se make you heir to a' my lan'.

O sister, sister, take my middle,
And ye's get my gold and my golden girdle.

O sister, sister, save my life,
And I swear I'se never be nae man's wife.

'Foul fa' the han' that I should take,
It twin'd[2] me an' my wardles' make.'[3]

'Your cherry cheeks and yallow hair,
Gars me gae maiden for evermair.'

Sometimes she sank, an' sometimes she swam,
Till she cam down yon bonny mill dam;

O out it came the miller's son,
An' saw the fair maid swimmin' in.

'O father, father, draw your dam!
Here's either a mermaid, or a swan.'

The miller quickly drew the dam,
An' there he found a drown'd woman;

You couldna see her yallow hair,
For gold and pearl that were sae rare;

You couldna see her middle sma',
For golden girdle that was sae braw;

Ye couldna see her fingers white
For golden rings that was sae gryte.

And by there came a harper fine,
That harped to the king at dine.

When he did look that lady upon,
He sigh'd and made a heavy moan;

He's taen three locks o' her yallow hair,
And wi' them strung his harp sae fair.

The first tune he did play and sing
Was—'Farewell to my father the king.'

The nexten tune that he played syne
Was—'Farewell to my mother the queen.'

The lasten tune that he play'd then
Was—'Wae to my sister, fair Ellen!'

Anonymous

1 wave   2 deprived   3 life-mate

43   *Helen of Kirconnell*

I wish I were where Helen lies,
Night and day on me she cries;
O that I were where Helen lies,
   On fair Kirconnell Lee!

Curst be the heart that thought the thought,
And curst the hand that fired the shot,
When in my arms burd[1] Helen dropt,
   And died to succour me!

O think na ye my heart was sair,
When my love dropt down and spak nae mair,
There did she swoon wi' mickle care,
   On fair Kirconnell Lee.

As I went down the water side,
None but my foe to be my guide,
None but my foe to be my guide,
   On fair Kirconnell Lee;

I lighted down my sword to draw,
I hacked him in pieces sma',
I hacked him in pieces sma',
   For her sake that died for me.

I wish my grave were growing green,
A winding-sheet drawn ower my een,
And I in Helen's arms lying,
   On fair Kirconnell Lee.

I wish I were where Helen lies!
Night and day on me she cries;
And I am weary of the skies,
   For her sake that died for me.

Anonymous

1 maid

44 *Lamkin*

It's Lamkin was a mason good
   As ever built with stane,
He built Lord Wearie's castle,
   But payment gat he nane.

'O pay me, Lord Wearie;
  Come pay me my fee.'
'I canna pay you, Lamkin,
  For I maun gang o'er the sea.'

'O pay me now, Lord Wearie;
  Come, pay me out o' hand.'
'I canna pay you, Lamkin,
  Unless I sell my land.'

'O gin ye winna pay me,
  I here sall mak a vow,
Before that ye come hame again,
  Ye sall ha'e cause to rue.'

Lord Wearie got a bonny ship,
  To sail the saut sea faem;[1]
Bade his lady weel the castle keep,
  Ay till he should come hame.

But the nourice[2] was a fause limmer[3]
  As e'er hung on a tree;
She laid a plot wi' Lamkin,
  When her lord was o'er the sea.

She laid a plot wi' Lamkin,
  When the servants were awa';
Let him in at a little shot window,[4]
  And brought him to the ha'.

'O where's a' the men o' this house,
  That ca' me Lamkin?'
'They're at the barn well thrashing,
  'Twill be lang ere they come in.'

'And where's the women o' this house,
  That ca' me Lamkin?'
'They're at the far well washing;
  'Twill be lang ere they come in.'

'And where's the bairns o' this house,
    That ca' me Lamkin?'
'They're at the school reading;
    'Twill be night or they come hame.'

'O where's the lady o' this house,
    That ca's me Lamkin?'
'She's up in her bower sewing,
    But we soon can bring her down.'

Then Lamkin's tane a sharp knife,
    That hang down by his gair,[5]
And he has gi'en the bonny babe
    A deep wound and a sair.

Then Lamkin he rocked,
    And the fause nourice sang,
Till frae ilka bore[6] o' the cradle
    The red blood out sprang.

Then out it spak the lady,
    As she stood on the stair,
'What ails my bairn, nourice,
    That he's greeting[7] sae sair?

'O still my bairn, nourice;
    O still him wi' the pap!'
'He winna still, lady,
    For this, nor for that.'

'O still my bairn, nourice;
    O still him wi' the wand!'
'He winna still, lady,
    For a' his father's land.'

'O still my bairn, nourice,
    O still him wi' the bell!'
'He winna still, lady,
    Till ye come down yoursel'.'

O the firsten step she steppit,
   She steppit on a stane;
But the neisten step she steppit,
   She met him, Lamkin.

'O mercy, mercy, Lamkin!
   Ha'e mercy upon me!
Though you've ta'en my young son's life,
   Ye may let mysel' be.'

'O sall I kill her, nourice?
   Or sall I lat her be?'
'O kill her, kill her, Lamkin,
   For she ne'er was good to me.'

'O scour the basin, nourice,
   And mak it fair and clean,
For to keep this lady's heart's blood,
   For she's come o' noble kin.'

'There need nae basin, Lamkin;
   Let it run through the floor;
What better is the heart's blood
   O' the rich than o' the poor?'

But ere three months were at an end,
   Lord Wearie came again;
But dowie, dowie[8] was his heart
   When first he came hame.

'O wha's blood is this,' he says,
   'That lies in the châmer?'
'It is your lady's heart's blood;
   'Tis as clear as the lamer.'[9]

'And wha's blood is this,' he says,
   'That lies in my ha?''
'It is your young son's heart's blood;
   'Tis the clearest ava'.'

O sweetly sang the black-bird
　　That sat upon the tree;
But sairer grat Lamkin,
　　When he was condemn'd to die.

And bonny sang the mavis
　　Out o' the thorny brake;
But sairer grat the nourice,
　　When she was tied to the stake.

Anonymous

1 foam　2 nurse　3 wretch　4 projecting window　5 skirt
6 hole　7 crying　8 gloomy　9 amber

45　*The dæmon lover*

'O where have you been, my long, long love,
　　This long seven years and more?'—
'O I'm come to seek my former vows
　　Ye granted me before.'—

'O hold your tongue of your former vows,
　　For they will breed sad strife;
O hold your tongue of your former vows,
　　For I am become a wife.'

He turn'd him right and round about,
　　And the tear blinded his ee;
'I wad never hae trodden on Irish ground,
　　If it had not been for thee.

'I might hae had a king's daughter,
　　Far, far beyond the sea;
I might have had a king's daughter,
　　Had it not been for love o' thee.'—

'If ye might have had a king's daughter,
　　Yoursel' ye had to blame;
Ye might have taken the king's daughter,
　　For ye kenned that I was nane.'—

['O false are the vows of womankind,
    But fair is their false body;
I never wad hae trodden on Irish ground,
    Had it not been for love o' thee.'—]

'If I was to leave my husband dear,
    And my two babes also,
O what have you to take me to,
    If with you I should go?'—

'I hae seven ships upon the sea,
    The eighth brought me to land;
With four and twenty bold mariners,
    And music on every hand.'

She has taken up her two little babes,
    Kiss'd them baith cheek and chin;
'O fair ye weel, my ain two babes,
    For I'll never see you again.'

She set her foot upon the ship,
    No mariners could she behold;
But the sails were o' the taffety,
    And the masts o' the beaten gold.

She had not sail'd a league, a league,
    A league but barely three,
When dismal grew his countenance,
    And drumlie[1] grew his ee.

[The masts that were like the beaten gold,
    Bent not on the heaving seas;
But the sails, that were o' the taffety,
    Fill'd not in the east land-breeze.—]

They had not sailed a league, a league,
    A league but barely three,
Until she espied his cloven foot,
    And she wept right bitterly.

'O hold your tongue of your weeping,' says he,
    'Of your weeping now let me be;
I will show you how the lilies grow
    On the banks of Italy.'—

'O what hills are yon, yon pleasant hills,
    That the sun shines sweetly on?'—
'O yon are the hills of heaven,' he said,
    'Where you will never win.'—

'O whaten a mountain is yon,' she said,
    'All so dreary wi' frost and snow?'
'O yon is the mountain of hell,' he cried,
    'Where you and I will go.'

[And aye when she turn'd her round about,
    Aye taller he seem'd for to be;
Until that the tops o' that gallant ship
    Nae taller were than he.

The clouds grew dark, and the wind grew loud,
    And the levin² fill'd her ee;
And waesome wail'd the snaw-white sprites
    Upon the gurlie³ sea.]

He strack the tap-mast wi' his hand,
    The fore-mast wi' his knee;
And he brake that gallant ship in twain,
    And sank her in the sea.

Anonymous

1 gloomy   2 lightning   3 stormy

46   *Fine flowers in the valley*

She sat down below a thorn,
    Fine flowers in the valley;
And there she has her sweet babe born,
    And the green leaves they grow rarely.

'Smile na sae sweet, my bonny babe,
  Fine flowers in the valley,
And ye smile sae sweet, ye'll smile me dead.'
  And the green leaves they grow rarely.

She's ta'en out her little penknife,
  Fine flowers in the valley,
And twinn'd the sweet babe o' its life,
  And the green leaves they grow rarely.

She's howket[1] a grave by the light o' the moon,
  Fine flowers in the valley,
And there she's buried her sweet babe in,
  And the green leaves they grow rarely.

As she was going to the church,
  Fine flowers in the valley,
She saw a sweet babe in the porch,
  And the green leaves they grow rarely.

'O sweet babe, and thou were mine,
  Fine flowers in the valley,
I wad clead thee in the silk so fine,'
  And the green leaves they grow rarely.

'O mother dear, when I was thine,
  Fine flowers in the valley,
Ye did na prove to me sae kind,'
  And the green leaves they grow rarely.

Anonymous

1 digged

47   *Græme and Bewick*

Gude Lord Græme is to Carlisle gane,
  Sir Robert Bewick there met he,
And arm in arm to the wine they did go,
  And they drank till they were baith merry.

Gude Lord Græme has ta'en up the cup,
  'Sir Robert Bewick, and here's to thee!
And here's to our twa sons at hame!
  For they like us best in our ain country.'—

'O were your son a lad like mine,
  And learn'd some books that he could read,
They might hae been twa brethren bold,
  And they might hae bragged[1] the Border side.

'But your son's a lad, and he is but bad,
  And billy to my son he canna be;'

'[I] sent him to the schools, and he wadna learn;
  [I] bought him books, and he wadna read;
But my blessing shall he never earn,
  Till I see how his arm can defend his head.'—

Gude Lord Græme has a reckoning call'd,
  A reckoning then called he;
And he paid a crown, and it went roun',
  It was all for the gude wine and free.

And he has to the stable gane,
  Where there stood thirty steeds and three;
He's ta'en his ain horse amang them a',
  And hame he rade sae manfully.

'Welcome, my auld father!' said Christie Græme,
  'But where sae lang frae hame were ye?'—
'It's I hae been at Carlisle town,
  And a baffled man by thee I be.

'I hae been at Carlisle town,
  Where Sir Robert Bewick he met me;
He says ye're a lad, and ye are but bad,
  And billy to his son ye canna be.

'I sent ye to the schools, and ye wadna learn;
  I bought ye books, and ye wadna read;
Therefore my blessing ye shall never earn,
  Till I see with Bewick thou save my head.'

'Now, God forbid, my auld father,
    That ever sic a thing should be!
Billy Bewick was my master, and I was his scholar,
    And aye sae weel as he learned me.'

'O hold thy tongue, thou limmer² loon,
    And of thy talking let me be!
If thou does na end me this quarrel soon,
    There is my glove, I'll fight wi' thee.'

Then Christie Græme he stooped low
    Unto the ground, you shall understand;—
'O father, put on your glove again,
    The wind has blown it from your hand?'

'What's that thou says, thou limmer loon?
    How dares thou stand to speak to me?
If thou do not end this quarrel soon,
    There's my right hand, thou shalt fight with me.'—

Then Christie Græme's to his chamber gane,
    To consider weel what then should be;
Whether he should fight with his auld father,
    Or with his billy Bewick, he.

'If I should kill my billy dear,
    God's blessing I shall never win;
But if I strike at my auld father,
    I think 'twould be a mortal sin.

'But if I kill my billy dear,
    It is God's will, so let it be;
But I make a vow, ere I gang frae hame,
    That I shall be the next man's die.'—

Then he's put on's back a gude auld jack,³
    And on his head a cap of steel,
And sword and buckler by his side;
    O gin he did not become them weel!

We'll leave off talking of Christie Græme,
    And talk of him again belive;[4]
And we will talk of bonny Bewick,
    Where he was teaching his scholars five.

When he had taught them well to fence,
    And handle swords without any doubt,
He took his sword under his arm,
    And he walk'd his father's close about.

He look'd atween him and the sun,
    And a' to see what there might be,
Till he spied a man in armour bright,
    Was riding that way most hastily.

'O wha is yon, that came this way,
    Sae hastily that hither came?
I think it be my brother dear,
    I think it be young Christie Græme.

'Ye're welcome here, my billy dear,
    And thrice ye're welcome unto me!'—
'But I'm wae to say, I've seen the day,
    When I am come to fight wi' thee.

'My father's gane to Carlisle town,
    Wi' your father Bewick there met he:
He says I'm a lad, and I am but bad,
    And a baffled man I trow I be.

'He sent me to schools, and I wadna learn;
    He gae me books, and I wadna read;
Sae my father's blessing I'll never earn,
    Till he see how my arm can guard my head.'

'O God forbid, my billy dear,
    That ever such a thing should be!
We'll take three men on either side,
    And see if we can our fathers agree.'

'O hold thy tongue, now, billy Bewick,
    And of thy talking let me be!
But if thou'rt a man, as I'm sure thou art,
    Come o'er the dyke, and fight wi' me.'

'But I hae nae harness, billy, on my back,
    As weel I see is on thine.'—
'But as little harness as is on thy back,
    As little, billy, shall be on mine.'—

Then he's thrown off his coat o' mail,
    His cap of steel away flung he;
He stuck his spear into the ground,
    And he tied his horse unto a tree.

Then Bewick has thrown off his cloak,
    And's psalter-book frae's hand flung he;
He laid his hand upon the dyke,
    And ower he lap most manfully.

O they hae fought for twa lang hours;
    When twa lang hours were come and gane,
The sweat drapp'd fast frae off them baith,
    But a drap of blude could not be seen.

Till Græme gae Bewick an awkward stroke,
    Ane awkward stroke strucken sickerly;[5]
He has hit him under the left breast,
    And dead-wounded to the ground fell he.

'Rise up, rise up, now, billy dear,
    Arise and speak three words to me!
Whether thou's gotten thy deadly wound,
    Or if God and good leeching may succour thee?'

'O horse, O horse, now, billy Græme,
    And get thee far from hence with speed;
And get thee out of this country,
    That none may know who has done the deed.'—

'O I have slain thee, billy Bewick,
    If this be true thou tellest to me;
But I made a vow, ere I came frae hame,
    That aye the next man I wad be.'

He has pitch'd his sword in a moodie-hill,[6]
    And he had leap'd twenty lang feet and three,
And on his ain sword's point he lap,
    And dead upon the ground fell he.

'Twas then came up Sir Robert Bewick,
    And his brave son alive saw he;
'Rise up, rise up, my son,' he said,
    'For I think ye hae gotten the victory.'

'O hold your tongue, my father dear,
    Of your prideful talking let me be!
Ye might hae drunken your wine in peace,
    And let me and my billy be.

'Gae dig a grave, baith wide and deep,
    And a grave to hold baith him and me;
But lay Christie Græme on the sunny side,
    For I'm sure he won the victory.'

'Alack! a wae!' auld Bewick cried,
    'Alack! was I not much to blame?
I'm sure I've lost the liveliest lad
    That e'er was born unto my name.'

'Alack! a wae!' quo' gude Lord Græme,
    'I'm sure I hae lost the deeper lack!
I durst hae ridden the Border through,
    Has Christie Græme been at my back

'Had I been led through Liddesdale,
    And thirty horsemen guarding me,
And Christie Græme been at my back,
    Sae soon as he had set me free!

'I've lost my hopes, I've lost my joy,
    I've lost the key but and the lock;
I durst hae ridden the world round,
    Had Christie Græme been at my back.'

Anonymous

1 defied   2 rascal   3 coat of mail   4 soon   5 surely
6 mole-hill

48   *The gardener*

The gardener stands in his bower door
    With a primrose in his hand;
And by there came a true maiden
    As slim as a willow wand.

'O lady, can you fancy me
    And will you be my bride!
You shall have all the flowers in my garden
    To be to you a weed.¹

'The lily white to be your smock,
    It becomes your body best;
Your head shall be dressed with gillyglower
    With the red rose in your breast.

'Your gown shall be the sweet william,
    Your coat the camovine,
Your apron of the salads neat
    That taste both sweet and fine.

'Your gloves shall be the marigold
    All glittering to your hand;
Well dropped o'er with blue blaewort
    That grows among corn land.'

'Young man, you've shaped a weed for me
    Among your summer flowers!
Now I will shape another for you
    Among the winter showers.

'The new-fall'n snow to be your smock,
    It becomes your body best;
Your head shall be wrapped with the eastern wind
    And the cold rain on your breast.'

Anonymous

1 dress

49   *The Laird o' Logie*

I will sing, if ye will hearken,
    If ye will hearken unto me;
The king has ta'en a poor prisoner,
    The wanton laird o' young Logie.

Young Logie's laid in Edinburgh chapel,
    Carmichael's the keeper o' the key;
And May Margaret's lamenting sair,
    A' for the love o' young Logie.

'Lament, lament na, May Margaret,
    And of your weeping let me be;
For ye maun to the king himsel',
    To seek the life o' young Logie.'

May Margaret has kilted her green cleiding,
    And she has curl'd back her yellow hair,—
'If I canna get young Logie's life,
    Farewell to Scotland for evermair.'

When she came before the king,
    She kneelit lowly on her knee.
'O what's the matter, May Margaret?
    And what needs a' this courtesy?'

'A boon, a boon, my noble liege,
    A boon, a boon, I beg o' thee!
And the first boon that I come to crave
    Is to grant me the life o' young Logie.'

'O na, O na, May Margaret,
  Forsooth, and so it mauna be;
For a' the gowd o' fair Scotland
  Shall not save the life o' young Logie.'

But she has stown[1] the king's redding kaim,[2]
  Likewise the queen her wedding knife;
And sent the tokens to Carmichael,
  To cause young Logie get his life.

She sent him a purse o' the red gowd,
  Another o' the white money;
She sent him a pistol for each hand,
  And bade him shoot when he gat free.

When he came to the Tolbooth stair,
  Then he let his volley flee;
It made the king in his chamber start,
  E'en in the bed where he might be.

'Gae out, gae out, my merry men a',
  And bid Carmichael come speak to me;
For I'll lay my life the pledge o' that,
  That yon's the shot o' young Logie.'

When Carmichael came before the king,
  He fell low down upon his knee;
The very first word that the king spake
  Was,—'Where's the laird of young Logie?'

Carmichael turn'd him round about
  (I wot the tear blinded his e'e)—
'There came a token frae your grace
  Has ta'en away the laird frae me.'

'Hast thou play'd me that, Carmichael?
  And hast thou play'd me that?' quoth he;
'The morn the Justice Court's to stand,
  And Logie's place ye maun supply.'

Carmichael's awa to Margaret's bower,
    Even as fast as he may dri'e,³—
'O if young Logie be within,
    Tell him to come and speak with me!'

May Margaret turn'd her round about
    (I wot a loud laugh laughed she)—
'The egg is chipp'd, the bird is flown,
    Ye'll see nae mair of young Logie.'

The tane is shipped at the pier of Leith,
    The t'other at the Queen's Ferry;
And she's gotten a father to her bairn,
    The wanton laird of young Logie.

Anonymous

1 stolen 2 hair comb 3 drive

50 *Kemp Owyne*

Her mother died when she was young,
    Which gave her cause to make great moan;
Her father married the worst woman
    That ever lived in Christendom.

She served her with foot and hand,
    In everything that she could dee;
Till once, in an unlucky time,
    She threw her in ower Craigy's sea.

Says, 'Lie you there, dove Isabel,
    And all my sorrows lie with thee;
Till Kemp Owyne come ower the sea,
    And borrow¹ you with kisses three,
Let all the world do what they will,
    Oh borrowed shall you never be.'

Her breath grew strang, her hair grew lang,
    And twisted thrice about the tree,

And all the people, far and near,
  Thought that a savage beast was she;
This news did come to Kemp Owyne,
  Where he lived far beyond the sea.

He hasted him to Craigy's sea,
  And on the savage beast look'd he;
Her breath was strang, her hair was lang,
  And twisted was about the tree,
And with a swing she came about;
  'Come to Craigy's sea, and kiss with me.'

'Here is a royal belt,' she cried,
  'That I have found in the green sea:
And while your body it is on,
  Drawn shall your blood never be;
But if you touch me, tail or fin,
  I vow my belt your death shall be.'

He stepped in, gave her a kiss,
  The royal belt he brought him wi';
Her breath was strang, her hair was lang,
  And twisted twice about the tree,
And with a swing she came about:
  'Come to Craigy's sea, and kiss with me.'

'Here is a royal ring,' she said,
  'That I have found in the green sea;
And while your finger it is on,
  Drawn shall your blood never be;
But if you touch me, tail or fin,
  I swear my ring your death shall be.'

He stepped in, gave her a kiss,
  The royal ring he brought him wi';
Her breath was strang, her hair was lang,
  And twisted aince around the tree,
And with a swing she came about:
  'Come to Craigy's sea, and kiss with me.'

'Here is a royal brand,' she said,
    'That I have found in the green sea;
And while your body it is on,
    Drawn shall your blood never be:
But if you touch me, tail or fin,
    I swear my brand your death shall be.'

He stepped in, gave her a kiss,
    The royal brand he brought him wi';
Her breath was sweet, her hair grew short,
    And twisted nane about the tree;
And smilingly she came about,
    As fair a woman as fair could be.

Anonymous

1 redeem

51   The unquiet grave

The wind doth blow to-day, my love,
    And a few small drops of rain;
I never had but one true-love,
    In cold grave she was lain.

I'll do as much for my true-love
    As any young man may;
I'll sit and mourn all at her grave
    For a twelvemonth and a day.

The twelvemonth and a day being up,
    The dead began to speak:
'Oh, who sits weeping on my grave,
    And will not let me sleep?'

''Tis I, my love, sits on your grave,
    And will not let you sleep;
For I crave one kiss of your clay-cold lips,
    And that is all I seek.'

'You crave one kiss of my clay-cold lips,
  But my breath smells earthy strong;
If you have one kiss of my clay-cold lips,
  Your time will not be long.

''Tis down in yonder garden green,
  Love, where we used to walk;
The finest flower that ere was seen
  Is withered to a stalk.

'The stalk is withered dry, my love,
  So will our hearts decay;
So make yourself content, my love,
  Till God call you away!'

O wet and weary is the night,
  And even down pours the rain,
And he that was sae true to me,
  Lies in the greenwood slain.

Anonymous

52   The false knight on the road

'O where are you going?'
  Quoth the false knight on the road.
'I am going to the school,'
  Quoth the wee boy, and still he stood.

'What's that upon your back?'
  Quoth the false knight on the road.
'Wot well it is my books,'
  Quoth the wee boy, and still he stood.

'What's that upon your arm?'
  Quoth the false knight on the road.
'Wot well it is my peat,'
  Quoth the wee boy, and still he stood.

'Who owns they sheep?'
  Quoth the false knight on the road.
'They are mine and my mother's,'
  Quoth the wee boy, and still he stood.

'How many of them are mine?'
  Quoth the false knight on the road.
'All they that have blue tails,'
  Quoth the wee boy, and still he stood.

'I wish you were on yonder tree,'
  Quoth the false knight on the road.
'And a good ladder under me,'
  Quoth the wee boy, and still he stood.

'And the ladder for to break,'
  Quoth the false knight on the road.
'And you for to fall down,'
  Quoth the wee boy, and still he stood.

'I wish you were in yonder sea,'
  Quoth the false knight on the road.
'And a good bottom[1] under me,'
  Quoth the wee boy, and still he stood.

'And the bottom for to break,'
  Quoth the false knight on the road.
'And you to be drowned,'
  Quoth the wee boy, and still he stood.

Anonymous

1 ship

53 *The cherry-tree carol*

Joseph was an old man
  And an old man was he,
When he married Maid Mary
  The Queen of Galilee.

Joseph and Mary walkéd
   Through an orchard green,
Where was berries and cherries
   As thick as might be seen.

O then bespoke Mary
   So meek and so mild,
'Pluck me a cherry, Joseph,
   For I am with child.'

O then bespoke Joseph
   So wilful and wild,
'Let him pluck thee cherries
   That got thee with child.'

O then bespoke the Babe
   Within his mother's womb,
'Bow down, then, the tallest tree,
   For my mother to have some.'

Then bowed down the tallest tree
   Unto this mother's hand;
Then she cried: 'See, Joseph,
   I have cherries at command!'

As Joseph was a-walking
   He heard angels sing:
'This night shall be born to us
   Our heavenly king.'

'He neither shall be born to us
   In house nor in hall,
Nor in the place of Paradise,
   But in an ox's stall.

'He neither shall be clothéd
   In purple nor in pall,
But all in fair linen
   Such as babies wear all.

'He neither shall be rockéd
　　In silver nor in gold
But all in a wooden cradle
　　That stands on the mould.'

Then Mary took her babe
　　Up on her left knee:
With, 'Dear child, I pray thee now,
　　Tell how this world shall be.'

'On the fifth day of January
　　Three kings shall draw near,
While the stars in the heaven
　　Do tremble for fear.

'Upon the Good Friday
　　I will hang on a rood
And all the seed of Adam
　　I'll buy with my blood.

'For I will be so dead, Mother,
　　As stones in the wall:
O the stones in the street, Mother,
　　Shall mourn for me all.

'Upon Easter day, Mother,
　　My rising shall be:
O, the sun and the moon then
　　Shall uprise with me.'

Anonymous

54　*A lyke-wake dirge*

This ae nighte, this ae nighte,
　　Every nighte and alle,
Fire and fleet and candle-lighte,
　　And Christe receive thy saule.

When thou from hence away art past,
   Every nighte and alle,
To Whinny-muir thou com'st at last;
   And Christe receive thy saule.

If ever thou gavest hosen and shoon,
   —*Every nighte and alle,*
Sit thee down and put them on;
   And Christe receive thy saule.

If hosen and shoon thou ne'er gav'st nane
   —*Every nighte and alle,*
The whinnes sall prick thee to the bare bane;
   And Christe receive thy saule.

From Whinny-muir when thou may'st pass,
   —*Every nighte and alle,*
To Brig o' Dread thou com'st at last;
   And Christe receive thy saule.

If ever thou gavest meat or drink,
   —*Every nighte and alle,*
The fire sall never make thee shrink;
   And Christe receive thy saule.

If meat or drink thou ne'er gav'st nane,
   —*Every nighte and alle,*
The fire will burn thee to the bare bane;
   And Christe receive thy saule.

This ae nighte, this ae nighte,
   —*Every nighte and alle,*
Fire and fleet and candle-lighte,
   And Christe receive thy saule.

Anonymous

55   *The twa corbies*

As I was walking all alane
   I heard twa corbies making a mane:[1]

The tane unto the tother say,
'Whar sall we gang and dine to-day?'

'In behint yon auld fail-dyke,
I wot there lies a new-slain knight;
And naebody kens that he lies there
But his hawk, his hound, and his lady fair

'His hound is to the hunting gane,
His hawk to fetch the wild-fowl hame,
His lady's ta'en anither mate,
So we may mak our dinner sweet.

'Ye'll sit on his white hause-bane,[2]
And I'll pike out his bonnie blue e'en;
Wi' ae lock o' his gowden hair
We'll theek our nest when it grows bare.

'Mony a one for him maks mane,
But nane sall ken what he is gane;
O'er his white banes, when they are bare,
The wind sall blaw for evermair.'

Anonymous

1 moan   2 neck-bone

56 *Terly terlow*

Terly terlow,
Terly terlow,
So merrily the shepherds began to blow!
About the field they piped full right,
Even about the middès of the night;
Adown from Heaven they saw come a light.
    Terly terlow.

Of angels there came a company
With merry songs and melody;
The shepherds anon gan them espy.
    Terly terlow.

'Gloria in excelsis' the angels sang
And said that peace was present among
To every man that to the faith would belong.
  Terly terlow.

The shepherds hied them to Bethlem,
To see that blessed sunnës beam;
And there they found that glorious stream.
  Terly terlow.

Now pray we to that meekë child,
And to his mother that is so mild
The which was never defiled.
  Terly terlow.

Anonymous

57   *To Rosamund*

Madam, ye ben of all beauty shrine
As far as circled is the mappëmound,[1]
For as the crystal glorious ye shine
And like ruby ben your cheekës round.
Therewith ye ben so merry and so jocund,
That at a revel when that I see you dance,
It is an oinëment unto my wound,
Though ye to me ne do no dalliance.

For though I weep of tearës full a tune,[2]
Yet may that woe mine heartë not confound;
Your seemly voice that ye so small outtwine[3]
Maketh my thought in joy and bliss abound.
So courteously I go with lovë bound
That to myself I say in my penance
Sufficeth me to love you, Rosamund,
Though ye to me ne do no dalliance.

Was never pike wallowed in galantine[4]
As I in love am wallowed and y-wound;[5]
For which full oft I of myself divine

Than I am true Tristan the Second.
My love may not refreyed[6] be nor afound;[7]
I brennë ay[8] in an amorous pleasance.
Do what you list, I will your thrall be found,
Though ye to me ne do no dalliance.

Geoffrey Chaucer

1 map of the world   2 barrel   3 utter   4 sauce   5 wound
up   6 cooled down   7 founder   8 burn for ever

58   *Now welcome summer*

Now welcome summer with thy sunnë soft
That hast this winter's weathers overshake
And driven away the longë nightës black.

Saint Valentine that art full high aloft—
Thus singen smallë foulës for thy sake:
Now welcome summer with thy sunnë soft
That hast this winter's weathers overshake.

Well have they causë for to gladden oft,
Since each of them recovered hath his make;[1]
Full blissful may they singen when they wake:
Now welcome summer with thy sunnë soft
That hast this winter's weathers overshake
And driven away the longë nightës black.

Geoffrey Chaucer

1 mate

59   *Merciless beauty*

A Triple Roundel

I. CAPTIVITY

Your eyën two will slay me suddenly,
I may the beauty of them not sustain,
So woundeth it throughout my heartë keen.

And but your word will healen hastily
My heartës woundë, while that it is green.
Your eyën two will slay me suddenly,
I may the beauty of them not sustain.

Upon my truth I say you faithfully,
That ye ben of my life and death the queen;
For with my death the truthë shall be seen.
Your eyën two will slay me suddenly,
I may the beauty of them not sustain,
So woundeth it throughout my heartë keen.

2. REJECTION

So hath your beauty from your heartë chased
Pity, that me ne availeth not to plain;[1]
For Danger[2] holds your mercy in his chain.

Guiltless my death thus have ye me purchased;
I say you sooth, me needeth not to feign;
So hath your beauty from your heartë chased
Pity, that me ne availeth not to plain.

Alas! that nature hath in you compassed
So great beauty, that no man may attain
To mercy, though he starvë[3] for the pain.
So hath your beauty from your heartë chased
Pity, that me ne availeth not to plain;
For Danger holds your mercy in his chain.

3. ESCAPE

Since I from love escapëd am so fat,
I never think to be in his prison lean;
Since I am free, I count him not a bean.

He may answer and sayë this or that;
I do not force,[4] I speak right as I mean.
Since I from love escapëd am so fat,
I never think to be in his prison lean.

Love hath my name ystruck out of his slate,
And he is struck out of my bookës clean
For evermore; there is no other mean.
Since I from love escapëd am so fat,
I never think to be in his prison lean;
Since I am free, I count him not a bean.

Geoffrey Chaucer

1 complain   2 pride   3 die   4 I care not

60   *Truth*

Flee from the press and dwell with soothfastness,[1]
Suffice unto thy good, though it be small;
For hoard[2] hath hate and climbing tickleness,[3]
Press hath envy and weal blent overall;[4]
Savour no more than thee behovë shall;
Work well, thyself that other folk canst rede;[5]
And truthë shall deliver, it is no dread.

Tempest[6] thee not all crooked to redress,
In trust of her[7] that turneth as a ball:
Great rest stands in little business;
And eke beware to spurn against an awl;[8]
Strive not as does the crockë with the well.
Dauntë thyself, that dauntest others' deed;
And truthë shall deliver, it is no dread.

That thee is sent, receive in buxomness,
The wrestling for this world asketh a fall.
She is no home, she is but wilderness:
Forth, pilgrim, forth! forth, beast, out of thy stall!
Know thy country, look up, thank God of all;
Hold the high way, and let thy ghost thee lead,
And truthë shall deliver, it is no dread.

ENVOY

Therefore, thou vache, leave thine old wretchedness
Unto the worldë; leave now to be thrall;

Cry him mercy, that of his high goodness
Made thee of nought, and in especial
Draw unto him and pray in general
For thee, and eke for other, heavenly maid;
And truthë shall deliver, it is no dread.

Geofffrey Chaucer

1 love of truth 2 avarice 3 instability 4 competition
breeds malice and prosperity makes men blind 5 advise
6 distress 7 i.e. Fortune 8 i.e. beware of opposing adver-
sity

61   Gentilesse

The firstë stock, father of gentilesse—
What man that claimeth gentle for to be,
Must follow his trace, and all his wittës dress
Virtue to suë[1] and vicës for to flee.
For unto virtue longeth dignity,
And not the reverse, safely dare I deem,
All were he mitre, crown or diadem.

This firstë stock was full of righteousness,
True of his word, sober, piteous and free.
Clean of his ghost and lovëd business,
Against the vice of sloth in honesty:
And, but his heir love virtue as did he,
He is not gentil, though he richë seem,
All were he mitre, crown or diadem.

Vicë may well be heir to old richesse;
But there may no man, as men wel may see,
Bequeath his heir his virtuous noblesse
That is appropred unto no degree,
But to the firstë Father in majesty,
That maketh him his heir, that can him queme,[2]
All were he mitre, crown or diadem.

Geoffrey Chaucer

1 pursue 2 please

BALADE

Sometime this world was so steadfast and stable
That mannës word was obligation,
And now it is so false and deceivable
That word and deed, as in conclusion,
Ben nothing like, for turnëd up so down
Is all this world for mead and wilfulness,
That all is lost for lack of steadfastness.

What maketh this world to be so variable
But lust that folk have in dissension?
Among us now a man is held unable
But—if he can by some collusion
Do his neighbour wrong or oppression.
What causeth this but wilful wretchedness,
That all is lost for lack of steadfastness?

Truth is put down, reason is holden fable;
Virtue hath now no domination,
Pity exiled, no man is merciable.
Through covetise is blent[1] discretion;
The world hath made a permutation
From right to wrong, from truth to fickleness,
That all is lost for lack of steadfastness.

LENVOY TO KING RICHARD

O Prince, desirë to be honourable,
Cherish thy folk and hate extortion!
Suffer no thing that may be reprovable
To thine estate, done in thy region.
Show forth thy sword of castigation,
Dread God, do law, love truth and worthiness,
And wed thy folk again to steadfastness.

Geoffrey Chaucer

[1] blinded

63 Hide, Absolon

Hide, Absolon, thy giltë tresses clear;
Esther, lay thou thy meekness all adown;
Hide, Jonathas, all thy friendly manner;
Penelope and Marcia Catoun,
Make of your wifehood no comparison;
Hide ye your beauties, Isoud and Elaine;
My lady cometh, that all this may distain.[1]

Thy fairë body, let it not appear,
Lavine; and thou, Lucrece of Romë town,
And Polixene that boughten love so dear,
And Cleopatre with all thy passion,
Hide ye your troth of love and your renown;
And thou, Thisbe, that hast of love such pain;
My lady cometh, that all this may distain.

Hero, Dido, Laodamia all y-fere,[2]
And Phyllis, hanging for thy Demophon,
And Canacë, espiëd by thy cheer,
Ysiphile, betraysëd with Jason,
Maketh of your troth neither boast nor soun;
Nor Ypermestre or Adriane, ye twain;
My lady cometh that all this may distain.

Geoffrey Chaucer

1 stain, bedim   2 together

64 Though ye suppose

Though ye suppose all jeopardies are past,
    And all is done ye looked for before,
Ware yet, I rede you, of Fortune's double cast,
    For one false point she is wont to keep in store,
    And under the fell oft festered is the sore:
That when ye think all danger for to pass
Ware of the lizard lieth lurking in the grass.

John Skelton

By Saint Mary, my lady,
Your mammy and your daddy
Brought forth a goodly baby.

My maiden Isabel,
Reflaring rosabel,[1]
The fragrant camamel,

The ruddy rosary,
The sovereign rosemary,
The pretty strawberry,

The columbine, the nept,[2]
The jeloffer[3] well set,
The proper violet;

Ennewèd[4] your colour
Is like the daisy flower
After the April shower.

Star of the morrow grey,
The blossom on the spray,
The freshest flower of May,

Maidenly demure,
Of womanhood the lure;
Wherefore I you assure,

It were an heavenly health,
It were an endless wealth,
A life for God himself,

To hear this nightingale
Among the birdës smale
Warbling in the vale,

'Dug, dug! jug, jug!
Good year and good luck!'
With 'Chuck, chuck, chuck, chuck!'

John Skelton

1 scented rose   2 catmint   3 pink   4 tinted

Merry Margaret,
As midsummer flower,
Gentle as falcon
Or hawk of the tower;
With solace and gladness,
Much mirth and no madness,
All good and no badness;
So joyously,
So maidenly,
So womanly
Her demeaning,
In every thing
Far, far passing
That I can indite,
Or suffice to write,
Of Merry Margaret,
As midsummer flower,
Gentle as falcon
Or hawk of the tower;
As patient and still
And as full of good will
As fair Isiphil,
Coliander,
Sweet pomander,
Good Cassander;
Stedfast of thought,
Well made, well wrought,
Far may be sought,
Erst that ye can find
So courteous, so kind,
As Merry Margaret
This midsummer flower,
Gentle as falcon
Or hawk of the tower.

John Skelton

With margerain gentle,
The flower of goodlihead,
Embroidered the mantle is
Of your maidenhead.
Plainly I cannot glose;
Ye be, as I divine,
The pretty primërose,
The goodly columbine.
With margerain gentle,
The flower of goodlihead,
Embroidered the mantle is
Of your maidenhead.
Benign, courteous and meek,
With words well devised;
In you who list to seek
Be virtues well comprised.
With margerain gentle,
The flower of goodlihead,
Embroidered the mantle is
Of your maidenhead.

John Skelton

68   *Woefully arrayed*

Woefully arrayed,
      My blood, man,
      For thee ran,
   It may not be nayed:
      My body blue and wan,
      Woefully arrayed.

Behold me, I pray thee, with thy whole reason,
And be not so hard-hearted, and for this encheason,[1]
Sith I for thy soul sake was slain in good season,
Beguiled and betrayed by Judas' false treason:
   Unkindly entreated,
   With sharp cord sore fretted,
   The Jewes me threated:

They mowéd[2], they grinned, they scornéd me,
Condemned to death, as thou may'st see,
    Woefully arrayed.

Thus naked am I nailéd, I man, for thy sake!
I love thee, then love me; why sleepest thou? awake!
Remember my tender heart-root for thee brake,
With painës my veinës constrained to crake:[3]
    Thus tuggéd to and fro,
    Thus wrappéd all in woe,
    Whereas never man was so,
Entreated thus in most cruel wise,
Was like a lamb offered in sacrifice,
    Woefully arrayed.

Of sharp thorn I have worn a crown on my head,
So painéd, so strainéd, so rueful, so red,
Thus bobbéd,[4] thus robbéd, thus for thy love dead,
Unfeignéd I deignéd my blood for to shed:
    My feet and handes sore
    The sturdy nailes bore:
    What might I suffer more
Than I have done, O man, for thee?
Come when thou list, welcome to me,
    Woefully arrayed.

Of record thy good Lord I have been and shall be:
I am thine, thou art mine, my brother I call thee.
Thee love I entirely—see what is bafall'n me!
Sore beating, sore threating, to make thee, man, all free:
    Why art thou unkind?
    Why has not me in mind?
    Come yet and thou shalt find
Mine endléss mercie and grace—
See how a spear my heart did race,[5]
    Woefully arrayed.

Dear brother, no other thing I of thee desire
But give me thine heart free to reward mine hire:

I wrought thee, I bought thee from eternal fire:
I pray thee array thee toward my high empire
  Above the orient
  Whereof I am regent,
  Lord God omnipotent,
With me to reign in endless wealth:
Remember, man, thy soul's health.

    Woefully arrayed,
     My blood, man,
     For thee ran,
    It may not be nayed:
     My body blue and wan,
    Woefully arrayed.

John Skelton

1 cause   2 mocked   3 crack   4 scourged   5 wound

69   *To his wife*

'Petually
Constrained am I
With weeping eye
  To mourn and 'plain,

That we so nigh
Of progeny[1]
So suddenly
  Should part in twain.

When ye are gone
Come forth is none
But all alone
  Endure must I.

With grievly groan
Making my moan,
As it were one
  That should needs die.

What chance suddein
So doth me stay'n
In every way'n
　That for no thing

I cannot lay'n,
Nor yet refrain
Mine eyes twain
　From sore weeping!

John Skelton

1 so soon to have a child

70　*Amends to the tailors and soutars*[1]

Betwixt twelve hours and eleven
I dreamed an angel came from Heaven
With pleasant stevin[2] saying on high,
'Tailors and soutars, blest be ye.'

In Heaven high ordained is your place
Above all saints in great solace,
Next God greatest in dignity:
Tailors and soutars, blest be ye.

The cause to you is not unkenned.
That God mismakes ye do amend[3]
By craft and great agility:
Tailors and soutars, blest be ye.

Soutars, with shoon well made and meet
Ye mend the faults of ill-made feet.
Wherefore to Heaven your souls will flee:
Tailors and soutars, blest be ye.

And ye, tailors, with well made clothes
Can mend the worst made man that goes
And make him seemly for to see:
Tailors and soutars, blest be ye.

Though God make a misfashioned swain,
Ye can him all shape new again
And fashion him better by such three:[4]
Tailors and soutars, blest be ye.

Though a man have a broken back,
Have he a good tailor, what reck?[5]
That can it cover with craftes slee:[6]
Tailors and soutars, blest be ye.

Of God great kindness may ye claim
That help his people from crook and lame,
Supporting faultes with your supply:
Tailors and soutars, blest be ye.

In earth ye kith[7] such miracles here;
In Heaven ye shall be saints full clear,
Though ye be knaves in this country:
Tailors and soutars, blest be ye.

William Dunbar

1 shoemakers   2 voice   3 you correct the errors made by
God   4 i.e. by three times   5 what does it matter?   6 sly
7 cause

71   *Lament for the makers*

WHEN HE WAS SICK

I that in health was and gladness
Am troublit now with great sickness
And feblit[1] with informity:
   Timor mortis conturbat me.[2]

Our pleasance here is all vainglory,
This false world is but transitory,
The flesh is bruckle[3], the fiend is slee:[4]
   Timor mortis conturbat me.

The state of man does change and vary,
Now sound, now sick, now blithe, now sary,[5]

Now dansand merry, now like to die:
   Timor mortis conturbat me.

No state in earth here standis sicker;[6]
As with the wind wavis the wicker,[7]
So wannis[8] the worlds vanity:
   Timor mortis conturbat me.

Unto the death goes all estates,
Princes, prelates, and potestates,
Baith rich and poor of all degree:
   Timor mortis conturbat me.

He takis the knightes into the field
Enarmit[9] under helm and shield;
Victor he is at all melee:[10]
   Timor mortis conturbat me.

That strong unmerciful tyrand
Takis on the mothers breast soukand[11]
The babe full of benignity:
   Timor mortis conturbat me.

He takis the campion[12] in the stour,[13]
The captain closit in the tower,
The lady in bower full of beauty:
   Timor mortis conturbat me.

He sparis no lord for his puissance,[14]
Nor clerk for his intelligence;
His awful stroke may no man flee:
   Timor mortis conturbat me.

Art magicians and astrologgis,
Rhethoris, loggicians and theologgis,
Them helps no conclusions slee:
   Timor mortis conturbat me.

In medicine the most practicianis,
Leechis, surgeons and physicianis,
Themself fra death may not supplee,[15]
    Timor mortis conturbat me.

I see that makers among the lave[16]
Plays here their pagents, syne[17] goes to grave;
Sparit is nocht their facultee:
    Timor mortis conturbat me.

He has done piteously devour
The noble Chaucer of makers flower,
The Monk of Bury, and Gower all three:
    Timor mortis conturbat me.

The good Sir Hugh of Iglintoun,
Ettric, Herriot, and Wintoun,
He has taen out of this country:
    Timor mortis conturbat me.

That scorpios fell has done infeck
Maister John Clerk, and James Affleck,
Fra ballat making and tragedie:
    Timor mortis conturbat me.

Holland and Barbour he has berevit;
Alas! that he not with us levit
Sir Mungo Lockart of the Lee:
    Timor mortis conturbat me.

Clerk of Tranent eke he has tane,
That made the anteris[18] of Gawaine;
Sir Gilbert Hay endit has he:
    Timor mortis conturbat me.

He has Blind Harry and Sandy Traill
Slain with his schour of mortal hail,
Which Patrick Johnstoun might nocht flee:
    Timor mortis conturbat me.

He has reft Merseir his endite,[19]
That did in love so lively write,
So short, so quick, of sentence high:
   Timor mortis conturbat me.

He has tane Rowll of Aberdeen,
And gentil Rowll of Corstorphine;
Two better fellows did no man see:
   Timor mortis conturbat me.

In Dunfermline he has tane Broun
With Maister Robert Henrysoun;
Sir John the Ross enbrast has he:
   Timor mortis conturbat me.

And he has now tane, last of a',
Good gentil Stobo and Quintin Shaw,
Of whom all wichtis has pitie:
   Timor mortis conturbat me.

Good Maister Walter Kennedy
In point of death lies verily;
Great ruth it were that so should be:
   Timor mortis conturbat me.

Since he has all my brether tane,
He will nocht let me live alane;
Of force I must his next prey be:
   Timor mortis conturbat me.

Since for the death remeid is none,
Best is that we for death dispone,
After our death that live may we:
   Timor mortis conturbat me.

                        William Dunbar

1 enfeebled   2 the fear of death distresses me   3 frail   4 sly
5 sorry   6 secure   7 willow   8 wanes   9 armed   10 battle
11 sucking   12 champion   13 battle   14 power   15 save
16 rest   17 then   18 adventures   19 power of composition

72 An Epitaph

O mortal folk, you may behold and see
   How I lie here, sometime a mighty knight:
The end of joy and all prosperity
   Is death at last, thorough his course and might:
     For though the day be never so long
     At last the bells ringeth to evensong.

Stephen Hawes

73 Love continual

If love, for love of long time had,
   May join with joy, and care hence cast,
Then may remembrance make me glad.
   Days, weeks, and years, in all time past
My Love hath loved me so lovingly,
And I will love her as truly.

And as we twain have loved and do,
   So be we fixed to love even still;
The law of love hath made us two
   To work two willës in one will:
My Love will love me so lovingly,
And I will love her as truly.

Ye lovers all in present place
   That long for love continual,
I wish to you like pleasant case
   As ye perceive by me doth fall,
And yours to love as lovingly.

John Heywood

Whoso list to hunt, I know where is an hind,
  But as for me, alas, I may no more:
  The vain travail hath wearied me so sore.
I am of them that farthest cometh behind;
Yet may I by no means my wearied mind
  Draw from the deer: but as she fleeth afore,
Fainting I follow. I leave off therefore,
  Since in a net I seek to hold the wind.
Who list her hunt, I put him out of doubt,
  As well as I may spend his time in vain:
  And, graven with diamonds, in letters plain
There is written her fair neck round about:
  Noli me tangere,[1] for Caesar's I am;
  And wild for to hold, though I seem tame.

                           Sir Thomas Wyatt

1 Touch me not

75 *Madam, withouten many words*

Madam, withouten many words
  Once I am sure ye will or no;
And if you will, then leave your bawds,[1]
  And use your wit and show it so.

And with a beck ye shall me call,
  And if of one that burneth alway
Ye have any pity at all,
  Answer him fair with Yea or Nay.

If it be Yea, I shall be fain;
  If it be Nay, friends as before;
Ye shall another man obtain,
  And I mine own and yours no more.

                           Sir Thomas Wyatt

1 jests

They flee from me that sometime did me seek
  With naked foot stalking in my chamber.
I have seen them gentle, tame and meek
    That now are wild and do not remember
    That sometime they put themself in danger
To take bread at my hand; and now they range
Busily seeking with a continual change.

Thankèd be fortune it hath been otherwise
    Twenty times better: but once in special,
In thin array after a pleasant guise,
    When her loose gown from her shoulders did fall,
    And she me caught in her arms long and small;
Therewithal sweetly did me kiss,
And softly said, 'Dear heart, how like you this?'

It was no dream: I lay broad waking.
    But all is turnèd through my gentleness
Into a strange fashion of forsaking;
    And I have leave to go of her goodness,
    And she also to use new-fangledness.
But since that I so kindly am served,
I would fain know what she hath deserved.

                                        Sir Thomas Wyatt

77   *There was never nothing more me pained*

There was never nothing more me pained,
    Nor nothing more me moved,
As when my sweetheart her complained
    That ever she me loved.
        Alas the while!

With piteous look she said and sighed:
    'Alas, what aileth me

To love and set my wealth so light
    On him that loveth not me?
        Alas the while!

'Was I not well void of all pain,
    When that nothing me grieved?
And now with sorrows I must complain,
    And cannot be relieved.
        Alas the while!

'My restful nights and joyful days
    Since I began to love
Be take from me; all thing decays,
    Yet can I not remove.
        Alas the while!'

She wept and wrung her hands withal,
    The tears fell in my neck;
She turned her face and let it fall;
    Scarcely therewith could speak.
        Alas the while!

Her pains tormented me so sore
    That comfort had I none,
But cursed my fortune more and more
    To see her sob and groan:
        Alas the while!

Sir Thomas Wyatt

78   *Who hath heard of such cruelty before?*

Who hath heard of such cruelty before?
    That when my plaint remembered her my woe
That caused it, she, cruel more and more,
    Wishèd each stitch, as she did sit and sew,
Had pricked mine heart, for to increase my sore;
    And, as I think, she thought it had been so:
For as she thought 'This is his heart indeed',
She prickèd hard and made herself to bleed.

Sir Thomas Wyatt

79 *The wandering gadling*

The wandering gadling[1] in the summer tide,
   That finds the adder with his reckless foot,
Starts not dismayed so suddenly aside
   As jealous despite did, though there were no boot,[2]
When that he saw me sitting by her side,
   That of my health is very crop and root.
It pleased me then to have so fair a grace
   To sting that heart that would have my place.

Sir Thomas Wyatt

1 boy   2 remedy

80 *My lute awake!*

My lute awake! perform the last
Labour that thou and I shall waste,
   And end that I have now begun;
For when this song is sung and past,
   My lute be still, for I have done.

As to be heard where ear is none,
As lead to grave in marble stone,
   My song may pierce her heart as soon;
Should we then sigh, or sing, or moan?
   No, no, my lute, for I have done.

The rocks do not so cruelly
Repulse the waves continually,
   As she my suit and affection;
So that I am past remedy,
   Whereby my lute and I have done.

Proud of the spoil that thou hast got
Of simple hearts thorough love's shot,
   By whom, unkind, thou hast them won,
Think not he hath his bow forgot
   Although my lute and I have done.

Vengeance shall fall on thy disdain,
That makest but game on earnest pain;
  Think not alone under the sun
Unquit to cause thy lover's plain,
  Although my lute and I have done.

Perchance thee lie withered and old,
The winter nights that are so cold,
  Plaining in vain under the moon;
Thy wishes then dare not be told.
  Care then who list, for I have done.

And then may chance thee to repent
The time that thou has lost and spent
  To cause thy lovers sigh and swoon;
Then shalt thou know beauty but lent,
  And wish and want as I have done.

Now cease my lute, this is the last
Labour that thou and I shall waste,
  And ended is that we begun;
Now is this song both sung and past;
  My lute be still, for I have done.

Sir Thomas Wyatt

81   *Marvel no more*

Marvel no more although
  The songs I sing do moan,
For other life than woe
  I never provèd none.
And in my heart also
  Is graven with letters deep
A thousand sighs and mo,
  A flood of tears to weep.

How may a man in smart
    Find matter to rejoice?
How may a mourning heart
    Set forth a pleasant voice?
Play who that can that part:
    Needs must in me appear
How fortune overthwart
    Doth cause my mourning cheer.

Perdy, there is no man
    If he never saw sight
That perfectly tell can
    The nature of the light.
Alas, how should I then,
    That never tasted but sour,
But do as I began,
    Continually to lour?

But yet perchance some chance
    May chance to change my tune:
And when such chance doth chance,
    Then shall I thank fortune.
And if I have such chance,
    Perchance ere it be long
For such a pleasant chance
    To sing some pleasant song.

                              Sir Thomas Wyatt

82   *The enemy of life*

The enemy of life, decayer of all kind,
    That with his cold weathers away the green,
This other night me in my bed did find,
    And offered me to rid my fever clean;
And I did grant, so did despair me blind.
    He drew his bow with arrow sharp and keen,
And struck the place where love had hit before,
And drove the first dart deeper more and more.

                              Sir Thomas Wyatt

Once as methought fortune me kissed
   And bade me ask what I thought best;
And I should have it as me list,
   Therewith to set my heart in rest.

I askèd nought but my dear heart
   To have for ever more mine own:
Then at an end were all my smart,
   Then should I need no more to moan.

Yet for all that a stormy blast
   Had overturned this goodly day;
And fortune seemèd at the last
   That to her promise she said nay.

But like as one out of despair
   To sudden hope revivèd I;
Now fortune showest herself so fair
   That I content me wonderly.

My most desire my hand may reach,
   My will is alway at my hand;
Me need not long for to beseech
   Her that hath power me to command.

What earthly thing more can I crave?
   What would I wish more at my will?
No thing on earth more would I have,
   Save that I have to have it still.

For fortune hath kept her promise
   In granting me my most desire:
Of my suffrance I have redress,
   And I content me with my hire.

                        Sir Thomas Wyatt

84 *Nature, that gave the bee*

Nature, that gave the bee so feat a grace
　　To find honey of so wondrous fashion,
Hath taught the spider out of the same place
　　To fetch poison by strange alteration.
Though this be strange, it is a stranger case
　　With one kiss by secret operation
Both these at once in those your lips to find,
In change whereof I leave my heart behind.

Sir Thomas Wyatt

85 *And wilt thou leave me thus?*

And wilt thou leave me thus?
Say nay, say nay, for shame,
To save thee from the blame
Of all my grief and grame;[1]
And wilt thou leave me thus?
　　Say nay, say nay!

And wilt thou leave me thus,
That hath loved thee so long,
In wealth and woe among?
And is thy heart so strong
As for to leave me thus?
　　Say nay, say nay!

And wilt thou leave me thus,
That hath given thee my heart,
Never for to depart,
Neither for pain nor smart;
And wilt thou leave me thus?
　　Say nay, say nay!

And wilt thou leave me thus
And have no more pity
Of him that loveth thee?

Alas thy cruelty!
And wilt thou leave me thus?
    Say nay, say nay!

Sir Thomas Wyatt

1 sorrow

86   *Forget not yet*

Forget not yet the tried intent
Of such a truth as I have meant,
My great travail so gladly spent
    Forget not yet.

Forget not yet when first began
The weary life ye know since when,
The suit, the service none tell can,
    Forget not yet.

Forget not yet the great assays,
The cruel wrong, the scornful ways,
The painful patience in denays,[1]
    Forget not yet.

Forget not yet, forget not this,
How long ago hath been and is
The mind that never meant amiss,
    Forget not yet.

Forget not yet thine own approved,
The which so long hath thee so loved,
Whose steadfast faith yet never moved,
    Forget not this.

Sir Thomas Wyatt

1 denials

I am as I am and so will I be,
But how that I am none knoweth truly,
Be it evil, be it well, be I bound, be I free,
I am as I am and so will I be.

I lead my life indifferently,
I mean no thing but honestly,
And though folks judge full diversely,
I am as I am and so will I die.

I do not rejoice nor yet complain,
Both mirth and sadness I do refrain,
And use the mean since folks will feign,
Yet I am as I am, be it pleasure or pain.

Divers do judge as they do trow,
Some of pleasure and some of woe,
Yet for all that no thing they know,
But I am as I am wheresoever I go.

But since judgers do thus decay,
Let every man his judgement say;
I will it take in sport and play,
For I am as I am whosoever say nay.

Who judgeth well, well God him send;
Who judgeth evil, God them amend;
To judge the best therefore intend,
For I am as I am and so will I end.

Yet some there be that take delight
To judge folks' thought for envy and spite,
But whether they judge me wrong or right,
I am as I am and so do I right.

Praying you all that this do read
To trust it as you do your creed,
And not to think I change my wede,[1]
For I am as I am however I speed.

But how that is I leave to you;
Judge as ye list false or true;
Ye know no more than afore ye knew;
Yet I am as I am, whatever ensue.

And from this mind I will not flee;
But to you all that misjudge me
I do protest as ye may see
That I am as I am and so will I be.

Sir Thomas Wyatt

1 clothing

88 *He is not dead*

He is not dead that sometime hath a fall.
    The sun returneth that was under the cloud;
And when fortune hath spit out all her gall,
    I trust good luck to me shall be allowed.
For I have seen a ship into haven fall
    After the storm hath broke both mast and shroud;
And eke the willow that stoppeth with the wind
Doth rise again, and greater wood doth bind.

Sir Thomas Wyatt

89 *My galley*

My galley, chargèd with forgetfulness,
    Thorough sharp seas in winter nights doth pass
    'Tween rock and rock; and eke mine enemy, alas!
That is my Lord, steereth with cruelness;
And every oar a thought in readiness,
    As though that death were light in such a case.
    And endless wind doth tear the sail apace
Of forcèd sights, and trusty fearfulness;

A rain of tears, a cloud of dark disdain,
  Hath done the wearèd cords great hinderance,
  Wreathed with error and eke with ignorance.
The stars be hid that led me to this pain.
  Drownèd is reason that should me comfort,
  And I remain despairing of the port.

Sir Thomas Wyatt

90 *You that in love find luck*

You that in love find luck and abundance,
  And live in lust and joyful jollity,
  Arise, for shame, do away your sluggardy;
  Arise, I say, do May some observance!
Let me in bed lie dreaming in mischance;
  Let me remember the haps most unhappy
  That me betide in May most commonly,
As one whom love list little to advance.
  Sepham said true that my nativity
Mischanced was with the ruler of the May:
  He guessed, I prove, of that the verity.
In May my wealth and eke my life, I say,
  Have stood so oft in such perplexity:
  Rejoice! Let me dream of your felicity.

Sir Thomas Wyatt

91 *Tagus, farewell*

Tagus, farewell, that westward with thy streams
  Turns up the grains of gold already tried:
With spur and sail for I go seek the Thames,
  Gainward the sun that showeth her wealthy pride;
And to the town which Brutus sought by dreams
  Like bended moon doth lend her lusty side.
My king, my country alone for whom I live,
Of mighty love the wings for this me give.

Sir Thomas Wyatt

My pen, take pain a little space
To follow that which doth me chase,
  And hath in hold my heart so sore;
But when thou hast this brought to pass,
  My pen, I prithee, write no more.

 Remember, oft thou hast me eased,
And all my pain full well appeased,
  But now I know, unknown before,
For where I trust I am deceived:
  And yet, my pen, thou canst no more.

A time thou hadst as other have
To write which way my hope to crave;
  That time is past: withdraw, therefore.
Since we do lose that other save,
  As good leave off and write no more.

In worth to use another way,
Not as we would but as we may;
  For once my loss is past restore,
And my desire is my decay,
  My pen, yet write a little more.

To love in vain whoever shall
Of worldly pain it passeth all.
  As in like case I find. Wherefore
To hold so fast and yet to fall?
  Alas, my pen, now write no more.

Since thou hast taken pain this space
To follow that which doth me chase,
  And hath in hold my heart so sore,
Now hast thou brought my mind to pass:
  My pen, I prithee, write no more.

Sir Thomas Wyatt

It is possible
That so high debate,
So sharp, so sore, and of such rate,
Should end so soon as was begun so late?
Is it possible?

Is it possible
So cruel intent,
So hasty heat and so soon spent,
From love to hate, and thence for to relent?
Is it possible?

Is it possible
That any may find
Within one heart so diverse kind,
To change or turn as weather and wind?
Is it possible?

Is it possible
To spy it in any eye
That turns as oft as chance in die?
The troth whereof can any try?
Is it possible?

Is it possible
For to turn so oft,
To bring that lowest that was most aloft,
And to fall highest yet to light soft:
Is it possible?

All is possible,
Whoso list believe;
Trust therefore first, and after preve:
As men wed ladies by licence and leave
All is possible.

Sir Thomas Wyatt

In faith methinks it is no right
　To hate me thus for loving thee;
So fair a face, so full of spite,
　Who would have thought such cruelty?
　But since there is no remedy
That by no means ye can me love,
I shall you leave and other prove.

For if I have for my good will
　No reward else but cruelty,
In faith thereof I can no skill
　Since that I loved ye honestly;
　But take heed I will till I die
Or that I love so well again,
Since women use so much to feign.

Sir Thomas Wyatt

95   Throughout the world

Throughout the world, if it were sought,
Fair words enough a man shall find:
They be good cheap, they cost right nought,
Their substance is but only wind:
　But well to say and so to mean,
　That sweet accord is seldom seen.

Sir Thomas Wyatt

96   You and I and Amyas

You and I and Amyas,
Amyas and you and I,
To the green wood must we go, alas!
You and I, my life, and Amyas.

The knight knocked at the castle gate;
The lady marvelled who was thereat.

To call the porter he would not blin;[1]
The lady said he should not come in.

The portress was a lady bright;
Strangeness that lady hight.

She askèd him what was his name;
He said, 'Desire, your man, Madame.'

She said, 'Desire, what do ye here?'
He said, 'Madame, as your prisoner.'

He was counselled to brief a bill,
And show my lady his own will.

'Kindness,' said she, 'would it bear,
And Pity,' said she, 'would be there.'

Thus how they did we cannot say;
We left them there and went our way.

William Cornish

1 cease

97 *Pleasure it is*

    Pleasure it is
To hear, iwis,
The birdës sing.
The deer in the dale,
The sheep in the vale,
The corn springing—
God's purveyance
For sustenance
It is for man.

Then we always
To give him praise,
And thank him then,
And thank him then.

William Cornish

98   *Set me whereas the sun*

Set me whereas the sun doth parch the green,
   Or where his beams may not dissolve the ice,
In temperate heat where he is felt and seen,
   With proud people, in presence sad and wise;
Set me in base or yet in high degree,
   In the long night or in the shortest day,
In clear weather or where mists thickest be,
   In lofty youth or when my hairs be grey;
Set me in earth, in heaven, or yet in hell,
   In hill, in dale, or in the foaming flood,
Thrall or at large, alive whereso I dwell,
   Sick or in health, in ill fame or in good;
     Yours will I be, and with that only thought
     Comfort myself when that my hap is nought.

Henry Howard, Earl of Surrey

99   *Spring*

The softë season, that bud and bloom forth brings,
   With green hath clad the hill and eke the vale;
The nightingale with feathers new she sings;
   The turtle to her mate hath told her tale.
Summer is come, for every spray now springs;
   The hart hath hung his old head on the pale;
The buck in break his winter coat he flings;
   The fishes fleet with new repairèd scale.
The adder all her slough away she slings;
   The swift swallow pursueth the fliës small;

The busy bee her honey now she mings;[1]
   Winter is worn that was the flowers' bale.
And thus I see among these pleasant things
Each care decays, and yet my sorrow springs.

Henry Howard, Earl of Surrey

1 mixes

100   *An epitaph on Clere*

Norfolk spring thee, Lambeth holds thee dead;
Clere, of the Count of Cleremont, thou hight;
Within the womb of Ormond's race thou bred,
And saw'st thy cousin crowned in thy sight.
Shelton for love, Surrey for lord thou chase;[1]
(Aye me! whilst life did last that league was tender)
Tracing whose steps thou sawest Kelsal blaze,
Landrecy burnt, and battered Boulogne render.
At Montreuil gates, hopeless of all recure,
Thine Earl, half dead, gave in thy hand his will;
Which cause did thee this pining death procure,
Ere summers four times seven thou couldst fulfill.
   Ah! Clere! if love had booted, care, or cost,
   Heaven had not won nor earth so timely lost.

Henry Howard, Earl of Surrey

1 chose

101   *On the death of Sir Thomas Wyatt*

Wyatt resteth here that quick could never rest,
   Whose heavenly gifts increasèd by disdain
And virtue sank the deeper in his breast
   Such profit he by envy could obtain.

A head where wisdom mysteries did frame,
   Whose hammers beat still in that lively brain,
As on a stithe where that some work of fame
   Was daily wrought, to turn to Britain's gain.

A visage stern and mild, where both did grow
    Vice to contemn, in virtue to rejoice;
Amid great storms whom grace assurèd so
    To live upright, and smile at fortune's choice.

A hand that taught what might be said in rhyme;
    That reft Chaucer the glory of his wit;
A mark, the which (unperfected for time)
    Some may approach, but never none shall hit.

A tongue that served in foreign realms his king;
    Whose courteous talk to virtue did inflame
Each noble heart; a worthy guide to bring
    Our English youth by travail unto fame.

An eye whose judgement none affect could blind,
    Friends to allure and foes to reconcile,
Whose piercing look did represent a mind
    With virtue fraught reposèd void of guile.

A heart where dread was never so imprest
    To hide the thought that might the truth advance;
In neither fortune loft,[1] nor yet represt
    To swell in wealth or yield unto mischance.

A valiant corpse, where force and beauty met,
    Happy alas, too happy but for foes,
Lived, and ran the race that nature set;
    Of manhood's shape where she the mould did lose.

But to the heavens that simple soul is fled,
    Which left, with such as covert Christ to know,
Witness of faith that never could be dead;
    Sent for our health, but not receivèd so.

Thus for our guilt this jewel have we lost;
The earth his bones, the heavens possess his ghost.

Henry Howard, Earl of Surrey

1 praise

In going to my naked bed as one that would have slept,
I heard a wife sing to her child, that long before had wept;
She sighèd sore and sang full sore, to bring the babe to
  rest,
That would not rest but crièd still, in sucking at her
  breast.
She was full weary of her watch, and grievèd with her
  child,
She rockèd it and ratèd it until on her it smiled.
Then did she say, Now have I found the proverb true to
  prove,
The falling out of faithful friends renewing is of love.

Then took I paper, pen, and ink, this proverb for to
  write,
In register for to remain of such a worthy wight:
As she proceeded thus in song unto her little brat,
Much matter uttered she of weight, in place whereas she
  sat:
And provèd plain there was no beast, nor creature bear-
  ing life,
Could well be known to live in love without discord
  and strife:
Then kissèd she her little babe and sware by God above,
The falling out of faithful friends renewing is of love.

She said that neither king nor prince nor lord could live
  aright,
Until their puissance they did prove, their manhood and
  their might.
When manhood shall be matchèd so that fear can take
  no place,
Then weary works make warriors each other to embrace,
And left their force that failèd them, which did consume
  the rout,
That might before have lived their time, their strength
  and nature out:

Then did she sing as one that thought no man could her
    reprove,
The falling out of faithful friends renewing is of love.

She said she saw no fish nor fowl, nor beast within her
    haunt,
That met a stranger in their kind, but could give it a
    taunt:
Since flesh might not endure, but rest must wrath
    succeed,
And force the fight to fall to play in pasture where they
    feed,
So noble nature can well end the work she hath begun,
And bridle well that will not cease her tragedy in some:
Thus in song she oft rehearsed, as did her well behove,
The falling out of faithful friends renewing is of love.

I marvel much pardy (quoth she) for to behold the rout,
To see man, woman boy and beast, to toss the world
    about:
Some kneel, some crouch, some beck, some check, and
    some can smoothly smile,
And some embrace others in arms and there think many
    a wile,
Some stand aloof at cap and knee, some humble and
    some stout,
Yet are they never friends in deed until they once fall
    out:
Thus ended she her song and said, before she did
    remove,
The falling out of faithful friends renewing is of love.

Richard Edwards

103   *Lines before execution*

My prime of youth is but a frost of cares;
My feast of joy is but a dish of pain;
My crop of corn is but a field of tares;

And all my good is but vain hope of gain:
    The day is fled, and yet I saw no sun;
    And now I live, and now my life is done!

The spring is past, and yet it hath not sprung;
The fruit is dead, and yet the leaves are green;
My youth is gone, and yet I am but young;
I saw the world, and yet I was not seen:
    My thread is cut, and yet it is not spun;
    And now I live, and now my life is done!

I sought my death, and found it in my womb;
I looked for life, and saw it was a shade;
I trod the earth, and knew it was my tomb;
And now I die, and now I am but made:
    The glass is full, and now my glass is run;
    And now I live, and now my life is done!

Chidiock Tychborn

BOOK TWO

The Elizabethans to the Restoration

INTRODUCTION

The period covered by Book Two is the hundred years having as its central point the death of Queen Elizabeth I in 1603. It is the richest in lyric poetry in the whole course of English literature. Although the period is one of great names—Spenser, Ralegh, Shakespeare, Donne, Jonson, Marvell—it is one in which the minor poets also were brilliant and talented. To read the anonymous poems alone in this section is to be aware of the richness, variety and subtlety of the lyric art. The age of Elizabeth I was an age of song. Love is the most universal theme, but religion, humour and sheer *joie de vivre* all play their part. During Elizabeth's reign the madrigal—that form of chamber music in which extreme artificiality is uniquely combined with extreme spontaneity—was brought from Italy by the pioneer, Nicholas Yonge. We may never know for certain whether the lutenist composers made up their own lyrics or employed anonymous poets. Songs are also a part of Elizabethan drama, and some of the loveliest short poems in the language, notably those of Shakespeare, are embedded in stage plays.

The sonnet, introduced from Italy, as we have seen, by Sir Thomas Wyatt, became all the rage, and every courtier, every aspiring lover, was expected to be able to compose a woeful sonnet to his mistress. The most famous sonnet-sequences were written by Sir Philip Sidney, Edmund Spenser, Michael Drayton, Samuel Daniel, and—the greatest of all—William Shakespeare.

John Donne, one of the most intense and original of love poets, shows in his work the change that took place in the spirit of the age between the reigns of Elizabeth I and James I.

There is little in his love poems of the care-free spirit of other poets of his youthful days; there is something tortured and restless, both in his language and in his thought, which is intensified in the religious poetry of his later years. He was the founder of what has been called the 'Metaphysical' school of poets, of whom Herbert, Vaughan and Crashaw were the most notable members. Meanwhile, Ben Jonson took over the tradition of smooth and mellifluous verse associated with the name of Spenser. His followers, Herrick and the Cavaliers, continued this tradition into the troubled times of the Stuart kings. Andrew Marvell, writing at the time when the Civil War gave way to the Cromwellian interregnum, combined in his passionate, yet witty, lyrics both traditions, the Cavalier and the Metaphysical.

With Marvell the Renaissance tradition, as formed under the early Tudors and brought to its triumphant fulfilment under the last Tudor and the first Stuart, died. When England recovered from the political and religious upheaval of the mid-seventeenth century, and the reaction against Puritan repression had set in, her poetry had lost something for ever. History does not stand still, and the wounds left by the Civil War were slow to heal. Of course the brief account given here is far tidier than the full story would be. But when you come to read Book Three, which begins with the restoration of the monarchy in 1660, you will notice the change. In Book Two, however, you have the record in lyric poetry of the English spirit at the time when we achieved our national majority, a self-conscious nationhood expressing itself in many ways, not least in the realization of the poetic potentialities of our language.

CONTENTS

ANONYMOUS

JOHN DAVIES OF HEREFORD 1565–1618

THOMAS DEKKER 1570–1632

MADRIGALISTS AND OTHERS OF
DOUBTFUL DATE

JOHN MARSTON 1576–1634

JOHN FLETCHER 1579–1625

JOHN WEBSTER 1580–1625

ANDREW MARVELL 1621–1678

HENRY VAUGHAN 1622–1695

WILLIAM HAMMOND c. 1655

104 *What dreamed I?*

Benedicite, what dreamèd I this night?
Methought the world was turnèd up so down;
The sun, the moon, had lost their force and light;
The sea also drownèd both tower and town.
Yet more marvel how that I heard the sound
Of onës voice saying 'Bear in thy mind,
Thy lady hath forgotten to be kind.'

To complain me, alas, why should I so,
For my complaint it did me never good?
But by constraint now must I show my woe
To her only which is mine eyës food,
Trusting sometime that she will change her mood,
And let me not alway be guerdonless,
Since for my truth she needeth no witness.

Anonymous

105 *O death, rock me asleep*

O death, rock me asleep,
  Bring me to quiet rest,
Let pass my weary guiltless ghost
  Out of my careful breast.
Toll on, thou passing bell;
Ring out my doleful knell;
Let thy sound my death tell.
  Death doth draw nigh;
  There is no remedy.

My pains who can express?
  Alas, they are so strong;
My dolour will not suffer strength
  My life for to prolong.
Toll on, thou passing bell;
Ring out my doleful knell;
Let thy sound my death tell.

Death doth draw nigh;
There is no remedy.

Alone in prison strong
    I wait my destiny.
Woe worth this cruel hap that I
    Should taste this misery!
Toll on, thou passing bell;
Ring out my doleful knell;
Let thy sound my death tell.
    Death doth draw nigh;
    There is no remedy.

Farewell, my pleasures past,
    Welcome, my present pain!
I feel my torments so increase
    That life cannot remain.
Cease now, thou passing bell;
Rung is my doleful knell;
For the sound my death doth tell.
    Death doth draw nigh;
    There is no remedy.

Anonymous

106 *Greensleeves*

Greensleeves was all my joy,
    Greensleeves was my delight;
Greensleeves was my heart of gold,
    And who but Lady Greensleeves.

Alas, my love! ye do me wrong
    To cast me off discourteously;
And I have lovèd you so long,
    Delighting in your company.

I have been ready at your hand,
  To grant whatever you would crave;
I have both wagered life and land
  Your love and goodwill for to have.

I bought thee kerchers to thy head,
  That were wrought fine and gallantly;
I kept thee both at board and bed,
  Which cost my purse well favouredly.

Thy girdle of gold so red,
  With pearls bedeckèd sumptuously,
The like no other lasses had,
  And yet thou wouldst not love me.

Thy purse and eke thy gay gilt knives,
  Thy pincase gallant to the eye;
No better wore the burgess wives,
  And yet thou wouldst not love me.

Thy crimson stockings all of silk,
  With gold all wrought above the knee;
Thy pumps as white as was the milk,
  And yet thou wouldst not love me.

Thy gown was of the grassy green,
  Thy sleeves of satin hanging by,
Which made thee be our harvest queen,
  And yet thou wouldst not love me.

My gayest gelding I thee gave,
  To ride wherever likèd thee;
No lady ever was so brave,
  And yet thou wouldst not love me.

My men were clothèd all in green,
  And they did ever wait on thee;
All this was gallant to be seen,
  And yet thou wouldst not love me.

They set thee up, they took thee down,
  They served thee with humility;
Thy foot might not once touch the ground,
  And yet thou wouldst not love me.

For every morning when thou rose
   I sent thee dainties orderly
To cheer thy stomach from all woes,
   And yet thou wouldst not love me.

Thou couldst desire no earthly thing
   But still thou hadst it readily;
Thy music still to play and sing,
   And yet thou wouldst not love me.

And who did pay for all this gear
   That thou didst spend when pleasèd thee?
Even I that am rejected here,
   And thou disdain'st to love me.

Well, I will pray to God on high
   That thou my constancy mayst see,
And that yet once before I die
   Thou wilt vouchsafe to love me.

   Greensleeves was all my joy,
      Greensleeves was my delight;
   Greensleeves was my heart of gold,
      And who but Lady Greensleeves.

Anonymous

107   Beauty, a silver dew

Beauty, a silver dew that falls in May;
   Love is an egg-shell with that humour filled;
Desire, a wingèd boy coming that way,
   Delights and dallies with it in the field.
      The fiery sun draws up the shell on high;
      Beauty decays, love dies, desire doth fly.

Anonymous

Jerusalem, my happy home,
  When shall I come to thee?
When shall my sorrows have an end;
  Thy joys when shall I see?

O happy harbour of the saints,
  O sweet and pleasant soil,
In thee no sorrow may be found,
  No grief, no care, no toil.

There lust and lucre cannot dwell,
  There envy bears no sway;
There is no hunger, heat, nor cold,
  But pleasure every way.

Thy walls are made of precious stones,
  Thy bulwarks diamonds square;
Thy gates are of right orient pearl,
  Exceeding rich and rare.

Thy turrets and thy pinnacles
  With carbuncles do shine;
Thy very streets are paved with gold,
  Surpassing clear and fine.

Ah, my sweet home, Jerusalem,
  Would God I were in thee!
Would God my woes were at an end,
  Thy joys that I might see!

Thy gardens and thy gallant walks
  Continually are green;
There grows such sweet and pleasant flowers
  As nowhere else are seen.

Quite through the streets, with silver sound,
  The flood of life doth flow;
Upon whose banks on every side
  The wood of life doth grow.

There trees for evermore bear fruit,
    And evermore do spring;
There evermore the angels sit,
    And evermore do sing.

Our Lady sings Magnificat
    With tune surpassing sweet;
And all the virgins bear their part,
    Sitting about her feet.

Jerusalem, my happy home,
    Would God I were in thee!
Would God my woes were at an end,
    Thy joys that I might see!

Anonymous

109   *Since first I saw your face*

Since first I saw your face I resolved to honour and
    renown ye;
If now I be disdained, I wish my heart had never known
    ye.
What, I that loved and you that liked, shall we begin to
    wrangle?
No, no, no, my heart is fast and cannot disentangle.

If I admire or praise you too much, that fault you may
    forgive me
Or if my hands had strayed but a touch, then justly
    might you leave me.
I asked you leave, you bade me love; is't now a time to
    chide me?
No, no, no, I'll love you still, what fortune e'er betide
    me.

The sun, whose beams most glorious are, rejecteth no
    beholder,
And your sweet beauty past compare made my poor
    eyes the bolder.

Where beauty moves and wit delights, and signs of
    kindness bind me,
There, O there, where'er I go, I'll leave my heart
    behind me.

Anonymous

110   *Brown is my love*

Brown is my love but graceful;
And each renownèd whiteness
Matched with thy lovely brown loseth its brightness.

Fair is my love but scornful;
Yet have I seen despisèd
Dainty white lilies and sad flowers well prizèd.

Anonymous

111   *Dear, if you change*

Dear, if you change, I'll never choose again;
    Sweet, if you shrink, I'll never think of love;
Fair, if you fail, I'll judge all beauty vain;
    Wise, if too weak, more wits I'll never prove.
Dear, sweet, fair, wise, change, shrink, nor be not weak;
And on my faith, my faith shall never break.

Earth with her flowers shall sooner heaven adorn;
    Heaven her bright stars through earth's dim globe
                                        shall move;
Fire heat shall lose, and frosts of flames be born;
    Air, made to shine, as black as hell shall prove.
Earth, heaven, fire, air, the world transformed shall
                                        view,
Ere I prove false to faith or strange to you.

Anonymous

I saw my lady weep
  And sorrow proud to be advancèd so
In those fair eyes where all perfections keep.
  Her face was full of woe;
But such a woe, believe me, as wins more hearts
Than mirth can do with her enticing parts.

  Sorrow was there made fair
  And passion wise, tears a delightful thing;
Silence beyond all speech a wisdom rare.
  She made her sighs to sing,
And all things with so sweet a sadness move
As made my heart at once both grieve and love.

  O fairer than aught else
  The world can show, leave off in time to grieve.
Enough, enough your joyful look excels;
  Tears kills the heart, believe.
  O! strive not to be excellent in woe,
Which only breeds your beauty's overthrow.

Anonymous

113   Fine knacks for ladies

Fine knacks for ladies, cheap, choice, brave and new!
Good pennyworths, but money cannot move.
I keep a fair but for the fair to view;
A beggar may be liberal of love.
Though all my wares be trash, the heart is true.

Great gifts are guiles and look for gifts again;
My trifles come as treasures from my mind.
It is a precious jewel to be plain;
Sometimes in shell the orient pearls we find.
Of others take a sheaf, of me a grain.

Within this pack pins, points, laces and gloves,
And divers toys fitting a country fair,
But in my heart, where duty serves and loves,
Turtles and twins, court's brood, a heavenly pair.
Happy the heart that thinks of no removes.

Anonymous

114   *Tom o'Bedlam's song*

From the hag and hungry goblin
That into rags would rend ye,
All spirits that stand
By the naked man,
In the book of moons defend ye!
That of your five sound senses
You never be forsaken;
Nor travel from
Yourselves with Tom
Abroad, to beg your bacon.

Nor never sing any food and feeding,
Money, drink, or clothing;
Come dame or maid,
Be not afraid,
For Tom will injure nothing.

Of thirty bare years have I
Twice twenty been engaged;
And of forty been
Three times fifteen
In durance soundly caged.

In the lovely lofts of Bedlam,
In stubble soft and dainty,
Brave bracelets strong,
Sweet whips ding, dong,
And a wholesome hunger plenty.

With a thought I took for Maudlin,
And a cruse of cockle pottage,
And a thing thus—tall,
Sky bless you all
I fell into this dotage.

I sleep not till the Conquest;
Till then I never wakèd;
Till the roguish boy
Of love, when I lay,
Me found and stripped me naked.

When short I have shorn my sow's face,
And swigged my hornèd barrel;
In an oaken inn
Do I pawn my skin,
As a sort of gilt apparel:
The moon's my constant mistress,
And the lovely owl my marrow;
The flaming drake
And the night-crow make
Me music, to my sorrow.

The palsy plague there pounces,
When I prig your pigs or pullen;
Your culvers take
Or mateless make
Your chanticleer, and sullen;
When I want provant with Humphrey I sup,
And when benighted,
To repose in Paul's,
With waking souls,
I never am affrighted.

I know more than Apollo.
For oft when he lies sleeping,
I behold the stars
At mortal wars,
And the rounded welkin weeping;
The moon embraces her shepherd,

And the Queen of Love her warrior;
While the first doth horn
The stars of the morn,
And the next heavenly farrier.

The Gypsy Snap and Tedro
Are none of Tom's comradoes.
The punk I scorn
And the cutpurse sworn
Are the roaring boys bravadoes.
The sober, white, and gentle,
Me trace, or touch and spare not;
But those that cross
Tom's rhinoceros
Do what the panther dare not.

With a host of furious fancies
Whereof I am commander,
With a burning spear,
And a horse of air,
To the wilderness I wander;
By a knight of ghosts and shadows
I summoned am to tourney
Ten leagues beyond
The wide world's end;
Methinks it is no journey.

Anonymous

115 *Lament for Walsingham*

In the wracks of Walsingham
Whom should I choose
But the Queen of Walsingham
To be guide to my Muse?

Then, thou Prince of Walsingham,
Grant me to frame
Bitter plaints to rue thy wrong,
Bitter woe for thy name.

Bitter was it, O to see
The silly sheep
Murdered by the ravening wolves
While the shepherds did sleep.

Bitter was it, O to view
The sacred vine,
Which the gardeners placed all close,
Rooted up by the swine.

Bitter, bitter, O to behold
The grape to grow
Where the walls of Walsingham
So stately did show.

Such were the works of Walsingham
While she did stand:
Such are the wracks as now do show
Of that holy land.

Level, level with the ground
The towers do lie,
Which with their golden glittering tops
Pierced once to the sky.

Where were gates no gates are now;
The ways unknown,
While the press of peers did pass,
While her fame was far blown.

Owls do scrike where the sweetest hymns
Lately were sung;
Toads and serpents hold their dens
Where the palmers did throng.

Weep, weep, O Walsingham,
Whose days are nights;
Blessing turn to blasphemies,
Holy deeds to despite.

Sin is where Our Lady sat;
Heaven is turned to Hell;
Satan sits where our Lord did sway.
Walsingham, O, farewell.

Anonymous

The shrine of Our Lady at Walsingham in Norfolk was
destroyed at the Reformation.

116   Preparations

Yet if His Majesty, our sovereign lord,
Should of his own accord
Friendly himself invite,
And say, 'I'll be your guest to-morrow night,'
How should we stir ourselves, call and command
All hands to work! 'Let no man idle stand!
Set me fine Spanish tables in the hall,
See they be fitted all;
Let there be room to eat,
And order taken that there want no meat;
See every sconce and candlestick made bright,
That without tapers they may give a light.
Look to the presence; are the carpets spread,
The dais overhead,
The cushions in the chairs,
And all the candles lighted on the stairs?
Perfume the chambers, and in any case
Let each man give attendance in his place.'
Thus if a king were coming would we do,
And 'twere good reason too;
For 'tis a duteous thing
To show all honour to an earthly king,
And after all our travail and our cost,
So he be pleased to think no labour lost.
But at the coming of the King of Heaven
All's set at six and seven:

We wallow in our sin,
Christ cannot find a chamber in the inn,
We entertain him always like a stranger,
And, as at first, still lodge him in a manger.

Anonymous

117 *Love me little, love me long*

Love me little, love me long,
Is the burden of my song;
Love that is too hot and strong
   Burneth all to waste;
Still I would not have thee cold,
Or backward or too bold,
For love that lasteth till 'tis old
   Fadeth not in haste.

Winter's cold or summer's heat,
Autumn tempests on it beat,
It can never know defeat,
   Never can rebel;
Such the love that I would gain,
Such love, I tell thee plain,
That thou must give or love in vain,
   So to thee farewell.

Anonymous

118 *For her love I cark and care*

For her love I cark[1] and care;
For her love I droop and dare[2];
For her all my bliss is bare,
   And I wax wan.
For her love in sleep I slake;
For her love all night I wake;
For her love I mourning make,
   More than any man.

Anonymous

1 worry 2 am dazed

119   *Two rivers*

Says Tweed to Till:
'What gars ye rin so still?'[1]
Says Till to Tweed:
'Though ye rin with speed,
And I rin slaw,
For ae man that ye drown,
I drown twa.'

Anonymous

1 Why do you run so slowly?

120   *Mounsier Mingo*

Mounsier Mingo for quaffing doth pass
In cup, cruse, can or glass;
In cellar never was his fellow found
To drink profound,
By task and turn so round
To quaff, carouse so sound
And yet bear so fresh a brain
Sans taint or stain
Or foil, refoil or quarrel
But to the beer and barrel
Where he works to win his name,
Where he works to win his name!
And stout doth stand
In Bacchus' band
With pot in hand
To purchase fame,
For he calls with cup and can:
'Come, try my courage, man to man,
And let him conquer me that can
And spare not.
I care not;
While hands can heave the pot
No fear falls to my lot.

God Bacchus do me right
And dub me knight
Domingo.'

Anonymous

121 *Like flowers we spring*

Like flowers we spring up fair but soon decaying;
Our days and years are in their prime declining;
Man's life on such uncertainties is founded:
The wheel of fickle fate is never staying;
Time every hour our thread of life untwining:
He that ere now with store of wealth abounded,
Anon through want is wounded.
Wayfaring men we are, pilgrims and strangers,
On earth we have no certain habitation,
Nor keep one constant station;
But, through a multitude of fears and dangers,
We travel up and down towards our ending,
Unto our silent graves mournfully wending.

Anonymous

122 *Do not, oh do not prize*

Do not, oh do not prize thy beauty at too high a rate;
Love to be loved while thou art lovely, lest thou love
too late:
  Frowns paint wrinkles in thy brows
    At which spiteful age doth smile,
  Women in their froward vows
    Glorying to beguile.

Wert thou the only world's admirèd, thou canst love
but one;
And many have before been loved, thou art not loved
alone:

Couldst thou speak with heavenly grace
   Sappho might with thee compare;
Blush the roses in thy face,
   Rosamund was as fair.

Pride is the canker that consumeth beauty in her prime;
They that delight in long debating feel the curse of time:
   All things with the time do change
     That will not the time obey;
   Some even to themselves seem strange
     Thorough their own delay.

Anonymous

123 *Mortality*

Grass of levity,
Span in brevity,
Flowers' felicity,
Fire of misery,
Wind's stability,
Is mortality.

Anonymous

Inscription in the churchyard of St Mary Magdalene, Milk
Street, London.

124 *On Sir Francis Drake*

Sir Drake, whom well the world's end knew,
   Which thou didst compass round,
And whom both poles of heaven once saw,
   Which north and south do bound,
The stars above would make thee known,
   If men here silent were;
The sun himself cannot forget
   His fellow-traveller.

Anonymous

'Turn, Willie Macintosh,
    Turn, I bid you;
Gin ye burn Auchindown,
    Huntly will head you.'

'Head me or hang me,
    That canna fley¹ me;
I'll burn Auchindown
    Ere the life leave me.'

Coming down Deeside,
    In a clear morning,
Auchindown was in flame,
    Ere the cock-crowing.

But coming o'er Cairn Croom,
    And looking down, man,
I saw Willie Macintosh
    Burn Auchindown, man.

'Bonny Willie Macintosh,
    Where left ye your men?'—
'I left them in the Stapler,
    But they 'll come hame.'

'Bonny Willie Macintosh,
    Where now is your men?'—
'I left them in the Stapler,
    Sleeping in their sheen.'²

Anonymous

1 frighten   2 shoes

126   *Love is a babel*

Love is a babel,
    No man is able
To say 'tis this or 'tis that;

So full of passions,
Of sundry fashions,
'Tis like I cannot tell what.

Love's fair in cradle,
Foul in fable,
'Tis either too cold or too hot.
An arrant liar,
Fed by desire,
It is—and yet it is not.

Love is a fellow
Clad oft in yellow,
The canker worm of the mind,
A privy mischief
And such a sly thief,
No man knows which way to find.

Love is a wonder
That's here and yonder,
As common to one as to moe;
A monstrous cheater,
Every man's debtor;
Hang him, and so let him go.

Anonymous

127 *My dancing day*

To-morrow shall be my dancing day;
    I would my true love did so chance
To see the legend of my play,
    To call my true love to the dance.
    Sing O my love, my love, my love
    This have I done for my true love.

In a manger laid and wrapt I was,
    So very poor, this was my chance.
Betwixt an ox and a silly poor ass,
    To call my true love to my dance.
    Sing O my love, my love, my love—
    This have I done for my true love.

Into the desert I was led,
  Where I fasted without substance,
The devil bade me make stones my bread,
  To have me break my true love's dance.
    Sing O my love, my love, my love—
    This have I done for my true love.

For thirty pence Judas me sold
  His covetousness for to advance;
'Mark whom I kiss, the same do hold,'
  The same is he shall lead the dance.
    Sing O my love, my love, my love—
    This have I done for my true love.

Then on a cross hangèd I was,
  Where a spear to my heart did glance;
There issued forth both water and blood,
  To call my true love to my dance.
    Sing O my love, my love, my love—
    This have I done for my true love.

Then down to Hell I took my way
  For my true love's deliverance,
And rose again on the third day
  Up to my true love and the dance.
    Sing O my love, my love, my love—
    This have I done for my true love.

Anonymous

128   *Faradiddle dyno*

Ha ha! ha ha! this world doth pass
  Most merrily, I'll be sworn,
For many an honest Indian ass
  Goes for a unicorn.
Faradiddle dyno,
This is idle fyno.

Tie hie! tie hie! O sweet delight!
    He tickles this age that can
Call Tullia's ape a marmosite
    And Leda's goose a swan.
Faradiddle dyno,
This is idle fyno.

So so! so so! fine English days!
    For false play is no reproach,
For he that doth the coachman praise
    May safely use the coach.
Faradiddle dyno,
This is idle fyno.

Anonymous

129   *I will lift up mine eyes*

I will lift up mine eyes unto the hills, from whence
cometh my help. My help cometh from the Lord, which
made Heaven and earth.

He will not suffer thy foot to be moved: he that
keepeth thee will not slumber. Behold, he that keepeth
Israel shall neither slumber nor sleep.

The Lord is thy keeper: the Lord is thy shade upon
thy right hand.

The sun shall not smite thee by day, nor the moon by
night. The Lord shall preserve thee from evil: he shall
preserve thy soul.

The Lord shall preserve thy going out and thy coming
in from this time forth, and even for evermore.

Psalm 121

130   *The Lord is my shepherd*

The Lord is my shepherd; I shall not want.
He maketh me to lie down in green pastures:
He leadeth me beside the still waters.

He restoreth my soul:

He leadeth me in the paths of righteousness for his name's sake.

Yea, though I walk through the valley of the shadow of death,

I will fear no evil: for thou art with me; thy rod and thy staff they comfort me.

Thou preparest a table before me in the presence of mine enemies:

Thou anointest my head with oil; my cup runneth over.

Surely goodness and mercy shall follow me all the days of my life:

And I will dwell in the house of the Lord for ever.

Psalm 23

131   *Mary Hamilton*

There were ladies, they lived in a bower,
    And oh they were fair!
The youngest of them is to the king's court,
    To learn some onco lair.[1]

She hadna been in the king's court
    A twelvemonth and a day,
Till of her they could get no work,
    For wantonness and play.

Word is to the kitchen gone,
    And word is to the hall,
And word is up to Madam the Queen
    And that is worst of all,
That Mary Hamilton has born a bairn,
    To the highest stewart of all.

'O rise, O rise, Mary Hamilton,
    O rise, and tell to me
What thou did with thy sweet babe
    We sair heard weep by thee.'

'Hold your tongue, Madam,' she said,
  'And let your folly be;
It was a shower of sad sickness
  Made me weep so bitterly.'

'O rise, O rise, Mary Hamilton,
  O rise, and tell to me
What thou did with thy sweet babe
  We sair heard weep by thee.'

'I put it in a pinafore
  And set it on the sea;
I bade it sink or it might swim,
  It should ne'er come home to me.'

'O rise, O rise, Mary Hamilton,
  Arise and go with me;
There is a wedding in Glasgow town
  This day we'll go and see.'

She put not on her black clothing,
  She put not on her brown,
But she put on the glistering gold,
  To shine through Edinburgh town.

As they came into Edinburgh town,
  The city for to see,
The bailie's wife and the provost's wife
  Said, 'Och and alas for thee!'

'Give never alas for me,' she said,
  'Give never alas for me;
It's all for the sake of my poor babe,
  This death that I must die.'

As they went up the Tolbuith stair,
  The stair it was so high,
The bailie's son and the provost's son
  Said, 'Och and alas for thee!'

'Give never alas for me,' she said,
  'Give never alas for me!
It's all for the sake of my poor babe,
  This death that I must die.

'But bring to me a cup,' she said,
  'A cup but and a can,
And I will drink to all my friends
  And they will drink to me again.'

'Here's to you all, travellers,
  Who travel by land or sea;
Let na wit to my father nor mother
  The death that I must die.

'Here's to you all, travellers,
  That travel on dry land;
Let na wit to my father nor mother
  But I am coming home.

'Little did my mother think,
  First time she cradled me,
What land I was to travel on,
  Or what death I would die.

'Little did my mother think,
  First time she tied my head,
What land I was to tread upon,
  Or where I would win my bread.

'Yestreen Queen Mary had four Maries,
  This night she'll have but three;
She had Mary Seaton, and Mary Beaton,
  And Mary Carmichael and me.

'Yestreen I washed Queen Mary's feet
  And bore her to her bed;
This day she's given me my reward,
  This gallows tree to tread.

'Cast off, cast off my gown,' she said,
   'But let my petticoat be,
And tie a napkin on my face,
   For that gallows I darena see.'

By and came the King himself,
   Looked up with a pitiful eye:
'Come down, come down, Mary Hamilton,
   This day thou wilt dine with me.'

'Hold your tongue, my sovereign liege,
   And let your folly be;
And ye had a mind to save my life,
   Ye shouldna shamed me here.'

Anonymous

1 unusual learning

132 *Love will find out the way*

Over the mountains
   And under the waves,
Over the fountains
   And under the graves;
Over floods which are the deepest,
   Which do Neptune obey,
Over rocks which are the steepest
   Love will find out the way.

Where there is no place
   For the glow-worm to lie;
Where there is no space
   For the receipt of a fly;
Where the gnat she dares not venter,
   Lest herself fast she lay;
But if Love come, he will enter
   And will find out the way.

You may esteem him
   A child by his force;
Or you may deem him
   A coward, which is worse;

But if she whom Love doth honour
  Be concealed from the day,
Set a thousand guards upon her,
  Love will find out the way.

Some think to lose him,
  Which is too unkind;
And some do suppose him,
  Poor heart! to be blind;
If that he were hidden,
  Do the best that you may,
Blind Love, if so you call him,
  Will find out the way.

Well may the eagle
  Stoop down to the fist;
Or you may inveigle
  The phoenix of the east;
With fear the tiger's movèd
  To give over his prey;
But never stop a lover,
  He will post on his way.

If the earth should part him,
  He would gallop it o'er;
If the seas should o'erthwart him,
  He would swim to the shore.
Should his love become a swallow,
  Through the air to stray,
Love would lend wings to follow,
  And will find out the way.

There is no striving
  To cross his intent,
There is no contriving
  His plots to prevent;
But if once the message greet him,
  That his true love doth stay,
If death should come and meet him,
  Love will find out the way.

Anonymous

Like as the damask rose you see,
Or like the blossom on the tree,
Or like the dainty flower of May,
Or like the morning to the day,
Or like the sun, or like the shade,
Or like the gourd which Jonas had—
Even such is man, whose thread is spun,
Drawn out, and cut, and so is done.
The rose withers, the blossom blasteth,
The flower fades, the morning hasteth,
The sun sets, the shadow flies,
The gourd consumes; and man he dies.

Like to the grass that's newly sprung,
Or like a tale that's new begun,
Or like the bird that's here to-day.
Or like the pearlèd dew of May,
Or like an hour, or like a span,
Or like the singing of a swan—
Even such is man, who lives by breath,
Is here, now there: so life, and death.
The grass withers, the tale is ended,
The bird is flown, the dew's ascended,
The hour is short, the span not long,
The swan's near death; man's life is done.

Like to the bubble in the brook,
Or, in a glass, much like a look,
Or like a shuttle in weaver's hand,
Or like a writing on the sand,
Or like a thought, or like a dream,
Or like the gliding of the stream—
Even such is man, who lives by breath,
Is here, now there: so life, and death.
The bubble's cut, the look's forgot,
The shuttle's flung, the writing's blot,
The thought is past, the dream is gone,
The water glides; man's life is done.

Like to an arrow from the bow,
Or like swift course of watery flow,
Or like the time 'twixt flood and ebb,
Or like the spider's tender web,
Or like a race, or like a goal,
Or like the dealing of a dole—
Even such is man, whose brittle state
Is always subject unto fate.
The arrow's shot, the flood soon spent,
The time no time, the web soon rent,
The race soon run, the goal soon won,
The dole soon dealt; man's life first done.

Like to the lightning from the sky,
Or like a post that quick doth hie,
Or like a quaver in short song,
Or like a journey three days long,
Or like the snow when summer's come,
Or like the pear, or like the plum—
Even such is man, who heaps up sorrow,
Lives but this day and dies to-morrow.
The lightning's past, the post must go.
The song is short, the journey's so,
The pear doth rot, the plum doth fall,
The snow dissolves, and so must all.

Anonymous

134 *Down in a garden*

Down in a garden sat my dearest Love,
Her skin more soft and white than down of swan,
More tender-hearted than the turtle-dove,
And far more kind than bleeding pelican.
I courted her; she rose and blushing said,
'Why was I born to live and die a maid?'
With that I plucked a pretty marigold,
Whose dewy leaves shut up when day is done:
'Sweeting,' I said, 'arise, look and behold,
A pretty riddle I'll to thee unfold:

These leaves shut in as close as cloistered nun,
Yet will they open when they see the sun.'
'What mean you by this riddle, sir?' she said,
'I pray expound it.' Then I thus began:
'Know maids are made for men, man for a maid.'
With that she changed her colour and grew wan:
'Since that this riddle you so well unfold,
Be you the sun, I'll be the marigold.'

Anonymous

135 *To Celia*

When, Celia, I intend to flatter you,
And tell you lies to make you true,
    I swear
 There's none so fair—
 And you believe it too.

Oft have I matched you with the rose, and said
No twins so like hath nature made:
    But 'tis
 Only in this—
 You prick my hand, and fade.

Oft have I said, there is no precious stone
But may be found in you alone;
    Though I
 No stone espy
 Unless your heart be one.

When I praise your skin, I quote the wool
That silkworms from their entrails pull,
    And show
 That new-fall'n snow
 Is not more beautiful.

Yet grow not proud by such hyperboles:
Were you as excellent as these,
                              Whilst I
     Before you lie—
     They might be had with ease.

Anonymous

136   *A question*

          I ask thee, whence those ashes were
          Which shrine themselves in plaits of hair?
          Unknown to me; sure, each morn, dies
          A phoenix for a sacrifice.

          I ask, whence are those airs that fly
          From birds in sweetest harmony?
          Unknown to me; but sure the choice
          Of accents echoed from her voice.

          I ask thee, whence those active fires
          Take light, which glide through burnished air?
          Unknown to me; unless there flies
          A flash of lightning from her eyes.

          I ask thee, whence those ruddy blooms
          Pierce on her cheeks on scarlet gowns?
          Unknown to me; sure that which flies
          From fading roses her cheek dyes.

          I'll ask thee of the lily, whence
          It gained that type of innocence?
          Unknown to me; sure Nature's deck
          Was ravished from her snowy neck.

Anonymous

137 *Song*

So have I seen a silver swan,
    As in a watery looking-glass,
Viewing her whiter form, and then
    Courting herself with lovely grace:
        As now she doth herself admire,
        Being at once the fuel and the fire.

Anonymous

138   *The mad-merry pranks of Robin Good-Fellow*

From Oberon in fairyland,
    The king of ghosts and shadows there,
Mad Robin I, at his command,
    Am sent to view the night-sports here.
What revel rout is kept about,
    In every corner where I go
I will o'er-see, and merry be,
    And make good sport, with ho, ho, ho!

More swift than lightning can I fly
    About this airy welkin soon,
And in a minute's space descry
    Each thing that's done beneath the moon.
There's not a hag nor ghost shall wag,
    Nor cry 'Goblin!' where I do go,
But Robin I their feats will spy,
    And fear them home, with ho, ho, ho!

If any wanderers I meet,
    That from their night-sports do trudge home,
With counterfeiting voice I greet
    And cause them on with me to roam,
Through woods, through lakes, through bogs, through
                                        brakes,
    O'er bush and brier, with them I go,
I call upon them to come on,
    And wend me laughing, ho, ho, ho!

Sometimes I meet them like a man;
    Sometimes an ox, sometimes a hound;
And to a horse I turn me can,
    To trip and trot about them round.
But if to ride, my back they stride,
    More swift than wind away I go,
O'er hedge and lands, through pools and ponds
    I whirry, laughing, ho, ho, ho!

When lazy queans have naught to do,
    But study how to cog and lie;
To make debate and mischief too
    'Twixt one another secretly;
I mark their glose and do disclose
    To them that they had wrongèd so;
When I have done, I get me gone,
    And leave them scolding, ho, ho, ho!

From hag-bred Merlin's time have I
    Thus nightly revelled to and fro,
And for my pranks men call me by
    The name of Robin Good-fellow.
Fiends, ghosts and sprites, that haunt the nights,
    The hags and goblins, do me know;
And beldams old my feats have told,
    So *vale*, *vale*; ho, ho, ho!

Anonymous

139 *If all the world were paper*

If all the world were paper,
    And all the sea were ink,
And all the trees were bread and cheese,
    How should we do for drink?

If all the world were sand-o,
    Oh, then what should we lack-o?
If, as they say, there were no clay,
    How should we take tobacco?

If friars had no bald pates,
  Nor nuns had no dark cloisters;
If all the seas were beans and peas,
  How should we do for oysters?

If there had been no projects,
  Nor none that did great wrongs;
If fiddlers shall turn players all,
  How should we do for songs?

If all things were eternal,
  And nothing their end bringing;
If this should be, then how should we
  Here make an end of singing?

Anonymous

140 *England*

Oh, England!
  Sick in head and sick in heart,
  Sick in whole and every part:
  And yet sicker thou art still
  For thinking that thou art not ill.

Anonymous

141 *The wandering spectre*

Wae's me, wae's me,
The acorn's not yet
Fallen from the tree
That's to grow the wood,
That's to make the cradle,
That's to rock the bairn,
That's to grow a man,
That's to lay me.

Anonymous

I am of Ireland
And of the holy land
   Of Ireland.
Good sir, pray I thee,
For of saint charity,
Come and dance with me
   In Ireland.

Anonymous

143   In youth is pleasure

In an arbour green asleep whereas I lay,
The birds sang sweet in the middës of the day,
I dreamèd fast of mirth and play:
   In youth is pleasure, in youth is pleasure.

Methought I walked still to and fro,
And from her company I could not go,
But when I waked it was not so:
   In youth is pleasure, in youth is pleasure.

Therefore my heart is surely pight[1]
Of her alone to have a sight
Which is my joy and heart's delight:
   In youth is pleasure, in youth is pleasure.

Robert Wever

1 set

144   Fair is my love

Fair is my love that feeds among the lilies,
The lilies growing in that pleasant garden
Where Cupid's mount, that well-beloved hill, is,
And where that little God himself is warden.

See where my love sits in the beds of spices,
Beset all round with camphor, myrrh and roses,
And interlaced with curious devices
Which her apart from all the world encloses;
There doth she tune her lute for her delight,
And with sweet music makes the ground to move,
Whilst I, poor I, do sit in heavy plight,
Wailing alone my unrespected love:
  Not daring rush into so rare a place,
  That gives to her, and she to it, a grace.

Bartholomew Griffin

145 *Inscription in a garden*

If any flower that here is grown
  Or any herb may ease your pain,
Take and accompt it as your own,
  But recompense the like again;
    For some and some is honest play,
    And so my wife taught me to say.

If here to walk you take delight,
  Why, come and welcome when you will;
If I bid you sup here this night,
  Bid me another time, and still
    Think some and some is honest play,
    For so my wife taught me to say.

Thus if you sup or dine with me,
  If you walk here or sit at ease,
If you desire the thing you see,
  And have the same your mind to please,
    Think some and some is honest play,
    And so my wife taught me to say.

George Gascoigne

When I was fair and young, and favour gracèd me,
Of many was I sought, their mistress for to be;
But I did scorn them all and answered them therefore,
'Go, go, go, seek some other where,
Importune me no more!'

How many weeping eyes I made to pine with woe,
How many sighing hearts I have no skill to show;
Yet I the prouder grew, and answered them therefore,
'Go, go, go, seek some other where,
Importune me no more!'

Then spake fair Venus' son, that proud victorious boy,
And said: 'Fine dame, since that you be so coy,
I will so pluck your plumes that you shall say no more,
Go, go, go, seek some other where,
Importune me no more!'

When he had spake these words, such change grew
in my breast
That neither night nor day since that, I could take any
rest.
Then lo! I did repent that I had said before,
'Go, go, go, seek some other where,
Importune me no more!'

Queen Elizabeth I

147   *The lowest trees have tops*

The lowest trees have tops; the ant her gall;
The fly her spleen; the little sparks their heat;
The slender hairs cast shadows, though but small;
And bees have stings, although they be not great.
Seas have their source, and so have shallow springs;
And love is love, in beggars as in kings.

Where rivers smoothest run, deep are the fords;
    The dial stirs, yet none perceives it move;
The firmest faith is in the fewest words;
    The turtles cannot sing, and yet they love.
True hearts have eyes and ears, no tongues to speak;
They hear and see, and sigh; and then they break.

Sir Edward Dyer

148   *The country lad*

Who can live in heart so glad
As the merry country lad?
Who upon a fair green balk[1]
May at pleasure sit and walk,
And amid the azure skies
See the morning sun arise,
While he hears in every spring
How the birds do chirp and sing:
Or before the hounds in cry
See the hare go stealing by:
Or along the shallow brook,
Angling with a baited hook,
See the fishes leap and play
In a blessed sunny day:
Or to hear the partridge call
Till she have her covey all:
Or to see the subtle fox,
How the villain plies the box;[2]
After feeding on his prey,
How he closely sneaks away,
Through the hedge and down the furrow
Till he gets into his burrow:
Then the bee to gather honey;
And the little black-haired coney,[3]
On a bank for sunny place,
With her forefeet wash her face,—

Are not these, with thousands moe
Than the courts of kings do know,
The true pleasing spirit's sights
That may breed true love's delights?

Nicholas Breton

1 Bank   2 Raids the chicken run   3 Rabbit

149   *The passionate shepherd to his love*

Come live with me and be my love,
And we will all the pleasures prove
That hills and valleys, dales and fields
And all the craggy mountains yields.

There we will sit upon the rocks
And see the shepherds feed their flocks,
By shallow rivers to whose falls
Melodious birds sing madrigals.

And I will make thee beds of roses
With a thousand fragrant posies,
A cap of flowers and a kirtle
Embroidered all with leaves of myrtle.

A gown made of the finest wool
Which from our pretty lambs we pull;
Fair linèd slippers for the cold,
With buckles of the purest gold;

A belt of straw and ivy buds,
With coral clasps and amber studs:
And if these pleasures may thee move,
Come live with me and be my love.

The shepherds' swains shall dance and sing
For thy delight each May morning:
If these delights thy mind may move,
Then live with me and be my love.

Christopher Marlowe

If all the world and love were young,
And truth in every shepherd's tongue,
These pretty pleasures might me move
To live with thee and be thy love.

Time drives the flocks from field to fold
When rivers rage and rocks grow cold,
And Philomel becometh dumb,
The rest complain of cares to come.

The flowers do fade, and wanton fields
To wayward winter reckoning yields;
A honey tongue, a heart of gall
Is fancy's spring, but sorrow's fall.

Thy gowns, thy shoes, thy beds of roses,
Thy cap, thy kirtle and thy posies
Soon break, soon wither, soon forgotten,
In folly ripe, in reason rotten.

Thy belt of straw and ivy buds,
Thy coral clasps and amber studs,
All these in me no means can move
To come to thee and be thy love.

But could youth last and love still breed,
Had joys no date nor age no need,
Then these delights my mind might move
To live with thee and be thy love.

Sir Walter Ralegh

151   *False Love*

Farewell false love, the oracle of lies,
    A mortal foe and enemy to rest,
An envious boy, from whom all cares arise,

A bastard vile, a beast with rage possessed,
    A way of error, a temple full of treason,
    In all effects contrary unto reason;

A poisoned serpent covered all with flowers,
    Mother of sighs and murderer of repose,
A sea of sorrows from whence are drawn such showers
    As moisture lend to every grief that grows,
        A school of guile, a net of deep deceit,
        A gilded hook that holds a poisoned bait;

A fortress foiled which reason did defend,
    A siren song, a fever of the mind,
A maze wherein affection finds no end,
    A raging cloud that runs before the wind,
        A substance like the shadow of the sun,
        A goal of grief for which the wisest run;

A quenchless fire, a nurse of trembling fear,
    A path that leads to peril and mishap,
A true retreat of sorrow and despair,
    An idle boy that sleeps in pleasure's lap,
        A deep mistrust of that which certain seems,
        A hope of that which reason doubtful deems.

Sith then thy trains my younger years betrayed
    And for my faith ingratitude I find,
And sith repentance hath my wrongs bewrayed
    Whose course was ever contrary to kind,
        False love, desire, and beauty frail, adieu!
        Dead is the root whence all these fancies grew.

Sir Walter Ralegh

152   *A description of love*

Now what is love? I pray thee tell.
It is that fountain and that well
Where pleasure and repentance dwell.
It is perhaps that sauncing[1] bell
That tolls all in to heaven or hell:
And this is love, as I hear tell.

Yet what is love? I pray thee say.
It is a work on holy-day;
It is December matched with May;
When lusty bloods in fresh array
Hear ten months after of the play:
And this is love, as I hear say.

Yet what is love? I pray thee sayn.
It is a sunshine mixed with rain;
It is a toothache or like pain;
It is a game where none doth gain;
The lass saith no and would full fain:
And this is love, as I hear sayn.

Yet what is love? I pray thee say.
It is a yea, it is a nay,
A pretty kind of sporting fray;
It is a thing will soon away;
Then take the vantage while you may:
And this is love, as I hear say.

Yet what is love? I pray thee show.
A thing that creeps, it cannot go;
A prize that passeth to and fro;
A thing for one, a thing for mo;
And he that proves must find it so:
And this is love, sweet friend, I trow.

Sir Walter Ralegh

1 sacring

153 *Farewell to the court*

Like truthless dreams so are my joys expired,
   And past return are all my dandled days;
My love misled, and fancy quite retired,
   Of all which past the sorrow only stays.

My lost delights, now clean from sight of land,
   Have left me all alone in unknown ways;
My mind to woe, my life in fortune's hand,
   Of all which past the sorrow only stays.

As in a country strange without companion,
  I only wail the wrong of death's delays,
Whose sweet spring spent, whose summer well-nigh
                                              done,
  Of all which past the sorrow only stays;

    Whom care forewarns ere age and winter cold,
    To haste me hence, to find my fortune's fold.

Sir Walter Ralegh

154 *Walsinghame*

As you came from the holy land
  Of Walsinghame,
Met you not with my true love
  By the way as you came?

How should I know your true love,
  That have met many a one
As I came from the holy land,
  That have come, that have gone?

She is neither white nor brown,
  But as the heavens fair;
There is none that hath her form divine
  In the earth or the air.

Such a one did I meet, good sir,
  Such an angelic face,
Who like a nymph, like a queen, did appear
  In her gait, in her grace.

She hath left me here alone
  All alone, as unknown,
Who sometime did me lead with herself,
  And me loved as her own.

What's the cause that she leaves you alone
    And a new way doth take,
That sometime did love you as her own,
    And her joy did you make?

I have loved her all my youth,
    But now am old, as you see:
Love likes not the falling fruit,
    Nor the withered tree.

Know that love is a careless child,
    And forgets promise past:
He is blind, he is deaf when he list,
    And in faith never fast.

His desire is a dureless content,
    And a trustless joy;
He is won with a world of despair,
    And is lost with a toy.

Of womenkind such indeed is the love,
    Or the word love abused,
Under which many childish desires
    And conceits are excused.

But true love is a durable fire,
    In the mind over burning,
Never sick, never old, never dead,
    From itself never turning.

Sir Walter Ralegh

155   *To the Queen*

Our passions are most like to floods and streams;
    The shallow murmur, but the deep are dumb.
So when affections yield discourse, it seems
    The bottom is but shallow whence they come.
        They are rich in words must needs discover
        That they are poor in that which makes a lover.

Wrong not, dear empress of my heart,
　　The merit of true passion,
With thinking that he feels no smart
　　That sues for no compassion;
Since, if my plaints serve not to prove
　　The conquest of your beauty,
It comes not from defect of love,
　　But from excess of duty.

For knowing that I sue to serve
　　A saint of such perfection
As all desire but none deserve
　　A place in her affection,
I rather choose to want relief
　　Than venture the revealing;
When glory recommends the grief,
　　Despair distrusts the healing.

Thus those desires that aim too high
　　For any mortal lover,
When reason cannot make them die
　　Discretion will them cover.
Yet when discretion doth bereave
　　The plaints that they should utter,
Then your discretion may perceive
　　That silence is a suitor.

Silence in love bewrays more woe
　　Than words, though ne'er so witty;
A beggar that is dumb, ye know,
　　Deserveth double pity.
Then misconceive not, dearest heart,
　　My true though secret passion,
He smarteth most that hides his smart
　　And sues for no compassion.

Sir Walter Ralegh

Conceit[1] begotten by the eyes
Is quickly born and quickly dies,
For while it seeks our hearts to have,
Meanwhile there reason makes his grave;
For many things the eyes approve
Which yet the heart doth seldom love.

For as the seeds in springtime sown
Die in the ground ere they be grown,
Such is conceit, whose rooting fails,
As child that in the cradle quails,
Or else within the mother's womb
Hath his beginning and his tomb.

Affection follows fortune's wheels
And soon is shaken from her heels;
For following beauty or estate
Her liking still is turned to hate;
For all affections have their change
And fancy only loves to range.

Desire himself runs out of breath,
And getting, does but gain his death;
Desire nor reason hath nor rest,
And blind doth seldom choose the best;
Desire attained is not desire,
But as the cinders of the fire.

As ships in port desired are drowned,
As fruit once ripe then falls to ground,
As flies that seek for flames are brought
To cinders by the flames they sought,
So fond desire when it attains
The life expires, the woe remains.

And yet some poets fain would prove
Affection to be perfect love,
And that desire is of that kind,

No less a passion of the mind,
As if wild beasts and men did seek
To like, to love, to choose alike.

Sir Walter Ralegh

1 imagination

157   *The lie*

Go, soul, the body's guest,
Upon a thankless arrant;
Fear not to touch the best;
The truth shall be thy warrant.
Go, since I needs must die,
And give the world the lie.

Say to the court, it glows,
And shines like rotten wood;
Say to the church, it shows
What's good, and doth no good.
If church and court reply,
Then give them both the lie.

Tell potentates they live
Acting by others' action;
Not loved unless they give,
Not strong but by a faction.
If potentates reply,
Give potentates the lie.

Tell men of high condition
That manage the estate
Their purpose is ambition,
Their practice only hate;
And if they once reply,
Then give them all the lie.

Tell them that brave it most
They beg for more by spending
Who, in their greatest cost,

Seek nothing but commending;
And if they make reply,
Then give them all the lie.

Tell zeal it wants devotion;
Tell love it is but lust;
Tell time it is but motion;
Tell flesh it is but dust;
And wish them not reply,
For thou must give the lie.

Tell age it daily wasteth;
Tell honour how it alters;
Tell beauty how she blasteth;
Tell favour how it falters;
And as they shall reply,
Give every one the lie.

Tell wit how much it wrangles
In tickle points of niceness;
Tell wisdom she entangles
Herself in over-wiseness;
And when they do reply,
Straight give them both the lie.

Tell physic of her boldness;
Tell skill it is pretension;
Tell charity of coldness;
Tell law it is contention;
And as they do reply,
So give them still the lie.

Tell fortune of her blindness;
Tell nature of decay;
Tell friendship of unkindness;
Tell justice of delay;
And if they will reply,
Then give them all the lie.

Tell arts they have no soundness,
But vary by esteeming;
Tell schools they want profoundness,
And stand too much on seeming.
If arts and schools reply,
Give arts and schools the lie.

Tell faith it's fled the city;
Tell how the country erreth;
Tell, manhood shakes off pity;
Tell, virtue least preferreth;
And if they do reply,
Spare not to give the lie.

So when thou hast, as I
Commanded thee, done blabbing,
Although to give the lie
Deserves no less than stabbing,
Stab at thee he that will,
No stab the soul can kill.

Sir Walter Ralegh

158 *The passionate man's pilgrimage*

Give me my scallop-shell of quiet,
My staff of faith to walk upon,
My scrip of joy, immortal diet,
My bottle of salvation,
My gown of glory, hope's true gage;
And thus I'll take my pilgrimage.

Blood must be my body's balmer;
No other balm will there be given;
Whilst my soul, like a white palmer,
Travels to the land of heaven;
Over the silver mountains,
Where spring the nectar fountains;
  There will I kiss
  The bowl of bliss,

And drink my everlasting fill
On every milken hill.
My soul will be a-dry before,
But after it will thirst no more.

Then by that happy blissful day
More peaceful pilgrims I shall see,
That have cast off their rags of clay
And walk apparelled fresh like me.
   I'll take them first
   To quench their thirst
And taste of nectar suckets
   At those clear wells
   Where sweetness dwells
Drawn up by saints in crystal buckets.

And when our bottles and all we
Are filled with immortality,
Then the blest paths we'll travel,
Strowed with rubies, thick as gravel;
Ceilings of diamonds, sapphire floors,
High walls of coral and pearly bowers.
From thence to heaven's bribless hall
Where no currupted voices brawl,
No conscience molten into gold,
No forged accuser bought and sold,
No cause deferred, no vain-spent journey,
For there Christ is the king's attorney,
Who pleads for all without degrees,
And he hath angels but no fees.
And when the grand twelve-million jury
Of our sins with direful fury
Against our souls black verdicts give,
Christ pleads his death and then we live.

Be thou my speaker, taintless pleader,
Unblotted lawyer, true proceeder!
Thou givest salvation even for alms,
Not with a bribèd lawyer's palms;
And this is mine eternal plea
To him that made heaven, earth and sea,

That since my flesh must die so soon
And want a head to dine next noon,
Just at the stroke when my veins start and spread
Set on my soul an everlasting head!
Then am I ready, like a palmer fit,
To tread those blest paths which before I writ.

Sir Walter Ralegh

159 *The wood, the weed, the wag*

Three things there be that prosper all apace
And flourish while they are asunder far,
But on a day they meet all in a place,
And when they meet they one another mar.

And they be these: the wood, the weed, the wag.
The wood is that that makes the gallows tree;
The weed is that that strings the hangman's bag;
The wag, my pretty knave, betokens thee.

Now mark, dear boy, while these assemble not,
Green springs the tree, hemp grows, the wag is wild;
But when they meet it makes the timber rot,
It frets the halter and it chokes the child.
  God bless the child!

Sir Walter Ralegh

160 *My body in the walls*

My body in the walls captivèd
Feels not the wounds of spiteful envy;
But my thralled mind, of liberty deprivèd,
Fast fettered in her ancient memory,
Doth nought behold but sorrow's dying face.
Such prison erst was so delightful
As it desired no other dwelling-place,
But time's effects and destinies despiteful

Have changèd both my keeper and my fare.
Love's fire and beauty's light I then had store,
But now, close kept as captives wonted are,
That food, that heat, that light I find no more.

Despair bolts up my doors and I alone
Speak to dead walls, but these hear not my moan.

Sir Walter Ralegh

161   *One day I wrote her name*

One day I wrote her name upon the strand,
But came the waves and washèd it away:
Again I wrote it with a second hand,
But came the tide and made my pains his prey.
'Vain man,' said she, 'that dost in vain assay
A mortal thing so to immortalise,
For I myself shall like to this decay,
And eek my name be wipèd out likewise.'
'Not so,' quod I, 'let baser things devise
To die in dust, but you shall live by fame:
My verse your virtues rare shall eternise,
And in the heavens write your glorious name.
Where whenas death shall all the world subdue,
    Our love shall live and later life renew.'

Edmund Spenser

162   *Fidele's song*

I serve a mistress whiter than the snow,
    Straighter than cedar, brighter than the glass,
Finer in trip and swifter than the roe,
    More pleasant than the field of flowering grass;
More gladsome to my withering joys that fade,
Than winter's sun or summer's cooling shade.

Sweeter than swelling grape of ripest wine,
  Softer than feathers of the fairest swan,
Smoother than jet, more stately than the pine,
  Fresher than poplar, smaller than my span,
Clearer than beauty's fiery pointed beam,
Or icy crust of crystal's frozen stream.

Yet she is curster than the bear by kind,
  And harder-hearted than the aged oak,
More glib than oil, more fickle than the wind,
  Stiffer than steel, no sooner bent but broke.
Lo! thus my service is a lasting sore;
Yet will I serve, although I die therefore.

Anthony Munday

163   *Dirge for Robin Hood*

Weep, weep, ye woodmen, wail;
  Your hands with sorrow wring!
Your master Robin Hood lies dead,
  Therefore sigh as you sing.

Here lies his primer and his beads,
  His bent bow and his arrows keen,
His good sword and his holy cross.
  Now cast on flowers fresh and green;

And, as they fall, shed tears and say
  Well-a, well-a-day! well-a, well-a-day!
Thus cast ye flowers and sing,
  And on to Wakefield take your way.

Anthony Munday

164   *Beauty sat bathing*

Beauty sat bathing by a spring
  Where fairest shades did hide her;
The winds blew calm, the birds did sing,
  The cool streams ran beside her.

My wanton thoughts enticed mine eye
    To see what was forbidden:
But memory said, fie!
    So vain desire was chidden:—
        Hey nonny nonny O!
        Hey nonny nonny!

Into a slumber then I fell,
    When fond imagination
Seemèd to see, but could not tell
    Her feature or her fashion.
But even as babes in dreams do smile,
    And sometimes fall a-weeping,
So I awaked, as wise this while
    As when I fell a-sleeping:—
        Hey nonny nonny O!
        Hey nonny nonny!

Anthony Munday

165   *O wearisome condition*

O wearisome condition of humanity!
Born under one law, to another bound;
Vainly begot, and yet forbidden vanity,
Created sick, commanded to be sound;
What meaneth Nature by these diverse laws?
Passion and reason self-division cause;
Is it the mark or majesty of power
To make offences that it may forgive?
Nature herself doth her own self deflower
To hate those errors which herself doth give.

Fulke Greville, Lord Brooke

166   *You little stars*

You little stars that live in skies
    And glory in Apollo's glory,
In whose aspect conjoinèd lies
    The Heaven's will and Nature's story,

Joy to be likened to those eyes,
    Which eyes make all eyes glad or sorry;
For when you force thoughts from above,
These overrule your force by love.

And thou, O love, which in these eyes
    Hast married reason with affection,
And made them saints of beauty's skies,
    Where joys are shadows of perfection,
Lend me thy wings that I may rise
    Up not by worth but thy election;
For I have vowed in strangest fashion
To love and never seek compassion.

Fulke Greville, Lord Brooke

167 *Myra*

I, with whose colours Myra dressed her head,
    I, that wore posies of her own hand-making,
I, that mine own name in the chimneys[1] read
    By Myra finely wrought ere I was waking:
Must I look on, in hope time coming may
With change bring back my turn again to play?

I, that on Sunday at the church-stile found
    A garland sweet with true-love-knots in flowers,
Which I to wear about my arms was bound
    That each of us might know that all was ours:
Must I lead now an idle life in wishes,
And follow Cupid for his loaves and fishes?

I, that did wear the ring her mother left,
    I, for whose love she gloried to be blamèd,
I, with whose eyes her eyes committed theft,
    I, who did make her blush when I was namèd:
Must I lose ring, flowers, blush, theft, and go naked,
Watching with sighs till dead love be awakèd?

Was it for this that I might Myra see
  Washing the water with her beauty's white?
Yet would she never write her love to me.
  Thinks wit of change when thoughts are in delight?
Mad girls may safely love as they may leave;
No man can print a kiss: lines may deceive.

                              Fulke Greville, Lord Brooke

1 i.e. tapestry screens

168 *My true love hath my heart*

My true love hath my heart and I have his,
  By just exchange one for another given:
    I hold his dear and mine he cannot miss;
  There never was a better bargain driven:
    My true love hath my heart and I have his.

My heart in me keeps him and me in one;
  My heart in him his thoughts and senses guides;
    He loves my heart for once it was his own;
  I cherish his because in me it bides:
    My true love hath my heart and I have his.

                              Sir Philip Sidney

169 *Loving in truth*

Loving in truth, and fain in verse my love to show,
  That she, dear she, might take some pleasure of my
                                              pain,
Pleasure might cause her read, reading might make her
                                              know,
  Knowledge might pity win and pity grace obtain—
I sought fit words to paint the blackest face of woe,
  Studying inventions fine, her wits to entertain,
Oft turning others' leaves to see if thence would flow
  Some fresh and fruitful showers upon my sunburned
                                              brain.

But words came halting forth, wanting Invention's stay;
    Invention, Nature's child, fled stepdame Study's
                        blows,
And others' feet still seemed but strangers in my way.
    Thus, great with child to speak, and helpless in my
                        throes,
    Biting my truant pen, beating myself for spite,
    'Fool,' said my Muse to me, 'look in thy heart and
                        write.'

Sir Philip Sidney

170   *Come sleep*

Come sleep, O sleep, the certain knot of peace,
    The baiting-place of wit, the balm of woe,
The poor man's wealth, the prisoner's release,
    Th'indifferent judge between the high and low;
With shield of proof shield me from out the press
    Of those fierce darts despair at me doth throw;
O make me in those civil wars to cease;
    I will good tribute pay, if thou do so.
Take thou of me smooth pillows, sweetest bed,
    A chamber deaf to noise and blind to light,
A rosy garland and a weary head;
    And if these things, as being thine by right,
      Move not thy heavy grace, thou shalt in me,
      Livelier than elsewhere, Stella's image see.

Sir Philip Sidney

171   *A very phoenix*

A very phoenix, in her radiant eyes
    I leave mine age, and get my life again;
True Hesperus, I watch her fall and rise
    And with my tears extinguish all my pain.

My lips for shadows shield her springing roses,
   Mine eyes for watchmen guard her while she sleepeth,
My reasons serve to 'quite her faint supposes;
   Her fancy, mine; my faith her fancy keepeth;
She flower, I branch; her sweet my sour supporteth,
O happy Love, where such delights consorteth!

Thomas Lodge

172   *Weep not, my wanton*

Weep not, my wanton, smile upon my knee;
When thou art old there's grief enough for thee.
   Mother's wag, pretty boy,
   Father's sorrow, father's joy.
   When thy father first did see
   Such a boy by him and me,
   He was glad, I was woe:
   Fortune changèd made him so,
   When he left his pretty boy,
   Last his sorrow, first his joy.

Weep not, my wanton, smile upon my knee;
When thou art old there's grief enough for thee.
   Streaming tears that never stint,
   Like pearl drops from a flint,
   Fell by course from his eyes,
   That one another's place supplies:
   Thus he grieved in every part,
   Tears of blood fell from his heart,
   When he left his pretty boy,
   Father's sorrow, father's joy.

Weep not, my wanton, smile upon my knee;
When thou art old there's grief enough for thee.
   The wanton smiled, father wept;
   Mother cried, baby leapt;
   More he crowed, more we cried;
   Nature could not sorrow hide.

He must go, he must kiss
Child and mother, baby bliss;
For he left his pretty boy,
Father's sorrow, father's joy.

Weep not, my wanton, smile upon my knee;
When thou art old there's grief enough for thee.

Robert Greene

173 *The old knight*

His golden locks time hath to silver turned;
   O time too swift, O swiftness never ceasing!
His youth 'gainst time and age hath ever spurned,
   But spurned in vain; youth waneth by increasing:
Beauty, strength, youth, are flowers by fading seen;
Duty, faith, love, are roots, and ever green.

His helmet now shall make a hive for bees;
   And, lovers' sonnets turned to holy psalms,
A man-at-arms must now serve on his knees,
   And feed on prayers, which are age's alms:
But though from court to cottage he depart,
His saint is sure of his unspotted heart.

And when he saddest sits in homely cell,
   He'll teach his swains this carol for a song:
'Blest be the hearts that wish my sovereign well,
   Curst be the souls that think her any wrong.'
Goddess, allow this aged man his right,
To be your beadsman now that was your knight.

George Peele

174 *Bethsabe's song*

Hot sun, cool fire, tempered with sweet air,
Black shade, fair nurse, shadow my white hair:
Shine, sun; burn, fire; breathe, air, and ease me;
Black shade, fair nurse, shroud me and please me:

Shadow, my sweet nurse, keep me from burning,
Make not my glad cause, cause of mourning.
    Let not my beauty's fire
    Inflame unstaid desire,
    Nor pierce any bright eye
    That wandereth lightly.

                  George Peele

175   *Whenas the rye*

Whenas the rye reach to the chin,
   And chopcherry, chopcherry ripe within,
Strawberries swimming in the cream,
And schoolboys playing in the stream;
    Then O, then O, then O my true love said,
      Till that time come again,
    She could not live a maid.

                  George Peele

176   *A voice from the well*

Fair maiden, white and red,
Comb me smooth and stroke my head
And thou shalt have some cockle bread.
Gently dip but not too deep,
For fear thou make the golden beard to weep.
Fair maid, white and red,
Comb me smooth and stroke my head;
And every hair a sheave shall be,
And every sheave a golden tree.

                  George Peele

177   *Treason*

Treason doth never prosper; what's the reason?
For if it prosper, none dare call it treason.

               Sir John Harington

As I in hoary winter's night
　　Stood shivering in the snow,
Surprised I was with sudden heat
　　Which made my heart to glow;
And lifting up a fearful eye
　　To view what fire was near,
A pretty babe all burning bright
　　Did in the air appear;
Who, scorchèd with excessive heat,
　　Such floods of tears did shed,
As though his floods should quench his flames,
　　Which with his tears were bred:
'Alas!' quoth he, 'but newly born
　　In fiery heats I fry,
Yet none approach to warm their hearts
　　Or feel my fire but I!
My faultless breast the furnace is;
　　The fuel, wounding thorns;
Love is the fire, and sighs the smoke;
　　The ashes, shames and scorns;
The fuel justice layeth on,
　　And mercy blows the coals,
The metal in this furnace wrought
　　Are men's defilèd souls:
For which, as now on fire I am
　　To work them to their good,
So will I melt into a bath,
　　To wash them in my blood.'
With this he vanished out of sight
　　And swiftly shrunk away,
And straight I callèd unto mind
　　That it was Christmas day.

Robert Southwell

179   *Diaphenia*

　　Diaphenia like a daffadowndilly,
　　　White as the sun, fair as the lily,

Heigh ho, how I do love thee!
  I do love thee as my lambs
  Are belovèd of their dams;
How blest were I if thou woulds't prove me.

  Diaphenia like the spreading roses,
  That in thy sweets all sweets encloses,
Fair sweet, how I do love thee!
  I do love thee as each flower
  Loves the sun's life-giving power;
For dead, thy breath to life might move me.

  Diaphenia like to all things blessed
  When all thy praises are expressèd,
Dear joy, how I do love thee!
  As the birds do love the spring,
  Or the bees their careful king:
Then in requite, sweet virgin, love me!

Henry Constable

180   *Care-charmer sleep*

Care-charmer sleep, son of the sable night,
  Brother to death, in silent darkness born,
Relieve my anguish and restore the light,
  With dark forgetting of my cares return.
And let the day be time enough to mourn
  The shipwreck of my ill-adventured youth;
Let waking eyes suffice to wail their storm,
  Without the torment of the night's untruth.
Cease, dreams, the images of day-desires,
  To model forth the passions of the morrow;
Never let rising sun approve you liars,
  To add more grief to aggravate my sorrow.
    Still let me sleep, embracing clouds in vain;
    And never wake to feel the day's disdain.

Samuel Daniel

181 *Love is a sickness*

Love is a sickness full of woes,
   All remedies refusing;
A plant that with most cutting grows,
   Most barren with best using.
      Why so?
More we enjoy it, more it dies;
   If not enjoyed, it sighing cries,
      Heigh ho!

Love is a torment of the mind,
   A tempest everlasting;
And Jove hath made it of a kind
   Not well, nor full, nor fasting.
      Why so?
More we enjoy it, more it dies;
   If not enjoyed, it sighing cries,
      Heigh ho!

Samuel Daniel

182 *How many foolish things*

How many paltry, foolish, painted things
That now in coaches trouble every street
Shall be forgotten whom no poet sings
Ere they be well wrapped in their winding sheet!
Where I to thee eternity shall give,
When nothing else remaineth of these days,
And queens hereafter shall be glad to live
Upon the alms of thy superfluous praise.
Virgins and matrons, reading these my rhymes,
Shall be so much delighted with thy story,
That they shall grieve they lived not in these times,
To have seen thee, thy sex's only glory:
   So shalt thou fly above the vulgar throng,
   Still to survive in my immortal song.

Michael Drayton

Fair stood the wind for France
When we our sails advance,
Nor now to prove our chance
   Longer will tarry;
But putting to the main
At Caux, the mouth of Seine,
With all his martial train
   Landed King Harry.

And taking many a fort,
Furnish'd in warlike sort,
Marcheth tow'rds Agincourt
   In happy hour;
Skirmishing day by day
With those that stopp'd his way,
Where the French Gen'ral lay
   With all his power.

Which, in his height of pride,
King Henry to deride,
His ransom to provide
   Unto him sending;
Which he neglects the while
As from a nation vile,
Yet with an angry smile
   Their fall portending.

And turning to his men,
Quoth our brave Henry then,
'Though they to one be ten
   Be not amazèd:
Yet have we well begun;
Battles so bravely won
Have ever to the sun
   By fame been raisèd.

'And for myself (quoth he)
This my full rest shall be:
England ne'er mourn for me
   Nor more esteem me:

Victor I will remain
Or on this earth lie slain,
Never shall she sustain
    Loss to redeem me.

'Poitiers and Cressy tell,
When most their pride did swell,
Under our swords they fell:
    No less our skill is
Than when our grandsire great,
Claiming the regal seat,
By many a warlike feat
    Lopp'd the French lilies.'

The Duke of York so dread
The eager vaward led;
With the main Henry sped
    Among his henchmen.
Excester had the rear,
A braver man not there;
O Lord how hot they were
    On the false Frenchmen!

They now to fight are gone,
Armour on armour shone,
Drum now to drum did groan,
    To hear was wonder;
That with the cries they make
The very earth did shake:
Trumpet to trumpet spake,
    Thunder to thunder.

Well it thine age became,
O noble Erpingham,
Which didst the signal aim
    To our hid forces!
When from a meadow by,
Like a storm suddenly
The English archery
    Stuck the French horses.

With Spanish yew so strong,
Arrows a cloth-yard long
That like to serpents stung,
    Piercing the weather;
None from his fellow starts,
But playing manly parts,
And like true English hearts
    Stuck close together.

When down their bows they threw,
And forth their bilbos[1] drew,
And on the French they flew,
    Not one was tardy;
Arms were from shoulders sent,
Scalps to the teeth were rent,
Down the French peasants went—
    Our men were hardy.

This while our noble king,
His broadsword brandishing,
Down the French host did ding
    As to o'erwhelm it;
And many a deep wound lent,
His arms with blood besprent,
And many a cruel dent
    Bruisèd his helmet.

Gloster, that duke so good,
Next of the royal blood,
For famous England stood
    With his brave brother;
Clarence, in steel so bright,
Though but a maiden knight,
Yet in that furious fight
    Scarce such another.

Warwick in blood did wade,
Oxford the foe invade,
And cruel slaughter made
    Still as they ran up;

Suffolk his axe did ply,
Beaumont and Willoughby
Bare them right doughtily,
   Ferrers and Fanhope.

Upon Saint Crispin's Day
Fought was this noble fray,
Which fame did not delay
   To England to carry.
O when shall English men
With such acts fill a pen?
Or England breed again
   Such a King Harry?

Michael Drayton

1 bilbos—swords, from Bilbao

184   *To the Virginian voyage*

You brave heroic minds
   Worthy your country's name,
     That honour still pursue;
     Go and subdue!
Whilst loitering hinds
   Lurk here at home with shame.

Britons, you stay too long:
   Quickly aboard bestow you,
     And with a merry gale
     Swell your stretch'd sail
With vows as strong
   As the winds that blow you.

Your course securely steer,
   West and by south forth keep!
     Rocks, lee-shores, nor shoals
     When Eolus scowls
You need not fear;
   So absolute the deep.

And cheerfully at sea
  Success you still entice
    To get the pearl and gold,
    And ours to hold
Virginia,
  Earth's only paradise.

Where nature hath in store
  Fowl, venison, and fish,
    And the fruitfull'st soil
    Without your toil
Three harvests more,
  All greater than your wish.

And the ambitious vine
  Crowns with his purple mass
    The cedar reaching high
    To kiss the sky,
The cypress, pine,
  And useful sassafras.

To whom the Golden Age
  Still nature's laws doth give,
    No other cares attend,
    But them to defend
From winter's rage,
  That long there doth not live.

When as the luscious smell
  Of that delicious land
    Above the seas that flows
    The clear wind throws,
Your hearts to swell
  Approaching the dear strand;

In kenning of the shore
  (Thanks to God first given)
    O you the happiest men,
    Be frolic then!
Let cannons roar,
  Frighting the wide heaven.

And in regions far,
  Such heroes bring ye forth
    As those from whom we came;
    And plant our name
Under that star
  Not known unto our North.

And as there plenty grows
Of laurel everywhere—
    Apollo's sacred tree—
    You it may see
A poet's brows
  To crown, that may sing there.

Thy *Voyages* attend,
  Industrious Hakluyt,
    Whose reading shall inflame
    Men to seek fame,
And much commend
  To after times thy wit.

                Michael Drayton

185   *Sirena*

Near to the silver *Trent*
  Sirena dwelleth;
She to whom Nature lent
  All that excelleth;
By which the Muses late
  And the neat Graces
Have for their greater state
  Taken their places;
Twisting an anadem
  Wherewith to crown her,
As it belong'd to them
  Most to renown her.
        On thy bank,
        In a rank,
        Let thy swans sing her,
      And with their music
      Along let them bring her.

Tagus and *Pactolus*
  Are to thee debtor,
Nor for their gold to us
  Are they the better:
Henceforth of all the rest
  Be thou the River
Which, as the daintiest,
  Puts them down ever.
For as my precious one
  O'er thee doth travel,
She to pearl paragon
  Turneth thy gravel.
          On thy bank . . .

Our mournful Philomel,
  That rarest tuner,
Henceforth in Aperil
  Shall wake the sooner,
And to her shall complain
  From the thick cover,
Redoubling every strain
  Over and over:
For when my Love too long
  Her chamber keepeth,
As though it suffer'd wrong,
  The Morning weepeth.
          On thy bank . . .

Oft have I seen the Sun,
  To do her honour,
Fix himself at his noon
  To look upon her;
And hath gilt every grove,
  Every hill near her,
With his flames from above
  Striving to cheer her:
And when she from his sight
  Hath herself turnèd,
He, as it had been night,
  In clouds hath mournèd.
          On thy bank . . .

The verdant meads are seen,
  When she doth view them,
In fresh and gallant green
  Straight to renew them;
And every little grass
  Broad itself spreadeth,
Proud that this bonny lass
  Upon it treadeth:
Nor flower is so sweet
  In this large cincture,
But it upon her feet
  Leaveth some tincture.
        On thy bank . . .

The fishes in the flood,
  When she doth angle,
For the hook strive a-good
  Them to entangle;
And leaping on the land,
  From the clear water,
Their scales upon the sand
  Lavishly scatter;
Therewith to pave the mould
  Whereon she passes,
So herself to behold
  As in her glasses.
        On thy bank . . .

When she looks out by night,
  The stars stand gazing,
Like comets to our sight
  Fearfully blazing;
As wond'ring at her eyes
  With their much brightness
Which so amaze the skies,
  Dimming their lightness.
The raging tempests are calm
  When she speaketh,
Such most delightsome balm
  From her lips breaketh.
        On thy bank . . .

In all our *Brittany*
　　There's not a fairer,
Nor can you fit any
　　Should you compare her.
Angels her eyelids keep,
　　All hearts surprising;
Which look whilst she doth sleep
　　Like the sun's rising:
She alone of her kind
　　Knoweth true measure,
And her unmatchèd mind
　　Is heavens' treasure.
　　　　　On thy bank . . .

Fair *Dove* and *Darwen* clear,
　　Boast ye your beauties,
To *Trent* your mistress here
　　Yet pay your duties:
My Love was higher born
　　Tow'rds the full fountains,
Yet she doth moorland scorn
　　And the *Peak* mountains;
Nor would she none should dream
　　Where she abideth,
Humble as is the stream
　　Which by her slideth.
　　　　　On thy bank . . .

Yet my poor rustic Muse
　　Nothing can move her,
Nor the means I can use,
　　Though her true lover:
Many a long winter's night
　　Have I waked for her,
Yet this my piteous plight
　　Nothing can stir her.
All thy sands, silver *Trent*,
　　Down to the *Humber*,
The sighs that I have spent
　　Never can number.

On thy bank,
In a rank,
Let thy swans sing her,
And with their music
Along let them bring her.

Michael Drayton

186 *Since there's no help*

Since there's no help, come let us kiss and part—
Nay, I have done, you get no more of me;
And I am glad, yea, glad with all my heart,
That thus so cleanly I myself can free.
Shake hands for ever, cancel all our vows,
And when we meet at any time again,
Be it not seen in either of our brows
That we one jot of former love retain.
Now at the last gasp of Love's latest breath,
When, his pulse failing, Passion speechless lies,
When Faith is kneeling by his bed of death,
And Innocence is closing up his eyes,
   —Now if thou woulds't, when all have given him
    over,
   From death to life thou might'st him yet recover.

Michael Drayton

187 *The garden*

The world's a garden; pleasures are the flowers,
  Of fairest hues, in form and number many:
  The lily, first, pure-whitest flower of any,
Rose sweetest rare, with pinkèd gilliflowers,
The violet, and double marigold,
  And pansy too: but after all mischances,
Death's winter comes and kills with sudden cold
  Rose, lily, violet, marigold, pink, pansies.

Joshua Sylvester

188 Go, silly worm

Go, silly worm, drudge, trudge and travel,
  Despising pain;
    So thou mayst gain
Some honour, or some golden gravel:
But death the while (to fill his number)
    With sudden call
    Takes thee from all
To prove thy days but dream and slumber.

Joshua Sylvester

189 When daisies pied

When daisies pied and violets blue
  And lady-smocks all silver-white
And cuckoo-buds of yellow hue
  Do paint the meadows with delight,
The cuckoo then, on every tree,
Mocks married men; for thus sings he,
    Cuckoo!
Cuckoo, cuckoo! O word of fear,
Unpleasing to a married ear!

When shepherds pipe on oaten straws,
  And merry larks are ploughmen's clocks,
When turtles tread, and rooks, and daws,
  And maidens bleach their summer smocks,
The cuckoo then, on every tree,
Mocks married men; for thus sings he,
    Cuckoo!
Cuckoo, cockoo! O word of fear,
Unpleasing to a married ear!

William Shakespeare

When icicles hang by the wall
  And Dick the shepherd blows his nail
And Tom bears logs into the hall
  And milk comes frozen home in pail,
When blood is nipped and ways be foul,
Then nightly sings the staring owl,
    To-whit!
To-who!—a merry note,
While greasy Joan doth keel the pot.

When all aloud the wind doth blow
  And coughing drowns the parson's saw
And birds sit brooding in the snow
  And Marian's nose looks red and raw,
When roasted crabs hiss in the bowl,
Then nightly sings the staring owl,
    Tu-whit!
To-who!—a merry note,
While greasy Joan doth keel the pot.

William Shakespeare

191   *Come unto these yellow sands*

Come unto these yellow sands,
And then take hands,
Curtsied when you have, and kissed,
The wild waves whist,
Foot it featly here and there;
And, sweet sprites, the burthen bear.
    Hark, hark!
      Bow, wow,
    The watch-dogs bark:
      Bow, wow.
Hark, hark! I hear
The strain of strutting chanticleer
Cry, Cock-a-diddle-dow!

William Shakespeare

Where the bee sucks, there suck I:
In a cowslip's bell I lie;
There I couch when owls do cry.
On the bat's back I do fly
After summer merrily:
Merrily, merrily shall I live now,
Under the blossom that hangs on the bough.

William Shakespeare

193 *Full fathom five*

Full fathom five thy father lies;
  Of his bones are coral made;
Those are pearls that were his eyes:
  Nothing of him that doth fade
But doth suffer a sea-change
Into something rich and strange.
Sea-nymphs hourly ring his knell:
    Ding-dong.
  Hark! now I hear them—
    Ding-dong, bell!

William Shakespeare

194 *O mistress mine*

O mistress mine, where are you roaming?
O stay and hear! Your true love's coming,
That can sing both high and low:
Trip no further, pretty sweeting;
Journey's end in lovers meeting,
Every wise man's son doth know.

What is love? 'Tis not hereafter;
Present mirth hath present laughter;
What's to come is still unsure:
In delay there lies no plenty;
Then come kiss me, sweet-and-twenty!
Youth's a stuff will not endure.

William Shakespeare

195   *Come away, come away, death*

Come away, come away, death,
And in sad cypress let me be laid;
Fly away, fly away, breath;
I am slain by a fair cruel maid.
My shroud of white, stuck all with yew,
      O prepare it!
My part of death, no one so true
      Did share it.

Not a flower, not a flower sweet,
On my black coffin let there be strown;
Not a friend, not a friend greet
My poor corse, where my bones shall be thrown:
A thousand thousand sighs to save,
      Lay me O where
Sad true lover never find my grave
      To weep there!

William Shakespeare

196   *Under the greenwood tree*

Under the greenwood tree,
Who loves to lie with me,
And turn his merry note
Unto the sweet bird's throat,

Come hither, come hither, come hither;
  Here shall he see
  No enemy
But winter and rough weather.

Who doth ambition shun,
And loves to lie i' the sun,
Seeking the food he eats
And pleased with what he gets,
Come hither, come hither, come hither:
  Here shall he see
  No enemy
But winter and rough weather.

William Shakespeare

197 *Blow, blow, thou winter wind*

Blow, blow, thou winter wind,
Thou art not so unkind,
  As man's ingratitude;
Thy tooth is not so keen,
Because thou art not seen,
  Although thy breath be rude.
Heigh ho! sing heigh ho! unto the green holly:
Most friendship is feigning, most loving mere folly:
  Then heigh ho, the holly!
  This life is most jolly.

Freeze, freeze, thou bitter sky,
That dost not bite so nigh
  As benefits forgot:
Though thou the waters warp,
Thy sting is not so sharp
  As friend remembered not.
Heigh ho! sing heigh ho! unto the green holly:
Most friendship is feigning, most loving mere folly:
  Then heigh ho, the holly!
  This life is most jolly.

William Shakespeare

It was a lover and his lass,
  With a hey and a ho and a hey nonino,
That o'er the green cornfield did pass,
  In the spring time, the only pretty ring time,
When birds do sing, hey ding a ding, ding;
Sweet lovers love the spring.

Between the acres of the rye,
  With a hey and a ho and a hey nonino,
These pretty country folks would lie,
  In the spring time, the only pretty ring time,
When birds do sing, hey ding a ding, ding;
Sweet lovers love the spring.

This carol they began that hour,
  With a hey and a ho and a hey nonino,
How that life was but a flower,
  In the spring time, the only pretty ring time,
When birds do sing, hey ding a ding, ding;
Sweet lovers love the spring.

And therefore take the present time,
  With a hey and a ho and a hey nonino,
For love is crownèd with the prime,
  In the spring time, the only pretty ring time,
When birds do sing, hey ding a ding, ding;
Sweet lovers love the spring.

William Shakespeare

199   Take, O take those lips away

Take, O take those lips away,
  That so sweetly were forsworn;
And those eyes, the break of day,
  Lights that do mislead the morn!

But my kisses bring again,
 Bring again;
Seals of love, but sealed in vain,
 Sealed in vain!

William Shakespeare

200 *Hark, hark! the lark*

Hark, hark, the lark at Heaven's gate sings,
 And Phoebus 'gins arise,
His steeds to water at those springs
 In chaliced flowers that lies;
And winking Mary-buds begin
 To ope their golden eyes;
With everything that pretty bin
My lady sweet, arise!
 Arise, arise!

William Shakespeare

201 *Fear no more the heat o' the sun*

Fear no more the heat o' the sun,
 Nor the furious winter's rages;
Thou thy worldly task hast done,
 Home art gone and ta'en thy wages;
Golden lads and girls all must
As chimney-sweepers come to dust.

Fear no more the frown o' the great,
 Thou art past the tyrant's stroke;
Care no more to clothe and eat;
 To thee the reed is as the oak;
The sceptre, learning, physic must
All follow this and come to dust.

Fear no more the lightning-flash,
  Nor the all-dreaded thunder-stone;
Fear not slander, censure rash;
  Thou hast finished joy and moan;
All lovers young, all lovers must
Consign to thee and come to dust.

William Shakespeare

202 *Orpheus with his lute*

Orpheus with his lute made trees
And the mountain tops that freeze
  Bow themselves when he did sing:
To his music plants and flowers
Ever sprung; as sun and showers
  There had made a lasting spring.

Every thing that heard him play,
Even the billows of the sea,
  Hung their heads and then lay by.
In sweet music is such art,
Killing care and grief of heart
  Fall asleep, or hearing die.

William Shakespeare

203 *Sigh no more, ladies*

Sigh no more, ladies, sigh no more;
  Men were deceivers ever;
One foot in sea and one on shore,
  To one thing constant never.
Then sigh not so, but let them go,
  And be you blithe and bonny,
Converting all your sounds of woe
  Into Hey nonny nonny!

Sing no more ditties, sing no mo,
    Of dumps so dull and heavy;
The fraud of men was ever so,
    Since summer first was leavy.
Then sigh not so, but let them go,
    And be you blithe and bonny,
Converting all your sounds of woe
    Into Hey nonny nonny!

William Shakespeare

204   *The wind and the rain*

When that I was and a little tiny boy,
    With hey ho, the wind and the rain,
A foolish thing was but a toy,
    For the rain it raineth every day.

But when I came to man's estate,
    With hey ho, the wind and the rain,
'Gainst knaves and thieves men shut their gate,
    For the rain it raineth every day.

But when I came, alas! to wive,
    With hey ho, the wind and the rain,
By swaggering could I never thrive,
    For the rain it raineth every day.

But when I came unto my beds,
    With hey ho, the wind and the rain,
With toss-pots still had drunken heads,
    For the rain it raineth every day.

A great while ago the world begun,
    With hey ho, the wind and the rain,
But that's all one, our play is done,
    And we'll strive to please you every day.

William Shakespeare

205 *When daffodils begin to peer*

When daffodils begin to peer,
   With hey! the doxy over the dale,
Why, then comes in the sweet o' the year;
   For the red blood reigns in the winter's pale.

The white sheet bleaching on the hedge,
   With hey! the sweet birds O how they sing!
Doth set my pugging tooth on edge;
   For a quart of ale is a dish for a king.

The lark, that tirra-lirra chants,
   With hey, with hey! the thrush and the jay;
Are summer songs for me and my aunts,
   While we lie tumbling in the hay.

William Shakespeare

206 *Jog on, jog on*

Jog on, jog on, the footpath way,
   And merrily hent the stile-a;
A merry heart goes all the day,
   Your sad tires in a mile-a.

William Shakespeare

Sonnets by William Shakespeare

207   SONNET 12

When I do count the clock that tells the time,
And see the brave day sunk in hideous night;
When I behold the violet past prime,
And sable curls all silver'd o'er with white;

When lofty trees I see barren of leaves,
Which erst from heat did canopy the herd,
And summer's green, all girded up in sheaves,
Borne on the bier with white and bristly beard;
Then of thy beauty do I question make,
That thou among the wastes of time must go,
Since sweets and beauties do themselves forsake,
And die as fast as they see others grow;
    And nothing 'gainst Time's scythe can make defence
    Save breed, to brave him when he takes thee hence.

SONNET 18

Shall I compare thee to a summer's day?
Thou art more lovely and more temperate:
Rough winds do shake the darling buds of May,
And summer's lease hath all too short a date:
Sometime too hot the eye of heaven shines,
And often is his gold complexion dimm'd;
And every fair from fair sometime declines,
By chance, or nature's changing course, untrimm'd;
But thy eternal summer shall not fade,
Nor lose possession of that fair thou ow'st;
Nor shall Death brag thou wander'st in his shade,
When in eternal lines to time thou grow'st:
    So long as men can breathe, or eyes can see,
    So long lives this, and this gives life to thee.

SONNET 19

Devouring Time, blunt thou the lion's paws,
And make the earth devour her own sweet brood;
Pluck the keen teeth from the fierce tiger's jaws,
And burn the long-lived phoenix in her blood;
Make glad and sorry seasons as thou fleets,
And do whate'er thou wilt, swift-footed Time,
To the wide world and all her fading sweets;
But I forbid thee one most heinous crime:
O, carve not with thy hours my love's fair brow,
Nor draw no lines there with thine antique pen;

Him in thy course untainted do allow
For beauty's pattern to succeeding men.
 Yet, do thy worst, old Time: despite thy wrong,
 My love shall in my verse ever live young.

A womans' face, with Nature's own hand painted,
Hast thou, the master-mistress of my passion;
A woman's gentle heart, but not acquainted
With shifting change, as is false women's fashion;
An eye more bright than theirs, less false in rolling,
Gilding the object whereupon it gazeth;
A man in hew all *Hews* in his controlling,
Which steals men's eyes, and women's souls amazeth.
And for a woman wert thou first created;
Till Nature, as she wrought thee, fell a-doting,
And by addition me of thee defeated,
By adding one thing to my purpose nothing.
 But since she prick't thee out for women's pleasure,
 Mine be thy love, and thy love's use their treasure.

Let those who are in favour with their stars
Of public honour and proud titles boast,
Whilst I, whom fortune of such triumph bars,
Unlookt for joy in that I honour most.
Great princes' favourites their fair leaves spread
But as the marigold at the sun's eye;
And in themselves their pride lies buried,
For at a frown they in their glory die.
The painful warrior famoused for fight,
After a thousand victories once foil'd,
Is from the book of honour razed quite,
And all the rest forgot for which he toil'd:
 Then happy I, that love and am beloved
 Where I may not remove nor be removed.

SONNET 29

When, in disgrace with fortune and men's eyes,
I all alone beweep my outcast state,
And trouble deaf heaven with my bootless cries,
And look upon myself, and curse my fate,
Wishing me like to one more rich in hope,
Featured like him, like him with friends possest,
Desiring this man's art, and that man's scope,
With what I most enjoy contented least;
Yet in these thoughts myself almost despising,
Haply I think on thee, —and then my state,
Like to the lark at break of day arising
From sullen earth, sings hymns at heaven's gate;
    For thy sweet love remember'd such wealth brings,
    That then I scorn to change my state with kings.

SONNET 30

When to the sessions of sweet silent thought
I summon up remembrance of things past,
I sigh the lack of many a thing I sought,
And with old woes new wail my dear time's waste:
Then can I drown an eye, unused to flow,
For precious friends hid in death's dateless night,
And weep afresh love's long-since cancell'd woe,
And moan the expense of many a vanisht sight:
Then can I grieve at grievances foregone,
And heavily from woe to woe tell o'er
The sad account of fore-bemoaned moan,
Which I new pay as if not paid before.
    But if the while I think on thee, dear friend,
    All losses are restored, and sorrows end.

SONNET 32

If thou survive my well-contented day,
When that churl Death my bones with dust shall cover,
And shalt by fortune once more re-survey
These poor rude lines of thy deceased lover:
Compare them with the bettering of the time,

And though they be outstript by every pen,
Reserve them for my love, not for their rime,
Exceeded by the height of happier men.
O, then vouchsafe me but this loving thought:
'Had my friend's Muse grown with this growing age,
A dearer birth than this his love had brought,
To march in ranks of better equipage:
  But since he died, and poets better prove,
  Theirs for their style I'll read, his for his love.'

215   SONNET 33

Full many a glorious morning have I seen
Flatter the mountain-tops with sovereign eye,
Kissing with golden face the meadows green,
Gilding pale streams with heavenly alchemy;
Anon permit the basest clouds to rise
With ugly rack on his celestial face,
And from the forlorn world his visage hide,
Stealing unseen to west with this disgrace:
Even so my sun one early morn did shine
With all-triumphant splendour on my brow;
But, out, alack! he was but one hour mine,
The region cloud hath maskt him from me now.
  Yet him for this my love no whit disdaineth;
  Suns of the world may stain when heaven's sun
    staineth.

216   SONNET 34

Why didst thou promise such a beauteous day,
And make me travel forth without my cloak,
To let base clouds o'ertake me in my way,
Hiding thy bravery in their rotten smoke?
'Tis not enough that through the cloud thou break,
To dry the rain on my storm-beaten face,
For no man well of such a salve can speak
That heals the wound, and cures not the disgrace:
Nor can thy shame give physic to my grief;
Though thou repent, yet I have still the loss:
The offender's sorrow lends but weak relief

To him that bears the strong offence's cross.
 Ah, but those tears are pearl which thy love sheds,
 And they are rich, and ransom all ill deeds.

      SONNET 35

No more be grieved at that which thou hast done:
Roses have thorns, and silver fountains mud;
Clouds and eclipses stain both moon and sun,
And loathsome canker lives in sweetest bud.
All men make faults, and even I in this,
Authorizing thy trespass with compare,
Myself corrupting, salving thy amiss,
Excusing 'their sins more than thy sins are';
For to thy sensual fault I bring in sense,—
Thy adverse party is thy advocate,—
And 'gainst myself a lawful plea commence:
Such civil war is in my love and hate,
 That I an accessary needs must be,
 To that sweet thief which sourly robs from me.

      SONNET 36

Let me confess that we two must be twain,
Although our undivided loves are one:
So shall those blots that do with me remain,
Without thy help, by me be borne alone.
In our two loves there is but one respect,
Though in our lives a separable spite,
Which though it alter not love's sole effect,
Yet doth it steal sweet hours from love's delight.
I may not evermore acknowledge thee,
Lest my bewailed guilt should do thee shame;
Nor thou with public kindness honour me,
Unless thou take that honour from thy name:
 But do not so; I love thee in such sort,
 As, thou being mine, mine is thy good report.

Take all my loves, my love, yea, take them all;
What hast thou then more than thou hadst before?
No love, my love, that thou mayst true love call;
All mine was thine before thou hadst this more.
Then, if for my love thou my love receivest,
I cannot blame thee for my love thou usest;
But yet be blamed, if thou this self deceivest
By wilful taste of what thyself refusest.
I do forgive thy robbery, gentle thief,
Although thou steal thee all my poverty;
And yet, love knows, it is a greater grief
To bear love's wrong than hate's known injury.
  Lascivious grace, in whom all ill well shows,
  Kill me with spites; yet we must not be foes.

Those pretty wrongs that liberty commits,
When I am sometime absent from thy heart,
Thy beauty and thy years full well befits,
For still temptation follows where thou art.
Gentle thou art, and therefore to be won,
Beauteous thou art, therefore to be assailed;
And when a woman woos, what woman's son
Will sourly leave her till she have prevailed?
Ay me! but yet thou mightest my seat forbear,
And chide thy beauty and thy straying youth,
Who lead thee in their riot even there
Where thou art forced to break a twofold truth,—
  Hers, by thy beauty tempting her to thee,
  Thine, by thy beauty being false to me.

That thou hast her, it is not all my grief,
And yet it may be said I loved her dearly;
That she hath thee, is of my wailing chief,
A loss in love that touches me more nearly
Loving offenders, thus I will excuse ye:—

Thou dost love her, because thou know'st I love her;
And for my sake even so doth she abuse me,
Suff'ring my friend for my sake to approve her.
If I lose thee, my loss is my love's gain,
And losing her, my friend hath found that loss;
Both find each other, and I lose both twain,
And both for my sake lay on me this cross:
    But here's the joy; my friend and I are one;
    Sweet flattery! then she loves but me alone.

SONNET 43

When most I wink, then do mine eyes best see,
For all the day they view things unrespected;
But when I sleep, in dreams they look on thee,
And, darkly bright, are bright in dark directed.
Then thou, whose shadow shadows doth make bright,
How would thy shadow's form form happy show
To the clear day with thy much clearer light,
When to unseeing eyes thy shade shines so!
How would, I say, mine eyes be blessed made
By looking on thee in the living day,
When in dead night thy fair imperfect shade
Through heavy sleep on sightless eyes doth stay!
    All days are nights to see till I see thee,
    And nights bright days when dreams do show thee
    me.

SONNET 44

If the dull substance of my flesh were thought,
Injurious distance should not stop my way;
For then, despite of space, I would be brought,
From limits far remote, where thou dost stay.
No matter then although my foot did stand
Upon the farthest earth removed from thee;
For nimble thought can jump both sea and land,
As soon as think the place where he would be.
But, ah, thought kills me, that I am not thought,
To leap large lengths of miles when thou art gone,
But that, so much of earth and water wrought,

I must attend time's leisure with my moan;
  Receiving naught by elements so slow
  But heavy tears, badges of either's woe.

SONNET 55

Not marble, nor the gilded monuments
Of princes, shall outlive this powerful rime;
But you shall shine more bright in these contents
Than unswept stone, besmear'd with sluttish time.
When wasteful war shall statues overturn,
And broils root out the work of masonry,
Nor Mars his sword nor war's quick fire shall burn
The living record of your memory.
'Gainst death and all-oblivious enmity
Shall you pace forth; your praise shall still find room
Even in the eyes of all posterity
That wears this world out to the ending doom.
  So, till the judgement that yourself arise,
  You live in this, and dwell in lovers' eyes.

SONNET 56

Sweet love, renew thy force; be it not said
Thy edge should blunter be than appetite,
Which but to-day by feeding is allay'd,
To-morrow sharpen'd in his former might:
So, love, be thou; although to-day thou fill
Thy hungry eyes even till they wink with fullness,
To-morrow see again, and do not kill
The spirit of love with a perpetual dullness.
Let this sad int'rim like the ocean be
Which parts the shore, where two contracted new
Come daily to the banks, that, when they see
Return of love, more blest may be the view;
  Or call it winter, which, being full of care,
  Makes summer's welcome thrice more wisht, more
    rare.

Like as the waves make towards the pebbled shore,
So do our minutes hasten to their end;
Each changing place with that which goes before,
In sequent toil all forwards do contend.
Nativity, once in the main of light,
Crawls to maturity, wherewith being crown'd,
Crooked eclipses 'gainst his glory fight,
And Time that gave both now his gift confound.
Time doth transfix the flourish set on youth,
And delves the parallels in beauty's brow;
Feeds on the rarities of nature's truth,
And nothing stands but for his scythe to mow:
    And yet, to times in hope my verse shall stand,
    Praising thy worth, despite his cruel hand.

Tired with all these, for restful death I cry,—
Ask to behold Desert a beggar born,
And needy Nothing trimm'd in jollity,
And purest Faith unhappily forsworn,
And gilded Honour shamefully misplaced,
And maiden Virtue rudely strumpeted,
And right Perfection wrongfully disgraced,
And Strength by limping Sway disabled,
And Art made tongue-tied by Authority,
And Folly, doctor-like, controlling Skill,
And simple Truth miscall'd Simplicity,
And captive Good attending captain Ill:
    Tired with all these, from these would I be gone,
    Save that, to die, I leave my love alone.

Those parts of thee that the world's eye doth view
Want nothing that the thought of hearts can mend;
All tongues, the voice of souls, give thee that due,
Uttering bare truth, even so as foes commend.
Thy outward thus with outward praise is crown'd;

But those same tongues, that give thee so thine own,
In other accents do this praise confound
By seeing further than the eye hath shown.
They look into the beauty of thy mind,
And that, in guess, they measure by thy deeds;
Then, churls, their thoughts, although their eyes were
    kind,
To thy fair flower add the rank smell of weeds:
    But why thy odour matcheth not thy show,
    The soil is this, that thou dost common grow.

229   SONNET 71

No longer mourn for me when I am dead
Than you shall hear the surly sullen bell
Give warning to the world that I am fled
From this vile world, with vilest worms to dwell;
Nay, if you read this line, remember not
The hand that writ it; for I love you so,
That I in your sweet thoughts would be forgot,
If thinking on me then should make you woe.
O, if, I say, you look upon this verse
When I perhaps compounded am with clay,
Do not so much as my poor name rehearse;
But let your love even with my life decay;
    Lest the wise world should look into your moan,
    And mock you with me after I am gone.

230   SONNET 73

That time of year thou mayst in me behold
When yellow leaves, or none, or few, do hang
Upon those boughs which shake against the cold,
Bare ruin'd choirs, where late the sweet birds sang.
In me thou see'st the twilight of such day
As after sunset fadeth in the west;
Which by and by black night doth take away,
Death's second self, that seals up all in rest.
In me thou see'st the glowing of such fire,
That on the ashes of his youth doth lie,

As the death-bed whereon it must expire,
Consumed with that which it was nourisht by.
  This thou perceivest, which makes thy love more
    strong,
  To love that well which thou must leave ere long.

SONNET 74

But be contented: when that fell arrest
Without all bail shall carry me away,
My life hath in this line some interest,
Which for memorial still with thee shall stay.
When thou reviewest this, thou dost review
The very part was consecrate to thee:
The earth can have but earth, which is his due;
My spirit is thine, the better part of me:
So, then, thou hast but lost the dregs of life,
The prey of worms, my body being dead;
The coward conquest of a wretch's knife,
Too base of thee to be remembered.
  The worth of that is that which it contains,
  And that is this, and this with thee remains.

SONNET 82

I grant thou wert not married to my Muse,
And therefore mayst without attaint o'erlook
The dedicated words which writers use
Of their fair subject, blessing every book.
Thou art as fair in knowledge as in hue,
Finding thy worth a limit past my praise;
And therefore art enforced to seek anew
Some fresher stamp of the time-bettering days.
And do so, love; yet when they have devised
What strained touches rhetoric can lend,
Thou truly fair wert truly sympathized
In true plain words by thy true-telling friend;
  And their gross painting might be better used
  Where cheeks need blood; in thee it is abused.

Was it the proud full sail of this great verse,
Bound for the prize of all-too-precious you,
That did my ripe thoughts in my brain inhearse,
Making their tomb the womb wherein they grew?
Was it his spirit, by spirits taught to write
Above a mortal pitch, that struck me dead?
No, neither he, nor his compeers by night
Giving him aid, my verse astonished.
He, nor that affable familiar ghost
Which nightly gulls him with intelligence,
As victors, of my silence cannot boast;
I was not sick of any fear from thence:
    But when your countenance fill'd up his line,
    Then lackt I matter; that enfeebled mine.

Some glory in their birth, some in their skill,
Some in their wealth, some in their bodies' force;
Some in their garments, though new-fangled ill;
Some in their hawks and hounds, some in their horse;
And every humour hath his adjunct pleasure,
Wherein it finds a joy above the rest:
But these particulars are not my measure;
All these I better in one general best.
Thy love is better than high birth to me,
Richer than wealth, prouder than garments' cost,
Of more delight than hawks or horses be;
And having thee, of all men's pride I boast:
    Wretched in this alone, that thou mayst take
    All this away, and me most wretched make.

They that have power to hurt and will do none,
That do not do the thing they most do show,
Who, moving others, are themselves as stone,
Unmoved, cold, and to temptation slow;

They rightly do inherit heaven's graces,
And husband nature's riches from expense;
They are the lords and owners of their faces,
Others but stewards of their excellence.
The summer's flower is to the summer sweet,
Though to itself it only live and die;
But if that flower with base infection meet,
The basest weed outbraves his dignity:
    For sweetest things turn sourest by their deeds;
    Lilies that fester smell far worse than weeds.

SONNET 95

How sweet and lovely dost thou make the shame
Which, like a canker in the fragrant rose,
Doth spot the beauty of thy budding name!
O, in what sweets doth thou thy sins enclose!
That tongue that tells the story of thy days,
Making lascivious comments on thy sport,
Cannot dispraise but in a kind of praise;
Naming thy name blesses an ill report.
O, what a mansion have those vices got
Which for their habitation chose out thee,
Where beauty's veil doth cover every blot,
And all things turn to fair that eyes can see!
    Take heed, dear heart, of this large privilege;
    The hardest knife ill-used doth lose his edge.

SONNET 97

How like a winter hath my absence been
From thee, the pleasure of the fleeting year!
What freezings have I felt, what dark days seen!
What old December's bareness every where!
And yet this time removed was summer's time;
The teeming autumn, big with rich increase,
Bearing the wanton burden of the prime,
Like widow'd wombs after their lords' decease:
Yet this abundant issue seem'd to me
But hope of orphans and unfather'd fruit;

For summer and his pleasures wait on thee,
And, thou away, the very birds are mute;
   Or, if they sing, 'tis with so dull a cheer,
   That leaves look pale, dreading the winter's near.

SONNET 106

When in the chronicle of wasted time
I see descriptions of the fairest wights,
And beauty making beautiful old rime
In praise of ladies dead and lovely knights,
Then, in the blazon of sweet beauty's best,
Of hand, of foot, of lip, of eye, of brow,
I see their antique pen would have exprest
Even such a beauty as you master now.
So all their praises are but prophecies
Of this our time, all you prefiguring;
And, for they lookt but with divining eyes,
They had not skill enough your worth to sing:
   For we, which now behold these present days,
   Have eyes to wonder, but lack tongues to praise.

SONNET 107

Not mine own fears, nor the prophetic soul
Of the wide world dreaming on things to come,
Can yet the lease of my true love control,
Supposed as forfeit to a confined doom.
The mortal moon hath her eclipse endured,
And the sad augurs mock their own presage;
Incertainties now crown themselves assured,
And peace proclaims olives of endless age.
Now with the drops of this most balmy time
My love looks fresh, and Death to me subscribes,
Since, spite of him, I'll live in this poor rime,
While he insults o'er dull and speechless tribes:
   And thou in this shalt find thy monument,
   When tyrants' crests and tombs of brass are spent.

Alas, 'tis true I have gone here and there,
And made myself a motley to the view,
Gored mine own thoughts, sold cheap what is most
      dear,
Made old offences of affections new;
Most true it is that I have lookt on truth
Askance and strangely: but, by all above,
These blenches gave my heart another youth,
And worse essays proved thee my best of love.
Now all is done, have what shall have no end:
Mine appetite I never more will grind
On newer proof, to try an older friend,
A god in love, to whom I am confined.
      Then give me welcome, next my heaven the best,
      Even to thy pure and most loving breast.

Let me not to the marriage of true minds
Admit impediments. Love is not love
Which alters when it alteration finds,
Or bends with the remover to remove:
O, no! it is an ever-fixed mark,
That looks on tempests, and is never shaken,
It is the star to every wandering bark,
Whose worth's unknown, although his height be taken.
Love's not Time's fool, though rosy lips and cheeks
Within his bending sickle's compass come;
Love alters not with his brief hours and weeks,
But bears it out even to the edge of doom.
      If this be error, and upon me proved,
      I never writ, nor no man ever loved.

Like as, to make out appetites more keen,
With eager compounds we our palate urge;
As, to prevent our maladies unseen,
We sicken to shun sickness when we purge;

Even so, being full of your ne'er-cloying sweetness,
To bitter sauces did I frame my feeding;
And, sick of welfare, found a kind of meetness
To be diseased, ere that there was true needing.
Thus policy in love, t'anticipate
The ills that were not, grew to faults assured,
And brought to medicine a healthful state,
Which, rank of goodness, would by ill be cured:
  But thence I learn, and find the lesson true,
  Drugs poison him that so fell sick of you.

SONNET 119

What potions have I drunk of Siren tears,
Distill'd from limbecks foul as hell within,
Applying fears to hopes, and hopes to fears,
Still losing when I saw myself to win!
What wretched errors hath my heart committed,
Whilst it hath thought itself so blessed never!
How have mine eyes out of their spheres been fitted
In the distraction of this madding fever!
O benefit of ill! now I find true
That better is by evil still made better;
And ruin'd love, when it is built anew,
Grows fairer than at first, more strong, far greater.
  So I return rebuked to my content,
  And gain by ill thrice more than I have spent.

SONNET 121

'Tis better to be vile than vile esteemed,
When not to be receives reproach of being;
And the just pleasure lost, which is so deemed
Not by our feeling, but by others' seeing:
For why should others' false adulterate eyes
Give salutation to my sportive blood?
Or on my frailties why are frailer spies,
Which in their wills count bad what I think good?
No, I am that I am; and they that level
At my abuses reckon up their own:
I may be straight, though they themselves be bevel;

By their rank thoughts my deeds must not be shown;
   Unless this general evil they maintain—
   All men are bad, and in their badness reign.

SONNET 127

In the old age black was not counted fair,
Or if it were, it bore not beauty's name;
But now is black beauty's successive heir,
And beauty slander'd with a bastard shame:
For since each hand hath put on nature's power,
Fairing the foul with art's false borrow'd face,
Sweet beauty hath no name, no holy bower,
But is profaned, if not lives in disgrace.
Therefore my mistress' eyes are raven black,
Her eyes so suited, and they mourners seem
At such who, not born fair, no beauty lack,
Slandering creation with a false esteem:
   Yet so they mourn, becoming of their woe,
   That every tongue says beauty should look so.

SONNET 129

The expense of spirit in a waste of shame
Is lust in action; and till action, lust
Is perjured, murd'rous, bloody, full of blame,
Savage, extreme, rude, cruel, not to trust;
Enjoy'd no sooner but despised straight;
Past reason hunted; and no sooner had,
Past reason hated, as a swallow'd bait,
On purpose laid to make the taker mad:
Mad in pursuit, and in possession so;
Had, having, and in quest to have, extreme;
A bliss in proof, and proved, a very woe;
Before, a joy proposed; behind, a dream.
   All this the world well knows; yet none knows well
   To shun the heaven that leads men to this hell.

SONNET 130

My mistress' eyes are nothing like the sun;
Coral is far more red than her lips' red:
If snow be white, why then her breasts are dun;
If hairs be wires, black wires grow on her head.
I have seen roses damaskt, red and white,
But no such roses see I in her cheeks;
And in some perfumes is there more delight
Than in the breath that from my mistress reeks.
I love to hear her speak, yet well I know
That music hath a far more pleasing sound:
I grant I never saw a goddess go;
My mistress, when she walks, treads on the ground.
    And yet, by heaven, I think my love as rare
    As any she belied with false compare.

SONNET 133

Beshrew that heart that makes my heart to groan
For that deep wound it gives my friend and me!
Is't not enough to torture me alone,
But slave to slavery my sweet'st friend must be?
Me from myself thy cruel eye hath taken,
And my next self thou harder hast engrossed:
Of him, myself, and thee, I am forsaken:
A torment thrice threefold thus to be crossed.
Prison my heart in thy steel bosom's ward,
But then my friend's heart let my poor heart bail;
Whoe'er keeps me, let my heart be his guard;
Thou canst not then use rigour in my jail:
    And yet thou wilt; for I, being pent in thee,
    Perforce am thine, and all that is in me.

SONNET 134

So, now I have confest that he is thine,
And I myself am mortgaged to thy will,
Myself I'll forfeit, so that other mine
Thou wilt restore, to be my comfort still:

But thou wilt not, nor he will not be free,
For thou art covetous, and he is kind;
He learn'd but, surety-like, to write for me,
Under that bond that him as fast doth bind.
The statute of thy beauty thou wilt take,
Thou usurer, that putt'st forth all to use,
And sue a friend came debtor for my sake;
So him I lose through my unkind abuse.
 Him have I lost; thou hast both him and me:
 He pays the whole, and yet am I not free.

SONNET 141

In faith, I do not love thee with mine eyes,
For they in thee a thousand errors note;
But 'tis my heart that loves what they despise,
Who, in despite of view, is pleased to dote;
Nor are mine ears with thy tongue's tune delighted;
Nor tender feeling to base touches prone,
Nor taste, nor smell, desire to be invited
To any sensual feast with thee alone:
But my five wits nor my five senses can
Dissuade one foolish heart from serving thee,
Who leaves unsway'd the likeness of a man,
Thy proud heart's slave and vassal wretch to be:
 Only my plague thus far I count my gain,
 That she that makes me sin awards me pain.

SONNET 143

Lo, as a careful housewife runs to catch
One of her feather'd creatures broke away,
Sets down her babe, and makes all swift dispatch
In pursuit of the thing she would have stay;
Whilst her neglected child holds her in chase,
Cries to catch her whose busy care is bent
To follow that which flies before her face,
Not prizing her poor infant's discontent:

So runn'st thou after that which flies from thee,
Whilst I thy babe chase thee afar behind;
But if thou catch thy hope, turn back to me,
And play the mother's part, kiss me, be kind:
    So will I pray that thou mayst have thy *Will*,
    If thou turn back, and my loud crying still.

SONNET 144

Two loves I have of comfort and despair,
Which like two spirits do suggest me still:
The better angel is a man right fair,
The worser spirit a woman colour'd ill.
To win me soon to hell, my female evil
Tempteth my better angel from my side,
And would corrupt my saint to be a devil,
Wooing his purity with her foul pride.
And whether that my angel be turn'd fiend
Suspect I may, yet not directly tell;
But being both from me, both to each friend,
I guess one angel in another's hell:
    Yet this shall I ne'er know, but live in doubt,
    Till my bad angel fire my good one out.

SONNET 146

Poor soul, the centre of my sinful earth—
My sinful earth these rebel powers array—
Why dost thou pine within and suffer dearth,
Painting thy outward walls so costly gay?
Why so large cost, having so short a lease,
Dost thou upon thy fading mansion spend?
Shall worms, inheritors of this excess,
Eat up thy charge? is this thy body's end?
Then, soul, live thou upon thy servant's loss,
And let that pine to aggravate thy store;
Buy terms divine in selling hours of dross;
Within be fed, without be rich no more:
    So shalt thou feed on Death, that feeds on men,
    And Death once dead, there's no more dying then.

My love is as a fever, longing still
For that which longer nurseth the disease;
Feeding on that which doth preserve the ill,
The uncertain sickly appetite to please.
My reason, the physician to my love,
Angry that his prescriptions are not kept,
Hath left me, and I desperate now approve
Desire is death, which physic did except.
Past cure I am, now reason is past care,
And frantic-mad with evermore unrest;
My thoughts and my discourse as madmen's are,
At random from the truth vainly exprest;
　　For I have sworn thee fair, and thought thee bright,
　　Who art as black as hell, as dark as night.

Love is too young to know what conscience is;
Yet who knows not conscience is born of love?
Then, gentle cheater, urge not my amiss,
Lest guilty of my faults thy sweet self prove:
For, thou betraying me, I do betray
My nobler part to my gross body's treason;
My soul doth tell my body that he may
Triumph in love; flesh stays no farther reason;
But, rising at thy name, doth point out thee
As his triumphant prize. Proud of this pride,
He is contented thy poor drudge to be,
To stand in thy affairs, fall by thy side.
　　No want of conscience hold it that I call
　　Her 'love' for whose dear love I rise and fall.

256　*The phoenix and the turtle*

Let the bird of loudest lay,
On the sole Arabian tree,
Herald sad and trumpet be,
To whose sound chaste wings obey.

But thou shrieking harbinger,
Foul precurrer of the fiend,
Augur of the fever's end,
To this troop come thou not near!

From this session interdict
Every fowl of tyrant wing,
Save the eagle, feather'd king:
Keep the obsequy so strict.

Let the priest in surplice white,
That defunctive music can,
Be the death-divining swan,
Lest the requiem lack his right.

And thou treble-dated crow,
That thy sable gender makest
With the breath thou givest and takest,
'Mongst our mourners shalt thou go.

Here the anthem doth commence:
Love and constancy is dead;
Phoenix and the turtle fled
In a mutual flame from hence.

So they loved, as love in twain
Had the essence but in one;
Two distincts, division none:
Number there in love was slain.

Hearts remote, yet not asunder;
Distance, and no space was seen
'Twixt the turtle and his queen:
But in them it were a wonder.

So between them love did shine,
That the turtle saw his right
Flaming in the phoenix' sight;
Either was the other's mine.

Property was thus appalled,
That the self was not the same;
Single nature's double name
Neither two nor one was called.

Reason, in itself confounded,
Saw division grow together,
To themselves yet either neither,
Simple were so well compounded,

That it cried, How true a twain
Seemeth this concordant one!
Love hath reason, reason none,
If what parts can so remain.

Whereupon it made this threne
To the phoenix and the dove,
Co-supremes and stars of love,
As chorus to their tragic scene.

THRENOS

Beauty, truth, and rarity,
Grace in all simplicity,
Here enclosed in cinders lie.

Death is now the phoenix' nest;
And the turtle's loyal breast
To eternity doth rest,

Leaving no posterity:
'Twas not their infirmity,
It was married chastity.

Truth may seem, but cannot be;
Beauty brag, but 'tis not she;
Truth and beauty buried be.

To this urn let those repair
That are either true or fair;
For these dead birds sigh a prayer.

William Shakespeare

257 *In rainy-gloomy weather*

This weather's like my troubled mind and eyes:
The one being sad, the other full of tears;
And as wind oft the often showering dries,
So sighs my tears dry up, and kindle cares.
Sighs please and pain the displeased painful heart;
They please in giving vent to griefs up-pent;
And yet the heart they ease, they cause to smart:
So griefs increase as sighs do give them vent.
But were my mind thus sad but for my crimes,
And mine eyes turned to tears for cause so dear;
Or, did my heart for that sigh oftentimes,
My sighs, my tears, my sadness blessed were:
  But 'tis, sith hope, my ship, through fate's cross-wave,
  Now grates upon the gravel of my grave.

John Davies of Hereford

258 *Art thou poor?*

Art thou poor, yet hast thou golden slumbers?
    O sweet content!
Art thou rich, yet is thy mind perplex'd?
    O punishment!
Dost thou laugh to see how fools are vex'd
To add to golden numbers golden numbers?
    O sweet content! O sweet, O sweet content!
Work apace, apace, apace, apace;
Honest labour bears a lovely face;
Then hey nonny nonny—hey nonny nonny!

Canst drink the waters of the crispèd spring?
    O sweet content!
Swim'st thou in wealth, yet sink'st in thine own tears?
    O punishment!
Then he that patiently want's burden bears,
No burden bears, but is a king, a king!
    O sweet content! O sweet, O sweet content!

Work apace, apace, apace, apace;
Honest labour bears a lovely face;
Then hey nonny nonny—hey nonny nonny!

Thomas Dekker

259   *Fain would I change that note*

Fain would I change that note
    To which fond love hath charmed me,
Long, long to sing by rote,
    Fancying that that harmed me:
Yet when this thought doth come,
Love is the perfect sum
    Of all delight,
I have no other choice
Either for pen or voice
    To sing or write.

O love, they wrong thee much
    That say thy sweet is bitter,
When thy ripe fruit is such
    As nothing can be sweeter.
Fair house of joy and bliss,
Where truest pleasure is,
    I do adore thee;
I know thee what thou art;
I serve thee with my heart,
    And fall before thee.

Tobias Hume

260   *There is a lady sweet and kind*

There is a lady sweet and kind,
Was never face so pleased my mind;
I did but see her passing by,
And yet I love her till I die.

Her gesture, motion and her smiles,
Her wit, her voice, my heart beguiles,
Beguiles my heart, I know not why,
And yet I love her till I die.

Her free behaviour, winning looks,
Will make a lawyer burn his books.
I touched her not, alas, not I,
And yet I love her till I die.

Had I her fast betwixt mine arms,
Judge you that think such sports were harms,
Wer't any harm? No, no, fie, fie!
For I will love her till I die.

Should I remain confinèd there,
So long as Phoebus in her sphere,
I to request, she to deny,
Yet would I love her till I die.

Cupid is wingèd and doth range,
Her country so my love doth change,
But change she earth, or change she sky,
Yet will I love her till I die.

Thomas Ford

261   *On a child beginning to talk*

Methinks 'tis pretty sport to hear a child
Rocking a word in mouth yet undefiled.
The tender racket rudely plays the sound,
Which, weakly bandied, cannot back rebound,
And the soft air the softer roof doth kiss,
With a sweet dying and a pretty miss,
Which hears no answer yet from the white rank
Of teeth not risen from their coral bank.
The alphabet is searched for letters soft

To try a word before it can be wrought;
And, when it slideth forth, it goes as nice
As when a man doth walk upon the ice.

Thomas Bastard

262 *Sweet Suffolk owl*

Sweet Suffolk owl, so trimly dight
With feathers like a lady bright,
Thou sing'st alone, sitting by night,
    Te whit, te whoo.
The note that forth so freely rolls
With shrill command the mouse controls
And sings a dirge for dying souls,
    Te whit, te whoo.

Thomas Vautor

263 *Elegy on Shakespeare*

Renownèd Spenser, lie a thought more nigh
To learned Chaucer, and rare Beaumont lie
A little nearer Spenser, to make room
For Shakespeare in your threefold, fourfold tomb.
To lodge all four in one bed make a shift
Until Doomsday, for hardly will a fifth
Betwixt this day and that by fate be slain,
For whom your curtains may be drawn again.
If your precedency in death doth bar
A fourth place in your sacred sepulchre,
Under this carvèd marble of thine own,
Sleep, rare tragedian, Shakespeare, sleep alone;
Thy unmolested peace, unshared cave
Possess as lord, not tenant, of thy grave,
    That unto us and others it may be
    Honour hereafter to be laid by thee.

William Basse

My sweetest Lesbia, let us live and love;
And though the sager sort our deeds reprove,
Let us not weigh them. Heaven's great lamps do dive
Into their west, and straight again revive.
But soon as once set is our little light,
Then must we sleep one ever-during night.

If all would lead their lives in love like me,
Then bloody swords and armour should not be;
No drum nor trumpet peaceful sleeps should move,
Unless alarm came from the camp of love.
But fools do live and waste their little light,
And seek with pain their ever-during night.

When timely death my life and fortune ends,
Let not my hearse be vexed with mourning friends
But let all lovers, rich in triumph, come
And with sweet pastimes grace my happy tomb.
And, Lesbia, close up thou my little light,
And crown with love my ever-during night.

Thomas Campion

265 *Youth and age*

Though you are young and I am old,
Though your veins hot and my blood cold,
Though youth is moist and age is dry,
Yet embers live when flames do die.

The tender graft is easily broke,
But who shall shake the sturdy oak?
You are more fresh and fair than I,
Yet stubs do live when flowers do die.

Thou that thy youth dost vainly boast
Know, buds are soonest nipped with frost.
Think that thy fortune still doth cry:
'Thou fool, to-morrow thou must die.'

Thomas Campion

266 *Dido*

Dido was the Carthage Queen
    And loved the Trojan knight
That wandering many coasts had seen
    And many a dreadful sight;
As they on hunting rode, a shower
Drave them in a loving hour
    Down to a darksome cave
Where Aeneas with his charms
Locked Queen Dido in his arms
    And had what he could have.

Dido Hymen's rites forgot,
    Her love was winged with haste,
Her honour she considered not
    But in her breast him placed.
And when her love was new begun
Jove sent down his wingèd son
    To fright Aeneas' sleep;
Bade him by the break of day
From Queen Dido steal away,
    Which made her wail and weep.

Dido wept, but what of this?
    The Gods would have it so:
Aeneas nothing did amiss,
    For he was forced to go.
Learn, lordings, then, no faith to keep
With your loves, but let them weep:
    'Tis folly to be true.
Let this story serve your turn,
And let twenty Didos burn
    So you get daily new.

Thomas Campion

There is a garden in her face
  Where roses and white lilies blow;
A heavenly paradise is that place,
  Wherein all pleasant fruits do flow:
    There cherries grow which none may buy
    Till 'Cherry-ripe' themselves do cry.

Those cherries fairly do enclose
  Of orient pearl a double row,
Which when her lovely laughter shows,
  They look like rose-buds fill'd with snow;
    Yet them nor peer nor prince can buy
    Till 'Cherry-ripe' themselves do cry.

Her eyes like angels watch them still;
  Her brows like bended bows do stand,
Threat'ning with piercing frowns to kill
  All that attempt with eye or hand
    Those sacred cherries to come nigh,
    Till 'Cherry-ripe' themselves do cry.

                                    Thomas Campion

268   *Follow thy fair sun*

Follow thy fair sun, unhappy shadow!
  Though thou be black as night,
  And she made all of light,
Yet follow thy fair sun, unhappy shadow!

Follow her, whose light thy light depriveth!
  Though here thou liv'st disgraced,
  And she in heaven is placed,
Yet follow her whose light the world reviveth!

Follow those pure beams, whose beauty burneth!
  That so have scorchèd thee
  As thou still black must be,
Till her kind beams thy black to brightness turneth.

Follow her, while yet her glory shineth!
  There comes a luckless night
  That will dim all her light;
And this the black unhappy shade divineth.

Follow still, since so thy fates ordainèd!
  The sun must have his shade,
  Till both at once do fade,—
The sun still proud, the shadow still disdainèd.

Thomas Campion

269   *Follow your saint*

Follow your saint, follow with accents sweet!
Haste you, sad notes, fall at her flying feet!
There, wrapt in cloud of sorrow, pity move,
And tell the ravisher of my soul I perish for her love:
But if she scorns my never-ceasing pain,
Then burst with sighing in her sight, and ne'er return
  again!

All that I sung still to her praise did tend;
Still she was first, still she my songs did end;
Yet she my love and music both doth fly,
The music that her echo is and beauty's sympathy:
Then let my notes pursue her scornful flight!
It shall suffice that they were breathed and died for her
  delight.

Thomas Campion

270   *When thou must home*

When thou must home to shades of underground,
And there arrived, a new admirèd guest,
The beauteous spirits do engirt thee round,
White Iope, blithe Helen, and the rest,
To hear the stories of thy finish'd love
From that smooth tongue whose music hell can move;

Then wilt thou speak of banqueting delights,
Of masques and revels which sweet youth did make,
Of tourneys and great challenges of knights,
And all these triumphs for thy beauty's sake:
When thou hast told these honours done to thee,
Then tell, O tell, how thou didst murder me!

Thomas Campion

271 *In praise of Neptune*

Of Neptune's empire let us sing,
At whose command the waves obey;
To whom the rivers tribute pay,
Down the high mountains sliding:
To whom the scaly nation yields
Homage for the crystal fields
    Wherein they dwell:
And every sea-dog pays a gem
Yearly out of his wat'ry cell
To deck great Neptune's diadem.

The Tritons dancing in a ring
Before his palace gates do make
The water with their echoes quake,
Like the great thunder sounding:
The sea-nymphs chant their accents shrill,
And the sirens, taught to kill
    With their sweet voice,
Make ev'ry echoing rock reply
Unto their gentle murmuring noise
The praise of Neptune's empery.

Thomas Campion

272 *Winter nights*

Now winter nights enlarge
    The number of their hours,
And clouds their storms discharge
    Upon the airy towers.

Let now the chimneys blaze
    And cups o'erflow with wine;
Let well-tuned words amaze
    With harmony divine.
Now yellow waxen lights
    Shall wait on honey love,
While youthful revels, masques, and courtly sights
    Sleep's leaden spells remove.

This time doth well dispense
    With lovers' long discourse;
Much speech hath some defence,
    Though beauty no remorse.
All do not all things well;
    Some measures comely tread,
Some knotted riddles tell,
    Some poems smoothly read.
The summer hath his joys,
    And winter his delights;
Though love and all his pleasures are but toys,
    They shorten tedious nights.

Thomas Campion

273   *Integer vitæ*

The man of life upright,
    Whose guiltless heart is free
From all dishonest deeds,
    Or thought of vanity;

The man whose silent days
    In harmless joys are spent,
Whom hopes cannot delude,
    Nor sorrow discontent;

That man needs neither towers
    Nor armour for defence,
Nor secret vaults to fly
    From thunder's violence:

He only can behold
  With unaffrighted eyes
The horrors of the deep
  And terrors of the skies.

Thus, scorning all the cares
  That fate or fortune brings,
He makes the heaven his book,
  His wisdom heavenly things;

Good thoughts his only friends,
  His wealth a well-spent age,
The earth his sober inn
  And quiet pilgrimage.

Thomas Campion

274 *Never weather-beaten sail*

Never weather-beaten sail more willing bent to shore,
Never tirèd pilgrim's limbs affected slumber more,
Than my wearied sprite now longs to fly out of my
    troubled breast:
O come quickly, sweetest Lord, and take my soul to
    rest!

Ever blooming are the joys of heaven's high Paradise,
Cold age deafs not there our ears nor vapour dims our
    eyes:
Glory there the sun outshines; whose beams the Blessèd
    only see:
O come quickly, glorious Lord, and raise my sprite to
    Thee!

Thomas Campion

Spring, the sweet spring, is the year's pleasant king;
Then blooms each thing, then maids dance in a ring,
Cold doth not sting, the pretty birds do sing—
    Cuckoo, jug-jug, pu-we, to-witta-woo!

The palm and may make country houses gay,
Lambs frisk and play, the shepherds pipe all day,
We hear aye birds tune this merry lay:
    Cuckoo, jug-jug, pu-we, to-witta-woo!

The fields breathe sweet, the daisies kiss our feet,
Young lovers meet, old wives a-sunning sit;
In every street these tunes our ears do greet:
    Cuckoo, jug-jug, pu-we, to-witta-woo!
       Spring, the sweet spring!

Thomas Nashe

276   *In time of pestilence 1593*

Adieu, farewell earth's bliss,
This world uncertain is;
Fond are life's lustful joys,
Death proves them all but toys,
None from his darts can fly.
I am sick, I must die.
   Lord, have mercy on us!

Rich men, trust not in wealth,
Gold cannot buy you health;
Physic himself must fade,
All things to end are made.
The plague full swift goes by.
I am sick, I must die.
   Lord, have mercy on us!

Beauty is but a flower
Which wrinkles will devour;
Brightness falls from the air,
Queens have died young and fair,
Dust hath closed Helen's eye.
I am sick, I must die.
  Lord, have mercy on us!

Strength stoops unto the grave,
Worms feed on Hector brave,
Swords may not fight with fate,
Earth still holds ope her gate.
Come! come! the bells do cry.
I am sick, I must die.
  Lord, have mercy on us!

Wit with his wantonness
Tasteth death's bitterness;
Hell's executioner
Hath no ears for to hear
What vain art can reply.
I am sick, I must die.
  Lord, have mercy on us!

Haste, therefore, each degree,
To welcome destiny.
Heaven is our heritage,
Earth but a player's stage;
Mount we unto the sky.
I am sick, I must die.
  Lord, have mercy on us!

Thomas Nashe

277 *Epitaph on Sir Albert Morton's wife*

He first deceased; she for a little tried
To live without him, liked it not, and died.

Sir Henry Wotton

You meaner beauties of the night,
    Which poorly satisfy our eyes
More by your number than your light,
    You common people of the skies,
What are you, when the moon shall rise?

Ye violets that first appear,
    By your pure purple mantles known
Like the proud virgins of the year
    As if the spring were all your own,—
What are you, when the rose is blown?

Ye curious chanters of the wood
    That warble forth Dame Nature's lays,
Thinking your passions understood
    By your weak accents; what's your praise
When Philomel her voice doth raise?

So when my mistress shall be seen
    In sweetness of her looks and mind,
By virtue first, then choice, a queen,
    Tell me, if she were not designed
Th'eclipse and glory of her kind?

Sir Henry Wotton

279   *Parthenope*

I wish no rich-refined Arabian gold,
Nor Orient Indian pearl, rare nature's wonder,
No diamonds the Egyptian surges under,
No rubies of America, dear sold,
Nor sapphires which rich Afric's sands enfold,
Treasures far distant from this isle asunder;
Barbarian ivories in contempt I hold,
But only this, this only, Venus grant:

That I my sweet Parthenope may get.
Her hairs no grace of golden tires want,
Pure pearls with perfect rubies are inset,
True diamonds in eyes, sapphires in veins,
Nor can I that soft ivory skin forget;
England, in one small subject, such contains.

Barnaby Barnes

280 *On a pair of garters*

Go, loving woodbine, clip with lovely grace
Those two sweet plants which bear the flowers of love;
Go, silken vines, those tender elms embrace
Which flourish still, although their roots do move.
As soon as you possess your blessed places
You are advancèd and ennobled more
Than diadems, which were white silken laces
That ancient kings about their forehead wore.
Sweet bands, take heed lest you ungently bind,
Or with your strictness make too deep a print:
Was never tree had such a tender rind,
Although her inward heart be hard as flint.
    And let your knots be fast and loose at will:
    She must be free, though I stand bound and still.

Sir John Davies

281 *Queen and huntress*

Queen and huntress, chaste and fair,
Now the sun is laid to sleep,
Seated in thy silver chair,
State in wonted manner keep:
    Hesperus entreats thy light,
    Goddess excellently bright.

Earth, let not thy envious shade
Dare itself to interpose;
Cynthia's shining orb was made
Heaven to clear, when day did close:
  Bless us then with wishèd sight,
  Goddess excellently bright.

Lay thy bow of pearl apart,
And thy crystal shining quiver;
Give unto the flying hart
Space to breathe, how short soever:
  Thou that mak'st a day of night,
  Goddess excellently bright.

Ben Jonson

282 *Still to be neat*

Still to be neat, still to be drest
As you were going to a feast;
Still to be powdered, still perfumed:
Lady, it is to be presumed,
Though art's hid causes are not found,
All is not sweet, all is not sound.

Give me a look, give me a face,
That makes simplicity a grace;
Robes loosely flowing, hair as free:
Such sweet neglect more taketh me
Than all the adulteries af art;
They strike mine eyes, but not my heart.

Ben Jonson

283 *The triumph of Charis*

See the chariot at hand here of love,
  Wherein my lady rideth!
Each that draws is a swan or a dove
  And well the car love guideth.

As she goes, all hearts do duty
 Unto her beauty;
And enamoured do wish, so they might
 But enjoy such a sight,
That they still were to run by her side,
Through swords, through seas, whither she would ride.

Do but look on her eyes, they do light
 All that love's world compriseth!
Do but look on her hair, it is bright
 As love's star when it riseth!
Do but mark, her forehead's smoother
 Than words that soothe her!
And from her arched brows such a grace
 Sheds itself through the face,
As alone there triumphs to the life
All the gain, all the good of the elements' strife.

Have you seen but a bright lily grow
 Before rude hands have touched it?
Have you marked but the fall of the snow
 Before the soil hath smutched it?
Have you felt the wool of beaver?
 Or swan's down ever?
Or have smelt of the bud of the briar?
 Or the nard in the fire?
Or have tasted the bag of the bee?
O so white, O so soft, O so sweet is she!

Ben Jonson

284 *The hour-glass*

Do but consider this small dust
Here running in the glass
By atoms moved;
Could you believe that this
The body was
Of one that loved?

And in his mistress's flame, playing like a fly,
Turned to cinders by her eye?
Yes, and in death as life unblest,
To have't expressed,
Even ashes of lovers find no rest.

Ben Jonson

285 *A little shrub growing by*

Ask not to know this man. If fame should speak
His name in any metal, it would break.
Two letters were enough the plague to tear
Out of his grave, and poison every ear.
A parcel of court-dirt, a heap, and mass
Of all vice hurled together, there he was,
Proud, false, and treacherous, vindictive, all
That thought can add, unthankful, the lay-stall[1]
Of putrid flesh! of blood the sink!
And so I leave to stir him, lest he stink.

Ben Jonson

1 refuse-heap

286 *To Celia*

Drink to me only with thine eyes
    And I will pledge with mine;
Or leave a kiss but in the cup
    And I'll not look for wine.
The thirst that from the soul doth rise
    Doth ask a drink divine;
But might I of Jove's nectar sup
    I would not change for thine.

I sent thee late a rosy wreath
    Not so much honouring thee
As giving it a hope that there
    It could not withered be.

But thou thereon didst only breathe
    And sent'st it back to me;
Since when it grows and smells, I swear,
    Not of itself but thee.

Ben Jonson

287   *That women are but men's shadows*

Follow a shadow, it still flies you,
    Seem to fly it, it will pursue;
So court a mistress, she denies you;
    Let her alone, she will court you.
Say are not women truly then
Styled but the shadows of us men?

At morn and even, shades are longest;
    At noon they are or short or none;
So men at weakest, they are strongest,
    But grant us perfect, they're not known.
Say are not women truly then
Styled but the shadows of us men?

Ben Johnson

288   *Love and death*

Though I am young and cannot tell
Wither what Death or Love is well,
Yet I have heard they both bear darts,
And both do aim at human hearts:
And then again, I have been told,
Love wounds with heat, as Death with cold;
So that I fear they do but bring
Extremes to touch, and mean one thing.
As in a ruin we it call
One thing to be blown up, or fall;
Or to our end like way may have
By a flash of lightning, or a wave:

So Love's inflamèd shaft or brand,
May kill as soon as Death's cold hand;
Except Love's fires the virtue have
To fright the frost out of the grave.

Ben Jonson

289 *The good-morrow*

I wonder, by my troth, what thou and I
Did till we loved. Were we not weaned till then,
But sucked on country pleasures, childishly?
Or snorted we in the seven sleepers' den?
'Twas so; but this, all pleasures fancies be.
If ever any beauty I did see,
Which I desired and got, 'twas but a dream of thee.

And now good-morrow to our waking souls,
Which watch not one another out of fear;
For love all love of other sights controls
And makes one little room an everywhere.
Let sea-discoverers to new worlds have gone,
Let maps to others worlds on worlds have shown,
Let us possess one world, each hath one, and is one.

My face in thine eye, thine in mine appears,
And true plain hearts do in the faces rest,
Where can we find two better hemispheres
Without sharp North, without declining West?
Whatever dies was not mixed equally;
If our two loves be one, or thou and I
Love so alike that none do slacken, none can die.

John Donne

290 *Song*

Go, and catch a falling star;
    Get with child a mandrake root;
Tell me, where all past years are,
    Or who cleft the devil's foot.

Teach me to hear mermaids singing
Or to keep off envy's stinging,
    And find
    What wind
Serves to advance an honest mind.

If thou beest born to strange sights,
   Things invisible to see,
Ride ten thousand days and nights
   Till age snow white hairs on thee.
Thou, when thou return'st, wilt tell me
All strange wonders that befell thee,
    And swear
    No where
Lives a woman true, and fair.

If thou find'st one, let me know;
   Such a pilgrimage were sweet.
Yet do not, I would not go:
   Though at next door we might meet,
Though she were true when you met her,
And last till you write your letter,
    Yet she
    Will be
False, ere I come, to two, or three.

John Donne

291   *The undertaking*

I have done one braver thing
   Than all the worthies did,
And yet a braver thence doth spring,
   Which is to keep that hid.

It were but madness now t'impart
   The skill of specular stone,
When he which can have learned the art
   To cut it, can find none.

So, if I now should utter this,
    Others (because no more
Such stuff to work upon there is)
    Would love but as before.

But he who loveliness within
    Hath found, all outward loathes,
For he who colour loves and skin
    Loves but their oldest clothes.

If, as I have, you also do
    Virtue attired in woman see,
And dare love that, and say so too,
    And forget the he and she;

And if this love, though placèd so,
    From profane men you hide,
Which will no faith on this bestow,
    Or if they do, deride:

Then you have done a braver thing
    Than all the worthies did,
And a braver thence will spring,
    Which is to keep that hid.

John Donne

292   *The sun rising*

        Busy old fool, unruly sun,
            Why dost thou thus
Through windows and through curtains call on us?
Must to thy motions lovers' seasons run
        Saucy pedantic wretch, go chide
        Late schoolboys and sour prentices,
    Go tell court-huntsmen that the king will ride,
        Call country ants to harvest offices;
Love, all alike, no season knows nor clime,
Nor hours, days, months, which are the rags of time.

Thy beams, so reverent and strong,
Why shouldst thou think?
I could eclipse and cloud them with a wink,
But that I would not lose her sight so long;
If her eyes have not blinded thine,
Look, and to-morrow late tell me
Whether both the Indias of spice and mine
Be where thou left'st them or lie here with me.
Ask for those kings whom thou saw'st yesterday,
And thou shalt hear all here in one bed lay.

She is all states and all princes I;
Nothing else is.
Princes do but play us; compared to this,
All honour's mimic; all wealth alchemy.
Thou sun art half as happy as we,
In that the world's contracted thus;
Thine age asks ease, and since thy duties be
To warm the world, that's done in warming us.
Shine here to us, and thou art everywhere;
This bed thy centre is, these walls thy sphere.

John Donne

293   *The canonization*

For God's sake hold your tongue, and let me love,
Or chide my palsy or my gout,
My five grey hairs, or ruined fortune flout.
With wealth your state, your mind with arts improve,
Take you a course, get you a place,
Observe his honour or his grace,
Or the king's real or his stampèd face
Contemplate; what you will, approve,
So you will let me love.

Alas, alas, who's injured by my love?
What merchant's ships have my sighs drowned?
Who says my tears have overflowed his ground?
When did my cold a forward spring remove?

When did the heats which my veins fill
    Add one more to the plaguey bill?
Soldiers find wars, and lawyers find out still
    Litigious men, which quarrels move,
    Though she and I do love.

Call us what you will, we are made such by love;
    Call her one, me another fly,
We are tapers too and at our own cost die,
    And we in us find the eagle and the dove.
        The phoenix riddle hath more wit
        By us, we two being one, are it.
So to one neutral thing both sexes fit;
    We die and rise the same, and prove
    Mysterious by this love.

We can die by it, if not live by love,
    And if unfit for tombs and hearse
Our legend be, it will be fit for verse;
    And if no piece of chronicle we prove,
        We'll build in sonnets' pretty rooms;
        As well a well-wrought urn becomes
The greatest ashes as half-acre tombs,
    And by these hymns all shall approve
    Us canonised for love:

And thus invoke us, you whom reverent love
    Made one another's hermitage;
You, to whom love was peace, that now is rage;
Who did the whole world's soul contract, and drove
        Into the glasses of your eyes
        (So made such mirrors, and such spies,
That they did all to you epitomise)
    Countries, towns, courts: beg from above,
    A pattern of your love!

John Donne

Sweetest love, I do not go
   For weariness of thee,
Nor in hope the world can show
   A fitter love for me;
     But since that I
Must die at last, 'tis best
To use myself in jest,
   Thus by feigned deaths to die;

Yesternight the sun went hence,
   And yet is here to-day;
He hath no desire nor sense,
   Nor half so short a way:
     Then fear not me,
But believe that I shall make
Speedier journeys, since I take
   More wings and spurs than he.

O how feeble is man's power,
   That if good fortune fall,
Cannot add another hour
   Nor a lost hour recall!
     But come bad chance,
And we join to it our strength,
And we teach it art and length
   Itself o'er us to advance.

When thou sigh'st, thou sigh'st not wind
   But sigh'st my soul away;
When thou weep'st, unkindly kind,
   My life's blood doth decay.
     It cannot be
That thou lov'st me, as thou say'st,
If in thine my life thou waste
   That art the best of me.

Let not thy divining heart
   Forethink me any ill;
Destiny may take thy part,
   And may thy fears fulfil;

But think that we
Are but turned aside to sleep;
They who one another keep
    Alive, ne'er parted be.

John Donne

295   *Air and angels*

Twice and thrice had I loved thee
Before I knew thy face or name;
So in a voice, so in a shapeless flame
Angels affect us oft and worshipped be;
   Still when to where thou wert I came,
Some lovely glorious nothing I did see.
   But since my soul, whose child love is,
Takes limbs of flesh and else could nothing do,
   More subtle than the parent is,
Love must not be, but take a body too,
   And therefore what thou wert, and who,
     I bid love ask, and now
That it assume thy body I allow,
And fix itself in thy lip, eye and brow.

While thus to ballast love I thought,
And so more steadily to have gone,
With wares which would sink admiration,
I saw I had love's pinnace overfraught,
Every thy hair for love to work upon
Is much too much, some fitter must be sought;
   For nor in nothing, nor in things
Extreme, and scattering bright, can love inhere;
   Then, as an angel, face and wings
Of air, not pure as it, yet pure doth wear,
   So thy love may be my love's sphere;
     Just such disparity
As is 'twixt air and angels' purity,
'Twixt women's love and men's will ever be.

John Donne

All kings and all their favourites,
    All glory of honours, beauties, wits,
The sun itself, which makes time as they pass,
Is older by a year now than it was
When thou and I first one another saw;
All other things to their destruction draw;
    Only our love hath no decay.
This no to-morrow hath nor yesterday;
Running, it never runs from us away
But truly keeps his first, last, everlasting day

Two graves must hide thine and my corse;
    If one might, death were no divorce.
Alas, as well as other princes we
(Who prince enough in one another be)
Must leave at last in death these eyes and ears,
Oft fed with true oaths and with sweet salt tears;
    But souls where nothing dwells but love
(All other thoughts being inmates) then shall prove
This or a love increasèd there above,
When bodies to their graves, souls from their graves
                                    remove.

And then we shall be throughly blest,
    But we no more than all the rest;
Here upon earth we are kings, and none but we
Can be such kings, nor of such subjects be.
Who is so safe as we where none can do
Treason to us except one of us two?
    True and false fears let us refrain;
Let us love nobly and live and add again
Years and years unto years, till we attain
To write three score: this is the second of our reign.

John Donne

Blasted with sighs and surrounded with tears,
   Hither I come to seek the spring,
    And at mine eyes and at mine ears
Receive such balms as else cure every thing;
   But O self-traitor, I do bring
The spider love, which transubstantiates all
   And can convert manna to gall;
And that this place may thoroughly be thought
   True paradise, I have the serpent brought.

'Twere wholesomer for me that winter did
   Benight the glory of this place,
    And that a grave frost did forbid
These trees to laugh and mock me to my face;
   But that I may not this disgrace
Endure nor yet leave loving, love, let me
   Some senseless piece of this place be;
Make me a mandrake so I may grow here
   Or a stone fountain weeping out my year.

Hither with crystal vials lovers come,
   And take my tears which are love's wine,
   And try your mistress' tears at home;
For all are false that taste not just like mine;
   Alas, hearts do not in eyes shine,
Nor can you more judge woman's thoughts by tears
   Than by her shadow what she wears.
O perverse sex, where none is true but she
   Who's therefore true because her truth kills me.

John Donne

298   *A valediction: of weeping*

   Let me pour forth
My tears before thy face whilst I stay here;
For thy face coins them and thy stamp they bear,
And by this mintage they are something worth,

For thus they be
Pregnant of thee;
Fruits of much grief they are, emblems of more.
When a tear falls, that thou falls which it bore;
So thou and I are nothing then, when on a divers shore.

On a round ball
A workman that hath copies by can lay
An Europe, Afric and an Asia,
And quickly make that which was nothing, all.
So doth each tear
Which thee doth wear
A globe, yea world, by that impression grow,
Till thy tears mixed with mine do overflow
This world, by water sent from thee my heaven dis-
solvèd so.

O more than moon,
Draw not up seas to drown me in thy sphere;
Weep me not dead in thine arms, but forbear
To teach the sea what it may do too soon;
Let not the wind
Example find
To do me more harm that it purposeth;
Since thou and I sigh one another's breath
Whoe'er sighs most is cruellest, and hastes the other's
death.

John Donne

299   *The flea*

Mark but this flea, and mark in this
How little that which thou deni'st me is;
It sucked me first and now it sucks thee,
And in this flea our two loves mingled be.
Thou knowst that this cannot be said
A sin, nor shame, nor loss of maidenhead.
Yet this enjoys before it woo,
And pampered swells with one blood made of two,
And this, alas! is more than we would do.

O stay! three lives in one flea spare
Where we almost, yea more than married are.
This flea is you and I, and this
Our marriage-bed and marriage-temple is;
Though parents grudge, and you, we're met
And cloistered in these living walls of jet.
　　Though use make you apt to kill me,
　　Let not to that self-murder added be,
　　And sacrilege three sins in killing three.

Cruel and sudden, hast thou since
Purpled thy nail in blood of innocence?
Wherein could this flea guilty be
Except in that drop which it sucked from thee?
Yet thou triumph'st and say'st that thou
Findst not thyself nor me the weaker now;
　　'Tis true, then learn how false fears be;
　　Just so much honour when thou yield'st to me
　　Will waste as this flea's death took life from thee.

John Donne

300　*The curse*

Whoever guesses, thinks, or dreams he knows
Who is my mistress, wither by this curse;
　　His only, and only his purse
　　May some dull heart to love dispose,
And she yield then to all that are his foes;
　　May he be scorned by one whom all else scorn,
　　Forswear to others what to her he hath sworn
　　With fear of missing, shame of getting, torn:

Madness his sorrow, gout his cramp may he
Make by but thinking who hath made him such:
　　And may he feel no touch
　　Of conscience, but of fame, and be

Anguished, not that 'twas sin but that 'twas she;
    In early and long scarceness may he rot,
    For land which had been his if he had not
    Himself incestuously an heir begot;

May he dream treason, and believe that he
Meant to perform it, and confess and die
        And no record tell why:
    His sons, which none of his may be,
Inherit nothing but his infamy.
    Or may he so long parasites have fed,
    That he would fain be theirs whom he hath bred,
    And at the last is circumcised for bread:

The venom of all stepdames, gamesters' gall,
What tyrants and their subjects interwish,
        What plants, mine, beasts, fowl, fish
        Can contribute, all ill which all
Prophets or poets spake; and all which shall
    Be annexed in schedules unto this by me,
    Fall on that man; for if it be a she,
    Nature beforehand hath outcursed me.

John Donne

301   *A nocturnal upon Saint Lucy's Day*

BEING THE SHORTEST DAY

'Tis the year's midnight and it is the day's,
Lucy's, who scarce seven hours herself unmasks;
    The sun is spent, and now his flasks
    Send forth light squibs, no constant rays;
        The world's whole sap is sunk:
The general balm th'hydroptic earth hath drunk,
Whither, as to the bed's feet, life is shrunk,
Dead and interred; yet all these seem to laugh
Compared with me, who am their epitaph.

Study me then, you who shall lovers be
At the next world, that is at the next spring:
  For I am every dead thing,
  In whom love wrought new alchemy,
    For his art did express
A quintessence even from nothingness,
From dull privations and lean emptiness:
He ruined me, and I am rebegot
Of absence, darkness, death; things which are not.

All others from all things draw all that's good,
Life, soul, form, spirit, whence they being have;
  I by love's limbecke am the grave
  Of all that's nothing. Oft a flood
    Have we two wept, and so
Drowned the whole world, us two; oft did we grow
To be two chaoses, when we did show
Care to aught else; and often absences
Withdrew our souls and made us carcases.

But I am by her death (which word wrongs her)
Of the first nothing the elixir grown;
  Were I a man, that I were one
  I needs must know; I should prefer,
    If I were any beast,
Some ends, some means; yea, plants, yea, stones detest
And love; all some properties invest;
If I an ordinary nothing were,
As shadow, a light and body must be here.

But I am none; nor will my sun renew.
You lovers, for whose sake the lesser sun
  At this time to the goat is run
  To fetch new lust and give it you,
    Enjoy your summer all;
Since she enjoys her long night's festival
Let me prepare towards her and let me call
This hour her vigil and her eve, since this
Both the year's and the day's deep midnight is.

John Donne

When by thy scorn, O murderess, I am dead
And that thou think'st thee free
From all solicitation from me,
Then shall my ghost come to thy bed
And thee, fained vestal, in worse arms shall see;
Then thy sick taper will begin to wink,
And he whose thou art then, being tired before,
Will, if thou stir or pinch to wake him, think
   Thou call'st for more;
And in full sleep will from thee shrink;
And then, poor aspen wretch, neglected thou
Bathed in a cold quicksilver sweat wilt lie,
   A verier ghost than I;
What I will say, I will not tell thee now
Lest that preserve thee; and since my love is spent
I'd rather thou shouldst painfully repent
Than by my threatenings rest still innocent.

John Donne

303 *The extasy*

Where like a pillow on a bed
   A pregnant bank swelled up, to rest
The violet's reclining head,
   Sat we two, one another's best.
Our hands were firmly cemented
   With a fast balm which thence did spring;
Our eye-beams twisted and did thread
   Our eyes upon one double string;
So to intergraft our hands as yet
   Was all the means to make us one,
And pictures in our eyes to get
   Was all our propagation.
As 'twixt two equal armies fate
   Suspends uncertain victory,

Our souls (which to advance their state
   Were gone out) hung 'twixt her and me.
And whilst our souls negotiate there,
   We like sepulchral statues lay;
All day the same our postures were,
   And we said nothing all the day.
If any so by love refined
   That he soul's language understood
And by good love were grown all mind
   Within convenient distance stood,
He (though he knew not which soul spake
   Because both meant, both spake the same)
Might thence a new concoction take
   And part far purer than he came.
This extasy doth unperplex
   (We said) and tell us what we love;
We see by this it was not sex;
   We see, we saw not what did move:
But as all several souls contain
   Mixture of things they know not what,
Love these mixed souls doth mix again
   And makes both one, each this and that.
A single violet transplant:
   The strength, the colour and the size
(All which before was poor and scant)
   Redoubles still and multiplies.
When love with one another so
   Interinanimates two souls
That abler soul which thence doth flow
   Defects of loneliness controls.
We then, who are this new soul, know
   Of what we are composed and made,
For the atomies of which we grow
   Are souls whom no change can invade.
But O alas, so long, so far
   Our bodies why do we forbear?
They are ours, though they are not we; we are
   The intelligences, they the spheres.
We owe them thanks because they thus
   Did us to us at first convey,

Yielded their forces, sense, to us
    Nor are dross to us but allay.
On man heaven's influence works not so,
    But that it first imprints the air
So soul into the soul may flow,
    Though it to body first repair,
As our blood labours to beget
    Spirits as like souls as it can
Because such fingers need to knit
    That subtle knot which makes us man:
So must pure lovers' souls descend
    To affections and to faculties,
Which sense may reach and apprehend
    Else a great prince in prison lies.
To our bodies turn we then, that so
    Weak men on love revealed may look;
Love's mysteries in souls do grow,
    But yet the body is his book.
And if some lover such as we
    Have heard this dialogue of one,
Let him still mark us, he shall see
    Small change when we are to bodies gone.

                                        John Donne

304   *The funeral*

Whoever comes to shroud me, do not harm
    Nor question much
That subtle wreath of hair which crowns my arm,
The mystery, the sign you must not touch.
    For 'tis my outward soul,
Viceroy to that which then to heaven being gone
    Will leave this to control
And keep these limbs her provinces from dissolution.

For if the sinewy thread my brain lets fall
    Through every part
Can tie those parts and make me one of all;
These hairs which upward grew, and strength and art

Have from a better brain,
Can better do it; except she meant that I
  By this should know my pain,
As prisoners then are manacled when they are con-
                              demned to die.

Whate'er she meant by it, bury it with me;
  For since I am
Love's martyr, it might breed idolatry
If into others' hands these relics came;
  As 'twas humility
To afford to it all that a soul can do,
  So 'tis some bravery
That since you would save none of me, I bury some of
                                            you.

                                    John Donne

305   *The relic*

When my grave is broke up again
Some second guest to entertain
(For graves have learned that womanhead
To be to more than one a bed)
    And he that digs it spies
A bracelet of bright hair about the bone,
    Will he not let us alone
And think that there a loving couple lies
Who thought that this device might be some way
To make their souls at the last busy day
Meet at this grave and make a little stay?

If this fall in a time or land
Where misdevotion doth command,
Then he that digs us up will bring
Us to the bishop and the king
    To make us relics; then
Thou shalt be a Mary Magdalen and I
    A something else thereby;

All women shall adore us and some men;
And since at such times miracles are sought,
I would have that age by this paper taught
What miracles we harmless lovers wrought.

First, we loved well and faithfully
Yet knew not what we loved nor why;
Difference of sex no more we knew
Than our guardian angels do;
    Coming and going, we
Perchance might kiss, but not between those meals;
    Our hands n'er touched the seals
Which nature, injured by late law, sets free:
These miracles we did; but now alas
All measure and all language I should pass
Should I tell what a miracle she was.

John Donne

306   *The expiration*

So, so, break off this last lamenting kiss,
    Which sucks two souls and vapours both away;
Turn thou, ghost, that way and let me turn this,
    And let ourselves benight our happiest day.
We asked none leave to love; nor will we owe
    Any so cheap a death as saying, Go:

Go—and if that word hath not quite killed thee,
    Ease me with death by bidding me go too.
O if it have, let my word work on me
    And a just office on a murderer do,
Except it be too late to kill me so,
    Being double dead, going and bidding go.

John Donne

307 *His picture*

Here take my picture; though I bid farewell,
Thine in my heart, where my soul dwells, shall dwell.
'Tis like me now; but I dead will be more,
When we are shadows both, than 'twas before.
When weather-beaten I come back, my hand
Perhaps with rude oars torn or sunbeams tanned,
My face and breast of haircloth, and my head
With care's rash sudden storms being o'erspread;
My body's a sack of bones, broken within,
And powder's blue stains scattered on my skin;
If rival fools tax thee to have loved a man
So foul and coarse as O I may seem then,
This shall say what I was, and thou shalt say:
Do his hurts reach me? Doth my worth decay?
Or do they reach his judging mind that he
Should now love less what he did love to see?
That which in him was fair and delicate
Was but the milk which in love's childish state
Did nurse it, who now is grown strong enough
To feed on that which to disused tastes seems tough.

John Donne

308 *At the round earth's imagined corners*

At the round earth's imagined corners blow
Your trumpets, angels, and arise, arise
From death, you numberless infinities
Of souls, and to your scattered bodies go,
All whom the flood did, and fire shall o'erthrow,
All whom war, dearth, age, agues, tyrannies,
Despair, law, chance hath slain, and you whose eyes
Shall behold God and never taste death's woe.
But let them sleep, lord, and me mourn a space
For if above all these my sins abound
'Tis late to ask abundance of thy grace

When we are there; here on this lowly ground
Teach me how to repent; for that's as good
As if thou hadst sealed my pardon with thy blood.

John Donne

309 *Death, be not proud*

Death, be not proud, though some have callèd thee
Mighty and dreadful, for thou art not so;
For those whom thou think'st thou dost overthrow
Die not, poor death, nor yet canst thou kill me.
From rest and sleep, which yet thy pictures be,
Much pleasure, then from thee much more, must flow
And soonest our best men with thee do go,
Rest of their bones and soul's delivery.
Thou art slave to fate, chance, kings and desperate men
And dost with poison, war and sickness dwell,
And poppy or charms can make us sleep as well
And better than thy stroke; why swell'st thou then?
One short sleep past, we wake eternally,
And death shall be no more; death, thou shalt die.

John Donne

310 *Batter my heart*

Batter my heart, three-personed God; for you
As yet but knock, breathe, shine, and seek to mend;
That I may rise and stand, o'erthrow me and bend
Your force to break, blow, burn and make me new.
I, like a usurped town to another due,
Labour to admit you, but O to no end.
Reason, your viceroy in me, me should defend
But is captived, and proves weak or untrue.
Yet dearly I love you and would be lovèd fain,
But am betrothed unto your enemy:
Divorce me, untie, or break that knot again;
Take me to you, imprison me, for I,
Except you enthrall me, never shall be free,
Nor ever chaste except you ravish me.

John Donne

Thou mighty gulf, insatiate cormorant,
Deride me not, though I seem petulant
To fall into thy chops. Let others pray
For ever their fair poems flourish may.
But as for me, hungry oblivion,
Devour me quick, accept my orison,
   My earnest prayers, which do importune thee,
   With gloomy shade of thy still empery
   To veil both me and my rude poesy.

Far worthier lines in silence of thy state
Do sleep securely, free from love or hate,
From which this living ne'er can be exempt,
But whilst it breathes will hate and fury tempt.
Then close his eyes with thy all-dimming hand,
Which not right glorious actions can withstand.
Peace, hateful tongues, I now in silence pace;
Unless some hound do wake me from my place,
   I with this sharp, yet well-meant poesy,
   Will sleep secure, right free from injury
   Of cankered hate or rankest villainy.

John Marston

Do not fear to put thy feet
Naked in the river sweet;
Think not leech or newt or toad
Will bite thy foot when thou hast trod;
Nor let the water rising high
As thou wad'st in make thee cry
And sob; but ever live with me
And not a wave shall trouble thee.

John Fletcher

Beauty clear and fair
    Where the air
Rather like a perfume dwells,
    Where the violet and the rose
    The blue veins in blush disclose
And come to honour nothing else.

Where to live near
    And planted there
Is to live, and still live new;
    Where to gain a favour is
    More than light, perpetual bliss;
Make me live by serving you.

Dear again, back recall
    To this light,
A stranger to himself and all;
    Both the wonder and the story
    Shall be yours, and eke the glory;
I am your servant and your thrall.

John Fletcher

314 *Bridal song*

Roses, their sharp spines being gone,
Not royal in their smells alone
    But in their hue;
Maiden-pinks of odour faint,
Daisies smell-less yet most quaint
    And sweet thyme true.

Primrose, first-born child of Ver,
Merry springtime's harbinger,
    With her bells dim;
Oxlips in their cradles growing,
Marigolds on death-beds blowing,
    Larks'-heels trim.

All, dear nature's children's sweet,
Lie 'fore bride and bridegroom's feet,
   Blessing their sense!
Not an angel of the air,
Bird melodious or bird fair,
   Be absent hence!

The crow, the slanderous cuckoo, nor
The boding raven, nor chough hoar,
   Nor chattering pie,
May on our bride-house perch or sing,
Or with them any discord bring,
   But from it fly!

John Fletcher

315 *Call for the robin redbreast*

Call for the robin redbreast and the wren
Since o'er shady groves they hover
And with leaves and flowers do cover
The friendless bodies of unburied men.
Call unto his funeral dole
The ant, the fieldmouse and the mole
To rear him hillocks that shall keep him warm
And (when gay tombs are robbed) sustain no harm;
But keep the wolf far thence, that's foe to men
For with his nails he'll dig them up again.

John Webster

316 *A dirge*

Hark, now everything is still,
The screech-owl and the whistler shrill
Call upon our dame aloud
And bid her quickly don her shroud.
Much you had of land and rent;
Your length in clay's now competent:

A long war disturbed your mind,
Here your perfect peace is signed.
Of what is't fools make such vain keeping?
Sin their conception, their birth weeping,
Their life a general mist of error,
Their death a hideous storm of terror.
Strew your hair with powders sweet,
Don clean linen, bathe your feet,
And (the foul fiend more to check)
A crucifix let bless your neck.
'Tis now full tide 'tween night and day.
End your groan and come away.

John Webster

317   *All the flowers of the spring*

All the flowers of the spring
Meet to perfume our burying.
These have but their growing prime
And man does flourish but his time.
Survey our progress from our birth:
We are set, we grow, we turn to earth.
Courts adieu, and all delights,
All bewitching appetites!
Sweetest breath and clearest eye
Like perfumes go out and die;
And consequently this is done
As shadows wait upon the sun.
Vain the ambition of kings
Who seek by trophies and dead things
To leave a living name behind
And weave but nets to catch the wind.

John Webster

318   *Of seals and arms*

Eagles and lions, kings of birds and beasts
Adorn men's seals and arms with honoured crests;

But beasts are beasts, and fairest fowls are foul,
And many a knave's seal's better than his soul.

John Taylor

319   *Sonnet*

MACKADO, FUSTIAN AND MOTLEY

Sweet semi-circled Cynthia played at maw,[1]
The whilst Endymion ran the wild-goose chase;
Great Bacchus with his crossbow killed a daw,
And sullen Saturn smiled with pleasant face.
The ninefold Bugbears of the Caspian lake
Sat whistling ebon hornpipes to their ducks;
Madge-owlet straight for joy her girdle brake,
And rugged Satyrs frisked like stags and bucks;
The untamed tumbling fifteen-footed Goat
With promulgation of the Lesbian shores
Confronted Hydra in a sculler boat,
At which the mighty mountain Taurus roars.
    Meantime great Sultan Soliman was born,
    And Atlas blew his rustic rumbling horn.

John Taylor

1 cards

320   *A hymn*

Drop, drop, slow tears,
    And bathe those beauteous feet,
Which brought from heaven
    The news and prince of peace.
Cease not, wet eyes,
    His mercies to entreat;
To cry for vengeance
    Sin doth never cease.

In your deep floods
    Drown all my faults and fears;
Nor let his eye
    See sin, but through my tears.

Phineas Fletcher

321   *The fairies' farewell*

Farewell, rewards and fairies,
    Good housewives now may say,
For now foul sluts in dairies
    Do fare as well as they;
And though they sweep their hearths no less
    Than maids were wont to do,
Yet who of late for cleanliness
    Finds sixpence in her shoe?

Lament, lament, old abbeys,
    The fairies' lost command,
They did but change priests' babies,
    But some have changed your land;
And all your children stol'n from thence
    Are now grown puritanes
Who live as changelings ever since
    For love of your domains.

At morning and at evening both
    You merry were and glad;
So little care of sleep and sloth
    These pretty ladies had;
When Tom came home from labour,
    Or Ciss to milking rose,
Then merrily went their tabor
    And nimbly went their toes.

Witness those rings and roundelays
    Of theirs which yet remain,
Were footed in Queen Mary's days
    On many a grassy plain.

But since of late Elizabeth
    And later James came in,
They never dance on any heath
    As when the time had been.

By which we note the fairies
    Were of the old profession,
Their songs were Ave Maries,
    Their dances were procession;
But now alas, they all are dead
    Or gone beyond the seas,
Or further from religion fled,
    Or else they take their ease.

                                    Richard Corbet

322 *To his son*

VINCENT CORBET, on his birthday, November 10, 1630,
            being then three years old.

What I shall leave thee none can tell,
    But all shall say I wish thee well;
I wish thee, Vin, before all wealth,
    Both bodily and ghostly[1] health:
Not too much wealth, nor wit, come to thee,
    So much of either may undo thee.
I wish thee learning, not for show,
    Enough for to instruct, and know;
Not such as gentlemen require,
    To prate at table, or at fire.
I wish thee all thy mother's graces,
    Thy father's fortunes, and his places.
I wish thee friends, and one at Court.
    Not to build on, but support;
To keep thee, not in doing many
    Oppressions, but from suffering any.
I wish thee peace in all thy ways,
    Nor lazy nor contentious days;
And when thy soul and body part,
    As innocent as now thou art.

                                    Richard Corbet

1 spiritual

Tears, flow no more, or if you needs must flow,
    Fall yet more slow,
  Do not the world invade,
From smaller springs than yours rivers have grown
    And they again a sea have made,
Brackish like you, and which like you have flown.

Ebb to my heart, and on the burning fires
    Of my desires,
  O let your torrents fall,
From smaller heat than theirs such sparks arise
    As into flame converting all,
This world might be but my love's sacrifice.

Yet if the tempests of my sighs so blow
    You both must flow
  And my desires still burn;
Since that in vain all help my love requires,
    Why may not yet their rages turn
To dry those tears, and to blow out those fires?

Lord Herbert of Cherbury

324 *Kind and true*

'Tis not how witty nor how free,
Nor yet how beautiful she be,
But how much kind and true to me.
Freedom and wit none can confine
And beauty like the sun doth shine,
But kind and true are only mine.

Let others with attention sit
To listen, and admire her wit,
That is a rock where I'll not split.
Let others dote upon her eyes
And burn their hearts for sacrifice,
Beauty's a calm where danger lies.

But kind and true have been long tried
A harbour where we may confide,
And safely there at anchor ride.
From change of winds there we are free
And need not fear storms' tyranny,
Nor pirate though a prince he be.

Aurelian Townshend

325   *The relief on Easter Eve*

Like an hart, the live-long day
That in thorns and thickets lay,
Rouse thee, soul, thy flesh forsake,
Get to rèlief from thy brake;
Shuddering I would have thee part,
And at every motion start.
Look behind thee still to see
If thy frailties follow thee.
Deep in silence of the night
Take a sweet and stol'n delight;
Graze on clover by this calm
Precious spring of bleeding balm:
Thou rememberest how it ran
From his side, that's God and man.
Taste the pleasures of this stream,
Thou wilt think thy flesh a dream.
Nightly this repast go take,
Get to rèlief from thy brake.

Thomas Pestel

326   *Shake off your heavy trance*

Shake off your heavy trance
    And leap into a dance

Such as no mortals use to tread;
   Fit only for Apollo
To play to for the moon to lead
   And all the stars to follow.

Francis Beaumont

327   *In this world's raging sea*

In this world's raging sea
Where many Scyllas bark,
Where many sirens are,
Save, and not cast away;
He only saves his barge
With too much ware who doth it not o'ercharge;
Or when huge storms arise,
And waves menace the skies,
Gives what he got with no deploring show,
And doth again in seas his burden throw.

William Drummond

328   *My thoughts hold mortal strife*

My thoughts hold mortal strife,
I do detest my life
And with lamenting cries
(Peace to my soul to bring)
Oft calls that prince which here doth monarchize,
But he grim-grinning king,
Who caitiffs scorns, and doth the blest surprise,
   Late having decked with beauty's rose his tomb,
   Disdains to crop a weed, and will not come.

William Drummond

329   *This world a hunting is*

This world a hunting is,
The prey poor man, the Nimrod fierce is death;
His speedy greyhounds are
Lust, sickness, envy, care,
Strife that ne'er fails amiss,
With all those ills which haunt us while we breathe.

Now, if by chance we fly
Of these the eager chase,
Old age with stealing pace
Casts up his net, and there we panting die.

William Drummond

330   *Saint John the Baptist*

The last and greatest herald of Heaven's King
Girt with rough skins, hies to the desert wild,
Among that savage brood the woods forth bring,
Which he more harmless found than man, and mild.
His food was locusts, and what there doth spring
With honey that from virgin hives distilled;
Parched body, hollow eyes, some uncouth thing
Made him appear, long since from earth exiled.
There burst he forth: All ye whose hopes rely
On God, with me amidst these deserts mourn,
Repent, repent, and from old errors turn!
—Who listened to his voice, obeyed his cry?
Only the echoes, which he made relent,
Rung from their flinty caves, Repent! Repent!

William Drummond

331   *If crossed with all mishaps*

If crossed with all mishaps be my poor life,
If one short day I never spent in mirth,
If my sprite with itself holds lasting strife,
If sorrow's death is but new sorrow's birth;

If this vain world be but a sable stage
Where slave-born man plays to the scoffing stars;
If youth be tossed with love, with weakness age,
If knowledge serve to hold our thoughts in wars;
If time can close the hundred mouths of fame,
And make what long since passed like that to be;
If virtue only be an idle name,
If I, when I was born, was born to die—
    Why seek I to prolong these loathsome days?
    The fairest rose in shortest time decays.

William Drummond

332   Can you paint a thought?

Can you paint a thought, or number
Every fancy in a slumber?
Can you count soft minutes roving
From a dial's point by moving?
Can you grasp a sigh, or lastly
Rob a virgin's honour chastely?
No, O no! yet you may
Sooner do both that and this,
This and that, and never miss,
Than by any praise display
Beauty's beauty; such a glory
As beyond all fate, all story,
    All arms, all arts,
    All loves, all hearts,
Greater than those, or they,
Do, shall and must obey.

John Ford

333   The marigold

When with a serious musing I behold
The grateful and obsequious marigold,
How duly, every morning, she displays
Her open breast, when Titan spreads his rays;

How she observes him in his daily walk,
Still bending towards him her tender stalk;
How when he down declines she droops and mourns,
Bedewed (as 'twere) with tears till he returns;
And how she veils her flowers when he is gone
As if she scorned to be looked on
By an inferior eye; or did contemn
To wait upon a meaner life than him.
When this I meditate methinks the flowers
Have spirits far more generous than ours
And give us fair examples to despise
The servile fawnings and idolatries
Wherewith we court these earthly things below
Which merit not the service we bestow.
But O my God! though grovelling I appear
Upon the ground (and have a rooting here
Which hales me downwards) yet in my desire,
To that which is above me I aspire.
And all my best affections I profess
To him that is the sun of righteousness.
Oh! keep the morning of his incarnation,
The burning noontide of his bitter passion,
The night of his descending, and the height
Of his ascension ever in my sight:
    That imitating him, in what I may,
    I never follow an inferior way.

George Wither

334   *To Anthea who may command him anything*

Bid me to live, and I will live
   Thy Protestant to be:
Or bid me love, and I will give
   A loving heart to thee.

A heart as soft, a heart as kind,
   A heart as sound and free
As in the whole world thou canst find,
   That heart I'll give to thee.

Bid that heart stay, and it will stay,
    To honour thy decree:
Or bid it languish quite away,
    And 't shall do so for thee.

Bid me weep, and I will weep
    While I have eyes to see:
And, having none, yet I will keep
    A heart to weep for thee.

Bid me despair, and I'll despair
    Under that cypress tree:
Or bid me die, and I will dare
    E'en death to die for thee.

Thou art my life, my love, my heart,
    The very eyes of me,
Thou hast command of every part,
    To live and die for thee.

                                Robert Herrick

335   *To Dianeme*

Sweet, be not proud of those two eyes
Which starlike sparkle in their skies;
Nor be you proud, that you can see
All hearts your captives; yours yet free:
Be you not proud of that rich hair
Which wantons with the lovesick air;
Whenas that ruby which you wear,
Sunk from the tip of your soft ear,
Will last to be a precious stone
When all your world of beauty's gone.

                                Robert Herrick

Get up, get up for shame, the blooming morn
   Upon her wings presents the god unshorn.
     See how Aurora throws her fair
     Fresh-quilted colours through the air:
     Get up, sweet slug-a-bed, and see
     The dew-bespangled herb and tree.
Each flower has wept and bowed toward the east,
Above an hour since, yet you not dressed;
     Nay! not so much as out of bed?
     When all the birds have matins said,
     And sung their thankful hymns, 'tis sin,
     Nay, profanation to keep in,
Whenas a thousand virgins on this day
Spring, sooner than the lark to fetch in May.

Rise, and put on your foliage, and be seen
To come forth, like the spring-time, fresh and green,
     And sweet as Flora. Take no care
     For jewels for your gown or hair:
     Fear not; the leaves will strew
     Gems in abundance upon you:
Besides, the childhood of the day has kept,
Against you come, some orient pearls unwept.
     Come and receive them while the light
     Hangs on the dew-locks of the night,
     And Titan on the eastern hill
     Retires himself, or else stands still
Till you come forth. Wash, dress, be brief in praying:
Few beads are best when once we go a Maying.

Come, my Corinna, come; and coming mark
How each field turns a street, each street a park,
     Made green and trimmed with trees: see how
     Devotion gives each house a bough
     Or branch: each porch, each door, ere this
     An ark, a tabernacle is,

Made up of white-thorn neatly interwove,
As if here were those cooler shades of love.
　　Can such delights be in the street
　　And open fields, and we not see 't?
　　Come, we'll abroad: and let's obey
　　The proclamation made for May,
And sin no more, as we have done, by staying;
But, my Corinna, come, let's go a Maying.

There's not a budding boy or girl this day
But is got up and gone to bring in May.
　　A deal of youth, ere this, is come
　　Back, and with white-thorn laden home.
　　Some have dispatched their cake and cream,
　　Before that we have left to dream:
And some have wept and woo'd, and plighted troth,
And chose their priest, ere we can cast off sloth:
　　Many a green-gown has been given,
　　Many a kiss, both odd and even:
　　Many a glance too, has been sent
　　From out the eye, love's firmament:
Many a jest told of the keys betraying
This night, and locks picked: yet y'are not a Maying.

Come, let us go, while we are in our prime,
And take the harmless folly of the time:
　　We shall grow old apace, and die
　　Before we know our liberty.
　　Our life is short, and our days run
　　As fast away as doth the sun.
And as a vapour or a drop of rain,
Once lost, can ne'er be found again,
　　So when or you or I are made
　　A fable, song, or fleeting shade,
　　All love, all liking, all delight
　　Lies drowned with us in endless night.
Then, when time serves, and we are but decaying,
Come, my Corinna, come, let's go a Maying.

Robert Herrick

337   *Upon Julia's clothes*

Whenas in silks my Julia goes,
Then, then, methinks, how sweetly flows
That liquefaction of her clothes.

Next, when I cast mine eyes and see
That brave vibration each way free,
O how that glittering taketh me!

Robert Herrick

338   *Love dislikes nothing*

Whatsoever thing I see,
Rich or poor although it be,
'Tis a mistress unto me.

Be my girl or fair or brown,
Does she smile or does she frown,
Shall I write a sweetheart down.

Be she rough or smooth of skin,
When I touch I then begin
For to let affection in.

Be she bald, or does she wear
Locks incurled of others' hair,
I shall find enchantment there.

Be she whole or be she rent,
So my fancy be content,
She's to me most excellent.

Be she fat or be she lean,
Be she sluttish, be she clean,
I'm a man for every scene.

Robert Herrick

A sweet disorder in the dress
Kindles in clothes a wantonness;
A lawn about the shoulders thrown
Into a fine distraction,
An erring lace which here and there
Enthrals the crimson stomacher,
A cuff neglectful and thereby
Ribbons to flow confusedly,
A winning wave, deserving note,
In the tempestuous petticoat,
A careless shoestring in whose tie
I see a wild civility,
Do more bewitch me than when art
Is too precise in every part.

Robert Herrick

340 To meadows

Ye have been fresh and green,
    Ye have been filled with flowers,
And ye the walks have been
    Where maids have spent their hours.

You have beheld how they
    With wicker arks did come
To kiss, and bear away
    The richer cowslips home.

You've heard them sweetly sing,
    And seen them in a round,
Each virgin like a spring
    With honeysuckles crowned.

But now we see none here
    Whose silvery feet did tread
And with dishevelled hair
    Adorned this smoother mead.

Like unthrifts having spent
   Your stock and needy grown,
You're left here to lament
   Your poor estates alone.

Robert Herrick

341   *The bellman*

From noise of scare-fires rest ye free,
From murder's benedicitie,
From all mischances that may fright
Your pleasing slumbers in the night,
Mercy secure ye all and keep
The goblin from ye while ye sleep.
Past one o'clock, and almost two,
My masters all, good day to you.

Robert Herrick

342   *To daffodils*

Fair daffodils, we weep to see
   You haste away so soon;
As yet the early rising sun
   Has not attained his noon.
      Stay, stay,
   Until the hasting day
         Has run
   But to the evensong;
And having prayed together we
   Will go with you along.

We have short time to stay as you,
   We have as short a spring;
As quick a growth to meet decay,
   As you or anything.

We die,
As your hours do, and dry
   Away
Like to the summer's rain;
Or as the pearls of morning's dew
Ne'er to be found again.

Robert Herrick

343   *Chop-cherry*

Thou gav'st me leave to kiss;
Thou gav'st me leave to woo;
Thou mad'st me think, by this
And that, thou lov'dst me too.

But I shall ne'er forget
How for to make thee merry
Thou mad'st me chop, but yet
Another snapped the cherry.

Robert Herrick

344   *In the dark none dainty*

Night hides our thefts; all faults then pardoned be:
All are alike fair when no spots we see.
Lais and Lucretia in the night-time are
Pleasing alike; alike both singular:
Joan and my lady have at that time one,
One and the self-same prized complexion.
Then please alike the pewter and the plate,
The chosen ruby and the reprobate.

Robert Herrick

345   *The vision*

Methought I saw, as I did dream in bed,
A crawling vine about Anacreon's head;

Flushed was his face; his hairs with oil did shine;
And as he spake, his mouth ran o'er with wine.
Tippled he was, and tippling lisped withal;
And lisping reeled, and reeling like to fall.
A young enchantress close by him did stand
Tapping his plump thighs with a myrtle wand;
She smiled; he kissed; and kissing, culled her too;
And being cup-shot, more he could not do.
For which methought in pretty anger she
Snatched off his crown and gave the wreath to me;
Since when methinks about my brains do swim,
And I am wild and wanton like to him.

Robert Herrick

346   The coming of good luck

So good luck came, and on my roof did light
Like noiseless snow, or as the dew of night:
Not all at once, but gently, as the trees
Are by the sunbeams tickled by degrees.

Robert Herrick

347   A compass needle

Behold this needle: when the Arctic stone
Had touched it, how it trembles up and down,
Hunts for the Pole, and cannot be possessed
Of peace until it find that point, that rest.

Such is the heart of man, which when it hath
Attained the virtue of a lively faith,
It finds no rest on earth, makes no abode
In any object but his heaven, his God.

Francis Quarles

Underneath this sable hearse
Lies the subject of all verse:
Sidney's sister, Pembroke's mother;
Death, ere thou hast slain another,
Fair and learn'd and good as she,
Time shall throw a dart at thee.

William Browne

349 *Love's epitaph*

My epitaph write on your heart,
Since we did part,
For I dare swear I once lay there,
I was so near;
But time that all things doth consume,
I now presume
Hath wasted me so that I'm gone,
Both flesh and bone,
And every letter without doubt
Is quite rased out;
Next lover may he be love-curst,
As I the first.

William Cavendish, Duke of Newcastle

350 *A contemplation upon flowers*

Brave flowers, that I could gallant it like you
And be as little vain,
You come abroad, and make a harmless show,
And to your beds of earth again;
You are not proud, you know your birth
For your embroidered garments are from earth:

You do obey your months, and times, but I
Would have it ever spring,
My fate would know no winter, never die
Nor think of such a thing;
Oh that I could my bed of earth but view
And smile, and look as cheerfully as you:

O teach me to see death, and not to fear
But rather to take truce:
How often have I seen you at a bier,
And there look fresh and spruce;
You fragrant flowers, then teach me that my breath
Like yours may sweeten, and perfume my death.

Henry King

351　*The church windows*

Lord, how can man preach thy eternal word?
　　He is a brittle crazy glass:
Yet in thy temple thou dost him afford
　　This glorious and transcendent place
　　To be a window through thy grace.

But when thou dost anneal in glass thy story
　　Making thy life to shine within
The holy preachers; then the light and glory
　　More reverent grows and more doth win;
　　Which else shows waterish, bleak and thin.

Doctrine and life, colours and light in one
　　When they combine and mingle, bring
A strong regard and awe: but speech alone
　　Doth vanish like a flaring thing,
　　And in the ear, not conscience, ring.

George Herbert

Sweet day, so cool, so calm, so bright,
The bridal of the earth and sky:
The dew shall weep thy fall to-night;
    For thou must die.

Sweet rose, whose hue, angry and brave,
Bids the rash gazer wipe his eye:
Thy root is ever in its grave
    And thou must die.

Sweet spring, full of sweet days and roses,
A box where sweets compacted lie:
My music shows ye have your closes,
    And all must die.

Only a sweet and virtuous soul,
Like seasoned timber, never gives;
But though the whole world turn to coal,[1]
    Then chiefly lives.

George Herbert

1 fuel

353 *Life*

I made a posy while the day ran by:
Here will I smell my remnant out and tie
    My life within this band.
But time did beckon to the flowers, and they
By noon most cunningly did steal away,
    And withered in my hand.

My hand was next to them, and then my heart:
I took, without more thinking, in good part
    Time's gentle admonition:
Who did so sweetly death's sad taste convey,
Making my mind to smell my fatal day;
    Yet sugaring the suspicion.

Farwell dear flowers, sweetly your time ye spent,
Fit, while ye lived, for smell or ornament,
   And after death for cures.
I follow straight without complaints or grief,
Since if my scent be good, I care not, if
   It be as short as yours.

George Herbert

354   The quip

The merry world did on a day
   With his train-bands and mates agree
To meet together where I lay,
   And all in sport to jeer at me.

First beauty crept into a rose;
   Which when I plucked not, Sir, said she,
Tell me, I pray, whose hands are those?
   But thou shalt answer, Lord, for me.

Then money came, and chinking still,
   What tune is this, poor man? said she,
I heard in music you had skill.
   But thou shalt answer, Lord, for me.

Then came brave glory, puffing by
   In silks that whistled, who but he?
He scarce allowed me half an eye.
   But thou shalt answer, Lord, for me.

Then came quick wit and conversation
   And he would needs a comfort be,
And, to be short, make an oration.
   But thou shalt answer, Lord, for me.

Yet when the hour of thy design
   To answer these fine things shall come,
Speak not at large, say, I am thine;
   And then they have their answer home.

George Herbert

I struck the board, and cried, No more.
I will abroad.
What? shall I ever sigh and pine?
My lines and life are free; free as the road,
Loose as the wind, as large as store.
Shall I be still in suit?
Have I no harvest but a thorn
To let me blood, and not restore
What I have lost with cordial fruit.
    Sure there was wine
Before my sighs did dry it: there was corn
Before my tears did drown it.
Is the year only lost to me?
Have I no bays to crown it?
No flowers, no garlands gay? all blasted?
    All wasted?
Not so, my heart: but there is fruit,
    And thou hast hands.
Recover all thy sigh-blown age
On double pleasures: leave thy cold dispute
Of what is fit, and not; forsake thy cage,
    Thy rope of sands,
Which petty thoughts have made, and made to thee
Good cable, to enforce and draw,
    And be thy law,
While thou didst wink and wouldst not see.
    Away; take heed:
    I will abroad.
All in thy death's head there: tie up thy fears.
    He that forbears
To suit and serve his need,
    Deserves his load.
But as I raved and grew more fierce and wild
    At every word,
Methought I heard one calling, Child:
And I replied, My Lord.

George Herbert

When God at first made man,
Having a glass of blessings standing by,
Let us, said he, pour on him all we can;
Let the world's riches which dispersèd lie
    Contract into a span.

So strength first made a way,
Then beauty flowed, then wisdom, honour, pleasure:
When almost all was out, God made a stay,
Perceiving that, alone of all his treasure,
    Rest in the bottom lay.

For if I should, said he,
Bestow this jewel also on my creature,
He would adore my gifts instead of me,
And rest in nature, not the God of nature:
    So both should losers be.

Yet let him keep the rest,
But keep them with repining restlessness;
Let him be rich and weary, that at least,
If goodness lead him not, yet weariness
    May toss him to my breast.

George Herbert

357 *And now in age I bud again*

And now in age I bud again;
After so many deaths I live and write;
I once more smell the dew and rain,
And relish versing: O my only Light,
    It cannot be
    That I am he
On whom Thy tempests fell all night.

George Herbert

Gaze not on thy beauty's pride,
Tender maid, in the false tide
That from lovers' eyes doth slide.

Let thy faithful crystal show,
How thy colours come and go,
Beauties take a foil from woe.

Love, that in those smooth streams lies,
Under pity's fair disguise,
Will thy melting heart surprise.

Nets, of passion's finest thread,
Snaring poems, will be spread
All, to catch thy maidenhead.

Then beware, for those that cure
Love's disease, themselves endure
For reward a calenture.[1]

Rather let the lover pine,
Than his pale cheek should assign
A perpetual blush to thine.

Thomas Carew

1 deluding dream

359 *Victorious men of earth*

Victorious men of earth, no more
    Proclaim how wide your empires are;
Though you bind in every shore
    And your triumphs reach as far
        As night or day;
    Yet you proud monarchs must obey
And mingle with forgotten ashes, when
Death calls ye to the crowd of common men.

Devouring famine, plague, and war,
  Each able to undo mankind,
Death's servile emissaries are:
  Nor to these alone confined:
    He hath at will
  More quaint and subtle ways to kill;
A smile, a miss, as he will use the art,
Shall have the cunning skill to break a heart.

James Shirley

360   *The glories of our blood and state*

The glories of our blood and state
Are shadows, not substantial things;
There is no armour against fate:
Death lays his icy hand on kings.
      Sceptre and crown
      Must tumble down
And in the dust be equal made
With the poor crooked scythe and spade.

Some men with swords may reap the field
And plant with laurels where they kill;
But their strong nerves at last must yield,
They tame but one another still;
      Early or late
      They stoop to fate
And must give up their murmuring breath
When they, pale captives, creep to death.

The garlands wither on your brow;
Then boast no more your mighty deeds;
Upon death's purple altar now
See where the victor-victim bleeds.
      All heads must come
      To the cold tomb;
Only the actions of the just
Smell sweet and blossom in the dust.

James Shirley

My limbs I will fling
Out of joint and sing,
And dancing will shake my hair:
  Not bow at each beck,
  Nor break my neck
With sorrow and deep despair.

Such a chirping din,
With mirth within,
And a head not needing a clout,
  Is much better far
  Than a careful chair
And a wreath of thorns without.

William Strode

362 *On Westwell Downs*

When Westwell Downs I 'gan to tread,
Where cleanly winds the green did sweep,
Methought a landscape there was spread,
Here a bush and there a sheep;
  The pleated wrinkles on the face
  Of wave-swoln earth did lend such grace,
  As shadowings in imagery
  Which both deceive and please the eye.

The sheep sometimes did tread a maze
By often winding in and in,
And sometimes round about they trace
Which milkmaids call a fairy ring.
  Such semi-circles have they run,
  Such lines across so trimly spun,
  That shepherds learn, whene'er they please,
  A new geometry with ease.

Here and there two hilly crests
Amidst them hug a pleasant green,
And these are like two swelling breasts
That close a tender fall between.
  Here could I read or sleep or pray
  From early morn till flight of day:
  But hark! a sheep's bell calls me up,
  Like Oxford college bells, to sup.

William Strode

363   *Upon his picture*

When age hath made me what I am not now:
And every wrinkle tells me where the plough
Of time hath furrowed; when an ice shall flow
Through every vein, and all my head be snow:
When death displays his coldness in my cheek,
And I myself in my own picture seek,
Not finding what I am, but what I was;
In doubt which to believe, this or my glass;
Yet though I alter, this remains the same
As it was drawn: retains the primitive frame
And first complexion; here will still be seen
Blood on the cheek, and down upon the chin,
Here the smooth brow will stay, the lively eye,
The ruddy lip, and hair of youthful dye.
Behold what frailty we in man can see,
Whose shadow is less given to change than he.

Thomas Randolph

364   *To the younger Lady Lucy Sydney*

Why came I so untimely forth
Into a world which, wanting thee,
Could entertain us with no worth,
Or shadow of felicity?

That time should me so far remove
From that which I was born to love!

Yet, fairest blossom, do not slight
That age which you may know so soon.
The rosy morn resigns her light
And milder splendours to the noon:
    If such thy dawning beauty's power,
    Who shall abide its noontide hour?

Edmund Waller

365   *Go, lovely rose*

        Go, lovely rose
Tell her that wastes her time and me,
    That now she knows,
When I resemble her to thee,
    How sweet and fair she seems to be.

    Tell her that's young,
And shuns to have her graces spied,
    That hadst thou sprung
In deserts where no men abide,
    Thou must have uncommended died.

    Small is the worth
Of beauty from the light retired:
    Bid her come forth,
Suffer herself to be desired,
    And not blush so to be admired.

    Then die, that she
The common fate of all things rare
    May read in thee,
How small a part of time they share,
    That are so wondrous sweet and fair.

Edmund Waller

Wake all the dead! what ho! what ho!
How soundly they sleep whose pillows lie low!
They mind not poor lovers who walk above
On the decks of the world in storms of love.
    No whisper now nor glance can pass
    Through wickets or through panes of glass;
For our windows and doors are shut and barred.
Lie close in the church and in the churchyard.
    In every grave make room, make room!
    The world's at an end, and we come, we come.

The state is now love's foe, love's foe;
Has seized on his arms, his quiver and bow;
Has pinioned his wings, and fettered his feet,
Because he made way for lovers to meet.
    But O sad chance, his judge was old;
    Hearts cruel grow when blood grows cold.
No man being young his process would draw.
O heavens, that love should be subject to law!
    Lovers go woo the dead, the dead!
    Lie two in a grave, and to bed, to bed!

Sir William Davenant

O thou that sleep'st like pig in straw,
    Thou lady dear, arise!
Open, to keep the sun in awe,
    Thy pretty pinking eyes:
And, having stretched each leg and arm,
    Put on your clean white smock,
And then, I pray, to keep you warm,
    A petticoat on dock.

Arise, arise! Why should you sleep
    When you have slept enough?
Long since, French boys cried 'Chimney-sweep,'
    And damsels 'Kitchen-stuff.'
The shops were opened long before,
    And youngest prentice goes
To lay at's mistress' chamber-door
    His master's shining shoes.

Arise, arise! Your breakfast stays—
    Good water-gruel warm,
Or sugar-sops, which Galen says
    With mace will do no harm.
Arise, arise! When you are up
    You'll find more to your cost—
For morning's-draught in caudle-cup,
    Good nut-brown ale and toast.

                                    Sir William Davenant

368 *Hope*

To hope is good, but with such wild applause
    Each promise Fabius thou dost entertain;
As if decreed thee by Fate's certain laws,
    Or in possession now it did remain.

Wisdom is armed 'gainst all that can succeed,
    Time's changes and his stratagems: for such
His nature is, that when his wings we need,
    He will come creeping on his halting crutch.

Do not, if wise, then to thyself assure
    The future, nor on present goods rely,
    Or think there's any time from time secure:
    For then when patience sees her harvest nigh,

That mocking tyrant in an instant rears
A wall between the sickle and the ears.

                                    Sir Richard Fanshawe

Hence, loathed Melancholy,
  Of Cerberus and blackest Midnight born
In Stygian cave forlorn
  'Mongst horrid shapes, and shrieks, and sights unholy!
Find out some uncouth cell,
  Where brooding Darkness spreads his jealous wings,
And the night raven sings;
  There, under ebon shades and low-browed rocks,
As ragged as thy locks,
  In dark Cimmerian desert ever dwell.
But come, thou Goddess fair and free,
In heaven yclept Euphrosyne,
And by men heart-easing Mirth;
Whom lovely Venus, at a birth,
With two sister Graces more,
To ivy-crownèd Bacchus bore:
Or whether (as some sager sing)
The frolic wind that breathes the spring,
Zephyr, with Aurora playing,
As he met her once a-Maying,
There, on beds of violets blue,
And fresh-blown roses washed in dew,
Filled her with thee, a daughter fair,
So buxom, blithe, and debonair.
Haste thee, Nymph, and bring with thee
Jest, and youthful Jollity,
Quips and Cranks and Wanton Wiles,
Nods and Becks and wreathèd Smiles,
Such as hang on Hebe's cheek,
And love to live in dimple sleek;
Sport that wrinkled Care derides,
And Laughter holding both his sides.
Come, and trip it, as you go,
On the light fantastic toe;
And in thy right hand lead with thee
The mountain-nymph, sweet Liberty;
And, if I give thee honour due,
Mirth, admit me of thy crew,

To live with her, and live with thee,
In unreproved pleasures free;
To hear the lark begin his flight,
And, singing, startle the dull night,
From his watch-tower in the skies,
Till the dappled dawn doth rise;
Then to come, in spite of sorrow,
And at my window bid good-morrow,
Through the sweet-briar or the vine,
Or the twisted eglantine;
While the cock, with lively din,
Scatters the rear of darkness thin;
And to the stack, or the barn-door,
Stoutly struts his dames before:
Oft listening how the hounds and horn
Cheerly rouse the slumbering morn,
From the side of some hoar hill,
Through the high wood echoing shrill:
Sometime walking, not unseen,
By hedgerow elms, on hillocks green,
Right against the eastern gate
Where the great Sun begins his state,
Robed in flames and amber light,
The clouds in thousand liveries dight;
While the ploughman, near at hand,
Whistles o'er the furrowed land,
And the milkmaid singeth blithe,
And the mower whets his scythe,
And every shepherd tells his tale
Under the hawthorn in the dale.
Straight mine eye hath caught new pleasures,
Whilst the landskip round it measures:
Russet lawns, and fallows grey,
Where the nibbling flocks do stray;
Mountains on whose barren breast
The labouring clouds do often rest;
Meadows trim, with daisies pied;
Shallow brooks, and rivers wide;

Towers and battlements it sees
Bosomed high in tufted trees,
Where perhaps some beauty lies,
The cynosure of neighbouring eyes.
Hard by a cottage chimney smokes
From betwixt two aged oaks,
Where Corydon and Thyrsis met
Are at their savoury dinner set
Of herbs and other country messes,
Which the neat-handed Phillis dresses;
And then in haste her bower she leaves,
With Thestylis to bind the sheaves;
Or, if the earlier season lead,
To the tanned haycock in the mead.
  Sometimes, with secure delight,
The upland hamlets will invite,
When the merry bells ring round,
And the jocund rebecks sound
To many a youth and many a maid
Dancing in the chequered shade,
And young and old come forth to play
On a sunshine holiday,
Till the livelong daylight fail:
Then to the spicy nut-brown ale,
With stories told of many a feat,
How Faery Mab the junkets eat.
She was pinched and pulled, she said;
And he, by Friar's lantern led,
Tells how the drudging goblin sweat
To earn his cream-bowl duly set,
When in one night, ere glimpse of morn,
His shadowy flail hath threshed the corn
That ten day-labourers could not end;
Then lies him down, the lubber fiend,
And, stretched out all the chimney's length,
Basks at the fire his hairy strength,
And crop-full out of doors he flings,
Ere the first cock his matin rings.

Thus done the tales, to bed they creep,
By whispering winds soon lulled asleep.
Towered cities please us then,
And the busy hum of men,
Where throngs of knights and barons bold,
In weeds of peace, high triumphs hold,
With store of ladies, whose bright eyes
Rain influence, and judge the prize
Of wit or arms, while both contend
To win her grace whom all commend.
There let Hymen oft appear
In saffron robe, with taper clear,
And pomp, and feast, and revelry,
With mask and antique pageantry;
Such sights as youthful poets dream
On summer eves by haunted stream.
Then to the well-trod stage anon,
If Jonson's learned sock be on,
Or sweetest Shakespeare, Fancy's child,
Warble his native wood-notes wild,
And ever, against eating cares,
Lap me in soft Lydian airs,
Married to immortal verse,
Such as the meeting soul may pierce,
In notes with many a winding bout
Of linkèd sweetness long drawn out
With wanton heed and giddy cunning,
The melting voice through mazes running,
Untwisting all the chains that tie
The hidden soul of harmony;
That Orpheus' self may heave his head
From golden slumber on a bed
Of heaped Elysian flowers, and hear
Such strains as would have won the ear
Of Pluto to have quite set free
His half-regained Eurydice.
These delights if thou canst give,
Mirth, with thee I mean to live.

John Milton

Hence, vain deluding Joys,
    The brood of Folly without father bred!
How little you bested,
    Or fill the fixèd mind with all your toys!
Dwell in some idle brain.
    And fancies fond with gaudy shapes possess,
As thick and numberless
    As the gay motes that people the sun-beams,
Or likest hovering dreams,
The fickle pensioners of Morpheus' train.
But, hail! thou Goddess sage and holy!
Hail, divinest Melancholy!
Whose saintly visage is too bright
To hit the sense of human sight,
And therefore to our weaker view
O'erlaid with black, staid Wisdom's hue;
Black, but such as in esteem
Prince Memnon's sister might beseem,
Or that starred Ethiop queen that strove
To set her beauty's praise above
The Sea-Nymphs, and their powers offended,
Yet thou art higher far descended:
Thee bright-haired Vesta long of yore
To solitary Saturn bore;
His daughter she; in Saturn's reign
Such mixture was not held a stain.
Oft in glimmering bowers and glades
He met her, and in secret shades
Of woody Ida's inmost grove,
Whilst yet there was no fear of Jove.
Come, pensive Nun, devout and pure,
Sober, steadfast, and demure,
All in a robe of darkest grain,
Flowing with majestic train,
And sable stole of cypress lawn
Over thy decent shoulders drawn.
Come; but keep thy wonted state,
With even step, and musing gait,

And looks commercing with the skies,
Thy rapt soul sitting in thine eyes:
There, held in holy passion still,
Forget thyself to marble, till
With a sad leaden downward cast
Thou fix them on the earth as fast.
And join with thee calm Peace and Quiet,
Spare Fast, that oft with Gods doth diet,
And hears the Muses in a ring
Aye round about Jove's alter sing;
And add to those retired Leisure,
That in trim gardens takes his pleasure;
But, first and chiefest, with thee bring
Him that yon soars on golden wing,
Guiding the fiery-wheelèd throne,
The Cherub Contemplation;
And the mute Silence hist along,
'Less Philomel will deign a song,
In her sweetest saddest plight,
Smoothing the rugged brow of Night,
While Cynthia checks her dragon yoke
Gently o'er the accustomed oak.
Sweet bird, that shunn'st the noise of folly,
Most musical, most melancholy!
Thee, chauntress, oft the woods among
I woo, to hear thy even-song;
And, missing thee, I walk unseen
On the dry smooth-shaven green,
To behold the wandering moon,
Riding near her highest noon,
Like one that had been led stray
Through the heaven's wide pathless way,
And oft, as if her head she bowed,
Stooping through a fleecy cloud.
Oft, on a plat of rising ground,
I hear the far-off curfew sound,
Over some wide-watered shore,
Swinging slow with sullen roar;
Or, if the air will not permit,
Some still removèd place will fit,

Where glowing embers through the room
Teach light to counterfeit a gloom,
Far from all resort of mirth,
Save the cricket on the hearth,
Or the bellman's drowsy charm
To bless the doors from nightly harm.
Or let my lamp, at midnight hour,
Be seen in some high lonely tower,
Where I may oft outwatch the Bear,
With thrice great Hermes, or unsphere
The spirit of Plato, to unfold
What worlds or what vast regions hold
The immortal mind that hath forsook
Her mansion in this fleshly nook;
And of those demons that are found
In fire, air, flood, or underground,
Whose power hath a true consent
With planet or with element.
Sometime let gorgeous Tragedy
In sceptred pall come sweeping by,
Presenting Thebes, or Pelops' line,
Or the tale of Troy divine,
Or what (though rare) of later age
Ennobled hath the buskined stage.
But, O sad Virgin! that thy power
Might raise Musaeus from his bower;
Or bid the soul of Orpheus sing
Such notes as, warbled to the string,
Drew iron tears down Pluto's cheek,
And made Hell grant what love did seek;
Or call up him that left half-told
The story of Cambuscan bold,
Of Camball, and of Algarsife,
And who had Canace to wife,
That owned the virtuous ring and glass,
And of the wondrous horse of brass
On which the Tartar king did ride;
And if aught else great bards beside
In sage and solemn tunes have sung,
Of turneys, and of trophies hung,

Of forests, and enchantments drear,
Where more is meant than meets the ear.
Thus, Night, oft see me in thy pale career,
Till civil-suited Morn appear,
Not tricked and frounced, as she was wont
With the Attic boy to hunt,
But kerchieft in a comely cloud,
While rocking winds are piping loud,
Or ushered with a shower still,
When the gust hath blown his fill,
Ending on the rustling leaves,
With minute-drops from off the eaves.
And, when the sun begins to fling
His flaring beams, me, Goddess, bring
To archèd walks of twilight groves,
And shadows brown, that Sylvan loves,
Of pine, or monumental oak,
Where the rude axe with heavèd stroke
Was never heard the nymphs to daunt,
Or fright them from their hallowed haunt.
There, in close covert, by some brook,
Where no profaner eye may look,
Hide me from day's garish eye,
While the bee with honeyed thigh,
That at her flowery work doth sing,
And the waters murmuring,
With such consort as they keep,
Entice the dewy-feathered Sleep.
And let some strange mysterious dream
Wave at his wings in airy stream
Of lively portraiture displayed,
Softly on my eyelids laid;
And, as I wake, sweet music breathe
Above, about, or underneath,
Sent by some Spirit to mortals good,
Or the unseen Genius of the wood.
But let my due feet never fail
To walk the studious cloister's pale,
And love the high embowèd roof,
With antique pillars massy-proof,

And storied windows richly dight,
Casting a dim religious light.
There let the pealing organ blow,
To the full-voiced quire below,
In service high and anthems clear,
As may with sweetness through mine ear
Dissolve me into ecstasies,
And bring all Heaven before mine eyes.
And may at last my weary age
Find out the peaceful hermitage,
The hairy gown and mossy cell,
Where I may sit and rightly spell
Of every star that heaven doth shew,
And every herb that sips the dew,
Till old experience do attain
To something like prophetic strain.
These pleasures, Melancholy, give;
And I with thee will choose to live.

John Milton

371   Echo

Sweet Echo, sweetest nymph, that liv'st unseen
    Within thy airy shell
  By slow Meander's margent green,
And in the violet-embroidered vale
  Where the love-lorn nightingale
Nightly to thee her sad song mourneth well:
Canst thou not tell me of a gentle pair
  That likest thy Narcissus are?
    O, if thou have
  Hid them in some flowery cave,
    Tell me but where,
  Sweet Queen of Parley, Daughter of the Sphere!
  So may'st thou be translated to the skies,
And give resounding grace to all Heaven's harmonies!

John Milton

Sabrina fair,
    Listen where thou art sitting
Under the glassy, cool, translucent wave,
    In twisted braids of lilies knitting
The loose train of thy amber-dropping hair;
    Listen for dear honour's sake,
    Goddess of the silver lake,
        Listen and save!

Listen, and appear to us,
In name of great Oceanus,
By the earth-shaking Neptune's mace,
And Tethys' grave majestic pace;
By hoary Nereus' wrinkled look,
And the Carpathian wizard's hook;
By scaly Triton's winding shell,
And old soothsaying Glaucus' spell;
By Leucothea's lovely hands,
And her son that rules the strands;
By Thetis' tinsel-slippered feet,
And the songs of Sirens sweet;
By dead Parthenope's dear tomb,
And fair Ligea's golden comb,
Wherewith she sits on diamond rocks
Sleeking her soft alluring locks;
By all the nymphs that nightly dance
Upon thy streams with wily glance;
Rise, rise, and heave thy rosy head
From thy coral-paven bed,
And bridle in thy headlong wave,
Till thou our summons answered have.
                        Listen and save!

John Milton

373 *Nymphs and shepherds, dance no more*

Nymphs and shepherds, dance no more
    By sandy Ladon's lilied banks;

On old Lycaeus, or Cyllene hoar,
    Trip no more in twilight ranks;
Though Erymanth your loss deplore,
    A better soil shall give ye thanks.
From the stony Maenalus
Bring your flocks, and live with us;
Here ye shall have greater grace,
To serve the Lady of this place.
Though Syrinx your Pan's mistress were,
Yet Syrinx well might wait on her.
    Such a rural Queen
    All Arcadia hath not seen.

John Milton

374   *On his blindness*

When I consider how my light is spent
    Ere half my days in this dark world and wide,
    And that one talent which is death to hide
    Lodged with me useless, though my soul more bent
To serve therewith my Maker, and present
    My true account, lest He returning chide,
    'Doth God exact day-labour, light denied?'
    I fondly ask. But Patience, to prevent
That murmur, soon replies, 'God doth not need
    Either man's work or his own gifts. Who best
    Bear his mild yoke, they serve him best. His state
Is kingly: thousands at his bidding speed,
    And post o'er land and ocean without rest;
    They also serve who only stand and wait.'

John Milton

375   *On his deceased wife*

Methought I saw my late espoused saint
    Brought to me like Alcestis from the grave,
    Whom Jove's great son to her glad husband gave,
    Rescued from Death by force, though pale and faint.

Mine, as whom washed from spot of child-bed taint
　　Purification in the Old Law did save,
　　And such as yet once more I trust to have
　　Full sight of her in Heaven without restraint,
Came vested all in white, pure as her mind.
　　Her face was veiled; yet to my fancied sight
　　Love, sweetness, goodness, in her person shined
So clear as in no face with more delight.
　　But, oh! as to embrace me she inclined,
　　I waked, she fled, and day brought back my night.

John Milton

376   *On the late massacre in Piedmont*

Avenge, O Lord, thy slaughtered saints, whose bones
　　Lie scattered on the Alpine mountains cold;
　　Even them who kept thy truth so pure of old,
　　When all our fathers worshipped stocks and stones,
Forget not: in thy book record their groans
　　Who were thy sheep, and in their ancient fold
　　Slain by the bloody Piemontese, that rolled
　　Mother with infant down the rocks. Their moans
The vales redoubled to the hills, and they
　　To heaven. Their martyred blood and ashes sow
　　O'er all the Italian fields, where still doth sway
The triple Tyrant; that from these may grow
　　A hundredfold, who, having learnt thy way,
　　Early may fly the Babylonian woe.

John Milton

377   *An epitaph for a godly man's tomb*

Here lies a piece of Christ; a star in dust;
A vein of gold; a china dish that must
Be used in heaven, when God shall feast the just.

Robert Wild

Why so pale and wan fond lover?
   Prithee why so pale?
Will, when looking well can't move her
   Looking ill prevail?
   Prithee why so pale?

Why so dull and mute young sinner?
   Prithee why so mute?
Will, when speaking well can't win her
   Saying nothing do't?
   Prithee why so mute?

Quit, quit for shame, this will not move,
   This cannot take her;
If of herself she will not love,
   Nothing can make her:
   The devil take her.

                                        Sir John Suckling

379   *No, no, fair heretic*

No, no, fair heretic, it needs must be
   But an ill love in me,
   And worse for thee;
For were it in my power,
To love thee now this hour
   More than I did the last;
I would then so fall
   I might not love at all;
Love that can flow, and can admit increase,
Admits as well an ebb, and may grow less.

True love is still the same; the Torrid Zones,
   And those more frigid ones
   It must not know:

For love grown cold or hot,
   Is lust or friendship, not
      The thing we have.
For that's a flame would die
      Held down, or up too high:
Then think I love more than I can express,
And would love more could I but love thee less.

Sir John Suckling

380   *To Cupid*

Of thee kind boy I ask no red and white
   To make up my delight,
      No odd becoming graces,
Black eyes, or little know-not-whats in faces;
Make me but mad enough, give me good store
Of Love, for her I court,
      I ask no more,
'Tis love in love that makes the sport.

There's no such thing as that we beauty call,
   It is mere cosenage all;
      For though some time ago
Liked certain colours mingled so and so,
That doth not tie me now from choosing new,
If I a fancy take
      To black and blue,
That fancy doth it beauty make.

'Tis not the meat, but 'tis the appetite
   Makes eating a delight,
      And if I like one dish
More than another, that a pheasant is;
What in our watches, that in us is found,
So to the height and nick
      We up be wound,
No matter by what hand or trick.

Sir John Suckling

O for some honest lover's ghost,
  Some kind unbodied post
  Sent from the shades below.
  I strangely long to know
Whether the nobler Chaplets wear,
Those that their mistress scorn did bear,
  Or those that were used kindly.

For what-so-e'er they tell us here
  To make those sufferings dear,
  'Twill there I fear be found,
  That to the being crowned
T'have loved alone, will not suffice
Unless we also have been wise,
  And have our loves enjoyed.

What posture can we think him in,
  That here unloved again
  Departs and's thither gone
  Where each sits by his own?
Or how can that Elysium be
Where I my mistress still can see
  Circled in another's arms?

For there the Judges all are just,
  And Sophonisba must
  Be his whom she held dear;
  Not his who loved her here:
The sweet Philoclea since she died
Lies by her Pirocles his side,
  Not by Amphialus.

Some bays perchance or myrtle bough
  For difference crowns the brow
  Of those kind souls that were
  The noble martys here;
And if that be only odds
As, who can tell, ye kinder gods,
  Give me the woman here.

                    Sir John Suckling

I tell thee Dick where I have been,
Where I the rarest things have seen;
    O things without compare!
Such sights again cannot be found
In any place on English ground,
    Be it at Wake, or Fair.

At Charing Cross, hard by the way
Where we (thou knowest) do sell our hay,
    There is a house with stairs;
And there did I see coming down
Such folk as are not in our town,
    Vorty at least, in Pairs.

Amongst the rest, one pestilent fine,
(His beard no bigger though than mine)
    Walked on before the rest:
Our Landlord looks like nothing to him:
The King (God bless him) 'twould undo him,
    Should he go still so dressed.

At Course-a-Park, without all doubt,
He should have just been taken out
    By all the maids i' the town:
Though lusty Roger there had been,
Or little George upon the Green,
    Or Vincent of the Crown.

But wot you what? the youth was going
To make an end for all his wooing;
    The parson for him stayed;
Yet by his leave, for all his haste,
He did not so much wish all past,
    Perchance, as did the maid.

The maid (and thereby hangs a tale)
For such a maid no Whitsun ale
    Could ever yet produce:
No grape that's kindly ripe, could be
So sound, so plump, so soft as she,
    Nor half so full of juice.

Her finger was so small, the ring
Would not stay on, which they did bring,
   It was too wide a peck;
And to say truth, for out it must,
It looked like a great collar, just
   About our young colt's neck.

Her feet beneath her petticoat,
Like little mice stole in and out,
   As if they feared the light:
But O she dances such a way
No sun upon an Easter day
   Is half so fine a sight.

He would have kissed her once or twice,
But she would not, she was so nice,
   She would not do't in sight,
And then she looked as who should say
I will do what I list today;
   And you shall do't at night.

Her cheeks so rare a white was on,
No daisy makes comparison,
   Who sees them is undone,
For streaks of red were mingled there,
Such as are on a Catherine pear,
   The side that's next to the sun.

Her lip's were red, and one was thin,
Compared to that was near her chin,
   (Some bee had stung it newly).
But, Dick, her eyes so guard her face,
I durst no more upon them gaze,
   Than on the sun in July.

Her mouth so small when she does speak,
Thou'dst swear her teeth her words did break,
   That they might passage get,
But she so handled still the matter,
They came as good as ours, or better,
   And are not spent a whit.

If wishing should be any sin,
The parson himself had guilty been,
  She looked that day so purely;
And did the youth so oft the feat
At night, as some did in conceit,
  It would have spoiled him, surely.

Just in the nick the cook knocked thrice,
And all the waiters in a trice
  His summons did obey,
Each serving man with dish in hand,
Marched boldly up, like our Trained Band,
  Presented, and away.

When all the meat was on the table,
What man of knife, or teeth, was able
  To stay to be entreated?
And this the very reason was,
Before the parson could say Grace,
  The company was seated.

The business of the kitchen's great,
For it is fit that men should eat;
  Nor was it there denied:
Passion o' me! How I run on!
There's that that would be thought upon,
  I trow, besides the bride.

Now hats fly off, and youths carouse;
Healths first go round, and then the house,
  The bride's came thick and thick;
And when 'twas named another's health,
Perhaps he made it hers by stealth.
  And who could help it, Dick?

O' the sudden up they rise and dance;
Then sit again, and sigh, and glance:
  Then dance again and kiss:
Thus several ways the time did pass,
Till every woman wished her place,
  And every man wished his.

By this time all were stol'n aside
To counsel and undress the bride;
  But that he must not know;
But yet 'twas thought he guessed her mind,
And did not mean to stay behind
  Above an hour or so.

When in he came, Dick, there she lay
Like new-fall'n snow melting away
  ('Twas time I trow to part);
Kisses were now the only stay,
Which soon she gave, as who would say,
  Good Boy! with all my heart.

But just as heavens would have to cross it,
In came the bridesmaids with the posset;
  The bridegroom eat in spite;
For he had left the women to't
It would have cost two hours to do't,
  Which were too much that night.

At length the candles out and out,
All that they had not done, they do't:
  What that is, who can tell?
But I believe it was no more
Than thou and I have done before
  With Briget, and with Nell.

Sir John Suckling

383 *On Ben Jonson*

The Muse's fairest light in no dark time,
The wonder of a learned age; the line
Which none can pass; the most proportioned wit
To nature, the best judge of what was fit;
The deepest, plainest, highest, clearest pen;
The voice most echoed by consenting men,
The soul which answered best to all well said
By others, and which most requital made,

Tuned to the highest key of ancient Rome,
Returning all her music with his own,
In whom with nature study claimed a part
And yet who to himself owed all his art.
　　Here lies Ben Jonson, every age will look
　　With sorrow here, with wonder on his book.

Sidney Godolphin

384　*On a virtuous young gentlewoman that died
　　suddenly*

When the old flaming prophet climbed the sky,
Who, at one glimpse, did vanish, and not die,
He made more preface to a death than this:
So far from sick, she did not breathe amiss.
She, who to Heaven more heaven doth annex,
Whose lowest thought was above all our sex,
Accounted nothing death but to be reprieved,
And died as free from sickness as she lived.
Others are dragged away, or must be driven,
She only saw her time and stepped to Heaven,
Where Seraphims view all her glories o'er
As one returned, that had been there before.
For while she did this lower world adorn
Her body seemed rather assumed than born:
So rarefied, advanced, so pure and whole,
That body might have been another's soul;
And equally a miracle it were,
That she could die, or that she could live here.

William Cartwright

385　*To my dear and loving husband*

If ever two were one, then surely we.
If ever man were lov'd by wife, then thee.
If ever wife was happy in a man,
Compare with me, ye women, if you can.

I prize thy love more than whole mines of gold,
Or all the riches that the east doth hold.
My love is such that rivers cannot quench,
Nor ought but love from thee give recompence.
Thy love is such I can no way repay;
The heavens reward thee manifold I pray.
Then while we live, in love lets so persever,
That when we live no more, we may live ever.

Anne Bradstreet

386   *A letter to her husband, absent upon publick
employment*

As loving hind that (hartless) wants her deer,
Scuds through the woods and fern with harkning ear,
Perplext, in every bush and nook doth pry
Her dearest deer might answer ear or eye:
So doth my anxious soul, which now doth miss
A dearer dear (far dearer heart) than this,
Still wait with doubts, and hopes, and failing eye,
His voice to hear or person to discry.
Or as the pensive dove doth all alone
On withered bough most uncouthly bemoan
The absence of her love and loving mate,
Whose loss hath made her so unfortunate:
Ev'n thus do I, with many a deep sad groan,
Bewail my turtle true, who now is gone,
His presence and his safe return still woo
With thousand doleful sighs and mournful coo.
Or as the loving mullet, that true fish,
Her fellow lost, nor joy nor life doth wish,
But lanches on that shore, there for to die
Where she her captive husband doth espy.
Mine being gone, I lead a joyless life,
I have a loving fere, yet seem no wife:
But worst of all. to him can't steer my course,
I here, he there, alas, both kept by force.
Return my dear, my joy, my only love,

Unto thy hind, thy mullet and thy dove,
Who neither joys in pasture, house nor streams;
The substance gone, O me, these are but dreams.
Together at one tree, oh let us brouze,
And like two turtles roost within one house,
And like the mullets in one river glide,
Let's still remain but one, till death divide.
 Thy loving love and dearest dear,
 'At home, abroad, and every where,

A. B.

Anne Bradstreet

387 *Love*

All love at first, like generous wine,
Ferments and frets, until 'tis fine;
But when 'tis settled on the lee,
And from the impurer matter free,
Becomes the richer still, the older,
And proves the pleasanter, the colder.

Samuel Butler

388 *On himself, on hearing what was his sentence*

Let them bestow on every earth a limb;
Open all my veins that I may swim
To Thee my Saviour, in that Crimson Lake;
Then place my purboiled head upon a stake;
Scatter my ashes, throw them in the air:
Lord, since Thou knowest where all these atoms are,
I'm hopeful, once Thou'lt recollect my dust,
And confident Thou'lt raise me with the Just.

James Graham, Marquis of Montrose

My dear and only love, I pray
    That little world of thee
Be governed by no other sway
    Than purest monarchy;
For if confusion have a part,
    Which virtuous souls abhor,
And hold a synod in thine heart,
    I'll never love thee more.

Like Alexander I will reign,
    And I will reign alone;
My thoughts did evermore disdain
    A rival on my throne.
He either fears his fate too much,
    Or his deserts are small,
That dares not put it into touch,
    To gain or lose it all.

And in the empire of thine heart,
    Where I should solely be,
If others do pretend a part
    Or dare to vie with me,
Or if committees thou erect,
    And go on such a score,
I'll laugh and sing at thy neglect,
    And never love thee more.

But if thou wilt prove faithful then,
    And constant to thy word,
I'll make thee glorious by my pen
    And famous by my sword;
I'll serve thee in such noble ways
    Was never heard before;
I'll crown and deck thee all with bays,
    And love thee more and more.

James Graham, Marquis of Montrose

Love making all things else his foes
Like a fierce torrent overflows
Whatever doth his course oppose.

This was the cause the poets sung,
Thy mother from the sea was sprung,
But they were mad to make thee young.

Her father, not her son, art thou;
From our desires our actions grow
And from the cause the effect must flow.

Love is as old as place or time;
'Twas he the fatal tree did climb,
Grandsire of Father Adam's crime.

Love drowsy days and stormy nights
Makes, and breaks friendship, whose delights
Feed, but not glut our appetites.

How happy he that loves not lives!
Him neither hope nor fear deceives
To Fortune who no hostage gives.

How unconcerned in things to come!
If here he frets, he finds at Rome,
At Paris or Madrid his home.

Secure from low and private ends,
His life, his zeal, his wealth attends
His prince, his country and his friends.

Sir John Denham

391   *The gnat*

One night, all tired with the weary day,
And with my tedious self, I went to lay

My fruitless cares
And needless fears
    Asleep.
The curtains of the bed, and of mine eyes
Being drawn, I hoped no trouble would surprise
    That rest which now
    'Gan on my brow
        To creep.

When lo a little fly, less than it's name
(It was a gnat) with angry murmer came.
    About she flew
    And louder grew
        Whilst I
Fain would have scorned the silly thing, and slept
Out all its noise; I resolute silence kept,
    And laboured so
    To overthrow
        The fly.

But still with sharp alarms vexatious she
Or challenged, or rather mocked me.
    Angry at last
    About I cast
        My hand.
'Twas well night would not let me blush, nor see
With whom I fought; and yet though feeble she
    Nor her nor my
    Own wrath could I
        Command.

Away she flies, and her own triumph sings
I being left to fight with idler things,
    A feeble pair
    Myself and air.
        How true
A worm is man, whom flies their sport can make!
Poor worm; true rest in no bed can he take,
    But one of earth
    Whence he came forth
        And grew.

For there none but his silent sisters be,
Worms of as true and genuine earth as he,
  Which from the same
  Corruption came:
    And there
Though on his eyes they feed, though on his heart,
They neither vex nor wake him; every part
  Rests in sound sleep,
  And out doth keep
    All fear.

Joseph Beaumont

392   *To Lucasta, going to the wars*

Tell me not, Sweet, I am unkind,
  That from the nunnery
Of thy chaste breast and quiet mind
  To war and arms I fly.

True, a new mistress now I chase,
  The first foe in the field;
And with a stronger faith embrace
  A sword, a horse, a shield.

Yet this inconstancy is such
  As thou too shalt adore;
I could not love thee, Dear, so much,
  Loved I not honour more.

Richard Lovelace

393   *Gratiana dancing and singing*

She beat the happy pavèment—
By such a star made firmament,
  Which now no more the roof envìes!
    But swells up high, with Atlas even,
    Bearing the brighter nobler heaven,
  And, in her, all the deities.

Each step trod out a lover's thought,
And the ambitious hopes he brought
  Chained to her brave feet with such arts,
    Such sweet command and gentle awe,
    As, when she ceased, we sighing saw
  The floor lay paved with broken hearts.

                              Richard Lovelace

394   *To Althea, from prison*

When love with unconfinèd wings
  Hovers within my gates,
And my divine Althea brings
  To whisper at the grates;
When I lie tangled in her hair
  And fettered to her eye,
The birds that wanton in the air
  Know no such liberty.

When flowing cups run swiftly round
  With no allaying Thames,
Our careless heads with roses bound,
  Our hearts with loyal flames;
When thirsty grief in wine we steep,
  When healths and draughts go free—
Fishes that tipple in the deep
  Know no such liberty.

When like committed linnets, I
  With shriller notes shall sing
The sweetness, mercy, majesty,
  And glories of my king;
When I shall voice aloud how good
  He is, how great should be,
Enlarged winds, that curl the flood,
  Know no such liberty.

Stone walls do not a prison make,
    Nor iron bars a cage;
Minds innocent and quiet take
    That for an hermitage;
If I have freedom in my love
    And in my soul am free,
Angels alone, that soar above,
    Enjoy such liberty.

Richard Lovelace

395 *On the death of Mr. William Hervey*

It was a dismal and a fearful night:
Scarce could the morn drive on th' unwilling light,
When sleep, death's image, left my troubled breast
    By something liker death possessed.
My eyes with tears did uncommanded flow,
    And on my soul hung the dull weight
    Of some intolerable fate.
What bell was that? Ah me! too much I know!

My sweet companion and my gentle peer,
Why hast thou left me thus unkindly here,
Thy end for ever and my life to moan?
    O, thou hast left me all alone!
Thy soul and body, when death's agony
    Besieged around thy noble heart,
    Did not with more reluctance part
Than I, dearest friend, do part from thee.

My dearest friend, would I had died for thee!
Life and this world henceforth will tedious be:
Nor shall I know hereafter what to do
    If once my griefs prove tedious too.
Silent and sad I walk about all day,
    As sullen ghosts stalk speechless by
    Where their hid treasures lie;
Alas! my treasures gone; why do I stay?

Say, for you saw us, ye immortal lights,
How oft unwearied have we spent the nights,
Till the Ledaen stars, so famed for love,
   Wondered at us from above!
We spent them not in toys, in lusts, or wine;
   But search of deep philosophy,
   Wit, eloquence, and poetry—
Arts which I loved, for they, dear friend, were thine.

Ye fields of Cambridge, our dear Cambridge, say
Have ye not seen us walking every day?
Was there a tree about which did not know
   The love betwixt us two?
Henceforth, ye gentle trees, forever fade;
   Or your sad branches thicker join
   And into darksome shades combine,
Dark as the grave wherein my friend is laid!

Large was his soul: as large a soul as e'er
Submitted to inform a body here;
High as the place 'twas shortly in heaven to have,
   But low and humble as his grave.
So high that all the virtues there did come,
   As to their chiefest seat
   Conspicuous and great;
So low, that for me too it made a room.

Knowledge he only sought, and so soon caught
As if for him knowledge had rather sought;
Nor did more learning ever crowded lie
   In such a short mortality.
Whene'er the skilful youth discoursed or writ,
   Still did the notions throng
   About his eloquent tongue;
Nor could his ink flow faster than his wit.

His mirth was the pure spirits of various wit,
Yet never did his God or friends forget;
And when deep talk and wisdom came in view,
   Retired, and gave to them their due.

For the rich help of books he always took,
   Though his own searching mind before
   Was so with notions written o'er,
As if wise Nature had made that her book.

With as much zeal, devotion, piety,
He always lived, as other saints do die.
Still with his soul severe account he kept,
   Weeping all debts out e'er he slept.
Then down in peace and innocence he lay,
   Like the sun's laborious light,
   Which still in water sets at night,
Unsullied with his journey of the day.

But happy thou, ta'en from this frantic age,
Where ignorance and hypocrisy does rage!
A fitter time for heaven no soul e'er chose—
   The place now only free from those.
There 'mong the blest thou dost for ever shine;
   And wheresoe'er thou casts thy view
   Upon that white and radiant crew,
See'st not a soul clothed with more light than thine.

Abraham Cowley

396 *And she washed his feet with her tears, and wiped*
     them with the hairs of her head

The proud Egyptian queen, her Roman guest,
(To express her love in height of state, and pleasure)
   With pearl dissolved in gold, did feast,
      Both food, and treasure.

And now, dear Lord, thy lover, on the fair
And silver tables of thy feet, behold!
   Pearl in her tears, and in her hair
      Offers thee gold.

Sir Edward Sherburne

I am returned, my fair, but see
Perfectïon in none but thee:
  Yet many beauties have I seen,
  And in that search a truant been,
Through fruitless curiosity.

I've been to see each blear-eyed star,
Fond men durst with thy light compare;
  And, to my admiration, find
  That all, but I, in love are blind,
And none but thee divinely fair.

Here then I fix, and now grown wise,
All objects, but thy face, despise;
  Taught by my folly, now I swear,
  If you forgive me, ne'er to err,
Nor seek impossibilities.

                              Charles Cotton

I have been in love, and in debt, and in drink,
  This many and many a year;
And those three plagues enough, one would think,
  For one poor mortal to bear.
'Twas drink made me fall into love,
  And love made me run into debt,
And though I have struggled and struggled and strove.
  I cannot get out of them yet.

  There's nothing but money can cure me,
    And rid me of all my pain;
      'Twill pay all my debts,
      And remove all my lets,
  And my mistress, that cannot endure me,
    Will love me, and love me again:
Then I'll fall to loving and drinking amain.

                              Alexander Brome

Where the remote bermudas ride,
In the ocean's bosom unespied,
From a small boat, that rowed along,
The listening winds received this song:
'What should we do but sing His praise,
That led us through the watery maze,
Unto an isle so long unknown,
And yet far kinder than our own?
Where He the huge sea-monsters wracks,
That lift the deep upon their backs;
He lands us on a grassy stage,
Safe from the storms, and prelate's rage.
He gave us this eternal spring,
Which here enamels every thing,
And sends the fowls to us in care,
On daily visits through the air;
He hangs in shades the orange bright,
Like golden lamps in a green night,
And does in the pomegranates close
Jewels more rich than Ormus shows;
He makes the figs our mouths to meet,
And throws the melons at our feet;
But apples plants of such a price,
No tree could ever bear them twice;
With cedars chosen by His hand,
From Lebanon He stores the land,
And makes the hollow seas that roar,
Proclaim the Ambergris on shore;
He cast (of which we rather boast)
The Gospel's pearl upon our coast,
And in these rocks for us did frame
A temple where to sound His name.
Oh! let our voice His praise exalt,
Till it arrive at Heaven's vault,
Which, thence (perhaps) rebounding, may
Echo, beyond the Mexique Bay.'

Thus sang they, in the English boat,
An holy and a cheerful note;
And all the way, to guide their chime,
With falling oars they kept the time.

Andrew Marvell

400   *To his coy mistress*

Had we but world enough, and time,
This coyness, lady, were no crime.
We would sit down, and think which way
To walk, and pass our long love's day.
Thou by the Indian Ganges' side
Shouldst rubies find: I by the tide
Of Humber would complain. I would
Love you ten years before the flood,
And you should, if you please, refuse
Till the conversion of the Jews;
My vegetable love should grow
Vaster than empires and more slow;
An hundred years should go to praise
Thine eyes, and on thy forehead gaze;
Two hundred to adore each breast,
But thirty thousand to the rest;
An age at least to every part,
And the last age should show your heart.
For, lady, you deserve this state,
Nor would I love at lower rate.
    But at my back I always hear
Time's wingèd chariot hurrying near,
And yonder all before us lie
Deserts of vast eternity.
Thy beauty shall no more be found,
Nor, in thy marble vault shall sound
My echoing song; then worms shall try
That long-preserved virginity,
And your quaint honour turn to dust,
And into ashes all my lust:

The graves a fine and private place,
But none I think do there embrace.
    Now therefore, while the youthful hue
Sits on thy skin like morning dew,
And while thy willing soul transpires
At every pore with instant fires,
Now let us sport us while we may,
And now, like amorous birds of prey,
Rather at once our time devour,
That languish in this slow-chapt power.
Let us roll all our strength and all
Our sweetness up into one ball,
And tear our pleasures with rough strife,
Through the iron gates of life;
Thus, though we cannot make our sun
Stand still, yet we will make him run.

Andrew Marvell

401   *The mower to the glow-worms*

Ye living lamps by whose dear light
The nightingale does sit so late,
And studying all the summer night,
Her matchless songs does meditate;

Ye country comets, that portend
No war nor prince's funeral,
Shining unto no higher end
Than to presage the grass's fall;

Ye glow-worms, whose officious flame
To wandering mowers shows the way,
That in the night have lost their aim,
And after foolish fires do stray;

Your courteous lights in vain you waste,
Since Juliana here is come,
For she my mind hath so displaced,
That I shall never find my home.

Andrew Marvell

The wanton troopers riding by
Have shot my fawn, and it will die.
Ungentle men! they cannot thrive
Who killed thee. Thou ne'er didst alive
Them any harm, alas! nor could
Thy death yet do them any good.
I'm sure I never wished them ill;
Nor do I for all this, nor will:
But, if my simple prayers may yet
Prevail with heaven to forget
Thy murder, I will join my tears,
Rather than fail. But, O my fears!
It cannot die so. Heaven's king
Keeps register of everything,
And nothing may we use in vain;
Even beasts must be with justice slain,
Else men are made their deodands.
Though they should wash their guilty hands
In this warm life-blood which doth part
From thine, and wound me to the heart
Yet could they not be clean; their stain
Is dyed in such a purple grain.
There is not such another in
The world, to offer for their sin.

   Unconstant Sylvio, when yet
I had not found him counterfeit,
One morning (I remember well),
Tied in this silver chain and bell,
Gave it to me: nay, and I know
What he said then, I'm sure I do:
Said he, 'Look how your huntsmen here
Hath taught a fawn to hunt his deer.'
But Sylvio soon had me beguiled;
This waxèd tame, while he grew wild
And quite regardless of my smart,
Left me his fawn, but took his heart.

   Thenceforth I set myself to play
My solitary time away

With this; and very well content,
Could so my idle life have spent;
For it was full of sport, and light
Of foot and heart, and did invite
Me to its game: it seemed to bless
Itself in me; how could I less
Than love it? O, I cannot be
Unkind to a beast that loveth me.
Had it lived long, I do not know
Whether it too might have done so
As Sylvio did; his gifts might be
Perhaps as false, or more, than he;
But I am sure, for aught that I
Could in so short a time espy,
Thy love was far more better than
The love of false and cruel men.

    With sweetest milk and sugar first
I it at my own fingers nursed;
And as it grew, so every day
It waxed more white and sweet than they.
It had so sweet a breath! And soft
And white, shall I say than in my hand?
Nay, any lady's of the land.

    It is a wondrous thing how fleet
'Twas on those little silver feet;
With what a pretty skipping grace
It oft would challenge me the race;
And when't had left me far away,
'Twould stay, and run again, and stay;
For it was nimbler much than hinds,
And trod as if on the four winds.

    I have a garden of my own,
But so with roses overgrown,
And lilies, that you would it guess
To be a little wilderness;
And all the spring-time of the year
It only lovèd to be there.
Among the beds of lilies I
Have sought it oft, where it should lie,
Yet could not, till itself would rise,

Find it, although before my eyes;
For, in the flaxen lilies' shade
It like a bank of lilies laid.
Upon the roses it would feed,
Until its lips e'en seem to bleed.
And then to me 'twould boldly trip,
And print those roses on my lip.
But all its chief delight was still
On roses thus itself to fill,
And its pure virgin limbs to fold
In whitest sheets of lilies cold:
Had it lived long, it would have been
Lilies without, roses within.

    O help! O help! I see it faint
And die as calmly as a saint!
See how it weeps! the tears do come
Sad, slowly, dropping like a gum.
So weeps the wounded balsam; so
Thy holy frankincense doth flow;
The brotherless Heliades
Melt in such amber tears as these.

    I in a golden vial will
Keep these two crystal tears, and fill
It till it do o'erflow with mine,
Then place it in Diana's shrine.

    Now my sweet fawn is vanished to
Whither the swans and turtles go;
In fair Elysium to endure,
With milk-like lambs, and ermines pure.
O do not run too fast: for I
Will but bespeak thy grave, and die.

    First, my unhappy statue shall
Be cut in marble; and withal,
Let it be weeping too; but there
The engraver sure his art may spare;
For I so truly thee bemoan,
That I shall weep, though I be stone,
Until my tears, still dropping, wear
My breast, themselves engraving there;
There at my feet shalt thou be laid,

Of purest alabaster made;
For I would have thine image be
White as I can, though not as thee.

Andrew Marvell

403   The garden

How vainly men themselves amaze,
To win the palm, the oak, or bays;
And their incessant labour see
Crowned from some single herb, or tree,
Whose short and narrow-vergèd shade
Does prudently their toils upbraid;
While all the flowers and trees do close,
To weave the garlands of respose!

Fair Quiet, have I found thee here,
And Innocence, thy sister dear?
Mistaken long, I sought you then
In busy companies of men.
Your sacred plants, if here below,
Only among the plants will grow;
Society is all but rude
To this delicious solitude.

No white nor red was ever seen
So amorous as this lovely green.
Fond lovers, cruel as their flame,
Cut in these trees their mistress' name:
Little, alas! they know or heed,
How far these beauties hers exceed!
Fair trees! wheres' e'er your bark I wound,
No name shall but your own be found.

When we have run our passion's heat,
Love hither makes his best retreat.
The gods, that mortal beauty chase,
Still in a tree did end their race;

Apollo hunted Daphne so,
Only that she might laurel grow;
And Pan did after Syrinx speed,
Not as a nymph, but for a reed.

What wondrous life is this I lead!
Ripe apples drop about my head;
The luscious clusters of the vine
Upon my mouth do crush their wine;
The nectarine, and curious peach,
Into my hands themselves do reach;
Stumbling on melons, as I pass,
Insnared with flowers, I fall on grass.

Meanwhile the mind, from pleasure less,
Withdraws into its happiness;
The mind, that ocean where each kind
Does straight its own resemblance find;
Yet it creates, transcending these,
Far other worlds, and other seas,
Annihilating all that's made
To a green thought in a green shade.

Here at the fountain's sliding foot,
Or at some fruit-tree's mossy root,
Casting the body's vest aside,
My soul into the boughs does glide:
There, like a bird, it sits and sings,
Then whets and claps it silver wings,
And, till prepared for longer flight,
Waves in its plumes the various light.

Such was the happy garden-state,
While man there walked without a mate:
After a place so pure and sweet,
What other help could yet be meet!
But 'twas beyond a mortal's share
To wander solitary there:
Two paradises 'twere in one,
To live in paradise alone.

How well the skilful gardener drew
Of flowers, and herbs, this dial new;
Where from above, the milder sun
Does through a fragrant zodiac run,
And, as it works, the industrious bee
Computes its times as well as we!
How could such sweet and wholesome hours
Be reckoned but with herbs and flowers?

Andrew Marvell

404   *The fair singer*

To make a final conquest of all me,
Love did compose so sweet an enemy,
In whom both beauties to my death agree,
Joining themselves in fatal harmony,
That, while she with her eyes my heart does bind,
She with her voice might captivate my mind.

I could have fled from one but singly fair;
My disentangled soul itself might save,
Breaking the curlèd trammels of her hair;
But how should I avoid to be her slave,
Whose subtle art invisibly can wreathe
My fetters of the very air I breathe?

It had been easy fighting in some plain,
Where victory might hang in equal choice,
But all resistance against her is vain,
Who has the advantage both of eyes and voice;
And all my forces needs must be undone,
She having gainèd both the wind and sun.

Andrew Marvell

405   *The definition of love*

My love is of a birth as rare
   As 'tis, for object, strange and high
It was begotten by Despair,
   Upon Impossibility.

Magnanimous Despair alone
  Could show me so divine a thing,
Where feeble Hope could ne'er have flown,
  But vainly flapped its tinsel wing.

And yet I quickly might arrive
  Where my extended soul is fixed;
But Fate does iron wedges drive,
  And always crowds itself betwixt.

For Fate with jealous eye does see
  Two perfect loves, nor lets them close;
Their union would her ruin be,
  And her tyrannic power depose.

And therefore her decrees of steel
  Us as the distant poles have placed,
(Though Love's whole world on us does wheel),
  Not by themselves to be embraced,

Unless the giddy heaven fall,
  And earth some new convulsion tear,
And, us to join, the world should all
  Be cramped into a planisphere.

As lines, so loves oblique, may well
  Themselves into every angle greet:
But ours, so truly parallel,
  Though infinite, can never meet.

Therefore, the love which us doth bind,
  But Fate so enviously debars,
Is the conjunction of the mind,
  And opposition of the stars.

                              Andrew Marvell

406 *The picture of little T. C. in a prospect of flowers*

See with what simplicity
This nymph begins her golden days!
In the green grass she loves to lie,
And there with her fair aspect tames

The wilder flowers and gives them names,
But only with the roses plays,
       And them does tell
What colour best becomes them and what smell.

Who can fortell for what high cause
This darling of the gods was born?
Yet this is she whose chaster laws
The wanton Love shall one day fear,
And, under her command severe,
See his bow broke, his ensigns torn.
       Happy who can
Appease this virtuous enemy of man!

O then let me in time compound
And parley with those conquering eyes,
Ere they have tried force to wound;
Ere with their glancing wheels they drive
In triumph over hearts that stive,
And them that yield but more despise:
       Let me be laid
Where I may see the glories from some shade.

Meantime, whilst every verdant thing
Itself does at thy beauty charm,
Reform the errors of the spring;
Make that the tulips may have share
Of sweetness seeing they are fair;
And roses of their thorns disarm;
       But most procure
That violets may a longer age endure.

But O young beauty of the woods,
Whom Nature courts with fruit and flowers,
Gather the flowers, but spare the buds,
Lest Flora, angry at thy crime
To kill her infants in their prime,
Do quickly make the example yours;
       And ere we see,
Nip in the blossom all our hopes and thee.

Andrew Marvell

Fancy, and I, last evening walked,
And, Amoret, of thee we talked;
The west just then had stoln the sun,
And his last blushes were begun:
We sat, and marked how every thing
Did mourn his absence; how the spring
That smiled, and curled about his beams,
Whilst he was here, now checked her streams:
The wanton eddies of her face
Were taught less noise, and smoother grace;
And in a slow, sad channel went,
Whispering the banks their discontent:
The careless ranks of flowers that spread
Their perfumed bosoms to his head,
And with an open, free embrace,
Did entertain his beamy face;
Like absent friends point to the west,
And on that weak reflection feast.
If creatures then that have no sense,
But the loose tie of influence,
(Though fate, and time each day remove
Those things that element their love)
At such vast distance can agree,
Why, Amoret, why should not we?

Henry Vaughan

408 *The retreat*

Happy those early days when I
Shined in my angel-infancy.
Before I understood this place
Appointed for my second race,
Or taught my soul to fancy aught
But a white, celestial thought,
When yet I had not walked above
A mile or two from my first love,

And looking back, at a short space,
Could see a glimpse of his bright face;
When on some guilded cloud, or flower,
My gazing soul would dwell an hour,
And in those weaker glories spy
Some shadows of eternity;
Before I taught my tongue to wound
My conscience with a sinful sound,
Or had the black art to dispense
A several sin to every sense,
But felt through all this fleshly dress
Bright shoots of everlastingness.

  O how I long to travel back
And tread again that ancient track!
That I might once more reach that plain,
Where first I felt my glorious train,
From whence th'enlightened spirit sees
That shady city of palm trees;
But, ah! my soul with too much stay
Is drunk, and staggers in the way.
Some men a forward motion love,
But I by backward steps would move,
And when this dust falls to the urn
In that state I came, return.

Henry Vaughan

409 *Peace*

My Soul, there is a country
  Far beyond the stars,
Where stands a wingèd sentry
  All skilful in the wars,
There, above noise, and danger
  Sweet peace sits crowned with smiles,
And one born in a manger
  Commands the beauteous files,
He is thy gracious friend,

And, oh my soul awake!
Did in pure love descend
  To die here for thy sake;
If thou can get but thither,
  There grows the flower of peace,
The rose that cannot wither,
  Thy fortress, and thy ease;
Leave then thy foolish ranges;
  For none can thee secure,
But one, who never changes,
  Thy God, thy life, thy Cure.

Henry Vaughan

410 The world

I saw Eternity the other night
Like a great ring of pure and endless light,
  All calm, as it was bright,
And round beneath it, time, in hours, days, years
  Driven by the spheres
Like a vast shadow moved, in which the world
  And all her train were hurled;
The doting lover in his quaintest strain
  Did there complain,
Near him, his lute, his fancy, and his flights,
  Wit's sour delights,
With gloves, knots the silly snares of pleasure;
  Yet his dear treasure
All scattered lay, while he his eyes did pour
  Upon a flower.

The darksome statesman, hung with weights and woe,
Like a thick midnight fog moved there so slow
  He did not stay, nor go;
Condemning thoughts, like sad eclipses, scowl
  Upon his soul,

And crowds of crying witnesses without
   Pursued him with one shout.
Yet digged the mole, and lest his ways be found
   Worked underground,
Where he did clutch his prey, but one did see
   That policy;
Churches and altars fed him, perjuries
   Were gnats and flies,
It rained about him blood and tears, but he
   Drank them as free.

The fearful miser on a heap of rust
Sat pining all his life there, did scarce trust
   His own hands with the dust,
Yet would not place one piece above, but lives
   In fear of thieves.
Thousands there were as frantic as himself
   And hugged each one his pelf,
The downright Epicure placed heaven in sense
   And scorned pretence
While others, slipped into wide excess
   Said little less;
The weaker sort slight, trivial wares enslave
   Who think them brave,
And poor, despisèd truth sat counting by
   Their victory.

Yet some, who all this while did weep and sing,
And sing, and weep, soared up into the ring,
   But most would use no wing.
O fools, said I, thus to prefer dark night
   Before true light,
To live in grots, and caves, and hate the day
   Because it shows the way,
The way which from this dead and dark abode
   Leads up to God,
A way where you might tread the sun, and be
   More bright than he.

But as I did there madness so discuss
    One whispered thus,
This ring the bridegroom did for none provide
    But for his bride.

Henry Vaughan

411 *The world of light*

They are all gone into the world of light!
    And I alone sit lingering here;
Their very memory is fair and bright,
    And my sad thoughts doth clear.

It glows and glitters in my cloudy breast
    Like stars upon some gloomy grove,
Or those faint beams in which this hill is dressed,
    After the sun's remove.

I see them walking in an air of glory,
    Whose light doth trample on my days:
My days which are at best but dull and hoary,
    Mere glimmering and decays.

O holy hope! and high humility,
    High as the heavens above!
These are your walks and you have shown them me
    To kindle my cold love.

Dear, beauteous death, the jewel of the just,
    Shining nowhere but in the dark:
What mysteries do lie beyond thy dust;
    Could man out-look that mark!

He that hath found some fledged bird's nest may know,
    At first sight, if the bird be flown;
But what fair well or grove he sings in now,
    That is to him unknown.

And yet, as angels in some brighter dreams
    Call to the soul when man doth sleep,
So some strange thoughts transcend our wonted themes,
    And into glory peep.

If a star were confined into a tomb
    Her captive flames must needs burn there;
But when the hand that locked her up, gives room,
    She'll shine through all the sphere.

O father of eternal life, and all
    Created glories under thee!
Resume thy spirit from this world of thrall
    Into true liberty.

Either disperse these mists, which blot and fill
    My perspective still as they pass,
Or else remove me whence unto that hill,
    Where I shall need no glass.

Henry Vaughan

412 Man

    Weighing the steadfastness and state
Of some mean things which here below reside,
Where birds like watchful clocks the noiseless date
    And intercourse of times divide,
Where bees at night get home and give, and flowers
    Early as well as late,
Rise with the sun and set in the same bowers;

    I would, said I, my God would give
The staidness of these things to man! for these
To his divine appointments ever cleave,
    And no new business breaks their peace;
The birds nor sow, nor reap, yet sup and dine,
    The flowers without their clothes live,
Yet Solomon was never dressed so fine.

Man hath still either toys or care;
He hath no root, nor to one place is tied,
But ever restless and irregular
    About this earth doth run and ride,
He knows he hath a home but scarce knows where,
        He says it is so far
That he hath quite forgot how to go there.

He knocks at all doors, strays and roams,
Nay, hath not so much wit as some stones have
Which in the darkest nights point to their homes,
    By some hid sense their maker gave;
Man is the shuttle, to whose winding quest
    And passage through these looms
God ordered motion but ordained no rest.

                                        Henry Vaughan

413 *The storm*

I see the use; and know my blood
    Is not a sea,
But a shallow, bounded flood,
    Though red as he;
Yet I have flows as strong as his
    And boiling streams that rave
With the same curling force and hiss
    As doth the mountained wave.

But when his waters billow thus,
    Dark storms and wind
Incite them to that fierce discuss,
    Else not inclined.
Thus the enlarged, enragèd air
    Uncalms these to a flood;
But still the weather that's most fair
    Breeds tempests in my blood.

Lord, then round me with weeping clouds,
   And let my mind
In quick blasts sigh beneath those shrouds,
   A spirit-wind;
So shall that storm purge this recluse
   Which sinful ease made foul,
And wind and water to thy use
   Both wash and wing my soul.

Henry Vaughan

414   *Tell me, O Love*

Tell me, O Love, why Celia, smooth
As seas when winds forbear to soothe
Their waves to wanton curls, than down
More soft, which doth the thistle crown,
Whiter than is the milky road
That leads to Jove's supreme abode,
Should harder far and rougher be
Than most obdurate rocks to me?
Sheds on my hopes as little day
As the pale moon's eclipsèd ray?
My heart would break, but that I hear
Love gently whisper in my ear,
   'Actions of women, by affection led,
   Must backward, like the sacred tongue, be read.'

William Hammond

BOOK THREE

The Restoration to the Romantics

INTRODUCTION

The period we have to consider in this part is one of the poorest in lyric poetry in the whole of English literature. It has been called the 'age of prose and reason'. Both of these are enemies to poetry. The first great name after the Restoration was that of John Dryden, the creator of modern English prose. The debt owed to him by prose is immense; his effect on poetry is more questionable. For Dryden believed that it was the business of poetry, not to sing, but to argue and persuade. His most characteristic poems, such as *The Hind and the Panther* and *Absalom and Achitophel*, are long satirical and persuasive discourses; because of their length alone, they are outside the scope of this book. His most famous follower, Alexander Pope, is also at his most characteristic in long pieces, such as *The Rape of the Lock* or the *Essay on Man*. His short poems are mostly epigrams and lampoons. Pope's aim was summed up in the word 'correctness': he believed that poetry should be smooth, regular and mellifluous. Like most of his contemporaries he undervalued Elizabethan poetry and thought that the highest potentialities of English poetry had not been achieved until the Restoration and the maturity of Dryden. He himself was considered by many during the eighteenth century to be the greatest poet England had ever known. To him the purpose of poetry was to reform by satire and to preach morality through didactic verse. Such ideals cannot produce the highest poetry. We shall find more enjoyment in the less ambitious verse of Jonathan Swift, John Gay and some of the lesser known poets of the time.

Some who managed to achieve a different strain were Thomas Gray, who tried to get away from social satire, and

Christopher Smart, who wrote his best poems in a madhouse. William Collins was something of a Romantic before his time, and the descriptive poems of James Thomson and Mark Akenside were also aimed at an advance on the ideals of the Restoration and the Augustans. These poets are not at their most typical in short poems. It is also worth mentioning that some of the best hymns in our language were composed during the eighteenth century, notably by Isaac Watts, Samuel Wesley and William Cowper.

If the Restoration and the eighteenth century are seen at their best in long poems, and the most famous writers of the time were concerned more with satire than with lyric, there is a refreshing background of anonymous verse which is well worth knowing. It is not easy to date traditional verse with any accuracy, and it is not certain that all the poems in the anonymous section should really be placed in this part. However ancient some of our ballads and folk songs may be, it is probable that many of the versions in which they have come down to us date from this period. Here you will find some of the glees and rounds of the Restoration period, such as *White Sand and Grey Sand*; versions of such ballads as *Barbara Allen* and *Bonnie James Campbell*; folk songs such as *The Seeds of Love* and *I Will Give my Love an Apple*, and lastly, a few of the best of the old nursery rhymes which seem to belong to all time rather than to any particular century. It is in such songs and verses of humble, anonymous origin that we find the true spirit of poetry preserved during the age of reason. Even at our most prosaic we scarcely ever lost the love of the ancient ballads; it was this, rather than a taste for satire and moralizing, that kept alive the lyrical tradition which was reawakened with such astonishing results in the later eighteenth century.

CONTENTS

ANONYMOUS

SAMUEL HARDING *c.* 1640

JOHN BUNYAN 1628–1688

JOHN DRYDEN 1631–1700

WILLIAM CONGREVE 1670–1729

HENRY CAREY ?1687–1743

ISAAC WATTS 1674–1748

THOMAS PARNELL 1679–1718

ABEL EVANS 1679–1737

WILLIAM COWPER 1731–1800

415 *On Thomas Carew*

Two bodies lie beneath this stone
Whom love and marriage both made one.
One soul conjoined them by a force
Above the power of death's divorce;
One flame of life their lives did burn
Even to ashes in their urn.
They die but not depart who meet
In wedding and in winding sheet:
Whom God hath knit so firm in one
Admit no separation.
Therefore unto one marble trust
We leave their now united dust
As roots on earth embrace to rise
Most lovely flowers in Paradise.

Anonymous

416 *On Susan Pattison*

To free me from domestic strife
Death called at my house, but he spake with my wife.
Susan, wife of David Pattison lies here,
Stop, Reader, and if not in a hurry, shed a tear.

Anonymous, 1706

417 *I saw a peacock*

I saw a peacock with a fiery tail
I saw a blazing comet drop down hail
I saw a cloud with ivy circled round
I saw a sturdy oak creep on the ground

I saw a pismire swallow up a whale
I saw a raging sea brim full of ale
I saw a Venice glass sixteen foot deep
I saw a well full of men's tears that weep
I saw their eyes all in a flame of fire
I saw a house as big as the moon and higher
I saw the sun even in the midst of night
I saw the Man that saw this wondrous sight.

Anonymous

418   *The Cutty Wren*

O where are you going? says Milder to Malder,
O I cannot tell, says Festel to Fose,
We're going to the woods, says John the Red Nose,
We're going to the woods, says John the Red Nose.

O what will you do there? says Milder to Malder,
O I cannot tell, says Festel to Fose,
We'll shoot the Cutty Wren, says John the Red Nose,
We'll shoot the Cutty Wren, says John the Red Nose.

O how will you shoot her? says Milder to Malder,
O I cannot tell, says Festel to Fose,
With bows and arrows, says John the Red Nose,
With bows and arrows, says John the Red Nose.

O that will not do, says Milder to Malder,
O, what will do then? says Festel to Fose,
Big guns and cannons, says John the Red Nose,
Big guns and cannons, says John the Red Nose.

O how will you bring her home? says Milder to Malder,
O, I cannot tell, says Festel to Fose,
On four strong men's shoulders, says John the Red
    Nose,
On four strong men's shoulders, says John the Red
    Nose.

O that will not do, says Milder to Malder,
O what will do then? says Festel to Fose.
Big carts and wagons, says John the Red Nose,
Big carts and wagons, says John the Red Nose.

O what will you cut her up with? says Milder to Malder,
O I cannot tell, says Festel to Fose,
With knives and with forks, says John the Red Nose,
With knives and with forks, says John the Red Nose.

O that will not do, says Milder to Malder,
O what will do then? says Festel to Fose,
Hatchets and cleavers, says John the Red Nose,
Hatchets and cleavers, says John the Red Nose.

O how will you boil her? says Milder to Malder,
O I cannot tell, says Festel to Fose,
In pots and in kettles, says John the Red Nose,
In pots and in kettles, says John the Red Nose.

O that will not do, says Milder to Malder,
O what will do then? says Festel to Fose,
Brass pans and cauldrons, says John the Red Nose.
Brass pans and cauldrons, says John the Red Nose.

O who'll have the spare ribs? says Milder to Malder,
O I cannot tell, says Festel to Fose,
We'll give them to the poor, says John the Red Nose,
We'll give them to the poor, says John the Red Nose.

Anonymous

419 *Bonnie James Campbell*

High upon highlands
   And low upon Tay,
Bonnie James Campbell
   Rode out on a day.

Saddled and bridled
  And booted rode he;
Home came horse, home came saddle,
  But ne'er home came he.

Home came his saddle,
  All bloody to see,
O home came his good horse,
  But never came he.

Out came his mother dear,
  Greeting fu' sair;
And out came his bonny bride
  Riving her hair.

'My meadow lies green,
  My corn is unshorn,
My house is to build
  And my babe is unborn.'

Anonymous

420   *Admiral Benbow*

Come, all ye seamen bold
  And draw near, and draw near,
Come, listen to my song
  And have no fear:
'Tis of an Admiral's fame,
And John Benbow was his name—
How unto his end he came
  You shall hear, you shall hear.

John Benbow he set sail
  For to fight, for to fight.
Until Du Casse's ships
  They hove in sight.
He after them made sail
With a fine and pleasant gale,
But his captains they turned tail,
  In affright, in affright.

Said Kirby unto Wade:
  'Let us run! Let us run!'
To Kirby, Wade replied:
  'Ay, let's have done,
For I value no disgrace
Nor the losing of my place
But I swear I will not face
  Shot of gun, shot of gun!'

So brave Benbow sailed alone
  On that day, on that day.
Alone against the French,
  Where they lay;
He fought them with a frown,
Till the blood came trickling down—
And he earned a great renown
  On that day, on that day.

Brave Benbow lost his leg
  By chain shot, by chain shot;
Yet all the pain he bore
  He valued not;
Brave Benbow lost his leg
But his company he did beg:
'Fight on lads, don't reneg[1]!
  'Tis our lot, 'tis our lot!'

A surgeon dressed his wound;
  Cried Benbow, cried Benbow:
'Nay to my cabin, faith,
  I will not go!
Let a cradle[2] now in haste
On the quarter-deck be placed!'
And with a fury still he faced
  England's foe, England's foe.

Anonymous

1 break your oath of loyalty 2 a support for his shattered
leg

421 *Slaves to the world*

Slaves to the world should be tossed in a blanket,
   If I might have my will,
Like to the wheel that's turning up
   So fast on yonder hill,
And falling down and down again
   The ground it touch until.

Anonymous

422 *White sand and grey sand*

White sand and grey sand!
Who'll buy my grey sand?
Who'll buy my white sand?

Anonymous

423 *Wilt thou lend me thy mare?*

Wilt thou lend me thy mare to go a mile?
No, she's lamed leaping over a stile.
   But if thou wilt her to me spare,
   Thou shalt have money for thy mare.
      O, O, say you so?
      Money will make the mare to go,
      Money will make the mare to go.

Anonymous

424 *Wind, gentle evergreen*

Wind, gentle evergreen, to form a shade
Around the tomb where Sophocles is laid;
Sweet ivy, bend thy boughs and intertwine
With blushing roses and the clustering vine;
Thus will thy lasting leaves, with beauties hung,
Prove grateful emblems of the lays he sung.

Anonymous

425 *A boat, a boat*

A boat, a boat, haste to the ferry,
For we'll go over to be merry,
And laugh and quaff and drink old sherry.

Anonymous

426 *Gabriel John*

Under this stone lies Gabriel John
In the year of Our Lord one thousand and one.
Cover his head with turf or stone,
'Tis all one, 'tis all one,
With turf or stone 'tis all one.
Pray for the soul of gentle John;
If you please you may, or let it alone,
　　'Tis all one.

Anonymous

427 *The wench in the street*

Have you observed the wench in the street,
She's scarce any hose or shoes to her feet,
Yet she is very merry, and when she cries she sings,
I ha' hot codlins, hot codlins;
Or have you ever seen or heard
The mortal with a Lyon Tawny beard,
He lives as merrily as any heart can wish,
And still he cries, buy a brish, buy a brish.
Since these are merry, why should we take care,
Musicians like chameleons must live by the air:
Then let's be blithe and bonny, and no good meeting
　　baulk,
For when we have no money, we shall find chalk.

Anonymous

I sowed the seeds of love
And I sowed them in the spring,
I planted them in my garden fair
While the small birds they did sing.

My garden was well planted
With flowers everywhere,
But I had not the liberty to choose for myself
The flower that I loved so dear.

The gardener standing by
I asked him to choose for me;
He chose me the violet, the lily and the pink,
But these I refused all three.

The violet I did not like
Because it fades so soon;
The lily and the pink I did overthink,
But vowed I would wait till June.

In June is the red, red rose,
And that's the flower for me;
I plucked and I pulled at the red rosy bud
Till I gained the willow tree.

The willow tree will twist,
And the willow tree will twine,
And I wish I were in that young man's arms
That first had this heart of mine.

Anonymous

429   *I will give my love an apple*

I will give my love an apple without any core,
I will give my love a house without any door.
I will give my love a palace wherein she may be,
And she may unlock it without any key.

My head is the apple without any core,
My mind is the house without any door,
My heart is the palace wherein she may be
And she may unlock it without any key.

I will give my love a cherry without any stone,
I will give my love a chick without any bone,
I will give my love a ring, not a rent to be seen,
I will get my love children without any crying.

When the cherry's in blossom there's never a stone,
When the chick's in the egg there is never a bone,
When the ring is a-running there's not a rent to be seen,
And when they're child-making they're seldom crying.

Anonymous

430 *Hares on the mountain*

If all those pretty maidens were as hares on the mountain,
Then all those young men would get guns, go a-hunting.

If all those pretty maidens were as rushes a-growing,
Then all those young men would get scythes, go a-
     mowing.

If all those pretty maidens were as ducks in the water,
Then all those young men would strip and swim after.

If all those pretty maidens were as birds in the bushes,
Then all those young men would go bang those bushes.

Anonymous

431 *Died of love*

A brisk young lover came a-courting me,
He stole away my liberty.
He stole it away with a free good will,
And though he's false, I love him still.

All in the meadows and I did run,
A-gathering flowers as they sprung;
Of every sort I plucked and pulled
Until I got my apron full.

When I wore my apron low,
My love followed me through frost and snow;
But when I wore it up to my chin,
My love passed by and never looked in.

There is a bird in yonder tree;
Some say he's blind and cannot see.
I wish it had been the same with me
Before I gained his company.

I wish to God my babe was born,
Sat smiling on its daddy's arms,
And I myself all in the cold clay
And the green grass growing over me.

There is an ale house in yonder town,
Where my love goes and sits him down;
He takes some strange girl on his knee
And tells her what he doesn't tell me.

A grief to me and I'll tell you why:
Because she's got more gold than I.
Her gold will waste and her beauty pass
And she will come like me at last.

Anonymous

432   *Deep in love*

Down in the meadows fresh and gay
Picking lilies all the day,
Picking flowers both red and blue,
I little thought what love could do.

I put my hand into the bush,
Thinking the sweetest flower to find,
I pricked my finger to the bone
And left the sweetest flower alone.

If roses be such a prickly flower,
They ought to be gathered while they are green;
And he loves an unkind lover,
I'm sure he striveth against the stream.

I leaned my back up against some oak,
Thinking it was a trusty tree;
First it bended, then it broke,
And so did my false love to me.

There is a ship sails on the sea,
It's loaded deep as deep can be,
But not so deep as the love I'm in:
I care not if I sink or swim.

Love is handsome and love is fine,
Love is charming when it is new;
As it grows older, it grows colder,
And fades away like the morning dew.

Anonymous

433 *The cuckoo*

O meeting is a pleasure, but parting is grief,
An inconstant lover is worse than a thief.
A thief can but rob you of all that you have,
But an inconstant lover will send you to the grave.

The grave it will rot you and bring you to dust,
An inconstant lover no maiden can trust.
They'll kiss you and court you, poor maids to deceive,
There's not one in twenty that you may believe.

Come all you fair maidens, wherever you be,
Don't hang your poor hearts on the sycamore tree.
The leaf it will wither, the roots will decay,
And if you're forsaken, you perish away.

The cuckoo is a pretty bird, he sings as he flies,
He bringeth good tidings, he telleth no lies.
He sucketh sweet flowers to keep his voice clear,
And when he sings Cuckoo, the summer draweth near.

Anonymous

434   *Barbara Allen*

'Twas early in the month of May
    When green leaves they were springing
When a young man on his deathbed lay
    For the love of Barbara Allen.

He sent to her his servant-man
    To the place where she was dwelling,
Saying, Fair maid, you must come to my master
    If your name is Barbara Allen.

Slowly, slowly she walked along
    And slowly she got to him,
And when she got to his bedside,
    Young man, says she, you're dying.

Dying, dying? O don't say so!
    One kiss from you will cure me.
One kiss from me you never shall have,
    If your poor heart is breaking.

Don't you remember the other day
    When in the city dwelling
You gave kind words to other girls,
    And none to Barbara Allen?

As she was walking through the fields
    She heard the bells a-ringing
And as they rang they seemed to say
    Hard-hearted Barbara Allen.

As she was walking up the town
    She saw the corpse a-coming.
Put him down, put him down, you six young men,
    And let me gaze upon him.

The more she looked, the more she laughed,
    And the further she got from him,
Till all her friends cried out, For shame,
    Hard-hearted Barbara Allen!

Hard-hearted creature sure was I
    To him that loved me dearly;
I wish I had more kinder been
    In life when he was near me.

'Twas he that died on one good day,
    And she died on the morrow.
'Twas him that only died for love
    And she that died for sorrow.

Anonymous

435 *High Germany*

O Polly, love, O Polly, the rout has just begun,
And we must march away at the beating of the drum;
Go dress yourself all in your best and come along with
    me,
I'll take you to the cruel wars in High Germany.

O Billy, dearest Billy, you mind what I do say,
My feet they are so tender, I cannot march away;
Besides, my dearest Billy, I am with child by thee;
I am not fit for cruel wars in High Germany.

I'll buy you a horse, my love, and on it you shall ride,
And all my heart's delight shall be riding by your side;
We'll call at every alehouse and drink when we are dry,
We'll sweetheart on the road, my love, get married by
    and by.

O cursèd were the cruel wars, that ever they should rise,
And out of merry England press many a lad likewise;
They pressed young Billy from me, likewise my
    brothers three,
And sent them to the cruel wars in High Germany.

Anonymous

436   *The raggle taggle gypsies*

Three gypsies stood at the castle gate,
They sang so high, they sang so low,
The lady sate in her chamber late,
Her heart it melted away as snow.

They sang so sweet, they sang so shrill,
That fast her tears began to flow.
And she laid down her silken gown,
Her golden rings and all her show.

She plucked off her high-heeled shoes,
A-made of Spanish leather, O!
She would in the street, with her bare, bare feet,
All out in the wind and weather, O!

It was late last night, when my lord came home,
Enquiring for his a-lady, O!
The servants said on every hand,
'She's gone with the raggle taggle gypsies, O!'

'O saddle to me my milk-white steed.
Go and fetch me my pony, O!
That I may ride and seek my bride,
Who is gone with the raggle taggle gypsies, O!'

O he rode high and he rode low,
He rode through woods and copses too.
Until he came to an open field,
And there he espied his a-lady, O!

'What makes you leave your house and land?
What makes you leave your money, O?
What makes you leave your new-wedded lord,
To go with the raggle taggle gypsies, O?'

'What care I for my house or my land
What care I for my money, O?
What care I for my new-wedded lord?
I'm off with the raggle taggle gypsies, O!'

'Last night you slept on a goose-feather bed,
With the sheet turned down so bravely, O!
And tonight you'll sleep in a cold open field,
Along with the raggle taggle gypsies, O!'

'What care I for a goose-feather bed,
With the sheet turned down so bravely, O?
For tonight I shall sleep in a cold open field,
Along with the raggle-taggle gypsies, O!'

Anonymous

437 *The croppy boy*

It was early, early in the spring,
The birds did whistle and sweetly sing,
Changing their notes from tree to tree
And the song they sang was Old Ireland Free.

It was early, early in the night,
The yeoman cavalry gave me a fright;
The yeoman cavalry was my downfall,
And taken was I by Lord Cornwall.

'Twas in the guard-house where I was laid
And in a parlour where I was tried;
My sentence passed and my courage low
When to Dungannon I was forced to go.

As I was passing my father's door
My brother William stood at the door,
My aged father stood at the door
And my tender mother her hair she tore.

As I was walking up Wexford Street
My own first cousin I chanced to meet;
My own first cousin did me betray
And for one bare guinea swore my life away.

My sister Mary heard the express,
She ran upstairs in her morning dress:
Five hundred guineas I will lay me down
To see my brother safe in Wexford town.

As I was walking up Wexford Hill
Who could blame me to cry my fill?
I looked behind and I looked before
But my tender mother I shall ne'er see more.

As I was mounted on the scaffold high,
My aged father was standing by;
My aged father did me deny,
And the name he gave me was the croppy boy.

It was in Dungannon this young man died
And in Dungannon his body lies.
All you good people that do pass by
Just drop a tear for the croppy boy.

Anonymous

438   *The Golden Vanity*

There was a ship came from the north country,
And the name of the ship was the Golden Vanity,

And they feared she might be taken by the Turkish
  enemy,
That sails upon the Lowland, Lowland,
That sails upon the Lowland sea.

Then up came a little cabin boy,
And he said to the skipper, 'What will you give to me,
If I swim along-side of the Turkish enemy,
And sink her in the Lowland, Lowland,
And sink her in the Lowland sea?'

'O I will give you silver and I will give you gold,
And my only daughter your bride-to-be,
If you'll swim along-side of the Turkish enemy,
And sink her in the Lowland, Lowland,
And sink her in the Lowland sea.'

Then the boy made him ready, and overboard sprang he,
And he swam along-side of the Turkish enemy;
And with his auger sharp in her side he bored holes three,
And he sank her in the Lowland, Lowland,
And he sank her in the Lowland sea.

Anonymous

439 *Henry Martyn*

In merry Scotland, in merry Scotland
  There lived brothers three;
They all did cast lots which of them should go
  A-robbing upon the salt sea.

The lot it fell on Henry Martyn,
  The youngest of the three;
That he should go rob on the salt, salt sea,
  To maintain his brothers and he.

He had not sailed a long winter's night,
  Nor yet a short winter's day,
Before that he met with a lofty old ship,
  Come sailing along that way.

'Stand off! stand off!' said Henry Martyn,
  'For you shall not pass by me;
For I am a robber all on the salt seas,
  To maintain us brothers three.'

'Stand off! stand off!' the captain he cried,
  'The life-guards they are aboard.
My cannons are loaden with powder and shot;
  And every man hath a sword.'

For three long hours they merrily fought,
  For hours they fought full three;
At last a deep wound got Henry Martyn,
  And down by the mast fell he.

'Twas broadside against a broadside then,
  And at it the which should win,
A shot in the gallant ship bored a hole,
  And then did the water rush in.

Bad news, bad news for old England,
  Bad news has come to the town,
For a rich merchant's vessel is cast away
  And all her brave seamen drown.

Bad news, bad news through the London street,
  Bad news has come to the King!
The lives of his guard they be all a-lost,
  O the tidings be sad that I bring.

Anonymous

440   *At the setting of the sun*

Come all you young fellows that carry a gun,
Beware of late shooting when daylight is done,
For 'tis little you reckon what hazards you run,
I shot my true love at the setting of the sun.

In a shower of rain as my darling did hie
All under the bushes to keep herself dry,
With her head in her apron I thought her a swan,
And I shot my true love at the setting of the sun.

I'll fly from my country, I nowhere find rest,
I've shot my true love like a bird in her nest.
Like lead on my heart lies the deed I have done,
I shot my true love at the setting of the sun.

In the night the fair maid as a white swan appears,
She says, O my true love, quick dry up your tears,
I freely forgive you, I have Paradise won,
I was shot by my love at the setting of the sun.

O the years as they pass leave me lonely and sad,
I can ne'er love another and naught makes me glad.
I wait and expect till life's little span done
I meet my true love at the rising of the sun.

Anonymous

441   *The crocodile*

Now listen you landsmen unto me, to tell you the truth
    I'm bound,
What happened to me by going to sea, and the wonders
    that I found;
Shipwrecked I was once off Perouse and cast upon the
    shore,
So then I did resolve to roam, the country to explore.

'Twas far I had not scouted out, when close alongside
    the ocean,
I saw something move which at first I thought was all
    the world in motion;
But steering up close alongside, I found 'twas a croco-
    dile,
And from his nose to the tip of his tail he measured five
    hundred mile.

While up aloft the wind was high, it blew a gale from
the south,
I lost my hold and away did fly right into the crocodile's
mouth,
He quickly closed his jaws on me and thought he'd got
a victim,
But I ran down his throat, d'ye see, and that's the way
I tricked him.

I travelled on for a month or two, till I got into his maw,
Where I found of rum-kegs not a few, and a thousand
fat bullocks in store.
Of life I banished all my care, for of grub I was not
stinted,
And in this crocodile I lived ten years, and very well
contented.

This crocodile being very old, one day, alas, he died;
He was ten long years a-getting cold, he was so long
and wide,
His skin was eight miles thick, I'm sure, or very near
about,
For I was full ten years or more a-cutting my way out.

And now I've once more got on earth, I've vow'd no
more to roam,
In a ship that passed I got a berth, and now I'm safe at
home.
And if my story you should doubt, should you ever
travel the Nile,
It's ten to one you'll find the shell of the wonderful
crocodile.

Anonymous

442   *Sir John Barleycorn*

There came three men from out the West
Their victory to try;
And they have ta'en a solemn oath,
Poor Barleycorn should die.

They took a plough and ploughed him in,
Clods harrowed on his head;
And then they took a solemn oath
John Barleycorn was dead.

There he lay sleeping in the ground
Till rain did on him fall;
Then Barleycorn sprung up his head,
And so amazed them all.

There he remained till Midsummer
And looked both pale and wan;
Then Barleycorn he got a beard
And so became a man.

Then they sent men with scythes so sharp
To cut him off at knee;
And then poor Johnny Barleycorn
They served most barbarously.

Then they sent men with pitchforks strong
To pierce him through the heart;
And like a doleful Tragedy
They bound him in a cart.

And then they brought him to a barn
A prisoner to endure;
And so they fetched him out again,
And laid him on the floor.

Then they set men with holly clubs,
To beat the flesh from th' bones;
But the miller served him worse than that
He ground him 'twixt two stones.

O! Barleycorn is the choicest grain
That ere was sown on land,
It will do more than any grain,
By turning of your hand.

It will make a boy into a man,
A man into an ass;
To silver it will change your gold,
Your silver into brass.

It will make the huntsman hunt the fox,
That never wound a horn;
It will bring the tinker to the stocks
That people may him scorn.

O! Barleycorn is th' choicest grain
That ere was sown on land.
And it will cause a man to drink
Till he neither can go nor stand.

Anonymous

443   *The British Grenadiers*

Some talk of Alexander, and some of Hercules,
Of Conon and Lysander, and some Miltiades;
But of all the world's brave Heroes, there's none that
    can compare,
With a tow, row, row, row, row, to the British Grena-
    diers.
    Chorus. But of all the world's brave Heroes, etc.

None of those ancient Heroes ever saw a cannon ball,
Or knew the force of powder to slay their foes with all;
But our brave boys do know it, and banish all their fears,
With a tow, row, row, row, row, the British Grena-
    diers.
    Chorus. But our brave boys, etc.

When ever we are commanded to storm the palisades,
Our leaders march with fuses and we with hand
    grenades;
We throw them from the Glacis about our enemies ears,
With a tow, row, row, row, row, the British Grena-
    diers.
    Chorus. We throw them, etc.

The God of War was pleased and great Bellona smiles,
To see these nobles Heroes of our British Isles;
And all the Gods celestial, descending from their spheres,
Beheld with admiration the British Grenadiers.
    Chorus. And all the Gods celestial, etc.

Then let us crown a Bumper, and drink a health to those
Who carry caps and pouches, that wear the louped
    clothes;
May they and their commanders live happy all their
    years,
With a tow, row, row, row, row, the British Grena-
    diers.
    Chorus. May they and their commanders, etc.

Anonymous

444   *Riddle of snow and sun*

White bird featherless
Flew from Paradise,
Pitched on the castle wall;
Along came Lord Landless,
Took it up handless,
And rode away horseless to the King's white hall.

Anonymous

445   *Brandy Hill*

As I went up the Brandy Hill
I met my father with good will;
He had jewels, he had rings,
He had many pretty things;
He'd a cat with nine tails,
He'd a hammer wanting nails.
Up Jock!
Down Tom!
Blow the bellows, old man.

Anonymous

Can you make me a cambric shirt,
  Parsley, sage, rosemary and thyme,
Without any seam or needlework?
  And you shall be a true lover of mine.

Can you wash it in yonder well,
Where never sprung water or rain ever fell?

Can you dry it on yonder thorn,
Which never bore blossom since Adam was born?

Now you have asked me questions three,
I hope you'll answer as many for me.

Can you find me an acre of land
Between the salt water and the sea sand?

Can you plough it with a ram's horn
And sow it all over with one peppercorn?

Can you reap it with a sickle of leather
And bind it up with a peacock's feather?

When you have done and finished your work,
  Parsley, sage, rosemary and thyme,
Then come to me for your cambric shirt,
  And you shall be a true lover of mine.

Anonymous

447 *Charing Cross*

I cry my matches at Charing Cross,
Where sits a black man on a black horse.
They told me it was Charles the First—
Oh dear, my heart was ready to burst!

Anonymous

448 *Hart and hare*

The hart he loves the high wood,
  The hare she loves the hill;
The knight he loves his bright sword,
  The lady loves her will.

Anonymous

449 *Ladybird, ladybird*

Ladybird, ladybird, fly away home;
Your house is on fire, your children all gone;
All except one, and that's little Ann,
And she has crept under the warming pan.

Anonymous

450 *A man of words*

A man of words and not of deeds
Is like a garden full of weeds;
And when the weeds begin to grow,
It's like a garden full of snow;
And when the snow begins to fall,
It's like a bird upon the wall;
And when the bird away does fly,
It's like an eagle in the sky;
And when the sky begins to roar,
It's like a lion at the door;
And when the door begins to crack,
It's like a stick across your back;
And when your back begins to smart,
It's like a penknife in your heart;
And when your heart begins to bleed,
You're dead, and dead, and dead indeed.

Anonymous

Matthew, Mark, Luke and John,
Bless the bed that I lie on.
Four corners to my bed,
Four angels round my head;
One to watch and one to pray
And two to bear my soul away.

Anonymous

452 *Birthdays*

Monday's child is fair of face,
Tuesday's child is full of grace,
Wednesday's child is full of woe,
Thursday's child has far to go,
Friday's child is loving and giving,
Saturday's child works hard for his living,
And the child that is born on the Sabbath day
Is bonny and blithe and good and gay.

Anonymous

453 *I had a little nut tree*

I had a little nut tree,
    Nothing would it bear
But a silver nutmeg
    And a golden pear;
The King of Spain's daughter
    Came to visit me,
And all for the sake
    Of my little nut tree.

Anonymous

454　Rock, ball, fiddle

He that lies at the stock[1]
Shall have a gold rock;
He that lies at the wall
Shall have a gold ball;
He that lies in the middle
Shall have a gold fiddle.

Anonymous

1 the outside of the bed

455　*A man of Thessaly*

There was a man of Thessaly,
　And he was wondrous wise,
He jumped into a bramble bush
　And scratched out both his eyes.
And when he saw his eyes were out,
　With all his might and main
He jumped into another bush
　And scratched them in again.

Anonymous

456　*Babylon*

How many miles to Babylon?
　Threescore and ten.
Can I get there by candlelight?
　Yes, and back again.

Then open the gates without more ado
And let the King and his men pass through.

Anonymous

There was a crooked man,
    And he went a crooked mile;
He found a crooked sixpence
    Upon a crooked stile:
He bought a crooked cat,
    Which caught a crooked mouse,
And they all lived together
    In a little crooked house.

Anonymous

458   Of death

Noblest bodies are but gilded clay:
                Put away
    But the precious shining rind,
The inmost rottenness remains behind.
Kings, on earth though gods they be,
Yet in death are vile as we;
He, a thousands' king before,
Now is vassal unto more.
Vermin now insulting lie,
And dig for diamonds in each eye:
Whilst the sceptre-bearing hand
Cannot their inroads withstand.
Here doth one in odours wade
By the regal unction made,
While another dares to gnaw
On that tongue, his people's law.
Fools! ah, fools are we, who so contrive,
                And do strive,
    In each gaudy ornament,
Who shall his corpse in the best dish present.

Samuel Harding

He that is down, needs fear no fall,
He that is low, no pride:
He that is humble, ever shall
Have God to be his guide.

I am content with what I have,
Little be it, or much:
And, Lord, contentment still I crave,
Because thou savest such.

Fulness to such a burden is
That go on pilgrimage;
Here little, and hereafter bliss,
Is best from age to age.

John Bunyan

460 *The pilgrim song*

Who would true valour see,
Let him come hither;
One here will constant be,
Come wind, come weather.
There's no discouragement,
Shall make him once relent,
His first avowed intent,
To be a pilgrim.

Who so beset him round,
With dismal stories,
Do but themselves confound;
His strength the more is.
No lion can him fright,
He'll with a giant fight,
But he will have a right,
To be a pilgrim.

Hobgoblin, nor foul fiend,
Can daunt his spirit:
He knows he at the end,
Shall life inherit.
Then fancies fly away,
He'll fear not what men say,
He'll labour night and day,
To be a pilgrim.

John Bunyan

461   *Of the child with the bird at the bush*

My little bird, how canst thou sit
    And sing amidst so many thorns?
Let me but hold upon thee get,
    My love with honour thee adorns.

Thou art at present little worth,
    Five farthings none will give for thee;
But prithee, little bird, come forth,
    Thou of more value art to me.

'Tis true it is sun-shine to-day,
    To-morrow birds will have a storm;
My pretty one, come thou away,
    My bosom then shall keep thee warm.

Thou subject art to cold o'nights,
    When darkness is thy covering;
At days thy danger's great by kites,
    How canst thou then sit there and sing?

Thy food is scarce and scanty too,
    'Tis worms and trash which thou dost eat;
Thy present state I pity do,
    Come, I'll provide thee better meat.

I'll feed thee with white bread and milk,
     And sugar-plums, if them thou crave;
I'll cover thee with finest silk,
     That from the cold I may thee save.

My father's palace shall be thine,
     Yea, in it thou shalt sit and sing;
My little bird, if thou'lt be mine,
     The whole year round shall be thy spring.

I'll teach thee all the notes at court;
     Unthought-of music thou shalt play;
And all that thither do resort
     Shall praise thee for it every day.

I'll keep thee safe from cat and cur,
     No manner o' harm shall come to thee:
Yea, I will be thy succourer,
     My bosom shall thy cabin be.

But lo! behold, the bird is gone;
     These charmings would not make her yield:
The child's left at the bush alone,
     The bird flies yonder o'er the field.

John Bunyan

462 *Farewell, ungrateful traitor*

Farewell, ungrateful traitor!
     Farewell, my perjured swain!
Let never injured creature
     Believe a man again.
The pleasure of possessing
Surpasses all expressing,
But 'tis too short a blessing,
     And love too long a pain.

'Tis easy to deceive us,
    In pity of your pain;
But when we love, you leave us
    To rail at you in vain.
Before we have descried it,
There is no bliss beside it;
But she that once has tried it,
    Will never love again.

The passion you pretended,
    Was only to obtain;
But when the charm is ended,
    The charmer you disdain.
Your love by ours we measure,
Till we have lost our treasure;
But dying is a pleasure,
    When living is a pain.

John Dryden

463   *Why should a foolish marriage vow?*

Why should a foolish marriage vow,
    Which long ago was made,
Oblige us to each other now,
    When passion is decayed?
We loved, and we loved, as long as we could,
    Till our love was loved out in us both;
But our marriage is dead, when the pleasure is fled:
    'Twas pleasure first made it an oath.

If I have pleasures for a friend,
    And farther love in store,
What wrong has he whose joys did end,
    And who could give no more?
'Tis a madness that he should be jealous of me,
    Or that I should bar him of another:
For all we can gain is to give ourselves pain,
    When neither can hinder the other.

John Dryden

Our author, by experience, finds it true,
'Tis much more hard to please himself than you;
And out of no feigned modesty, this day
Damns his laborious trifle of a play:
Not that it's worse than what before he writ,
But he has now another taste of wit;
And, to confess a truth, (tho' out of time,)
Grows weary of his long-loved mistress, Rhyme.
Passion's too fierce to be in fetters bound,
And nature flies him like enchanted ground.
What verse can do, he has performed in this,
Which he presumes the most correct of his;
But spite of all his pride, a secret shame
Invades his breast at Shakespeare's sacred name:
Awed when he heard his godlike Romans rage,
He, in just despair, would quit the stage;
And to an age less polished, more unskilled,
Does, with disdain, the foremost honours yield.
As with the greater dead he dare not strive,
He would not match his verse with those who live:
Let him retire, betwixt two ages cast,
The first of this, and hindmost of the last.
A losing gamester, let him sneak away;
He bears no ready money from the play.
The fate which governs poets thought it fit
He should not raise his fortunes by his wit.
The clergy thrive, and the litigious bar;
Dull heroes fatten with the spoils of war:
All southern vices, Heaven be praised, are here;
But wit's a luxury you think too dear.
When you to cultivate the plant are loth,
'Tis a shrewd sign 'twas never of your growth;
And wit in northern climates will not blow,
Except, like orange trees, 'tis housed from snow.
There needs no care to put a playhouse down,
'Tis the most desert place of all the town:

We and our neighbours, to speak proudly, are,
Like monarchs, ruined with expensive war;
While, like wise English, unconcerned you sit,
And see us play the tragedy of wit.

John Dryden

465   *Sylvia the fair*

Sylvia, the fair, in the bloom of fifteen,
Felt an innocent warmth as she lay on the green;
She had heard of a pleasure, and something she guessed
By the towzing, and tumbling, and touching her breast.
She saw the men eager, but was at a loss,
What they meant by their sighing, and kissing so close;
    By their praying and whining
    And clasping and twining,
    And panting and wishing,
    And sighing and kissing,
  And sighing and kissing so close.

'Ah!' she cried, 'ah! for a languishing maid,
In a country of Christians, to die without aid!
Not a Whig, or a Tory, or Trimmer at least,
Or a Protestant parson, or Catholic priest,
To instruct a young virgin, that is at a loss,
What they meant by their sighing and kissing so close!
    By their praying and whining,
    And clasping and twining,
    And panting and wishing,
    And sighing and kissing,
  And sighing and kissing so close.'

Cupid, in shape of a swain did appear,
He saw the sad wound, and in pity drew near;
Then showed her his arrow, and bid her not fear,
For the pain was no more than a maiden may bear.
When the balm was infused, she was not at a loss,

What they meant by their sighing and kissing so close;
    By their praying and whining,
    And clasping and twining,
    And panting and wishing,
    And sighing and kissing,
And sighing and kissing so close.

John Dryden

466   *A song for St. Cecilia's Day, 1687*

From harmony, from heavenly harmony
  This universal frame began;
   When Nature underneath a heap
    Of jarring atoms lay,
  And could not heave her head,
The tuneful voice was heard from high:
  'Arise ye more than dead.'
Then cold, and hot, and moist, and dry,
In order to their stations leap,
  And Music's power obey.
From harmony, from heavenly harmony
  This universal frame began:
  From harmony to harmony
Thro' all the compass of the notes it ran,
The diapason closing full in man.

What passion cannot music raise and quell!
  When Jubal struck the corded shell,
  His listening brethren stood around,
And, wondering, on their faces fell
  To worship that celestial sound.
Less than a god they thought there could not dwell
  Within the hollow of that shell
  That spoke so sweetly and so well.
What passion cannot music raise and quell!

  The Trumpet's loud clangour
    Excites us to arms,
  With shrill notes of anger,
    And mortal alarms.

The double double double beat
    Of the thundering drum
Cries: 'Hark! the foes come;
Charge, charge, 'tis too late to retreat.'

    The soft complaining Flute
    In dying notes discovers
    The woes of hopeless lovers,
Whose dirge is whispered by the warbling Lute.

    Sharp Violins proclaim
Their jealous pangs, and desperation,
Fury, frantic indignation,
Depth of pains, and height of passion,
    For the fair, disdainful dame.

    But O! what art can teach,
    What human voice can reach,
The sacred Organ's praise
    Notes inspiring holy love,
Notes that wing their heavenly ways
    To mend the choirs above.

Orpheus could lead the savage race;
And trees uprooted left their place,
    Sequacious of the lyre;
But bright Cecilia raised the wonder higher:
When to her Organ vocal breath was given,
An angel heard, and straight appeared,
    Mistaking earth for heaven.

GRAND CHORUS

As from the power of sacred lays
    The spheres began to move,
And sung the great Creator's praise
So, when the last and dreadful hour
This crumbling pageant shall devour,
The Trumpet shall be heard on high,
The dead shall live, the living die,
And Music shall untune the sky.

                                        John Dryden

467   *Fairest isle*

Fairest isle, all isles excelling,
    Seat of pleasures and of loves;
Venus here will chose her dwelling,
    And forsake her Cyprian groves.

Cupid from his favourite nation
    Care and envy will remove;
Jealousy, that poisons passion,
    And despair, that dies for love.

Gentle murmurs, sweet complaining,
    Sighs that blow the fire of love;
Soft repulses, kind disdaining,
    Shall be all the pains you prove.

Every swain shall pay his duty,
    Grateful every nymph shall prove;
And as these excel in beauty,
    Those shall be renowned for love.

John Dryden

468   *The song of Momus to Mars*

Thy sword within the scabbard keep,
    And let mankind agree;
Better world were fast asleep,
    Than kept awake by thee.
The fools are only thinner,
    With all our cost and care;
But neither side a winner,
    For things are as they were.

John Dryden

469 *All, all of a piece throughout*

All, all of a piece throughout:
Thy chase had a beast in view;
Thy wars brought nothing about;
Thy lovers were all untrue.
'Tis well an old age is out,
And time to begin a new.

John Dryden

470 *An epitaph on his grandfather*

Here lies an aged corpse, which late
Incaged a soul, whom neither fate
Nor times could change from its first state.

Oppressèd more with age than cares;
Respected more for silver hairs
Than gold; for wisdom more than years.

Happy in every child he had;
Happy in self; and only sad
Being born in good days, but deceased in bad.

Thomas Shipman

471 *The review*

My childhood is a sphere
Wherein ten thousand heavenly joys appear:
Those thoughts it doth include
And those affections, which reviewed,
Again present to me
In better sort the things that I did see.
Imaginations real are,
Unto my mind again repair:
Which makes my life a circle of delights;
A hidden sphere of obvious benefits;
An earnest that the actions of the just
Shall still revive and flourish in the dust.

Thomas Traherne

How like an angel came I down!
  How bright are all things here!
When first among his works I did appear
  Oh, how their glory did me crown!
The world resembled his eternity,
    In which my soul did walk;
  And every thing that I did see
      Did with me talk.

The skies in their magnificence,
  The lovely, lively air,
Oh, how divine, how soft, how sweet, how fair!
  The stars did entertain my sense,
And all the works of God so bright and pure,
    So rich and great, did seem
  As if they ever must endure
      In my esteem.

A native health and innocence
  Within my bones did grow,
And while my God did all his glories show,
  I felt a vigour in my sense
That was all spirit: I within did flow
    With seas of life like wine;
  I nothing in the world did know
      But 'twas divine.

Harsh rugged objects were concealed,
  Oppressions, tears and cries,
Sins, griefs, complaints, dissensions, weeping eyes
  Were hid, and only things revealed
Which heavenly spirits and the angels prize.
    The state of innocence
  And bliss, not trades and poverties,
      Did fill my sense.

The streets seemed paved with golden stones,
  The boys and girls all mine;
To me how did their lovely faces shine!
  The sons of men all holy ones,

In joy and beauty, then appeared to me;
     And every thing I found
 (While like an angel I did see)
     Adorned the ground.

   Rich diamonds, and pearl, and gold
     Might every where be seen;
Rare colours, yellow, blue, red, white and green,
     Mine eyes on every side behold:
All that I saw, a wonder did appear,
     Amazement was my bliss:
   That and my wealth met every where:
         No joy to this!

   Cursed, ill-devised proprieties,
     With envy, avarice
And fraud (those fiends that spoil ev'n Paradise),
     Were not the object of mine eyes,
Nor hedges, ditches, limits, narrow bounds:
     I dreamt not aught of those,
   But in surveying all men's grounds
         I found repose.

   For property its self was mine,
     And hedges, ornaments;
Walls, houses, coffers, and their rich contents,
     To make me rich combine.
Clothes, costly jewels, laces, I esteemed
     My wealth by others worn;
   For me they all to wear them seemed
         When I was born.

                              Thomas Traherne

473   *Love in fantastic triumph*

   Love in fantastic triumph sate,
     Whilst bleeding hearts around him flowed,
 For whom fresh pains he did create,
     And strange tyrannic power he showed;

From thy bright eyes he took his fire,
    Which round about in sport he hurled;
But 'twas from mine he took desire,
    Enough to undo the amorous world.

From me he took his sighs and tears,
    From thee his pride and cruelty;
From me his languishments and fears,
    And every killing dart from thee;
Thus thou and I the god have armed,
    And set him up a deity;
But my poor heart alone is harmed,
    Whilst thine the victor is, and free.

                                        Aphra Behn

474   *Upon a wasp chilled with cold*

    The bear that breathes the northern blast
Did numb, torpedo-like, a wasp
Whose stiffened limbs encrampt; lay bathing
In Sol's warm breath and shine as saving,
Which with her hands she chafes and slams
Rubbing her legs, shanks, thighs, and hands.
Her petty toes and fingers' ends
Nipped with this breath, she out extends
Unto the sun in great desire
To warm her digits at that fire:
Doth hold her temples in this state
Where pulse doth beat and head doth ache,
Doth turn and stretch her body small,
Doth comb her velvet capitol
As if her little brain-pan were
A volume of choice precepts clear;
As if her satin jacket hot
Contained Apothecary's shop
Of nature's receipts, that prevails
To remedy all her sad ails,
As if her velvet helmet high

Did turret rationality.
She fans her wing up to the wind
As if her petticoat were lined
With reason's fleece and hoists sail
And humming flies in thankful gale
Unto her dun curled palace hall,
Her warm thanks offering for all.

Lord, clear my misted sight, that I
May hence view thy divinity,
Some sparks whereof thou up dost hasp
Within this little downy wasp,
In whose small corporation we
A school and a schoolmaster see:
Where we may learn, and easily find
A nimble spirit, bravely mind
Her work in every limb; and lace
It up neat with a vital grace,
Acting each part though ne'er so small,
Here of this fustian animal,
Till I enravished climb into
The godhead on this ladder do:
Where all my pipes inspired upraise
And heavenly music, furred with praise.

Edward Taylor

475   *The joy of church fellowship rightly attended*

In Heaven soaring up, I dropt an ear
    On earth: and oh! sweet melody!
And listening, found it was the saints who were
    Encoacht for Heaven that sang for joy.
        For in Christs coach they sweetly sing,
        As they to glory ride therein.

Oh! joyous hearts! Enfir'd with holy flame!
    Is speech thus tasselled with praise?
Will not your inward fire of joy contain,
    That it in open flames doth blaze?
        For in Christs coach saints sweetly sing,
        As they to glory ride therein.

And if a string do slip by chance, they soon
    Do screw it up again: whereby
They set it in a more melodious tune
    And a diviner harmony.
    For in Christs coach they sweetly sing,
    As they to glory ride therein.

In all their acts, public and private, nay,
    And secret too, they praise impart.
But in their acts divine, and worship, they
    With hymns do offer up their heart.
    Thus in Christs coach they sweetly sing,
    As they to glory ride therein.

Some few not in; and some whose time and place
    Block up this coach's way, do go
As travellers afoot: and so do trace
    The road that gives them right thereto;
    While in this coach these sweetly sing,
    As they to glory ride therein.

Edward Taylor

476   *Upon a spider catching a fly*

Thou sorrow, venom elf:
    Is this thy play,
To spin a web out of thyself
    To catch a fly?
        For why?

I saw a pettish wasp
    Fall foul therein:
Whom yet thy whorle pins did not hasp
    Let he should fling
        His sting.

But as afraid, remote
    Didst stand hereat,
And with thy little fingers stroke
    And gently tap
        His back.

Thus gently him didst treat
   Lest he should pet,
And in a froppish, aspish heat
   Should greatly fret
      Thy net.

Whereas the silly fly,
   Caught by its leg,
Thou by the throat took'st hastily,
   And 'hind the head
      Bite dead.

This goes to pot, that not
   Nature doth call.
Strive not above what strength hath got,
   Lest in the brawl
      Thou fall.

This fray seems thus to us:
   Hells spider gets
His intrails spun to whip cords thus,
   And wove to nets,
      And sets.

To tangle Adams race
   In's stratagems
To their destructions, spoil'd, made base
   By venom things,
      Damn'd sins.

But mighty, gracious Lord,
   Communicate
Thy grace to breake the cord; afford
   Us glorys gate
      And state.

We'll nightingaile sing like,
   When pearcht on high
In glories cage, thy glory, bright:
   Yea, thankfully,
      For joy.

                              Edward Taylor

As some brave admiral, in former war
  Deprived of force, but pressed with courage still,
Two rival fleets arriving from afar,
  Crawls to the top of an adjacent hill,

From whence (with thoughts full of concern) he views
  The wise and daring conduct of the fight,
And each bold action to his mind renews
  His present glory, and his past delight:

From his fierce eyes flashes of rage he throws
  As from black clouds when lightning breaks away,
Transported thinks himself amidst his foes,
  And absent yet enjoys the bloody day:

So, when my days of impotence approach,
  And I'm by love and wine's unlucky chance
Driven from the pleasing billows of debauch
  On the dull shore of lazy temperance,

My pains at last some respite shall afford
  While I behold the battles you maintain;
When fleets of glasses sail around the board,
  From whose broadside volleys of wit shall rain.

Nor shall the sight of honourable scars,
  Which my too forward valour did procure,
Frighten new-listed soldiers from the wars;
  Past joys have more than paid what I endure.

Should some brave youth (worth being drunk) prove
                            nice
  And from his fair inviter meanly shrink,
'Twould please the ghost of my departed vice
  If at my counsel he repent and drink.

Or should some cold-complexioned sot forbid,
  With his dull morals, our night's brisk alarms,
I'll fire his blood by telling what I did
  When I was strong and able to bear arms.

I'll tell of whores attacked, their lords at home,
  Bawds' quarters beaten up, and fortress won,
Windows demolished, watches overcome,
  And handsome ills by my contrivance done.

With tales like these I will such heat inspire
  As to important mischief shall incline;
I'll make him long some ancient church to fire
  And fear no lewdness they're called to by wine.

Thus bravo-like I'll saucily impose,
  And, safe from danger, valiantly advise;
Sheltered in impotence, urge you to blows,
  And, being good for nothing else, be wise.

John Wilmot, Earl of Rochester

478   *The bully*

Room, room for a Blade of the Town
  That takes delight in roaring,
And daily rambles up and down,
  And at night in the street lies snoring:
That for the noble name of Spark
  Dares his companions rally;
Commits an outrage in the dark,
  Then slinks into an alley.

To every female that he meets
  He swears he bears affection,
Defies all laws, arrests, and 'cheats,
  By the help of a kind protection.
Then he, intending further wrongs,
  By some resenting cully
Is decently run through the lungs,
  And there's an end of bully.

John Wilmot, Earl of Rochester

While on those lovely looks I gaze,
    To see a wretch pursuing,
In raptures of a blest amaze,
    His pleasing, happy ruin;
'Tis not for pity that I move:
    His fate is too aspiring,
Whose heart, broke with a load of love,
    Dies wishing and admiring.

But if this murder you'd forgo,
    Your slave from death removing,
Let me your art of charming know,
    Or learn you mine of loving.
But, whether life or death betide,
    In love 'tis equal measure;
The victor lives with empty pride,
    The vanquished die with pleasure.

John Wilmot, Earl of Rochester

480   Christ Church bells

O the bonny Christ Church bells!
    One, two, three, four, five, six;
They sound so wondrous great,
    So woundy sweet,
    And they troll so merrily, merrily.
    O the first and second bell!
    That every day at four and ten
Cry, Come, come, come, come, come to prayers;
And the verger troops before the dean:
Tinkle, tinkle, ting, goes the small bell at nine
    To call the beerers home,
        But the devil a man
        Will leave his can
    Till he hears the mighty *Tom.*

Henry Aldrich

481 *I'll sail upon the dog-star*

I'll sail upon the dog-star,
And then pursue the morning;
I'll chase the moon till it be noon
But I'll make her leave her horning.

I'll climb the frosty mountain
And there I'll coin the weather;
I'll tear the rainbow from the sky
And tie both ends together.

The stars pluck from their orbs too
And crowd them in my budget;
And whether I'm a roaring boy,
Let all the nation judge it.

Thomas Durfey

482 *The South Sea bubble*

Ombre and basset laid aside,
  New games employ the fair;
And brokers all those hours divide
  Which lovers used to share.

The court, the park, the foreign song
  And harlequin's grimace
Forlorn; amidst the city throng
  Behold each blooming face.

With Jews and Gentiles undismayed
  Young tender virgins mix;
Of whiskers nor of beards afraid,
  Nor all the cozening tricks.

Bright jewels, polished once to deck
  The fair one's rising breast,
Or sparkle round her ivory neck
  Lie pawned in iron chest.

The gayer passions of the mind
    How avarice controls!
Even love does now no longer find
    A place in female souls.

Anne, Countess of Winchilsea

483 *Death*

What has this bugbear Death that's worth our care?
    After a life in pain and sorrow passed,
After deluding hope and dire despair,
    Death only gives us quiet at the last.

How strangely are our love and hate misplaced!
    Freedom we seek, and yet from freedom flee!
Courting those tyrant sins that chain us fast,
    And shunning Death, that only sets us free.

'Tis not a foolish fear of future pains,
(Why should they fear who keep their souls from
                                                    stains?)
    That makes us dread thy terrors, Death, to see:
'Tis not the loss of riches, or of fame,
Or the vain toys the vulgar pleasures name;
    'Tis nothing, Caelia, but losing thee.

William Walsh

484 *An ode*

The merchant, to secure his treasure,
    Conveys it in a borrowed name:
Euphelia serves to grace my measure,
    But Cloe is my real flame.

My softest verse, my darling lyre,
    Upon Euphelia's toilet lay—
When Cloe noted her desire
    That I should sing, that I should play.

My lyre I tune, my voice I raise,
　　But with my numbers mix my sighs;
And whilst I sing Euphelia's praise,
　　I fix my soul on Cloe's eyes.

Fair Cloe blushed: Euphelia frowned:
　　I sung, and gazed; I played, and trembled:
And Venus to the Loves around
　　Remarked how ill we all dissembled.

Matthew Prior

485　*To a child of quality, five years old, the author then*
forty

Lords, knights, and squires, the numerous band
　　That wear the fair Miss Mary's fetters,
Were summoned by her high command
　　To show their passions by their letters.

My pen amongst the rest I took,
　　Lest those bright eyes, that cannot read,
Should dart their kindling fires, and look
　　The power they have to be obeyed.

Nor quality, nor reputation,
　　Forbid me yet my flame to tell;
Dear Five-years-old befriends my passion,
　　And I may write till she can spell.

For, while she makes her silk-worms' beds
　　With all the tender things I swear;
While all the house my passion reads,
　　In papers round her baby's hair;

She may receive and own my flame,
　　For, though the strictest prudes should know it,
She'll pass for a most virtuous dame,
　　And I for an unhappy poet.

Then too, alas! when she shall tear
   The rhymes some younger rival sends,
She'll give me leave to write, I fear,
   And we shall still continue friends.

For, as our different ages move,
   'Tis so ordained (would fate but mend it!),
That I should be past making love
   When she begins to comprehend it.

Matthew Prior

486   *The new year's gift to Phyllis*

The circling months begin this day
   To run their yearly ring,
And long-breathed time, which ne'er will stay,
   Refits his wings and shoots away,
     It round again to bring.

Who feels the force of female eyes
   And thinks some nymph divine,
Now brings his annual sacrifice,
   Some pretty toy or neat device
     To offer at her shrine.

But I can pay no offering
   To show how I adore,
Since I have but a heart to bring—
   A downright foolish, faithful thing,
     And that you had before.

Yet we may give, for custom sake,
   What will to both be new:
My constancy a gift I'll make
   And in return of it will take
     Some levity from you.

Matthew Prior

Venus, take my votive glass:
Since I am not what I was,
What from this day I shall be,
Venus, let me never see.

Matthew Prior

488   *A maypole*

Deprived of root, and branch and rind,
Yet flowers I bear of every kind:
And such is my prolific power,
They bloom in less than half an hour;
Yet standers-by may plainly see
They get no nourishment from me.
My head with giddiness goes round,
And yet I firmly stand my ground:
All over naked I am seen,
And painted like an Indian queen.
No couple-beggar in the land
E'er joined such numbers hand in hand.
I joined them fairly with a ring;
Nor can our parson blame the thing.
And though no marriage words are spoke,
They part not till the ring is broke;
Yet hypocrite fanatics cry,
I'm but an idol raised on high;
And once a weaver in our town,
A damned Cromwellian, knocked me down.
I lay a prisoner twenty years
And then the jovial Cavaliers
To their old post restored all three—
I mean the church, the king, and me.

Jonathan Swift

To their Excellencies the Lords Justices of Ireland,

The humble petition of Frances Harris,

Who must starve and die a maid if it miscarries;

Humbly showeth, that I went to warm myself in Lady
Betty's chamber because I was cold;

And I had in purse seven pounds, four shillings, and
sixpence, (besides farthings) in money and gold;

So because I had been buying things for my lady last
night,

I was resolved to tell my money, to see if it was
right.

Now, you must know, because my trunk has a very
bad lock,

Therefore, all the money I have, which, God knows, is
a very small stock,

I keep in my pocket, tied about my middle, next my
smock.

So when I went to put up my purse, as God would have
it, my smock was unripped,

And instead of putting it into my pocket, down it
slipped;

Then the bell rung, and I went down to put my lady to
bed;

And, God knows, I thought my money was as safe as
my maidenhead.

So, when I came up again, I found my pocket feel very
light;

But when I searched, and missed my purse, Lord! I
thought I should have sunk outright.

'Lord! madam,' says Mary, 'how d'ye do?'—'Indeed,'
says I, 'never worse:

But pray, Mary, can you tell what I have done with
my purse?'

'Lord help me!' says Mary, 'I never stirred out of this
place!'

'Nay,' said I, 'I had it in Lady Betty's chamber, that's a
plain case.'

So Mary got me to bed, and covered me up warm:

However, she stole away my garters, that I might do myself no harm.

So I tumbled and tossed all night, as you may very well think,

But hardly ever set my eyes together, or slept a wink.

So I was a-dreamed, methought, that I went and searched the folks around,

And in a corner of Mrs. Duke's box, tied in a rag, the money was found.

So next morning we told Whittle, and he fell a swearing:

Then my dame Wadgar came, and she, you know, is thick of hearing.

'Dame,' said I, as loud as I could bawl, 'do you know what a loss I have had?'

'Nay,' says she, 'my Lord Colway's folks are all very sad:

For my Lord Dromedary comes a Tuesday without fail.'

'Pugh!' said I, 'but that's not the business that I ail.'

Says Cary, says he, 'I have been a servant this five and twenty years come spring,

And in all the places I have lived I never heard of such a thing.'

'Yes,' says the steward, 'I remember when I was at my Lord Shrewsbury's,

Such a thing as this happened, just about the time of gooseberries.'

So I went to the party suspected, and found her full of grief:

(Now you must know, of all things in the world I hate a thief:)

However I was resolved to bring the discourse slily about:

'Mrs. Duke,' said I, 'here's an ugly accident has happened out:

'Tis not that I value the money three skips of a louse:

But the thing I stand upon is the credit of the house.

'Tis true, seven pounds, four shillings, and sixpence makes a great hole in my wages:

Besides as they say, service is no inheritance in these ages.

Now, Mrs. Duke, you know, and everybody under-
stands,
That though 'tis hard to judge, yet money can't go
without hands.'
'The *devil* take me!' said she, blessing herself, 'if ever I
saw 't!'
So she roared like a bedlam, as though I had called her all
to nought.
So, you know, what could I say to her any more?
I e'en left her, and came away as wise as I was before.
Well; but then they would have had me gone to the
cunning man:
'No,' said I, ''tis the same thing, the Chaplain will be
here anon!'
So the Chaplain came in. Now the servants say he is
my sweetheart,
Because he's always in my chamber, and I always take
his part.
So, as the devil would have it, before I was aware, out
I blundered,
'Parson,' said I, 'can you cast a nativity when a body's
plundered?'
(Now you must know he hates to be called *Parson* like
the devil!)
'Truly,' says he, 'Mrs. Nab, it might become you to be
more civil;
If your money be gone, as the learned Divine says, d'ye
see,
You are no text for my handling; so take that from me:
I was never a conjurer before, I'd have you to know.'
'Lord,' said I, 'don't be angry, I am sure I never thought
you so;
You know I honour the cloth: I design to be a parson's
wife;
I never took one in your coat to be a conjurer in all my
life.'
With that he twisted his girdle at me like a rope, as who
should say,
'Now you may go hang yourself for me!' and so went
away.

Well: I thought I should have swooned. 'Lord!' said I,
    'what shall I do?
I have lost my money, and shall lose my true love too!'
Then my lord called me: 'Harry,' said my lord, 'don't
    cry;
I'll give you something toward thy loss:' 'And,' says
    my lady, 'so will I.'
Oh! but, said I, what if, after all, the Chaplain won't
    come to?
For that, he said (an't please your Exellencies), I must
    petition you.
The premises tenderly considered, I desire your
    Exellencies' protection,
And that I may have a share in next Sunday's collec-
    tion;
And, over and above, I may have your Exellencies'
    letter,
With an order for the Chaplain aforesaid, or, instead of
    him, a better:
And then your poor petitioner, both night and day,
Or the Chaplain (for 'tis his trade,) as in duty bound,
    shall ever pray.

Jonathan Swift

490 *A description of a city shower*

Careful observers may fortell the hour,
By sure prognostics, when to dread a shower.
While rain depends, the pensive cat gives o'er
Her frolics, and pursues her tail no more.
Returning home at night, you'll find the sink
Strike your offended sense with double stink.
If you be wise, then go not far to dine:
You'll spend in coach-hire more than save in wine.
A coming shower your shooting corns presage,
Old aches will throb, your hollow tooth will rage:
Sauntering in coffee-house is Dulman seen;
He damns the climate, and complains of spleen.

Meanwhile the South, rising with dabbled wings,
A sable cloud athwart the welkin flings,
That swilled more liquor than it could contain,
And, like a drunkard, gives it up again.
Brisk Susan whips her linen from the rope,
While the first drizzling shower is borne aslope;
Such is that sprinkling which some careless queen
Flirts on you from her mop, but not so clean:
You fly, invoke the gods; then, turning, stop
To rail; she singing, still whirls on her mop.
Not yet the dust had shunned the unequal strife,
But, aided by the wind, fought still for life,
And wafted with its foe by violent gust,
'Twas doubtful which was rain, and which was dust.
Ah! where must needy poet seek for aid,
When dust and rain at once his coat invade?
Sole coat! where dust, cemented by the rain,
Erects the nap, and leaves a cloudy stain!
Now in contiguous drops the flood comes down,
Threatening with deluge this devoted town.
To shops in crowds the daggled females fly,
Pretend to cheapen goods, but nothing buy.
The Templar spruce, while every spout's abroach,
Stays till 'tis fair, yet seems to call a coach.
The tucked-up sempstress walks with hasty strides,
While streams run down her oiled umbrella's sides.
Here various kinds, by various fortunes led,
Commence acquaintance underneath a shed.
Triumphant Tories, and desponding Whigs,
Forget their feuds, and join to save their wigs.
Boxed in a chair the beau impatient sits,
While spouts run clattering o'er the roof by fits,
And ever and ever and anon with frightful din
The leather sounds; he trembles from within.
So when Troy chairmen bore the wooden steed,
Pregnant with Greeks impatient to be freed,
(Those bully Greeks, who, as the moderns do,
Instead of paying chairmen, ran them through,)
Laocoon struck the outside with his spear,
And each imprisoned hero quaked for fear.

Now from all parts the swelling kennels flow,
And bear their trophies with them as they go:
Filth of all hues and odour, seem to tell
What street they sailed from, by their sight and smell.
They, as each torrent drives with rapid force,
From Smithfield to St. Pulchre's shape their course,
And in huge confluence joined at Snowhill ridge,
Fall from the conduit prone to Holborn bridge.
Sweeping from butcher's stalls, dung, guts, and blood,
Drowned puppies, stinking sprats, all drenched in mud,
Dead cats, and turnip tops, come tumbling down the
    flood.

Jonathan Swift

491 *The progress of poetry*

The farmer's goose, who in the stubble
Has fed without restraint or trouble,
Grown fat with corn and sitting still,
Can scarce get o'er the barn-door sill;
And hardly waddles forth to cool
Her belly in the neighbouring pool!
Nor loudly cackles at the door,
For cackling shows the goose is poor.

  But, when she must be turned to graze,
And round the barren common strays,
Hard exercise, and harder fare,
Soon make my dame grow lank and spare;
Her body light, she tries her wings,
And scorns the ground and upward springs;
While all the parish, as she flies,
Hear sounds harmonious from the skies.

  Such is the poet fresh in pay,
The third night's profit of his play,
His morning draughts till noon can swill,
Among his brethren of the quill:
With good roast beef his belly full,
Grown foggy lazy, fat and dull,

Deep sunk in plenty and delight,
What poet e'er could take his flight?
Or, stuffed with phlegm up to the throat,
What poet e'er could sing a note?
Nor Pegasus could bear the load
Along the high celestial road:
The steed oppressed, would break his girth,
To raise the lumber from the earth.
    But view him in another scene,
When all his drink is Hippocrene,
His money spent, his patron fail,
His credit out for cheese and ale;
His two-years coat so smooth and bare,
Through every thread it lets in air;
With hungry meals his body pined,
His guts and belly full of wind;
And, like a jockey for a race,
His flesh brought down to flying case:
Now his exalted spirit loathes
Encumbrances of food and clothes;
And up he rises like a vapour,
Supported high on wings of paper.
He singing flies, and flying sings,
While from below all Grub-Street rings.

Jonathan Swift

492   *On Gaulstown House*

'Tis so old and ugly, and yet so convenient,
You're sometimes in pleasure, though often in pain in't;
'Tis so large, you may lodge a few friends in ease in't,
You turn and stretch at your length if you please in't;
'Tis so little, the family live in a press in't,
And poor Lady Betty has scarce room to dress in't;
'Tis so cold in the winter, you can't bear to lie in't,
And so hot in summer, you're ready to fry in't;
'Tis so brittle, 'twould scarce bear the weight of a ton,
Yet so staunch that it keeps out a great deal of sun;

'Tis so crazy, the weather with ease beats quite through
     it,
And you're forced every year in some part to renew it;
'Tis so ugly, so useful, so big, and so little,
'Tis so staunch and so crazy, so strong and so brittle,
'Tis at one time so hot, and another so cold,
It is part of the new, and part of the old;
It is just half a blessing, and just half a curse—
I wish then, dear George, it were better or worse.

Jonathan Swift

493   *A quiet life and a good name*

Nell scolded in so loud a din,
That Will durst hardly venture in:
He marked the conjugal dispute;
Nell roared incessant, Dick sat mute;
But, when he saw his friend appear,
Cried bravely, 'Patience, good my dear!'
At sight of Will she bawled no more,
But hurried out and clapped the door.
     Why, Dick! the devil's in thy Nell,
Quoth Will, thy house is worse than Hell.
Why what a peal the jade has rung!
Damn her, why don't you slit her tongue?
For nothing else will make it cease.
Dear Will, I suffer this for peace:
I never quarrel with my wife;
I bear it for a quiet life.
Scripture, you know, exhorts us to it;
Bids us to seek peace, and ensue it.
     Will went again to visit Dick;
And entering in the very nick,
He saw virago Nell belabour,
With Dick's own staff, his peaceful neighbour.
Poor Will, who needs must interpose,
Received a brace or two of blows.
But now, to make my story short,

Will drew out Dick to take a quart.
Why Dick, thy wife has devilish whims;
Ods-buds! why don't you break her limbs?
If she were mine, and had such tricks,
I'd teach her how to handle sticks:
Zounds! I'd ship her to Jamaica,
Or truck the carrion for tobacco:
I'd send her far enough away—
Dear Will, but what would people say?
Lord! I should get so ill a name,
The neighbours sound would cry out shame.

Dick suffered for his peace and credit;
But who believed him when he said it?
Can he, who makes himself a slave,
Consult his peace, or credit save?
Dick found it by his ill success,
His quiet small, his credit less.
She served him at the usual rate;
She stunned, and then she broke his pate:
And what he thought the hardest case,
The parish jeered him to his face;
Those men who wore the breeches least,
Called him a cuckold, fool, and beast.
At home he was pursued with noise,
Abroad was pestered by the boys:
Within, his wife would break his bones:
Without, they pelted him with stones;
False patience and mistaken pride!
There are ten thousand Dicks beside;
Slaves to their quiet and good name,
Are used like Dick, and bear the blame.

Jonathan Swift

494 *On censure*

Ye wise, instruct me to endure
An evil which admits no cure;
Or, how this evil can be borne,
Which breeds at once both hate and scorn.

Bare innocence is no support,
When you are tried in Scandal's court.
Stand high in honour, wealth, or wit,
All others, who inferior sit,
Conceive themselves in conscience bound
To join, and drag you to the ground.
Your altitude offends the eyes
Of those who want the power to rise.
The world, a willing stander-by,
Inclines to aid a specious lie:
Alas! they would not do you wrong;
But all appearances are strong.

Yet whence proceeds this weight we lay
On what detracting people say!
For let mankind discharge their tongues
In venom, till they burst their lungs,
Their utmost malice cannot make
Your head, or tooth, or finger ache;
Nor spoil your shape, distort your face,
Or put one feature out of place.
Nor will you find your fortune sink
By what they speak, or what they think.
Nor can ten hundred thousand lies
Make you less virtuous, learn'd, or wise.

The most effectual way to balk
Their malice, is—to let them talk.

Jonathan Swift

495   *The power of time*

If neither brass nor marble can withstand
The mortal force of Time's destructive hand;
If mountains sink to vales, if cities die,
And lessening rivers mourn their fountains dry;
When my old cassock (said a Welsh divine)
Is out at elbows, why should I repine?

Jonathan Swift

496 *Catullus de Lesbia*

Lesbia forever on me rails,
To talk of me she never fails.
Now, hang me, but for all her art,
I find that I have gained her heart.
My proof is this: I plainly see,
The case is just the same with me.
I curse her every hour sincerely,
Yet, hang me, but I love her dearly.

Jonathan Swift

497 *False though she be to me*

False though she be to me and love,
   I'll ne'er pursue revenge;
For still the charmer I approve,
   Though I deplore her change.

In hours of bliss we oft have met:
   They could not always last;
And though the present I regret,
   I'm grateful for the past.

William Congreve

498 *Sally in our alley*

Of all the girls that are so smart
   There's none like pretty Sally;
She is the darling of my heart,
   And she lives in our alley.
There is no lady in the land
   Is half so sweet as Sally;
She is the darling of my heart,
   And she lives in our alley.

Her father he makes cabbage-nets
   And through the streets does cry 'em;
Her mother she sells laces long
   To such as please to buy 'em;
But sure such folks could ne'er beget
   So sweet a girl as Sally!
She is the darling of my heart,
   And she lives in our alley.

When she is by, I leave my work,
   I love her so sincerely;
My master comes like any Turk,
   And bangs me most severely—
But let him bang his bellyful,
   I'll bear it all for Sally;
She is the darling of my heart,
   And she lives in our alley.

Of all the days that's in the week
   I dearly love but one day—
And that's the day that comes betwixt
   A Saturday and Monday;
For then I'm dressed all in my best
   To walk abroad with Sally:
She is the darling of my heart,
   And she lives in our alley.

My master carried me to church,
   And often I am blamèd
Because I leave him in the lurch
   As soon as text is namèd;
I leave the church in sermon-time
   And slink away to Sally;
She is the darling of my heart,
   And she lives in our alley.

When Christmas comes about again
   O, then I shall have money;
I'll hoard it up, and box it all,
   I'll give it to my honey:

I would it were ten thousand pound,
    I'd give it all to Sally;
She is the darling of my heart,
    And she lives in our alley.

My master and the neighbours all
    Make game of me and Sally,
And, but for her, I'd better be
    A slave and row a galley;
But when my seven long years are out,
    O, then I'll marry Sally,—
O, then we'll wed, and then we'll bed,
    But not in our alley!

Henry Carey

499   *Man frail, and God eternal*

Our God, our help is ages past,
    Our hope for years to come,
Our shelter from the stormy blast,
    And our eternal home.

Under the shadow of Thy throne
    Thy Saints have dwelt secure;
Sufficient is Thine arm alone,
    And our defence is sure.

Before the hills in order stood,
    Or earth received her frame,
From everlasting Thou art God,
    To endless years the same.

Thy word commands our flesh to dust,
    Return, ye sons of men:
All nations rose from earth at first,
    And turn to earth again.

A thousand ages in Thy sight
    Are like an evening gone;
Short as the watch that ends the night
    Before the rising sun.

The busy tribes of flesh and blood
   With all their lives and cares
Are carried downwards by Thy flood,
   And lost in following years.

Time like an ever-rolling stream
   Bears all its sons away;
They fly forgotten as a dream
   Dies at the opening day.

Like flowery fields the nations stand
   Pleased with the morning-light;
The flowers beneath the mower's hand
   Lie withering e'er 'tis night.

Our God, our help in ages past,
   Our hope for years to come,
Be Thou our guard while troubles last,
   And our eternal home.

Isaac Watts

500   *When thy beauty appears*

When thy beauty appears
In its graces and airs,
   All bright as an angel new dropped from the sky,
At distance I gaze, and am awed by my fears,
   So strangely you dazzle my eye!

But when, without art,
Your kind thoughts you impart,
   When your love runs in blushes through every vein;
When it darts from your eyes, when it pants in your
                                 heart,
   Then I know you're a woman again.

There's a passion and pride
In our sex, she replied,
   And thus, might I gratify both, I would do:
Still an angel appear to each lover beside,
   But still be a woman to you.

Thomas Parnell

501 On Blenheim House

See, Sir, here's the grand approach,
   This way is for his Grace's coach;
There lies the bridge, and here's the clock:
Observe the lion and the cock,
The spacious court, the colonade,
And mark how wide the hall is made!
The chimneys are so well designed,
They never smoke in any wind.
This gallery's contrived for walking,
The windows to retire and talk in;
The council-chamber for debate,
And all the rest are rooms of state.
   Thanks, Sir, cried I, 'tis very fine,
But where d'ye sleep, or where d'ye dine?
I find, by all you have been telling,
That 'tis a house, but not a dwelling.

Abel Evans

502 When none shall rail

While malice, Pope, denies thy page
   It's own celestial fire;
While critics, and while bards in rage
   Admiring, won't admire;

While wayward pens thy worth assail,
   And envious tongues decry,
These times tho' many a friend bewail,
   These times bewail not I.

But when the world's loud praise is thine,
   And spleen no more shall blame,
When with thy Homer thou shalt shine
   In one established fame,

When none shall rail, and every lay
    Devote a wreath to thee;
That day (for come it will) that day
    Shall I lament to see.

David Lewis

503   *The tame stag*

As a young stag the thicket past
The branches held his antlers fast,
A clown, who saw the captive hung,
Across the horns his halter flung.
   Now safely hampered in the cord,
He bore the present to his lord:
His lord was pleased: as was the clown,
When he was tipped with half a crown.
The stag was brought before his wife,
The tender lady begged his life,
How sleek the skin! how specked like ermine!
Sure never creature was so charming!
   At first within the yard confined,
He flies and hides from all mankind;
Now bolder grown, with fixed amaze
And distant awe presumes to gaze,
Munches the linen on the lines,
And on a hood or apron dines;
He steals my little master's bread,
Follows the servants to be fed,
Nearer and nearer now he stands,
To feel the praise of patting hands,
Examines every fist for meat,
And though repulsed disdains retreat,
Attacks again with levelled horns,
And man, that was his terror, scorns.

   Such is the country maiden's fright,
When first a redcoat is in sight,
Behind the door she hides her face,
Next time at distance eyes the lace,

She now can all his terrors stand,
Nor from his squeeze withdraws her hand;
She plays familiar in his arms,
And every soldier hath his charms;
From tent to tent she spreads her flame:
For custom conquers fear and shame.

John Gay

504 *If the heart of a man*

If the heart of man is depressed with cares,
The mist is dispelled when a woman appears;
Like the notes of a fiddle, she sweetly, sweetly
Raises the spirits and charms our ears
   Roses and lilies her cheeks disclose,
   But her ripe lips are more sweet than those,
   Press her,
   Caress her,
   With blisses
   Her kisses
Dissolve us in pleasure, and soft repose.

John Gay

505 *Before the barn-door crowing*

Before the barn-door crowing,
   The cock by hens attended,
His eyes around him throwing,
   Stands for a while suspended:
Then one he singles from the crew,
   And cheers the happy hen;
With how do you do, and how do you do,
   And how do you do again.

John Gay

506 *Were I laid on Greenland's coast*

Were I laid on Greenland's coast,
  And in my arms embraced my lass;
Warm amidst eternal frost,
  Too soon the half-year's night would pass.

Were I sold on Indian soil,
  Soon as the burning day was closed,
I could mock the sultry toil,
  When on my charmer's breast reposed.

  And I would love you all the day,
  Every night would kiss and play,
  If with me you'd fondly stray
  Over the hills and far away.

John Gay

507 *Go, rose*

Go, rose, my Cloe's bosom grace.
  How happy should I prove,
Might I supply that envied place
  With never-fading love!
There, Phoenix-like, beneath her eye,
Involved in fragrance, burn and die.

Know, hapless flower, that thou shalt find
  More fragrant roses there,
I see thy withering head reclined
  With envy and despair;
One common fate we both must prove:
You die with envy, I with love.

John Gay

508 *Engraved on the collar of a dog*

I am his Highness' dog at Kew;
Pray tell me, sir, whose dog are you?

Alexander Pope

Lest you should think that verse shall die,
Which sounds the silver Thames along,
Taught on the wings of truth to fly
Above the reach of vulgar song;

Though daring Milton sits sublime,
In Spenser native Muses play;
Nor yet shall Waller yield to time,
Nor pensive Cowley's moral lay.

Sages and chiefs long since had birth
Ere Caesar was or Newton named;
These raised new empires o'er the earth,
And those, new heavens and systems framed.

Vain was the chief's, the sage's pride!
They had no poet, and they died.
In vain they schemed, in vain they bled!
They had no poet, and are dead.

Alexander Pope

510   Solitude

Happy the man, whose wish and care
A few paternal acres bound,
Content to breathe his native air
    In his own ground.

Whose herds with milk, whose fields with bread,
Whose flocks supply him with attire;
Whose trees in summer yield him shade,
    In winter, fire.

Blest, who can unconcern'dly find
Hours, days, and years, slide soft away
In health of body, peace of mind,
    Quiet by day,

Sound sleep by night; study and ease
Together mixed; sweet recreation,
And innocence, which most does please
　　With meditation.

Thus let me live, unseen, unknown;
Thus unlamented let me die;
Steal from the world, and not a stone
　　Tell where I lie.

Alexander Pope

511　*Elegy to the memory of an unfortunate lady*

What beckoning ghost along the moonlight shade
Invites my steps, and points to yonder glade?
'Tis she!—but why that bleeding bosom gored,
Why dimly gleams the visionary sword!
Oh, ever beauteous, ever friendly, tell,
Is it, in heaven, a crime to love too well?
To bear too tender or too firm a heart,
To act a lover's or a Roman's part?
Is there no bright reversion in the sky
For those who greatly think, or bravely die?
　　Why bade ye else, ye powers, her soul aspire
Above the vulgar flight of low desire?
Ambition first sprung from your blest abodes,
The glorious fault of angels and of gods:
Thence to their images on earth it flows,
And in the breast of kings and heroes glows.
Most souls, 'tis true, but peep out once an age,
Dull, sullen prisoners in the body's cage:
Dim lights of life, that burn a length of years,
Useless, unseen, as lamps in sepulchres;
Like eastern kings a lazy state they keep,
And, close confined to their own palace, sleep.
　　From these perhaps (ere Nature bade her die)
Fate snatched her early to the pitying sky.

As into air the purer spirits flow,
And separate from their kindred dregs below;
So flew the soul to its congenial place,
Nor left one virtue to redeem her race.

But thou, false guardian of a charge too good,
Thou, mean deserter of thy brother's blood!
See on these ruby lips the trembling breath,
These cheeks now fading at the blast of death;
Cold is that breast which warmed the world before,
And those love-darting eyes must roll no more.
Thus, if eternal justice rules the ball,
Thus shall your wives, and thus your children, fall:
On all the line a sudden vengeance waits,
And frequent hearses shall besiege your gates;
There passengers shall stand, and pointing say,
(While the long funerals blacken all the way),
'Lo! these were they whose souls the furies steeled,
And with hearts unknowing how to yield.'
Thus unlamented pass the proud away,
The gaze of fools, and pageant of a day!
So perish all whose breast ne'er learned to glow
For others' good, or melt at others' woe.

What can atone (oh ever-injured shade!)
Thy fate unpitied, and thy rites unpaid?
No friends' complaint, no kind domestic tear
Pleased thy pale ghost, or graced thy mournful bier.
By foreign hands thy dying eyes were closed,
By foreign hands thy decent limbs composed,
By foreign hands thy humble grave adorned,
By strangers honoured, and by strangers mourned!
What, though no friends in sable weeds appear,
Grieve for an hour, perhaps then mourn a year,
And bear about the mockery of woe
To midnight dances, and the public show?
What, though no weeping loves thy ashes grace,
Nor polished marble emulate thy face?
What, though no sacred earth allow thee room,
Nor hallowed dirge be muttered o'er the tomb?
Yet shall thy grave with rising flowers be dressed,
And the green turf lie lightly on thy breast:

There shall the morn her earliest tears bestow,
There the first roses of the year shall blow;
While angels with their silver wings o'er shade
The ground now sacred by thy reliques made.
  So peaceful rests, without a stone, a name,
What once had beauty, titles, wealth and fame.
How loved, how honoured once, avails thee not,
To whom related, or by whom begot;
A heap of dust alone remains of thee,
'Tis all thou art and all the proud shall be!
  Poets themselves must fall, like those they sung,
Deaf the praised ear, and mute the tuneful tongue.
Even he, whose soul now melts in mournful lays,
Shall shortly want the generous tear he pays;
Then from his closing eyes thy form shall part,
And the last pang shall tear thee from his heart,
Life's idle business at one gasp be o'er,
The Muse forgot, and thou beloved no more!

Alexander Pope

512   *On a certain lady at court*

I know the thing that's most uncommon;
    (Envy be silent and attend!)
I know a reasonable woman,
    Handsome and witty, yet a friend.

Not warped by passion, awed by rumour,
    Nor grave through pride, or gay through folly;
An equal mixture of good humour
    And sensible soft melancholy.

' Has she no faults then, (Envy says), sir?
    Yes, she has one I must aver:
When all the world conspires to praise her,
    The woman's deaf, and does not hear.

Alexander Pope

Dear, damned, distracted town, farewell!
   Thy fools no more I'll tease:
This year in peace, ye critics, dwell,
   Ye harlots, sleep at ease!

Soft B——s and rough C——s, adieu,
   Earl Warwick, make your moan,
The lively H——k and you
   May knock up whores alone.

To drink and droll be Rowe allowed
   Till the third watchman's toll;
Let Jervas gratis paint, and Frowde
   Save threepence and his soul.

Farewell Arbuthnot's raillery
   On every learned sot;
And Garth, the best good Christian be,
   Although he knows it not.

Lintot, farewell! thy bard must go;
   Farewell unhappy Tonson!
Heaven gives thee for thy loss of Rowe,
   Lean Philips and fat Johnson.

Why should I stay? Both parties rage;
   My vixen mistress squalls;
The wits in envious feuds engage:
   And Homer (damn him!) calls.

The love of arts lies cold and dead
   In Halifax's urn;
And not one Muse of all he fed
   Has yet the grace to mourn.

My friends, by turns, my friends confound,
   Betray, and are betrayed:
Poor Y——r's sold for fifty pounds,
   And B——ll is a jade.

Why make I friendships with the great,
    When I no favour seek?
Or follow girls, seven hours in eight,
    I need but once a week?

Still idle, with a busy air,
    Deep whimsies to contrive;
The gayest valetudinaire,
    Most thinking rake, alive.

Solicitous for other ends,
    Though fond of dear repose;
Careless or drowsy with my friends,
    And frolic with my foes.

Luxurious lobster-nights, farewell,
    For sober, studious days;
And Burlingtons' delicious meal,
    For salads, tarts, and pease!

Adieu to all, but Gay alone,
    Whose soul, sincere and free,
Loves all mankind, but flatters none,
    And so may starve with me.

                                        Alexander Pope

514   *Love thy country*

Love thy country, wish it well,
    Not with too intense a care,
'Tis enough, that when it fell,
    Thou, it's ruin, didst not share.

Envy's censure, flattery's praise,
    With unmoved indifference, view;
Learn to tread life's dangerous maze,
    With unerring virtue's clue.

Void of strong desires, and fear,
    Life's wide ocean trust no more;
Strive thy little bark to steer,
    With the tide, but near the shore.

Thus prepared, thy shortened sail
    Shall, whene'er the winds increase,
Seizing each propitious gale,
    Waft thee to the Port of Peace.

Keep thy conscience from offence,
    And tempestuous passions, free,
So, when thou art called from hence,
    Easy shall thy passage be;

Easy shall thy passage be,
    Cheerful, thy allotted stay;
Short the account twixt God and thee;
    Hope shall meet thee, on the way;

Truth shall lead thee to the gate,
    Mercy's self shall let thee in;
Where it's never-changing state
    Full perfection shall begin.

George Bubb Dodington, Lord Melcombe

515   *From a hint in the minor poets*

No! not for those of women born,
    Not so unlike the die is cast;
For after all our vaunt and scorn
    How very small the odds at last!

Him, raised to Fortune's utmost top,
    With him beneath her feet compare;
And one has nothing more to hope,
    And one has nothing more to fear.

Samuel Wesley

516 *On the setting up of Mr. Butler's monument in Westminster Abbey*

While Butler, needy wretch! was yet alive,
No generous patron would a dinner give:
See him, when starv'd to death and turn'd to dust,
Presented with a monumental bust!
The poet's fate is here in emblem shown,
He ask'd for bread, and he received a stone!

Samuel Wesley

517 *Epigram on Handel and Bononcini*

Some say, compared to Bononcini
  That Mynheer Handel's but a ninny;
Others aver, that he to Handel
Is scarcely fit to hold a candle.
Strange all this difference should be
'Twixt Tweedledum and Tweedledee!

John Byrom

518 *Mistaken fair*

Mistaken fair, lay Sherlock by,
  His doctrine is deceiving;
For whilst he teaches us to die,
  He cheats us of our living.

To die's a lesson we shall know
  Too soon without a master;
Then only let us study now
  How we may live the faster.

To live's to love, to bless, be blest
  With mutual inclination;
Share then my ardour in your breast,
  And kindly meet my passion.

But if thus blest I may not live,
    And pity you deny,
To me at least your Sherlock give,
    'Tis I must learn to die.

Philip Stanhope, Earl of Chesterfield

519   *The fly*

Busy, curious, thirsty fly,
Gently drink, and drink as I;
Freely welcome to my cup,
Could'st thou sip, and sip it up;
Make the most of life you may,
Life is short and wears away.

Just alike, both mine and thine,
Hasten quick to their decline;
Thine's a summer, mine's no more,
Though repeated to threescore;
Threescore summers when they're gone,
Will appear as short as one.

William Oldys

520   *The bastard's lot*

In gayer hours, when high my fancy run,
The muse, exulting, thus her lay begun.
   Blest be the bastard's birth! through wondrous ways
He shines eccentric like a comet's blaze!
No sickly fruit of faint compliance he!
He! stamped in nature's mint of ecstasy!
He lives to build, not boast a generous race:
No tenth transmitter of a foolish face.
His daring hope, no sire's example bounds;
His first-born lights no prejudice confounds.
He, kindling from within, requires no flame;

He glories in a bastard's glowing name.

  Born to himself, by no possession led,
In freedom fostered, and by fortune fed;
Nor guides, nor rules, his Sovereign Choice control,
His body independent, as his soul.
Loosed to the world's wide range,—enjoyed no aim
Prescribed no duty, and assigned no name:
Nature's unbounded Son, he stands alone,
His heart unbiased, and his mind his own.

  O Mother, yet no Mother!—'tis to you
My thanks for such distinguished claims are due.
You, unenslaved to nature's narrow laws,
Warm championess for freedom's sacred cause,
From all the dry devoirs of blood and line,
From ties maternal, moral and divine,
Discharged my grasping Soul; pushed me from shore,
And launched me into Life without an oar.

  What had I lost, if conjugally kind,
By nature hating, yet by vows confined,
Untaught the Matrimonial Bounds to slight,
And coldly conscious of a husband's right,
You had faint-drawn me with a form alone,
A lawful lump of life by force your own!
Then, while your backward will retrenched desire,
And unconcurring spirits lent no fire,
I had been born your dull, domestic Heir;
Load of your life, and motive of your care;
Perhaps been poorly rich and meanly great;
The slave of pomp, a cypher in the state;
Lordly neglectful of a worth unknown,
And slumbering in a seat, by chance my own.

  Far nobler Blessings wait the bastard's lot;
Conceived in rapture, and with fire begot!
Strong as necessity, he starts away,
Climbs against wrongs, and brightens into day.

  Thus unprophetic, lately misinspired,
I sang: Gay flattering hope my fancy fired;
Inly secure, through conscious scorn of ill,
Nor taught by wisdom, how to balance will,
Rashly deceived, I saw no pits to shun;

But thought to Purpose, and to Act were One;
Heedless what pointed cares pervert his way,
Whom caution arms not, and whom woes betray;
But now exposed and shrinking from distress,
I fly to shelter, while the tempests press;
My muse to grief resigns the varying tone,
The raptures languish, and the numbers groan.

Richard Savage

521   *To a young lady*

Polly, from me, though now a love-sick youth,
Nay, though a poet, hear the voice of truth!
Polly, you're not a beauty, yet you're pretty;
So grave, yet gay; so silly, yet so witty;
A heart of softness, yet a tongue of satire;
You've cruelty, yet, even in that, good-nature:
Now you are free, and now reserved a while;
Now a forced frown betrays a willing smile.
Reproached for absence, yet your sight denied;
My tongue you silence, yet my silence chide.
How would you praise me, should your sex defame!
Yet, should they praise, grow jealous, and exclaim.
If I despair, with some kind look you bless;
But if I hope, at once all hope suppress.
You scorn; yet should my passion change or fail,
Too late you'd whimper out a softer tale.
You love; yet from your lover's wish retire;
Doubt, yet discern; deny, and yet desire,
Such, Polly, are your sex—part truth, part fiction,
Some thought, much whim, and all a contradiction.

Richard Savage

522   *For ever, Fortune, wilt thou prove*

For ever, Fortune, wilt thou prove
An unrelenting foe to love,
And when we meet a mutual heart
Come in between, and bid us part?

Bid us sigh on from day to day,
And wish and wish the soul away;
Till youth and genial years are flown,
And all the life of life is gone?

But busy, busy, still art thou,
To bind the loveless joyless vow,
The heart from pleasure to delude,
To join the gentle to the rude.

For once, O Fortune, hear my prayer,
And I absolve thy future care;
All other blessings I resign,
Make thou but dear Amanda mine.

James Thomson

523   *Man's a bubble*

Man's a poor deluded bubble
    Wandering in a mist of lies,
Seeing false or seeing double.
    Who would trust to such weak eyes?

Yet presuming on his senses
    On he goes most wondrous wise:
Doubts of truth, believes pretences;
    Lost in error, lives and dies.

Robert Dodsley

524   *On a halfpenny which a young lady gave a beggar,*
       and which the author redeemed for half-a-crown

Dear little, pretty, favourite ore,
That once increased Gloriana's store;
That lay within her bosom blest,
Gods might have envied thee thy rest!

I've read, imperial Jove of old
For love transformed himself to gold:
And why for a more lovely lass
May he not now have lurked in brass?
O, rather than from her he'd part
He'd shut that charitable heart,
That heart whose goodness nothing less
Than this vast power could dispossess.
For Gloriana's gentle touch
Thy mighty value now is such,
That thou to me art worth alone
More than his medals are to Sloane.

Henry Fielding

525   *On the death of Mr. Robert Levet a Practiser in Physic*

Condemned to hope's delusive mine,
    As on we toil from day to day,
By sudden blasts, or slow decline,
    Or social comforts drop away.

Well tried through many a varying year,
    See Levet to the grave descend;
Officious, innocent, sincere,
    Of every friendless name the friend.

Yet still he fills affection's eye,
    Obscurely wise, and coarsely kind;
Nor, lettered arrogance, deny
    Thy praise to merit unrefined.

When fainting nature called for aid,
    And hovering death prepared the blow,
His vigorous remedy displayed
    The power of art without the show.

In misery's darkest caverns known,
    His useful care was ever nigh,
Where hopeless anguish poured his groan,
    And lonely want retired to die.

No summons mocked by chill delay,
  No petty gain disdained by pride,
The modest wants of every day
  The toil of every day supplied.

His virtues walked their narrow round,
  Nor made a pause, nor left a void;
And sure the Eternal Master found
  The single talent well employed.

The busy day, the peaceful night,
  Unfelt, uncounted, glided by;
His frame was firm, his powers were bright,
  Though now his eightieth year was nigh.

Then with no fiery throbbing pain,
  No cold gradations of decay,
Death broke at once the vital chain,
  And freed his soul the nearest way.

Samuel Johnson

526   *The winter's walk*

Behold, my fair, where'er we rove,
  What dreary prospects round us rise:
The naked hills, the leafless grove,
  The hoary ground, the frowning skies.

Nor only through the wasted plain,
  Stern Winter, is thy force confessed;
Still wider spreads thy horrid reign,
  I feel thy power usurp my breast.

Enlivening hope and fond desire
  Resign the heart to spleen and care:
Scarce frighted Love maintains his fire
  And rapture saddens to despair.

In groundless hope, and causeless fear,
    Unhappy man! behold thy doom,
Still changing with the changeful year
    The slave of sunshine and of gloom,

Tired with vain joys, and false alarms,
    With mental and corporeal strife,
Snatch me, my Stella, to thy arms,
    And hide me from the sight of life.

Samuel Johnson

527   *An epitaph upon the celebrated Claudy Philips,
musician, who died very poor*

Philips, whose touch harmonious could remove
The pangs of guilty power and hapless love,
Rest here, distressed by poverty no more,
Here find that calm, thou gavest so oft before.
Sleep, undisturbed, within this peaceful shrine,
Till angels wake thee, with a note like thine.

Samuel Johnson

528   *When Delia on the plain appears*

When Delia on the plain appears,
Awed by a thousand tender fears
I would approach but dare not move:
Tell me, my heart, if this be love?

Whene'er she speaks, my ravished ear
No other voice than hers can hear,
No other wit but hers approve:
Tell me, my heart, if this be love?

If she some other youth commend,
Though I was once his fondest friend,
His instant enemy I prove:
Tell me, my heart, if this be love?

When she is absent, I no more
Delight in all that pleased before—
The clearest spring, or shadiest grove:
Tell me, my heart, if this be love?

When fond of power, of beauty vain,
Her nets she spread for every swain,
I strove to hate, but vainly strove:
Tell me, my heart, if this be love?

George Lyttelton

529   *The landskip*

How pleased within my native bowers
   Erewhile I passed the day!
Was ever scene so decked with flowers?
   Were ever flowers so gay?

How sweetly smiled the hill, the vale,
   And all the landskip round!
The river gliding down the dale!
   The hill with beeches crowned!

But now, when urged by tender woes
   I speed to meet my dear,
That hill and stream my zeal oppose,
   And check my fond career.

No more, since Daphne was my theme,
   Their wonted charms I see:
That verdant hill, and silver stream,
   Divide my love and me.

William Shenstone

At length, my friends, the feast of life is o'er;
I've eat sufficient—and I'll drink no more:
My night is come; I've spent a jovial day;
'Tis time to part, but oh! what is to pay?

Richard Graves

531   *Ode on the death of a favourite cat drowned in a tub
of gold fishes*

'Twas on a lofty vase's side,
Where China's gayest art had dyed
    The azure flowers, that blow;
Demurest of the tabby kind,
The pensive Selima reclined,
    Gazed on the lake below.

Her conscious tail her joy declared;
The fair round face, the snowy beard,
    The velvet of her paws,
Her coat, that with the tortoise vies,
Her ears of jet, and emerald eyes,
    She saw; and purred applause.

Still had she gazed; but amidst the tide
Two angel forms were seen to glide,
    The Genii of the stream:
Their scaly armour's Tyrian hue
Through richest purple to the view
    Betrayed a golden gleam.

The hapless Nymph with wonder saw:
A whisker first and then a claw,
    With many an ardent wish,
She stretched in vain to reach the prize.
What female heart can gold despise?
    What cat's averse to fish?

Presumptuous maid! with looks intent
Again she stretched, again she bent,
    Nor knew the gulf between.
(Malignant Fate sat by, and smiled.)
The slippery verge her feet beguiled,
    She tumbled headlong in.

Eight times emerging from the flood
She mewed to every watery God,
    Some speedy aid to send.
No dolphin came, no nereid stirred:
Nor cruel Tom, nor Susan heard.
    A favourite has no friend!

From hence, ye beauties, undeceived,
Know, one false step is ne'er retrieved,
    And be with caution bold.
Not all that tempts your wandering eyes
And heedless hearts, is lawful prize;
    Nor all, that glisters, gold.

Thomas Gray

532   *The progress of poesy*

I—1

Awake, Æolian lyre, awake,
And give to rapture all thy trembling strings.
From Helicon's harmonious springs
A thousand rills their mazy progress take:
The laughing flowers, that round them blow,
Drink life and fragrance as they flow.
Now the rich stream of music winds along
Deep, majestic, smooth, and strong,
Through verdant vales, and Ceres' golden reign:
Now rolling down the steep amain,
Headlong, impetuous, see it pour:
The rocks, and nodding groves rebellow to the roar.

Oh! Sovereign of the willing soul,
Parent of sweet and solemn-breathing airs,
Enchanting shell! the sullen Cares,
And frantic Passions hear thy soft control.
On Thracia's hills the Lord of War,
Has curbed the fury of his car,
And dropped his thirsty lance at thy command.
Perching on the sceptred hand
Of Jove, thy magic lulls the feathered king
With ruffled plumes, and flagging wing:
Quenched in dark clouds of slumber lie
The terror of his beak, and lightnings of his eye.

Thee the voice, the dance, obey,
Tempered to thy warbled lay.
O'er Idalia's velvet-green
The rosy-crowned loves are seen
On Cytherea's day
With antic sports, and blue eyed pleasures,
Frisking light in frolic measures;
Now pursuing, now retreating,
Now in circling troops they meet:
To brisk notes in cadence beating
Glance their many-twinkling feet.
Slow melting strains their Queen's approach declare:
Where'er she turns the Graces homage pay.
With arms sublime, that float upon the air,
In gliding state she wins her easy way:
O'er her warm cheek, and rising bosom, move
The bloom of young desire, and purple light of love.

Man's feeble race what ills await,
Labour, and penury, the racks of pain,
Disease, and sorrow's weeping train,
And death, and refuge from the storms of fate!
The fond complaint, my song, disprove,

And justify the laws of Jove.
Say, has he given in vain the heavenly Muse?
Night, and all her sickly dews,
Her spectres wan, and birds of boding cry,
He gives to range the dreary sky:
Till down the eastern cliffs afar
Hyperion's march they spy, and glittering shafts of war.

II—2

In climes beyond the solar road,
When shaggy forms o'er ice-built mountains roam,
The Muse has broke the twilight-gloom
To cheer the shivering native's dull abode.
And oft, beneath the oderous shade
Of Chili's boundless forests laid,
She deigns to hear the savage youth repeat
In loose numbers wildly sweet
Their feather-cinctured chiefs, and dusky loves.
Her track where'er the Goddess roves,
Glory pursue, and generous shame,
The unconquerable mind, and freedom's holy flame.

II—3

Woods, that wave o'er Delphi's steep
Isles, that crown the Ægean deep,
Fields, that cool Ilissus laves,
Or where Maeander's amber waves
In lingering labyrinths creep,
How do your tuneful echoes languish,
Mute, but to the voice of anguish?
Where each old poetic mountain
Inspiration breathed around:
Every shade and hallowed fountain
Murmured deep a solemn sound:
Till the sad Nine in Greece's evil hour
Left their Parnassus for the Latian plains.
Alike they scorn the pomp of tyrant-power,
And coward vice, that revels in her chains.
When Latium had her lofty spirit lost,
They sought, oh Albion! next thy sea-encircled coast.

Far from the sun and summer-gale,
In thy green lap was nature's darling laid,
What time, where lucid Avon strayed,
To him the mighty mother did unveil
Her aweful face: the dauntless child
Stretched forth his little arms, and smiled.
This pencil take (she said) whose colours clear
Richly paint the vernal year:
Thine too these golden keys, immortal boy!
This can unlock the gates of joy;
Of horror that, and thrilling fears,
Or ope the sacred source of sympathetic tears.

Nor second he, that rode sublime
Upon the seraph-wings of ecstasy,
The secrets of the abyss to spy.
He passed the flaming bounds of place and time:
The living throne, the sapphire-blaze,
Where Angels tremble, while they gaze,
He saw; but blasted with excess of light,
Closed his eyes in endless night.
Behold, where Dryden's less presumptuous car,
Wide o'er the fields of Glory bear
Two coursers of ethereal race,
With necks in thunder clothed, and long-resounding
    pace.

Hark, his hands the lyre explore!
Bright-eyed fancy hovering o'er
Scatters from her pictured urn
Thoughts, that breathe, and words, that burn.
But ah! 'tis heard no more——
Oh! Lyre divine, what daring Spirit
Wakes thee now? though he inherit

Nor the pride, nor ample pinion,
That the Theban Eagle bear,
Sailing with supreme dominion
Through the azure deep of air:
Yet oft before his infant eyes would run
Such forms, as glitter in the Muse's ray
With orient hues, unborrowed of the sun:
Yet shall he mount, and keep his distant way
Beyond the limits of a vulgar fate,
Beneath the Good how far—but far above the Great.

Thomas Gray

533 *Elegy written in a country churchyard*

The curfew tolls the knell of parting day,
    The lowering herd wind slowly o'er the lea,
The plowman homeward plods his weary way,
    And leaves the world to darkness and to me.

Now fades the glimmering landscape on the sight,
    And all the air a solemn stillness holds,
Save where the beetle wheels his droning flight,
    And drowsy tinklings lull the distant folds:

Save that from yonder ivy-mantled tower
    The moping owl does to the moon complain
Of such as wand'ring near her secret bower
    Molest her ancient solitary reign.

Beneath those rugged elms, that yew-tree's shade,
    Where heaves the turf in many a mould'ring heap
Each in his narrow cell for ever laid,
    The rude forefathers of the hamlet sleep.

The breezy call of incense-breathing morn,
    The swallow twitt'ring from the straw-built shed,
The cock's shrill clarion, or the echoing horn,
    No more shall rouse them from their lowly bed.

For them no more the blazing hearth shall burn,
  Or busy housewife ply her evening care:
No children run to lisp their sire's return,
  Or climb his knees the envied kiss to share.

Oft did the harvest to their sickle yield,
  Their furrow oft the stubborn glebe has broke;
How jocund did they drive their team afield!
  How bow'd the woods beneath their sturdy stroke!

Let not ambition mock their useful toil,
  Their homely joys, and destiny obscure;
Nor grandeur hear with a disdainful smile
  The short and simple annals of the poor.

The boast of heraldry, the pomp of power,
  And all that beauty, all that wealth e'er gave,
Await alike th' inevitable hour:
  The paths of glory lead but to the grave.

Nor you, ye proud, impute to these the fault,
  If memory o'er their tomb no trophies raise,
Where through the long-drawn aisle and fretted vault
  The pealing anthem swells the note of praise.

Can storied urn or animated bust
  Back to its mansion call the fleeting breath?
Can honour's voice provoke the silent dust,
  Or flattery soothe the dull cold ear of death?

Perhaps in this neglected spot is laid
  Some heart once pregnant with celestial fire;
Hands that the rod of empire might have sway'd,
  Or waked to ecstasy the living lyre:

But knowledge to their eyes her ample page
  Rich with the spoils of time did ne'er unroll;
Chill penury repress'd their noble rage,
  And froze the genial current of the soul.

Full many a gem of purest ray serene
  The dark unfathom'd caves of ocean bear:
Full many a flower is born to blush unseen,
  And waste its sweetness on the desert air.

Some village-Hampden, that with dauntless breast
    The little tyrant of his fields withstood,
Some mute inglorious Milton here may rest,
    Some Cromwell, guiltless of his country's blood.

Th' applause of list'ning senates to command,
    The threats of pain and ruin to despise
To scatter plenty o'er a smiling land,
    And read their history in a nation's eyes.

Their lot forbad: nor circumscrib'd alone
    Their growing virtues, but their crimes confined;
Forbad to wade through slaughter to a throne,
    And shut the gates of mercy on mankind;

The struggling pangs of conscious truth to hide,
    To quench the blushes of ingenuous shame,
Or heap the shrine of luxury and pride
    With incense kindled at the muse's flame.

Far from the madding crowd's ignoble strife,
    Their sober wishes never learn'd to stray;
Along the cool sequester'd vale of life
    They kept the noiseless tenour of their way.

Yet ev'n these bones from insult to protect
    Some frail memorial still erected nigh,
With uncouth rhymes and shapeless sculpture deck'd,
    Implores the passing tribute of a sigh.

Their name, their years, spelt by th' unletter'd Muse,
    The place of fame and elegy supply:
And many a holy text around she strews
    That teach the rustic moralist to die.

For who, to dumb forgetfulness a prey,
    This pleasing anxious being e'er resign'd,
Left the warm precincts of the cheerful day,
    Nor cast one longing lingering look behind?

On some fond breast the parting soul relies,
　　Some pious drops the closing eye requires;
Ev'n from the tomb the voice of nature cries,
　　Ev'n in our ashes live their wonted fires.

For thee, who, mindful of th' unhonour'd dead,
　　Dost in these lines their artless tale relate;
If chance, by lonely contemplation led,
　　Some kindred spirit shall inquire thy fate,—

Haply some hoary-headed swain may say,
　　'Oft have we seen him at the peep of dawn
Brushing with hasty steps the dews away
　　To meet the sun upon the upland lawn.

'There at the foot of yonder nodding beech
　　That wreathes its old fantastic roots so high,
His listless length at noontide would he stretch,
　　And pore upon the brook that babbles by.

'Hard by yon wood, now smiling as in scorn,
　　Mutt'ring his wayward fancies he would rove,
Now drooping, woeful wan, like one forlorn,
　　Or crazed with care, or cross'd in hopeless love.

'One morn I miss'd him on the custom'd hill,
　　Along the heath, and near his favourite tree;
Another came; nor yet beside the rill,
　　Nor up the lawn, nor at the wood was he;

'The next, with dirges due in sad array
　　Slow through the church-way path we saw him
　　　　　　　　　　　　　　　　　borne:—
Approach and read (for thou canst read) the lay
　　Graved on the stone beneath yon aged thorn.'

The Epitaph

Here rests his head upon the lap of Earth
　　A Youth, to Fortune and to Fame unknown;
Fair Science frown'd not on his humble birth,
　　And Melancholy mark'd him for her own

Large was his bounty, and his soul sincere;
　　Heaven did a recompense as largely send:
He gave to Misery all he had, a tear,
　　He gain'd from Heaven, 'twas all he wish'd, a friend.

No farther seek his merits to disclose,
　　Or draw his frailties from their dread abode,
(There they alike in trembling hope repose,)
　　The bosom of his Father and his God.

Thomas Gray

534　*The brown jug*

Dear Tom, this brown jug that now foams with mild
　　ale,
(In which I will drink to sweet Nan of the Vale)
Was once Tony Fillpot, a thirsty old soul
As e'er drank a bottle, or fathomed a bowl;
In boozing about 'twas his praise to excel,
—And among jolly topers he bore off the bell.

It chanced, as in dog-days he sat at his ease
In his flower-woven arbour as gay as you please,
With a friend and a pipe puffing sorrows away
And with honest old stingo was soaking his clay,
His breath-doors of life on a sudden were shut
And he died full as big as a Dorchester butt.

His body, when long in the ground it had lain
And time into clay had resolved it again,
A potter found out in its covert so snug
And with part of fat Toby he formed this brown jug,
Now sacred to friendship, and mirth, and mild ale;
So here's to my lovely sweet Nan on the Vale.

Francis Fawkes

Ye powers unseen, to whom the bards of Greece
Erected altars; ye who to the mind
More lofty views unfold, and prompt the heart
With more divine emotions, if erewhile
Not quite unpleasing have my votive rites
Of you been deemed when oft this lonely seat
To you I consecrated; then vouchsafe
Here with your instant energy to crown
My happy solitude. It is the hour
When most I love to invoke you, and have felt
Most frequent your glad ministry divine.
The air is calm: the sun's unveiled orb
Shines in the middle heaven: the harvest round
Stands quiet, and among the golden sheaves
The reapers lie reclined. The neighbouring groves
Are mute; nor even a linnet's random strain
Echoeth amid the silence. Let me feel
Your influence, ye kind powers. Aloft in heaven
Abide ye? or on those transparent clouds
Pass ye from hill to hill? or on those shades
Which yonder elms cast o'er the lake below
Do you converse retired? From what loved haunt
Shall I expect you? Let me once more feel
Your influence, O ye kind inspiring powers:
And I will guard it well, nor shall a thought
Rise in my mind, nor shall a passion move
Across my bosom unobserved, unstored
By faithful memory: and then at some
More active moment, will I call them forth
Anew; and join them in majestic forms,
And give them utterance in harmonious strains;
That all mankind shall wonder at your sway.

Mark Akenside

536   *How sleep the brave*

How sleep the brave, who sink to rest,
By all their Country's wishes blest!

When Spring, with dewy fingers cold,
Returns to deck their hallowed mold,
    She there shall dress a sweeter sod,
    Than fancy's feet have ever trod.

By fairy hands their knell is rung,
By forms unseen their dirge is sung;
There Honour comes, a Pilgrim grey,
To bless the turf that wraps their clay,
And freedom shall a-while repair,
To dwell a weeping hermit there!

William Collins

537   *Ode to evening*

If aught of oaten stop, or pastoral song,
May hope, chaste Eve, to sooth thy modest ear,
    Like thy own solemn springs,
    Thy springs, and dying gales,
O Nymph reserved, while now the bright-haired sun
Sits in yon western tent, whose cloudy skirts,
    With brede ethereal wove,
    O'erhang his wavy bed:
Now air is hushed, save where the weak-eyed bat,
With short shrill shriek flits by on leathern wing,
    Or where the beetle winds
    His small but sullen horn,
As oft he rises 'midst the twilight path,
Against the pilgrim born in heedless hum:
    Now teach me, maid composed,
    To breathe some softened strain,
Whose numbers stealing through thy darkning vale,
May not unseemly with its stillness suit,
    As musing slow, I hail
    Thy genial loved return!
For when thy folding star arising shews
His paly circlet, at his warning lamp
    The fragrant hours, and Elves

Who slept in flowers the day,
And many a Nymph who wreaths her brows with
sedge,
And sheds the freshening dew, and lovelier still,
  The pensive pleasures sweet
  Prepare thy shadowy car.
Then lead, calm Vot'ress, where some sheety lake
Cheers the lone heath, or some time-hallowed pile,
  Or up-land fallows grey
  Reflect it's last cool gleam.
But when chill blustering winds, or driving rain,
Forbid my willing feet, be mine the hut,
  That from the mountain's side,
  Views wilds, and swelling floods,
And hamlets brown, and dim-discovered spires,
And hears their simple bell, and marks o'er all
  Thy dewy fingers draw
  The gradual dusky veil.
While Spring shall pour his showers, as oft he wont,
And bathe thy breathing tresses, meekest Eve!
  While Summer loves to sport
  Beneath thy lingering light;
While sallow Autumn fills thy lap with leaves;
Or Winter yelling through the troublous air,
  Affrights thy shrinking train,
  And rudely rends thy robes;
So long, sure-found beneath the Sylvan shed,
Shall fancy, friendship, science, rose-lipped health,
  Thy gentlest influence own,
  And hymn thy favourite name!

William Collins

538   *Ode on the death of Thomson*

In yonder grave a Druid lies
  Where slowly winds the stealing wave!
The year's best sweets shall duteous rise
  To deck it's Poet's sylvan grave!

In yon deep bed of whispering reeds
    His airy harp shall now be laid,
That he, whose heart in sorrow bleeds,
    May love through life the soothing shade.

Then maids and youths shall linger here,
    And while it's sounds at distance swell,
Shall sadly seem in pity's ear
    To hear the Woodland Pilgrim's Knell.

Remembrance oft shall haunt the shore
    When Thames in Summer-wreaths is dressed,
And oft suspend the dashing oar
    To bid his gentle Spirit rest!

And oft as ease and health retire
    To breezy lawn, or forest deep,
The friend shall view yon whitening spire,
    And 'mid the varied Landscape weep.

But Thou, who own'st that earthly bed,
    Ah! what will every dirge avail?
Or tears, which love and pity shed,
    That mourn beneath the gliding sail!

Yet lives there one, whose heedless eye
    Shall scorn thy pale shrine glimmering near?
With Him, sweet bard, may fancy die,
    And joy desert the blooming year.

But thou, lorn stream, whose sullen tide
    No sedge-crowned sisters now attend,
Now waft me from the green hill's side
    Whose cold turf hides the buried friend!

And see, the fairy valleys fade,
    Dun night has veiled the solemn view!
—Yet once again, dear parted shade,
    Meek nature's child, again adieu!

The genial meads assigned to bless
  Thy life, shall mourn thy early doom;
Their hinds, and shepherd-girls shall dress
  With simple hands thy rural tomb.

Long, long, thy stone and pointed clay
  Shall melt the musing Briton's eyes,
O! vales, and wild woods, shall He say
  In yonder grave your Druid lies!

William Collins

539   *Hymn for Saturday*

Now's the time for mirth and play,
Saturday's an holiday;
Praise to Heav'n unceasing yield,
I've found a lark's nest in the field.

A lark's nest, then your playmate begs
You'd spare herself and speckled eggs;
Soon she shall ascend and sing
Your praises to th'eternal King.

Christopher Smart

540   *Elegy on the death of a mad dog*

Good people all, of every sort,
  Give ear unto my song;
And if you find it wondrous short,—
  It cannot hold you long.

In Islington there was a man,
  Of whom the world might say,
That still a godly race he ran,—
  Whene'er he went to pray.

A kind and gentle heart he had,
  To comfort friends and foes;
The naked every day he clad,—
  When he put on his clothes.

And in that town a dog was found,
  As many dogs there be,
Both mongrel, puppy, whelp, and hound,
  And curs of low degree.

This dog and man at first were friends;
  But when a pique began,
The dog, to gain some private ends,
  Went mad, and bit the man.

Around from all the neighbouring streets,
  The wondering neighbours ran,
And swore the dog had lost his wits,
  To bite so good a man.

The wound it seemed both sore and sad
  To every Christian eye;
And while they swore the dog was mad,
  They swore the man would die.

But soon a wonder came to light,
  That showed the rogues they lied;
The man recovered of the bite,
  The dog it was that died.

Oliver Goldsmith

541 *An elegy on that glory of her sex Mrs. Mary Blaize*

Good people all, with one accord,
  Lament for Madam Blaize,
Who never wanted a good word—
  From those who spoke her praise.

The needy seldom passed her door,
  And always found her kind;
She freely lent to all the poor,—
  Who left a pledge behind.

She strove the neighbourhood to please,
  With manners wonderous winning,
And never followed wicked ways,—
  Unless when she was sinning.

At church, in silks and satins new,
  With hoop of monstrous size,
She never slumbered in her pew,—
  But when she shut her eyes.

Her love was sought, I do aver,
  By twenty beaus and more;
The king himself has followed her,—
  When she has walked before.

But now her wealth and finery fled,
  Her hangers-on cut short all;
The doctors found, when she was dead,—
  Her last disorder mortal.

Let us lament, in sorrow sore,
  For Kent-street well may say,
That had she lived a twelve-month more,
  She had not died to-day.

Oliver Goldsmith

542 *When lovely woman stoops*

When lovely woman stoops to folly,
  And finds too late that men betray,
What charm can sooth her melancholy,
  What art can wash her guilt away?

The only art her guilt to cover,
   To hide her shame from every eye,
To give repentance to her lover,
   And wring his bosom—is to die.

Oliver Goldsmith

543   *David Garrick*

Here lies David Garrick, describe me who can,
An abridgement of all that was pleasant in man;
As an actor, confessed without rival to shine,
As a wit, if not first, in the very first line,
Yet with talents like these, and an excellent heart,
The man had his failings, a dupe to his art;
Like an ill judging beauty, his colours he spread,
And beplastered, with rouge, his own natural red.
On the stage he was natural, simple, affecting,
'Twas only that, when he was off, he was acting:
With no reason on earth to go out of his way,
He turned and he varied full ten times a day;
Though secure of our hearts, yet confoundedly sick,
If they were not his own by finessing and trick,
He cast off his friends, as a huntsman his pack,
For he knew when he pleased he could whistle them
   back.
Of praise, a mere glutton, he swallowed what came,
And the puff of a dunce, he mistook it for fame,
'Till his relish grown callous, almost to disease,
Who peppered the highest, was surest to please.
But let us be candid, and speak out our mind,
If dunces applauded, he paid them in kind.
Ye Kenricks, ye Kellys, and Woodfalls so grave,
What a commerce was yours, while you got and you
   gave?
How did Grub-street re-echo the shouts that you raised,
While he was berosciused, and you were bepraised?
But peace to his spirit, wherever it flies,
To act as an angel, and mix with the skies:

Those poets, who owe their best fame to his skill,
Shall still be his flatterers, go where he will.
Old Shakespeare, receive him, with praise and with
    love,
And Beaumonts and Bens be his Kellys above.

Oliver Goldsmith

544   *Verses written during the war, 1756–1763*

Go, lovely boy! to yonder tower,
    The fane of Janus, ruthless King!
And shut, O! shut the brazen door,
    And here the keys in triumph bring.

Full many a tender heart hath bled,
    Its joys in Belgia's soil entombed:
Which thou to Hymen's smiling bed,
    And length of sweetest hours, had doomed.

Oh glory! you to ruin owe
    The fairest plume the hero wears:
Raise the bright helmet from his brow;
    You'll mock, beneath, the manly tears.

Who does not burn to place the crown
    Of conquest on his Albion's head?
Who weeps not at her plaintive moan,
    To give her hapless orphans bread?

Forgive, ye brave, the generous fault,
    If thus my virtue fails; alone
My Delia stole my earliest thought,
    And framed its feelings by her own.

Her mind so pure, her face so fair;
    Her breast the seat of softest love;
It seemed her words an angel's were,
    Her gentle precepts from above.

My mind thus formed, to misery gave
    The tender tribute of a tear:
O! Belgia, open thy vast grave,
    For I would pour an ocean there.

When first you showed me at your feet
    Pale liberty, religion tied,
I flew to shut the glorious gate
    Of freedom on a tyrant's pride.

Though great the cause, so wore with woes,
    I cannot but lament the deed:
My youth to melancholy bows,
    And Clotho trifles with my thread.

But stop, my Clio, wanton muse,
    Indulge not this unmanly strain:
Beat, beat the drums, my ardour rouse,
    And call the soldier back again.

Sound, sound the clarion, fill the fife,
    Throughout the sensual world proclaim,
One crowded hour of glorious life
    Is worth an age without a name.

Go then, thou little lovely boy,
    I cannot, must not, hear thee now;
And all thy soothing arts employ
    To cheat my Delia of her woe.

If the gay flower, in all its youth,
    The scythe of glory here must meet;
Go, bear my laurel, pledge of truth,
    And lay it at my Delia's feet.

Her tears shall keep it ever green,
    To crown the image in her breast;
Till death doth close the hapless scene,
    And calls its angel home to rest.

Thomas Osbert Mordaunt

545 *The drum*

I hate that drum's discordant sound,
Parading round, and round, and round:
To thoughtless youth it pleasure yields,
And lures from cities and from fields,
To sell their liberty for charms
Of tawdry lace, and glittering arms;
And when ambition's voice commands,
To march, and fight, and fall, in foreign lands.

I hate that drum's discordant sound,
Parading round, and round, and round:
To me it talks of ravaged plains,
And burning towns, and ruined swains,
And mangled limbs, and dying groans,
And widow's tears, and orphans' moans;
And all that misery's hand bestows,
To fill the catalogue of human woes.

John Scott

546 *The rights of women*

Hath woman then no rights, presumptuous Paine?
Is man thy idol, arrogant and vain?
Woman be mine, but still on reason's plan
Her rights I raise above the rights of man.
'Tis hers to rule with absolute control
Each rude excess of his too lordly soul;
Yet rule with such a just, persuasive sway,
That man shall be both proud and happy to obey.

William Cowper

547 *The shrubbery*

Oh happy shades! to me unblest,
    Friendly to peace, but not to me,
How ill the scene that offers rest,
    And heart that cannot rest, agree!

This glassy stream, that spreading pine,
    Those alders quivering to the breeze,
Might sooth a soul less hurt than mine,
    And please, if any thing could please.

But fixed unalterable care
    Foregoes not what she feels within,
Shows the same sadness every where,
    And slights the season and the scene.

For all that pleased in wood or lawn,
    While peace possessed these silent bowers,
Her animating smile withdrawn,
    Has lost its beauties and its powers.

The saint or moralist should tread
    This moss-grown alley, musing, slow;
They seek, like me, the secret shade,
    But not, like me, to nourish woe.

Me fruitful scenes and prospects waste
    Alike admonish not to roam;
These tell me of enjoyments past,
    And those of sorrows yet to come.

William Cowper

548   *The poplar-field*

The poplars are felled, farewell to the shade
And the whispering sound of the cool colonnade,
The winds play no longer, and sing in the leaves,
Nor Ouse on his bosom their image receives.

Twelve years have elapsed since I first took a view
Of my favourite field and the bank where they grew,
And now in the grass behold they are laid,
And the tree is my seat that once lent me a shade.

The blackbird has fled to another retreat
Where the hazels afford him a screen from the heat,
And the scene where his melody charmed me before,
Resounds with his sweet-flowing ditty no more.

My fugitive years are all hasting away,
And I must ere long lie as lowly as they,
With a turf on my breast, and a stone at my head,
Ere another such grove shall arise in its stead.

'Tis a sight to engage me, if any thing can,
To muse on the perishing pleasures of man;
Though his life be a dream, his enjoyments, I see,
Have a being less durable even than he.

William Cowper

549 *God moves in a mysterious way*

God moves in a mysterious way,
   His wonders to perform;
He plants his footsteps in the sea,
   And rides upon the storm.

Deep in unfathomable mines
   Of never failing skill,
He treasures up his bright designs,
   And works his sovereign will.

Ye fearful saints fresh courage take,
   The clouds ye so much dread
Are big with mercy, and shall break
   In blessings on your head.

Judge not the Lord by feeble sense,
   But trust him for his grace;
Behind a frowning providence,
   He hides a smiling face.

His purposes will ripen fast,
    Unfolding every hour;
The bud may have a bitter taste,
    But sweet will be the flower.

Blind unbelief is sure to err,
    And scan his work in vain;
God is his own interpreter,
    And he will make it plain.

William Cowper

550   *To Mary*

The twentieth year is well-nigh past,
Since first our sky was overcast;
Ah would that this might be the last!
        My Mary!

Thy spirits have a fainter flow,
I see thee daily weaker grow—
'Twas my distress that brought thee low,
        My Mary!

Thy needles, once a shining store,
For my sake restless heretofore,
Now rust disused, and shine no more,
        My Mary!

For though thou gladly wouldst fulfil
The same kind office for me still,
Thy sight now seconds not thy will,
        My Mary!

But well thou played'st the housewife's part,
And all thy threads with magic art
Have wound themselves about this heart,
        My Mary!

Thy indistinct expressions seem
Like language uttered in a dream;
Yet me they charm, whate'er the theme,
      My Mary!

Thy silver locks, once auburn bright,
Are still more lovely in my sight
Than golden beams of orient light,
      My Mary!

For could I view nor them nor thee,
What sight worth seeing could I see?
The sun would rise in vain for me,
      My Mary!

Partakers of thy sad decline,
Thy hands their little force resign;
Yet, gently pressed, press gently mine,
      My Mary!

And then I feel that still I hold
A richer store ten thousandfold
Than misers fancy in their gold,
      My Mary!

Such feebleness of limbs thou prov'st,
That now at every step thou mov'st
Upheld by two; yet still thou lov'st,
      My Mary!

And still to love, though pressed with ill,
In wintry age to feel no chill,
With me is to be lovely still,
      My Mary!

But ah! by constant heed I know,
How oft the sadness that I show
Transforms thy smiles to looks of woe,
      My Mary!

And should my future lot be cast
With much resemblance of the past,
Thy worn-out heart will break at last,
      My Mary!

William Cowper

Obscurest night involved the sky,
  Th' Atlantic billows roared,
When such a destined wretch as I,
  Washed headlong from on board,
Of friends, of hope, of all bereft,
His floating home for ever left.

No braver chief could Albion boast
  Than he with whom he went,
Nor ever ship left Albion's coast,
  With warmer wishes sent.
He loved them both, but both in vain,
Nor him beheld, nor her again.

Not long beneath the whelming brine,
  Expert to swim, he lay;
Nor soon he felt his strength decline,
  Or courage die away;
But waged with death a lasting strife,
Supported by despair of life.

He shouted: nor his friends had failed
  To check the vessel's course,
But so the furious blast prevailed,
  That, pitiless perforce,
They left their outcast mate behind,
And scudded still before the wind.

Some succour yet they could afford;
  And, such as storms allow,
The cask, the coop, the floated cord,
  Delayed not to bestow.
But he (they knew) nor ship, nor shore,
Whate'er they gave, should visit more.

Nor, cruel as it seemed, could he
  Their haste himself condemn,
Aware that flight, in such a sea,
  Alone could rescue them;
Yet bitter felt it still to die
Deserted, and his friends so nigh.

He long survives, who lives an hour
    In ocean, self-upheld:
And so long he, with unspent power,
    His destiny repelled;
And ever, as the minutes flew,
Entreated help, or cried—Adieu!

At length, his transient respite past,
    His comrades, who before
Had heard his voice in every blast,
    Could catch the sound no more.
For then, by toil subdued, he drank
The stifling wave, and then he sank.

No poet wept him: but the page
    Of narrative sincere,
That tells his name, his worth, his age,
    Is wet with Anson's tear.
And tears by bards or heroes shed
Alike immortalize the dead.

I therefore purpose not, or dream,
    Descanting on his fate,
To give the melancholy theme
    A more enduring date:
But misery still delights to trace
Its 'semblance in another's case.

No voice divine the storm allayed,
    No light propitious shone;
When, snatched from all effectual aid,
    We perished, each alone:
But I beneath a rougher sea,
And whelmed in deeper gulfs than he.

William Cowper

552   *The loss of the 'Royal George'*

Toll for the brave!
    The brave that are no more:
All sunk beneath the wave
    Fast by their native shore!

Eight hundred of the brave,
    Whose courage well was tried,
Had made the vessel heel,
    And laid her on her side.

A land-breeze shook the shrouds,
    And she was overset;
Down went the *Royal George*,
    With all her crew complete.

Toll for the brave!
    Brave Kempenfelt is gone;
His last sea-fight is fought,
    His work of glory done.

It was not in the battle;
    No tempest gave the shock;
She sprang no fatal leak;
    She ran upon no rock.

His sword was in its sheath,
    His fingers held the pen,
When Kempenfelt went down
    With twice four hundred men.

Weigh the vessel up
    Once dreaded by our foes!
And mingle with our cup
    The tear that England owes.

Her timbers yet are sound,
    And she may float again
Full charted with England's thunder,
    And plough the distant main.

But Kempenfelt is gone,
    His victories are o'er;
And he and his eight hundred
    Shall plough the wave no more.

William Cowper

BOOK FOUR
The Romantics

INTRODUCTION

The half-century beginning about 1780 is called by literary historians the Romantic period, and the word Romantic will do well enough to sum up the spirit of that age. Politically it was an age of revolution, succeeding a time of stagnation; it was a time of rebellion, and poetry was infected by this tendency. William Blake grew up to find himself, at the beginning of this period, in an age of poetic and emotional aridity; Wordsworth and Coleridge strove also to break away from the traditionalism which depressed the work of their elders. Sir Walter Scott and Coleridge found inspiration in medieval romance and balladry. A world of sensation was opened up to poets which had been closed to the eighteenth century.

Rebellion, however, was not simply against literary fashions, but to some extent against society itself and the tyranny of custom. Rebels are individualists, and perhaps the greatest discovery of the Romantic poets was themselves. It was the age of Jean-Jacques Rousseau, of American Independence and the French Revolution: everywhere the rights of nations, classes and individuals were being asserted.

In such an age it is natural that the reader of poetry should notice the differences which divide the poets, rather than the similarities which, in another age, unite them. The great figures of the time—Keats and Clare, Shelley and Byron, besides those already named—have little in common apart from their romanticism. Each was out to discover or re-discover poetic territory peculiarly his own. The major poetry of the period is among the best known in English literature. So strong was the influence of Wordsworth in the Victorian period that the Wordsworthian lyric became almost the type of English poetry; but Wordsworth was not the only poet to rediscover wild nature. None has celebrated the beauty of rural England more lovingly and intimately than John Clare.

But the minor poetry of this period is also worthy of closer attention than it sometimes receives. It is interesting to notice that the present part contains poems by no less than three children of Coleridge; the sonnets of his eldest son, Hartley, are quite undeservedly neglected. There are also short poems by Charles Lamb and even his sister Mary—certainly no major poet—and by George Darley and Thomas Lovell Beddoes which present various aspects of the spirit of romanticism. All were interested as much in formal perfection and verbal music as in romantic self-exploration. All the Romantics, like other poets, were concerned with problems and form and diction, but only in the case of a thorough-going classic like Landor do we feel that formal considerations actually dictate meaning.

It is worth noting, again, that the present period sees, if not quite the beginnings of American poetry, at least its achievement of something like majority. We shall hear much more of it in the next part; meanwhile Philip Freneau, William Cullen Bryant, Ralph Waldo Emerson, Henry Wadsworth Longfellow and John Greenleaf Whittier may stand as pioneers in the establishment of a true transatlantic tradition.

Enough has been said to suggest that this is a period of change and variety, of formal experiment and individual assertion. We think of it not so much as an age of poetry as an age of poets. Blake—Coleridge—Shelley: each is in his own way a portentous figure; the difficulty is to think of them as contemporaries, their deaths occurring within ten years of each other. In a conspectus of poets so various, then, it may not be out of place to conclude by returning to the beginning of our period and singling out the Scotsman Burns, whose achievement is so hard to define, so impossible to relate to his age. Burns was of humble birth and preferred the native tradition of local balladry to the elegances of refined poetry: in both these respects he was a forerunner and a portent. At the same time it was his unique quality to seem less like the pioneer of a new spirit of rebellious romanticism than one of the minstrels of the Middle Ages, whose name, though not his songs, if he had lived then, might have been forgotten.

CONTENTS

PHILIP FRENEAU 1752–1832

GEORGE CRABBE 1754–1832

WILLIAM BLAKE 1757–1827

ROBERT BURNS 1759–1796

SAMUEL ROGERS 1763–1855

MARY LAMB 1764–1847

RICHARD ALFRED MILLIKIN 1767–1815

WILLIAM WORDSWORTH 1770–1850

SIR WALTER SCOTT 1771–1832

GEORGE GORDON, LORD BYRON 1788-1824

CHARLES WOLFE 1791-1823

PERCY BYSSHE SHELLEY 1792-1822

JOHN KEATS 1795-1821

GEORGE DARLEY 1795-1846

HARTLEY COLERIDGE 1796-1849

JOHN GREENLEAF WHITTIER 1807–1892

CHARLES TENNYSON TURNER 1808–1879

553 *Ballade: To a fish of the brooke*

Why flyest thou away with fear?
Trust me, there's nought of danger near,
   I have no wicked hooke
All covered with a snaring bait,
Alas, to tempt thee to thy fate,
   And dragge thee from the brooke.

O harmless tenant of the flood,
I do not with to spill thy blood,
   For Nature unto thee
Perchance hath given a tender wife,
And children dear, to charme thy life,
   As she hath done for me.

Enjoy thy streame, O harmless fish;
And when an angler, for his dish,
   Through gluttony's vile sin,
Attempts, a wretch, to pull thee *out*,
God give thee strength, O gentel trout,
   To pull the raskall *in!*!

              John Wolcot

554 *Rock of ages*

Rock of ages, cleft for me,
Let me hide myself in Thee!
Let the Water and the Blood,
From thy riven side which flowed,
Be of sin the double cure;
Cleanse me from it's guilt and power.

Not the labours of my hands
Can fulfil thy law's demands:
Could my zeal no respite know,
Could my tears for ever flow,

All for sin could not atone:
Thou must save, and Thou alone.
Nothing in my hand I bring;
Simply to thy Cross I cling;
Naked, come to Thee for dress;
Helpless, look to Thee for grace;
Foul, I to the fountain fly:
Wash me, Saviour, or I die!

While I draw this fleeting breath—
When my eye-strings break in death—
When I soar to worlds unknown—
See Thee on thy judgment-throne—
Rock of ages, cleft for me,
Let me hide myself in Thee.

Augustus Montague Toplady

555   *My mother bids me bind my hair*

My mother bids me bind my hair
    With bands of rosy hue,
Tie up my sleeves with ribbons rare,
    And lace my bodice blue.

'For why,' she cries, 'sit still and weep,
    While others dance and play?'
Alas! I scarce can go or creep,
    While Lubin is away.

'Tis sad to think the days are gone,
    When those we love were near;
I sit upon this mossy stone,
    And sigh when none can hear.

And while I spin my flaxen thread,
    And sing my simple lay,
The village seems asleep or dead,
    Now Lubin is away.

Anne Hunter

Here, a sheer hulk, lies poor Tom Bowling,
    The darling of our crew;
No more he'll hear the tempest howling,
    For death has broached him to.
His form was of the manliest beauty,
    His heart was kind and soft,
Faithful below he did his duty,
    And now he's gone aloft.

Tom never from his word departed,
    His virtues were so rare,
His friends were many, and true hearted,
    His Poll was kind and fair:
And then he'd sing so blithe and jolly,
    Ah many's the time and oft!
But mirth is turned to melancholy,
    For Tom is gone aloft.

Yet shall Poor Tom find pleasant weather,
    When he who all commands
Shall give, to call life's crew together,
    The word to pipe all hands.
Thus death, who Kings and Tars dispatches,
    In vain Tom's life has doffed,
For though his body's under hatches,
    His soul is gone aloft.

Charles Dibdin

557 *Here's to the maiden*

Here's to the maiden of bashful fifteen;
    Here's to the widow of fifty;
Here's to the flaunting extravagant queen,
    And here's to the housewife that's thrifty.

Let the toast pass,—
Drink to the lass,
I'll warrant she'll prove an excuse for the glass.

Here's to the charmer whose dimples we prize;
   Now to the maid who has none, sir:
Here's to the girl with a pair of blue eyes,
   And here's to the nymph with but one, sir.
     Chorus. Let the toast pass, etc.

Here's to the maid with a bosom of snow;
   Now to her that's as brown as a berry:
Here's to the wife with a face full of woe,
   And now to the girl that is merry.
     Chorus. Let the toast pass, etc.

For let 'em be clumsy, or let 'em be slim,
   Young or ancient, I care not a feather;
So fill a pint bumper quite up to the brim,
   And let us e'en toast them together.
     Chorus. Let the toast pass, etc.

Richard Brinsley Sheridan

558   *The wild honeysuckle*

Fair flower, that dost so comely grow,
Hid in this silent, dull retreat,
Untouched thy honied blossoms blow,
Unseen thy little branches greet:
     No roving foot shall crush thee here,
     No busy hand provoke a tear.

By Nature's self in white arrayed,
She bade thee shun the vulgar eye,
And planted here the guardian shade,
And sent soft waters murmuring by;
     Thus quietly thy summer goes,
     Thy days declining to repose.

Smit with those charms, that must decay,
I grieve to see your future doom;
They died—nor were those flowers more gay,
The flowers that did in Eden bloom;
    Unpitying frosts, and Autumn's power
    Shall leave no vestige of this flower.

From morning suns and evening dews
At first thy little being came:
If nothing once, you nothing lose,
For when you die you are the same;
    The space between is but an hour,
    The frail duration of a flower.

Philip Freneau

559   *The Indian burying ground*

In spite of all the learned have said,
   I still my old opinion keep;
The posture, that we give the dead,
   Points out the soul's eternal sleep.

No so the ancients of these lands—
   The Indian, when from life released,
Again is seated with his friends,
   And shares again the joyous feast.

His imaged birds, and painted bowl,
   And venison, for a journey dressed,
Bespeak the nature of the soul,
   Activity, that knows no rest.

His bow, for action ready bent,
   And arrows, with a head of stone,
Can only mean that life is spent,
   And not the old ideas gone.

Thou, stranger, that shalt come this way,
  No fraud upon the dead commit—
Observe the swelling turf, and say
  They do not lie, but here they sit.

Here still a lofty rock remains,
  On which the curious eye may trace
(Now wasted, half, by wearing rains)
  The fancies of a ruder race.

Here still an aged elm aspires,
  Beneath whose far-projecting shade
(And which the shepherd still admires)
  The children of the forest played!

There oft a restless Indian queen
  (Pale Shebah, with her braided hair)
And many a barbarous form is seen
  To chide the man that lingers there.

By midnight moons, o'er moistening dews;
  In habit for the chase arrayed,
The hunter still the deer pursues,
  That hunter and the deer, a shade!

And long shall timorous fancy see
  The painted chief, and pointed spear,
And Reason's self shall bow the knee
  To shadows and delusions here.

                                    Philip Freneau

560 *His wife's wedding ring*

The ring so worn, as you behold,
So thin, so pale, is yet of gold:
The passion such it was to prove;
Worn with life's cares, love yet was love.

                                    George Crabbe

Whether on Ida's shady brow,
Or in the chambers of the East,
The chambers of the sun, that now
From ancient melody have ceased;

Whether in Heaven ye wander fair,
Or the green corners of the earth,
Or the blue regions of the air
Where the melodious winds have birth;

Whether on crystal rocks ye rove,
Beneath the bosom of the sea
Wandering in many a coral grove,
Fair Nine, forsaking Poetry!

How have you left the ancient love
That bards of old enjoyed in you!
The languid strings do scarcely move!
The sound is forced, the notes are few!

William Blake

562 *My silks and fine array*

My silks and fine array,
My smiles and languished air,
By love are driven away;
And mournful lean Despair
Brings me yew to deck my grave;
Such end true lovers have.

His face is fair as heaven
When springing buds unfold;
O! why to him was't given
Whose heart is wintry cold?
His breast is love's all-worshipped tomb,
Where all love's pilgrims come.

Bring me an axe and spade,
Bring me a winding sheet;
When I my grave have made
Let winds and tempests beat:
Then down I'll lay as cold as clay.
True love does pass away!

William Blake

563   *To spring*

O thou with dewy locks, who lookest down
Thro' the clear windows of the morning, turn
Thine angel eyes upon our western isle,
Which in full choir hails thy approach, O Spring!

The hills tell each other, and the listening
Valleys hear; all our longing eyes are turned
Up to thy bright pavilions: issue forth,
And let thy holy feet visit our clime.

Come o'er the eastern hills, and let our winds
Kiss thy perfumed garments; let us taste
Thy morn and evening breath; scatter thy pearls
Upon our love-sick land that mourns for thee.

O deck her forth with thy fair fingers; pour
Thy soft kisses on her bosom; and put
Thy golden crown upon her languished head,
Whose modest tresses were bound up for thee.

William Blake

564   *Mad song*

The wild winds weep,
And the night is a-cold;
Come hither, Sleep,
And my griefs enfold:

But lo! the morning peeps
Over the eastern steeps,
And the rustling birds of dawn
The earth do scorn.

Lo! to the vault
Of paved heaven,
With sorrow fraught
My notes are driven:
They strike the ear of night,
Make weep the eyes of day;
They make mad the roaring winds,
And with tempests play,

Like a fiend in a cloud,
With howling woe
After night I do crowd,
And with night will go;
I turn my back to the east
From whence comforts have increased;
For light doth seize my brain
With frantic pain.

William Blake

565 *How sweet I roamed*

How sweet I roamed from field to field
And tasted all the summer's pride,
Till I the Prince of Love beheld
Who in the sunny beams did glide!

He showed me lilies for my hair,
And blushing roses for my brow;
He led me through his gardens fair
Where all his golden pleasures grow.

With sweet May dews my wings were wet,
And Phoebus fired my vocal rage;
He caught me in his silken net,
And shut me in his golden cage.

He loves to sit and hear me sing,
Then, laughing, sports and plays with me;
Then stretches out my golden wing,
And mocks my loss of liberty.

William Blake

566   *Piping down the valleys wild*

Piping down the valleys wild,
Piping songs of pleasant glee,
On a cloud I saw a child,
And he laughing said to me:

'Pipe a song about a lamb!'
So I piped with merry cheer.
'Piper pipe that song again.'
So I piped: he wept to hear.

'Drop thy pipe, thy happy pipe;
Sing thy songs of happy cheer.'
So I sung the same again,
While he wept with joy to hear.

'Piper, sit thee down and write
In a book, that all may read.'
So he vanished from my sight,
And I plucked a hollow reed,

And I made a rural pen,
And I stained the water clear,
And I wrote my happy songs
Every child may joy to hear.

William Blake

Hear the voice of the Bard!
Who present, past, and future sees;
Whose ears have heard
The Holy Word,
That walked among the ancient trees,

Calling the lapsèd soul,
And weeping in the evening dew;
That might control
The starry pole,
And fallen, fallen, light renew!

'O Earth, O Earth, return!
Arise from out the dewy grass;
Night is worn,
And the morn
Rises from the slumberous mass.

'Turn away no more;
Why wilt thou turn away?
The starry floor,
The watery shore,
Is given thee till the break of day.'

William Blake

568 Earth's answer

Earth raised up her head
From the darkness dread and drear,
Her light fled
(Stony dread!)
And her locks covered with grey despair.

'Prisoned on watery shore,
Starry Jealousy does keep my den:
Cold and hoar,
Weeping o'er,
I hear the Father of the Ancient Men.

'Selfish Father of Men!
Cruel, jealous, selfish Fear!
Can delight,
Chained in night,
The virgins of youth and morning bear?

'Does spring hide its joy
When buds and blossoms grow?
Does the sower
Sow by night,
Or the ploughman in darkness plough?

'Break this heavy chain
That does freeze my bones around.
Selfish! vain!
Eternal bane!
That free Love with bondage bound.'

William Blake

569 *A cradle song*

Sweet dreams form a shade
O'er my lovely infant's head;
Sweet dreams of pleasant streams
By happy, silent, moony beams.

Sweet sleep, with soft down
Weave thy brows an infant crown.
Sweet sleep, Angel mild,
Hover o'er my happy child.

Sweet smiles, in the night,
Hover over my delight;
Sweet smiles, mother's smiles,
All the livelong night beguiles.

Sweet moans, dovelike sighs,
Chase not slumber from thy eyes.
Sweet moans, sweeter smiles,
All the dovelike moans beguiles.

Sleep, sleep, happy child,
All creation slept and smiled;
Sleep, sleep, happy sleep,
While o'er the mother weep.

Sweet babe, in thy face
Holy image I can trace.
Sweet babe, once like thee,
Thy Maker lay and wept for me,

Wept for me, for thee, for all,
When he was an infant small.
Thou His image ever see,
Heavenly face that smiles on thee,

Smiles on thee, on me, on all;
Who became an infant small.
Infant smiles are His own smiles;
Heaven and earth to peace beguiles.

William Blake

570 *Sleep! sleep! beauty bright*

Sleep! sleep! beauty bright,
Dreaming o'er the joys of night;
Sleep! sleep! in thy sleep
Little sorrows sit and weep.

Sweet Babe, in thy face
Soft desires I can trace,
Secret joys and secret smiles,
Little pretty infant wiles.

As thy softest limbs I feel,
Smiles as of the morning steal
O'er thy cheek, and o'er thy breast
Where thy little heart does rest.

O! the cunning wiles that creep
In thy little heart asleep.
When thy little heart does wake
Then the dreadful lightnings break,

From thy cheek and from thy eye,
O'er the youthful harvests nigh.
Infant wiles and infant smiles
Heaven and Earth of peace beguiles.

William Blake

571   *Infant joy*

'I have no name:
I am but two days old.'
What shall I call thee?
'I happy am,
Joy is my name.'
Sweet joy befall thee!

Pretty Joy!
Sweet Joy, but two days old!
Sweet Joy I call thee.
Thou dost smile,
I sing the while,
Sweet joy befall thee!

William Blake

572   *Infant sorrow*

My mother groaned, my father wept,
Into the dangerous world I leapt;
Helpless, naked, piping loud,
Like a fiend hid in a cloud.

Struggling in my father's hands,
Striving against my swaddling-bands,
Bound and weary, I thought best
To sulk upon my mother's breast.

William Blake

573 *Nurse's song (Songs of innocence)*

When the voices of children are heard on the green,
And laughing is heard on the hill,
My heart is at rest within my breast,
And everything else is still.

'Then come home, my children, the sun is gone down,
And the dews of night arise;
Come, come, leave off play, and let us away
Till the morning appears in the skies.'

'No, no, let us play, for it is yet day,
And we cannot go to sleep;
Besides, in the sky the little birds fly,
And the hills are all covered with sheep.'

'Well, well, go and play till the light fades away,
And then go home to bed.'
The little ones leaped and shouted and laughed
And all the hills echoèd.

William Blake

574 *Nurse's song (Songs of experience)*

When the voices of children are heard on the green
And whisperings are in the dale,
The days of my youth rise fresh in my mind,
My face turns green and pale.

Then come home, my children, the sun is gone down
And the dews of night arise;
Your spring and your day are wasted in play,
And your winter and night in disguise.

William Blake

575   *The lamb*

Little Lamb, who made thee?
Dost thou know who made thee?
Gave thee life and bid thee feed,
By the stream and o'er the mead?
Gave thee clothing of delight,
Softest clothing, woolly, bright?
Gave thee such a tender voice,
Making all the vales rejoice?
Little Lamb, who made thee?
Dost thou know who made thee?

Little Lamb, I'll tell thee,
Little Lamb, I'll tell thee:
He is called by thy name,
For He calls Himself a Lamb.
He is meek, and He is mild;
He became a little child.
I a child, and thou a lamb,
We are called by His name.
Little Lamb, God bless thee!
Little Lamb, God bless thee!

William Blake

576   *The tiger*

Tiger! Tiger! burning bright
In the forests of the night,
What immortal hand or eye
Could frame thy fearful symmetry?

In what distant deeps or skies
Burnt the fire of thine eyes?
On what wings dare he aspire?
What the hand dare seize the fire?

And what shoulder, and what art,
Could twist the sinews of thy heart?
And when thy heart began to beat,
What dread hand, and what dread feet?

What the hammer? what the chain?
In what furnace was thy brain?
What the anvil? what dread grasp
Dare its deadly terrors clasp?

When the stars threw down their spears,
And watered heaven with their tears,
Did he smile his work to see?
Did he who made the lamb make thee?

Tiger! Tiger! burning bright
In the forests of the night,
What immortal hand or eye,
Dare frame thy fearful symmetry?

William Blake

577   *The blossom*

Merry, merry Sparrow!
Under the leaves so green,
A happy blossom
Sees you, swift as arrow,
Seek your cradle narrow
Near my bosom.

Pretty, pretty Robin!
Under leaves so green,
A happy blossom
Hears you sobbing, sobbing,
Pretty, pretty Robin,
Near my bosom.

William Blake

578   *The sick rose*

O Rose! thou art sick!
The invisible worm,
That flies in the night,
In the howling storm,

Had found out thy bed
Of crimson joy;
And his dark secret love
Does thy life destroy.

William Blake

579   *The chimney sweeper (Songs of innocence)*

When my mother died I was very young,
And my father sold me while yet my tongue
Could scarcely cry, ''weep! 'weep! 'weep! 'weep!''
So your chimneys I sweep, and in soot I sleep.

There's little Tom Dacre, who cried when his head,
That curled like a lamb's back, was shaved: so I said
'Hush Tom! never mind it, for when your head's bare
You know that the soot cannot spoil your white hair.'

And so he was quiet, and that very night,
As Tom was a sleeping, he had such a sight!—
That thousands of sweepers, Dick, Joe, Ned, and Jack,
Were all of them locked up in coffins of black.

And by came an Angel who had a bright key,
And he opened the coffins and set them all free;
Then down a green plain leaping, laughing, they run,
And wash in the river, and shine in the sun.

Then naked, and white, all their bags left behind,
They rise upon clouds and sport in the wind;
And the Angel told Tom, if he'd be a good boy,
He'd have God for his father and never want joy.

And so Tom awoke; and we rose in the dark,
And got with our bags and our brushes to work.
Tho' the morning was cold, Tom was happy and warm;
So if all do their duty they need not fear harm.

William Blake

580   *The chimney sweeper (Songs of experience)*

A little black thing among the snow,
Crying ''weep! 'weep!' in notes of woe!
'Where are thy father and mother, say?'—
'They are both gone up to the Church to pray.

'Because I was happy upon the heath,
And smiled among the winter's snow,
They clothed me in the clothes of death,
And taught me to sing the notes of woe.

'And because I am happy and dance and sing,
They think they have done me no injury,
And gone to praise God and His Priest and King,
Who make up a heaven of our misery.'

William Blake

581 Little boy lost

'Father! father! where are you going?
O do not walk so fast.
Speak, father, speak to your little boy,
Or else I shall be lost.'

The night was dark, no father was there;
The child was wet with dew;
The mire was deep, and the child did weep,
And away the vapour flew.

William Blake

582 The little boy found

The little boy lost in the lonely fen,
Led by the wandering light,
Began to cry; but God, ever nigh,
Appeared like his father in white.

He kissed the child, and by the hand led,
And to his mother brought,
Who in sorrow pale, thro' the lonely dale,
Her little boy weeping sought.

William Blake

583 A little boy lost

'Nought loves another as itself,
Nor venerates another so,
Nor is it possible to Thought
A greater than itself to know:

'And, Father, can I love you
Or any of my brothers more?
I loved you like the little bird
That picks up crumbs around the door.'

The Priest sat by and heard the child,
In trembling zeal he seized his hair:
He led him by his little coat,
And all admired the priestly care.

And standing on the altar, high,
'Lo! what a fiend is here,' said he,
'One who sets reason up for judge
Of our most holy Mystery.'

The weeping child could not be heard,
The weeping parents wept in vain;
They stripped him to his little shirt,
And bound him in an iron chain;

And burned him in a holy place,
Where many had been burned before:
The weeping parents wept in vain.
Are such things done on Albion's shore?

William Blake

584   *Holy Thursday*

'Twas on a Holy Thursday, their innocent faces clean,
The children walking two and two, in red and blue and
  green,
Grey-headed beadles walked before, with wands as white
  as snow,
Till into the high dome of Paul's they like Thames
  waters flow.

O what a multitude they seemed, these flowers of
  London town!
Seated in companies they sit with radiance all their own.

The hum of multitudes there, but multitudes of lambs,
Thousands of little boys and girls raising their innocent
    hands.

Now like a might wind they raise to Heaven the voice
    of song,
Or like harmonious thunderings the seats of Heaven
    among.
Beneath them sit the aged men, wise guardians of the
    poor;
Then cherish pity lest you drive an angel from your
    door.

William Blake

585   *A dream*

Once a dream did weave a shade
O'er my Angel-guarded bed,
That an emmet lost its way
Where on the grass methought I lay.

Troubled, 'wildered, and forlorn,
Dark, benighted, travel-worn,
Over many a tangled spray,
All heart-broke I heard her say:

'O, my children, do they cry?
Do they hear their father sigh?
Now they look abroad to see:
Now return and weep for me.'

Pitying, I dropped a tear;
But I saw a glow-worm near,
Who replied: 'What wailing wight
Calls the watchman of the night?

'I am set to light the ground,
While the beetle goes his round:
Follow now the beetle's hum;
Little wanderer, hie thee home.'

William Blake

586 *The divine image*

To Mercy, Pity, Peace, and Love
All pray in their distress;
And to these virtues of delight
Return their thankfulness.

For Mercy, Pity, Peace, and Love
Is God, our Father dear,
And Mercy, Pity, Peace, and Love
Is man, His child and care.

For Mercy has a human heart,
Pity a human face,
And Love, the human form divine,
And Peace, the human dress.

Then every man, of every clime,
That prays in his distress,
Prays to the human form divine,
Love, Mercy, Pity, Peace.

And all must love the human form,
In heathen, Turk, or Jew;
Where Mercy, Love, and Pity dwell
There God is dwelling too.

William Blake

587 *Laughing song*

When the green woods laugh with the voice of joy,
And the dimpling stream runs laughing by;

When the air does laugh with our merry wit,
And the green hill laughs with the noise of it;

When the meadows laugh with lively green,
And the grasshopper laughs in the merry scene,
When Mary and Susan and Emily
With their sweet round mouths sing 'Ha, Ha, He!'

When the painted birds laugh in the shade,
When our table with cherries and nuts is spread,
Come live, and be merry, and join with me,
To sing the sweet chorus of 'Ha, Ha, He!'

William Blake

588   *The shepherd*

How sweet is the shepherd's sweet lot!
From the morn to the evening he strays;
He shall follow his sheep all the day,
And his tongue shall be filled with praise.

For he hears the lamb's innocent call,
And he hears the ewe's tender reply;
He is watchful, while they are in peace,
For they know when their shepherd is nigh.

William Blake

589   *The echoing green*

The sun does arise,
And make happy the skies;
The merry bells ring
To welcome the spring;
The skylark and thrush,
The birds of the bush,
Sing louder around
To the bell's cheerful sound,
While our sports shall be seen
On the Echoing Green.

Old John with white hair,
Does laugh away care,
Sitting under the oak,
Among the old folk.
They laugh at our play,
And soon they all say:
'Such, such were the joys
When we all, girls and boys,
In our youth time were seen
On the Echoing Green.'

Till the little ones, weary,
No more can be merry;
The sun does descend,
And our sports have an end.
Round the laps of their mothers
Many sisters and brothers,
Like birds in their nest,
Are ready for rest,
And sport no more seen
On the darkening Green.

William Blake

590 *The little black boy*

My mother bore me in the southern wild,
And I am black, but O! my soul is white;
White as an angel is the English child,
But I am black, as if bereaved of light.

My mother taught me underneath a tree,
And, sitting down before the heat of day,
She took me on her lap and kissed me,
And, pointing to the east, began to say:

'Look on the rising sun, —there God does live,
And gives His light, and gives His heat away;
And flowers and trees and beasts and men receive
Comfort in morning, joy in the noonday.

'And we are put to earth a little space,
That we may learn to bear the beams of love;
And these black bodies and this sunburnt face
Is but a cloud, and like a shady grove.

'For when our souls have learned the heat to bear,
The cloud will vanish; we shall hear His voice,
Saying: "Come out from the grove My love and care,
And round my golden tent like lambs rejoice."'

Thus did my mother say, and kissed me;
And thus I say to little English boy.
When I from black and he from white cloud free,
And round the tent of God like lambs we joy,

I'll shade him from the heat, till he can bear
To lean in joy upon our Father's knee;
And then I'll stand and stroke his silver hair,
And be like him, and he will then love me.

William Blake

591   *On another's sorrow*

Can I see another's woe,
And be not in sorrow too?
Can I see another's grief,
And not seek for kind relief?

Can I see a falling tear,
And not feel my sorrow's share?
Can a father see his child
Weep, nor be with sorrow filled?

Can a mother sit and hear
An infant groan, an infant fear?
No, no! never can it be!
Never, never can it be!

And can He who smiles on all
Hear the wren with sorrows small,
Hear the small bird's grief and care,
Hear the woes that infants bear,

And not sit beside the nest,
Pouring pity in the breast;
And not sit the cradle near,
Weeping tear on infant's tear;

And not sit both night and day,
Wiping all our tears away?
O, no! never can it be!
Never, never can it be!

He doth give His joy to all;
He becomes an infant small;
He becomes a man of woe;
He doth feel the sorrow too.

Think not thou canst sigh a sigh,
And thy Maker is not by;
Think not thou canst weep a tear,
And thy Maker is not near.

O! He gives to us His joy
That our grief He may destroy;
Till our grief is fled and gone
He doth sit by us and moan.

William Blake

592   *Night*

The sun descending in the west,
The evening star does shine;
The birds are silent in their nest,
And I must seek for mine.

The moon, like a flower,
In heaven's high bower,
With silent delight
Sits and smiles on the night.

Farewell, green fields and happy groves,
Where flocks have took delight.
Where lambs have nibbled, silent moves
The feet of angels bright;
Unseen they pour blessing,
And joy without ceasing,
On each bud and blossom,
And each sleeping bosom.

They look in every thoughtless nest,
Where birds are covered warm;
They visit caves of every beast,
To keep them all from harm.
If they see any weeping
That should have been sleeping,
They pour sleep on their head,
And sit down by their bed.

When wolves and tigers howl for prey,
They pitying stand and weep;
Seeking to drive their thirst away,
And keep them from the sheep.
But if they rush dreadful,
The angels, most heedful,
Receive each mild spirit,
New worlds to inherit.

And there the lion's ruddy eyes
Shall flow with tears of gold,
And pitying the tender cries,
And walking round the fold,
Saying, 'Wrath, by His meekness,
And, by His health, sickness
Is driven away
From our immortal day.

'And now beside thee, bleating lamb,
I can lie down and sleep;
Or think on Him who bore thy name,
Graze after thee and weep.
For, washed in life's river,
My bright mane for ever
Shall shine like the gold
As I guard o'er the fold.'

William Blake

593   *The little girl found*

All the night in woe
Lyca's parents go
Over valleys deep,
While the deserts weep.

Tired and woe-begone,
Hoarse with making moan,
Arm in arm seven days
They traced the desert ways.

Seven nights they sleep
Among the shadows deep,
And dream they see their child
Starved in desert wild.

Pale, thro' pathless ways
The fancied image strays
Famished, weeping, weak,
With hollow piteous shriek.

Rising from unrest,
The trembling woman pressed
With feet of weary woe:
She could no further go.

In his arms he bore
Her, armed with sorrow sore;
Till before their way
A couching lion lay.

Turning back was vain:
Soon his heavy mane
Bore them to the ground.
Then he stalked around,

Smelling to his prey;
But their fears allay
When he licks their hands,
And silent by them stands.

They look upon his eyes
Filled with deep surprise;
And wondering behold
A spirit armed in gold.

On his head a crown;
On his shoulders down
Flowed his golden hair.
Gone was all their care.

'Follow me,' he said;
'Weep not for the maid;
In my palace deep
Lyca lies asleep.'

Then they followèd
Where the vision led,
And saw their sleeping child
Among tigers wild.

To this day they dwell
In a lonely dell;
Nor fear the wolfish howl
Nor the lion's growl.

William Blake

I love to rise in a summer morn
When the birds sing on every tree;
The distant huntsman winds his horn,
And the skylark sings with me.
O! what sweet company!

But to go to school on a summer morn,
O! it drives all joy away;
Under a cruel eye outworn,
The little ones spend the day
In sighing and dismay.

Ah! then at times I drooping sit,
And spend many an anxious hour,
Nor in my book can I take delight,
Nor sit in learning's bower,
Worn thro' with the dreary shower.

How can the bird that is born for joy
Sit in a cage and sing?
How can a child, when fears annoy,
But droop his tender wing,
And forget his youthful spring?

O! father and mother, if buds are nipped
And blossoms blown away,
And if the tender plants are stripped
Of their joy in the springing day,
By sorrow and care's dismay,

How shall the summer arise in joy,
Or the summer's fruits appear?
Or how shall we gather what griefs destroy,
Or bless the mellowing year,
When the blasts of winter appear?

William Blake

Never seek to tell thy love,
Love that never told can be;
For the gentle wind does move
Silently, invisibly.

I told my love, I told my love,
I told her all my heart;
Trembling, cold, in ghastly fears,
Oh! she doth depart.

Soon as she was gone from me,
A traveller came by,
Silently, invisibly:
He took her with a sigh.

William Blake

596   The clod and the pebble

'Love seeketh not itself to please,
Nor for itself hath any care,
But for another gives its ease,
And builds a Heaven in Hell's despair.'

So sung a little Clod of Clay,
Trodden with the cattle's feet;
But a Pebble of the brook
Warbled out these metres meet:

'Love seeketh only self to please,
To bind another to its delight,
Joy's in another's loss of ease,
And builds a Hell in Heaven's despite.'

William Blake

597 *I laid me down upon a bank*

I laid me down upon a bank,
Where Love lay sleeping;
I heard among the rushes dank
Weeping, weeping.

Then I went to the heath and the wild,
To the thistles and thorns of the waste;
And they told me how they were beguiled,
Driven out, and compelled to be chaste.

William Blake

598 *The garden of love*

I went to the Garden of Love,
And saw what I never had seen:
A Chapel was built in the midst,
Where I used to play on the green.

And the gates of this Chapel were shut,
And 'Thou shalt not' writ over the door;
So I turned to the Garden of Love
That so many sweet flowers bore;

And I saw it was filled with graves,
And tomb-stones where flowers should be;
And priests in black gowns were walking their rounds,
And binding with briars my joys and desires.

William Blake

599 *I saw a Chapel all of gold*

I saw a Chapel all of gold
That none did dare to enter in,
And many weeping stood without,
Weeping, mourning, worshipping.

I saw a Serpent rise between
The white pillars of the door,
And he forced and he forced and he forced;
Down the golden hinges tore,

And along the pavement sweet,
Set with pearls and rubies bright,
All his slimy length he drew,
Till upon the altar white

Vomiting his poison out
On the Bread and on the Wine.
So I turned into a sty,
And laid me down among the swine.

William Blake

600 *I asked a thief*

I asked a thief to steal me a peach:
He turned up his eyes.
I asked a lithe lady to lie her down:
Holy and meek, she cries.

As soon as I went
An Angel came:
He winked at the thief,
And smiled at the dame;

And without one word said
Had a peach from the tree,
And still as a maid
Enjoyed the lady.

William Blake

601 *I heard an Angel singing*

I heard an Angel singing
When the day was springing:
'Mercy, Pity, Peace
Is the world's release.'

Thus he sung all day
Over the new-mown hay,
Till the sun went down,
And haycocks looked brown.

I heard a Devil curse
Over the heath and the furze:
'Mercy could be no more
If there was nobody poor,

'And Pity no more could be,
If all were as happy as we.'
At his curse the sun went down,
And the heavens gave a frown.

Down poured the heavy rain
Over the new-reaped grain;
And Misery's increase
Is Mercy, Pity, Peace.

William Blake

602   *A poison tree*

I was angry with my friend:
I told my wrath, my wrath did end.
I was angry with my foe:
I told it not, my wrath did grow.

And I watered it in fears,
Night and morning with my tears:
And I sunned it with smiles,
And with soft deceitful wiles.

And it grew both day and night,
Till it bore an apple bright;
And my foe beheld it shine,
And he knew that it was mine,

And into my garden stole
When the night had veiled the pole:
In the morning glad I see
My foe outstretched beneath the tree.

William Blake

603   *Why should I care for the men of Thames?*

Why should I care for the men of Thames,
Or the cheating waves of chartered streams;
Or shrink at the little blasts of fear
That the hireling blows into my ear?

Tho' born on the cheating banks of Thames,
Tho' his waters bathed my infant limbs,
The Ohio shall wash his stains from me:
I was born a slave, but I go to be free!

William Blake

604   *Silent, silent night*

Silent, silent night,
Quench the holy light
Of thy torches bright;

For possessed of Day
Thousand spirits stray
That sweet joys betray.

Why should joys be sweet
Used with deceit,
Nor with sorrows meet?

But an honest joy
Does itself destroy
For a harlot coy.

William Blake

I wander thro' each chartered street,
Near where the chartered Thames does flow,
And mark in every face I meet
Marks of weakness, marks of woe.

In every cry of every man,
In every infant's cry of fear,
In every voice, in every ban
The mind-forged manacles I hear.

How the chimney-sweepers cry
Every blackening church appals;
And the hapless soldier's sigh
Runs in blood down palace walls.

But most thro' midnight streets I hear
How the youthful harlot's curse
Blasts the new-born infant's tear,
And blights with plague the marriage hearse.

William Blake

606   *The wild flower's song*

As I wandered the forest,
The green leaves among,
I heard a Wild Flower
Singing a song.

'I slept in the earth
In the silent night,
I murmured my fears
And I felt delight.

'In the morning I went,
As rosy as morn,
To seek for new joy;
But, oh! met with scorn.'

William Blake

607   *The little vagabond*

Dear mother, dear mother, the Church is cold,
But the Ale-house is healthy and pleasant and warm;
Besides I can tell where I am used well,
Such usage in Heaven will never do well.

But if at the Church they would give us some ale,
And a pleasant fire our souls to regale,
We'd sing and we'd pray all the livelong day,
Nor ever once wish from the Church to stray.

Then the Parson might preach, and drink, and sing,
And we'd be as happy as birds in the spring;
And modest Dame Lurch, who is always at Church,
Would not have bandy children, nor fasting, nor birch.

And God, like a father, rejoicing to see
His children as pleasant and happy as He,
Would have no more quarrel with the Devil or the
    barrel,
But kiss him, and give him both drink and apparel.

William Blake

608   *The fly*

Little Fly,
Thy summer's play
My thoughtless hand
Has brushed away.

Am not I
A fly like thee?
Or art not thou
A man like me?

For I dance,
And drink, and sing,
Till some blind hand
Shall brush my wing.

If thought is life
And strength and breath,
And the want
Of thought is death,

Then am I
A happy fly,
If I live
Or if I die.

William Blake

609 *Children of a future age*

Children of a future age,
Reading this indignant page,
Know that in former time,
Love, sweet Love, was thought a crime!

In the Age of Gold,
Free from winter's cold,
Youth and maiden bright
To the holy light,
Naked in the sunny beams delight.

Once a youthful pair,
Filled with softest care,
Met in a garden bright
Where the holy light
Had just removed the curtains of the night.

There, in rising day,
On the grass they play;
Parents were afar,
Strangers came not near,
And the maiden soon forgot her fear.

Tired with kisses sweet,
They agree to meet
When the silent sleep
Waves o'er heaven's deep,
And the weary tired wanderers weep.

To her father white
Came the maiden bright;
But his loving look,
Like the holy book,
All her tender limbs with terror shook.

'Ona! pale and weak!
To thy father speak:
O! the trembling fear,
O! the dismal care,
That shakes the blossoms of my hoary hair!'

William Blake

610   *Ah! sun-flower*

Ah! Sun-flower, weary of time,
Who countest the steps of the sun;
Seeking after that sweet golden clime,
Where the traveller's journey is done;

Where the Youth pined away with desire,
And the pale Virgin shrouded in snow,
Arise from their graves and aspire
Where my Sun-flower wishes to go.

William Blake

611   *My spectre around me*

My spectre around me night and day
Like a wild beast guards my way.
My emanation far within
Weeps incessantly for my sin.

A fathomless and boundless deep,
There we wander, there we weep;
On the hungry craving wind
My spectre follows thee behind.

He scents thy footsteps in the snow,
Wheresoever thou dost go
Through the wintry hail and rain.
When wilt thou return again?

Dost thou not in pride and scorn
Fill with tempests all my morn,
And with jealousies and fears
Fill my pleasant nights with tears?

Seven of my sweet loves thy knife
Has bereavèd of their life.
Their marble tombs I built with tears
And with cold and shuddering fears.

Seven more loves weep night and day
Round the tombs where my loves lay,
And seven more loves attend each night
Around my couch with torches bright.

And seven more loves in my bed
Crown with wine my mournful head,
Pitying and forgiving all
Thy transgressions, great and small.

William Blake

612   *And did those feet in ancient time?*

And did those feet in ancient time
    Walk upon England's mountains green?
And was the holy Lamb of God
    On England's pleasant pastures seen?

And did the Countenance Divine
   Shine forth upon our clouded hills?
And was Jerusalem builded here
   Among these dark Satanic Mills?

Bring me my bow of burning gold!
   Bring me my arrows of desire!
Bring me my spear! O clouds, unfold!
   Bring me my chariot of fire!

I will not cease from mental fight,
   Nor shall my sword sleep in my hand,
Till we have built Jerusalem
   In England's green and pleasant land.

William Blake

613   *A red, red rose*

O my love is like a red, red rose,
   That's newly sprung in June:
O my love is like the melody,
   That's sweetly played in tune.

As fair thou art, my bonnie lass,
   So deep in love am I;
And I will love thee still, my dear,
   Till a' the seas gang dry.

Till a' the seas gang dry, my dear,
   And the rocks melt wi' the sun;
And I will love thee still, my dear,
   While the sands o' life shall run.

And fare thee weel, my only love!
   And fare thee weel awhile!
And I will come again, my love,
   Tho' it were ten thousand mile.

Robert Burns

The lovely lass o' Inverness,
Nae joy nor pleasure can she see;
For e'en and morn she cries, Alas!
And aye the salt tear blinds her ee:
Drumossie moor—Drumossie day—
A waefu' day it was to me!
For there I lost my father dear,
My father dear, and brethren three.

Their winding sheet the bluidy clay,
Their graves are growing green to see:
And by them lies the dearest lad
That ever blest a women's ee!
Now wae to thee, thou cruel lord,
A bluidy man I trow thou be;
For mony a heart thou hast made sair
That ne'er did wrong to thine or thee.

Robert Burns

615 *Ye banks and braes*

Ye banks and braes o' bonnie Doon
    How can ye bloom sae fair!
How can ye chant, ye little birds,
    And I sae fu' o' care!

Thou'll break my heart, thou bonnie bird
    That sings upon the bough;
Thou minds me o' the happy days
    When my false Luve was true.

Thou'll break my heart, thou bonnie bird
    That sings beside thy mate;
For sae I sat, and sae I sang,
    And wist na o' my fate.

Aft hae I roved by bonnie Doon
   To see the woodbine twine,
And ilka bird sang o' its love;
   And sae did I o' mine.

Wi' lightsome heart I pu'd a rose,
   Frae aff its thorny tree;
And my false luver staw the rose,
   But left the thorn wi' me.

Robert Burns

616   *To a field mouse*

Wee, sleekit, cow'rin, tim'rous beastie,
O what a panic's in thy breastie!
Thou need na start awa sae hasty,
   Wi' bickering brattle!
I wad be laith to rin and chase thee
   Wi' murdering pattle!

I'm truly sorry man's dominion
Has broken nature's social union,
And justifies that ill opinion
   Which makes thee startle
At me, thy poor earth-born companion,
   And fellow-mortal!

I doubt na, whyles, but thou may thieve;
What then? poor beastie, thou maun live!
A daimen icker in a thrave
   'S a sma' request:
I'll get a blessing wi' the lave,
   And never miss't!

Thy wee bit housie, too, in ruin!
Its silly wa's the win's are strewin':

And naething, now, to big a new ane,
O' foggage green!
And bleak December's winds ensuin'
Baith snell and keen!

Thou saw the fields laid bare and waste
And weary winter comin' fast,
And cosy here, beneath the blast,
Thou thought to dwell,
Till crash! the cruel coulter passed
Out thro' thy cell.

That wee bit heap o' leaves and stibble
Has cost thee mony a weary nibble!
Now thou'd turned out for a' thy trouble
But house or hald,
To thole the winter's sleety dribble
And cranreuch cold?

But, Mousie, thou art no thy lane
In proving foresight may be vain:
The best laid schemes o' mice and men
Gang aft a-gley,
And lea'e us nought but grief and pain,
For promised joy.

Still thou art blest, compared wi' me!
The present only toucheth thee:
But, och! I backward cast my eye
On prospects drear!
And forward, tho' I canna see,
I guess and fear.

Robert Burns

617   *Corn rigs are bonny*

Corn rigs, an' barley rigs,
   An' corn rigs are bonny:
I'll ne'er forget that happy night,
   Amang the rigs wi' Annie.

It was upon a Lammas night,
    When corn rigs are bonny,
Beneath the moon's unclouded light,
    I held awa to Annie;
The time flew by, wi' tentless heed;
    Till, 'tween the late and early,
Wi' sma' persuasion she agreed
    To see me thro' the barley.

2

The sky was blue, the wind was still,
    The moon was shining clearly;
I set her down, wi' right good will,
    Amang the rigs o' barley:
I kent her heart was a' my ain;
    I lov'd her most sincerely;
I kiss'd her owre and owre again,
    Amang the rigs o' barley.

3

I lock'd her in my fond embrace;
    Her heart was beating rarely:
My blessings on that happy place,
    Amang the rigs o' barley!
But by the moon and stars so bright,
    That shone that hour so clearly!
She ay shall bless that happy night
    Amang the rigs o' barley.

4

I hae been blythe wi' comrades dear;
    I hae been merry drinking;
I hae been joufu' gath'ring gear;
    I hae been happy thinking:
But a' the pleasures e'er I saw,
    Tho' three times doubl'd fairly—
That happy night was worth them a',
    Amang the rigs o' barley.

                                    Robert Burns

I

I murder hate by field or flood,
    Tho' Glory's name may screen us.
In wars at hame I'll spend my blood—
    Life-giving wars of Venus.
The deities that I adore
    Are Social Peace and Plenty:
I'm better pleas'd to make one more
    Than be the death of twenty.

2

I would not die like Socrates,
    For all the fuss of Plato;
Nor would I with Leonidas,
    Nor yet would I with Cato;
The zealots of the Church and State
    Shall ne'er my mortal foes be;
But let me have bold Zimri's fate
    Within the arms of Cozbi.

Robert Burns

619   John Anderson my jo

I

John Anderson my jo, John,
    When we were first acquent,
Your locks were like the raven,
    Your bonny brow was brent;
But now your brow is beld, John,
    Your locks are like the snaw,
But blessings on your frosty pow,
    John Anderson my jo!

John Anderson my jo, John,
  We clamb the hill thegither,
And monie a cantie day, John,
  We've had wi' ane anither;
Now we maun totter down, John,
  And hand in hand we'll go,
And sleep thegither at the foot,
  John Anderson my jo!

Robert Burns

620 *On the author*

He who of Rankine sang, lies stiff and deid,
And a green, grassy hillock hides his heid:
Alas! alas! a devilish change indeed!

Robert Burns

621 *Composed in spring*

Again rejoicing Nature sees
  Her robe assume its vernal hues:
Her leafy locks wave in the breeze,
  All freshly steep'd in morning dews.

    Chorus: And maun I still on Menie doat,
           And bear the scorn that's in her e'e?
           For it's jet, jet black, an' it's like a hawk,
           An' it winna let a body be.

In vain to me the cowslips blaw,
  In vain to me the vi'lets spring;
In vain to me in glen or shaw,
  The mavis and the lintwhite sing.
        And maun I still . . .

The merry ploughboy cheers his team,
   Wi' joy the tentie seedsman stalks;
But life's to me a weary dream,
   A dream of ane that never wauks.
        And maun I still . . .

The wanton coot the water skims,
   Amang the reeds the ducklings cry,
The stately swan majestic swims,
   And ev'rything is blest but I.
        And maun I still . . .

The sheep-herd steeks his faulding slap,
   And o'er the moorlands whistles shill:
Wi' wild, unequal, wand'ring step,
   I meet him on the dewy hill.
        And maun I still . . .

And when the lark, 'tween light and dark,
   Blythe waukens by the daisy's side,
And mounts and sings on flittering wings,
   A woe-worn ghaist I hameward glide.
        And maun I still . . .

Come winter, with thine angry howl,
   And raging, bend the naked tree;
Thy gloom will soothe my cheerless soul,
   When nature all is sad like me!
        And maun I still . . .

Robert Burns

622   *I do confess thou art sae fair*

I do confess thou art sae fair,
   I wad been o'er the lugs in luve,
Had I na found the slightest prayer
   That lips could speak thy heart could muve.

I do confess thee sweet, but find
    Thou art so thriftless o' thy sweets,
Thy favours are the silly wind
    That kisses ilka things it meets.

See yonder rosebud, rich in dew,
    Amang its native briers sae coy;
How sune it tines its scent and hue,
    When pu'd and worn a common toy.

Sic fate ere lang shall thee betide,
    Tho' thou may gaily bloom awhile;
And sune thou shalt be thrown aside,
    Like ony common weed and vile.

Robert Burns

623 *To Miss Ferrier (enclosing the elegy on Sir J. H. Blair)*

Nae heathen name shall I prefix,
    Frae Pindus or Parnassus;
Auld Reekie dings them a' to sticks,
    For rhyme-inspiring lasses.

Jove's tunefu' dochters three times three
    Made Homer deep their debtor;
But, gien the body half an e'e,
    Nine Ferriers wad done better!

Last day my mind was in a bog,
    Down George's Street I stoited;
A creeping cauld prosaic fog
    My very senses doited.

Do what I dought to set her free,
   My saul lay in the mire;
Ye turned a neuk, I saw your e'e,
   She took the wing like fire!

The mournfu' sang I here enclose,
   In gratitude I send you,
And pray, in rhyme as well as prose,
   A' gude things may attend you!

Robert Burns

624   *The gowden locks of Anna*

Yestreen I had a pint o' wine,
   A place where body saw na;
Yestreen lay on this breast o' mine
   The gowden locks of Anna.

The hungry Jew in wilderness,
   Rejoicing o'er his manna,
Was naething to my hinnie bliss
   Upon the lips of Anna.

Ye monarchs, take the East and West
   Frae Indus to Savannah;
Gie me, within my straining grasp,
   The melting form of Anna.

There I'll despise Imperial charms,
   An Empress or Sultana,
While dying raptures in her arms
   I give and take wi' Anna!

Awa, thou flaunting God of Day!
   Awa, thou pale Diana!
Ilk Star, gae hide thy twinkling ray,
   When I'm to meet my Anna!

Come, in thy raven plumage, Night,
  (Sun, Moon, and Stars, withdrawn a';)
And bring an angel-pen to write
  My transports with my Anna!

POSTSCRIPT

The Kirk an' State may join, an' tell
  To do sic things I maunna:
The Kirk an' State may go to hell,
  An I'll gae to my Anna.

She is the sunshine o' my e'e,
  To live but here I canna;
Had I on earth but wishes three,
  The first should be my Anna.

Robert Burns

625   *Saw ye bonny Lesley?*

O saw ye bonny Lesley,
  As she gaed o'er the Border?
She's gane, like Alexander,
  To spread her conquests farther.

To see her is to love her,
  And love but her for ever;
For Nature made her what she is,
  And never made anither!

Thou art a queen, fair Lesley,
  Thy subjects, we before thee;
Thou art divine, fair Lesley,
  The hearts o' men adore thee.

The deil he could na scaith thee,
  Or aught that wad belang thee;
He'd look into thy bonie face,
  And say—'I canna wrang thee!'

The Powers aboon will tent thee,
   Misfortune sha'na steer thee;
Thou'rt like themselves sae lovely,
   That ill they'll ne'er let near thee.

Return again, fair Lesley,
   Return to Caledonie!
That we may brag we hae a lass
   There's nane again sae bonie.

Robert Burns

626   *There'll never be peace*

By yon castle wa', at the close of the day,
I heard a man sing, tho' his head it was grey;
And as he was singing, the tears fast down came,
There'll never be peace till Jamie comes hame.

The Church is in ruins, the State is in jars,
Delusions, oppressions, and murderous wars:
We darena weel say 't, tho' we ken wha 's to blame—
There'll never be peace till Jamie comes hame.

My seven braw sons for Jamie drew sword,
And now I greet[1] round their green beds in the yerd.
It brak the sweet heart of my faithful auld dame—
There'll never be peace till Jamie comes hame.

Now life is a burden that bows me down,
Sin' I tint[2] my bairns, and he tint his crown;
But till my last moments my words are the same—
There'll never be peace till Jamie comes hame.

Robert Burns

1 weep   2 lost

Tread lightly here, for here, 'tis said,
When piping winds are hushed around,
A small note wakes from underground,
Where now his tiny bones are laid.

No more in lone or leafless groves,
With ruffled wing and faded breast,
His friendless, homeless spirit roves;
Gone to the world where birds are blessed.

Where never cat glides o'er the green,
Or schoolboy's giant form is seen;
But love and joy and smiling Spring
Inspire their little souls to sing.

Samuel Rogers

I saw a boy with eager eye
Open a book upon a stall,
And read as he'd devour it all:
Which when the stall-man did espy,
Soon to the boy I heard him call,
'You, Sir, you never buy a book,
Therefore in one you shall not look.'
The boy passed slowly on, and with a sigh
He wished he never had been taught to read,
Then of the old churl's books he should have had no
    need.

Of sufferings the poor have many,
Which never can the rich annoy.
I soon perceived another boy
Who looked as if he'd not had any
Food for that day at least, enjoy

The sight of cold meat in a tavern larder.
This boy's case, thought I, is surely harder,
Thus hungry longing, thus without a penny,
Beholding choice of dainty dressèd meat:
No wonder if he wished he ne'er had learned to eat.

Mary Lamb

629   The groves of Blarney

The groves of Blarney they are so charming,
    All by the purling of sweet silent streams;
Being banked with posies that spontaneous grow there,
    Planted in order by the sweet rock close.
'Tis there's the daisy, and the sweet carnation,
    The blooming pink, and the rose so fair;
The daffodowndilly, besides the lily,—
    Flowers that scent the sweet fragrant air.

'Tis Lady Jeffreys that owns this station,
    Like Alexander, or Queen Helen fair;
There's no commander throughout the nation
    For emulation can with her compare.
She has castles round her, that no nine-pounder
    Could dare to plunder her place of strength:
But Oliver Cromwell he did her pummell,
    And made a breach in her battlement.

There's gravel walks there for speculation,
    And conversation in sweet solitude;
'Tis there the lover may hear the dove, or
    The gentle plover, in the afternoon.
And if a young lady should be so engaging
    As to walk alone in those shady bowers,
'Tis there her courtier he may transport her
    In some dark fort or under ground.

For 'tis there's the cave where no daylight enters,
   But bats and badgers are for ever bred;
Being mossed by natur', that makes it sweeter
   Than a coach and six or a feather bed.
'Tis there's the lake that is stored with perches,
   And comely eels in the verdant mud;
Besides the leeches and the groves of beeches,
   All standing in order for to guard the flood.

There's statues gracing this noble place in,
   All heathen goddesses so fair,—
Bold Neptune, Plutarch, and Nicodemus,
   All standing naked in the open air.
So now to finish this brave narration,
   Which my poor geni' could not entwine;
But were I Homer, or Nebuchadnezzar,
   'Tis in every feature I would make it shine.

                                        Richard Alfred Millikin

630   *Strange fits of passion have I known*

Strange fits of passion have I known:
And I will dare to tell,
But in the lover's ear alone,
What once to me befell.

When she I loved looked every day
Fresh as a rose in June,
I to her cottage bent my way,
Beneath an evening-moon.

Upon the moon I fixed my eye,
All over the wide lea;
With quickening pace my horse drew nigh
Those paths so dear to me.

And now we reached the orchard-plot;
And, as we climbed the hill,
The sinking moon to Lucy's cot
Came near, and nearer still.

In one of those sweet dreams I slept,
Kind Nature's gentlest boon!
And all the while my eyes I kept
On the descending moon.

My horse moved on; hoof after hoof
He raised, and never stopped:
When down behind the cottage roof,
At once, the bright moon dropped.

What fond and wayward thoughts will slide
Into a Lover's head!
'O mercy!' to myself I cried,
'If Lucy should be dead!'

William Wordsworth

631   *She dwelt among the untrodden ways*

She dwelt among the untrodden ways
    Beside the springs of Dove,
A maid whom there were none to praise
    And very few to love:

A violet by a mossy stone
    Half hidden from the eye!
—Fair as a star, when only one
    Is shining in the sky.

She lived unknown, and few could know
    When Lucy ceased to be;
But she is in her grave, and, oh,
    The difference to me!

William Wordsworth

I travelled among unknown men
  In lands beyond the sea;
Nor, England! did I know till then
  What love I bore to thee.

'Tis past, that melancholy dream!
  Nor will I quit thy shore
A second time; for still I seem
  To love thee more and more.

Among thy mountains did I feel
  The joy of my desire;
And she I cherished turned her wheel
  Beside an English fire.

Thy mornings showed, thy nights concealed
  The bowers where Lucy played;
And thine too is the last green field
  That Lucy's eyes surveyed.

William Wordsworth

---

633   *Lines written in early spring*

I heard a thousand blended notes
  While in a grove I sat reclined,
In that sweet mood when pleasant thoughts
  Bring sad thoughts to the mind.

To her fair works did Nature link
  The human soul that through me ran;
And much it grieved my heart to think
  What man has made of man.

Through primrose tufts, in that green bower,
  The periwinkle trailed its wreaths;
And 'tis my faith that every flower
  Enjoys the air it breathes.

The birds around me hopped and played,
    Their thoughts I cannot measure—
But the least motion which they made
    It seemed a thrill of pleasure.

The budding twigs spread out their fan
    To catch the breezy air;
And I must think, do all I can,
    That there was pleasure there.

If this belief from heaven be sent,
    If such be Nature's holy plan,
Have I not reason to lament
    What man has made of man?

William Wordsworth

634   *To the cuckoo*

O blithe new-comer! I have heard,
    I hear thee and rejoice.
O cuckoo! shall I call thee bird,
    Or but a wandering voice?

While I am lying on the grass
    Thy twofold shout I hear;
From hill to hill it seems to pass,
    At once far off, and near.

Though babbling only to the vale
    Of sunshine and of flowers,
Thou bringest unto me a tale
    Of visionary hours.

Thrice welcome, darling of the spring!
    Even yet thou art to me
No bird, but an invisible thing,
    A voice, a mystery;

The same whom in my schoolboy days
    I listened to; that cry
Which made me look a thousand ways
    In bush, and tree, and sky.

To seek thee did I often rove
    Through woods and on the green;
And thou wert still a hope, a love;
    Still longed for, never seen.

And I can listen to thee yet;
    Can lie upon the plain
And listen, till I do beget
    That golden time again.

O blessèd bird! the earth we pace
    Again appears to be
An unsubstantial, faery place,
    That is fit home for thee!

William Wordsworth

635   *The solitary reaper*

Behold her, single in the field,
Yon solitary Highland lass!
Reaping and singing by herself;
Stop here, or gently pass!
Alone she cuts and binds the grain,
And sings a melancholy strain;
O listen! for the vale profound
Is overflowing with the sound.

No nightingale did ever chaunt
More welcome notes to weary bands
Of travellers in some shady haunt,
Among Arabian sands:
A voice so thrilling ne'er was heard
In spring-time from the cuckoo-bird,
Breaking the silence of the seas
Among the farthest Hebrides.

Will no one tell me what she sings?—
Perhaps the plaintive numbers flow
For old, unhappy, far-off things,
And battles long ago:
Or is it some more humble lay,
Familiar matter of to-day?
Some natural sorrow, loss, or pain,
That has been, and may be again?

Whate'er the theme, the Maiden sang
As if her song could have no ending;
I saw her singing at her work,
And o'er the sickle bending;
I listen'd, motionless and still;
And, when I mounted up the hill,
The music in my heart I bore,
Long after it was heard no more.

William Wordsworth

636   *The world is too much with us*

The world is too much with us; late and soon,
Getting and spending, we lay waste our powers:
Little we see in Nature that is ours;
We have given our hearts away, a sordid boon!
This sea that bares her bosom to the moon;
The winds that will be howling at all hours,
And are up-gathered now like sleeping flowers;
For this, for everything, we are out of tune;
It moves us not.—Great God! I'd rather be
A Pagan suckled in a creed outworn;
So might I, standing on this pleasant lea,
Have glimpses that would make me less forlorn;
Have sight of Proteus rising from the sea;
Or hear old Triton blow his wreathèd horn.

William Wordsworth

. . . It seems a day
(I speak of one from many singled out)
One of those heavenly days that cannot die;
When, in the eagerness of boyish hope,
I left our cottage-threshold, sallying forth
With a huge wallet o'er my shoulders slung,
A nutting-crook in hand; and turned my steps
Tow'rd some far-distant wood, a figure quaint,
Tricked out in proud disguise of cast-off weeds
Which for that service had been husbanded,
By exhortation of my frugal dame—
Motley accoutrement, of power to smile
At thorns, and brakes, and brambles,—and in truth
More ragged than need was! O'er pathless rocks,
Through beds of matted fern, and tangled thickets,
Forcing my way, I came to one dear nook
Unvisited, where not a broken bough
Drooped with its withered leaves, ungracious sign
Of devastation; but the hazels rose
Tall and erect, with tempting clusters hung,
A virgin scene!—A little while I stood,
Breathing with such suppression of the heart
As joy delights in; and with wise restraint
Voluptuous, fearless of a rival, eyed
The banquet;—or beneath the trees I sate
Among the flowers, and with the flowers I played;
A temper known to those who, after long
And weary expectation, have been blest
With sudden happiness beyond all hope.
Perhaps it was a bower beneath whose leaves
The violets of five seasons re-appear
And fade, unseen by any human eye;
Where fairy water-breaks do murmur on
For ever; and I saw the sparkling foam,
And—with my cheek on one of those green stones
That, fleeced with moss, under the shady trees,
Lay round me, scattered like a flock of sheep—
I heard the murmur and the murmuring sound,

In that sweet mood when pleasure loves to pay
Tribute to ease; and of its joy secure,
The heart luxuriates with indifferent things,
Wasting its kindliness on stocks and stones,
And on the vacant air. Then up I rose,
And dragged to earth both branch and bough, with
    crash
And merciless ravage: and the shady nook
Of hazels, and the green and mossy bower,
Deformed and sullied, patiently gave up
Their quiet being: and unless I now
Confound my present feelings with the past,
Ere from the mutilated bower I turned
Exulting, rich beyond the wealth of kings,
I felt a sense of pain when I beheld
The silent trees, and saw the intruding sky.—
Then, dearest Maiden, move along these shades
In gentleness of heart; with gentle hand
Touch—for there is a spirit in the woods.

William Wordsworth

638   *She was a Phantom of delight*

She was a Phantom of delight
When first she gleamed upon my sight;
A lovely Apparition, sent
To be a moment's ornament;
Her eyes as stars of Twilight fair;
Like Twilight's too, her dusky hair:
But all things else about her drawn
From May-time and the cheerful Dawn;
A dancing shape, an Image gay,
To haunt, to startle, and way-lay.

I saw her upon nearer view,
A Spirit, yet a Woman too!
Her household motions light and free,
And steps of virgin-liberty;

A countenance in which did meet
Sweet records, promises as sweet;
A Creature not too bright or good
For human nature's daily food;
For transient sorrows, simple wiles,
Praise, blame, love, kisses, tears, and smiles.

And now I see with eye serene
The very pulse of the machine;
A Being breathing thoughtful breath,
A Traveller between life and death;
The reason firm, the temperate will,
Endurance, foresight, strength, and skill;
A perfect Woman, nobly planned,
To warn, to comfort, and command;
And yet a Spirit still, and bright
With something of angelic light.

William Wordsworth

639 *The reverie of poor Susan*

At the corner of Wood Street, when daylight appears,
Hangs a Thrush that sings loud, it has sung for three
    years:
Poor Susan has passed by the spot, and has heard
In the silence of morning the song of the Bird.

'Tis a note of enchantment; what ails her? She sees
A mountain ascending, a vision of trees;
Bright volumes of vapour through Lothbury glide,
And a river flows on through the vale of Cheapside.

Green pastures she views in the midst of the dale,
Down which she so often has tripped with her pail;
And a single small cottage, a nest like a dove's,
The one only dwelling on earth that she loves.

She looks, and her heart is in heaven: but they fade,
The mist and the river, the hill and the shade:
The stream will not flow, and the hill will not rise,
And the colours have all passed away from her eyes!

William Wordsworth

640   *Expostulation and reply*

'Why, William, on that old grey stone,
Thus for the length of half a day,
Why, William, sit you thus alone,
And dream your time away?

'Where are your books?—that light bequeathed
To Beings else forlorn and blind!
Up! up! and drink the spirit breathed
From dead men to their kind.

'You look round on your Mother Earth,
As if she for no purpose bore you;
As if you were her first-born birth,
And none had lived before you!'

One morning thus, by Esthwaite lake,
When life was sweet, I knew not why,
To me my good friend Matthew spake,
And thus I made reply:

'The eye—it cannot choose but see;
We cannot bid the ear be still;
Our bodies feel, where'er they be,
Against or with our will.

'Nor less I deem that there are Powers
Which of themselves our minds impress;
That we can feed this mind of ours
In a wise passiveness.

'Think you, 'mid all this mighty sum
Of things for ever speaking,
That nothing of itself will come,
But we must still be seeking?

'—Then ask not wherefore, here, alone,
Conversing as I may,
I sit upon this old grey stone,
And dream my time away.'

William Wordsworth

641   *The tables turned*

Up! up! my Friend, and quit your books;
Or surely you'll grow double:
Up! up! my Friend, and clear your looks;
Why all this toil and trouble?

The sun, above the mountain's head,
A freshening lustre mellow
Through all the long green fields has spread,
His first sweet evening yellow.

Books! 'tis a dull and endless strife:
Come, hear the woodland linnet,
How sweet his music! on my life,
There's more of wisdom in it.

And hark! how blithe the throstle sings!
He, too, is no mean preacher:
Come forth into the light of things,
Let Nature be your Teacher.

She has a world of ready wealth,
Our minds and hearts to bless—
Spontaneous wisdom breathed by health,
Truth breathed by cheerfulness.

One impulse from a vernal wood
May teach you more of man,
Of moral evil and of good,
Than all the sages can.

Sweet is the lore which Nature brings;
Our meddling intellect
Mis-shapes the beauteous forms of things:—
We murder to dissect.

Enough of Science and of Art;
Close up those barren leaves;
Come forth, and bring with you a heart
That watches and receives.

William Wordsworth

642   *Three years she grew in sun and shower*

Three years she grew in sun and shower,
Then Nature said, 'A lovelier flower
On earth was never sown;
This Child I to myself will take;
She shall be mine, and I will make
A Lady of my own.

'Myself will to my darling be
Both law and impulse: and with me
The Girl, in rock and plain,
In earth and heaven, in glade and bower,
Shall feel an overseeing power
To kindle or restrain.

'She shall be sportive as the fawn
That wild with glee across the lawn
Or up the mountain springs;
And hers shall be the breathing balm,
And hers the silence and the calm
Of mute insensate things.

'The floating clouds their state shall lend
To her; for her the willow bend;
Nor shall she fail to see
Even in the motions of the Storm
Grace that shall mould the Maiden's form
By silent sympathy.

'The stars of midnight shall be dear
To her; and she shall lean her ear
In many a secret place
Where rivulets dance their wayward round,
And beauty born of murmuring sound
Shall pass into her face.

'And vital feelings of delight
Shall rear her form to stately height,
Her virgin bosom swell;
Such thoughts to Lucy I will give
While she and I together live
Here in this happy dell.'

Thus Nature spake—The work was done—
How soon my Lucy's race was run!
She died, and left to me
This heath, this calm, and quiet scene;
The memory of what has been,
And never more will be.

William Wordsworth

643   *A slumber did my spirit seal*

A slumber did my spirit seal;
   I had no human fears:
She seemed a thing that could not feel
   The touch of earthly years.

No motion has she now, no force;
   She neither hears nor sees;
Rolled round in earth's diurnal course,
   With rocks, and stones, and trees.

William Wordsworth

644 The rainbow

My heart leaps up when I behold
   A rainbow in the sky:
So was it when my life began;
So is it now I am a man;
So be it when I shall grow old,
   Or let me die!
The Child is father of the Man;
And I could wish my days to be
Bound each to each by natural piety.

William Wordsworth

645 Composed upon Westminster Bridge, September 3, 1802

Earth has not anything to show more fair:
Dull would he be of soul who could pass by
A sight so touching in its majesty:
This City now doth, like a garment, wear
The beauty of the morning; silent, bare,
Ships, towers, domes, theatres, and temples lie
Open unto the fields, and to the sky;
All bright and glittering in the smokeless air.
Never did sun more beautifully steep
In his first splendour, valley, rock, or hill;
Ne'er saw I, never felt, a calm so deep!
The river glideth at his own sweet will:
Dear God! the very houses seem asleep;
And all that mighty heart is lying still!

William Wordsworth

It is a beauteous evening, calm and free,
The holy time is quiet as a Nun
Breathless with adoration; the broad sun
Is sinking down in its tranquillity;
The gentleness of heaven broods o'er the Sea:
Listen! the mighty Being is awake,
And doth with his eternal motion make
A sound like thunder—everlastingly.
Dear Child! dear Girl! that walkest with me here,
If thou appear untouched by solemn thought,
Thy nature is not therefore less divine:
Thou liest in Abraham's bosom all the year;
And worshipp'st at the Temple's inner shrine,
God being with thee when we know it not.

William Wordsworth

647 *Surprised by joy*

Surprised by joy—impatient as the Wind
I turned to share the transport—Oh! with whom
But Thee, deep buried in the silent tomb,
That spot which no vicissitude can find?
Love, faithful love, recalled thee to my mind—
But how could I forget thee? Through what power
Even for the least division of an hour,
Have I been so beguiled as to be blind
To my most grievous loss!—That thought's return
Was the worst pang that sorrow ever bore,
Save one, one only, when I stood forlorn,
Knowing my heart's best treasure was no more;
That neither present time, nor years unborn
Could to my sight that heavenly face restore.

William Wordsworth

When first descending from the moorlands
I saw the Stream of Yarrow glide
Along a bare and open valley,
The Ettrick Shepherd was my guide.

When last along its banks I wandered,
Through groves that had begun to shed
Their golden leaves upon the pathway,
My steps the Border-minstrel led.

The mighty Minstrel breathes no longer,
'Mid mouldering ruins low he lies;
And death upon the braes of Yarrow,
Has closed the Shepherd-poet's eyes.

Nor has the rolling year twice measured,
From sign to sign, its stedfast course,
Since every mortal power of Coleridge
Was frozen at its marvellous source;

The rapt One, of the godlike forehead,
The heaven-eyed creature sleeps in earth:
And Lamb, the frolic and the gentle,
Has vanished from his lonely hearth.

Like clouds that rake the mountain-summits,
Or waves that own no curbing hand,
How fast has brother followed brother,
From sunshine to the sunless land!

Yet I, whose lids from infant slumber
Were earlier raised, remain to hear
A timid voice, that asks in whispers,
'Who next will drop and disappear?'

Our haughty life is crowned with darkness,
Like London with its own black wreath,
On which with thee, O Crabbe! forth-looking,
I gazed from Hampstead's breezy heath.

As if but yesterday departed,
Thou too art gone before; but why,
O'er ripe fruit, seasonably gathered,
Should frail survivors heave a sigh?

Mourn rather for that holy Spirit,
Sweet as the spring, as ocean deep,
For Her who, ere her summer faded,
Has sunk into a breathless sleep.

No more of old romantic sorrows,
For slaughtered Youth or love-lorn Maid!
With sharper grief is Yarrow smitten,
And Ettrick mourns with her their Poet dead.

William Wordsworth

649   *A complaint*

There is a change—and I am poor;
Your love hath been, nor long ago,
A fountain at my fond heart's door,
Whose only business was to flow;
And flow it did; not taking heed
Of its own bounty, or my need.

What happy moments did I count!
Blest was I then all bliss above!
Now, for that consecrated fount
Of murmuring, sparkling, living love,
What have I? shall I dare to tell?
A comfortless and hidden well.

A well of love—it may be deep—
I trust it is,—and never dry;
What matter? if the waters sleep
In silence and obscurity.
—Such change, and at the very door
Of my fond heart, hath made me poor.

William Wordsworth

Beneath these fruit-tree boughs that shed
Their snow-white blossoms on my head,
With brightest sunshine round me spread
   Of spring's unclouded weather,
In this sequestered nook how sweet
To sit upon my orchard-seat!
And birds and flowers once more to greet,
   My last year's friends together.

One have I marked, the happiest guest
In all this covert of the blest:
Hail to Thee, far above the rest
   In joy of voice and pinion!
Thou, Linnet! in thy green array,
Presiding Spirit here to-day,
Dost lead the revels of the May;
   And this is thy dominion.

While birds, and butterflies, and flowers,
Make all one band of paramours,
Thou, ranging up and down the bowers,
   Art sole in thy employment:
A Life, a Presence like the Air,
Scattering thy gladness without care,
Too blest with any one to pair;
   Thyself thy own enjoyment.

Amid yon tuft of hazel trees,
That twinkle to the gusty breeze,
Behold him perched in ecstasies,
   Yet seeming still to hover;
There! where the flutter of his wings
Upon his back and body flings
Shadows and sunny glimmerings,
   That cover him all over.

My dazzled sight he oft deceives,
A Brother of the dancing leaves;
Then flits, and from the cottage eaves

Pours forth his song in gushes;
As if by that exulting strain
He mocked and treated with disdain
The voiceless Form he chose to feign,
  While fluttering in the bushes.

William Wordsworth

651   *Why art thou silent!*

Why art thou silent! Is thy love a plant
Of such weak fibre that the treacherous air
Of absence withers what was once so fair?
Is there no debt to pay, no boon to grant?
Yet have my thoughts for thee been vigilant—
Bound to thy service with unceasing care,
The mind's least generous wish a mendicant
For nought but what thy happiness could spare.
Speak—though this soft warm heart, once free to hold
A thousand tender pleasures, thine and mine,
Be left more desolate, more dreary cold
Than a forsaken bird's-nest filled with snow
'Mid its own bush of leafless eglantine—
Speak, that my torturing doubts their end may know!

William Wordsworth

652   *In these fair vales*

In these fair vales hath many a Tree
  At Wordsworth's suit been spared;
And from the builder's hand this Stone,
For some rude beauty of its own,
  Was rescued by the Bard:
So let it rest; and time will come
  When here the tender-hearted
May heave a gentle sigh for him,
  As one of the departed.

William Wordsworth

653   *To the moon*

With how sad steps, O Moon, thou climb'st the sky,
'How silently, and with how wan a face!'
Where art thou! Thou so often seen on high
Running among the clouds a Wood-nymph's race!
Unhappy Nuns, whose common breath's a sigh
Which they would stifle, move at such a pace!
The northern Wind, to call thee to the chase,
Must blow to-night his bugle horn. Had I
The power of Merlin, Goddess! this should be:
And all the stars, fast as the clouds were riven,
Should sally forth, to keep thee company,
Hurrying and sparkling through the clear blue heaven;
But, Cynthia! should to thee the palm be given,
Queen both for beauty and for majesty.

William Wordsworth

654   *Resolution and independence*

There was a roaring in the wind all night;
The rain came heavily and fell in floods;
But now the sun is rising calm and bright;
The birds are singing in the distant woods;
Over his own sweet voice the Stock-dove broods;
The Jay makes answer as the Magpie chatters;
And all the air is filled with pleasant noise of waters.

All things that love the sun are out of doors;
The sky rejoices in the morning's birth;
The grass is bright with rain-drops;—on the moors
The hare is running races in her mirth;
And with her feet she from the plashy earth
Raises a mist; that, glittering in the sun,
Runs with her all the way, wherever she doth run.

I was a Traveller then upon the moor;
I saw the hare that raced about with joy;
I heard the woods and distant waters roar;
Or heard them not, as happy as a boy:
The pleasant season did my heart employ:
My old remembrances went from me wholly;
And all the ways of men, so vain and melancholy.

But, as it sometimes chanceth, from the might
Of joy in minds that can no further go,
As high as we have mounted in delight
In our dejection do we sink as low;
To me that morning did it happen so;
And fears and fancies thick upon me came;
Dim sadness—and blind thoughts, I knew not, nor could
    name.

I heard the sky-lark warbling in the sky;
And I bethought me of the playful hare:
Even such a happy Child of earth am I;
Even as these blissful creatures do I fare;
Far from the world I walk, and from all care;
But there may come another day to me—
Solitude, pain of heart, distress, and poverty.

My whole life I have lived in pleasant thought,
As if life's business were a summer mood;
As if all needful things would come unsought
To genial faith, still rich in genial good;
But how can He expect that others should
Build for him, sow for him, and at his call
Love him, who for himself will take no heed at all?

I thought of Chatterton, the marvellous Boy,
The sleepless Soul that perished in his pride;
Of Him who walked in glory and in joy
Following his plough, along the mountain-side:
By our own spirits are we deified:
We Poets in our youth begin in gladness;
But thereof come in the end despondency and madness.

Now, whether it were by peculiar grace
A leading from above, a something given,
Yet it befell that, in this lonely place,
When I with these untoward thoughts had striven,
Beside a pool bare to the eye of heaven
I saw a Man before me unawares:
The oldest man he seemed that ever wore grey hairs.

As a huge stone is sometimes seen to lie
Couched on the bald top of an eminence;
Wonder to all who do the same espy,
By what means it could thither come, and whence;
So that it seems a thing endued with sense:
Like a sea-beast crawled forth, that on a shelf
Of rock or sand reposeth, there to sun itself;

Such seemed this Man, not all alive nor dead,
Nor all asleep—in his extreme old age:
His body was bent double, feet and head
Coming together in life's pilgrimage;
As if some dire constraint of pain, or rage
Of sickness felt by him in times long past,
A more than human weight upon his frame had cast.

Himself he propped, limbs, body and pale face,
Upon a long grey staff of shaven wood:
And, still as I drew near with gentle pace,
Upon the margin of that moorish flood
Motionless as a cloud the old Man stood,
That heareth not the loud winds when they call;
And moveth all together, if it move at all.

At length, himself unsettling, he the pond
Stirred with his staff, and fixedly did look
Upon the muddy water, which he conned,
As if he had been reading in a book:
And now a stranger's privilege I took;
And, drawing to his side, to him did say,
'This morning gives us promise of a glorious day'.

A gentle answer did the old Man make,
In courteous speech which forth he slowly drew:
And him with further words I thus bespake,
'What occupation do you there pursue?
This is a lonesome place for one like you'.
Ere he replied, a flash of mild surprise
Broke from the sable orbs of his yet-vivid eyes.

His words came feebly, from a feeble chest,
But each in solemn order followed each,
With something of a lofty utterance drest—
Choice word and measured phrase, above the reach
Of ordinary men; a stately speech;
Such as grave Livers do in Scotland use,
Religious men, who give to God and man their dues.

He told, that to these waters he had come
To gather leeches, being old and poor:
Employment hazardous and wearisome!
And he had many hardships to endure:
From pond to pond he roamed, from moor to moor;
Housing, with God's good help, by choice or chance;
And in this way he gained an honest maintenance.

The old Man still stood talking by my side;
But now his voice to me was like a stream
Scarce heard; nor word from word could I divide;
And the whole body of the Man did seem
Like one whom I had met with in a dream;
Or like a man from some far region sent,
To give me human strength, by apt admonishment.

My former thoughts returned: the fear that kills;
And hope that is unwilling to be fed;
Cold, pain, and labour, and all fleshly ills;
And mighty Poets in their misery dead.
—Perplexed, and longing to be comforted,
My question eagerly did I renew,
'How is it that you live, and what is it you do?'

He with a smile did then his words repeat;
And said that, gathering leeches, far and wide
He travelled; stirring thus about his feet
The waters of the pools where they abide.
'Once I could meet with them on every side;
But they have dwindled long by slow decay;
Yet still I persevere, and find them where I may'.

While he was talking thus, the lonely place,
The old Man's shape, and speech—all troubled me:
In my mind's eye I seemed to see him pace
About the weary moors continually,
Wandering about alone and silently.
While I these thoughts within myself pursued,
He, having made a pause, the same discourse renewed.

And soon with this he other matter blended,
Cheerfully uttered, with demeanor kind,
But stately in the main; and, when he ended,
I could have laughed myself to scorn to find
In that decrepit Man so firm a mind.
'God,' said I, 'be my help and stay secure;
I'll think of the Leech-gatherer on the lonely moor!'

William Wordsworth

655   *Proud Maisie*

Proud Maisie is in the wood,
     Walking so early;
Sweet Robin sits on the bush
     Singing so rarely.

'Tell me, thou bonny bird,
     When shall I marry me?'
—'When six braw gentlemen
     Kirkward shall carry ye.'

'Who make the bridal bed,
  Birdie, say truly?'
—'The grey-headed sexton
  That delves the grave duly.

'The glowworm o'er grave and stone
  Shall light thee steady;
The owl from the steeple sing
  Welcome, proud lady.'

Sir Walter Scott

656   *Look not thou*

Look not thou on beauty's charming,
Sit thou still when kings are arming,
Taste not when the wine-cup glistens,
Speak not when the people listens,
Stop thine ear against the singer,
From the red gold keep thy finger;
Vacant heart and hand and eye,
Easy live and quiet die.

Sir Walter Scott

657   *Kubla Khan*

In Xanadu did Kubla Khan
  A stately pleasure-dome decree:
Where Alph, the sacred river, ran
Through caverns measureless to man
  Down to a sunless sea.
So twice five miles of fertile ground
With walls and towers were girdled round:
And there were gardens bright with sinuous rills,
Where blossomed many an incense-bearing tree;
And here were forests ancient as the hills,
Enfolding sunny spots of greenery.

But oh! that deep romantic chasm which slanted
Down the green hill athwart a cedarn cover!
A savage place! as holy and enchanted
As e'er beneath a waning moon was haunted
By woman wailing for her demon-lover!
And from this chasm, with ceaseless turmoil seething,
As if this earth in fast thick pants were breathing,
A mighty fountain momently was forced:
Amid whose swift half-intermitted burst
Huge fragments vaulted like rebounding hail,
Or chaffy grain beneath the thresher's flail:
And 'mid these dancing rocks at once and ever
It flung up momently the sacred river.
Five miles meandering with a mazy motion
Through wood and dale the sacred river ran,
Then reached the caverns measureless to man,
And sank in tumult to a lifeless ocean:
And 'mid this tumult Kubla heard from far
Ancestral voices prophesying war!

　　The shadow of the dome of pleasure
　　Floated midway on the waves;
　　　Where was heard the mingled measure
　　　From the fountain and the caves.
　　It was a miracle of rare device,
　　A sunny pleasure-dome with caves of ice!

　　A damsel with a dulcimer
　　In a vision once I saw:
　　It was an Abyssinian maid,
　　And on her dulcimer she played,
　　Singing of Mount Abora.
　　Could I revive within me
　　Her symphony and song,
　　　To such a deep delight 'twould win me,
That with music loud and long,
I would build that dome in air,
That sunny dome! those caves of ice!
　　And all who heard should see them there,
　　And all should cry, Beware! Beware!

His flashing eyes, his floating hair!
  Weave a circle round him thrice,
And close your eyes with holy dread,
For he on honey-dew hath fed,
  And drunk the milk of Paradise.

Samuel Taylor Coleridge

658   *The rime of the ancient Mariner*

PART I

An ancient Mariner meeteth three gallants bidden to a wedding-feast and detaineth one.

It is an ancient Mariner,
And he stoppeth one of three.
'By thy long grey beard and glittering eye,
Now wherefore stopp'st thou me?

The Bridegroom's doors are open'd wide,
And I am next of kin;
The guests are met, the feast is set:
May'st hear the merry din.'

He holds him with his skinny hand,
'There was a ship,' quoth he.
'Hold off! unhand me, grey-beard loon!'
Eftsoons his hand dropt he.

The Wedding-Guest is spell-bound by the eye of the old sea-faring man, and constrained to hear his tale.

He holds him with his glittering eye—
The Wedding-Guest stood still,
And listens like a three years' child:
The Mariner hath his will.

The Wedding-Guest sat on a stone:
He cannot choose but hear;
And thus spake on that ancient man,
The bright-eyed Mariner:

'The ship was cheer'd, the harbour clear'd,
Merrily did we drop
Below the kirk, below the hill,
Below the lighthouse top.

The Mariner tells how the ship sailed southward with a good wind and fair weather, till it reached the Line.

The Sun came up upon the left,
Out of the sea came he!
And he shone bright, and on the right
Went down into the sea.

Higher and higher every day,
Till over the mast at noon——'
The Wedding-Guest here beat his breast,
For he heard the loud bassoon.

The Wedding-Guest heareth the bridal music; but the Mariner continueth his tale.

The bride hath paced into the hall,
Red as a rose is she;
Nodding their heads before her goes
The merry minstrelsy.

The Wedding-Guest he beat his breast,
Yet he cannot choose but hear;
And thus spake on that ancient man,
The bright-eyed Mariner:

The ship driven by a storm toward the South Pole.

'And now the Storm-blast came, and he
Was tyrannous and strong:
He struck with his o'ertaking wings,
And chased us south along.

With sloping masts and dipping prow,
As who pursued with yell and blow
Still treads the shadow of his foe,
And forward bends his head,
The ship drove fast, loud roar'd the blast,
And southward aye we fled.

And now there came both mist and snow
And it grew wondrous cold:
And ice, mast-high, came floating by,
As green as emerald.

And through the drifts the snowy clifts
Did send a dismal sheen;
Nor shapes of men nor beasts we ken—
The ice was all between.

The ice was here, the ice was there,
The ice was all around:
It crack'd and growl'd, and roar'd and howl'd,
Like noises in a swound!

At length did cross an Albatross,
Thorough the fog it came;
As if it had been a Christian soul,
We hail'd it in God's name.

It ate the food it ne'er had eat,
And round and round it flew.
The ice did split with a thunder-fit;
The helmsman steer'd us through!

And a good south wind sprung up behind;
The Albatross did follow,
And every day, for food or play,
Came to the mariners' hollo!

In mist or cloud, on mast or shroud,
It perch'd for vespers nine;
Whiles all the night, through fog-smoke white,
Glimmer'd the white moonshine.'

'God save thee, ancient Mariner,
From the fiends, that plague thee thus!—
Why look'st thou so?'—'With my crossbow
I shot the Albatross.

Part II

'The Sun now rose upon the right:
Out of the sea came he,
Still hid in mist, and on the left
Went down into the sea.

His shipmates cry out against the ancient Mariner for killing the bird of good luck.

And the good south wind still blew behind,
But no sweet bird did follow,
Nor any day for food or play
Came to the mariners' hollo!

And I had done a hellish thing,
And it would work 'em woe:
For all averr'd I had kill'd the bird
That made the breeze to blow.
Ah wretch! said they, the bird to slay
That made the breeze to blow!

But when the fog cleared off, they justify the same, and thus make themselves accomplices in the crime.

Nor dim nor red, like God's own head,
The glorious Sun uprist:
Then all averr'd I had kill'd the bird
That brought the fog and mist.
'Twas right, said they, such birds to slay,
That bring the fog and mist.

The fair breeze continues; the ship enters the Pacific Ocean, and sails northward, even till it reaches the Line.

The fair breeze blew, the white foam flew,
The furrow follow'd free;
We were the first that ever burst
Into that silent sea.

The ship hath been suddenly becalmed.

Down dropt the breeze, the sails dropt down,
'Twas sad as sad could be;
And we did speak only to break
The silence of the sea!

All in a hot and copper sky,
The bloody Sun, at noon,
Right up above the mast did stand,
No bigger than the Moon.

Day after day, day after day,
We stuck, nor breath nor motion;
As idle as a painted ship
Upon a painted ocean.

And the Albatross begins to be avenged.

Water, water, everywhere,
And all the boards did shrink;
Water, water, everywhere,
Nor any drop to drink.

The very deep did rot: O Christ!
That ever this should be!
Yea, slimy things did crawl with legs
Upon the slimy sea.

About, about, in reel and rout
The death-fires danced at night;
The water, like a witch's oils,
Burnt green, and blue, and white.

A Spirit had followed them: one of the invisible inhabitants of
this planet, neither departed souls nor angels; concerning whom
the learned Jew, Josephus, and the Platonic Constantinopolitan,
Michael Psellus, may be consulted. They are very numerous, and
there is no climate or element without one or more.

And some in dreams assurèd were
Of the Spirit that plagued us so;
Nine fathom deep he had follow'd us
From the land of mist and snow.

And every tongue, through utter drought,
Was wither'd at the root;
We could not speak, no more than if
We had been chok'd with soot.

The shipmates, in their sore distress, would fain throw the whole guilt on the ancient Mariner: in sign whereof they hang the dead sea-bird round his neck.

Ah! well-a-day! what evil looks
Had I from old and young!
Instead of the cross, the Albatross
About my neck was hung.

PART III

'There passed a weary time. Each throat
Was parch'd, and glazed each eye.
A weary time! a weary time!
How glazed each weary eye!
When looking westward, I beheld
A something in the sky.

The ancient Mariner beholdeth a sign in the element afar off.

At first it seem'd a little speck,
And then it seem'd a mist;
It mov'd and mov'd, and took at last
A certain shape, I wist.

A speck, a mist, a shape, I wist!
And still it near'd and near'd:
As if it dodg'd a water-sprite,
It plung'd, and tack'd, and veer'd.

At its nearer approach, it seemeth him to be a ship; and at a dear ransom he freeth his speech from the bonds of thirst.

With throats unslak'd, with black lips bak'd,
We could not laugh nor wail;
Through utter drought all dumb we stood!
I bit my arm, I suck'd the blood,
And cried, "A sail! a sail!"

With throats unslak'd, with black lips bak'd,
Agape they heard me call:
Gramercy! they for joy did grin,
And all at once their breath drew in,
As they were drinking all.

See! see! (I cried) she tacks no more
Hither to work us weal—
Without a breeze, without a tide,
She steadies with upright keel!

The western wave was all aflame,
The day was wellnigh done!
Almost upon the western wave
Rested the broad, bright Sun;
When that strange shape drove suddenly
Betwixt us and the Sun.

And straight the Sun was fleck'd with bars
(Heaven's Mother send us grace!)
As if through a dungeon-grate he peer'd
With broad and burning face.

Alas! (thought I, and my heart beat loud)
How fast she nears and nears!
Are those her sails that glance in the Sun,
Like restless gossameres?

Are those her ribs through which the Sun
Did peer, as through a grate?
And is that Woman all her crew?
Is that a Death? and are there two?
Is Death that Woman's mate?

Her lips were red, her looks were free,
Her locks were yellow as gold:
Her skin was as white as leprosy,
The Nightmare Life-in-Death was she,
Who thicks man's blood with cold.

Death and Life-in-Death have diced for the ship's crew, and she (the latter) winneth the ancient Mariner.

The naked hulk alongside came,
And the twain were casting dice;
"The game is done! I've won! I've won!"
Quoth she, and whistles thrice.

No twilight within the courts of the Sun.

The Sun's rim dips; the stars rush out:
At one stride comes the dark;
With far-heard whisper, o'er the sea,
Off shot the spectre-bark.

We listen'd and look'd sideways up!
Fear at my heart, as at a cup,
My life-blood seem'd to sip!
The stars were dim, and thick the night,
The steersman's face by his lamp gleam'd white;

At the rising of the Moon.

From the sails the dew did drip—
Till clomb above the eastern bar
The hornèd Moon, with one bright star
Within the nether tip.

One after another.

One after one, by the star-dogg'd Moon,
Too quick for groan or sigh,
Each turn'd his face with a ghastly pang,
And cursed me with his eye.

His shipmates drop down dead.

Four times fifty living men
(And I heard nor sigh nor groan),
With heavy thump, a lifeless lump,
They dropp'd down one by one.

The souls did from their bodies fly—
They fled to bliss or woe!
And every soul, it pass'd me by
Like the whizz of my crossbow!'

PART IV

The Wedding-Guest feareth that a spirit is talking to him.

'I fear thee, ancient Mariner!
I fear thy skinny hand!
And thou art long, and lank, and brown,
As is the ribb'd sea-sand.

But the ancient Mariner assureth him of his bodily life, and pro-
ceedeth to relate his horrible penance.

I fear thee and thy glittering eye,
And thy skinny hand so brown.'—
'Fear not, fear not, thou wedding guest!
This body dropt not down.

Alone, alone, all, all alone,
Alone on a wide, wide sea!
And never a saint took pity on
My soul in agony.

He despiseth the creatures of the calm.

The many men, so beautiful!
And they all dead did lie:
And a thousand thousand slimy things
Liv'd on; and so did I.

And envieth that they should live, and so many lie dead.

I look'd upon the rotting sea,
And drew my eyes away;
I look'd upon the rotting deck,
And there the dead men lay.

I look'd to heaven, and tried to pray;
But or ever a prayer had gusht,
A wicked whisper came, and made
My heart as dry as dust.

I clos'd my lids, and kept them close,
And the balls like pulses beat;
For the sky and the sea, and the sea and the sky,
Lay like a load on my weary eye,
And the dead were at my feet.

But the curse liveth for him in the eye of the dead men.
The cold sweat melted from their limbs,
Nor rot nor reek did they:
The look with which they look'd on me
Had never pass'd away.

An orphan's curse would drag to hell
A spirit from on high;
But oh! more horrible than that
Is the curse in a dead man's eye!
Seven days, seven nights, I saw that curse,
And yet I could not die.

In his loneliness and fixedness he yearneth towards the journeying Moon, and the stars that still sojourn, yet still move onward; and everywhere the blue sky belongs to them, and is their appointed rest and their native country and their own natural homes, which they enter unannounced, as lords that are certainly expected, and yet there is a silent joy at their arrival.
The moving Moon went up the sky,
And nowhere did abide;
Softly she was going up,
And a star or two beside—

Her beams bemock'd the sultry main,
Like April hoar-frost spread;
But where the ship's huge shadow lay,
The charmèd water burnt alway
A still and awful red.

By the light of the Moon he beholdeth God's creatures of the great calm.
Beyond the shadow of the ship,
I watch'd the water-snakes:
They moved in tracks of shining white,
And when they rear'd, the elfish light
Fell off in hoary flakes.

Within the shadow of the ship
I watch'd their rich attire:
Blue, glossy green, and velvet black,
They coil'd and swam; and every track
Was a flash of golden fire.

Their beauty and their happiness; he blesseth them in his heart.

O happy living things! no tongue
Their beauty might declare:
A spring of love gush'd from my heart,
And I bless'd them unaware:
Sure my kind saint took pity on me,
And I bless'd them unaware.

The Spell begins to break.

The self-same moment I could pray;
And from my neck so free
The Albatross fell off, and sank
Like lead into the sea.

PART V

'O sleep! it is a gentle thing,
Belov'd from pole to pole!
To Mary Queen the praise be given!
She sent the gentle sleep from Heaven,
That slid into my soul.

By grace of the holy Mother, the ancient Mariner is refreshed with rain.

The silly[1] buckets on the deck,
That had so long remain'd,
I dreamt that they were fill'd with dew;
And when I awoke, it rain'd.

My lips were wet, my throat was cold,
My garments all were dank;
Sure I had drunken in my dreams,
And still my body drank.

I mov'd, and could not feel my limbs:
I was so light—almost
I thought that I had died in sleep,
And was a blessèd ghost.

He heareth sounds and seeth strange sights and commotions in the sky and the element.

And soon I heard a roaring wind:
It did not come anear;
But with its sound it shook the sails,
That were so thin and sere.

The upper air burst into life!
And a hundred fire-flags sheen,
To and fro they were hurried about!
And to and fro, and in and out,
The wan stars danc'd between.

And the coming wind did roar more loud,
And the sails did sigh like sedge;
And the rain pour'd down from one black cloud;
The Moon was at its edge.

The thick black cloud was cleft, and still
The Moon was at its side;
Like waters shot from some high crag,
The lightning fell with never a jag,
A river steep and wide.

The bodies of the ship's crew are inspired, and the ship moves on.

The loud wind never reach'd the ship,
Yet now the ship mov'd on!
Beneath the lightning and the Moon
The dead men gave a groan.

They groan'd, they stirr'd, they all uprose,
Nor spake, nor mov'd their eyes;
It had been strange, even in a dream,
To have seen those dead men rise.

The helmsman steer'd, the ship mov'd on;
Yet never a breeze up-blew;
The mariners all 'gan work the ropes,
Where they were wont to do;
They rais'd their limbs like lifeless tools—
We were a ghastly crew.

The body of my brother's son
Stood by me, knee to knee:
The body and I pull'd at one rope,
But he said naught to me.'

But not by the souls of the men, nor by demons of earth or middle
air, but by a blessed troop of angelic spirits, sent down by the
invocation of the guardian saint.

'I fear thee, ancient Mariner!'
'Be calm, thou Wedding-Guest:
'Twas not those souls that fled in pain,
Which to their corses came again,
But a troop of spirits blest:

For when it dawn'd—they dropp'd their arms,
And cluster'd round the mast;
Sweet sounds rose slowly through their mouths,
And from their bodies pass'd.

Around, around, flew each sweet sound,
Then darted to the Sun;
Slowly the sounds came back again,
Now mix'd, now one by one.

Sometimes a-dropping from the sky
I heard the skylark sing;
Sometimes all little birds that are,
How they seem'd to fill the sea and air
With their sweet jargoning!

And now 'twas like all instruments,
Now like a lonely flute;
And now it is an angel's song,
That makes the Heavens be mute.

It ceas'd; yet still the sails made on
A pleasant noise till noon,
A noise like of a hidden brook
In the leafy month of June,
That to the sleeping woods all night
Singeth a quiet tune.

Till noon we quietly sail'd on,
Yet never a breeze did breathe:
Slowly and smoothly went the ship,
Mov'd onward from beneath.

The lonesome Spirit from the South Pole carries on the ship as far
as the Line, in obedience to the angelic troop, but still requireth
vengeance.

Under the keel nine fathom deep,
From the land of mist and snow,
The Spirit slid: and it was he
That made the ship to go.
The sails at noon left off their tune,
And the ship stood still also.

The Sun, right up above the mast,
Had fix'd her to the ocean;
But in a minute she 'gan stir,
With a short uneasy motion—
Backwards and forwards half her length
With a short uneasy motion.

Then like a pawing horse let go,
She made a sudden bound:
It flung the blood into my head,
And I fell down in a swound.

The Polar Spirit's fellow-demons, the invisible inhabitants of the
element, take part in his wrong; and two of them relate, one to the
other, that penance long and heavy for the ancient Mariner
hath been accorded to the Polar Spirit, who returneth southward.

How long in that same fit I lay,
I have not to declare;
But ere my living life return'd,
I heard, and in my soul discern'd
Two voices in the air.

"Is it he?" quoth one, "is this the man?
By Him who died on cross,
With his cruel bow he laid full low
The harmless Albatross.

The Spirit who bideth by himself
In the land of mist and snow,
He lov'd the bird that lov'd the man
Who shot him with his bow."

The other was a softer voice,
As soft as honey-dew:
Quoth he, "The man hath penance done,
And penance more will do."

PART VI

First Voice:

"But tell me, tell me! speak again,
Thy soft response renewing—
What makes that ship drive on so fast?
What is the Ocean doing?"

Second Voice:

"Still as a slave before his lord,
The Ocean hath no blast;
His great bright eye most silently
Up to the Moon is cast—

If he may know which way to go;
For she guides him smooth or grim.
See, brother, see! how graciously
She looketh down on him."

The Mariner hath been cast into a trance; for the angelic power
causeth the vessel to drive northward faster than human life could
endure.

First Voice:

"But why drives on that ship so fast,
Without or wave or wind?"

Second Voice:

"The air is cut away before,
And closes from behind.

Fly, brother, fly! more high, more high!
Or we shall be belated:
For slow and slow that ship will go,
When the Mariner's trance is abated."

The supernatural motion is retarded; the Mariner awakes, and his
penance begins anew.

I woke, and we were sailing on
As in a gentle weather:
'Twas night, calm night, the Moon was high;
The dead men stood together.

All stood together on the deck,
For a charnel-dungeon fitter:
All fix'd on me their stony eyes,
That in the Moon did glitter.

The pang, the curse, with which they died,
Had never pass'd away:
I could not draw my eyes from theirs,
Nor turn them up to pray.

The curse is finally expiated.

And now this spell was snapt: once more
I viewed the ocean green,
And look'd far forth, yet little saw
Of what had else been seen—

Like one that on a lonesome road
Doth walk in fear and dread,
And having once turn'd round, walks on,
And turns no more his head;
Because he knows a frightful fiend
Doth close behind him tread.

But soon there breath'd a wind on me,
Nor sound nor motion made:
Its path was not upon the sea,
In ripple or in shade.

It rais'd my hair, it fann'd my cheek
Like a meadow-gale of spring—
It mingled strangely with my fears,
Yet it felt like a welcoming.

Swiftly, swiftly flew the ship,
Yet she sail'd softly too:
Sweetly, sweetly blew the breeze—
On me alone it blew.

And the ancient Mariner beholdeth his native country.

O dream of joy! is this indeed
The lighthouse top I see?
Is this the hill? is this the kirk?
Is this mine own countree?

We drifted o'er the harbour-bar,
And I with sobs did pray—
O let me be awake, my God!
Or let me sleep alway.

The harbour-bay was clear as glass,
So smoothly it was strewn!
And on the bay the moonlight lay,
And the shadow of the Moon.

The rock shone bright, the kirk no less
That stands above the rock:
The moonlight steep'd in silentness
The steady weathercock.

The angelic spirits leave the dead bodies.

And the bay was white with silent light,
Till rising from the same,
Full many shapes, that shadows were,
In crimson colours came.

And appear in their own form of light.

A little distance from the prow
Those crimson shadows were:
I turn'd my eyes upon the deck—
O Christ! what saw I there!

Each corse lay flat, lifeless and flat,
And, by the holy rood!
A man all light, a seraph-man,
On every corse there stood.

This seraph-band, each wav'd his hand:
It was a heavenly sight!
They stood as signals to the land,
Each one a lovely light;

This seraph-band, each wav'd his hand,
No voice did they impart—
No voice; but O, the silence sank
Like music on my heart.

But soon I heard the dash of oars,
I heard the Pilot's cheer;
My head was turn'd perforce away,
And I saw a boat appear.

The Pilot and the Pilot's boy,
I heard them coming fast:
Dear Lord in Heaven! it was a joy
The dead men could not blast.

I saw a third—I heard his voice:
It is the Hermit good!
He singeth loud his godly hymns
That he makes in the wood.
He'll shrieve my soul, he'll wash away
The Albatross's blood.

PART VII

'This Hermit good lives in that wood
Which slopes down to the sea.
How loudly his sweet voice he rears!
He loves to talk with marineres
That come from a far countree.

He kneels at morn, and noon, and eve—
He hath a cushion plump:
It is the moss that wholly hides
The rotted old oak-stump.

The skiff-boat near'd: I heard them talk,
"Why, this is strange, I trow!
Where are those lights so many and fair,
That signal made but now?"

"Strange, by my faith!" the Hermit said—
"And they answer'd not our cheer!
The planks look warp'd! and see those sails,
How thin they are and sere!
I never saw aught like to them,
Unless perchance it were

Brown skeletons of leaves that lag
My forest-brook along;
When the ivy-tod is heavy with snow,
And the owlet whoops to the wolf below,
That eats the she-wolf's young."

"Dear Lord! it hath a fiendish look—
(The Pilot made reply)
I am a-fear'd."—"Push on, push on!"
Said the Hermit cheerily.

The boat came closer to the ship,
But I nor spake nor stirr'd;
The boat came close beneath the ship,
And straight a sound was heard.

Under the water it rumbled on,
Still louder and more dread:
It reach'd the ship, it split the bay;
The ship went down like lead.

Stunn'd by that loud and dreadful sound,
Which sky and ocean smote,
Like one that hath been seven days drown'd
My body lay afloat;
But swift as dreams, myself I found
Within the Pilot's boat.

Upon the whirl, where sank the ship
The boat spun round and round;
And all was still, save that the hill
Was telling of the sound.

I mov'd my lips—the Pilot shriek'd
And fell down in a fit;
The holy Hermit rais'd his eyes,
And pray'd where he did sit.

I took the oars: the Pilot's boy,
Who now doth crazy go,
Laugh'd loud and long, and all the while
His eyes went to and fro.
"Ha! ha!" quoth he, "full plain I see
The Devil knows how to row."

And now, all in my own countree,
I stood on the firm land!
The Hermit stepp'd forth from the boat,
And scarcely could he stand.

"O shrieve me, shrieve me, holy man!"
The Hermit cross'd his brow.
"Say quick," quoth he, "I bid thee say—
What manner of man art thou?"

Forthwith this frame of mine was wrench'd
With a woeful agony,
Which forc'd me to begin my tale;
And then it left me free.

And ever and anon throughout his future life an agony con-
straineth him to travel from land to land.

Since then, at an uncertain hour,
That agony returns:
And till my ghastly tale is told,
This heart within me burns.

I pass, like night, from land to land;
I have strange power of speech;
That moment that his face I see,
I know the man that must hear me:
To him my tale I teach.

What loud uproar bursts from that door!
The wedding-guests are there:
But in the garden-bower the bride
And bride-maids singing are:
And hark the little vesper bell,
Which biddeth me to prayer!

O Wedding-Guest! this soul hath been
Alone on a wide, wide sea:
So lonely 'twas, that God himself
Scarce seemèd there to be.

O sweeter than the marriage-feast,
'Tis sweeter far to me,
To walk together to the kirk
With a goodly company!—

To walk together to the kirk,
And all together pray,
While each to his great Father bends,
Old men, and babes, and loving friends,
And youths and maidens gay!

And to teach, by his own example, love and reverence to all
things that God made and loveth.

Farewell, farewell! but this I tell
To thee, thou Wedding-Guest!
He prayeth well, who loveth well
Both man and bird and beast.

He prayeth best, who loveth best
All things both great and small;
For the dear God who loveth us,
He made and loveth all.'

The Mariner, whose eye is bright,
Whose beard with age is hoar,
Is gone: and now the Wedding-Guest
Turn'd from the bridegroom's door.

He went like one that hath been stunn'd,
And is of sense forlorn:
A sadder and a wiser man
He rose the morrow morn.

Samuel Taylor Coleridge

¹ useless

659   I mix in life

I mix in life, and labour to seem free,
    With common persons pleased and common things,
While every thought and action tends to thee,
    And every impulse from thy influence springs.

Samuel Taylor Coleridge

660   This lime-tree bower my prison (*addressed to Charles
Lamb*)

Well, they are gone, and here must I remain,
This lime-tree bower my prison! I have lost
Beauties and feelings, such as would have been
Most sweet to my remembrance, even when age
Had dimmed mine eyes to blindness! They, meanwhile,

Friends, whom I never more may meet again,
On springy heath, along the hill-top edge,
Wander in gladness, and wind down, perchance,
To that still roaring dell, of which I told;
The roaring dell, o'erwooded, narrow, deep,
And only speckled by the mid-day sun;
Where its slim trunk the ash from rock to rock
Flings arching like a bridge; —That branchless ash,
Unsunned and damp, whose few poor yellow leaves
Ne'er tremble in the gale, yet tremble still,
Fanned by the water-fall! and there my friends
Behold the dark green file of long lank weeds,
That all at once (a most fantastic sight!)
Still nod and drip beneath the dripping edge
Of the blue clay-stone.

          Now, my friends emerge
Beneath the wide wide heaven—and view again
The many-steepled tract magnificent
Of hilly fields and meadows, and the sea,
With some fair bark, perhaps, whose sails light up
The slip of smooth clear blue betwixt two isles
Of purple shadow. Yes! they wander on
In gladness all; but thou, methinks, most glad,
My gentle-hearted Charles! for thou hast pined
And hungered after Nature, many a year,
In the great City pent, winning thy way
With sad yet patient soul, through evil and pain
And strange calamity. Ah! slowly sink
Behind the western ridge, thou glorious Sun!
Shine in the slant beams of the sinking orb,
Ye purple heath flowers! richlier burn ye clouds!
Live in the yellow light, ye distant groves!
And kindle, thou blue Ocean! So my friend
Struck with deep joy may stand, as I have stood,
Silent with swimming sense; yea, gazing round
On the wide landscape, gaze till all doth seem
Less gross than bodily; and of such hues
As veil the Almighty Spirit, when yet he makes
Spirits perceive his presence.

A delight
Comes sudden on my heart, and I am glad
As I myself were there! Nor in this bower,
This little lime-tree bower, have I not marked
Much that has soothed me. Pale beneath the blaze
Hung the transparent foliage; and I watched
Some broad and sunny leaf, and loved to see
The shadow of the leaf and stem above
Dappling its sunshine! And that walnut-tree
Was richly tinged, and a deep radiance lay
Full on the ancient ivy, which usurps
Those fronting elms, and now, with blackest mass
Makes their dark branches gleam a lighter hue
Through the late twilight: and though now the bat
Wheels silent by, and not a swallow twitters,
Yet still the solitary bumble-bee
Sings in the bean-flower! Henceforth I shall know
That Nature ne'er deserts the wise and pure;
No plot so narrow, be but Nature there,
No waste so vacant, but may well employ
Each faculty of sense, and keep the heart
Awake to love and beauty! And sometimes
'Tis well to be bereft of promised good,
That we may lift the soul, and contemplate
With lively joy the joys we cannot share.
My gentle-hearted Charles! when the last rook
Beat its straight path along the dusky air
Homewards, I blest it! deeming its black wing
(Now a dim speck, now vanishing in light)
Had crossed the mighty Orb's dilated glory,
While thou stood'st gazing; or, when all was still,
Flew creeking o'er thy head, and had a charm
For thee, my gentle-hearted Charles, to whom
No sound is dissonant which tells of Life.

Samuel Taylor Coleridge

661   *Frost at midnight*

The Frost performs its secret ministry,
Unhelped by any wind. The owlet's cry

Came loud—and hark, again! loud as before.
The inmates of my cottage, all at rest,
Have left me to that solitude, which suits
Abstruser musings: save that at my side
My cradled infant slumbers peacefully.
'Tis calm indeed! so calm, that it disturbs
And vexes meditation with its strange
And extreme silentness. Sea, hill, and wood,
This populous village! Sea, hill, and wood,
With all the numberless goings-on of life,
Inaudible as dreams! the thin blue flame
Lies on my low-burnt fire, and quivers not;
Only that film,[1] which fluttered on the grate,
Still flutters there, the sole unquiet thing.
Methinks, its motion in this hush of nature
Gives it dim sympathies with me who live,
Making it a companionable form,
Whose puny flaps and freaks the idling Spirit
By its own moods interprets, every where
Echo or mirror seeking of itself,
And makes a toy of Thought.

              But O! how oft,
How oft, at school, with most believing mind,
Presageful, have I gazed upon the bars,
To watch that fluttering stranger! and as oft
With unclosed lids, already had I dreamt
Of my sweet birth-place, and the old church tower,
Whose bells, the poor man's only music, rang
From morn to evening, all the hot Fair-day,
So sweetly, that they stirred and haunted me
With a wild pleasure, falling on mine ear
Most like articulate sounds of things to come!
So gazed I, till the soothing things I dreamt
Lulled me to sleep, and sleep prolonged my dreams!
And so I brooded all the following morn,
Awed by the stern preceptor's face, mine eye
Fixed with mock study on my swimming book;
Save if the door half opened, and I snatched
A hasty glance, and still my heart leaped up,

For still I hoped to see the stranger's face,
Townsman, or aunt, or sister more beloved,
My playmate when we both were clothed alike!

   Dear Babe, that sleepest cradled by my side,
Whose gentle breathings, heard in this deep calm,
Fill up the interspersèd vacancies
And momentary pauses of the thought!
My babe so beautiful! it thrills my heart
With tender gladness, thus to look at thee,
And think that thou shalt learn far other lore,
And in far other scenes! For I was reared
In the great city, pent mid cloisters dim,
And saw nought lovely but the sky and stars.
But thou, my babe! shalt wander like a breeze
By lakes and sandy shores, beneath the crags
Of ancient mountain, and beneath the clouds,
Which image in their bulk both lakes and shores
And mountain crags: so shalt thou see and hear
The lovely shapes and sounds intelligible
Of that eternal language, which thy God
Utters, who from eternity doth teach
Himself in all, and all things in himself.
Great universal Teacher! he shall mould
Thy spirit, and by giving make it ask.

   Therefore all seasons shall be sweet to thee,
Whether the summer clothe the general earth
With greenness, or the redbreast sit and sing
Betwixt the tufts of snow on the bare branch
Of mossy apple-tree, while the nigh thatch
Smokes in the sun-thaw; whether the eave-drops fall
Heard only in the trances of the blast,
Or if the secret ministry of frost
Shall hang them up in silent icicles,
Quietly shining to the moon.

Samuel Taylor Coleridge

1 *films* were called *strangers*, and portended the arrival of
some absent friend

Ere on my bed my limbs I lay,
It hath not been my use to pray
With moving lips or bended knees;
But silently, by slow degrees,
My spirits I to Love compose,
In humble trust mine eye-lids close,
With reverential resignation,
No wish conceived, no thought expressed,
Only a sense of supplication;
A sense o'er all my soul impressed
That I am weak, yet not unblest,
Since in me, round me, everywhere
Eternal Strength and Wisdom are.

But yesternight I prayed aloud
In anguish and in agony,
Up-starting from the fiendish crowd
Of shapes and thoughts that tortured me:
A lurid light, a trampling throng,
Sense of intolerable wrong,
And whom I scorned, those only strong!
Thirst of revenge, the powerless will
Still baffled, and yet burning still!
Desire with loathing strangely mixed
On wild or hateful objects fixed.
Fantastic passions! maddening brawl!
And shame and terror over all!
Deeds to be hid which were not hid,
Which all confused I could not know
Whether I suffered, or I did:
For all seemed guilt, remorse or woe,
My own or others still the same
Life-stifling fear, soul-stifling shame.

So two nights passed: the night's dismay
Saddened and stunned the coming day.
Sleep, the wide blessing, seemed to me
Distemper's worst calamity.

The third night, when my own loud scream
Had waked me from the fiendish dream,
O'ercome with sufferings strange and wild,
I wept as I had been a child;
And having thus by tears subdued
My anguish to a milder mood,
Such punishments, I said, were due
To natures deepliest stained with sin,—
For aye entempesting anew
The unfathomable hell within,
The horror of their deeds to view,
To know and loathe, yet wish and do!
Such griefs with such men well agree,
But wherefore, wherefore fall on me?
To be beloved is all I need,
And whom I love, I love indeed.

Samuel Taylor Coleridge

663   *On Donne's poetry*

With Donne, whose muse on dromedary trots,
Wreathe iron pokers into true-love knots;
Rhyme's sturdy cripple, fancy's maze and clue,
Wit's forge and fire-blast, meaning's press and screw.

Samuel Taylor Coleridge

664   *The knight's tomb*

Where is the grave of Sir Arthur O'Kellyn?
Where may the grave of that good man be?—
By the side of a spring, on the breast of Helvellyn,
Under the twigs of a young birch tree!
The oak that in summer was sweet to hear,
And rustled its leaves in the fall of the year,
And whistled and roared in the winter alone,

Is gone,—and the birch in its stead is grown.—
The Knight's bones are dust,
And his good sword rust;—
His soul is with the saints, I trust.

Samuel Taylor Coleridge

665 *Dejection (a letter to Sara Hutchinson, April 1802)*

Well, if the bard was weatherwise, who made
The grand old ballad of Sir Patrick Spence,
This night, so tranquil now, will not go hence
Unroused by winds, that ply a busier trade
Than that, which moulds yon clouds in lazy flakes,
Or the dull sobbing draft, that drones and rakes
Upon the strings of this Eolian lute,
      Which better far were mute.
For lo, the new moon, winter-bright!
And overspread with phantom light,
(With swimming phantom light o'erspread
But rimmed and circled with a silver thread)
I see the old moon in her lap foretelling
The coming-on of rain and squally blast—
O Sara! that the gust ev'n now were swelling,
And the slant night-shower driving loud and fast!

A grief without a pang, void, dark and drear,
A stifling, drowsy, unimpassioned grief
That finds no natural outlet, no relief
      In word, or sigh, or tear—
This Sara! well thou knowest,
Is that sore evil, which I dread the most,
And oft'nest suffer! In this heartless mood,
To other thoughts by yonder throstle wooed,
That pipes within the larch tree, not unseen,
(The larch, which pushes out in tassles green
Its bundled leafits) wooed to mild delights
By all the tender sounds and gentle sights
Of this sweet primrose-month—and vainly wooed

O dearest Sara, in this heartless mood
All this long eve, so balmy and serene,
Have I been gazing on the western sky
And its peculiar tint of yellow-green—
And still I gaze—and with how blank an eye!
And those thin clouds above, in flakes and bars,
That give away their motion to the stars;
Those stars, that glide behind them, or between,
Now sparkling, now bedimmed, but always seen;
Yon crescent moon, as fixed as if it grew
In its own cloudless, starless lake of blue—
A boat becalmed! dear William's Sky Canoe!
—I see them all, so excellently fair!
  I see, not feel, how beautiful they are.

      My genial spirits fail—
      And what can these avail
To lift the smothering weight from off my breast?
      It were a vain endeavour,
      Though I should gaze for ever
On that green light which lingers in the west!
I may not hope from outward forms to win
The passion and the life whose fountains are within!
These lifeless shapes, around, below, above,
      O what can they impart?
When even the gentle thought, that thou, my love
      Art gazing now, like me,
      And see'st the heaven I see—
Sweet thought it is—yet feebly stirs my heart!

      Feebly! O feebly!—Yet
      (I well remember it)
In my first dawn of youth that fancy stole
With many secret yearnings on my soul.
At eve, sky-gazing in 'ecstatic fit'
(Alas! for cloistered in a city school
The sky was all I knew of, beautiful)
At the barred window often did I sit,
And oft upon the leaded school roof lay,
      And to myself would say—

There does not live the man so stripped of good
       affections
As not to love to see a maiden's quiet eyes
Upraised, and linking on sweet dreams by dim connec-
       tions
To moon, or Evening Star, or glorious western skies—
While yet a boy this thought would so pursue me
That often it became a kind of vision to me.

    Sweet thought! and dear of old
    To hearts of finer mould;
Ten thousand times by friends and lovers blest.
    I spake with rash despair,
    And ere I was aware,
The weight was somewhat lifted from my breast.
O Sara, in that weather-fended wood,
Thy loved haunt, where the stock-doves coo at noon,
    I guess, that thou hast stood
And watched yon crescent, and its ghost-like moon.
And yet, far rather in my present mood
I would, that thou'dst been sitting all this while
Upon the sod-built Seat of Camomile—
And though thy robin may have ceased to sing,
Yet needs for my sake must thou love to hear
    The bee-hive murmuring near,
That ever-busy and most quiet thing
Which I have heard at midnight murmuring.

    I feel my spirit moved—
    And wheresoe'er thou be,
    O Sister! O Beloved!
    Those dear mild eyes, that see
    Even now the heaven I see—
There is a prayer in them: it is for me—
And I, dear Sara, I am blessing thee!

It was as calm as this, that happy night
When Mary, thou and I together were,
The low decaying fire our only light,
And listened to the stillness of the air.

O that affectionate and blameless maid,
Dear Mary! on her lap my head she laid—
    Her hand was on my brow,
    Even as my own is now;
And on my cheek I felt thy eye-lash play.
Such joy had I, that I may truly say,
My spirit was awe-stricken with the excess
And trance-like depth of its brief happiness.

Ah fair remembrances, that so revive
The heart, and fill it with a living power,
Where were they Sara?—or did I not strive
To win them to me?—on the fretting hour
Then when I wrote thee that complaining scroll
Which even to bodily sickness bruised thy soul!
And yet thou blam'st thyself alone; and yet
    Forbidd'st me all regret!

And I must not regret that I distressed
Thee, best beloved, who lovest me the best?
My better mind had fled, I know not wither,
For O! was this an absent friend's employ
To send from far both pain and sorrow thither
Where still his blessings should have called down joy!
I read thy guileless letter o'er again—
I hear thee of thy blameless self complain—
And only this I learn—and this alas, I know—
That thou art weak and pale with sickness, grief and
    pain—
    And I—I made thee so!

O for my own sake I regret perforce
Whatever turns thee, Sara, from the course
Of calm well-being and a heart at rest.
When thou, and with thee those whom thou lov'st best,
Shall dwell together in one happy home,
One house, the dear abiding home of all,
I too will crown me with a coronal—
Nor shall this heart in idle wishes roam

Morbidly soft!
No, let me trust that I shall wear away
In no inglorious toils the manly day,
And only now and then, and not too oft,
Some dear and memorable eve will bless
Dreaming of all your loves and quietness.
Be happy, and I need thee not in sight.
Peace in thy heart, and quiet in thy dwelling,
Health in thy limbs, and in thine eyes the light
Of love, and hope, and honourable feeling—
Where e'er I am I shall be well content!
Not near thee, haply shall be more content!
To all things I prefer the permanent.
And better seems it for a heart, like mine,
Always to know, than sometimes to behold,
        Their happiness, and thine—
For change doth trouble me with pangs untold!
To see thee, hear thee, feel thee—then to part,
        Oh! it weighs down the heart!
To visit those I love, as I love thee,
Mary, William, and dear Dorothy,
It is but a temptation to repine—
The transientness is poison in the wine,
Eats out the pith of joy, makes all joy hollow,
All pleasure a dim dream of pain to follow!
My own peculiar lot, my house-hold life
It is, and will remain, indifference or strife.
While ye are well and happy, 'twould but wrong you
If I should fondly yearn to be among you—
Wherefore, O wherefore should I wish to be
A withered branch upon a blossoming tree?

But, (let me say it, for I vainly strive
To beat away the thought) but if thou pined,
Whate'er the cause, in body or in mind,
I were the miserablest man alive
To know it and be absent! Thy delights
Far off, or near, alike I may partake—
But O, to mourn for thee, and to forsake

All power, all hope of giving comfort to thee—
To know that thou art weak and worn with pain,
And not to hear thee, Sara! not to view thee—
    Not to sit beside thy bed,
    Not to press thy aching head,
    Not to bring thee health again—
    At least to hope, to try—
By this voice, which thou lov'st, and by this earnest
    eye—
Nay, wherefore did I let it haunt my mind
    The dark distressful dream!
I turn from it, and listen to the wind
Which long has raved unnoticed. What a scream
Of agony by torture lengthened out
That lute sent forth! O thou wild storm without!
Jagg'd rock, or mountain pond, or blasted tree,
Or pine-grove, wither woodman never clomb,
Or lonely house, long held the witch's home,
Methinks were fitter instruments for thee,
Mad lutanist! that in this month of showers,
Of dark brown gardens, and of peeping flowers,
Mak'st Devil's Yule, with worse than wintry song
The blossoms, buds, and timorous leaves among.
Thou actor, perfect in all tragic sounds!
Thou mighty poet, even to frenzy bold!
    What tell'st thou now about?
'Tis of the rushing of an host in rout—
And many groans from men with smarting wounds—
At once they groan with smart, and shudder with the
    cold!
'Tis hushed: there is a trance of deepest silence,
Again! but all that sound, as of a rushing crowd,
And groans and tremulous shudderings, all are over—
And it has other sounds, all less deep, less loud!
    A tale of less affright,
    And tempered with delight,
As William's self had made the tender lay—
    'Tis of a little child
    Upon a heathy wild,
Not far from home—but it has lost its way—

And now moans low in utter grief and fear—
And now screams loud, and hopes to make its mother
      hear!

'Tis midnight, and small thoughts have I of sleep—
Full seldom may my friend such vigils keep—
O breathe she softly in her gentle sleep!
Cover her, gentle Sleep, with wings of healing.
And be this tempest but a mountain birth!
May all the stars hang bright above her dwelling,
Silent, as though they watched the sleeping earth!
Healthful and light, my darling, may'st thou rise
      With clear and cheerful eyes—
And of the same good tidings to me send!
      For O, beloved friend,
I am not the buoyant thing I was of yore:
When I like an own child, I to Joy belonged;
For others mourning oft, myself oft sorely wronged,
Yet bearing all things then, as if I nothing bore!

      Yes, dearest Sara, yes!
There was a time when though my path was rough
The joy within me dallied with distress;
And all misfortunes were but as the stuff
Whence fancy made me dreams of happiness:
For hope grew round me, like a climbing vine,
And leaves and fruitage, not my own, seemed mine!
But now ill-tidings bow me down to earth
Nor care I, that they rob me of my mirth;
      But O, each visitation
Suspends what Nature gave me at my birth,
      My shaping Spirit of Imagination!

I speak not now of those habitual ills
That wear out life, when two unequal minds
Meet in one house, and two discordant wills—
      This leaves me, where it finds,
Past cure, and past complaint—a fate austere
Too fixed and hopeless to partake of fear.

But thou, dear Sara (dear indeed thou art,
My comforter, my heart within my heart!)
Thou, and the few we love, though few ye be,
Make up a world of hopes and fears for me.
And if Affliction, or distempering Pain,
Or wayward Chance befall you, I complain
Not that I mourn—O friends most dear, most true,
    Methinks to weep with you
Were better far than to rejoice alone—
But that my coarse domestic life has known
No habits of heart-nursing sympathy,
No griefs, but such as dull and deaden me,
No mutual mild enjoyments of its own,
No hopes of its own vintage, none, O none—
Whence when I mourned for you, my heart might
    borrow
Fair forms and living motions for its sorrow.
For not to think of what I needs must feel,
But to be still and patient all I can;
And haply by abstruse research to steal
From my own nature all the natural man—
This was my sole resource, my wisest plan!
And that which suits a part, infects the whole,
And now is almost grown the temper of my soul.

  My little children are a joy, a love,
    A good gift from above!
But what is bliss that still calls up a woe,
    And makes it doubly keen
Compelling me to feel, as well as know,
What a most blessed lot mine might have been.
Those little angel children (woe is me!)
There have been hours, when feeling how they bind
And pluck out the wing-feathers of my mind,
Turning my error to necessity,
I have half wished they never had been born!
That, seldom! But sad thoughts they always bring,
And like a poet's Philomel, I sing
My love-song, with my breast against a thorn.

With no unthankful spirit I confess,
This clinging grief too, in its turn, awakes
That love, and father's joy; but O! it makes
The love the greater, and the joy far less.
These mountains too, these vales, these woods, these
    lakes,
Scenes full of beauty and of loftiness
Where all my life I fondly hoped to live—
I were sunk low indeed, did they no solace give;
But oft I seem to feel, and evermore I fear,
They are not to me now the things, which once they were.

O Sara, we receive but what we give,
And in our life alone does nature live.
Ours is her wedding garment, ours her shroud—
And would we aught behold of higher worth
Than that inanimate cold world allowed
To the poor loveless, ever-anxious crowd,
Ah! from the soul itself must issue forth
A light, a glory, and a luminous cloud
    Enveloping the earth!
And from the soul itself must there be sent
A sweet and potent voice, of its own birth,
Of all sweet sounds the life and element.

O pure of heart! thou needst not ask of me
What this strong music in the soul may be,
    What, and wherein it doth exist,
This light, this glory, this fair luminous mist,
This beautiful and beauty-making power!
Joy, innocent Sara: joy that ne'er was given
Save to the pure, and in their purest hour,
Joy Sara, is the spirit and the power,
That wedding nature to us gives in dower
    A new earth and new heaven,
Undreamt of by the sensual and the proud!
Joy is that strong voice, joy that luminous cloud—
    We, we ourselves rejoice!
And thence flows all that charms or ear or sight,
All melodies the echoes of that voice,
All colours a suffusion of that light.

Sister and friend of my devoutest choice!
Thou being innocent and full of love,
And nested with the darlings of thy love,
And feeling in thy soul, heart, lips, and arms
Even what the conjugal and mother dove
That borrows genial warmth from those she warms,
Feels in her thrilled wings, blessedly outspread—
Thou freed awhile from cares and human dread
By the immenseness of the good and fair
    Which thou see'st everywhere—
Thus, thus should'st thou rejoice!
To thee would all things live from pole to pole,
Their life the eddying of thy living soul—
    O dear! O innocent! O full of love!
A very friend! A sister of my choice—
O dear, as light and impulse from above,
Thus may'st thou ever, evermore rejoice!

Samuel Taylor Coleridge

666 *Well I remember how you smiled*

Well I remember how you smiled
    To see me write your name upon
The soft sea-sand . . . 'O! *what a child!*
    You think you're writing upon stone!

I have since written what no tide
    Shall ever wash away, what men
Unborn shall read o'er ocean wide
    And find Ianthe's name again.

Walter Savage Landor

667 *Rose Aylmer*

Ah what avails the sceptred race!
    Ah what the form divine!
What every virtue, every grace!
    Rose Aylmer, all were thine.

Rose Aylmer, whom these wakeful eyes
    May weep, but never see,
A night of memories and sighs
    I consecrate to thee.

Walter Savage Landor

668   *Dirce*

Stand close around, ye Stygian set,
    With Dirce in one boat conveyed!
Or Charon, seeing, may forget
    That he is old and she a shade.

Walter Savage Landor

669   *Mild is the parting year*

Mild is the parting year, and sweet
    The odour of the falling spray;
Life passes on more rudely fleet,
    And balmless is its closing day.

I wait its close, I court its gloom,
    But mourn that never must there fall
Or on my breast or on my tomb
    The tear that would have soothed it all.

Walter Savage Landor

670   *Past ruined Ilion Helen lives*

Past ruined Ilion Helen lives,
    Alcestis rises from the shades;
Verse calls them forth; 'tis verse that gives
    Immortal youth to mortal maids.

Soon shall Oblivion's deepening veil
  Hide all the peopled hills you see,
The gay, the proud, while lovers hail
  In distant ages you and me.

The tear for fading beauty's cheek,
  For passing glory cease to sigh;
One form shall rise above the wreck,
  One name, Ianthe, shall not die.

Walter Savage Landor

671   *Years*

Years, many parti-colour'd years,
  Some have crept on, and some have flown
Since first before me fell those tears
  I never could see fall alone.

Years, not so many, are to come,
  Years not so varied, when from you
One more will fall: when, carried home,
  I see it not, nor hear *Adieu*.

Walter Savage Landor

672   *The old familiar faces*

I have had playmates, I have had companions
In my days of childhood, in my joyful school-days;
All, all are gone, the old familiar faces.

I have been laughing, I have been carousing,
Drinking late, sitting late, with my bosom cronies;
All, all are gone, the old familiar faces.

I loved a love once, fairest among women:
Closed are her doors on me, I must not see her—
All, all are gone, the old familiar faces.

I have a friend, a kinder friend has no man:
Like an ingrate, I left my friend abruptly;
Left him, to muse on the old familiar faces.

Ghost-like I paced round the haunts of my childhood,
Earth seemed a desert I was bound to traverse,
Seeking to find the old familiar faces.

Friend of my bosom, thou more than a brother,
Why wert thou not born in my father's dwelling?
So we might talk of the old familiar faces.

How some they have died, and some they have left me,
And some are taken from me; all are departed;
All, all are gone, the old familiar faces.

Charles Lamb

673 *In my own album*

Fresh clad from heaven in robes of white,
A young probationer of light,
Thou wert, my soul, an album bright,

A spotless leaf; but thought, and care,
And friend and foe, in foul or fair,
Have 'written strange defeatures' there;

And Time, with heaviest hand of all,
Like that fierce writing on the wall.
Hath stamped sad dates—he can't recall;

And error, gliding worst designs—
Like speckled snake that strays and shines—
Betrays his path by crooked lines;

And vice hath left his ugly blot;
And good resolves, a moment hot,
Fairly began—but finished not;

And fruitless, late remorse doth trace—
Like Hebrew lore, a backward pace—
Her irrecoverable race.

Disjointed numbers; sense unknit;
Huge reams of folly; shreds of wit;
Compose the mingled mass of it.

My scalded eyes no longer brook
Upon this ink-blurred thing to look—
Go, shut the leaves, and clasp the book.

Charles Lamb

674 *To night*

Mysterious Night! when our first parent knew
Thee from report divine, and heard thy name,
Did he not tremble for this lovely frame,
This glorious canopy of light and blue?
Yet 'neath a curtain of translucent dew,
Bathed in the rays of the great setting flame,
Hesperus with the host of heaven came,
And lo! Creation widened in man's view.
Who could have thought such darkness lay concealed
Within thy beams, O sun! or who could find,
Whilst fly and leaf and insect stood revealed,
That to such countless orbs thou mad'st us blind!
Why do we then shun death with anxious strife?
If Light can thus deceive, wherefore not Life?

Joseph Blanco White

675 *The battle of the Baltic*

I

Of Nelson and the North,
Sing the glorious day's renown,
When to battle fierce came forth
All the might of Denmark's crown,

And her arms along the deep proudly shone;
By each gun the lighted brand,
In a bold determined hand,
And the Prince of all the land
Led them on.—

II

Like leviathans afloat,
Lay their bulwarks on the brine,
While the sign of battle flew
On the lofty British line:
It was ten of April morn by the chime:
As they drifted on their path,
There was silence deep as death;
And the boldest held his breath
For a time.—

III

But the might of England flush'd
To anticipate the scene;
And her van the fleeter rush'd
O'er the deadly space between.
'Hearts of oak!' our captains cried; when each gun
From its adamantine lips
Spread a death-shade round the ships,
Like the hurricane eclipse
Of the sun.

IV

Again! again! again!
And the havoc did not slack,
Till a feeble cheer the Dane,
To our cheering sent us back;—
Their shots along the deep slowly boom:—
Then ceased—and all is wail,
As they strike the shatter'd sail,
Or, in conflagration pale,
Light the gloom.—

Out spoke the victor then,
As he hail'd them o'er the wave:
'Ye are brothers! ye are men!
And we conquer but to save;—
So peace instead of death let us bring;
But yield, proud foe, thy fleet,
With the crews, at England's feet,
And make submission meet
To our King.'—

Then Denmark bless'd our chief,
That he gave her wounds repose;
And the sounds of joy and grief
From her people wildly rose,
As death withdrew his shades from the day.
While the sun look'd smiling bright
O'er a wide and woeful sight,
Where the fires of funeral light
Died away.

Now joy, old England, raise!
For the tidings of thy might,
By the festal cities' blaze,
While the wine-cup shines in light;
And yet amidst that joy and uproar,
Let us think of them that sleep,
Full many a fathom deep,
By thy wild and stormy steep,
Elsinore!

Brave hearts! to Britain's pride
Once so faithful and so true,
On the deck of fame that died,—
With the gallant good Riou;

Soft sigh the winds of heaven o'er their grave!
While the billow mournful rolls,
And the mermaid's song condoles,
Singing glory to the souls
Of the brave!—

Thomas Campbell

676 *Ye mariners of England*

Ye mariners of England
 That guard our native seas!
Whose flag has braved a thousand years,
The battle and the breeze!
Your glorious standard launch again
To match another foe:
And sweep through the deep,
While the stormy winds do blow;
While the battle rages loud and long
And the stormy winds do blow.

The spirits of your fathers
Shall start from every wave—
For the deck it was their field of fame,
And Ocean was their grave:
Where Blake and mighty Nelson fell
 Your manly hearts shall glow,
As ye sweep through the deep,
While the stormy winds do blow;
While the battle rages loud and long
And the stormy winds do blow.

Britannia needs no bulwarks,
No towers along the steep;
Her march is o'er the mountain waves,
Her home is on the deep.
With thunders from her native oak
She quells the floods below—
As they roar on the shore,
When the stormy winds do blow;
When the battle rages loud and long
And the stormy winds do blow.

The meteor flag of England
Shall yet terrific burn;
Till danger's troubled night depart
And the star of peace return.
Then, then, ye ocean-warriors!
Our song and feast shall flow
To the fame of your name,
When the storm has ceased to blow;
When the fiery fight is heard no more,
And the storm has ceased to blow.

Thomas Campbell

677   *Hohenlinden*

On Linden, when the sun was low,
All bloodless lay the untrodden snow;
And dark as winter was the flow
  Of Iser, rolling rapidly.

But Linden saw another sight,
When the drum beat at dead of night
Commanding fires of death to light
  The darkness of her scenery.

By torch and trumpet fast arrayed
Each horseman drew his battle blade,
And furious every charger neighed
  To join the dreadful revelry.

Then shook the hills with thunder riven;
Then rushed the steed, to battle driven
And louder than the bolts of heaven
  Far flashed the red artillery.

But redder yet that light shall glow
On Linden's hills of stainèd snow;
And bloodier yet the torrent flow
  Of Iser, rolling rapidly.

'Tis morn; but scarce yon level sun
Can pierce the war-clouds, rolling dun,
Where furious Frank and fiery Hun
   Shout in their sulphorous canopy.

The combat deepens. On ye Brave
Who rush to glory, or the grave!
Wave, Munich, all thy banners wave,
   And charge with all thy chivalry!

Few, few shall part, where many meet!
The snow shall be their winding sheet,
And every turf beneath their feet
   Shall be a soldier's sepulcre.

Thomas Campbell

678   *The harper*

On the green banks of Shannon, when Sheelah was
   nigh,
No blithe Irish lad was so happy as I;
No harp like my own could so cheerily play,
And wherever I went was my poor dog Tray.

When at last I was forced from my Sheelah to part,
She said (while the sorrow was big at her heart),
'Oh! remember your Sheelah when far, far away;
And be kind, my dear Pat, to our poor dog Tray.'

Poor dog! he was faithful, and kind, to be sure,
And he constantly loved me, although I was poor;
When the sour-looking folk sent me heartless away,
I had always a friend in my poor dog Tray.

When the road was so dark, and the night was so cold,
And Pat and his dog were grown weary and old,
How snugly we slept in my old coat of gray,
And he licked me for kindness—my poor dog Tray.

Though my wallet was scant I remembered his case,
Nor refused my last crust to his pitiful face;
But he died at my feet on a cold winter day,
And I played a sad lament for my poor dog Tray.

Where now shall I go, forsaken and blind?
Can I find one to guide me so faithful and kind?
To my sweet native village, so far, far away,
I can never more return with my poor dog Tray.

Thomas Campbell

679   *Echoes*

How sweet the answer echo makes
To music at night
When, roused by lute or horn, she wakes,
When far away o'er lawns and lakes
Goes answering light!

Yet love hath echoes truer far
And far more sweet
Than e'er, beneath the moonlight's star,
Of horn or lute or soft guitar
The songs repeat.

'Tis when the sigh,—in youth sincere
And only then,
The sigh that's breathed for one to hear—
Is by that one, that only dear
Breathed back again.

Thomas Moore

680   *Oft in the stilly night*

Oft in the stilly night
    Ere slumber's chain has bound me,
Fond Memory brings the light
    Of other days around me:

The smiles, the tears
    Of boyhood's years,
The words of love then spoken;
    The eyes that shone,
    Now dimmed and gone,
The cheerful hearts now broken!
Thus in the stilly night
    Ere slumber's chain has bound me,
Sad Memory brings the light
    Of other days around me.

When I remember all
    The friends so linked together
I've seen around me fall
    Like leaves in wintry weather,
        I feel like one
        Who treads alone
Some banquet-hall deserted,
        Whose lights are fled,
        Whose garlands dead,
And all but he departed!
Thus in the stilly night
    Ere slumber's chain has bound me,
Sad Memory brings the light
    Of other days around me.

Thomas Moore

681   *Believe me, if all those endearing young charms*

Believe me, if all those endearing young charms,
    Which I gaze on so fondly to-day,
Were to change by to-morrow, and fleet in my arms,
    Like fairy-gifts fading away,
Thou wouldst still be adored, as this moment thou art,
    Let thy loveliness fade as it will,
And around the dear ruin each wish of my heart
    Would entwine itself verdantly still.

It is not while beauty and youth are thine own,
  And thy cheeks unprofaned by a tear
That the fervour and faith of a soul can be known,
  To which time will but make thee more dear;
No, the heart that has truly loved never forgets,
  But as truly loves on to the close,
As the sun-flower turns on her god, when he sets,
  The same look which she turned when he rose.

Thomas Moore

682 *What's my thought like?*

  Ques. WHY is a pump like V–sc–nt C–stl–r–gh?
  Answ. Because it is a slender thing of wood,
    That up and down its awkward arm doth sway,
    And cooly spout and spout and spout away,
  In one weak, washy, everlasting flood!

Thomas Moore

683 *The Canadian boat song*

  Listen to me, as when ye heard our father
    Sing long ago the song of other shores—
  Listen to me, and then in chorus gather
    All your deep voices as ye pull your oars:
      Fair these broad meads—these hoary woods are
                                          grand;
      But we are exiles from our fathers' land.

  From the lone shieling of the misty island
    Mountains divide us, and the waste of seas—
  Yet still the blood is strong, the heart is Highland,
    And we in dreams behold the Hebrides:
      Fair these broad meads—these hoary woods are
                                          grand;
      But we are exiles from our fathers' land.

We ne'er shall tread the fancy-haunted valley,
  Where 'tween the dark hills creeps the small clear
                                           stream,
In arms around the patriarch banner rally,
  Nor see the moon on royal tombstones gleam:
    Fair these broad meads—these hoary woods are
                                           grand;
    But we are exiles from our fathers' land.

When the bold kindred, in the time long-vanished,
  Conquered the soil and fortified the keep,
No seer foretold the children should be banished,
  That a degenerate Lord should boast his sheep:
    Fair these broad meads—these hoary woods are
                                           grand;
    But we are exiles from our fathers' land.

Come foreign rage—let discord burst in slaughter!
  O then let clansmen true, and stern claymore—
The hearts that would have given their blood like
                                           water,
  Beat heavily beyond the Atlantic roar:
    Fair these broad meads—these hoary woods are
                                           grand;
    But we are exiles from our fathers' land.

John Galt

684   *A house and grounds*

Were this impossible, I know full well
What sort of house should grace my garden-bell—
A good, old country lodge, half hid with blooms
Of honied green, and quaint with straggling rooms,
A few of which, white-bedded and well swept,
For friends, whose names endeared them, should be
    kept.
Of brick I'd have it, far more broad than high,
With green up to the door, and elm trees nigh;

And the warm sun should have it in his eye.
The tiptoe traveller, peeping through the boughs
O'er my low wall, should bless the pleasant house,
And that my luck might not seem ill-bestowed,
A bench and spring should greet him on the road.
My grounds should not be large; I like to go
To Nature for a range, and prospect too,
And cannot fancy she'll comprise for me,
Even in a park, her all-sufficiency.
Besides, my thoughts fly far; and when at rest
Love, not to watch a tower, but a lulling nest.
But all the ground I had should keep a look
Of Nature still, have birds' nests and a brook;
One spot for flowers, the rest all turf and trees;
For I'd not grow my own bad lettuces.
I'd build a walk, however, against rain,
Long, peradventure as my whole domain,
And so be sure of generous exercise,
The youth of age, and medicine of the wise.
And this reminds me, that behind some screen
About my grounds, I'd have a bowling-green;
Such as in wits' and merry women's days
Suckling preferred before his walk of bays.
You may still see them, dead as haunts of fairies,
By the old seats of Killigrews and Careys,
Where all, alas, is vanished from the ring,
Wits and black eyes, the skittles, and the king!

James Henry Leigh Hunt

685   *The fate of a broom—an anticipation*

Lo! in Corruption's lumber room,
The remnants of a wondrous broom;
That walking, talking, oft was seen,
Making stout promise to sweep clean;
But evermore, at every push,
Proved but a stump without a brush.
Upon its handle-top, a sconce,

Like Brahma's, looked four ways at once,
Pouring on king, lords, church, and rabble,
Long floods of favour-currying gabble;
From fourfold mouthpiece always spinning
Projects of plausible beginning,
Whereof said sconce did ne'er intend
That any one should have an end;
Yet still, by shifts and quaint inventions,
Got credit for its good intentions,
Adding no trifle to the store,
Wherewith the devil paves his floor,
Worn out at last, found bare and scrubbish,
And thrown aside with other rubbish,
We'll e'en hand o'er the enchanted stick,
As a choice present for Old Nick,
To sweep, beyond the Stygian lake,
The pavement it has helped to make.

                                    Thomas Love Peacock

686   *The indignation of Taliesin*

False bards the sacred fire pervert,
Whose songs are won without desert;
Who falsehoods weave in specious lays,
To gild the base with virtue's praise.

From court to court, from tower to tower,
In warrior's tent, in lady's bower,
For gold, for wine, for food, for fire,
They tune their throats at all men's hire.

Their harps re-echo wide and far
With sensual love, and bloody war,
And drunkenness, and flattering lies:
Truth's light may shine for other eyes.

In palaces they still are found,
At feasts, promoting senseless sound:
He is their demigod at least,
Whose only virtue is his feast.

They love to talk; they hate to think;
All day they sing; all night they drink:
No useful toils their hands employ;
In boisterous throngs is all their joy.

The bird will fly, the fish will swim,
The bee the honeyed flowers will skim;
Its food by toil each creature brings,
Except false bards and worthless kings.

Learning and wisdom claim to find
Homage and succour from mankind;
But learning's right, and wisdom's due,
Are falsely claimed by slaves like you.

True bards know truth, and truth will show;
Ye know it not, nor care to know;
Your king's weak mind false judgment warps;
Rebuke his wrong, or break your harps.

I know the mountain and the plain;
I know where right and justice reign;
I from the tower will Elphin free;
Your king shall learn his doom from me.

A spectre of the marsh shall rise,
With yellow teeth, and hair, and eyes,
From whom your king in vain aloof
Shall crouch beneath the sacred roof.

He through the half-closed door shall spy
The Yellow Spectre sweeping by;
To whom the punishment belongs
Of Maelgon's crimes and Elphin's wrongs.

Thomas Love Peacock

687 *Beech and oak*

The slender beech and the sapling oak,
      That grow by the shadowy rill,
You may cut down both at a single stroke,
      You may cut down which you will.

But this you must know, that as long as they grow,
      Whatever change may be,
You never can teach either oak or beech
      To be aught but a greenwood tree.

Thomas Love Peacock

688 *She walks in beauty*

She walks in beauty, like the night
      Of cloudless climes and starry skies;
And all that's best of dark and bright
      Meet in her aspect and her eyes:
Thus mellow'd to that tender light
      Which heaven to gaudy day denies.

One shade the more, one ray the less,
      Had half impair'd the nameless grace
Which waves in every raven tress,
      Or softly lightens o'er her face;
Where thoughts serenely sweet express
      How pure, how dear their dwelling-place.

And on that cheek, and o'er that brow,
      So soft, so calm, yet eloquent,
The smiles that win, the tints that glow,
      But tell of days in goodness spent,
A mind at peace with all below,
      A heart whose love is innocent!

Lord Byron

689   *We'll go no more a-roving*

So, we'll go no more a-roving
    So late into the night,
Though the heart be still as loving
    And the moon be still as bright.

For the sword outwears its sheath,
    And the soul wears out the breast,
And the heart must pause to breathe,
    And love itself have rest.

Though the night was made for loving,
    And the day returns too soon,
Yet we'll go no more a-roving
    By the light of the moon.

Lord Bryon

690   *The isles of Greece*

The isles of Greece! the isles of Greece
    Where burning Sappho loved and sung,
Where grew the arts of war and peace,
    Where Delos rose and Phoebus sprung!
Eternal summer gilds them yet,
But all, except their sun, is set.

The Scian and the Teian muse,
    The hero's harp, the lover's lute,
Have found the fame your shores refuse:
    Their place of birth alone is mute
To sounds which echo further west
Than your sires' 'Islands of the Blest'.

The mountains look on Marathon—
    And Marathon looks on the sea;
And musing there an hour alone,
    I dream'd that Greece might still be free;
For standing on the Persians' grave,
I could not deem myself a slave.

A king sate on the rocky brow
   Which looks o'er sea-borne Salamis;
And ships, by thousands, lay below,
   And men in nations;—all were his!
He counted them at break of day—
And when the sun set, where were they?

And where are they? and where art thou
   My country? On thy voiceless shore
The heroic lay is tuneless now—
   The heroic bosom beats no more!
And must thy lyre, so long divine,
Degenerate into hands like mine?

'Tis something in the dearth of fame,
   Though link'd among a fetter'd race,
To feel at least a patriot's shame,
   Even as I sing, suffuse my face;
For what is left the poet here?
For Greeks a blush—for Greece a tear.

Must *we* but weep o'er days more blest?
   Must *we* but blush.—Our fathers bled.
Earth! render back from out thy breast
   A remnant of our Spartan dead!
Of the three hundred grant but three,
To make a new Thermopylae!

What, silent still? and silent all?
   Ah! no;—the voices of the dead
Sound like a distant torrent's fall,
   And answer, 'Let one living head,
But one, arise,—we come, we come!'
'Tis but the living who are dumb.

In vain—in vain: strike other chords;
   Fill high the cup with Samian wine!
Leave battles to the Turkish hordes,
   And shed the blood of Scio's vine!
Hark! rising to the ignoble call—
How answers each bold Bacchanal!

You have the Pyrrhic dance as yet;
   Where is the Pyrrhic phalanx gone?
Of two such lessons, why forget
   The nobler and the manlier one?
You have the letters Cadmus gave—
Think ye he meant them for a slave?

Fill high the bowl with Samian wine!
   We will not think of themes like these!
It made Anacreon's song divine:
   He served—but served Polycrates—
A tyrant; but our masters then
Were still, atl east, our countrymen.

The tyrant of the Chersonese
   Was freedom's best and bravest friend;
That tyrant was Miltiades!
   O that the present hour would lend
Another despot of the kind!
Such chains as his were sure to bind.

Fill high the bowl with Samian wine!
   On Suli's rock and Parga's shore,
Exists the remnant of a line
   Such as the Doric mothers bore;
And there, perhaps, some seed is sown,
The Heracleidan blood might own.

Trust not for freedom to the Franks—
   They have a king who buys and sells;
In native swords and native ranks
   The only hope of courage dwells:
But Turkish force and Latin fraud
Would break your shield, however broad.

Fill high the bowl with Samian wine!
   Our virgins dance beneath the shade—
I see their glorious black eyes shine;
   But gazing on each glowing maid,
My own the burning tear-drop laves,
To think such breasts must suckle slaves.

Place me on Sunium's marble steep,
   Where nothing, save the waves and I,
May hear our mutual murmurs sweep;
   There, swan-like, let me sing and die:
A land of slaves shall ne'er be mine—
Dash down yon cup of Samian wine!

Lord Byron

691   *For music*

There be none of Beauty's daughters
   With a magic like to thee;
And like music on the waters
   Is thy sweet voice to me:
When, as if its sound were causing
The charmèd ocean's pausing,
The waves lie still and gleaming,
And the loud winds seem dreaming:

And the midnight moon is weaving
   Her bright chain o'er the deep;
Whose breast is gently heaving,
   As an infant's asleep:
So the spirit blows before thee,
To listen and adore thee;
With a full but soft emotion,
Like the swell of Summer's ocean.

Lord Byron

692   *When we two parted*

When we two parted
   In silence and tears,
Half broken-hearted
   To sever for years,

Pale grew thy cheek and cold,
    Colder thy kiss;
Truly that hour foretold
    Sorrow to this.

The dew of the morning
    Sunk chill on my brow—
It felt like the warning
    Of what I feel now.
Thy vows are all broken,
    And light is thy fame:
I hear thy name spoken,
    And share in its shame.

They name thee before me,
    A knell to mine ear;
A shudder comes o'er me—
    Why wert thou so dear?
They know not I knew thee,
    Who knew thee too well:
Long, long shall I rue thee,
    Too deeply to tell.

In secret we met—
    I silence I grieve,
That thy heart could forget,
    Thy spirit deceive.
If I should meet thee
    After long years,
How should I greet thee?
    With silence and tears.

Lord Byron

693   *The burial of Sir John Moore at Corunna*

Not a drum was heard, not a funeral note,
    As his corpse to the rampart we hurried;
Not a soldier discharged his farewell shot
    O'er the grave where our hero we buried.

We buried him darkly at dead of night,
  The sods with our bayonets turning;
By the struggling moonbeams misty light
  And the lantern dimly burning.

No useless coffin enclosed his breast,
  Not in sheet nor in shroud we wound him:
But he lay like a warrior taking his rest,
  With his martial cloak around him.

Few and short were the prayers we said
  And we spoke not a word of sorrow,
But we steadfastly gazed on the face that was dead,
  And we bitterly thought of the morrow.

We thought as we hollowed his narrow bed
  And smoothed down his lonely pillow,
That the foe and the stranger would tread o'er his head,
  And we far away on the billow.

Lightly they'll talk of the spirit that's gone
  And o'er his cold ashes upbraid him,—
But little he'll reck, if they let him sleep on
  In the grave where a Briton has laid him.

But half of our heavy task was done
  When the clock struck the hour for retiring,
And we heard the distant and random gun
  That the foe was sullenly firing.

Slowly and sadly we laid him down,
  From the field of his fame fresh and gory:
We carved not a line, and we raised not a stone—
  But we left him alone with his glory.

Charles Wolfe

694   *A widow bird sate mourning for her love*

A widow bird sate mourning for her love
    Upon a wintry bough;
The frozen wind crept on above,
    The freezing stream below.

There was no leaf upon the forest bare,
    No flower upon the ground,
And little motion in the air
    Except the mill-wheel's sound.

                        Percy Bysshe Shelley

695   *Ozymandias*

I met a traveller from an antique land
Who said: Two vast and trunkless legs of stone
Stand in the desert. . . . Near them, on the sand,
Half sunk, a shattered visage lies, whose frown,
And wrinkled lip, and sneer of cold command,
Tell that its sculptor well those passions read
Which yet survive, stamped on these lifeless things,
The hand that mocked them, and the heart that fed:
And on the pedestal these words appear:
'My name is Ozymandias, king of kings:
Look on my works, ye Mighty, and despair!'
Nothing beside remains. Round the decay
Of that colossal wreck, boundless and bare
The lone and level sands stretch far away.

                        Percy Bysshe Shelley

696   *Ode to the west wind*

I

O wild West Wind, thou breath of Autumn's being,
Thou, from whose unseen presence the leaves dead
Are driven, like ghosts from an enchanter fleeing,

Yellow, and black, and pale, and hectic red,
Pestilence-stricken multitudes: O thou,
Who chariotest to their dark wintry bed

The wingèd seeds, where they lie cold and low,
Each like a corpse within its grave, until
Thine azure sister of the Spring shall blow

Her clarion o'er the dreaming earth, and fill
(Driving sweet buds like flocks to feed in air)
With living hues and odours plain and hill:

Wild Spirit, which art moving everywhere;
Destroyer and preserver; hear, O hear!

II

Thou on whose stream, mid the steep sky's commotion,
Loose clouds like earth's decaying leaves are shed,
Shook from the tangled boughs of Heaven and Ocean,

Angels of rain and lightning: there are spread
On the blue surface of thine aëry surge,
Like the bright hair uplifted from the head

Of some fierce Mænad, even from the dim verge
Of the horizon to the zenith's height,
The locks of the approaching storm. Thou dirge

Of the dying year, to which this closing night
Will be the dome of a vast sepulchre,
Vaulted with all thy congregated might

Of vapours, from whose solid atmosphere
Black rain, and fire, and hail will burst: O hear!

III

Thou who didst waken from his summer dreams
The blue Mediterranean, where he lay,
Lull'd by the coil of his crystàlline streams,

Beside a pumice isle in Baiæ's bay,
And saw in sleep old palaces and towers
Quivering within the wave's intenser day,

All overgrown with azure moss and flowers
So sweet, the sense faints picturing them! Thou
For whose path the Atlantic's level powers

Cleave themselves into chasms, while far below
The sea-blooms and the oozy woods which wear
The sapless foliage of the ocean, know

Thy voice, and suddenly grow gray with fear,
And tremble and despoil themselves: O hear!

IV

If I were a dead leaf thou mightest bear;
If I were a swift cloud to fly with thee;
A wave to pant beneath thy power, and share

The impulse of thy strength, only less free
Than thou, O uncontrollable! If even
I were as in my boyhood, and could be

The comrade of thy wanderings over Heaven,
As then, when to outstrip thy skiey speed
Scarce seem'd a vision; I would ne'er have striven

As thus with thee in prayer in my sore need.
O lift me as a wave, a leaf, a cloud!
I fall upon the thorns of life! I bleed!

A heavy weight of hours has chain'd and bow'd
One too like thee: tameless, and swift, and proud.

V

Make me thy lyre, even as the forest is:
What if my leaves are falling like its own!
The tumult of thy mighty harmonies

Will take from both a deep, autumnal tone,
Sweet though in sadness. Be thou, Spirit fierce,
My spirit! Be thou me, impetuous one!

Drive my dead thoughts over the universe
Like wither'd leaves to quicken a new birth!
And, by the incantation of this verse,

Scatter, as from an unextinguish'd hearth
Ashes and sparks, my words among mankind!
Be through my lips to unawaken'd earth

The trumpet of a prophecy! O Wind,
If Winter comes, can Spring be far behind?

Percy Bysshe Shelley

697   *Lines to a critic*

Honey from silkworms who can gather,
    Or silk from the yellow bee?
The grass may grow in winter weather
    As soon as hate in me.

Hate men who cant, and men who pray,
    And men who rail like thee;
An equal passion to repay
    They are not coy like me.

Or seek some slave of power and gold
    To be thy dear heart's mate;
Thy love will move that bigot cold
    Sooner than me, thy hate.

A passion like the one I prove
    Cannot divided be;
I hate thy want of truth and love—
    How should I then hate thee?

Percy Bysshe Shelley

As from an ancestral oak
  Two empty ravens sound their clarion,
Yell by yell, and croak by croak,
When they scent the noonday smoke
  Of fresh human carrion:—

As two gibbering night-birds flit
  From their bowers of deadly yew
Through the night to frighten it,
When the moon is in a fit,
  And the stars are none, or few:—

As a shark and dog-fish wait
  Under an Atlantic isle,
For the negro-ship, whose freight
Is the theme of their debate,
  Wrinkling their red gills the while—

Are ye, two vultures, sick for battle,
  Two scorpions under one wet stone,
Two bloodless wolves whose dry throats rattle,
Two crows perched on the murrained cattle,
  Two vipers tangled into one.

Percy Bysshe Shelley

699   *Sonnet: England in 1819*

An old, mad, blind, despised, and dying king,—
Princes, the dregs of their dull race, who flow
Through public scorn,—mud from a muddy spring,—
Rulers who neither see, nor feel, nor know,
But leech-like to their fainting country cling,
Till they drop, blind in blood, without a blow,—
A people starved and stabbed in the untilled field,—
An army, which liberticide and prey
Makes a two-edged sword to all who wield,—

Golden and sanguine laws which tempt and slay;
Religion Christless, Godless—a book sealed;
A Senate—Time's worst statute unrepealed,—
Are graves, from which a glorious phantom may
Burst, to illumine our tempestuous day.

Percy Bysshe Shelley

700   *To Coleridge*

Oh! there are spirits of the air,
    And genii of the evening breeze,
And gentle ghosts, with eyes as fair
    As star-beams among twilight trees:
Such lovely ministers to meet
Oft hast thou turned from men thy lonely feet.

With mountain winds, and babbling springs,
    And moonlight seas, that are the voice
Of these inexplicable things,
    Thou dost hold commune, and rejoice
When they did answer thee, but they
Cast, like a worthless boon, thy love away.

And thou hast sought in starry eyes
    Beams that were never meant for thine,
Another's wealth: tame sacrifice
    To a fond faith! still dost thou pine?
Still dost thou hope that greeting hands,
Voice, looks, or lips, may answer thy demands?

Ah! wherefore didst thou build thine hope
    On the false earth's inconstancy?
Did thine own mind afford no scope
    Of love, or moving thoughts to thee?
That natural scenes or human smiles
Could steal the power to wind thee in their wiles?

Yes, all the faithless smiles are fled
   Whose falsehood left thee broken-hearted;
The glory of the moon is dead;
   Night's ghosts and dreams have now departed;
Thine own soul still is true to thee,
But changed to a foul fiend through misery.

This fiend, whose ghastly presence ever
   Beside thee like thy shadow hangs,
Dream not to chase: the mad endeavour
   Would scourge thee to severer pangs.
Be as thou art. Thy settled fate,
Dark as it is, all change would aggravate.

                   Percy Bysshe Shelley

701   *Rarely, rarely comest thou*

Rarely, rarely, comest thou,
   Spirit of Delight!
Wherefore hast thou left me now
   Many a day and night?
Many a weary night and day
'Tis since thou art fled away.

How shall ever one like me
   Win thee back again?
With the joyous and the free
   Thou wilt scoff at pain.
Spirit false! thou hast forgot
All but those who need thee not.

As a lizard with the shade
   Of a trembling leaf,
Thou with sorrow art dismayed;
   Even the sighs of grief
Reproach thee, that thou art not near,
And reproach thou will not hear.

Let me set my mournful ditty
    To a merry measure;
Thou wilt never come for pity,
    Thou wilt come for pleasure;
Pity then will cut away
Those cruel wings, and thou wilt stay.

I love all that thou lovest,
    Spirit of Delight!
The fresh earth in new leaves dressed,
    And the starry night;
Autumn evening, and the morn
When the golden mists are born.

I love snow, and all the forms
    Of the radiant frost;
I love waves, and winds, and storms,
    Everything almost
Which is Nature's, and may be
Untainted by man's misery.

I love tranquil solitude,
    And such society
As is quiet, wise, and good;
    Between thee and me
What difference? but thou dost possess
The things I seek, not love them less.

I love Love—though he has wings,
    And like light can flee,
But above all other things,
    Spirit, I love thee—
Thou art love and life! Oh, come
Make once more my heart thy home.

                              Percy Bysshe Shelley

702   *To night*

    Swiftly walk o'er the western wave,
        Spirit of Night!
    Out of the misty eastern cave,
    Where, all the long and lone daylight,

Thou wovest dreams of joy and fear,
Which make thee terrible and dear—
    Swift be thy flight!

Wrap thy form in a mantle grey,
        Star-inwrought!
Blind with thine hair the eyes of Day;
Kiss her until she be wearied out,
Then wander o'er city, and sea, and land,
Touching all with thine opiate wand—
        Come long-sought!

When I arose and saw the dawn,
        I sighed for thee;
When light rode high, and the dew was gone,
And noon lay heavy on flower and tree,
And the weary day turned to his rest,
Lingering like an unloved guest,
        I sighed for thee.

Thy brother Death came, and cried,
        Wouldst thou me?
Thy sweet child Sleep, the filmy eyed,
Murmured like a noontide bee,
Shall I nestle near thy side?
Would thou me? And I replied,
        No, not thee!

Death will come when thou art dead,
        Soon, too soon—
Sleep will come when thou art fled;
Of neither would I ask the boon
I ask of thee, beloved Night—
Swift be thine approaching flight,
        Come soon, soon!

                                    Percy Bysshe Shelley

When the lamp is shattered
The light in the dust lies dead—
When the cloud is scattered
The rainbow's glory is shed.
When the lute is broken,
Sweet tones are remembered not;
When the lips have spoken,
Loved accents are soon forgot.

As music and splendour
Survive not the lamp and the lute,
The heart's echoes render
No song when the spirit is mute:
No song but sad dirges,
Like the wind through a ruined cell,
Or the mournful surges
That ring the dead seaman's knell.

When hearts have once mingled
Love first leaves the well-built nest;
The weak one is singled
To endure what it once possessed.
O Love! who bewailest
The frailty of all things here,
Why chose you the frailest
For your candle, your home, and your bier?

Its passions will rock thee
As the storms rock the ravens on high;
Bright reason will mock thee,
Like the sun from a wintry sky.
From thy nest every rafter
Will rot, and thine eagle come home
Leave thee naked to laughter,
When the leaves fall and the cold winds come.

Percy Bysshe Shelley

My faint spirit was sitting in the light
   Of thy looks, my love;
It panted for thee like the hind at noon
   For the brooks, my love.
Thy barb whose hoofs outspeed the tempest's flight
   Bore thee far from me;
My heart, for my weak feet were weary soon,
   Did companion thee.

Ah! fleeter far than fleetest storm or steed,
   Or the death they bear,
The heart which tender thought clothes like a dove
   With the wings of care;
In the battle, in the darkness, in the need,
   Shall mine cling to thee,
Nor claim one smile for all the comfort, love,
   It may bring to thee.

Percy Bysshe Shelley

705 *Mutability*

We are the clouds that veil the midnight moon;
   How restlessly they speed, and gleam, and quiver,
Streaking the darkness radiantly!—yet soon
   Night closes round, and they are lost for ever:

Or like forgotten lyres, whose dissonant strings
   Give various response to each varying blast,
To whose frail frame no second motion brings
   One mood or modulation like the last.

We rest.—A dream has power to poison sleep;
   We rise.—One wandering thought pollutes the day;
We feel, conceive or reason, laugh or weep;
   Embrace fond foe, or cast our cares away:

It is the same! —For, be it joy or sorrow,
     The path of its departure still is free:
Man's yesterday may ne'er be like his morrow;
     Nought may endure but Mutability.

Percy Bysshe Shelley

706   *One word is too often profaned*

One word is too often profaned
     For me to profane it,
One feeling too falsely disdained
     For thee to disdain it;
One hope is too like despair
     For prudence to smother,
And pity from thee more dear
     Than that from another.

I can give not what men call love,
     But wilt thou accept not
The worship the heart lifts above
     And the heavens reject not,—
The desire of the moth for the star,
     Of the night for the morrow,
The devotion to something afar
     From the sphere of our sorrow?

Percy Bysshe Shelley

707   *Stanzas written in dejection near Naples*

The sun is warm, the sky is clear,
     The waves are dancing fast and bright,
Blue isles and snowy mountains wear
     The purple noon's transparent might,
     The breath of the moist earth is light,
Around its unexpanded buds;
     Like many a voice of one delight,
The winds, the birds, the ocean floods,
The city's voice itself, is soft like Solitude's.

I see the deep's untrampled floor
    With green and purple seaweeds strown;
I see the waves upon the shore,
    Like light dissolved in star-showers, thrown:
    I sit upon the sands alone,—
The lightning of the noontide ocean
    Is flashing round me, and a tone
Arises from its measured motion,
How sweet! did any heart now share in my emotion.

Alas! I have nor hope nor health,
    Nor peace within nor calm around,
Nor that content surpassing wealth
    The sage in meditation found,
    And walked with inward glory crowned—
Nor fame nor power, nor love, nor leisure,
    Others I see whom these surround—
Smiling they live, and call life pleasure;—
To me that cup has been dealt in another measure.

Yet now despair itself is mild,
    Even as the winds and waters are;
I could lie down like a tired child,
    And weep away the life of care
    Which I have born and yet must bear,
Till death like sleep might steal on me,
    And I might feel in the warm air
My cheek grow cold, and hear the sea
Breathe o'er my dying brain its last monotony.

Some might lament that I were cold,
    As I, when this sweet day is gone,
Which my lost heart, too soon grown old,
    Insults with this untimely moan;
    They might lament—for I am one
Whom men love not,—and yet regret,
    Unlike this day, which, when the sun
Shall on its stainless glory set,
Will linger, though enjoyed, like joy in memory yet.

Percy Bysshe Shelley

I bring fresh showers for the thirsting flowers,
    From the seas and the streams;
I bear light shade for the leaves when laid
    In their noonday dreams.
From my wings are shaken the dews that waken
    The sweet buds every one,
When rocked to rest on their mother's breast,
    As she dances about in the sun.
I wield the flail of the lashing hail,
    And whiten the green plains under,
And then again I dissolve it in rain,
    And laugh as I pass in thunder.

I sift the snow on the mountains below,
    And their great pines groan aghast;
And all the night 'tis my pillow white,
    While I sleep in the arms of the blast.
Sublime on the towers of my skiey bowers,
    Lightning my pilot sits;
In a cavern under is fettered the thunder,
    It struggles and howls at fits;
Over earth and ocean, with gentle motion,
    This pilot is guiding me,
Lured by the love of the genii that move
    In the depths of the purple sea;
Over the rills, and the crags, and the hills,
    Over the lakes and the plains,
Wherever he dream, under mountain or stream,
    The Spirit he loves remains;
And I all the while bask in heaven's blue smile,
    Whilst he is dissolving in rains.

The sanguine sunrise, with meteor eyes,
    And his burning plumes outspread,
Leaps on the back of my sailing rack,
    When the morning star shines dead;
As on the jag of a mountain crag,
    Which an earthquake rocks and swings,

An eagle alit one moment may sit
  In the light of its golden wings.
And when sunset may breathe, from the lit sea beneath,
  Its ardours of rest and love,
And the crimson pall of eve may fall
  From the depth of heaven above,
With wings folded I rest, on mine aëry nest,
  As still as a brooding dove.

That orbèd maiden with white fire laden,
  Whom mortals call the moon,
Glides glimmering o'er my fleece-like floor,
  By the midnight breezes strewn;
And wherever the beat of her unseen feet,
  Which only the angels hear,
May have broken the woof of my tent's thin roof,
  The stars peep behind her and peer;
And I laugh to see them whirl and flee,
  Like a swarm of golden bees,
When I widen the rent in my wind-built tent,
  Till the calm rivers, lakes, and seas,
Like strips of the sky fallen through me on high,
  Are each paved with the moon and these.

I bind the Sun's throne with a burning zone,
  And the Moon's with a girdle of pearl;
The volcanoes are dim, and the stars reel and swim,
  When the whirlwinds my banner unfurl.
From cape to cape, with a bridge-like shape,
  Over a torrent sea,
Sunbeam-proof, I hang like a roof,—
  The mountains its columns be.
The triumphal arch through which I march
  With hurricane, fire, and snow,
When the Powers of the air are chained to my chair,
  Is the million-coloured bow;
The sphere-fire above its soft colours wove,
  While the moist earth was laughing below.

I am the daughter of Earth and Water,
    And the nursling of the Sky;
I pass through the pores of the ocean and shores;
    I change, but I cannot die.
For after the rain when with never a stain
    The pavilion of heaven is bare,
And the winds and sunbeams with their convex
                                    gleams
        Build up the blue dome of air,
I silently laugh at my own cenotaph,
    And out of the caverns of rain,
Like a child from the womb, like a ghost from the
                                    tomb,
    I arise and unbuild it again.

                                    Percy Bysshe Shelley

709   *Evening: Ponte al Mare, Pisa*

    The sun is set; the swallows are asleep;
        The bats are flitting fast in the grey air;
    The slow soft toads out of damp corners creep,
        And evening's breath, wandering here and there
    Over the quivering surface of the stream,
    Wakes not one ripple from its summer dream.

    There is no dew on the dry grass tonight,
        Nor damp within the shadow of the trees;
    The wind is intermitting, dry and light;
        And in the inconstant motion of the breeze,
    The dust and straws are driven up and down,
    And whirled about the pavement of the town.

    Within the surface of the fleeting river
        The wrinkled image of the city lay,
    Immovably unquiet, and forever
        It trembles, but it never fades away;
    Go to the [   ]
    You, being changed, will find it then as now.

The chasm in which the sun is sunk is shut
    By darkest barriers of cinereous cloud,
Like mountain over mountain huddled—but
    Growing and moving upwards in a crowd,
And over it a space of watery blue,
Which the keen evening star is shining through.

Percy Bysshe Shelley

710   *The Aziola*

'Do you not hear the Aziola cry?
    Methinks she must be nigh,'
        Said Mary, as we sate
In dusk, ere stars were lit, or candles brought;
        And I, who thought
    This Aziola was some tedious woman,
        Asked, 'Who is Aziola?' How elate
I felt to know that it was nothing human,
    No mockery of myself to fear or hate:
        And Mary saw my soul,
And laughed, and said, 'Disquiet yourself not;
    'Tis nothing but a little downy owl.'

Sad Aziola! many an eventide
    Thy music I had heard
By wood and stream, meadow and mountain-side,
    And fields and marshes wide,—
Such as nor voice nor lute, nor wind nor bird,
    The soul ever stirred;
Unlike and far sweeter than them all.
Sad Aziola! from that moment I
    Loved thee and thy sad cry.

Percy Bysshe Shelley

711 *Circumstance*

A man who was about to hang himself,
   Finding a purse, then threw away his rope;
The owner, coming to reclaim his pelf,
   The halter found, and used it. So is Hope
Changed for Despair—one laid upon the shelf,
   We take the other. Under Heaven's high cope
Fortune is God—all you endure and do
Depends on circumstance as much as you.

Percy Bysshe Shelley

712 *To the ivy*

Dark creeping Ivy, with thy berries brown,
   That fondly twists on ruins all thine own,
Old spire-points studding with a leafy crown
   Which every minute threatens to dethrone;
With fearful eye I view thy height sublime,
   And oft with quicker step retreat from thence
Where thou, in weak defiance, striv'st with Time,
   And hold'st his weapons in a dread suspense.
But, bloom of ruins, thou art dear to me,
   When, far from danger's way, thy gloomy pride
Wreathes picturesque around some ancient tree
   That bows his branches by some fountain-side:
Then sweet it is from summer suns to be,
With thy green darkness overshadowing me.

John Clare

713 *Nature*

O simple Nature, how I do delight
   To pause upon thy trifles—foolish things,
As some would call them. On the summer night,
   Tracing the lane-path where the dog-rose hings
     With dew-drops seeth'd, while chick'ring cricket
                  sings,

My eye can't help but glance upon its leaves,
  Where love's warm beauty steals her sweetest blush,
When, soft the while, the even silent heaves
  Her pausing breath just trembling thro' the bush,
  And then again dies calm, and all is hush.
Oh, how I feel, just as I pluck the flower
  And stick it to my breast—words can't reveal;
But there are souls that in this lovely hour
  Know all I mean, and feel whate'er I feel.

John Clare

714   *Summer morning*

I love to peep out on a summer's morn,
  Just as the scouting rabbit seeks her shed,
And the coy hare squats nestling in the corn,
  Frit at the bow'd ear tott'ring o'er her head;
And blund'ring pheasant, that from covert springs,
  His short sleep broke by early trampling feet,
Makes one to startle with his rustling wings,
  As through the boughs he seeks more safe retreat.
The little flower, begemm'd around with drops
  That shine at sunrise like to burnish'd gold,
'Tis sweet to view: the milk-maid often stops,
  And wonders much such spangles to behold;
The hedger, too, admires them deck the thorn,
And thinks he sees no beauties like the morn.

John Clare

715   *Sudden shower*

Black grows the southern sky, betokening rain,
  And humming hive-bees homeward hurry by:
They feel the change; so let us shun the grain,
  And take the broad road while our feet are dry.

Ay, there some dropples moistened on my face,
    And pattered on my hat—'tis coming nigh!
Let's look about, and find a sheltering place.
    The little things around, like you and I,
Are hurrying through the grass to shun the shower.
    Here stoops an ash-tree—hark! the wind gets high,
But never mind; this ivy, for an hour,
    Rain as it may, will keep us dryly here:
That little wren knows well his sheltering bower,
    Nor leaves his dry house though we come so near.

John Clare

716   *Summer images*

I love at early morn, from new-mown swath,
    To see the startled frog his route pursue,
And mark while, leaping o'er the dripping path,
    His bright sides scatter dew;
And early lark that from its bustle flies
    To hail his matin new;
        And watch him to the skies:

And note on hedgerow baulks, in moisture sprent,
    The jetty snail creep from the mossy thorn,
With earnest heed and tremulous intent,
    Frail brother of the morn,
That from the tiny bents and misted leaves
    Withdraws his timid horn,
        And fearful vision weaves:

Or swallow heed on smoke-tanned chimney-top,
    Wont to be first unsealing morning's eye,
Ere yet the bee hath gleaned one wayward drop
    Of honey on his thigh;
To see him seek morn's airy couch to sing,
    Until the golden sky
        Bepaint his russet wing:

And sawning boy by tanning corn espy,
  With clapping noise to startle birds away,
And hear him bawl to every passer-by
  To know the hour of day;
And see the uncradled breeze, refreshed and strong,
  With waking blossoms play,
    And breathe aeolian song.

I love the south-west wind, or low or loud,
  And not the less when sudden drops of rain
Moisten my pallid cheek from ebon cloud,
  Threatening soft showers again,
That over lands new ploughed and meadow grounds,
  Summer's sweet breath unchain,
    And wake harmonious sounds.

Rich music breathes in summer's every sound;
  And in her harmony of varied greens,
Woods, meadows, hedgerows, cornfields, all around
  Much beauty intervenes,
Filling with harmony the ear and eye;
  While o'er the mingling scenes
    Far spreads the laughing sky.

And wind-enamoured aspen—mark the leaves
  Turn up their silver lining to the sun,
And list! the brustling noise, that oft deceives,
  And makes the sheep-boy run:
The sound so mimics fast-approaching showers,
  He thinks the rain begun,
    And hastes to sheltering bowers.

John Clare

717   *Hares at play*

The birds are gone to bed, the cows are still,
And sheep lie panting on each old mole-hill;
And underneath the willow's grey-green bough,
Like toil a-resting, lies the fallow plough.

The timid hares throw daylight fears away
On the lane's road to dust and dance and play,
Then dabble in the grain by naught deterred
To lick the dew-fall from the barley's beard;
Then out they sturt again and round the hill
Like happy thoughts dance, squat, and loiter still,
Till milking maidens in the early morn
Jingle their yokes and sturt them in the corn;
Through well-known beaten paths each nimbling hare
Sturts quick as fear, and seeks its hidden lair.

John Clare

718 *Summer*

The woodman's axe renews its hollow stroke,
   And barkmen's noises in the woods awake,
Ripping the stained bark from the fallen oak,
   Where crumpled fox-fern and the branching brake
Fade 'neath their crushing feet. The timid hare
   Starts from its mossy root or sedgy seat,
And listening foxes leave their startled lair
   And to some blackthorn's spinney make retreat.
Haymakers with their shouldered rakes sojourn
   To hedgy closes, and amid the wheat
The schoolboy runs, while pleasures thickly burn
   Around his heart, to crop corn-bottle flowers,
Scaring the partridge from its quiet bourn,
   That hides for shelter from the summer heat.

John Clare

719 *Remembrances*

Summer's pleasures they are gone like to visions every
    one,
And the cloudy days of autumn and of winter cometh
    on.
I tried to call them back, but unbidden they are gone

Far away from heart and eye and for ever far away
Dear heart, and can it be that such raptures meet decay?
I thought them all eternal when by Langley Bush I lay,
I thought them joys eternal when I used to shout and
    play
On its bank at 'clink and bandy', 'chock' and 'taw' and
    'ducking-stone',
Where silence sitteth now on the wild heath as her own
Like a ruin of the past all alone.

When I used to lie and sing by old Eastwell's boiling
    spring,
When I used to tie the willow boughs together for a
    swing,
And fish with crooked pins and thread and never catch
    a thing,
With heart just like a feather, now as heavy as a stone;
When beneath old Lea Close Oak I the bottom branches
    broke
To make our harvest cart like so many working folk,
And then to cut a straw at the brook to have a soak.
Oh, I never dreamed of parting or that trouble had a
    sting,
Or that pleasures like a flock of birds would ever take to
    wing,
Leaving nothing but a little naked spring.

When jumping time away on old Crossberry Way,
And eating haws like sugarplums ere they had lost the
    may,
And skipping like a leveret before the peep of day
On the roly-poly up and downs of pleasant Swordy
    Well,
When in Round Oak's narrow lane as the south got
    black again
We sought the hollow ash that was shelter from the rain,
With our pockets full of peas we had stolen from the
    grain;

How delicious was the dinner-time on such a showery
    day!
Oh, words are poor receipts for what time hath stole
    away,
The ancient pulpit trees and the play.

When for school o'er Little Field with its brook and
    wooden brig,
Where I swaggered like a man though I was not half so
    big,
While I held my little plough though 'twas but a willow
    twig,
And drove my team along made of nothing but a name,
'Gee hep' and 'hoit' and 'woi'—oh, I never call to
    mind
These pleasant names of places but I leave a sigh behind,
While I see the little mouldiwarps hang sweeing to the
    wind
On the only aged willow that in all the field remains,
And nature hides her face while they're sweeing in their
    chains
And in a silent murmuring complains.

Here was commons for their hills, where they seek for
    freedom still,
Though every common's gone and though traps are set
    to kill
The little homeless miners—oh, it turns my bosom
    chill
When I think of old Sneap Green, Puddock's Nook and
    Hilly Snow,
Where bramble bushes grew and the daisy gemmed in
    dew
And the hills of silken grass like to cushions to the view,
Where we threw the pismire crumbs when we'd noth-
    ing else to do,
All levelled like a desert by the never-weary plough,
All vanished like the sun where that cloud is passing now
And settled here for ever on its brow.

Oh, I never thought that joys would run away from
  boys,
Or that boys would change their minds and forsake such
  summer joys;
But alack, I never dreamed that the world had other
  toys
To petrify first feeling like the fable into stone,
Till I found the pleasure past and a winter come at last,
Then the fields were sudden bare and the sky got over-
  cast,
And boyhood's pleasing haunts, like a blossom in the
  blast,
Was shrivelled to a withered weed and trampled down
  and done,
Till vanished was the morning spring and set the
  summer sun,
And winter fought her battle strife and won.

By Langley Bush I roam, but the bush hath left its hill,
On Cowper Green I stray, 'tis a desert strange and chill,
And the spreading Lea Close Oak, ere decay had penned
  its will,
To the axe of the spoiler and self-interest fell a prey,
And Crossberry Way and old Round Oak's narrow lane
With its hollow trees like pulpits I shall never see again,
Enclosure like a Buonaparte let not a thing remain,
It levelled every bush and tree and levelled every hill
And hung the moles for traitors—though the brook is
  running still
It runs a naked stream, cold and chill.

Oh, had I known as then joy had left the paths of men,
I had watched her night and day, be sure, and never
  slept agen,
And when she turned to go, Oh, I'd caught her mantle
  then,
And wooed her like a lover by my lonely side to stay;
Ay, knelt and worshipped on, as love in beauty's bower,
And clung upon her smiles as a bee upon a flower,
And gave her heart my posies, all cropt in a sunny hour,

As keepsakes and pledges all to never fade away;
But love never heeded to treasure up the may,
So it went the common road to decay.

John Clare

720   Badger

When midnight comes a host of dogs and men
Go out and track the badger to his den,
And put a sack within the hole, and lie
Till the old grunting badger passes by.
He comes and hears—they let the strongest loose.
The old fox hears the noise and drops the goose.
The poacher shoots and hurries from the cry,
And the old hare half wounded buzzes by.
They get a forkèd stick to bear him down
And clap the dogs and take him to the town,
And bait him all the way with many dogs,
And laugh and shout and fright the scampering hogs.
He runs along and bites at all he meets:
They shout and hollo down the noisy streets.

He turns about to face the loud uproar
And drives the rebels to their very door.
The frequent stone is hurled where'er they go;
When badgers fight, then everyone's a foe.
The dogs are clapt and urged to join the fray;
The badger turns and drives them all away.
Though scarcely half as big, demure and small,
He fights with dogs for hours and beats them all.
The heavy mastiff, savage in the fray,
Lies down and licks his feet and turns away.
The bulldog knows his match and waxes cold,
The badger grins and never leaves his hold.
He drives the crowd and follows at their heels
And bites them through—the drunkard swears and reels.

The frighted women take the boys away,
The blackguard laughs and hurries on the fray.
He tries to reach the woods, an awkward race,
But sticks and cudgels quickly stop the chase.

He turns agen and drives the noisy crowd
And beats the many dogs in noises loud.
He drives away and beats them every one,
And then they loose them all and set them on.
He falls as dead and kicked by boys and men,
Then starts and grins and drives the crowd agen;
Till kicked and torn and beaten out he lies
And leaves his hold and cackles, groans, and dies.

John Clare

721   *Gypsies*

The snow falls deep; the forest lies alone;
The boy goes hasty for his load of brakes,
Then thinks upon the fire and hurries back;
The gypsy knocks his hands and tucks them up,
And seeks his squalid camp, half hid in snow,
Beneath the oak which breaks away the wind,
And bushes close in snow like hovel warm;
There tainted mutton wastes upon the coals,
And the half-wasted dog squats close and rubs,
Then feels the heat too strong, and goes aloof;
He watches well, but none a bit can spare,
And vainly waits the morsel thrown away.
'Tis thus they live—a picture to the place,
A quiet, pilfering, unprotected race.

John Clare

722   *Song's eternity*

What is song's eternity?
    Come and see.
Can it noise and bustle be?
    Come and see.
Praises sung or praises said
    Can it be?

Wait awhile and these are dead—
    Sigh, sigh;
Be they high or lowly bred
    They die.

What is song's eternity?
    Come and see.
Melodies of earth and sky,
    Here they be.
Song once sung to Adam's ears
    Can it be?
Ballads of six thousand years
    Thrive, thrive;
Songs awakened with the spheres
    Alive.

Mighty songs that miss decay,
    What are they?
Crowds and cities pass away
    Like a day.
Books are writ and books are read;
    What are they?
Years will lay them with the dead—
    Sigh, sigh;
Trifles unto nothing wed,
    They die.

Dreamers, list the honey-bee;
    Mark the tree
Where the bluecap, 'tootle tee',
    Sings a glee
Sung to Adam and to Eve—
    Here they be.
When floods covered every bough,
    Noah's ark
Heard that ballad singing now;
    Hark, hark,

'Tootle tootle tootle tee'—
   Can it be
Pride and fame must shadows be?
   Come and see—
Every season owns her own;
   Bird and bee
Sing creation's music on;
   Nature's glee
Is in every mood and tone
   Eternity.

The eternity of song
   Liveth here;
Nature's universal tongue
   Singeth here
Songs I've heard and felt and seen
   Everywhere;
Songs like the grass are evergreen:
   The giver
Said 'Live and be'—and they have been,
   For ever.

John Clare

723 *Pleasant sounds*

   The rustling of leaves under the feet in woods and under
      hedges;
   The crumping of cat-ice and snow down wood-rides,
      narrow lanes, and every street causeway;
   Rustling through a wood or rather rushing, while the
      wind halloos in the oak-top like thunder;
   The rustle of birds' wings startled from their nests or
      flying unseen into the bushes;
   The whizzing of larger birds overhead in a wood, such
      as crows, puddocks, buzzards;
   The trample of robins and woodlarks on the brown
      leaves, and the patter of squirrels on the green moss;

The fall of an acorn on the ground, the pattering of nuts
    on the hazel branches as they fall from ripeness;
The flirt of the groundlark's wing from the stubbles—
    how sweet such pictures on dewy mornings, when
    the dew flashes from its brown feathers!

John Clare

724   *Little trotty wagtail*

Little trotty wagtail, he went in the rain,
And tittering, tottering sideways he ne'er got straight
    again,
He stooped to get a worm, and looked up to catch a fly,
And then he flew away ere his feathers they were dry.

Little trotty wagtail, he waddled in the mud,
And left his little footmarks, trample where he would.
He waddled in the water-pudge, and waggle went his
    tail.
And chirrupt up his wings to dry upon the garden rail.

Little trotty wagtail, you nimble all about,
And in the dimpling water-pudge you waddle in and
    out;
Your home is nigh at hand, and in the warm pigsty,
So, little Master Wagtail, I'll bid you a good-bye.

John Clare

725   *Clock-a-clay*

In the cowslip pips I lie,
Hidden from the buzzing fly,
While green grass beneath me lies,
Pearled with dew like fishes' eyes,
Here I lie, a clock-a-clay,
Waiting for the time of day.

While grassy forest quakes surprise,
And the wild wind sobs and sighs,
My gold home rocks as like to fall,
On its pillar green and tall;
When the pattering rain drives by
Clock-a-clay keeps warm and dry.

Day by day and night by night,
All the week I hide from sight;
In the cowslip pips I lie,
In rain and dew still warm and dry;
Day and night, and night and day,
Red, black-spotted clock-a-clay.

My home shakes in wind and showers,
Pale green pillar topped with flowers,
Bending at the wild wind's breath,
Till I touch the grass beneath;
Here I live, lone clock-a-clay,
Watching for the time of day.

John Clare

726   *The dying child*

He could not die when trees were green,
    For he loved the time too well.
His little hands, when flowers were seen,
    Were held for the bluebell,
        As he was carried o'er the green.

His eye glanced at the white-nosed bee;
    He knew those children of the spring:
When he was well and on the lea
    He held one in his hands to sing,
        Which filled his heart with glee.

Infants, the children of spring!
    How can an infant die
When butterflies are on the wing,
    Green grass, and such a sky?
        How can they die at spring?

He held his hands for daisies white,
    And then for violets blue,
And took them all to bed at night
    That in the green fields grew,
        As childhood's sweet delight.

And then he shut his little eyes,
    And flowers would notice not;
Birds' nests and eggs caused no surprise,
    He now no blossoms got:
        They met with plaintive sighs.

When winter came and blasts did sigh,
    And bare were plain and tree,
As he for ease in bed did lie
    His soul seemed with the free,
        He died so quietly.

John Clare

727   *Poets love nature*

Poets love nature, and themselves are love,
Though scorn of fools, and mock of idle pride.
The vile in nature worthless deeds approve,
They court the vile and spurn all good beside.
Poets love nature; like the calm of heaven,
Like heaven's own love, her gifts spread far and wide:
In all her works there are no signs of leaven;
Sorrow abashes from her simple pride.
Her flowers, like pleasures, have their season's birth,
They are her very scriptures upon earth,
And teach us simple mirth where'er we go.
Even in prison they can solace me,
For where they bloom God is, and I am free.

John Clare

I am: yet what I am none cares or knows,
    My friends forsake me like a memory lost;
I am the self-consumer of my woes,
    They rise and vanish in oblivious host,
Like shades in love and death's oblivion lost;
And yet I am, and live with shadows tost.

Into the nothingness of scorn and noise,
    Into the living sea of waking dreams,
Where there is neither sense of life nor joys,
    But the vast shipwreck of my life's esteems;
And e'en the dearest—that I loved the best—
Are strange—nay, rather stranger than the rest.

I long for scenes where man has never trod,
    A place where woman never smiled or wept;
There to abide with my Creator, God,
    And sleep as I in childhood sweetly slept:
Untroubling and untroubled where I lie,
The grass below—above the vaulted sky.

                                        John Clare

I lost the love of heaven above,
    I spurned the lust of earth below,
I felt the sweets of fancied love,
    And hell itself my only foe.

I lost earth's joys, but felt the glow
    Of heaven's flame about in me,
Till loveliness and I did grow
    The bard of immortality.

I loved, but women fell away;
    I hid me from her faded flame.
I snatched the sun's eternal ray
    And wrote till earth was but a name.

In every language upon earth,
   On every shore, o'er every sea,
I gave my name immortal birth
   And kept my spirit with the free.

John Clare

730   *Secret love*

I hid my love when young till I
Couldn't bear the buzzing of a fly;
I hid my love to my despite
Till I could not bear to look at light:
I dare not gaze upon her face
But left her memory in each place;
Where'er I saw a wild flower lie
I kissed and bade my love good-bye.

I met her in the greenest dells,
Where dewdrops pearl the wood bluebells;
The lost breeze kissed her bright blue eye,
The bee kissed and went singing by,
A sunbeam found a passage there,
A gold chain round her neck so fair;
As secret as the wild bee's song
She lay there all the summer long.

I hid my love in field and town
Till e'en the breeze would knock me down.
The bees seemed singing ballads o'er,
The fly's bass turned a lion's roar;
And even silence found a tongue,
To haunt me all the summer long;
The riddle nature could not prove
Was nothing else but secret love.

John Clare

The lark he rises early,
  And the ploughman goes away
Before it's morning fairly
  At the guessing break of day;
The fields lie in the dawning,
  And the valley's hid in gold,
At the pleasant time of morning
  When the shepherd goes to fold.

The maiden laughs and hollos
  When she sees the feeding cows;
They switch their tails and follow
  When she can't get over sloughs;
I love the gentle dawning,
  And the valleys hid in gold,
At the pleasant time of morning
  When the shepherd goes to fold.

John Clare

732 *Schoolboys in winter*

The schoolboys still their morning rambles take
To neighbouring village school with playing speed,
Loitering with pastime's leisure till they quake,
Oft looking up the wild-geese droves to heed,
Watching the letters which their journeys make;
Or plucking haws on which the fieldfares feed,
And hips, and sloes; and on each shallow lake
Making glib slides, where they like shadows go
Till some fresh pastimes in their minds awake.
Then off they start anew and hasty blow
Their numbed and clumpsing fingers till they glow;
Then races with their shadows wildly run
That stride huge giants o'er the shining snow
In the pale splendour of the winter sun.

John Clare

Dear brother Robin, this comes from us all
With our kind love, and could Gip write and all
Though but a dog he'd have his love to spare,
For still he knows, and by your corner chair
The moment he comes in he lies him down
And seems to fancy you are in the town.
This leaves us well in health, thank God for that!
For old acquaintance Sue has kept your hat
Which mother brushes ere she lays it by
And every Sunday goes upstairs to cry.
Jane still is yours till you come back agen
And ne'er so much as dances with the men;
And Ned the woodman every week comes in
And asks about you kindly as our kin;
And he with this and goody Thompson sends
Remembrances with those of all our friends.
Father with us sends love until he hears
And mother she has nothing but her tears,
Yet wishes you like us in health the same
And longs to see a letter with your name,
So, loving brother, don't forget to write.
Old Gip lies on the hearth stone every night;
Mother can't bear to turn him out of doors
And never noises now of dirty floors;
Father will laugh but lets her have her way,
And Gip for kindness get a double pay.
So Robin write and let us quickly see
You don't forget old friends no more than we,
Nor let my mother have so much to blame
To go three journeys ere your letter came.

John Clare

734   *To a waterfowl*

Whither, midst falling dew,
While glow the heavens with the last steps of day
Far, through their rosy depths, dost thou pursue
Thy solitary way?

Vainly the fowler's eye
Might mark thy distant flight to do thee wrong
As, darkly seen against the crimson sky,
    Thy figure floats along.

Seek'st thou the plashy brink
Of weedy lake, or marge of river wide,
Or where the rocking billows rise and sink
    On the chafed ocean-side?

There is a Power whose care
Teaches thy way along that pathless coast—
The desert and illimitable air—
    Lone wandering, but not lost.

All day thy wings have fanned,
At that far height, the cold, thin atmosphere,
Yet stoop not, weary, to the welcome land,
    Though the dark night is near.

And soon that toil shall end;
Soon shalt thou find a summer home, and rest,
And scream among thy fellows; reeds shall bend,
    Soon, o'er thy sheltered nest.

Thou'rt gone, the abyss of heaven
Hath swallowed up thy form; yet, on my heart
Deeply has sunk the lesson thou hast given,
    And shall not soon depart.

He who, from zone to zone,
Guides through the houndless sky thy certain flight,
In the long way that I must tread alone,
    Will lead my steps aright.

William Cullen Bryant

I

'O what can ail thee, knight-at-arms,
  Alone and palely loitering?
The sedge has wither'd from the lake,
  And no birds sing.

II

'O what can ail thee, knight-at-arms,
  So haggard and so woe-begone?
The squirrel's granary is full,
  And the harvest's done.

III

'I see a lily on thy brow
  With anguish moist and fever dew;
And on thy cheek a fading rose
  Fast withereth too.'

IV

'I met a lady in the meads,
  Full beautiful—a faery's child,
Her hair was long, her foot was light,
  And her eyes were wild.

V

'I made a garland for her head,
  And bracelets too, and fragrant zone;
She look'd at me as she did love,
  And made sweet moan.

VI

'I set her on my pacing steed,
  And nothing else saw all day long,
For sideways would she bend, and sing
  A faery's song.

'She found me roots of relish sweet,
  And honey wild, and manna dew,
And sure in language strange she said,
    "I love thee true."

'She took me to her elfin grot,
  And there she wept and sigh'd full sore,
And there I shut her wild, wild eyes
    With kisses four.

'And there she lulled me asleep,
  And there I dream'd—ah! woe betide!
The latest dream I ever dream'd
    On the cold hill's side.

'I saw pale kings and princes too,
  Pale warriors, death-pale were they all;
Who cry'd—"La belle Dame sans Merci
    Hath thee in thrall!"

'I saw their starv'd lips in the gloam,
  With horrid warning gaped wide,
And I awoke and found me here,
    On the cold hill's side.

'And this is why I sojourn here,
  Alone and palely loitering,
Though the sedge is withered from the lake,
    And no birds sing.'

John Keats

Season of mists and mellow fruitfulness,
  Close bosom-friend of the maturing sun;
Conspiring with him how to load and bless
  With fruit the vines that round the thatch-eaves run;
To bend with apples the moss'd cottage-trees,
  And fill all fruit with ripeness to the core;
    To swell the gourd, and plump the hazel shells
With a sweet kernel; to set budding more,
And still more, later flowers for the bees,
Until they think warm days will never cease,
    For Summer has o'er-brimm'd their clammy cells.

Who hath not seen thee oft amid thy store?
  Sometimes whoever seeks abroad may find
Thee sitting careless on a granary floor,
  Thy hair soft-lifted by the winnowing wind;
Or on a half-reap'd furrow sound asleep,
  Drowsed with the fume of poppies, while thy hook
    Spares the next swath and all its twinèd flowers:
And sometime like a gleaner thou dost keep
  Steady thy laden head across a brook;
  Or by a cider-press, with patient look,
    Thou watchest the last oozings hours by hours.

Where are the songs of Spring? Ay, where are they?
  Think not of them, thou hast thy music too,—
While barrèd clouds bloom the soft-dying day,
  And touch the stubble-plains with rosy hue;
Then in a wailful choir the small gnats mourn
  Among the river sallows, borne aloft
    Or sinking as the light wind lives or dies;

And full-grown lambs loud bleat from hilly bourn;
  Hedge-crickets sing; and now with treble soft
  The redbreast whistles from a garden-croft;
    And gathering swallows twitter in the skies.

John Keats

737 *In a drear-nighted December*

In a drear-nighted December,
  Too happy, happy tree,
Thy branches ne'er remember
  Their green felicity:
The north cannot undo them
With a sleety whistle through them,
Nor frozen thawings glue them
  From budding at the prime.

In a drear-nighted December,
  Too happy, happy brook,
Thy bubblings ne'er remember
  Apollo's summer look;
But with a sweet forgetting
They stay their crystal fretting,
Never, never petting
  About the frozen time.

Ah, would 'twere so with many
  A gentle girl and boy!
But were there ever any
  Writhed not at passèd joy?
To know the change and feel it,
When there is none to heal it
Nor numbèd sense to steel it—
  Was never said in rhyme.

John Keats

To one who has been long in city pent,
  'Tis very sweet to look into the fair
  And open face of heaven,—to breathe a prayer
Full in the smile of the blue firmament.
Who is more happy, when, with heart's content,
  Fatigued he sinks into some pleasant lair
  Of wavy grass, and reads a debonair
And gentle tale of love and languishment?
Returning home at evening, with an ear
  Catching the notes of Philomel,—an eye
Watching the sailing cloudlet's bright career,
He mourns that day so soon has glided by:
E'en like the passage of an angel's tear
  That falls through the clear ether silently.

John Keats

739 *On first looking into Chapman's Homer*

Much have I travell'd in the realms of gold;
  And many goodly states and kingdoms seen;
  Round many western islands have I been
Which bards in fealty to Apollo hold.
Oft of one wide expanse had I been told
  That deep-brow'd Homer ruled as his demesne;
  Yet did I never breathe its pure serene
Till I heard Chapman speak out loud and bold:
Then felt I like some watcher of the skies
  When a new planet swims into his ken;
Or like stout Cortez when with eagle eyes
  He star'd at the Pacific—and all his men
Look'd at each other with a wild surmise—
  Silent, upon a peak in Darien.

John Keats

Highmindedness, a jealousy for good,
  A loving-kindness for the great man's fame,
  Dwells here and there with people of no name,
In noisome alley, and in pathless wood:
And where we think the truth least understood,
  Oft may be found a 'singleness of aim,'
  That ought to frighten into hooded shame
A money-mong'ring, pitiable brood.
How glorious this affection for the cause
  Of steadfast genius, toiling gallantly!
What when a stout unbending champion awes
  Envy, and Malice to their native sty?
Unnumber'd souls breath out a still applause,
  Proud to behold him in his country's eye.

John Keats

741 *On the grasshopper and cricket*

The poetry of earth is never dead:
  When all the birds are faint with the hot sun,
  And hide in cooling trees, a voice will run
From hedge to hedge about the new-mown mead;
That is the grasshopper's—he takes the lead
  In summer luxury,—he has never done
  With his delights; for when tired out with fun
He rests at ease beneath some pleasant weed.
The poetry of earth is ceasing never:
  On a lone winter evening, when the frost
  Has wrought a silence, from the stove there shrills
The cricket's song, in warmth increasing ever,
  And seems to one in drowsiness half lost,
  The grasshopper's among some grassy hills.

John Keats

Thou still unravish'd bride of quietness,
  Thou foster-child of silence and slow time,
Sylvan historian, who canst thus express
  A flowery tale more sweetly than our rhyme:
What leaf-fring'd legend haunts about thy shape
  Of deities or mortals, or of both,
    In Tempe or the dales of Arcady?
What men or gods are these? What maidens loth?
  What mad pursuit? What struggle to escape?
    What pipes and timbrels? What wild ecstasy?

Heard melodies are sweet, but those unheard
  Are sweeter; therefore, ye soft pipes, play on;
Not to the sensual ear, but, more endear'd,
  Pipe to the spirit ditties of no tone:
Fair youth, beneath the trees, thou canst not leave
  Thy song, nor ever can those trees be bare;
    Bold lover, never, never canst thou kiss,
Though winning near the goal—yet, do not grieve;
  She cannot fade, though thou hast not thy bliss,
    For ever wilt thou love, and she be fair!

Ah, happy, happy boughs! that cannot shed
  Your leaves, nor ever bid the Spring adieu;
And, happy melodist, unwearied,
  For ever piping songs for ever new;
More happy love! more happy, happy love!
  For ever warm and still to be enjoy'd,
    For ever panting, and for ever young;
All breathing human passion far above,
  That leaves a heart high-sorrowful and cloy'd,
    A burning forehead, and a parching tongue.

Who are these coming to the sacrifice?
  To what green altar, O mysterious priest,
Leads't thou that heifer lowing at the skies,
  And all her silken flanks with garlands drest?

What little town by river or sea shore,
   Or mountain-built with peaceful citadel,
      Is emptied of this folk, this pious morn?
And little town, thy streets for evermore
   Will silent be; and not a soul to tell
      Why thou art desolate, can e'er return.

O Attic shape! Fair attitude! with brede
   Of marble men and maidens overwrought,
With forest branches and the trodden weed;
   Thou, silent form, dost tease us out of thought
As doth eternity: Cold Pastoral!
   When old age shall this generation waste,
      Thou shalt remain, in midst of other woe
Than ours, a friend to man, to whom thou say'st,
   Beauty is truth, truth beauty,—that is all
      Ye know on earth, and all ye need to know.

                                             John Keats

743   *Ode to psyche*

O Goddess! hear these tuneless numbers, wrung
   By sweet enforcement and remembrance dear.
And pardon that thy secrets should be sung
   Even into thine own soft-conched ear:
Surely I dreamt to-day; or did I see
   The winged Psyche with awaken'd eyes?
I wander'd in a forest thoughtlessly,
   And, on the sudden, fainting with surprise,
Saw two fair creatures, couched side by side
   In deepest grass, beneath the whisp'ring fan
   Of leaves and trembled blossoms, where there ran
      A brooklet, scarce espied:
'Mid hush'd, cool-rooted flowers, fragrant-eyed,
   Blue, freckle-pink, and budded Tyrian,
They lay calm-breathing on the bedded grass;
   Their arms embraced, and their pinions too;
   Their lips touch'd not, but had not bid adieu,
As if disjoined by soft-handed slumber,

And ready still past kisses to outnumber
    At tender eye-dawn of aurorean love:
        The winged boy I knew;
    But who wast thou, O happy, happy dove?
        His Psyche true!

O latest born and loveliest vision far
    Of all Olympus' faded hierarchy!
Fairer than Phoebe's sapphire-region'd star,
    Or Vesper, amorous glow-worm of the sky;
Fairer than these, though temple thou hast none,
        Nor altar heap'd with flowers;
Nor virgin choir to make delicious moan
        Upon the midnight hours;
No voice, no lute, no pipe, no incense sweet,
    From chain-swung censer teeming;
No shrine, no grove, no oracle, no heat
    Of pale-mouth'd prophet dreaming.
O brightest! though too late for antique vows,
    Too, too late for the fond believing lyre,
When holy were the haunted forest boughs,
    Holy the air, the water, and the fire;
Yet even in these days so far retir'd
    From happy pieties, thy lucent fans,
    Fluttering among the faint Olympians,
I see, and sing, by my own eyes inspired.
    So let me be thy choir, and make a moan
        Upon the midnight hours;
Thy voice, thy lute, thy pipe, thy incense sweet
    From swinged censer teeming;
Thy shrine, thy grove, thy oracle, thy heat
    Of pale-mouth'd prophet dreaming.

Yes, I will be thy priest, and build a fane
    In some untrodden region of my mind,
Where branched thoughts, new grown with pleasant
                                                    pain,
    Instead of pines shall murmur in the wind:
Far, far around shall those dark-cluster'd trees
    Fledge the wild-ridged mountains steep by steep;

And there by zephyrs, streams, and birds, and bees,
  The moss-lain Dryads shall be lull'd to sleep;
And in the midst of this wide quietness
A rosy sanctuary will I dress
With the wreath'd trellis of a working brain,
  With buds, and bells, and stars without a name,
With all the gardener Fancy e'er could feign,
  Who, breeding flowers, will never breed the same:
  And there shall be for thee all soft delight
    That shadowy thought can win,
  A bright torch, and a casement ope at night,
    To let the warm Love in!

                                        John Keats

744   *Ode on melancholy*

No, no, go not to Lethe, neither twist
  Wolf's-bane, tight-rooted, for its poisonous wine;
Nor suffer thy pale forehead to be kiss'd
  By nightshade, ruby grape of Proserpine;
Make not your rosary of yew-berries,
  Nor let the beetle, nor the death-moth be
    Your mournful Psyche, nor the downy owl
A partner in your sorrow's mysteries;
  For shade to shade will come too drowsily,
    And drown the wakeful anguish of the soul.

But when the melancholy fit shall fall
  Sudden from heaven like a weeping cloud,
That fosters the droop-headed flowers all,
  And hides the green hill in an April shroud;
Then glut thy sorrow on a morning rose,
  Or on the rainbow of the salt sand-wave,
    Or on the wealth of globed peonies;
Or if thy mistress some rich anger shows,
  Emprison her soft hand, and let her rave,
    And feed deep, deep upon her peerless eyes.

She dwells with Beauty—Beauty that must die;
　　And Joy, whose hand is ever at his lips
　Bidding adieu, and aching Pleasure nigh,
　　Turning to poison while the bee-mouth sips:
　Ay, in the very temple of Delight
　　Veil'd Melancholy has her sovran shrine,
　　　Though seen of none save him whose strenuous
　　　　　　　　　　　　　　　　　　　tongue
　Can burst Joy's grape against his palate fine,
　　His soul shall taste the sadness of her might,
　　And be among her cloudy trophies hung.

John Keats

745　*After dark vapours*

After dark vapours have oppress'd our plains
　　For a long dreary season, comes a day
　　Born of the gentle south, and clears away
From the sick heavens all unseemly stains.
The anxious mouth, relieving from its pains,
　　Takes as a long-lost right the feel of May,
　　The eyelids with the passing coolness play,
Like rose leaves with the drip of summer rains.
The calmest thoughts come round us—as of leaves
　　Budding,—fruit ripening in stillness,—autumn suns
Smiling at eve upon the quiet sheaves,—
Sweet Sappho's cheek,—a sleeping infant's breath,—
　　The gradual sand that through an hour-glass runs,—
A woodland rivulet,—a poet's death.

John Keats

746　*On an engraved gem of Leander*

Come hither all sweet maidens soberly,
　　Down-looking aye, and with a chasten'd light
　　Hid in the fringes of your eyelids white,

And meekly let your fair hands joined be,
As if so gentle that ye could not see,
   Untouch'd, a victim of your beauty bright,
   Sinking away to his young spirit's night,
Sinking bewilder'd 'mid the dreary sea:
'Tis young Leander toiling to his death.
   Nigh swooning, he doth purse his weary lips
      For Hero's cheek, and smiles against her smile.
   O horrid dream! see how his body dips,
      Dead-heavy; arms and shoulders gleam awhile:
He's gone: up bubbles all his amorous breath!

John Keats

747   *When I have fears*

When I have fears that I may cease to be
   Before my pen has glean'd my teeming brain,
Before high-piled books, in charact'ry,
   Hold like rich garners the full-ripen'd grain;
When I behold, upon the night's starr'd face,
   Huge cloudy symbols of a high romance,
And think that I may never live to trace
   Their shadows, with the magic hand of chance;
And when I feel, fair creature of an hour!
   That I shall never look upon thee more,
Never have relish in the faery power
   Of unreflecting love!—then on the shore
Of the wide world I stand alone, and think,
Till love and fame to nothingness do sink.

John Keats

748   *To Homer*

Standing aloof in giant ignorance,
   Of thee I hear and of the Cyclades,
As one who sits ashore and longs perchance
   To visit dolphin-coral in deep seas.

So thou wast blind!—but then the veil was rent;
  For Jove uncurtain'd Heaven to let thee live,
And Neptune made for thee a spumy tent,
  And Pan made sing for thee his forest-hive;
Aye, on the shores of darkness there is light,
  And precipices show untrodden green;
There is a budding morrow in midnight;
  There is a triple sight in blindness keen;
Such seeing hadst thou, as it once befel
To Dian, Queen of Earth, and Heaven, and Hell.

John Keats

749   *Meg Merrilies*

Old Meg she was a gipsy;
  And liv'd upon the moors:
Her bed it was the brown heath turf,
  And her house was out of doors.

Her apples were swart blackberries,
  Her currants, pods o' broom;
Her wine was dew of the wild white rose,
  Her book a church-yard tomb.

Her brothers were the craggy hills,
  Her sisters larchen trees;
Alone with her great family
  She liv'd as she did please.

No breakfast had she many a morn,
  No dinner many a noon,
And 'stead of supper she would stare
  Full hard against the moon.

But every morn, of woodbine fresh
  She made her garlanding,
And every night the dark glen yew
  She wove, and she would sing.

And with her fingers old and brown
    She plaited mats o' rushes,
And gave them to the cottagers
    She met among the bushes.

Old Meg was brave as Margaret Queen,
    And tall as Amazon:
An old red blanket cloak she wore,
    A chip hat had she on.
God rest her aged bones somewhere—
    She died full long agone!

John Keats

750   *On fame*

Fame, like a wayward girl, will still be coy
    To those who woo her with too slavish knees,
But makes surrender to some thoughtless boy,
    And dotes the more upon a heart at ease;
She is a gipsy, will not speak to those
    Who have not learnt to be content without her;
A jilt, whose ear was never whisper'd close,
    Who thinks they scandal her who talk about her;
A very gipsy is she, Nilus-born,
    Sister-in-law to jealous Potiphar;
Ye love-sick bards! repay her scorn for scorn;
    Ye artists lovelorn! madmen that ye are!
Make your best bow to her and bid adieu,
Then, if she likes it, she will follow you.

John Keats

751   *Why did I laugh to-night?*

Why did I laugh to-night? No voice will tell:
    No God, no demon of severe response,
Deigns to reply from heaven or from hell.
    Then to my human heart I turn at once.

Heart! Thou and I are here, sad and alone;
  Say, wherefore did I laugh? O mortal pain!
O darkness! darkness! ever must I moan,
  To question heaven and hell and heart in vain.
Why did I laugh? I know this being's lease,
  My fancy to its utmost blisses spreads;
Yet could I on this very midnight cease,
  And the world's gaudy ensigns see in shreds;
Verse, fame, and beauty are intense indeed,
But death intenser—death is life's high meed.

John Keats

752   *Modern love*

And what is love? It is a doll dressed up
For idleness to cosset, nurse, and dandle;
A thing of soft misnomers, so divine
That silly youth doth think to make itself
Divine by loving [too], and so goes on
Yawning and doting a whole summer long,
Till Miss's comb is made a pearl tiara,
And common Wellingtons turn Romeo boots;
Then Cleopatra lives at number seven,
And Antony resides in Brunswick Square.
Fools! if some passions high have warmed the world,
If queens and soldiers have played deep for hearts,
It is no reason why such agonies
Should be more common than the growth of weeds.
Fools! make me whole again that weighty pearl
The Queen of Egypt melted, and I'll say
That ye may love in spite of beaver hats.

John Keats

753   *Where didst thou find, young bard . . .*

Where didst thou find, young bard, thy sounding lyre?
  Where the bland accent, and the tender tone?
A-sitting snugly by thy parlour fire;
  Or didst thou with Apollo pick a bone?

The Muse will have a crow to pick with me
    For thus assaying in thy brightening path:
Who, that with his own brace of eyes can see,
    Unthunderstruck beholds thy gentle wrath?
Who from a pot of stout e'er blew the froth
    Into the bosom of the wandering wind,
Light as the powder on the back of moth,
    But drank thy Muses with a grateful mind?
Yea unto thee beldams drink metheglin,
    And anises, and caraway, and gin.

John Keats

754   *On a dream (after reading Dante's episode of Paolo and Francesca)*

As Hermes once took to his feathers light,
    When lulled Argus, baffled, swoon'd and slept,
So on a Delphic reed my idle spright,
    So play'd, so charm'd, so conquer'd, so bereft
The dragon-world of all its hundred eyes,
    And seeing it asleep so fled away,
Not to pure Ida with its snow-cold skies,
    Nor unto Tempe, where Jove grieved that day;
But to that second circle of sad Hell,
    Where in the gust, the whirlwind, and the flaw
Of rain and hail-stones, lovers need not tell
    Their sorrows,—pale were the sweet lips I saw,
Pale were the lips I kiss'd, and fair the form
I floated with, about that melancholy storm.

John Keats

755   *On the death of a recluse*

'Mid roaring brooks and dark moss-vales,
    Where speechless Thought abides,
Still her sweet spirit dwells,
    That knew no world besides.

Her form the woodland still retains—
    Wound but a creeping flower,
Her very life-blood stains
    Thee, in a falling shower.

Touch but the stream, drink but the air,
    Her cheek, her breath is known;
Ravish that red rose there,
    And she is all thine own.

George Darley

756   *The phoenix*

O blest unfabled Incense Tree,
That burns in glorious Araby,
With red scent chalicing the air,
Till earth-life grow Elysian there!

Half buried to her flaming breast
In this bright tree, she makes her nest,
Hundred-sunn'd Phoenix! when she must
Crumble at length to hoary dust!

Her gorgeous death-bed! her rich pyre
Burnt up with aromatic fire!
Her urn, sight high from spoiler men!
Her birthplace when self-born again!

The mountainless green wilds among,
Here ends she her unechoing song!
With amber tears and odorous sighs
Mourn'd by the desert where she dies!

Laid like the young fawn mossily
In sun-green vales of Araby,
I woke hard by the Phoenix tree
That with shadeless boughs flamed over me,
And upward call'd for a dumb cry.

With moonbroad orbs of wonder I
Beheld the immortal Bird on high
Glassing the great sun in her eye.
Stedfast she gazed upon his fire,
—Still her destroyer and her sire!—
As if to his her soul of flame
Had flown already whence it came;
Like those that sit and glare so still,
Intense with their death struggle, till
We touch, and curdle at their chill!—
But breathing yet while she doth burn,
　The deathless Daughter of the sun!
Slowly to crimson embers turn
　The beauties of the brightsome one.
O'er the broad nest her silver wings
Shook down their wasteful glitterings;
Her brinded neck high-arch'd in air
Like a small rainbow faded there;
But brighter glow'd her plumy crown
Mouldering to golden ashes down;
With fume of sweet woods, to the skies,
Pure as a Saint's adoring sighs,
Warm as a prayer in Paradise,
Her life-breath rose in sacrifice!
The while with shrill triumphant tone
Sounding aloud, aloft, alone,
Ceaseless her joyful deathwail she
Sang to departing Araby!

O, fast her amber blood doth flow
　From the heart-wounded Incense Tree,
Fast as earth's deep-embosom'd woe
　In silent rivulets to the sea!

Beauty may weep her fair first-born,
　Perchance in as resplendent tears,
Such golden dewdrops bow the corn
　When the stern sickleman appears:

But O! such perfume to a bower
    Never allured sweet-seeking bee,
As to sip fast that nectarous shower
    A thirstier minstrel drew in me!

George Darley

757   *To a friend*

When we were idlers with the loitering rills,
The need of human love we little noted:
Our love was nature, and the peace that floated
On the white mist, and dwelt upon the hills,
To sweet accord subdued our wayward wills:
One soul was ours, one mind, one heart devoted,
That, wisely doting, asked not why it doted,
And ours the unknown joy, which knowing kills.
But now I find how dear thou wert to me;
That man is more than half of nature's treasure,
Of that fair Beauty which no eye can see,
Of that sweet music which no ear can measure;
And now the streams may sing for others' pleasure,
The hills sleep on in their eternity.

Hartley Coleridge

758   *Long time a child*

Long time a child, and still a child, when years
Had painted manhood on my cheek, was I;
For yet I lived like one not born to die;
A thriftless prodigal of smiles and tears,
No hope I needed, and I knew no fears.
But sleep, though sweet, is only sleep, and waking,
I waked to sleep no more, at once o'ertaking
The vanguard of my age, with all arrears
Of duty on my back. Nor child, nor man,
Nor youth nor sage, I find my head is grey,

For I have lost the race I never ran:
A rathe December blights my lagging May;
And still I am a child though I be old,
Time is my debtor for my years untold.

Hartley Coleridge

759   *From country to town*

'Tis strange to me, who long have seen no face
That was not like a book whose every page
I knew by heart, a kindly common-place—
And faithful record of progressive age—
To wander forth and view an unknown race;
Of all that I have been to find no trace,
No footstep of my by-gone pilgrimage.
Thousands I pass, and no one stays his pace
To tell me that the day is fair, or rainy—
Each one his object seeks with anxious chase,
And I have not a common hope with any—
Thus like one drop of oil upon a flood,
In uncommunicating solitude—
Single am I amongst the countless many.

Hartley Coleridge

760   *An imitation of Wordsworth*

He lived amidst th'untrodden ways
    To Rydal Lake that lead;
A bard whom there were none to praise,
    And very few to read.

Behind a cloud his mystic sense,
    Deep hidden who can spy?
Bright as the night when not a star
    Is shining in the sky.

Unread his works—his 'Milk White Doe'
    With dust is dark and dim;
It's still in Longman's shop, and oh!
    The difference to him!

Hartley Coleridge

761   *I remember, I remember*

I remember, I remember
The house where I was born,
The little window where the sun
Came peeping in at morn;
He never came a wink too soon
Nor brought too long a day;
But now, I often wish the night
Had borne my breath away.

I remember, I remember
The roses, red and white,
The violets, and the lily-cups—
Those flowers made of light!
The lilacs where the robin built,
And where my brother set
The laburnum on his birthday,—
The tree is living yet!

I remember, I remember
Where I used to swing,
And thought the air must rush as fresh
To swallows on the wing;
My spirit flew in feathers then
That is so heavy now,
And summer pools could hardly cool
The fever on my brow.

I remember, I remember
The fir trees dark and high;
I used to think their slender tops
Were close against the sky:
It was a childish ignorance,
But now 'tis little joy
To know I'm farther off from heaven
That when I was a boy.

Thomas Hood

762   *Silence*

There is a silence where hath been no sound,
There is a silence where no sound may be,
In the cold grave—under the deep deep sea,
Or in the wide desert where no life is found,
Which hath been mute, and still must sleep profound;
No voice is hushed—no life treads silently,
But clouds and cloudy shadows wander free,
That never spoke, over the idle ground:
But in green ruins, in the desolate walls
Of antique palaces, where Man hath been,
Though the dun fox, or wild hyena, calls,
And owls, that flit continually between,
Shriek to the echo, and the low winds moan,
There the true silence is, self-conscious and alone.

Thomas Hood

763   *Ode on a distant prospect of Clapham Academy*

Ah me! those old familiar bounds!
That classic house, those classic grounds,
    My pensive thought recalls!
What tender urchins now confine,
What little captives now repine,
    Within yon irksome walls?

Ay, that's the very house! I know
Its ugly windows, ten a-row!
   Its chimneys in the rear!
And there's the iron rod so high,
That drew the thunder from the sky,
   And turn'd our table-beer!

There I was birch'd! there I was bred!
There like a little Adam fed
   From Learning's woeful tree!
The weary tasks I used to con!—
The hopeless leaves I wept upon!—
   Most fruitless leaves to me!—

The summon'd class!—the awful bow!—
I wonder who is master now
   And wholesome anguish sheds!
How many ushers now employs,
How many maids to see the boys
   Have nothing in their heads!

And Mrs. S——?—Doth she abet
(Like Pallas in the parlour) yet
   Some favour'd two or three,—
The little Crightons of the hour,
Her muffin-medals that devour,
   And swill her prize—bohea?

Ay, there's the play-ground! there's the lime
Beneath whose shade in summer's prime
   So wildly I have read!—
Who sits there *now*, and skims the cream
Of young Romance, and weaves a dream
   Of Love and Cottage-bread?

Who struts the Randall of the walk?
Who models tiny heads in chalk?
   Who scoops the light canoe?
What early genius buds apace?
Where's Poynter? Harris? Bowers? Chase?
   Hal Baylis? blithe Carew?

Alack! they're gone—a thousand ways!
And some are serving in 'the Greys',
   And some have perish'd young!—
Jack Harris weds his second wife;
Hal Baylis drives the *wane* of life;
   And blithe Carew—is hung!

Grave Bowers teaches A B C
To savages at Owhyee;
   Poor Chase is with the worms!—
All, all are gone—the olden breed!—
New crops of mushroom boys succeed,
   'And push us from our *forms!*'

Lo! where they scramble forth, and shout,
And leap, and skip, and mob about,
   At play where we have play'd!
Some hop, some run (some fall), some twine
Their crony arms; some in the shine,
   And some are in the shade!

Lo! there what mix'd conditions run!
The orphan lad; the widow's son;
   And Fortune's favour'd care—
The wealthy-born, for whom she hath
Mac-Adamised the future path—
   The Nabob's pamper'd heir!

Some brightly starr'd—some evil born,—
For honour some, and some for scorn,—
   For fair or foul renown!
Good, bad, indiff'rent—none may lack!
Look, here's a White, and there's a Black!
   And there's a Creole brown!

Some laugh and sing, some mope and weep,
And wish *their* frugal sires would keep
   Their only sons at home;—
Some tease the future tense, and plan
The full-grown doings of the man,
   And pant for years to come!

A foolish wish! There's one at hoop;
And four at *fives!* and five who stoop
   The marble taw to speed!
And one that curvets in and out,
Reining his fellow Cob about—
   Would I were in his *steed!*

Yet he would gladly halt and drop
That boyish harness off, to swop
   With this world's heavy van—
To toil, to tug. O little fool!
While thou canst be a horse at school
   To wish to be a man!

Perchance thou deem'st it were a thing
To wear a crown,—to be a king!
   And sleep on regal down!
Alas! thou know'st not kingly cares;
Far happier is thy head that wears
   That hat without a crown!

And dost thou think that years acquire
New added joys? Dost think thy sire
   More happy than his son?
That manhood's mirth?—Oh, go thy ways
To Drury Lane when —— *plays,*
   And see how *forced* our fun!

Thy taws are brave!—thy tops are rare!—
Our tops are spun with coils of care,
   Our *dumps* are no delight!—
The Elgin marbles are but tame,
And 'tis at best a sorry game
   To fly the Muse's kite!

Our hearts are dough, our heels are lead,
Our topmost joys fall dull and dead
   Like balls with no rebound!
And often with a faded eye
We look behind, and send a sigh
   Towards that merry ground!

Then be contented. Thou hast got
The most of heaven in thy young lot
   There's sky-blue in thy cup!
Thou'lt find thy Manhood all too fast—
Soon come, soon gone! and Age at last
   A sorry *breaking-up!*

Thomas Hood

764   *Our village—by a villager*

Our village, that's to say not Miss Mitford's village, but
   our village of Bullock Smithy,
Is come into by an avenue of trees, three oak pollards,
   two elders, and a withy;
And in the middle, there's a green of about not exceeding an acre and a half;
It's common to all, and fed off by nineteen cows, six
   ponies, three horses, five asses, two foals, seven pigs,
   and a calf!
Besides a pond in the middle, as is held by a similar sort
   of common law lease,
And contains twenty ducks, six drakes, three ganders,
   two dead dogs, four drown'd kittens, and twelve
   geese.
Of course the green's cropt very close, and does famous
   for bowling when the little village boys play at
   cricket;
Only some horse, or pig, or cow, or great jackass, is sure
   to come and stand right before the wicket.
There's fifty-five private houses, let alone barns and
   workshops, and pigstyes, and poultry huts, and such-
   like sheds;
With plenty of public-houses—two Foxes, one Green
   Man, three Bunch of Grapes, one Crown, and six
   King's Heads.
The Green Man is reckon'd the best, as the only one
   that for love or money can raise

A postilion, a blue jacket, two deplorable lame white horses, and a ramshackled 'neat postchaise'.

There's one parish church for all the people, whatsoever may be their ranks in life or their degrees,

Except one very damp, small, dark, freezing-cold, little Methodist chapel of Ease;

And close by the church-yard there's a stone-mason's yard, that when the time is seasonable

Will furnish with afflictions sore and marble urns and cherubims very low and reasonable.

There's a cage, comfortable enough; I've been in it with old Jack Jeffrey and Tom Pike;

For the Green Man next door will send you in ale, gin, or any thing else you like.

I can't speak of the stocks, as nothing remains of them but the upright post;

But the pound is kept in repairs for the sake of Cob's horse, as is always there almost.

There's a smithy of course, where that queer sort of chap in his way, Old Joe Bradley,

Perpetually hammers and stammers, for he stutters and shoes horses very badly.

There's a shop of all sorts, that sells every thing, kept by the widow of Mr. Task;

But when you go there it's ten to one she's out of every-thing you ask.

You'll know her house by the swarm of boys, like flies, about the old sugary cask:

There are six empty houses, and not so well paper'd inside as out,

For bill-stickers won't beware, but stick notices of sales and election placards all about.

That's the Doctor's with a green door, where the garden pots in the windows is seen;

A weakly monthly rose that don't blow, and a dead geranium, and a tea-plant with five black leaves and one green.

As for hollyoaks at the cottage doors, and honey-suckles and jasmines, you may go and whistle;

But the Tailor's front garden grows two cabbages, dock, a ha'porth of pennyroyal, two dandelions, and a thistle.

There are three small orchards—Mr. Busby's the school-master's is the chief—

With two pear-trees that don't bear; one plum and an apple, that every year is stripped by a thief.

There's another small day-school too, kept by the respectable Mrs. Gaby.

A select establishment, for six little boys and one big, and four little girls and a baby;

There's a rectory, with pointed gables and strange odd chimneys that never smokes,

For the rector don't live on his living like other Christian sort of folks;

There's a barber's, once a-week well filled with rough black-bearded, shock-headed churls,

And a window with two feminine men's heads, and two masculine ladies in false curls;

There's a butcher's, and a carpenter's, and a plumber's, and a small green-grocer's, and a baker,

But he won't bake on a Sunday, and there's a sexton that's a coal-merchant besides, and an undertaker;

And a toy-shop, but not a whole one, for a village can't compare with the London shops;

One window sells drums, dolls, kites, carts, bats, Clout's balls, and the other sells malt and hops.

And Mrs. Brown, in domestic economy not to be a bit behind her betters,

Lets her house to a milliner, a watchmaker, a rat-catcher, a cobler, lives in it herself, and it's the post-office for letters.

Now I've gone through all the village—ay, from end to end, save and except one more house,

But I haven't come to that—and I hope I never shall—and that's the Village Poor House!

Thomas Hood

And so men say, I love thee! hence thy eye
Meets mine so coldly, and thy little hand
Drops from my timid grasp so passively;
Hence that unlooked-for air of meek command,
With which thou check'st my ill-dissembled sigh,
As if e'en I forgot the sacred band
Thou wear'st so well, and would not rather die
Of grief, heart-broken, in some distant land.
It is most true I love thee,—love thee more
Than aught on this green earth—'tis a sad truth;
And I shall lose the best years of my youth
In a fond sorrow, with no better lore
   Sought or acquired than the poor minstrelsy
   With which I sing to sleep my restless love for thee!

Derwent Coleridge

766   *Melhill feast*

Aye, up at the feast, by Melhill's brow,
So softly below the clouds in flight,
There swept on the wood, the shade and light,
Tree after tree, and bough by bough.

And there, among girls on left and right,
On one with a winsome smile I set
My looks; and the more, the more we met
Glance upon glance, and sight by sight.

The road she had come by then was soon
The one of my paths that best I knew,
By glittering gossamer and dew,
Evening by evening, moon by moon.

Sweet were the hopes I found to cheer
My heart as I thought on time to come,
With one that would bless my happy home,
Moon upon moon, and year by year.

William Barnes

767   *The rwose in the dark*

In zummer, leäte at evenen tide,
    I zot to spend a moonless hour
'Ithin the window, wi' the zide
    A-bound wi' rwoses out in flow'r,
Bezide the bow'r, vorsook o' birds,
An' listen'd to my true-love's words.

A-risen to her comely height,
    She push'd the swingen ceäsement round;
And I could hear, beyond my zight,
    The win'-blow'd beech-tree softly sound,
On higher ground, a-swaÿen slow,
On drough my happy hour below.

An' tho the darkness then did hide
    The dewy rwose's blushen bloom,
He still did cast sweet aïr inside
    To Jeäne, a-chatten in the room;
An' though the gloom did hide her feäce,
Her words did bind me to the pleäce.

An' there, while she, wi' runnen tongue,
    Did talk unzeen 'ithin the hall,
I thought her like the rwose that flung
    His sweetness vrom his darken'd ball,
'Ithout the wall, an' sweet's the zight
Ov her bright feäce, by mornen light.

William Barnes

As day did darken on the dewless grass
   There still wi' nwone a-come by me,
   To stäy a-while at hwome by me;
   Within the house, all dumb by me,
A zot me sad as the eventide did pass.

An' there a win'-blast shook the rattlen door,
   An' seemed, as win' did mwone without,
   As if my Jeäne, alwone without,
   A-stannen on the stone without,
Wer there a-come wi' happiness oonce mwore.

I went to door; an' out vrom trees above
   My head, upon the blast by me,
   Sweet blossoms were a-cast by me,
   As if my love, a-past by me,
Did fling em down—a token ov her love.

'Sweet blossoms o' the tree where I do murn,'
   I thought, 'if you did blow vor her,
   Vor apples that should grow vor her,
   A-vallen down below vor her,
O then how happy I should zee you kern.'

But no. Too soon I voun' my charm abroke.
   Noo comely soul in white like her—
   Noo soul a-steppen light like her—
   An' nwone o' comely height like her—
Went by; but all my grief ageän awoke.

                    William Barnes

769   *Song*

He came unlook'd for, undesir'd,
A sun-rise in the northern sky:
More than the brightest dawn admir'd,
To shine and then for ever fly.

His love, conferr'd without a claim,
Perchance was like the fitful blaze,
Which lives to light a steadier flame,
And, while that strengthens, fast decays.

Glad fawn along the forest springing,
Gay birds that breeze-like stir the leaves,
Why hither haste, no message bringing
To solace one that deeply grieves?

Thou star that dost the skies adorn
So brightly heralding the day,
Bring one more welcome than the morn,
Or still in night's dark prison stay.

Sara Coleridge

770   *Gone in the wind*

Solomon, where is thy throne? It is gone in the wind.
Babylon, where is thy might? It is gone in the wind.
Like the swift shadows of noon, like the dreams of the
    blind,
Vanish the glories and pomps of the earth in the wind.

Man, canst thou build upon aught in the pride of thy
    mind?
Wisdom will teach thee that nothing can tarry behind:
Tho' there be thousand bright actions embalm'd and
    enshrined,
Myriads and millions of brighter are snow in the wind.

Solomon, where is thy throne? It is gone in the wind.
Babylon, where is thy might? It is gone in the wind.
All that the genius of man hath achieved or design'd
Waits but its hour to be dealt with as dust by the wind.

Say what is pleasure? A phantom, a mask undefined:
Science? An almond whereof we can pierce but the
rind:
Honour and affluence? Firmans that Fortune hath
sign'd,
Only to glitter and pass on the wings of the wind.

Solomon, where is thy throne? It is gone in the wind.
Babylon, where is thy might? It is gone in the wind.
Who is the fortunate? *He who in anguish hath pined!*
He shall rejoice when his relics are dust in the wind.

Mortal, be careful with what thy best hopes are en-
twined:
Woe to the miners for Truth, where the lampless have
mined!
Woe to the seekers on earth for what none ever find!
They and their trust shall be scatter'd like leaves to the
wind!

Solomon, where is thy throne? It is gone in the wind.
Babylon, where is thy might? It is gone in the wind.
Happy in death are they only whose hearts have con-
sign'd
All earth's affections and longings and cares to the wind.

Pity thou, reader, the madness of poor humankind
Raving of knowledge—and Satan so busy to blind!
Raving of glory, like me; for the garlands I bind,
Garlands of song, are but gather'd—and strewn in the
wind.

Solomon, where is thy throne? It is gone in the wind.
Babylon, where is thy might? It is gone in the wind.
I, Abul-Namez, must rest; for my fire is declined,
And I hear voices from Hades like bells on the wind.

James Clarence Mangan

The swallow leaves her nest,
The soul my weary breast;
But therefore let the rain
   On my grave
Fall pure; for why complain?
Since both will come again
   O'er the wave.

The wind dead leaves and snow
Doth hurry to and fro;
And, once, a day shall break
   O'er the wave,
When a storm of ghosts shall shake
The dead, until they wake
   In the grave.

            Thomas Lovell Beddoes

772 *Dream-pedlary*

If there were dreams to sell,
   What would you buy?
Some cost a passing bell;
   Some a light sigh,
That shakes from Life's fresh crown
Only a rose-leaf down.
If there were dreams to sell,
Merry and sad to tell,
And the crier rang the bell,
   What would you buy?

A cottage lone and still,
   With bowers nigh,
Shadowy, my woes to still,
   Until I die.

Such pearl from Life's fresh crown
Fain would I shake me down.
Were dreams to have at will,
This would best heal my ill,
    This would I buy.

Thomas Lovell Beddoes

773   *Wolfram's song*

Old Adam, the carrion crow,
    The old crow of Cairo;
He sat in the shower, and let it flow
    Under his tail and over his crest;
        And through every feather
        Leak'd the wet weather;
And the bough swung under his nest;
For his beak it was heavy with marrow.
    Is that the wind dying? O no;
    It's only two devils, that blow
    Through a murderer's bones, to and fro,
        In the ghosts' moonshine.

Ho! Eve, my grey carrion wife,
    When we have supped on king's marrow,
Where shall we drink and make merry our life?
    Our nest it is queen Cleopatra's skull,
        'Tis cloven and crack'd,
        And batter'd and hack'd,
But with tears of blue eyes it is full:
Let us drink then, my raven of Cairo!
    Is that the wind dying? O no;
    It's only two devils, that blow
    Through a murderer's bones, to and fro,
        In the ghosts' moonshine.

Thomas Lovell Beddoes

Strew not earth with empty stars,
  Strew it not with roses,
Nor feathers from the crest of Mars,
  Nor summer's idle posies.
'Tis not the primrose-sandalled moon,
  Nor cold and silent morn,
Nor he that climbs the dusty noon,
Nor mower war with scythe that drops,
Stuck with helmed and turbaned tops
  Of enemies new shorn.
Ye cups, ye lyres, ye trumpets know,
Pour your music, let it flow,
'Tis Bacchus' son who walks below.

Thomas Lovell Beddoes

775 *Days*

Daughters of Time, the hypocritic Days,
Muffled and dumb like barefoot dervishes
And marching single in an endless file,
Bring diadems and faggots in their hands.
To each they offer gifts after his will—
Bread, kingdoms, stars, and sky that holds them all.
I, in my pleachèd garden, watch'd the pomp,
Forgot my morning wishes, hastily
Took a few herbs and apples, and the Day
Turn'd and departed silent. I, too late,
Under her solemn fillet saw the scorn.

Ralph Waldo Emerson

If the red slayer think he slays,
  Or if the slain think he is slain,
They know not well the subtle ways
  I keep, and pass, and turn again.

Far or forgot to me is near;
  Shadow and sunlight are the same;
The vanish'd gods to me appear;
  And one to me are shame and fame.

They reckon ill who leave me out;
  When me they fly, I am the wings;
I am the doubter and the doubt,
  And I the hymn the Brahmin sings.

The strong gods pine for my abode,
  And pine in vain the sacred Seven;
But thou, meek lover of the good!
  Find me, and turn thy back on heaven.

Ralph Waldo Emerson

777 *The song of the western men*

A good sword and a trusty hand!
  A merry heart and true!
King James's men shall understand
  What Cornish lads can do.

And have they fix'd the where and when?
  And shall Trelawny die?
Here's twenty thousand Cornish men
  Will know the reason why!

Out spake their Captain brave and bold,
　A merry wight was he:
'If London Tower were Michael's Hold,
　We'll set Trelawny free!

'We'll cross the Tamar, land to land,
　The Severn is no stay;
With "One and All" and hand to hand
　And who shall bid us nay?

'And when we come to London Wall,
　A pleasant sight to view,
Come forth, come forth, ye cowards all!
　Here's men as good as you.

'Trelawny he's in keep and hold,
　Trelawny he may die:
But here's twenty thousand Cornish bold
　Will know the reason why!'
　　And shall Trelawny die?
　　And shall Trelawny die?
　　Here's twenty thousand Cornish men
　　Will know the reason why!

Robert Stephen Hawker

778　*The mask*

I have a smiling face, she said,
　I have a jest for all I meet,
I have a garland for my head
　And all its flowers are sweet,—
And so you call me gay, she said.

Grief taught to me this smile, she said,
　And Wrong did teach this jesting bold;
These flowers were pluck'd from garden-bed
　While a death-chime was toll'd.
And what now will you say?—she said.

Behind no prison-grate, she said,
    Which slurs the sunshine half a mile,
Live captives so uncomforted
    As souls behind a smile.
God's pity let us pray, she said.

I know my face is bright, she said,—
    Such brightness dying suns diffuse;
I bear upon my forehead shed
    The sign of what I lose,—
The ending of my day, she said.

If I dared leave this smile, she said,
    And take a moan upon my mouth,
And tie a cypress round my head,
    And let my tears run smooth,—
It were the happier way, she said.

And since that must not be, she said,
    I fain your bitter world would leave.
How calmly, calmly, smile the Dead,
    Who do not, therefore, grieve!
The yea of Heaven is yea, she said.

But in your bitter world, she said,
    Face-joy's a costly mask to wear.
'Tis bought with pangs long nourishèd,
    And rounded to despair.
Grief's earnest makes life's play, she said.

Ye weep for those who weep? she said—
    Ah fools! I bid you pass them by.
Go, weep for those whose hearts have bled
    What time their eyes were dry.
Whom sadder can I say? she said.

                                    Elizabeth Barrett Browning

779 *Grief*

I tell you, hopeless grief is passionless;
That only men incredulous of despair,
Half-taught in anguish, through the midnight air
Beat upward to God's throne in loud access
Of shrieking and reproach. Full desertness
In souls as countries lieth silent-bare
Under the blanching, vertical eye-glare
Of the absolute Heavens. Deep-hearted man, express
Grief for thy Dead in silence like to death—
Most like a monumental statue set
In everlasting watch and moveless woe
Till itself crumble to the dust beneath.
Touch it; the marble eyelids are not wet!
If it could weep, it could arise and go.

Elizabeth Barrett Browning

780 *Chaucer*

An old man in a lodge within a park;
The chamber walls depicted all around
With portraitures of huntsman, hawk, and hound,
And the hurt deer. He listeneth to the lark,
Whose song comes with the sunshine through the dark
Of painted glass in leaden lattice bound;
He listeneth and he laugheth at the sound,
Then writeth in a book like any clerk.
He is the poet of the dawn, who wrote
The Canterbury Tales, and his old age
Made beautiful with song; and as I read
I hear the crowing cock, I hear the note
Of lark and linnet, and from every page
Rise odours of plough'd field or flowery mead.

Henry Wadsworth Longfellow

When winter winds are piercing chill,
  And through the hawthorn blows the gale,
With solemn feet I tread the hill,
  That overbrows the lonely vale.

O'er the bare upland, and away
  Through the long reach of desert woods,
The embracing sunbeams chastely play,
  And gladden these deep solitudes.

Where, twisted round the barren oak,
  The summer vine in beauty clung,
And summer winds the stillness broke,
  The crystal icicle is hung.

Where, from their frozen urns, mute springs
  Pour out the river's gradual tide,
Shrilly the skater's iron rings,
  And voices fill the woodland side.

Alas! how changed from the fair scene,
  When birds sang out their mellow lay,
And winds were soft, and woods were green,
  And the song ceased not with the day!

But still wild music is abroad,
  Pale, desert woods! within your crowd;
And gathering winds, in hoarse accord,
  Amid the vocal reeds pipe loud.

Chill airs and wintry winds! my ear
  Has grown familiar with your song;
I hear it in the opening year,
  I listen, and it cheers me long.

Henry Wadsworth Longfellow

Half of my life is gone, and I have let
　　The years slip from me and have not fulfilled
　　The aspiration of my youth, to build
Some tower of song with lofty parapet.
Not indolence, nor pleasure, nor the fret
　　Of restless passions that would not be stilled,
　　But sorrow, and a care that almost killed,
Kept me from what I may accomplish yet;
Though, half-way up the hill, I see the Past
　　Lying beneath me with its sounds and sights,—
　　A city in the twilight dim and vast,
With smoking roofs, soft bells, and gleaming lights,—
　　And hear above me on the autumnal blast
　　The cataract of Death far thundering from the heights.

Henry Wadsworth Longfellow

783　*Hawthorne—May 23 1864*

How beautiful it was, that one bright day
　　In the long week of rain!
Though all its splendour could not chase away
　　The omnipresent pain.

The lovely town was white with apple-blooms,
　　And the great elms o'erhead
Dark shadows wove on their aerial looms
　　Shot through with golden thread.

Across the meadows, by the gray old manse,
　　The historic river flowed:
I was as one who wanders in a trance,
　　Unconscious of his road.

The faces of familiar friends seemed strange;
　　Their voices I could hear,
And yet the words they uttered seemed to change
　　Their meaning to my ear.

For the one face I looked for was not there,
   The one low voice was mute;
Only an unseen presence filled the air,
   And baffled my pursuit.

Now I look back, and meadow, manse, and stream
   Dimly my thought defines;
I only see—a dream within a dream—
   The hill-top hearsed with pines.

I only hear above his place of rest
   Their tender undertone,
The infinite longings of a troubled breast,
   The voice so like his own.

There in seclusion and remote from men
   The wizard hand lies cold,
Which at its topmost speed let fall the pen,
   And left the tale half told.

Ah! who shall lift that wand of magic power,
   And the lost clew regain?
The unfinished window in Aladdin's tower
   Unfinished must remain!

Henry Wadsworth Longfellow

784   *The tide rises, the tide falls*

The tide rises, the tide falls,
The twilight darkens, the curlew calls;
Along the sea-sands damp and brown
The traveller hastens toward the town,
   And the tide rises, the tide falls.

Darkness settles on roofs and walls,
But the sea, the sea in the darkness calls;
The little waves, with their soft, white hands,
Efface the footprints in the sands,
   And the tide rises, the tide falls.

The morning breaks; the steeds in their stalls
Stamp and neigh, as the hostler calls;
The day returns, but nevermore
Returns the traveller to the shore,
   And the tide rises, the tide falls.

Henry Wadsworth Longfellow

785 *All's well*

The clouds, which rise with thunder, slake
   Our thirsty souls with rain;
The blow most dreaded falls to break
   From off our limbs a chain;
And wrongs of man to man but make
   The love of God more plain.
As through the shadowy lens of even
The eye looks farthest into heaven
On gleams of star and depths of blue
The glaring sunshine never knew!

John Greenleaf Whittier

786 *Ichabod*

So fallen! so lost! the light withdrawn
   Which once he wore!
The glory from his gray hairs gone
   Forevermore!

Revile him not, the Tempter hath
   A snare for all;
And pitying tears, not scorn and wrath,
   Befit his fall!

Oh, dumb be passion's stormy rage,
    When he who might
Have lighted up and led his age,
    Falls back in night.

Scorn! would the angels laugh, to mark
    A bright soul driven,
Fiend-goaded, down the endless dark,
    From hope and heaven!

Let not the land once proud of him
    Insult him now,
Nor brand with deeper shame his dim,
    Dishonored brow.

But let its humbled sons, instead,
    From sea to lake,
A long lament, as for the dead,
    In sadness make.

Of all we loved and honored, naught
    Save power remains:
A fallen angel's pride of thought,
    Still strong in chains.

All else is gone; from those great eyes
    The soul has fled:
When faith is lost, when honor dies,
    The man is dead!

Then, pay the reverence of old days
    To his dead fame;
Walk backward, with averted gaze,
    And hide the shame!

John Greenleaf Whittier

When Letty had scarce pass'd her third glad year,
And her young artless words began to flow,
One day we gave the child a colour'd sphere
Of the wide earth, that she might mark and know,
By tint and outline, all its sea and land.
She patted all the world; old empires peep'd
Between her baby fingers; her soft hand
Was welcome at all frontiers. How she leap'd,
And laugh'd and prattled in her world-wide bliss;
But when we turn'd her sweet unlearnèd eye
On our own isle, she raised a joyous cry—
'Oh! yes, I see it, Letty's home is there!'
And while she hid all England with a kiss,
Bright over Europe fell her golden hair.

Charles Tennyson Turner

BOOK FIVE

The Victorians and the Twentieth Century

INTRODUCTION

Useful generalisations about nineteenth-century poetry are even harder to come by than generalisations about the poetry of any other period. It was an age of diverse influences and talents, an age when the many minor poets add up perhaps to something more impressive than the few major ones. By 1850 the great Romantics were all dead or silent. Their places were not adequately filled even by the dominating figures of Tennyson and Browning. Much of the work of these two masters which most appealed to their age ran to considerable length; they are accordingly not fully represented in these pages. Lyrics as interesting as theirs were being written by many others: by the Pre-Raphaelites (the Rossettis and William Morris), by Matthew Arnold, and by the Americans, whose poetry now became important both for quantity and for quality. The period of the American Civil War, fought to establish national unity, saw the fulfilment of two very different and opposed talents. Walt Whitman's voice was a loud one, and his large, diffuse, nationally conscious art was characteristic of one aspect of the American spirit. The other, Emily Dickinson, spoke with a quiet precision and a distaste for everything Whitman stood for; yet she is not less characteristic of another aspect of America. Later Americans—E. A. Robinson, Robert Frost, Wallace Stevens and John Crowe Ransom—remind us, now of one, now of the other side of the national genius.

Returning to Britain, we may make one fairly sound generalisation about the spirit of the Victorian age: it was highly serious and profoundly interested in social and ethical problems. But it had its lighter side, its reaction against solemnity. This is evident in the verse of Edward Lear and Lewis

Carroll. The later Victorian period was also one of rebellion against the stifling atmosphere of middle-class respectability. Among the poets of the nineties—Dowson, Henley and Housman, for instance—we notice the feeling of being social outlaws; we see also a reaction against length and heaviness in verse, so that once more poets began to do their best work in brief lyrics. Hardy, turning from the novel to verse about the end of the century, became perhaps the finest lyric poet of his time. The work of the Irishman, W. B. Yeats, had its greatest influence on the poets of today, as did that of the Jesuit, G. M. Hopkins, a lonely and unique figure, the effect of whose highly personal idiom is still being felt through the work of his disciple, Dylan Thomas.

The poetry of the first half of our own century is represented mainly by two 'schools': the Georgians and the poets of World War I—Davies, De la Mare, Edward Thomas, Siegfried Sassoon, Owen, Robert Graves and Edmund Blunden—are notable for the distinctively 'English' quality of their writing; by contrast, the movement which began as 'Imagism', and is represented by Ezra Pound and T. S. Eliot, though it became rooted in this country, and has had a fertilising effect on much of our present-day poetry, was American and European in origin.

In thus trying to suggest groupings among the seventy poets in this Part and to indicate the direction of some of the currents in their work, let us not forget that this is a book of poems, not of influences or even of poets. The effect produced by the book as a whole is one of diversity, not of sameness. It would be doing poetry a disservice if it were to be maintained that the stream flows regularly and tidily in neatly defined channels. On the contrary, its course is irregular and unpredictable, now flowing swiftly and abundantly, now spasmodically, at times almost disappearing underground, to re-emerge in new territory and under new appearances. It is the poems that matter.

CONTENTS

Much madness is divinest sense 899
I know some lonely houses 900
Pain has an element of blank 901
Belshazzar had a letter 902
Presentiment 903
The sky is low 904
There's a certain slant of light 905
Exultation is the going 906
I like a look of agony 907
I never saw a moor 908
The last night that she lived 909
The bustle in a house 910
Because I could not stop for death 911
I'm nobody! Who are you? 912
We play at paste 913
Hope is the thing with feathers 914
Surgeons must be very careful 915
Faith is a fine invention 916
I years had been from home 917
I gave myself to him 918
I dreaded that first robin so 919
I started early, took my dog 920
Essential oils are wrung 921
It was not death 922
I cannot live with you 923
Safe in their alabaster chambers 924

LEWIS CARROLL 1832-1898

Jabberwocky 925

RICHARD WATSON DIXON 1833-1900

Song (The feathers of the willow) 926

On a small six-acre farm dwelt John Grist the miller;
Near a pond not far beyond grew a drooping willer,
Underneath its spreading leaves sat Jane, his only
    daughter,
Meditating suicide in the muddy water,
Element aqua pura, aqua impura.
She sat by a duck pond of dark water,
Under the drooping willow tree.

She'd been jilted by a youth who had joined the Rifles,
A young man not worth a rap, who never stuck at
    trifles.
Though he promised to keep true, act like a faithful
    lover,
When his rifle suit he got, then leg bail he gave her,
Hooked it, stepped it, toddled, mizzled.
She sat by a duck pond of dark water,
Under the drooping willow tree.

'All alone I'm left,' says she, 'my poor heart is bustin;
Dearly did I love my Joe, though he wore plain fustin.
But my nose is out of joint, and don't it make me nettled.
In this pond I'll drown myself, then I shall be settled,
Bottled, finished, done for, flummoxed.'
She sat by a duck pond of dark water,
Under the drooping willow tree.

She'd no wish to spoil her clothes, so undressed that
    minute;
But the water felt so cold when her toes were in it.
'If it weren't so cold,' said she, 'I'd jump in like wink-
    ing.'
Then she wiped her nose, and sat upon the edge think-
    ing,
Pondering, puzzling, considering, ruminating.
She sat by a duck pond of dark water,
Under the drooping willow tree.

Like a Venus she sat in her nude state staying;
Presently she was frightened by a donkey braying.
Like a frog she gave a leap, but worse luck she stumbled,
Lost her equilibrium, and in the water tumbled,
Fell in, pitched in, dropped in, popped in.
She fell in the duck pond of dark water,
Under the drooping willow tree.

When she found she'd fallen in, she then took to
    swooning;
Very long it would not have been, before she took to
    drowning.
But her Joseph was close by, saw her in the water,
With his crooked walking stick by the wool he caught
    her,
Nabbed her, grabbed her, seized her, collared her,
From out of the duck pond of dark water,
Under the drooping willow tree.

He beheld her coming to with great acclamation,
And the tree bore witness to their reconciliation.
There it stands in all its pride, and will stand, moreover,
Unless the spot should be required by the London,
    Chatham and Dover
Railway, Company, Limited, good dividends.
They'll sit by the duck pond of dark water,
Under the drooping willow tree.

Anonymous

789   *Erith*

There are men in the village of Erith
Whom nobody seeth or heareth,
    And there looms on the marge
    Of the river a barge
That nobody roweth or steereth.

Anonymous

790 *Punch, brothers, punch!*

Punch, brothers, punch! punch the fare!
Punch in the presence of the passinjare!
A blue trip slip for an 8-cent fare,
A buff trip slip for a 6-cent fare,
A pink trip slip for a 3-cent fare,
All in the presence of the passinjare.

Anonymous (American)

791 *The splendour falls on castle walls*

The splendour falls on castle walls
    And snowy summits old in story:
The long light shakes across the lakes,
    And the wild cataract leaps in glory.
Blow, bugle, blow, set the wild echoes flying,
Blow, bugle; answer, echoes, dying, dying, dying.

O hark, O hear! how thin and clear,
    And thinner, clearer, farther going!
O sweet and far from cliff and scar
    The horns of Elfland faintly blowing!
Blow, let us hear the purple glens replying:
Blow, bugle; answer, echoes, dying, dying, dying,

O love, they die in yon rich sky,
    They faint on hill or field or river:
Our echoes roll from soul to soul,
    And grow for ever and for ever.
Blow, bugle, blow, set the wild echoes flying,
And answer, echoes, answer, dying, dying, dying.

Alfred, Lord Tennyson

The woods decay, the woods decay and fall,
The vapours weep their burthen to the ground,
Man comes and tills the field and lies beneath,
And after many a summer dies the swan.
Me only cruel immortality
Consumes: I wither slowly in thine arms,
Here at the quiet limit of the world,
A white-hair'd shadow roaming like a dream
The ever silent spaces of the East,
Far-folded mists, and gleaming halls of morn.
   Alas! for this grey shadow, once a man—
So glorious in his beauty and thy choice,
Who madest him thy chosen, that he seem'd
To his great heart none other than a God!
I ask'd thee, 'Give me immortality.'

   Then didst thou grant mine asking with a smile,
Like wealthy men who care not how they give.
But thy strong Hours indignant work'd their wills,
And beat me down and marr'd and wasted me,
And tho' they could not end me, left me maim'd
To dwell in presence of immortal youth,
Immortal age beside immortal youth,
And all I was, in ashes. Can thy love,
Thy beauty, make amends, tho' even now,
Close over us, the silver star, thy guide,
Shines in those tremulous eyes that fill with tears
To hear me? Let me go: take back thy gift:
Why should a man desire in any way
To vary from the kindly race of men,
Or pass beyond the goal of ordinance
Where all should pause, as is most meet for all?

   A soft air fans the cloud apart; there comes
A glimpse of that dark world where I was born.
Once more the old mysterious glimmer steals
From thy pure brows, and from thy shoulders pure,

And bosom beating with a heart renew'd.
Thy cheek begins to redden thro' the gloom,
Thy sweet eyes brighten slowly close to mine,
Ere yet they blind the stars, and the wild team
Which love thee, yearning for thy yoke, arise,
And shake the darkness from their loosen'd manes,
And beat the twilight into flakes of fire.

Lo! ever thus thou growest beautiful
In silence, then before thine answer given
Departest, and thy tears are on my cheek.

Why wilt thou ever scare me with thy tears,
And make me tremble lest a saying learnt,
In days far-off, on that dark earth, be true?
'The Gods themselves cannot recall their gifts.'

Ay me! ay me! with what another heart
In days far-off, and with what other eyes
I us'd to watch—if I be he that watch'd—
The lucid outline forming round thee; saw
The dim curls kindle into sunny rings;
Chang'd with thy mystic change, and felt my blood
Glow with the glow, that slowly crimson'd all
Thy presence and thy portals, while I lay,
Mouth, forehead, eyelids, growing dewy-warm
With kisses balmier than half-opening buds
Of April, and could hear the lips that kiss'd
Whispering I knew not what of wild and sweet,
Like that strange song I heard Apollo sing,
While Ilion like a mist rose into towers.

Yet hold me not for ever in thine East:
How can my nature longer mix with thine?
Coldly thy rosy shadows bathe me, cold
Are all thy lights, and cold my wrinkled feet
Upon thy glimmering thresholds, when the steam
Floats up from those dim fields about the homes

Of happy men that have the power to die,
And grassy barrows of the happier dead.
Release me, and restore me to the ground;
Thou seest all things, thou wilt see my grave:
Thou wilt renew thy beauty morn by morn;
I earth in earth forget these empty courts,
And thee returning on thy silver wheels.

Alfred, Lord Tennyson

793 Ulysses

It little profits that an idle king,
By this still hearth, among these barren crags,
Match'd with an aged wife, I mete and dole
Unequal laws unto a savage race,
That hoard, and sleep, and feed, and know not me.
I cannot rest from travel: I will drink
Life to the lees: all times I have enjoy'd
Greatly, have suffer'd greatly, both with those
That loved me, and alone; on shore, and when
Thro' scudding drifts the rainy Hyades
Vext the dim sea: I am become a name;
For always roaming with a hungry heart
Much have I seen and known; cities of men
And manners, climates, councils, governments,
Myself not least, but honour'd of them all;
And drunk delight of battle with my peers,
Far on the ringing plains of windy Troy.
I am a part of all that I have met;
Yet all experience is an arch wherethro'
Gleams that untravell'd world, whose margin fades
For ever and for ever when I move.
How dull it is to pause, to make an end,
To rust unburnish'd, not to shine in use!
As tho' to breathe were life. Life piled on life
Were all too little, and of one to me
Little remains: but every hour is sav'd

From that eternal silence, something more,
A bringer of new things; and vile it were
For some three suns to store and hoard myself,
And this gray spirit yearning in desire
To follow knowledge, like a sinking star,
Beyond the utmost bound of human thought.

This is my son, mine own Telemachus,
To whom I leave the sceptre and the isle—
Well-lov'd of me, discerning to fulfil
This labour, by slow prudence to make mild
A rugged people, and thro' soft degrees
Subdue them to the useful and the good.
Most blameless is he, centred in the sphere
Of common duties, decent not to fail
In offices of tenderness, and pay
Meet adoration to my household gods,
When I am gone. He works his work, I mine.

There lies the port: the vessel puffs her sail:
There gloom the dark broad seas. My mariners,
Souls that have toil'd, and wrought, and thought with
                                                    me—
That ever with a frolic welcome took
The thunder and the sunshine, and oppos'd
Free hearts, free foreheads—you and I are old;
Old age hath yet his honour and his toil;
Death closes all: but something ere the end,
Some work of noble note, may yet be done,
Not unbecoming men that strove with Gods.
The lights begin to twinkle from the rocks:
The long day wanes; the slow moon climbs: the deep
Moans round with many voices. Come, my friends,
'Tis not too late to seek a newer world.
Push off, and sitting well in order smite
The sounding furrows; for my purpose holds
To sail beyond the sunset, and the baths
Of all the western stars, until I die.
It may be that the gulfs will wash us down:
It may be we shall touch the Happy Isles,
And see the great Achilles, whom we knew.
Tho' much is taken, much abides; and tho'

We are not now that strength which in old days
Mov'd earth and heaven; that which we are, we are
One equal temper of heroic hearts,
Made weak by time and fate, but strong in will
To strive, to seek, to find, and not to yield.

Alfred, Lord Tennyson

794   *The owl*

When cats run home and light is come,
    And dew is cold upon the ground,
And the far-off stream is dumb,
    And the whirring sail goes round,
    And the whirring sail goes round;
        Alone and warming his five wits,
        The white owl in the belfry sits.

When merry milkmaids click the latch,
    And rarely smells the new-mown hay,
And the cock hath sung beneath the thatch
    Twice or thrice his roundelay,
    Twice or thrice his roundelay;
        Alone and warming his five wits,
        The white owl in the belfry sits.

Alfred, Lord Tennyson

795   *Mariana*

With blackest moss the flower-plots
    Were thickly crusted, one and all:
The rusted nails fell from the knots
    That held the pear to the gable-wall.
The broken sheds look'd sad and strange:
    Unlifted was the clinking latch;
    Weeded and worn the ancient thatch

Upon the lonely moated grange.
       She only said, 'My life is dreary,
           He cometh not,' she said;
       She said, 'I am aweary, aweary,
           I would that I were dead!'

Her tears fell with the dews at even;
   Her tears fell ere the dews were dried;
She could not look on the sweet heaven,
   Either at morn or eventide.
After the flitting of the bats,
   When thickest dark did trance the sky,
   She drew her casement-curtain by,
And glanced athwart the glooming flats.
       She only said, 'The night is dreary,
           He cometh not,' she said;
       She said, 'I am aweary, aweary,
           I would that I were dead!'

Upon the middle of the night,
   Waking she heard the night-fowl crow:
The cock sung out an hour ere light:
   From the dark fen the oxen's low
Came to her: without hope of change,
   In sleep she seem'd to walk forlorn,
   Till cold winds woke the gray-eyed morn
About the lonely moated grange.
       She only said, 'The day is dreary,
           He cometh not,' she said;
       She said, 'I am aweary, aweary,
           I would that I were dead!'

About a stone-cast from the wall
   A sluice with blacken'd waters slept,
And o'er it many, round and small,
   The cluster'd marish-mosses crept.
Hard by a poplar shook alway,
   All silver-green with gnarlèd bark:
   For leagues no other tree did mark

The level waste, the rounding gray.
     She only said, 'My life is dreary,
          He cometh not,' she said;
     She said, 'I am aweary, aweary,
          I would that I were dead!'

And ever when the moon was low,
     And the shrill winds were up and away
In the white curtain, to and fro,
     She saw the gusty shadow sway.
But when the moon was very low,
     And wild winds bound within their cell,
     The shadow of the poplar fell
Upon her bed, across her brow.
     She only said, 'The night is dreary,
          He cometh not,' she said;
     She said, 'I am aweary, aweary,
          I would that I were dead!'

All day within the dreamy house,
     The doors upon their hinges creak'd;
The blue fly sung in the pane; the mouse
     Behind the mouldering wainscot shriek'd,
Or from the crevice peer'd about.
     Old faces glimmer'd thro' the doors,
     Old footsteps trod the upper floors,
Old voices call'd her from without.
     She only said, 'My life is dreary,
          He cometh not,' she said;
     She said, 'I am aweary, aweary,
          I would that I were dead!'

The sparrow's chirrup on the roof,
     The slow clock ticking, and the sound
Which to the wooing wind aloof
     The poplar made, did all confound
Her sense; but most she loath'd the hour
     When the thick-moted sunbeam lay
     Athwart the chambers, and the day

Was sloping toward his western bower.
    Then, said she, 'I am very dreary,
      He will not come,' she said;
    She wept, 'I am aweary, aweary,
      O God, that I were dead!'

Alfred, Lord Tennyson

796   *The miller's daughter*

It is the miller's daughter,
   And she is grown so dear, so dear,
That I would be the jewel
   That trembles in her ear:
For hid in ringlets day and night,
I'd touch her neck so warm and white.

And I would be the girdle
   About her dainty dainty waist,
And her heart would beat against me,
   In sorrow and in rest:
And I should know if it beat right,
I'd clasp it round so close and tight.

And I would be the necklace,
   And all day long to fall and rise
Upon her balmy bosom,
   With her laughter or her sighs:
And I would lie so light, so light,
I scarce should be unclasp'd at night.

Alfred, Lord Tennyson

797   *Now sleeps the crimson petal*

Now sleeps the crimson petal, now the white;
Nor waves the cypress in the palace walk;
Nor winks the gold fin in the porphyry font:
The firefly wakens: waken thou with me.

Now droops the milk-white peacock like a ghost,
And like a ghost she glimmers on to me.

Now lies the Earth all Danae to the stars,
And all thy heart lies open unto me.

Now slides the silent meteor on, and leaves
A shining furrow, as thy thoughts in me.

Now folds the lily all her sweetness up,
And slips into the bosom of the lake:
So fold thyself, my dearest, thou, and slip
Into my bosom and be lost in me.

Alfred, Lord Tennyson

798 *Come down, O maid*

Come down, O maid, from yonder mountain height:
What pleasure lives in height (the shepherd sang),
In height and cold, the splendour of the hills?
But cease to move so near the Heavens, and cease
To glide a sunbeam by the blasted Pine,
To sit a star upon the sparkling spire:
And come, for Love is of the valley, come,
For Love is of the valley, come thou down
And find him; by the happy threshold, he,
Or hand in hand with Plenty in the maize,
Or red with spirted purple of the vats,
Or foxlike in the vine; nor cares to walk
With Death and Morning on the silver horns,
Nor wilt thou snare him in the white ravine,
Nor find him dropt upon the firths of ice,
That huddling slant in furrow-cloven falls
To roll the torrent out of dusky doors:
But follow; let the torrent dance thee down
To find him in the valley; let the wild
Lean-headed Eagles yelp alone, and leave
The monstrous ledges there to slope, and spill

Their thousand wreaths of dangling water-smoke,
That like a broken purpose waste in air:
So waste not thou; but come; for all the vales
Await thee; azure pillars of the hearth
Arise to thee; the children call, and I
Thy shepherd pipe, and sweet is every sound,
Sweeter thy voice, but every sound is sweet;
Myriads of rivulets hurrying thro' the lawn,
The moan of doves in immemorial elms,
And murmuring of innumerable bees.

Alfred, Lord Tennyson

799   *Come into the garden, Maud*

Come into the garden, Maud,
    For the black bat, Night, has flown,
Come into the garden, Maud,
    I am here at the gate alone;
And the woodbine spices are wafted abroad,
    And the musk of the roses blown.

For a breeze of morning moves,
    And the planet of Love is on high,
Beginning to faint in the light that she loves
    On a bed of daffodil sky,
To faint in the light of the sun she loves,
    To faint in his light, and to die.

All night have the roses heard
    The flute, violin, bassoon;
All night has the casement jessamine stirr'd
    To the dancers dancing in tune:
Till a silence fell with the waking bird,
    And a hush with the setting moon.

I said to the lily, 'There is but one
    With whom she has heart to be gay.
When will the dancers leave her alone?
    She is weary of dance and play.'

Now half to the setting moon are gone,
    And half to the rising day;
Low on the sand and loud on the stone
    The last wheel echoes away.

I said to the rose, 'The brief night goes
    In babble and revel and wine.
O young lord-lover, what sighs are those
    For one that will never be thine?
But mine, but mine,' so I sware to the rose,
    'For ever and ever, mine.'

And the soul of the rose went into my blood,
    As the music clash'd in the hall;
And long by the garden lake I stood,
    For I heard your rivulet fall
From the lake to the meadow and on to the wood,
    Our wood, that is dearer than all;

From the meadow your walks have left so sweet
    That whenever a March-wind sighs
He sets the jewel-print of your feet
    In violets blue as your eyes,
To the woody hollows in which we meet
    And the valleys of Paradise.

The slender acacia would not shake
    One long milk-bloom on the tree;
The white lake-blossom fell into the lake,
    As the pimpernel dozed on the lea;
But the rose was awake all night for your sake,
    Knowing your promise to me;
The lilies and roses were all awake,
    They sigh'd for the dawn and thee.

Queen rose of the rosebud garden of girls,
    Come hither, the dances are done,
In gloss of satin and glimmer of pearls,
    Queen lily and rose in one;
Shine out, little head, sunning over with curls,
    To the flowers, and be their sun.

There has fallen a splendid tear
  From the passion-flower at the gate.
She is coming, my dove, my dear;
  She is coming, my life, my fate;
The red rose cries, 'She is near, she is near;'
  And the white rose weeps, 'She is late;'
The larkspur listens, 'I hear, I hear;'
  And the lily whispers, 'I wait.'

She is coming, my own, my sweet;
  Were it ever so airy a tread,
My heart would hear her and beat,
  Were it earth in an earthy bed;
My dust would hear her and beat,
  Had I lain for a century dead;
Would start and tremble under her feet,
  And blossom in purple and red.

Alfred, Lord Tennyson

800   *O that 'twere possible*

O that 'twere possible
After long grief and pain
To find the arms of my true love
Round me once again! . . .

A shadow flits before me,
Not thou, but like to thee:
Ah, Christ! that it were possible
For one short hour to see
The souls we loved, that they might tell us
What and where they be!

Alfred, Lord Tennyson

801 *The eagle*

He clasps the crag with crooked hands;
Close to the sun in lonely lands,
Ring'd with the azure world, he stands.

The wrinkled sea beneath him crawls;
He watches from his mountain walls,
And like a thunderbolt he falls.

Alfred, Lord Tennyson

802 *To Helen*

Helen, thy beauty is to me
   Like those Nicèan barks of yore
That gently, o'er a perfumed sea,
   The weary way-worn wanderer bore
   To his own native shore.

On desperate seas long wont to roam,
   Thy hyacinth hair, thy classic face,
Thy Naiad airs have brought me home
   To the glory that was Greece,
And the grandeur that was Rome.

Lo, in yon brilliant window-niche
   How statue-like I see thee stand,
   The agate lamp within thy hand,
Ah! Psyche, from the regions which
   Are holy land!

Edgar Allan Poe

803 *Dreams*

Oh! that my young life were a lasting dream!
My spirit not awak'ning till the beam
Of an Eternity should bring the morrow.
Yes! tho' that long dream were of hopeless sorrow,

'T were better that the cold reality
Of waking life, to him whose heart must be,
And hath been still, upon the lovely earth,
A chaos of deep passion, from his birth.
But should it be—that dream eternally
Continuing—as dreams have been to me
In my young boyhood—should it thus be giv'n,
'T were folly still to hope for higher Heav'n.
For I have revell'd, when the sun was bright
I' the summer sky, in dreams of living light
And loveliness,—have left my very heart
In climes of mine imagining, apart
From mine own home, with beings that have been
Of mine own thought—what more could I have seen?
'T was once—and only once—and the wild hour
From my remembrance shall not pass—some pow'r
Or spell had bound me—'t was the chilly wind
Came o'er me in the night, and left behind
Its image on my spirit—or the moon
Shone on my slumbers in her lofty noon
Too coldly—or the stars—howe'er it was,
That dream was as that night-wind—let it pass.
I *have been* happy, tho' but in a dream.
I have been happy—and I love the theme:
Dreams! in their vivid coloring of life,
As in that fleeting, shadowy, misty strife
Of semblance with reality which brings
To the delirious eye, more lovely things
Of Paradise and Love—and all our own!
Than young Hope in his sunniest hour hath known.

Edgar Allan Poe

804   *A dream within a dream*

Take this kiss upon the brow!
And, in parting from you now,
Thus much let me avow:
You are not wrong, who deem

That my days have been a dream;
Yet if Hope has flown away
In a night, or in a day,
In a vision, or in none,
Is it therefore the less *gone*?
All that we see or seem
Is but a dream within a dream.

I stand amid the roar
Of a surf-tormented shore,
And I hold within my hand
Grains of the golden sand—
How few! yet how they creep
Through my fingers to the deep,
While I weep—while I weep!
O God! can I not grasp
Them with a tighter clasp?
O God! can I not save
One from the pitiless wave?
Is *all* that we see or seem
But a dream within a dream?

Edgar Allan Poe

805   *To science*

Science! true daughter of Old Time thou art!
    Who alterest all things with thy peering eyes.
Why preyest thou thus upon the poet's heart,
    Vulture, whose wings are dull realities?
How should he love thee? or how deem thee wise,
    Who wouldst not leave him in his wandering
To seek for treasure in the jewelled skies,
    Albeit he soared with an undaunted wing?
Hast thou not dragged Diana from her car,
    And driven the Hamadryad from the wood

To seek a shelter in some happier star?
    Hast thou not torn the Naiad from her flood,
The Elfin from the green grass, and from me
The summer dream beneath the tamarind tree?

Edgar Allan Poe

806   *Romance*

Romance, who loves to nod and sing,
With drowsy head and folded wing,
Among the green leaves as they shake
Far down within some shadowy lake,
To me a painted paroquet
Hath been—a most familiar bird—
Taught me my alphabet to say,
To lisp my very earliest word,
While in the wild wood I did lie,
A child—with a most knowing eye.

Of late, eternal Condor years
So shake the very Heaven on high
With tumult as they thunder by,
I have no time for idle cares
Through gazing on the unquiet sky.
And when an hour with calmer wings
Its down upon my spirit flings—
That little time with lyre and rhyme
To while away—forbidden things!
My heart would feel to be a crime
Unless it trembled with the strings.

Edgar Allan Poe

807   *The city in the sea*

Lo! Death has reared himself a throne
In a strange city lying alone

Far down within the dim West,
Where the good and the bad and the worst and the best
Have gone to their eternal rest.
There shrines and palaces and towers
(Time-eaten towers that tremble not!)
Resemble nothing that is ours.
Around, by lifting winds forgot,
Resignedly beneath the sky
The melancholy waters lie.

No rays from the holy heaven come down
On the long night-time of that town;
But light from out the lurid sea
Streams up the turrets silently—
Gleams up the pinnacles far and free—
Up domes—up spires—up kingly halls—

Up fanes—up Babylon-like walls—
Up shadowy long-forgotten bowers
Of sculptured ivy and stone flowers—
Up many and many a marvellous shrine
Whose wreathèd friezes intertwine
The viol, the violet, and the vine.

Resignedly beneath the sky
The melancholy waters lie.
So blend the turrets and shadows there
That all seem pendulous in air,
While from a proud tower in the town
Death looks gigantically down.

There open fanes and gaping graves
Yawn level with the luminous waves;
But not the riches there that lie
In each idol's diamond eye—
Not the gaily-jewelled dead
Tempt the waters from their bed;
For no ripples curl, alas!
Along the wilderness of glass—

No swellings tell that winds may be
Upon some far-off happier sea—
No heavings hint that winds have been
On seas less hideously serene.

But lo, a stir is in the air!
The wave—there is a movement there!
As if the towers had thrust aside,
In slightly sinking, the dull tide—
As if their tops had feebly given
A void within the filmy Heaven.
The waves have now a redder glow—
The hours are breathing faint and low—
And when, amid no earthly moans,
Down, down that town shall settle hence,
Hell, rising from a thousand thrones,
Shall do it reverence.

Edgar Allan Poe

808   *The sleeper*

At midnight, in the month of June,
I stand beneath the mystic moon.
An opiate vapor, dewy, dim,
Exhales from out her golden rim,
And softly dripping, drop by drop,
Upon the quiet mountain top,
Steals drowsily and musically
Into the universal valley.
The rosemary nods upon the grave;
The lily lolls upon the wave;
Wrapping the fog about its breast,
The ruin moulders into rest;
Looking like Lethe, see! the lake
A conscious slumber seems to take,
And would not, for the world, awake.
All Beauty sleeps!—and lo! where lies
Irene, with her Destinies!

Oh, lady bright! can it be right—
This window open to the night?
The wanton airs, from the tree-top,
Laughingly through the lattice drop—
The bodiless airs, a wizard rout,
Flit through thy chamber in and out,
And wave the curtain canopy
So fitfully—so fearfully—
Above the closed and fringèd lid
'Neath which thy slumb'ring soul lies hid,
That, o'er the floor and down the wall,
Like ghosts the shadows rise and fall!
Oh, lady dear, hast thou no fear?
Why and what art thou dreaming here?
Sure thou art come o'er far-off seas,
A wonder to these garden trees!
Strange is thy pallor! strange thy dress!
Strange, above all, thy length of tress,
And this all solemn silentness!

The lady sleeps! Oh, may her sleep,
Which is enduring, so be deep!
Heaven have her in its sacred keep!
This chamber changed for one more holy,
This bed for one more melancholy,
I pray to God that she may lie
Forever with unopened eye,
While the pale sheeted ghosts go by!

My love, she sleeps! Oh, may her sleep,
As it is lasting, so be deep!
Soft may the worms about her creep!
Far in the forest, dim and old,
For her may some tall vault unfold—
Some vault that oft hath flung its black
And wingèd pannels fluttering back,
Triumphant, o'er the crested palls
Of her grand family funerals—
Some sepulchre, remote, alone,

Against whose portal she hath thrown,
In childhood, many an idle stone—
Some tomb from out whose sounding door
She ne'er shall force an echo more,
Thrilling to think, poor child of sin!
It was the dead who groaned within.

Edgar Allan Poe

809   Dream-land

By a route obscure and lonely,
Haunted by ill angels only,
Where an Eidolon, named NIGHT,
On a black throne reigns upright,
I have reached these lands but newly
From an ultimate dim Thule—
From a wild weird clime that lieth, sublime,
    Out of SPACE—out of TIME.

Bottomless vales and boundless floods,
And chasms, and caves, and Titan woods,
With forms that no man can discover
For the tears that drip all over;
Mountains toppling evermore
Into seas without a shore;
Seas that restlessly aspire,
Surging, unto skies of fire;
Lakes that endlessly outspread
Their lone waters, lone and dead,—
Their still waters, still and chilly
With the snows of the lolling lily.

By the lakes that thus outspread
Their lone waters, lone and dead,—
Their sad waters, sad and chilly
With the snows of the lolling lily,—
By the mountains—near the river
Murmuring lowly, murmuring ever,—

By the grey woods,—by the swamp
Where the toad and the newt encamp,—
By the dismal tarns and pools
  Where dwell the Ghouls,—
By each spot the most unholy—
In each nook most melancholy,—
There the traveller meets, aghast,
Sheeted Memories of the Past—
Shrouded forms that start and sigh
As they pass the wanderer by—
White-robed forms of friends long given,
In agony, to the Earth—and Heaven.

For the heart whose woes are legion
'T is a peaceful, soothing region—
For the spirit that walks in shadow
'T is—oh, 't is an Eldorado!
But the traveller, travelling through it,
May not—dare not openly view it;
Never its mysteries are exposed
To the weak human eye unclosed;
So wills its King, who hath forbid
The uplifting of the fringèd lid;
And thus the sad Soul that here passes
Beholds it but through darkened glasses.

By a route obscure and lonely,
Haunted by ill angels only,
Where an Eidolon, named NIGHT,
On a black throne reigns upright,
I have wandered home but newly
From this ultimate dim Thule.

                                        Edgar Allan Poe

810 *How pleasant to know Mr. Lear*

  'How pleasant to know Mr. Lear!'
    Who has written such volumes of stuff!
  Some think him ill-tempered and queer,
    But a few think him pleasant enough.

His mind is concrete and fastidious,
   His nose is remarkably big;
His visage is more or less hideous,
   His beard it resembles a wig.

He has ears, and two eyes, and ten fingers,
   Leastways if you reckon two thumbs;
Long ago he was one of the singers,
   But now he is one of the dumbs.

He sits in a beautiful parlour,
   With hundreds of books on the wall;
He drinks a great deal of Marsala,
   But never gets tipsy at all.

He has many friends, laymen and clerical,
   Old Foss is the name of his cat:
His body is perfectly spherical,
   He weareth a runcible hat.

When he walks in a waterproof white,
   The children run after him so!
Calling out, 'He's come out in his night-
   Gown, that crazy old Englishman, oh!'

He weeps by the side of the ocean,
   He weeps on the top of the hill;
He purchases pancakes and lotion,
   And chocolate shrimps from the mill.

He reads but he cannot speak Spanish,
   He cannot abide ginger-beer:
Ere the days of his pilgrimage vanish,
   How pleasant to know Mr. Lear!

Edward Lear

811   *Calico pie*

Calico Pie,
The little birds fly
Down to the Calico tree.

Their wings were blue
And they sang 'Tilly-loo'—
Till away they all flew,
   And they never came back to me,
      They never came back,
      They never came back,
   They never came back to me.

Edward Lear

812   *The owl and the pussy-cat*

The Owl and the Pussy-Cat went to sea
In a beautiful pea-green boat;
They took some honey, and plenty of money,
Wrapped up in a five-pound note.
The Owl looked up to the stars above,
And sang to a small guitar,
'O lovely Pussy! O Pussy, my love,
What a beautiful Pussy you are,

            You are,
            You are!
What a beautiful Pussy you are!'

Pussy said to the Owl, 'You elegant fowl!
How charmingly sweet you sing!
O let us be married! too long we have tarried:
But what shall we do for a ring?'
They sailed away for a year and a day,
To the land where the Bong-tree grows,
And there in a wood a Piggy-wig stood,
With a ring at the end of his nose,

            His nose,
            His nose,
With a ring at the end of his nose.

'Dear Pig, are you willing to sell for one shilling
Your ring?' Said the Piggy, 'I will.'
So they took it away, and were married next day
By the Turkey who lives on the hill.

They dinèd on mince, and slices of quince,
Which they ate with a runcible spoon;
And hand in hand, on the edge of the sand,
They danced in the light of the moon,
                    The moon,
                    The moon,
They danced by the light of the moon.

Edward Lear

813   *The dong with a luminous nose*

When awful darkness and silence reign
Over the great Gromboolian plain,
    Through the long, long wintry nights;—
        When the angry breakers roar
        As they beat on the rocky shore;—
When Storm-clouds brood on the towering heights
    Of the Hills of the Chankly Bore:—

Then, through the vast and gloomy dark,
There moves what seems a fiery spark,
    A lonely spark with silvery rays
        Piercing the coal-black night,—
        A meteor strange and bright;—
Hither and thither the vision strays,
    A single lurid light.

Slowly it wanders,—pauses,—creeps,—
Anon it sparkles,—flashes and leaps;
And ever as onward it gleaming goes
A light on the Bong-tree stems it throws.

And those who watch at that midnight hour
From Hall or Terrace, or lofty Tower,
Cry, as the wild light passes along,—
        'The Dong!—the Dong!
    The wandering Dong through the forest goes!
        The Dong!—the Dong!
    The Dong with a luminous Nose!'

Long years ago
The Dong was happy and gay,
Till he fell in love with a Jumbly Girl
Who came to those shores one day.
For the Jumblies came in a Sieve, they did,—
Landing at eve near the Zemmery Fidd
Where the Oblong Oysters grow,
And the rocks are smooth and gray.
And all the woods and valleys rang
With the Chorus they daily and nightly sang,—

'Far and few, far and few,
Are the lands where the Jumblies live;
Their heads are green, and their hands are blue,
And they went to sea in a sieve.'

Happily, happily passed those days!
While the cheerful Jumblies staid;
They danced in circles all night long,
To the plaintive pipe of the lively Dong,
In moonlight, shine or shade.
For day and night he was always there
By the side of the Jumbly Girl so fair,
With her sky-blue hands, and her sea-green hair.

Till the morning came of that hateful day
When the Jumblies sailed in their sieve away,
And the Dong was left on the cruel shore
Gazing—gazing for evermore,—
Ever keeping his weary eyes on
That pea-green sail on the far horizon,—
Singing the Jumbly Chorus still
As he sate all day on the grassy hill,—

'Far and few, far and few,
Are the lands where the Jumblies live;
Their heads are green, and their hands are blue,
And they went to sea in a sieve.'

But when the sun was low in the West,
    The Dong arose and said,—
    'What little sense I once possessed
  Has quite gone out of my head!'
And since that day he wanders still
By lake and forest, marsh and hill,
Singing—'O somewhere, in valley or plain
Might I find my Jumbly Girl again!
For ever I'll seek by lake and shore
Till I find my Jumbly Girl once more!'

    Playing a pipe with silvery squeaks,
    Since then his Jumbly Girl he seeks.
    And because by night he could not see,
    He gathered the bark of the Twangum Tree
        On the flowery plain that grows.
        And he wove him a wondrous Nose,—
    A Nose as strange as a Nose could be!
Of vast proportions and painted red,
And tied with cords to the back of his head.
    —In a hollow rounded space it ended
    With a luminous lamp within suspended,
        All fenced about
        With a bandage stout
    To prevent the wind from blowing it out;—
    And with holes all round to send the light,
    In gleaming rays on the dismal night.

And now each night, and all night long,
Over those plains still roams the Dong;
And above the wail of the Chimp and Snipe
You may hear the squeak of his plaintive pipe
While ever he seeks, but seeks in vain
To meet with his Jumbly Girl again;
Lonely and wild—all night he goes.—
The Dong with a luminous Nose.
And all who watch at the midnight hour,
From Hall or Terrace, or lofty Tower,
Cry, as they trace the Meteor bright,
Moving along through the dreary night,—

'This is the hour when forth he goes,
The Dong with a luminous Nose!
Yonder—over the plain he goes;
  He goes!
  He goes;
The Dong with a luminous Nose!'

Edward Lear

814 *A toccata of Galuppi's*

Oh, Galuppi, Baldassaro, this is very sad to find!
I can hardly misconceive you; it would prove me deaf
  and blind;
But although I give you credit, 'tis with such a heavy
  mind!

Here you come with your old music, and here's all the
  good it brings.
What, they lived once thus at Venice, where the mer-
  chants were the kings,
Where St. Mark's is, where the Doges used to wed the
  sea with rings?

Ay, because the sea's the street there; and 'tis arched
  by . . . what you call
. . . Shylock's bridge with houses on it, where they kept
  the carnival!
I was never out of England—it's as if I saw it all!

Did young people take their pleasure when the sea was
  warm in May?
Balls and masks begun at midnight, burning ever to
  mid-day,
When they made up fresh adventures for the morrow,
  do you say?

Was a lady such a lady, cheeks so round and lips so
   red,—
On her neck the small face buoyant, like a bell-flower
   on its bed,
O'er the breast's superb abundance where a man might
   base his head?

Well (and it was graceful of them) they'd break talk off
   and afford
—She, to bite her mask's black velvet, he to finger on
   his sword,
While you sat and played Toccatas, stately at the clavi-
   chord?

What? Those lesser thirds so plaintive, sixths dimin-
   ished sigh on sigh,
Told them something? Those suspensions, those solu-
   tions—'Must we die?'
Those commiserating sevenths—'Life might last! we can
   but try!'

'Were you happy?'—'Yes.'—'And are you still as
   happy?'—'Yes—and you?'
—'Then more kisses'—'Did I stop them, when a million
   seemed so few?'
Hark—the dominant's persistence, till it must be
   answered to!

So an octave struck the answer. Oh, they praised you,
   I dare say!
'Brave Galuppi! that was music! good alike at grave
   and gay!
I can always leave off talking, when I hear a master play.'

Then they left you for their pleasure: till in due time,
   one by one,
Some with lives that came to nothing, some with deeds
   as well undone,
Death came tacitly and took them where they never see
   the sun.

But when I sit down to reason,—think to take my stand
    nor swerve
Till I triumph o'er a secret wrung from nature's close
    reserve,
In you come with your cold music, till I creep thro'
    every nerve.

Yes, you, like a ghostly cricket, creaking where a house
    was burned—
'Dust and ashes, dead and done with, Venice spent what
    Venice earned!
The soul doubtless, is immortal—where a soul can be
    discerned.

'Yours for instance, you know physics, something of
    geology,
Mathematics are your pastime; souls shall rise in their
    degree;
Butterflies may dread extinction,—you'll not die, it
    cannot be!

'As for Venice and its people, merely born to bloom
    and drop,
Here on earth they bore their fruitage, mirth and folly
    were the crop.
What of soul was left, I wonder, when the kissing had
    to stop?

'Dust and ashes!' So you creak it, and I want the heart
    to scold.
Dear dead women with such hair, too—what's become
    of all the gold
Used to hang and brush their bosoms? I feel chilly and
    grown old.

Robert Browning

815   *Love in a life*

Room after room,
I hunt the house through
We inhabit together.

Heart, fear nothing, for, heart, thou shalt find her,
Next time, herself!—not the trouble behind her
Left in the curtain, the couch's perfume!
As she brush'd it, the cornice-wreath blossom'd anew:
Yon looking-glass gleam'd at the wave of her feather.

Yet the day wears,
And door succeeds door;
I try the fresh fortune—
Range the wide house from the wing to the centre.
Still the same chance! she goes out as I enter.
Spend my whole day in the quest,—who cares?
But 'tis twilight, you see,—with such suites to explore,
Such closets to search, such alcoves to importune!

Robert Browning

816   *Pippa's song*

The year's at the spring
And day's at the morn;
Morning's at seven;
The hill-side's dew-pearled;
The lark's on the wing;
The snail's on the thorn:
God's in his heaven—
All's right with the world!

Robert Browning

817   *My last duchess*

FERRARA

That's my last Duchess painted on the wall,
Looking as if she were alive. I call
That piece a wonder, now: Frà Pandolf's hands
Worked busily a day, and there she stands.

Will't please you sit and look at her? I said
'Frà Pandolf' by design, for never read
Strangers like you that pictured countenance,
The depth and passion of its earnest glance,
But to myself they turned (since none puts by
The curtain I have drawn for you, but I)
And seemed as they would ask me, if they durst,
How such a glance came there; so, not the first
Are you to turn and ask thus. Sir, 'twas not
Her husband's presence only, called that spot
Of joy into the Duchess' cheek: perhaps
Frà Pandolf chanced to say 'Her mantle laps
Over my lady's wrist too much,' or 'Paint
Must never hope to reproduce the faint
Half-flush that dies along her throat:' such stuff
Was courtesy, she thought, and cause enough
For calling up that spot of joy. She had
A heart—how shall I say?—too soon made glad,
Too easily impressed; she liked whate'er
She looked on, and her looks went everywhere.
Sir, 'twas all one! My favour at her breast,
The dropping of the daylight in the West,
The bough of cherries some officious fool
Broke in the orchard for her, the white mule
She rode with round the terrace—all and each
Would draw from her alike the approving speech,
Or blush, at least. She thanked men,—good! but
    thanked
Somehow—I know not how—as if she ranked
My gift of a nine-hundred-years-old name
With anybody's gift. Who'd stoop to blame
This sort of trifling? Even had you skill
In speech—(which I have not)—to make your will
Quite clear to such an one, and say, 'Just this
Or that in you disgusts me; here you miss,
Or there exceed the mark'—and if she let
Herself be lessoned so, nor plainly set
Her wits to yours, forsooth, and made excuse,
—E'en then would be some stooping; and I choose

Never to stoop. Oh sir, she smiled, no doubt,
Whene'er I passed her; but who passed without
Much the same smile? This grew; I gave commands;
Then all smiles stopped together. There she stands
As if alive. Will't please you rise? We'll meet
The company below, then. I repeat,
The Count your master's known munificence
Is ample warrant that no just pretence
Of mine for dowry will be disallowed;
Though his fair daughter's self, as I avowed
At starting, is my object. Nay, we'll go
Together down, sir. Notice Neptune, though,
Taming a sea-horse, thought a rarity,
Which Claus of Innsbruck cast in bronze for me.

Robert Browning

818   *The lost mistress*

All's over, then: does truth sound bitter
    As one at first believes?
Hark, 'tis the sparrows' good-night twitter
    About your cottage eaves!

And the leaf-buds on the vine are woolly,
    I noticed that, to-day;
One day more bursts them open fully
    —You know the red turns grey.

To-morrow we meet the same then, dearest?
    May I take your hand in mine?
Mere friends are we,—well, friends the merest
    Keep much that I resign:

For each glance of the eye so bright and black,
    Though I keep with heart's endeavour,—
Your voice, when you wish the snowdrops back,
    Though it stay in my soul for ever!—

Yet I will but say what mere friends say,
  Or only a thought stronger;
I will hold your hand but as long as all may,
  Or so very little longer!

Robert Browning

819 *Meeting at night*

The grey sea and the long black land;
And the yellow half-moon large and low;
And the startled little waves that leap
In fiery ringlets from their sleep,
As I gain the cove with pushing prow,
And quench its speed i' the slushy sand.

Then a mile of warm sea-scented beach;
Three fields to cross till a farm appears;
A tap at the pane, the quick sharp scratch
And blue spurt of a lighted match,
And a voice less loud, thro' its joys and fears,
Than the two hearts beating each to each!

Robert Browning

820 *Parting at morning*

Round the cape of a sudden came the sea,
And the sun looked over the mountain's rim:
And straight was a path of gold for him,
And the need of a world of men for me.

Robert Browning

Oh, to be in England
Now that April's there,
And whoever wakes in England
Sees, some morning, unaware,
That the lowest boughs and the brushwood sheaf
Round the elm-tree bole are in tiny leaf,
While the chaffinch sings on the orchard bough
In England—now!
And after April, when May follows,
And the whitethroat builds, and all the swallows!
Hark, where my blossomed pear-tree in the hedge
Leans to the field and scatters on the clover
Blossoms and dewdrops—at the bent spray's edge—
That's the wise thrush; he sings each song twice over,
Lest you should think he never could recapture
The first fine careless rapture!
And though the fields look rough with hoary dew,
All will be gay when noon tide wakes anew
The buttercups, the little children's dower
—Far brighter than this gaudy melon-flower!

Robert Browning

Nobly, nobly Cape Saint Vincent to the North-west
died away;
Sunset ran, one glorious blood-red, reeking into Cadiz
Bay;
Bluish 'mid the burning water, full in face Trafalgar
lay—
In the dimmest North-east distance dawned Gibraltar
grand and gray;
'Here and here did England help me: how can I help
England?'—say,
Whoso turns as I, this evening, turn to God to praise
and pray,
While Jove's planet rises yonder, silent over Africa.

Robert Browning

Let's contend no more, Love,
    Strive nor weep:
All be as before, Love,
    —Only sleep!

What so wild as words are?
    I and thou
In debate, as birds are,
    Hawk on bough!

See the creature stalking
    While we speak!
Hush and hide the talking
    Cheek on cheek!

What so false as truth is,
    False to thee?
Where the serpent's tooth is
    Shun the tree—

Where the apple reddens
    Never pry—
Lest we lose our Edens,
    Eve and I.

Be a god and hold me
    With a charm!
Be a man and fold me
    With thine arm!

Teach me, only teach, Love!
    As I ought
I will speak thy speech, Love,
    Think thy thought—

Meet, if thou require it,
    Both demands,
Laying flesh and spirit
    In thy hands.

That shall be to-morrow
　　Not to-night:
I must bury sorrow
　　Out of sight:

—Must a little weep, Love,
　　(Foolish me!)
And so fall asleep, Love,
　　Loved by thee.

Robert Browning

824　*Up at a villa—down in the city (as distinguished by*
　　an Italian person of quality)

Had I but plenty of money, money enough and to spare,
The house for me, no doubt, were a house in the city-
　　square;
Ah, such a life, such a life, as one leads at the window
　　there!

Something to see, by Bacchus, something to hear, at
　　least!
There, the whole day long, one's life is a perfect feast;
While up at a villa one lives, I maintain it, no more than
　　a beast.

Well now, look at our villa! stuck like the horn of a bull
Just on a mountain-edge as bare as the creature's skull,
Save a mere shag of a bush with hardly a leaf to pull!
—I scratch my own, sometimes, to see if the hair's
　　turned wool.

But the city, oh the city—the square with the houses!
　　Why?
They are stone-faced, white as a curd, there's something
　　to take the eye!
Houses in four straight lines, not a single front awry;

You watch who crosses and gossips, who saunters, who
   hurries by;
Green blinds, as a matter of course, to draw when the
   sun gets high;
And the shops with fanciful signs which are painted
   properly.

What of a villa? Though winter be over in March by
   rights,
'Tis May perhaps ere the snow shall have withered well
   off the heights:
You've the brown ploughed land before, where the
   oxen steam and wheeze,
And the hills over-smoked behind by the faint grey
   olive-trees.

Is it better in May, I ask you? You've summer all at
   once;
In a day he leaps complete with a few strong April suns.
'Mid the sharp short emerald wheat, scarce risen three
   fingers well,
The wild tulip, at end of its tube, blows out its great red
   bell
Like a thin clear bubble of blood, for the children to
   pick and sell.

Is it ever hot in the square? There's a fountain to spout
   and splash!
In the shade it sings and springs; in the shine such foam-
   bows flash
On the horses with curling fish-tails, that prance and
   paddle and pash
Round the lady atop in her conch—fifty gazers do not
   abash,
Though all that she wears is some weeds round her waist
   in a sort of sash.

All the year long at the villa, nothing to see though you
   linger,
Except yon cypress that points like death's lean lifted
   forefinger.

Some think fireflies pretty, when they mix i' the corn
    and mingle,
Or thrid the stinking hemp till the stalks of it seem a-
    tingle.
Late August or early September, the stunning cicala is
    shrill,
And the bees keep their tiresome whine round the
    resinous firs on the hill.
Enough of the seasons,—I spare you the months of the
    fever and chill.

Ere you open your eyes in the city, the blessed church-
    bells begin:
No sooner the bells leave off than the diligence rattles
    in:
You get the pick of the news, and it costs you never a
    pin.
By-and-by there's the travelling doctor gives pills, lets
    blood, draws teeth;
Or the Pulcinello-trumpet breaks up the market be-
    neath.
At the post-office such a scene-picture—the new play,
    piping hot!
And a notice how, only this morning, three liberal
    thieves were shot.
Above it, behold the Archbishop's most fatherly of
    rebukes,
And beneath, with his crown and his lion, some little
    new law of the Duke's!
On a sonnet with flowery marge, to the Reverend Don
    So-and-so
Who is Dante, Boccaccio, Petrarca, Saint Jerome and
    Cicero,
'And moreover,' (the sonnet goes rhyming,) 'the skirts
    of Saint Paul has reached,
Having preached us those six Lent-lectures more
    unctuous than ever he preached.'
Noon strikes,—here sweeps the procession! our Lady
    borne smiling and smart

With a pink gauze gown all spangles, and seven swords
    stuck in her heart!
Bang-whang-whang goes the drum, *tootle-te-tootle* the fife;
No keeping one's haunches still: it's the greatest pleasure
    in life.

But bless you, it's dear—it's dear! fowls, wine, at double
    the rate.
They have clapped a new tax upon salt, and what oil
    pays passing the gate
It's a horror to think of. And so, the villa for me, not the
    city!
Beggars can scarcely be choosers: but still—ah, the pity,
    the pity!
Look, two and two go the priests, then the monks with
    cowls and sandals,
And the penitents dressed in white shirts, a-holding the
    yellow candles;
One, he carries a flag up straight, and another a cross
    with handles,
And the Duke's guard brings up the rear, for the better
    prevention of scandals:
Bang-whang-whang goes the drum, *tootle-te-tootle* the fife.
Oh, a day in the city-square, there is no such pleasure
    in life!

Robert Browning

825   *Misconceptions*

This is a spray the Bird clung to,
    Making it blossom with pleasure,
Ere the high tree-top she sprung to,
    Fit for her nest and her treasure.
    Oh, what a hope beyond measure
Was the poor spray's, which the flying feet hung to,—
So to be singled out, built in, and sung to!

This is a heart the Queen leant on,
  Thrilled in a minute erratic,
Ere the true bosom she bent on,
  Meet for love's regal dalmatic.
  Oh, what a fancy ecstatic
Was the poor heart's, ere the wanderer went on—
Love to be saved for it, proffered to, spent on!

Robert Browning

826 *Memorabilia*

Oh, did you once see Shelley plain,
  And did he stop and speak to you
And did you speak to him again?
  How strange it seems and new!

But you were living before that,
  And also you are living after;
And the memory I started at—
  My starting moves your laughter.

I crossed a moor, with a name of its own
  And a certain use in the world no doubt,
Yet a hand's-breadth of it shines alone
  'Mid the blank miles round about:

For there I picked up on the heather
  And there I put inside my breast
A moulted feather, an eagle-feather!
  Well, I forget the rest.

Robert Browning

827 *Appearances*

And so you found that poor room dull,
  Dark, hardly to your taste, my dear?
Its features seemed unbeautiful:
  But this I know—'twas there, not here,

You plighted troth to me, the word
Which—ask that poor room how it heard.

And this rich room obtains your praise
   Unqualified,—so bright, so fair,
So all whereat perfection stays?
   Ay, but remember—here, not there,
The other word was spoken! Ask
   This rich room how you dropped the mask!

Robert Browning

828   *Now*

Out of your whole life give but a moment!
All of your life that has gone before,
All to come after it,—so you ignore,
So you make perfect the present,—condense,
In a rapture of rage, for perfection's endowment,
Thought and feeling and soul and sense—
Merged in a moment which gives me at last
You around me for once, you beneath me, above me—
Me—sure that despite of time future, time past,—
This tick of our life-times' one moment you love me!
How long such suspension may linger? Ah, Sweet—
The moment eternal—just that and no more—
When ecstasy's utmost we clutch at the core
While cheeks burn, arms open, eyes shut and lips meet!

Robert Browning

829   *Prospice*

Fear death?—to feel the fog in my throat,
   The mist in my face,
When the snows begin, and the blasts denote
   I am nearing the place,

The power of the night, the press of the storm,
    The post of the foe;
Where he stands, the Arch Fear in a visible form,
    Yet the strong man must go:
For the journey is done and the summit attained,
    And the barriers fall,
Though a battle's to fight ere the guerdon be gained,
    The reward of it all.
I was ever a fighter, so—one fight more,
    The best and the last!
I would hate that death bandaged my eyes, and forbore,
    And bade me creep past.
No! let me taste the whole of it, fare like my peers
    The heroes of old,
Bear the brunt, in a minute pay glad life's arrears
    Of pain, darkness and cold.
For sudden the worst turns the best to the brave,
    The black minute's at end,
And the elements' rage, the fiend-voices that rave,
    Shall dwindle, shall blend,
Shall change, shall become first a peace out of pain,
    Then a light, then thy breast,
O thou soul of my soul! I shall clasp thee again,
    And with God be the rest!

                                            Robert Browning

830 *A pearl, a girl*

A simple ring with a single stone
    To the vulgar eye no stone of price:
Whisper the right word, that alone—
    Forth starts a sprite, like fire from ice,
And lo, you are lord (says an Eastern scroll)
Of heaven and earth, lord whole and sole
    Through the power in a pearl.

A woman ('tis I this time that say)
    With little the world counts worthy praise
Utter the true word—out and away
    Escapes her soul: I am wrapt in blaze,
Creation's lord, of heaven and earth
Lord whole and sole—by a minute's birth—
    Through the love in a girl!

Robert Browning

831   *The strangers*

Each care-worn face is but a book
    To tell of houses bought or sold;
Or filled with words that mankind took
    From those who lived and spoke of old.

I see none whom I know, for they
    See other things than him they meet;
And though they stop me by the way,
    'Tis still some other one to greet.

There are no words that reach my ear
    Those speak who tell of other things
Than what they mean for me to hear,
    For in their speech the counter rings.

I would be where each word is true,
    Each eye sees what it looks upon;
For here my eye has seen but few,
    Who in each act that act have done.

Jones Very

832   *Night of spring*

Slow, horses, slow,
    As thro' the wood we go—
We would count the stars in heaven,
    Hear the grasses grow:

Watch the cloudlets few
Dappling the deep blue,
In our open palms outspread
Catch the blessèd dew.

Slow, horses, slow,
As thro' the wood we go—
We would see fair Dian rise
With her huntress bow:

We would hear the breeze
Ruffling the dim trees,
Hear its sweet love-ditty set
To endless harmonies.

Slow, horses, slow,
As thro' the wood we go—
All the beauty of the night
We would learn and know!

Thomas Westwood

833 *Last lines*

No coward soul is mine,
No trembler in the world's storm-troubled sphere:
I see Heaven's glories shine,
And faith shines equal, arming me from fear.

O God within my breast,
Almighty, ever-present Deity!
Life—that in me has rest,
As I—undying Life—have power in Thee!

Vain are the thousand creeds
That move men's hearts: unutterably vain;
Worthless as wither'd weeds,
Or idlest froth amid the boundless main,

To waken doubt in one
Holding so fast by thine infinity;
    So surely anchor'd on
The steadfast rock of immortality.

    With wide-embracing love
Thy Spirit animates eternal years,
    Pervades and broods above,
Changes, sustains, dissolves, creates, and rears.

    Though earth and man were gone,
And suns and universes ceased to be,
    And Thou were left alone,
Every existence would exist in Thee.

    There is not room for Death,
Nor atom that his might could render void:
    Thou—Thou art Being and Breath,
And what Thou art may never be destroy'd.

Emily Brontë

834   *Love*

    Totus est Inermis Idem . . .

No show of bolts and bars
Can keep the foeman out,
Or 'scape this secret mine
Who enter'd with the doubt
That drew the line.
No warder at the gate
Can let the friendly in;
But, like the sun, o'er all
He will the castle win,
And shine along the wall.

Implacable is Love—
Foes may be bought or teased
From their hostile intent,
But he goes unappeased
Who is on kindness bent.

Henry David Thoreau

835   *Billy in the darbies*

Good of the Chaplain to enter Lone Bay
And down on his marrow-bones here and pray
For the like just o' me, Billy Budd.—
But look:
Through the port comes the moonshine astray!
It tips the guard's cutlass and silvers this nook;
But 'twill die in the dawning of Billy's last day.
A jewel-block they'll make of me to-morrow,
Pendant pearl from the yard-arm-end
Like the ear-drop I gave to Bristol-Molly—
Oh, 'tis me, not the sentence, they'll suspend.
Ay, ay, all is up; and I must up too
Early in the morning, aloft from alow.
On an empty stomach, now, never it would do.
They'll give me a nibble—bit of biscuit ere I go.
Sure, a messmate will reach me the last parting cup;
But turning heads away from the hoist and the belay,
Heaven knows who will have the running of me up!
No pipe to those halyards—But aren't it all sham?
A blur's in my eyes; it is dreaming that I am.
A hatchet to my panzer? all adrift to go?
The drum roll to grog, and Billy never know?
But Donald he has promised to stand by the plank;
So I'll shake a friendly hand ere I sink.
But—no! it is dead then I'll be, come to think.
I remember Taff the Welshman when he sank.
And his cheek it was like the budding pink.

But me, they'll lash me in hammock, drop me deep
Fathoms down, fathoms down, how I'll dream fast
   asleep.
I feel it stealing now. Sentry, are you there?
Just ease these darbies at the wrist,
And roll me over fair.
I am sleepy, and the oozy weeds about me twist.

Herman Melville

836   *The portent*

1859

Hanging from the beam,
   Slowly swaying (such the law),
Gaunt the shadow on your green,
   Shenandoah!
The cut is on the crown
(Lo, John Brown),
And the stabs shall heal no more.

Hidden in the cap
   Is the anguish none can draw;
So your future veils its face,
   Shenandoah!
But the streaming beard is shown
   (Weird John Brown),
The meteor of the war.

Herman Melville

837   *Misgivings*

1860

When ocean-clouds over inland hills
   Sweep storming in late autumn brown,
And horror the sodden valley fills,
   And the spire falls crashing in the town,
I muse upon my country's ills—
   The tempest bursting from the waste of Time
On the world's fairest hope linked with man's foulest
   crime.

Nature's dark side is heeded now—
    (Ah! optimist-cheer disheartened flown)—
A child may read the moody brow
    Of yon black mountain lone.
With shouts the torrents down the gorges go,
And storms are formed behind the storm we feel;
The hemlock shakes in the rafter, the oak in the driving
                keel.

Herman Melville

838   *Shiloh—a requiem*

April, 1862

Skimming lightly, wheeling still,
    The swallows fly low
Over the field in clouded days,
    The forest-field of Shiloh—
Over the field where April rain
Solaced the parched one stretched in pain
Through the pause of night
That followed the Sunday fight
    Around the church of Shiloh—
The church so lone, the log-built one,
That echoes to many a parting groan
      And natural prayer
    Of dying foemen mingled there—
Foemen at morn, but friends at eve—
    Fame or country least their care:
(What like a bullet can undeceive!)
    But now they lie low,
While over them the swallows skim,
    And all is hushed at Shiloh.

Herman Melville

About the Shark, phlegmatical one,
Pale sot of the Maldive sea,
The sleek little pilot-fish, azure and slim,
How alert in attendance be.
From his saw-pit of mouth, from his charnel of maw
They have nothing of harm to dread,
But liquidly glide on his ghastly flank
Or before his Gorgonian head;
Or lurk in the port of serrated teeth
In white triple tiers of glittering gates,
And there find a haven when peril's abroad,
An asylum in jaws of the Fates!
They are friends; and friendly they guide him to prey,
Yet never partake of the treat—
Eyes and brains to the dotard lethargic and dull,
Pale ravener of horrible meat.

Herman Melville

840 *The berg—a dream*

I saw a ship of martial build
(Her standards set, her brave apparel on)
Directed as by madness mere
Against a solid iceberg steer,
Nor budge it, though the infatuate ship went down.
The impact made huge ice-cubes fall
Sullen, in tons that crashed the deck;
But that one avalanche was all—
No other movement save the foundering wreck.

Along the spurs of ridges pale,
Not any slenderest shaft and frail,
A prism over glass-green gorges lone,
Toppled; nor lace of traceries fine,
Nor pendent drops in grot or mine
Were jarred, when the stunned ship went down,

Nor sole the gulls in cloud that wheeled
Circling one snow-flanked peak afar,
But nearer fowl the floes that skimmed
And crystal beaches felt no jar.
No thrill transmitted stirred the lock
Of jack-straw needle-ice at base;
Towers undermined by waves—the block
Atilt impending—kept their place.
Seals, dozing sleek on sliddery ledges
Slipt never, when by loftier edges
Through very inertia overthrown,
The impetuous ship in bafflement went down.

Hard Berg (methought), so cold, so vast,
With mortal damps self-overcast;
Exhaling still thy dankish breath—
Adrift dissolving, bound for death;
Though lumpish thou, a lumbering one—
A lumbering lubbard loitering slow,
Impingers rue thee and go down,
Sounding thy precipice below
Nor stir the slimy slug that sprawls
Along thy dead indifference of walls.

Herman Melville

841   *The latest decalogue*

Thou shalt have one God only; who
Would be at the expense of two?

No graven images may be
Worshipp'd, except the currency:

Swear not at all; for, for thy curse
Thine enemy is none the worse:

At church on Sunday to attend
Will serve to keep the world thy friend:

Honour thy parents; that is, all
From whom advancement may befall:

Thou shalt not kill; but need'st not strive
Officiously to keep alive:

Do not adultery commit;
Advantage rarely comes of it:

Thou shalt not steal; an empty feat,
When 'tis so lucrative to cheat:

Bear not false witness; let the lie
Have time on its own wings to fly:

Thou shalt not covet, but tradition
Approves all forms of competition.

Arthur Hugh Clough

842   *Say not the struggle nought availeth*

Say not the struggle naught availeth,
    The labour and the wounds are vain,
The enemy faints not, nor faileth,
    And as things have been they remain.

If hopes were dupes, fears may be liars;
    It may be, in yon smoke conceal'd,
Your comrades chase e'en now the fliers,
    And, but for you, possess the field.

For while the tired waves, vainly breaking,
    Seem here no painful inch to gain,
Far back, through creeks and inlets making,
    Comes silent, flooding in, the main.

And not by eastern windows only,
    When daylight comes, comes in the light;
In front the sun climbs slow, how slowly!
    But westward, look, the land is bright!

Arthur Hugh Clough

843   *The old song*

When all the world is young, lad,
    And all the trees are green;
And every goose a swan, lad,
    And every lass a queen;
Then hey for boot and horse, lad,
    And round the world away!
Young blood must have its course, lad,
    And every dog his day.

When all the world is old, lad,
    And all the trees are brown;
And all the sport is stale, lad,
    And all the wheels run down;
Creep home, and take your place there
    The spent and maim'd among;
God grant you find one face there
    You loved when all was young!

Charles Kingsley

844   *After the sea-ship*

After the sea-ship, after the whistling winds,
After the white-grey sails taut to their spars and ropes,
Below, a myriad myriad waves hastening, lifting up
    their necks,
Tending in ceaseless flow toward the track of the ship,
Waves of the ocean bubbling and gurgling, blithely
    prying,

Waves, undulating waves, liquid, uneven, emulous
   waves,
Toward that whirling current, laughing and buoyant,
   with curves,
Where the great vessel sailing and tacking displaced the
   surface,
Larger and smaller waves in the spread of the ocean
   yearnfully flowing,
The wake of the sea-ship after she passes, flashing and
   frolicsome under the sun,
A motley procession with many a fleck of foam and
   many fragments,
Following the stately and rapid ship, in the wake
   following.

Walt Whitman

845   *The beasts*

I think I could turn and live with animals, they are so
   placid and self-contain'd;
I stand and look at them long and long.
They do not sweat and whine about their condition;
They do not lie awake in the dark and weep for their
   sins;
They do not make me sick discussing their duty to God:
Not one is dissatisfied—not one is demented with the
    mania of owning things;
Not one kneels to another, nor to his kind that lived
   thousands of years ago;
Not one is respectable or industrious over the whole
   earth.

Walt Whitman

846   *The dismantled ship*

In some unused lagoon, some nameless bay,
On sluggish, lonesome waters, anchor'd near the shore,
An old, dismasted, gray and batter'd ship, disabled,
   done,

After free voyages to all the seas of earth, haul'd up at
    last and hawser'd tight,
Lies rusting, mouldering.

Walt Whitman

847 *Cavalry crossing a ford*

A line in long array where they wind betwixt green
    islands,
They take a serpentine course, their arms flash in the
    sun—hark to the musical clank,
Behold the silvery river, in it the splashing horses
    loitering stop to drink,
Behold the brown-faced men, each group, each person
    a picture, the negligent rest on the saddles,
Some emerge on the opposite bank, others are just
                      entering the ford—while,
    Scarlet and blue and snowy white,
    The guidon flags flutter gayly in the wind.
    To cheer one on the tedious way,
    To fetch one if one goes astray,
    To lift one if one totters down,
    To strengthen whilst one stands.

Walt Whitman

848 *Patrolling Barnegat*

Wild, wild the storm, and the sea high running,
Steady the roar of the gale, with incessant undertone
    muttering,
Shouts of demoniac laughter fitfully piercing and
    pealing,
Waves, air, midnight, their savagest trinity lashing,
Out in the shadows there milk-white combs careering,
On beachy slush and sand spurts of snow fierce slanting,
Where through the murk the easterly death-wind
    breasting,

Through cutting swirl and spray watchful and firm
   advancing,
(That in the distance! is that a wreck? is the red signal
   flaring?)
Slush and sand of the beach tireless till daylight wending,
Steadily, slowly, through hoarse roar never remitting,
Along the midnight edge by those milk-white combs
   careering,
A group of dim, weird forms, struggling, the night
   confronting,
That savage trinity warily watching.

Walt Whitman

849   *Sometimes with one I love*

Sometimes with one I love I fill myself with rage for
   fear I effuse unreturn'd love,
But now I think there is no unreturn'd love, the pay is
   certain one way or another,
(I loved a certain person ardently and my love was not
   return'd,
Yet out of that I have written these songs.)

Walt Whitman

850   *A hand-mirror*

Hold it up sternly—see this it sends back, (who is it, is
   it you?)
Outside fair costume, within ashes and filth,
No more a flashing eye, no more a sonorous voice or
   springy step,
Now some slave's eye, voice, hands, step,
A drunkard's breath, unwholesome eater's face, vene-
   realee's flesh,

Lungs rotting away piecemeal, stomach sour and canker-
  ous,
Joints rheumatic, bowels clogged with abomination,
Blood circulating dark and poisonous streams,
Words babble, hearing and touch callous,
No brain, no heart left, no magnetism of sex;
Such from one look in this looking-glass ere you go
  hence,
Such a result so soon—and from such a beginning!

Walt Whitman

851 *I sit and look out*

I sit and look out upon all the sorrows of the world, and
  upon all oppression and shame,
I hear secret convulsive sobs from young men at anguish
  with themselves, remorseful after deeds done,
I see in low life the mother misused by her children,
  dying, neglected, gaunt, desperate,
I see the wife misused by her husband, I see the treacherous seducer of young women,
I mark the ranklings of jealousy and unrequited love
  attempted to be hid, I see these sights on the earth,
I see the workings of battle, pestilence, tyranny, I see
  martyrs and prisoners,
I observe a famine at sea, I observe the sailors casting lots
  who shall be kill'd to preserve the lives of the rest,
I observe the slights and degradations cast by arrogant
  persons upon laborers, the poor, and upon negroes,
  and the like;
All these—all the meanness and agony without end I
  sitting look out upon,
See, hear, and am silent.

Walt Whitman

Hast never come to thee an hour,
A sudden gleam divine, precipitating, bursting all these
    bubbles, fashions, wealth?
These eager business aims—books, politics, art, amours,
To utter nothingness?

Walt Whitman

853 *You felons on trial in courts*

You felons on trial in courts,
You convicts in prison-cells, you sentenced assassins
    chain'd and hand-cuff'd with iron,
Who am I too that I am not on trial or in prison?
Me ruthless and devilish as any, that my wrists are not
    chain'd with iron, or my ankles with iron?

You prostitutes flaunting over the trottoirs or obscene
    in your rooms,
Who am I that I should call you more obscene than
    myself?
O culpable! I acknowledge—I exposé!
(O admirers, praise not me—compliment not me—you
    make me wince,
I see what you do not—I know what you do not.)

Inside these breast-bones I lie smutch'd and choked,
Beneath this face that appears so impassive hell's tides
    continually run,
Lusts and wickedness are acceptable to me,
I walk with delinquents with passionate love,
I feel I am of them—I belong to those convicts and
    prostitutes myself,
And henceforth I will not deny them—for how can I
    deny myself?

Walt Whitman

From all the rest I single out you, having a message for you,
You are to die—let others tell you what they please, I cannot prevaricate,
I am exact and merciless, but I love you—there is no escape for you.

Softly I lay my right hand upon you, you just feel it,
I do not argue, I bend my head close and half envelop it,
I sit quietly by, I remain faithful,
I am more than nurse, more than parent or neighbour,
I absolve you from all except yourself spiritual bodily, that is eternal, you yourself will surely escape,
The corpse you will leave will be but excrementitious.

The sun bursts through in unlooked-for directions,
Strong thoughts fill you and confidence, you smile,
You forget you are sick, as I forget you are sick,
You do not see the medicines, you do not mind the weeping friends, I am with you,
I exclude others from you, there is nothing to be commiserated,
I do not commiserate, I congratulate you.

Walt Whitman

855 *Ah, poverties, wincings, and sulky retreats*

Ah poverties, wincings, and sulky retreats,
Ah you foes that in conflict have overcome me,
(For what is my life or any man's life but a conflict with foes, the old, the incessant war?)
You degradations, you tussle with passions and appetites,
You smarts from dissatisfied friendships, (ah wounds the sharpest of all!)

You toil of painful and choked articulations, you mean-
nesses,
You shallow tongue-talks at tables, (my tongue the
shallowest of any;)
You broken resolutions, you racking angers, you
smother'd ennuis!
Ah think not you finally triumph, my real self has yet
to come forth,
It shall yet march forth o'ermastering, till all lies
beneath me,
It shall yet stand up the soldier of ultimate victory.

Walt Whitman

856   *You lingering sparse leaves of me*

You lingering sparse leaves of me on winter-nearing
boughs,
And I some well-shorn tree of field or orchard-row;
You tokens diminute and lorn—(not now the flush of
May, or July clover-bloom—no grain of August
now;)
You pallid banner-staves—you pennants valueless—you
overstay'd of time,
Yet my soul-dearest leaves confirming all the rest,
The faithfulest—hardiest—last.

Walt Whitman

857   *The ox-tamer*

In a far-away northern county in the placid pastoral
region,
Lives my farmer-friend, the theme of my recitative, a
famous tamer of oxen,
There they bring him the three-year-olds and the four-
year-olds to break them,

He will take the wildest steer in the world and break
   him and tame him,
He will go fearless without any whip where the young
   bullock chafes up and down the yard,
The bullock's head tosses restless high in the air with
   raging eyes,
Yet see you! how soon his rage subsides—how soon this
   tamer tames him;
See you! on the farms hereabouts a hundred oxen young
   and old, and he is the man who has tamed them,
They all know him, all are affectionate to him;
See you! some are such beautiful animals, so lofty looking;
Some are buff colour'd, some mottled, one has a white
   line running along his back, some are brindled.
Some have wide flaring horns (a good sign)—see you!
   the bright hides,
See, the two with stars on their foreheads—see, the
   round bodies and broad backs,
How straight and square they stand on their legs—what
   fine sagacious eyes!
How they watch their tamer—they wish him near them
   —how they turn to look after him!
What yearning expression! how uneasy they are when
   he moves away from them;
Now I marvel what it can be he appears to them, (books,
   politics, poems, depart—all else departs),
I confess I envy only his fascination—my silent, illiterate
   friend,
Whom a hundred oxen love there in his life on farms,
In the northern country far, in the placid pastoral region.

Walt Whitman

858 *I heard you solemn-sweet pipes of the organ*

I heard you solemn-sweet pipes of the organ as last
   Sunday morn I pass'd the church,

Winds of autumn, as I walk'd the woods at dusk I heard
   your long-stretch'd sighs up above so mournful,
I heard the perfect Italian tenor singing at the opera, I
   heard the soprano in the midst of the quartet singing;
Heart of my love! you too I heard murmuring low
   through one of the wrists around my head,
Heard the pulse of you when all was still ringing little
   bells last night under my ear.

Walt Whitman

859   *I saw in Louisiana a live-oak growing*

I saw in Louisiana a live-oak growing,
All alone stood it and the moss hung down from the
   branches,
Without any companion it grew there uttering joyous
   leaves of dark green,
And its look, rude, unbending, lusty, made me think of
   myself,
But I wonder'd how it could utter joyous leaves stand-
   ing alone there without its friend near, for I knew I
   could not,
And I broke off a twig with a certain number of leaves
   upon it, and twined around it a little moss,
And brought it away, and I have placed it in sight, in
   my room,
It is not needed to remind me as of my own dear friends,
(For I believe lately I think of little else than of them,)
Yet it remains to me a curious token, it makes me think
   of manly love;
For all that, and though the live-oak glistens there in
   Louisiana solitary in a wide flat space,
Uttering joyous leaves all its life without a friend a lover
   near,
I know very well I could not.

Walt Whitman

When I heard the learn'd astronomer,
When the proofs, the figures, were ranged in columns
   before me,
When I was shown the charts and diagrams, to add,
   divide, and measure them,
When I sitting heard the astronomer where he lectured
   with much applause in the lecture-room,
How soon unaccountable I became tired and sick,
Till rising and gliding out I wander'd off by myself,
In the mystical moist night-air, and from time to time,
Look'd up in perfect silence at the stars.

Walt Whitman

861 *Beginning my studies*

Beginning my studies the first step pleas'd me so much,
The mere fact consciousness, these forms, the power of
   motion,
The least insect or animal, the senses, eyesight, love,
The first step I say awed me and pleas'd me so much,
I have hardly gone and hardly wish'd to go any farther,
But stop and loiter all the time to sing it in ecstatic songs.

Walt Whitman

862 *The forsaken merman*

Come, dear children, let us away;
   Down and away below.
Now my brothers call from the bay;
   Now the great winds shorewards blow;
   Now the salt tides seawards flow;
Now the wild white horses play,
Champ and chafe and toss in the spray.
Children dear, let us away.
   This way, this way.

Call her once before you go.
  Call once yet.
In a voice that she will know:
  'Margaret! Margaret!'
Children's voices should be dear
(Call once more) to a mother's ear:
Children's voices, wild with pain.
Surely she will come again.
Call her once and come away.
  This way, this way.
'Mother dear, we cannot stay.'
The wild white horses foam and fret.
  Margaret! Margaret!

Come, dear children, come away down.
  Call no more.
One last look at the white-walled town,
And the little grey church on the windy shore.
  Then come down.
She will not come though you call all day.
  Come away, come away.

Children dear, was it yesterday
We heard the sweet bells over the bay?
In the caverns where we lay,
Through the surf and through the swell,
The far-off sound of a silver bell?
Sand-strewn caverns, cool and deep,
Where the winds are all asleep;
Where the spent lights quiver and gleam;
Where the salt weed sways in the stream;
Where the sea-beasts ranged all round
Feed in the ooze of their pasture-ground;
Where the sea-snakes coil and twine,
Dry their mail and bask in the brine;
Where great whales come sailing by,
Sail and sail, with unshut eye,
Round the world for ever and aye?
When did music come this way?
Children dear, was it yesterday?

Children dear, was it yesterday
(Call yet once) that she went away?

Once she sate with you and me,
On a red gold throne in the heart of the sea,
And the youngest sate on her knee.
She combed its bright hair, and she tended it well,
When down swung the sound of the far-off bell.
She sighed, she looked up through the clear green sea.
She said, 'I must go, for my kinsfolk pray
In the little grey church on the shore to-day.
'Twill be Easter-time in the world—ah me!
And I lose my poor soul, Merman, here with thee.'
I said, 'Go up, dear heart, through the waves;
Say thy prayer, and come back to the kind sea-caves.'
She smiled, she went up through the surf in the bay.
Children dear, was it yesterday?

Children dear, were we long alone?
'The sea grows stormy, the little ones moan.
Long prayers,' I said, 'in the world they say.
Come!' I said, and we rose through the surf in the bay.
We went up the beach, by the sandy down
Where the sea-stocks bloom, to the white-walled town.
Through the narrow paved streets, where all was still,
To the little grey church on the windy hill.
From the church came a murmur of folk at their prayers,
But we stood without in the cold-blowing airs.
We climbed on the graves, on the stones worn with
    rains,
And we gazed up the aisle through the small-leaded
    panes.
She sate by the pillar; we saw her clear:
'Margaret, hist! come quick, we are here.
Dear heart,' I said, 'we are long alone.
The sea grows stormy, the little ones moan.'
But ah, she gave me never a look,
For her eyes were sealed to the holy book.
Loud prays the priest; shut stands the door.
Come away, children, call no more!
Come away, come down, call no more!

Down, down, down.
Down to the depths of the sea.
She sits at her wheel in the humming town,
    Singing most joyfully.
Hark what she sings: 'O joy, O joy,
For the humming street, and the child with its toy.
For the priest, and the bell, and the holy well.
    For the wheel where I spun,
    And the blessed light of the sun.'
    And so she sings her fill,
    Singing most joyfully,
Till the shuttle falls from her hand,
    And the whizzing wheel stands still.
She steals to the window, and looks at the sand,
    And over the sand at the sea;
    And her eyes are set in a stare;
    And anon there breaks a sigh,
And anon there drops a tear,
    From a sorrow-clouded eye,
    And a heart sorrow-laden,
    A long, long sigh;
    For the cold, strange eyes of a little Mermaiden,
    And the gleam of her golden hair.

Come away, away, children!
    Come, children, come down!
The hoarse wind blows colder;
    Lights shine in the town.
    She will start from her slumber
    When gusts shake the door;
She will hear the winds howling,
    Will hear the waves roar.
We shall see, while above us
    The waves roar and whirl,
A ceiling of amber,
    A pavement of pearl.
Singing: 'Here came a mortal,
    But faithless was she.
And alone dwell for ever
    The kings of the sea.'

But, children, at midnight,
  When soft the winds blow,
When clear falls the moonlight,
  When spring-tides are low;
When sweet airs come seaward
  From heaths starred with broom,
And high rocks throw mildly
  On the blanched sands a gloom;
Up the still, glistening beaches,
  Up the creeks we will hie,
Over banks of bright seaweed
  The ebb-tide leaves dry.
We will gaze, from the sand-hills,
At the white, sleeping town;
At the church on the hillside—
  And then come back down.
  Singing: 'There dwells a loved one,
  But cruel is she!
She left lonely for ever
  The kings of the sea.'

Matthew Arnold

863   *Dover beach*

The sea is calm tonight,
The tide is full, the moon lies fair
Upon the Straits; —on the French coast, the light
Gleams, and is gone; the cliffs of England stand,
Glimmering and vast, out in the tranquil bay.
Come to the window, sweet is the night air!
Only, from the long line of spray
Where the ebb meets the moon-blanched sand,
Listen! you hear the grating roar
Of pebbles which the waves suck back, and fling,
At their return, up the high strand,
Begin, and cease, and then again begin
With tremulous cadence slow, and bring
The eternal note of sadness in.

Sophocles long ago
Heard it on the Aegean, and it brought
Into his mind the turbid ebb and flow
Of human misery; we
Find also in the sound a thought,
Hearing it by this distant northern sea.
The sea of faith
Was once, too, at the full, and round earth's shore
Lay like the folds of a bright girdle furled;
But now I only hear
Its melancholy, long, withdrawing roar,
Retreating to the breath
Of the night-wind down the vast edges drear
And naked shingles of the world.

Ah, love, let us be true
To one another! for the world, which seems
To lie before us like a land of dreams,
So various, so beautiful, so new,
Hath really neither joy, nor love, nor light,
Nor certitude, nor peace, nor help for pain;
And we are here as on a darkling plain
Swept with the confused alarms of struggle and flight,
Where ignorant armies clash by night.

Matthew Arnold

864   *Shakespeare*

Others abide our question. Thou art free.
We ask and ask: thou smilest and art still,
Out-topping knowledge. For the loftiest hill
That to the stars uncrowns his majesty,
Planting his steadfast footsteps in the sea,
Making the heaven of heavens his dwelling-place,
Spares but the cloudy border of his base
To the foiled searching of mortality:
And thou, who did the stars and sunbeams know,
Self-schooled, self-scanned, self-honoured, self-secure,

Didst walk on earth unguessed at. Better so!
All pains the immortal spirit must endure,
All weakness that impairs, all griefs that bow,
Find their sole voice in that victorious brow.

Matthew Arnold

865   S.S. 'Lusitania'

I read in Dante how that hornèd light,
Which hid Ulysses, waved itself and said:
'Following the sun, we set our vessel's head
To the great main; passed Seville on the right
And Ceuta on the left; then southward sped.
At last in air, far off, dim rose a Height.
We cheered; but from it rushed a blast of might,
And struck—and o'er us the sea-waters spread.'
I dropped the book, and of my child I thought
In his long black ship speeding night and day
O'er those same seas; dark Teneriffe rose, fraught
With omen; 'Oh! were that Mount passed,' I say.
Then the door opens and this card is brought:
'Reached Cape Verde Islands, "Lusitania."'

Matthew Arnold

866   The river

Still glides the stream, slow drops the boat
Under the rustling poplars' shade;
Silent the swans beside us float:
None speaks, none heeds—ah, turn thy head.

Let those arch eyes now softly shine,
That mocking mouth grow sweetly bland:
Ah, let them rest, those eyes, on mine;
On mine let rest that lovely hand.

My pent-up tears oppress my brain,
My heart is swoln with love unsaid:
Ah, let me weep, and tell my pain,
And on thy shoulder rest my head.

Before I die, before the soul,
Which now is mine, must re-attain
Immunity from my control,
And wander round the world again:

Before this teas'd o'erlabour'd heart
For ever leaves its vain employ,
Dead to its deep habitual smart,
And dead to hopes of future joy.

Matthew Arnold

867 *Longing*

Come to me in my dreams, and then
By day I shall be well again.
For then the night will more than pay
The hopeless longing of the day.

Come, as thou cam'st a thousand times,
A messenger from radiant climes,
And smile on thy new world, and be
As kind to others as to me.

Or, as thou never cam'st in sooth,
Come now, and let me dream it truth.
And part my hair, and kiss my brow,
And say—*My love! why sufferest thou?*

Come to me in my dreams, and then
By day I shall be well again.
For then the night will more than pay
The hopeless longing of the day.

Matthew Arnold

Again I see my bliss at hand;
The town, the lake are here.
My Marguerite smiles upon the strand
Unalter'd with the year.

I know that graceful figure fair,
That cheek of languid hue;
I know that soft enkerchief'd hair,
And those sweet eyes of blue.

Again I spring to make my choice;
Again in tones of ire
I hear a God's tremendous voice—
'Be counsell'd, and retire!'

Ye guiding Powers, who join and part,
What would ye have with me?
Ah, warn some more ambitious heart,
And let the peaceful be!

Matthew Arnold

869 *Absence*

In this fair stranger's eyes of grey
Thine eyes, my love, I see.
I shudder: for the passing day
Had borne me far from thee.

This is the curse of life: that not
A nobler calmer train
Of wiser thoughts and feelings blot
Our passions from our brain;

But each day brings its petty dust
Our soon-chok'd souls to fill,
And we forget because we must,
And not because we will.

I struggle towards the light; and ye,
Once-long'd-for storms of love!
If with the light ye cannot be,
I bear that ye remove.

I struggle towards the light; but oh,
While yet the night is chill,
Upon Time's barren, stormy flow,
Stay with me, Marguerite, still!

Matthew Arnold

870   *Youth's agitations*

When I shall be divorced, some ten years hence,
From this poor present self which I am now;
When youth has done its tedious vain expense
Of passions that for ever ebb and flow;
Shall I not joy youth's heats are left behind,
And breathe more happy in an even clime?
Ah no! for then I shall begin to find
A thousand virtues in this hated time.
Then I shall wish its agitations back,
And all its thwarting currents of desire;
Then I shall praise the heat which then I lack,
And call this hurrying fever, generous fire,
And sigh that one thing only has been lent
To youth and age in common—discontent.

Matthew Arnold

871   *A summer night*

In the deserted moon-blanch'd street
How lonely rings the echo of my feet!
Those windows, which I gaze at, frown,
Silent and white, unopening down,
Repellent as the world:—but see!
A break between the housetops shows

The moon, and, lost behind her, fading dim
Into the dewy dark obscurity
Down at the far horizon's rim,
   Doth a whole tract of heaven disclose.

And to my mind the thought
Is on a sudden brought
Of a past night, and a far different scene.
Headlands stood out into the moon-lit deep
As clearly as at noon;
The spring-tide's brimming flow
Heav'd dazzlingly between;
Houses with long white sweep
Girdled the glistening bay:
Behind, through the soft air,
The blue haze-cradled mountains spread away.
   That night was far more fair;
But the same restless pacings to and fro,
And the same vainly-throbbing heart was there,
And the same bright calm moon.

And the calm moonlight seems to say—
Hast thou then still the old unquiet breast
That neither deadens into rest
Nor ever feels the fiery glow
That whirls the spirit from itself away,
But fluctuates to and fro
Never by passion quite possess'd
And never quite benumb'd by the world's sway?—
And I, I know not if to pray
Still to be what I am, or yield, and be
Like all the other men I see.

For most men in a brazen prison live,
Where in the sun's hot eye,
With heads bent o'er their toil, they languidly
Their lives to some unmeaning taskwork give,
Dreaming of naught beyond their prison wall.
And as, year after year,
Fresh products of their barren labour fall

From their tired hands, and rest
Never yet comes more near,
Gloom settles slowly down over their breast.
And while they try to stem
The waves of mournful thought by which they are
                                                prest,
Death in their prison reaches them
Unfreed, having seen nothing, still unblest.

   And the rest, a few,
Escape their prison, and depart
On the wide Ocean of Life anew.
There the freed prisoner, where'er his heart
Listeth, will sail;
Nor does he know how there prevail,
Despotic on life's sea,
Trade-winds that cross it from eternity.
   Awhile he holds some false way, undebarr'd
By thwarting signs, and braves
The freshening wind and blackening waves.
And then the tempest strikes him, and between
The lightning bursts is seen
Only a driving wreck,
And the pale Master on his spar-strewn deck
With anguish'd face and flying hair
Grasping the rudder hard,
Still bent to make some port he knows not where,
Still standing for some false impossible shore.
   And sterner comes the roar
Of sea and wind, and through the deepening gloom
Fainter and fainter wreck and helmsman loom,
And he too disappears, and comes no more.

   Is there no life, but these alone?
Madman or slave, must man be one?

   Plainness and clearness without shadow of stain!
Clearness divine!
Ye Heavens, whose pure dark regions have no sign
Of languor, though so calm, and though so great

Are yet untroubled and unpassionate:
Who though so noble share in the world's toil,
And though so task'd keep free from dust and soil:
I will not say that your mild deeps retain
A tinge, it may be, of their silent pain
Who have long'd deeply once, and long'd in vain;
But I will rather say that you remain
A world above man's head, to let him see
How boundless might his soul's horizons be,
How vast, yet of what clear transparency.
How it were good to sink there, and breathe free.
How fair a lot to fill
Is left to each man still.

Matthew Arnold

872 *To Marguerite*

We were apart: yet, day by day,
I bade my heart more constant be;
I bade it keep the world away,
And grow a home for only thee:
Nor fear'd but thy love likewise grew,
Like mine, each day more tried, more true.

The fault was grave: I might have known,
What far too soon, alas, I learn'd—
The heart can bind itself alone,
And faith is often unreturn'd.—
    Self-sway'd our feelings ebb and swell:
Thou lov'st no more: Farewell! Farewell!

Farewell! and thou, thou lonely heart,
Which never yet without remorse
Even for a moment did'st depart
From thy remote and spherèd course
To haunt the place where passions reign,
Back to thy solitude again!

Back, with the conscious thrill of shame
Which Luna felt, that summer night,
Flash through her pure immortal frame,
When she forsook the starry height
To hang over Endymion's sleep
Upon the pine-grown Latmian steep;—

Yet she, chaste Queen, had never prov'd
How vain a thing is mortal love,
Wandering in Heaven, far remov'd.
But thou hast long had place to prove
This truth—to prove, and make thine own:
  Thou hast been, shalt be, art, alone.

Or, if not quite alone, yet they
Which touch thee are unmating things—
Ocean, and Clouds, and Night, and Day;
Lorn Autumns and triumphant Springs;
And life, and others' joy and pain,
And love, if love, of happier men.

Of happier men—for they, at least,
Have *dream'd* two human hearts might blend
In one, and were through faith releas'd
From isolation without end
Prolong'd, nor knew, although not less
Alone than thou, their loneliness.

Matthew Arnold

873   *A caution to poets*

What poets feel not, when they make,
   A pleasure in creating,
The world, in *its* turn, will not take
   Pleasure in contemplating.

Matthew Arnold

Coldly, sadly descends
The autumn evening. The Field
Strewn with its dank yellow drifts
Of wither'd leaves, and the elms,
Fade into dimness apace,
Silent;—hardly a shout
From a few boys late at their play!
The lights come out in the street,
In the school-room windows; but cold,
Solemn, unlighted, austere,
Through the gathering darkness, arise
The Chapel walls, in whose bound
Thou, my father! art laid.

There thou dost lie, in the gloom
Of the autumn evening. But ah!
That word, *gloom*, to my mind
Brings thee back in the light
Of thy radiant vigour again!
In the gloom of November we pass'd
Days not of gloom at thy side;
Seasons impair'd not the ray
Of thine even cheerfulness clear.
Such thou wast; and I stand
In the autumn evening, and think
Of bygone autumns with thee.

Fifteen years have gone round
Since thou arosest to tread,
In the summer morning, the road
Of death, at a call unforeseen,
Sudden. For fifteen years,
We who till then in thy shade
Rested as under the boughs
Of a mighty oak, have endured
Sunshine and rain as we might,
Bare, unshaded, alone,
Lacking the shelter of thee.

O strong soul, by what shore
Tarriest thou now? For that force,
Surely, has not been left vain!
Somewhere, surely, afar,
In the sounding labour-house vast
Of being, is practised that strength,
Zealous, beneficent, firm!

Yes, in some far-shining sphere,
Conscious or not of the past,
Still thou performest the word
Of the Spirit in whom thou dost live,
Prompt, unwearied, as here!
Still thou upraisest with zeal
The humble good from the ground,
Sternly repressest the bad.
Still, like a trumpet, dost rouse
Those who with half-open eyes
Tread the border-land dim
'Twixt vice and virtue; reviv'st,
Succourest;—this was thy work,
This was thy life upon earth.

What is the course of the life
Of mortal men of the earth?—
Most men eddy about
Here and there—eat and drink,
Chatter and love and hate,
Gather and squander, are raised
Aloft, are hurl'd in the dust,
Striving blindly, achieving
Nothing; and, then they die—
Perish; and no one asks
Who or what they have been,
More than he asks what waves
In the moonlit solitudes mild
Of the midmost Ocean, have swell'd,
Foam'd for a moment, and gone.

And there are some, whom a thirst
Ardent, unquenchable, fires,

Not with the crowd to be spent,
Not without aim to go round
In an eddy of purposeless dust,
Effort unmeaning and vain.
Ah yes, some of us strive
Not without action to die
Fruitless, but something to snatch
From dull oblivion, nor all
Glut the devouring grave!
We, we have chosen our path—
Path to a clear-purposed goal,
Path of advance! but it leads
A long, steep journey, through sunk
Gorges, o'er mountains in snow!
Cheerful, with friends, we set forth;
Then, on the height, comes the storm!
Thunder crashes from rock
To rock, the cataracts reply;
Lightnings dazzle our eyes;
Roaring torrents have breach'd
The track, the stream-bed descends
In the place where the wayfarer once
Planted his footstep—the spray
Boils o'er its borders; aloft,
The unseen snow-beds dislodge
Their hanging ruin;—alas,
Havoc is made in our train!
Friends who set forth at our side
Falter, are lost in the storm!
We, we only, are left!
With frowning foreheads, with lips
Sternly compress'd, we strain on,
On—and at nightfall, at last,
Come to the end of our way,
To the lonely inn 'mid the rocks;
Where the gaunt and taciturn Host
Stands on the threshold, the wind
Shaking his thin white hairs—
Holds his lantern to scan
Our storm-beat figures, and asks:

Whom in our party we bring?
Whom we have left in the snow?
Sadly we answer: We bring
Only ourselves; we lost
Sight of the rest in the storm.
Hardly ourselves we fought through,
Stripp'd, without friends, as we are.
Friends, companions, and train
The avalanche swept from our side.

But thou would'st not *alone*
Be saved, my father! *alone*
Conquer and come to thy goal,
Leaving the rest in the wild.
We were weary, and we
Fearful, and we, in our march,
Fain to drop down and to die.
Still thou turnedst, and still
Beckonedst the trembler, and still
Gavest the weary thy hand!
If, in the paths of the world,
Stones might have wounded thy feet,
Toil or dejection have tried
Thy spirit, of that we saw
Nothing! to us thou wert still
Cheerful, and helpful, and firm.
Therefore to thee it was given
Many to save with thyself;
And, at the end of thy day,
O faithful shepherd! to come,
Bringing thy sheep in thy hand.

And through thee I believe
In the noble and great who are gone;
Pure souls honour'd and blest
By former ages, who else—
Such, so soulless, so poor,
Is the race of men whom I see—
Seem'd but a cry of desire.
Yes! I believe that there lived

Others like thee in the past,
Not like the men of the crowd
Who all round me to-day
Bluster or cringe, and make life
Hideous, and arid, and vile;
But souls temper'd with fire,
Fervent, heroic, and good,
Helpers and friends of mankind.

Servants of God!—or sons
Shall I not call you? because
Not as servants ye knew
Your Father's innermost mind,
His, who unwillingly sees
One of his little ones lost—
Yours is the praise, if mankind
Hath not as yet in its march
Fainted, and fallen, and died!

See! in the rocks of the world
Marches the host of mankind,
A feeble, wavering line.
Where are they tending?—A God
Marshall'd them, gave them their goal.—
Ah, but the way is so long!
Years they have been in the wild!
Sore thirst plagues them; the rocks,
Rising all round, overawe.
Factions divide them; their host
Threatens to break, to dissolve.
Ah, keep, keep them combined!
Else, of the myriads who fill
That army, not one shall arrive!
Sole they shall stray; in the rocks
Labour for ever in vain.
Die one by one in the waste.

Then, in such hour of need
Of your fainting, dispirited race,

Ye, like angels, appear,
Radiant with ardour divine.
Beacons of hope, ye appear!
Languor is not in your heart,
Weakness is not in your word,
Weariness not on your brow.
Ye alight in our van; at your voice,
Panic, despair, flee away.
Ye move through the ranks, recall
The stragglers, refresh the outworn,
Praise, re-inspire the brave.
Order, courage, return.
Eyes rekindling, and prayers,
Follow your steps as ye go.
Ye fill up the gaps in our files,
Strengthen the wavering line,
Stablish, continue our march,
On, to the bound of the waste,
On, to the City of God.

Matthew Arnold

875   *Heraclitus*

They told me, Heraclitus, they told me you were dead,
They brought me bitter news to hear and bitter tears to
      shed.
I wept as I remember'd how often you and I
Had tired the sun with talking and sent him down the
      sky.

And now that thou art lying, my dear old Carian guest,
A handful of grey ashes, long, long ago at rest,
Still are thy pleasant voices, thy nightingales, awake;
For Death, he taketh all away, but them he cannot take.

William Cory

My little Son, who look'd from thoughtful eyes
And moved and spoke in quiet grown-up wise,
Having my law the seventh time disobey'd,
I struck him, and dismiss'd
With hard words and unkiss'd,
—His Mother, who was patient, being dead.
Then, fearing lest his grief should hinder sleep,
I visited his bed,
But found him slumbering deep,
With darken'd eyelids, and their lashes yet
From his late sobbing wet.
And I, with moan,
Kissing away his tears, left others of my own;
For, on a table drawn beside his head,
He had put, within his reach,
A box of counters and a red-vein'd stone,
A piece of glass abraded by the beach,
And six or seven shells,
A bottle with bluebells,
And two French copper coins, ranged there with careful
    art,
To comfort his sad heart.
So when that night I pray'd
To God, I wept, and said:
Ah! when at last we lie with trancèd breath,
Not vexing thee in death,
And Thou rememberest of what toys
We made our joys,
How weakly understood
Thy great commanded good,
Then, fatherly not less
Than I whom Thou hast moulded from the clay,
Thou'lt leave Thy wrath, and say,
'I will be sorry for their childishness.'

Coventry Patmore

Up the airy mountain,
  Down the rushy glen,
We daren't go a-hunting
  For fear of little men;
Wee folk, good folk,
  Trooping all together;
Green jacket, red cap,
  And white owl's feather!

Down along the rocky shore
  Some make their home,
They live on crispy pancakes
  Of yellow tide-foam;
Some in the reeds
  Of the black mountain lake,
With frogs for their watch-dogs
  All night awake.

High on the hill-top
  The old King sits;
He is now so old and gray
  He's nigh lost his wits.
With a bridge of white mist
  Columbkill he crosses,
On his stately journeys
  From Slieveleague to Rosses;
Or going up with music
  On cold starry nights
To sup with the Queen
  Of the gay Northern Lights.

They stole little Bridget
  For seven years long;
When she came down again
  Her friends were all gone;
They took her lightly back,
  Between the night and morrow,
They thought that she was fast asleep
  But she was dead with sorrow.

They have kept her ever since
    Deep within the lake,
On a bed of flag-leaves
    Watching till she wake.

By the craggy hill-side,
    Through the mosses bare,
They have planted thorn-trees
    For pleasure here and there.
If any man so daring
    As dig them up in spite,
He shall find their sharpest thorns
    In his bed at night.

Up the airy mountain,
    Down the rushy glen,
We daren't go a-hunting
    For fear of little men;
Wee folk, good folk,
    Trooping all together;
Green jacket, red cap,
    And white owl's feather!

William Allingham

878   *Mammon marriage*

The croak of a raven hoar!
    A dog's howl, kennel-tied!
Loud shuts the carriage-door:
    The two are away on their ghastly ride
To Death's salt shore!

Where are the love and the grace?
    The bridegroom is thirsty and cold!
The bride's skull sharpens her face!
    But the coachman is driving, jubilant, bold,
The devil's pace.

The horses shiver'd and shook
　　Waiting gaunt and haggard
With sorry and evil look;
　　But swift as a drunken wind they stagger'd
'Longst Lethe brook.

Long since, they ran no more;
　　Heavily pulling they died
On the sand of the hopeless shore
　　Where never swell'd or sank a tide,
And the salt burns sore.

Flat their skeletons lie,
　　White shadows on shining sand;
The crusted reins go high
　　To the crumbling coachman's bony hand.
On his knees awry.

Side by side, jarring no more,
　　Day and night side by side,
Each by a doorless door,
　　Motionless sit the bridegroom and bride
On the Dead-Sea-shore.

George MacDonald

879　*Desolate*

From the sad eaves the drip-drop of the rain!
The water washing at the latchet door;
A slow step plashing by upon the moor;
A single bleat far from the famished fold;
The clicking of an embered hearth and cold;
The rainy Robin tic-tac at the pane.

　So as it is with thee
　Is it with me,
So as it is and it used not to be,
With thee used not to be,

Nor me,'
So singeth Robin on the willow tree,
The rainy Robin tic-tac at the pane.

Here in this breast all day
The fire is dim and low,
Within I care not to stay,
Without I care not to go.

A sadness ever sings
Of unforgotten things,
And the bird of love is patting at the pane;
But the wintry water deepens at the door,
And a step is plashing by upon the moor
Into the dark upon the darkening moor,
And alas, alas, the drip-drop of the rain!

Sydney Dobell

880   *Lucifer in starlight*

On a starr'd night Prince Lucifer uprose.
Tired of his dark dominion swung the fiend
Above the rolling ball in cloud part screen'd,
Where sinners hugg'd their spectre of repose.
Poor prey to his hot fit of pride were those.
And now upon his western wing he lean'd,
Now his huge bulk o'er Afric's sands careen'd,
Now the black planet shadow'd Arctic snows.
Soaring through wide zones that prick'd his scars
With memory of the old revolt from Awe,
He reach'd a middle height, and at the stars,
Which are the brain of heaven, he look'd, and sank.
Around the ancient track march'd, rank on rank,
The army of unalterable law.

George Meredith

What of her glass without her? The blank grey
There where the pool is blind of the moon's face.
Her dress without her? The tossed empty space
Of cloud-rack whence the moon has passed away.
Her paths without her? Day's appointed sway
Usurped by desolate night. Her pillowed place
Without her? Tears, ah me! for love's good grace,
And cold forgetfulness of night or day.
What of the heart without her? Nay, poor heart,
Of thee what word remains ere speech be still?
A wayfarer by barren ways and chill,
Steep ways and weary, without her thou art,
Where the long cloud, the long wood's counterpart,
Sheds doubled darkness up the labouring hill.

Dante Gabriel Rossetti

882 *A superscription*

Look in my face; my name is Might-have-been;
I am also called No-more, Too-late, Farewell;
Unto thine ear I hold the dead-sea shell
Cast up thy Life's foam-fretted feet between;
Unto thine eyes the glass where that is seen
Which had Life's form and Love's, but by my spell
Is now a shaken shadow intolerable,
Of ultimate things unuttered the frail screen.
Mark me, how still I am! But should there dart
One moment through thy soul the soft surprise
Of that winged Peace which lulls the breath of sighs,—
Then shalt thou see me smile, and turn apart
Thy visage to mine ambush at thy heart
Sleepless with cold commemorative eyes.

Dante Gabriel Rossetti

The city's steeple-towers remove away,
Each singly; as each vain infatuate Faith
Leaves God in heaven, and passes. A mere breath
Each soon appears, so far. Yet that which lay
The first is now scarce further or more grey
That the last is. Now all are wholly gone.
The sunless sky has not once had the sun
Since the first weak beginning of the day.
The air falls back as the wind finishes,
And the clouds stagnate. On the water's face
The current breathes along, but is not stirred.
There is no branch that thrills with any bird.
Winter is to possess the earth a space,
And have its will upon the extreme seas.

Dante Gabriel Rossetti

884   *On the site of a mulberry-tree; planted by Wm.*
Shakespeare; felled by the Rev. F. Gastrell

This tree, here fall'n, no common birth or death
Shared with its kind. The world's enfranchised son,
Who found the trees of Life and Knowledge one,
Here set it, frailer than his laurel-wreath.
Shall not the wretch whose hand it fell beneath
Rank also singly—the supreme unhung?
Lo! Sheppard, Turpin, pleading with black tongue
This viler thief's unsuffocated breath!
We'll search thy glossary, Shakespeare! whence almost,
And whence alone, some name shall be reveal'd
For this deaf drudge, to whom no length of ears
Sufficed to catch the music of the spheres;
Whose soul is carrion now,—too mean to yield
Some Starveling's ninth allotment of a ghost.

Dante Gabriel Rossetti

I have been here before,
    But when or how I cannot tell:
I know the grass beyond the door,
    The sweet keen smell,
The sighing sound, the lights around the shore.

You have been mine before,—
    How long ago I may not know:
But just when at that swallow's soar
    Your neck turned so,
Some veil did fall,—I knew it all of yore.

Has this been thus before?
    And shall not thus time's eddying flight
Still with our lives our love restore
    In death's despite,
And day and night yield one delight once more?

Dante Gabriel Rossetti

886   *The woodspurge*

The wind flapped loose, the wind was still,
Shaken out dead from tree and hill
I had walked on at the wind's will,—
I sat now, for the wind was still.

Between my knees my forehead was,—
My lips, drawn in, said not Alas!
My hair was over in the grass,
My naked ears heard the day pass.

My eyes, wide open, had the run
Of some ten weeds to fix upon;
Among those few, out of the sun,
The woodspurge flowered, three cups in one.

From perfect grief there need not be
Wisdom or even memory:
One thing then learnt remains to me,—
The woodspurge has a cup of three.

Dante Gabriel Rossetti

887　*The honeysuckle*

I plucked a honeysuckle where
　　The hedge on high is quick with thorn,
　　And climbing for the prize, was torn,
And fouled my feet in quag-water;
　　And by the thorns and by the wind
　　The blossom that I took was thinn'd,
And yet I found it sweet and fair.

Thence to a richer growth I came,
　　Where, nursed in mellow intercourse,
　　The honeysuckles sprang by scores,
Not harried like my single stem,
　　All virgin lamps of scent and dew.
　　So from my hand that first I threw,
Yet plucked not any more of them.

Dante Gabriel Rossetti

888　*Winter*

How large that thrush looks on the bare thorn-tree!
A swarm of such, three little months ago,
Had hidden in the leaves and let none know
Save by the outburst of their minstrelsy.
A white flake here and there—a snow-lily
Of last night's frost—our naked flower-beds hold;
And for a rose-flower on the darkling mould
The hungry redbreast gleams. No bloom, no bee.

The current shudders to its ice-bound sedge:
Nipped in their bath, the stark reeds one by one
Flash each its clinging diamond in the sun:
'Neath winds which for this winter's sovereign pledge
Shall curb great king-masts to the ocean's edge
And leave memorial forest-kings o'erthrown.

Dante Gabriel Rossetti

889 *Memory*

Is Memory most of miseries miserable,
Or the one flower of ease in bitterest hell?

Dante Gabriel Rossetti

890 *Summer*

Winter is cold-hearted,
   Spring is yea and nay,
Autumn is a weathercock
   Blown every way:
Summer days for me
When every leaf is on its tree;

When Robin's not a beggar,
   And Jenny Wren's a bride,
And larks hang singing, singing, singing,
   Over the wheat-fields wide,
   And anchored lilies ride,
And the pendulum spider
   Swings from side to side,

And blue-black beetles transact business,
   And gnats fly in a host,
And furry caterpillars hasten
   That no time be lost,
And moths grow fat and thrive,
And ladybirds arrive.

Before green apples blush,
    Before green nuts embrown,
Why, one day in the country
    Is worth a month in town;
    Is worth a day and a year
Of the dusty, musty, lag-last fashion
    That days drone elsewhere.

Christina Rossetti

891   *Bread and milk*

Bread and milk for breakfast,
    And woollen frocks to wear,
And a crumb for robin redbreast
    On the cold days of the year.

Christina Rossetti

892   *Song*

When I am dead, my dearest,
    Sing no sad songs for me;
Plant thou no roses at my head,
    Nor shady cypress tree:
Be the green grass above me
    With showers and dewdrops wet;
And if thou wilt, remember,
    And if thou wilt, forget.

I shall not see the shadows,
    I shall not feel the rain;
I shall not hear the nightingale
    Sing on, as if in pain;
And dreaming through the twilight
    That doth not rise nor set,
Haply I may remember,
    And haply may forget.

Christina Rossetti

Before the paling of the stars,
　　Before the winter morn,
Before the earliest cock crow,
　　Jesus Christ was born:
Born in a stable,
　　Cradled in a manger,
In the world his hands had made
　　Born a stranger.

Priest and king lay fast asleep
　　In Jerusalem;
Young and old lay fast asleep
　　In crowded Bethlehem;
Saint and angel, ox and ass,
　　Kept a watch together
Before the Christmas daybreak
　　In the winter weather.

Jesus on his mother's breast
　　In the stable cold,
Spotless lamb of God was he,
　　Shepherd of the fold:
Let us kneel with Mary maid,
　　With Joseph bent and hoary,
With saint and angel, ox and ass,
　　To hail the King of Glory.

Christina Rossetti

894   *Parting*

My life closed twice before its close;
　　It yet remains to see
If Immortality unveil
　　A third event to me

So huge, so hopeless to conceive,
   As these that twice befell.
Parting is all we know of heaven,
   And all we need of hell.

Emily Dickinson

895   *The train*

I like to see it lap the miles,
And lick the valley's up,
And stop to feed itself at tanks;
And then, prodigious, step

Around a pile of mountains,
And, supercilious, peer
In shanties by the sides of roads;
And then a quarry pare

To fit its sides, and crawl between,
Complaining all the while
In horrid, hooting stanza;
Then chase itself down hill

And neigh like Boanerges:
Then, punctual as a star,
Stop—docile and omnipotent—
At its own stable door.

Emily Dickinson

896   *A narrow fellow in the grass*

A narrow fellow in the grass
Occasionally rides:
You may have met him—did you not?
His notice sudden is.

The grass divides as with a comb,
A spotted shaft is seen;
And then it closes at your feet
And opens further on.

He likes a boggy acre,
A floor too cool for corn.
Yet when a child, and barefoot,
I more than once, at morn,

Have passed, I thought, a whip-lash
Unbraiding in the sun—
When, stooping to secure it,
It wrinkled, and was gone.

Several of nature's people
I know, and they know me;
I feel for them a transport
Of cordiality;

But never met this fellow,
Attended or alone,
Without a tighter breathing,
And zero at the bone.

Emily Dickinson

897   *Success is counted sweetest*

Success is counted sweetest
By those who ne'er succeed,
To comprehend a nectar
Requires sorest need.

Not one of all the purple host
Who took the flag to-day
Can tell the definition,
So clear, of victory,

As he, defeated, dying,
On whose forbidden ear
The distant strains of triumph
Break, agonized and clear.

Emily Dickinson

898   *The heart asks pleasure first*

The heart asks pleasure first,
And then, excuse from pain;
And then, those little anodynes
That deaden suffering;

And then, to go to sleep;
And then, if it should be
The will of its Inquisitor,
The liberty to die.

Emily Dickinson

899   *Much madness is divinest sense*

Much madness is divinest sense
To a discerning eye;
Much sense the starkest madness.
'T is the majority
In this, as all, prevails.
Assent, and you are sane;
Demur,—You're straightway dangerous,
And handled with a chain.

Emily Dickinson

I know some lonely houses off the road
A robber'd like the look of,—
Wooden barred,
And windows hanging low,
Inviting to
A portico,
Where two could creep:
One hand the tools,
The other peep
To make sure all's asleep.
Old-fashioned eyes,
Not easy to surprise!

How orderly the kitchen'd look by night,
With just a clock,—
But they could gag the tick,
And mice won't bark;
And so the walls don't tell,
None will.

A pair of spectacles ajar just stir—
An almanac's aware.
Was it the mat winked,
Or a nervous star?
The moon slides down the stair
To see who's there.

There's plunder,—where?
Tankard, or spoon,
Earring, or stone,
A watch, some ancient brooch
To match the grandmamma,
Staid sleeping there.

Day rattles, too,
Stealth's slow;
The sun has got as far
As the third sycamore.

Screams chanticleer,
'Who's there?'
And echoes, trains away,
Sneer—'Where?'
While the old couple, just astir,
Fancy the sunrise left the door ajar!

Emily Dickinson

901   *Pain has an element of blank*

Pain has an element of blank;
It cannot recollect
When it began, or if there were
A day when it was not.

It has no future but itself,
Its infinite realms contain
Its past, enlightened to perceive
New periods of pain.

Emily Dickinson

902   *Belshazzar had a letter*

Belshazzar had a letter,—
He never had but one;
Belshazzar's correspondent
Concluded and begun
In that immortal copy
The conscience of us all
Can read without its glasses
On revelation's wall.

Emily Dickinson

903 Presentiment

Presentiment is that long shadow on the lawn
Indicative that suns go down;
The notice to the startled grass
That darkness is about to pass.

Emily Dickinson

904 The sky is low

The sky is low, the clouds are mean,
A travelling flake of snow
Across a barn or through a rut
Debates if it will go.

A narrow wind complains all day
How some one treated him;
Nature, like us, is sometimes caught
Without her diadem.

Emily Dickinson

905 There's a certain slant of light

There's a certain slant of light,
On winter afternoons,
That oppresses, like the weight
Of cathedral tunes.

Heavenly hurt it gives us;
We can find no scar,
But internal difference
Where the meanings are.

None may teach it anything,
'T is the seal, despair,—
An imperial affliction
Sent us of the air.

When it comes, the landscape listens,
Shadows hold their breath;
When it goes, 't is like the distance
On the look of death.

Emily Dickinson

906   *Exultation is the going*

Exultation is the going
Of an inland soul to sea,—
Past the houses, past the headlands,
Into deep eternity!

Bred as we, among the mountains,
Can the sailor understand
The divine intoxication
Of the first league out from land?

Emily Dickinson

907   *I like a look of agony*

I like a look of agony,
Because I know it's true;
Men do not sham convulsion,
Nor simulate a throe.

The eyes glaze once, and that is death.
Impossible to feign
The beads upon the forehead
By homely anguish strung.

Emily Dickinson

I never saw a moor,
I never saw the sea;
Yet know I how the heather looks,
And what a wave must be.

I never spoke with God,
Nor visited in heaven;
Yet certain am I of the spot
As if the chart were given.

Emily Dickinson

909 *The last night that she lived*

The last night that she lived,
It was a common night,
Except the dying; this to us
Made nature different.

We noticed smallest things,—
Things overlooked before,
By this great light upon our minds
Italicized, as 't were.

That others could exist
While she must finish quite,
A jealousy for her arose
So nearly infinite.

We waited while she passed;
It was a narrow time,
Too jostled were our souls to speak,
At length the notice came.

She mentioned, and forgot;
Then lightly as a reed
Bent to the water, shivered scarce,
Consented, and was dead.

And we, we placed the hair,
And drew the head erect;
And then an awful leisure was,
Our faith to regulate.

Emily Dickinson

910 *The bustle in a house*

The bustle in a house
The morning after death
Is solemnest of industries
Enacted upon earth,—

The sweeping up the heart,
And putting love away
We shall not want to use again
Until eternity.

Emily Dickinson

911 *Because I could not stop for death*

Because I could not stop for Death,
He kindly stopped for me;
The carriage held but just ourselves
And Immortality.

We slowly drove, he knew no haste,
And I had put away
My labor, and my leisure too,
For his civility.

We passed the school where children played,
Their lessons scarcely done;
We passed the fields of gazing grain,
We passed the setting sun.

We paused before a house that seemed
A swelling of the ground;
The roof was scarcely visible,
The cornice but a mound.

Since then 't is centuries; but each
Feels shorter than the day
I first surmised the horses' heads
Were toward eternity.

Emily Dickinson

912   *I'm nobody! Who are you?*

I'm nobody! Who are you?
Are you nobody, too?
Then there's a pair of us—don't tell!
They'd banish us, you know.

How dreary to be somebody!
How public, like a frog
To tell your name the livelong day
To an admiring bog!

Emily Dickinson

913   *We play at paste*

We play at paste,
Till qualified for pearl,
Then drop the paste,
And deem ourself a fool.
The shapes, though, were similar,
And our new hands
Learned gem-tactics
Practising sands.

Emily Dickinson

914   *Hope is the thing with feathers*

Hope is the thing with feathers
That perches in the soul,
And sings the tune without the words,
And never stops at all,

And sweetest in the gale is heard;
And sore must be the storm
That could abash the little bird
That kept so many warm.

I've heard it in the chillest land,
And on the strangest sea;
Yet, never, in extremity,
It asked a crumb of me.

Emily Dickinson

915   *Surgeons must be very careful*

Surgeons must be very careful
When they take the knife!
Underneath their fine incisions
Stirs the culprit,—Life!

Emily Dickinson

916   *Faith is a fine invention*

Faith is a fine invention
For gentlemen who see;
But microscopes are prudent
In an emergency!

Emily Dickinson

I years had been from home,
And now, before the door,
I dared not open, lest a face
I never saw before

Stare vacant into mine
And ask my business there.
My business,—just a life I left,
Was such still dwelling there?

I fumbled at my nerve,
I scanned the windows near;
The silence like an ocean rolled,
And broke against my ear.

I laughed a wooden laugh
That I could fear a door,
Who danger and the dead had faced,
But never quaked before.

I fitted to the latch
My hand, with trembling care,
Lest back the awful door should spring,
And leave me standing there.

I moved my fingers off
As cautiously as glass,
And held my ears, and like a thief
Fled gasping from the house.

Emily Dickinson

918   I gave myself to him

I gave myself to him,
And took himself for pay.
The solemn contract of a life
Was ratified this way.

The wealth might disappoint,
Myself a poorer prove
Than this great purchaser suspect,
The daily own of Love

Depreciate the vision;
But, till the merchant buy,
Still fable, in the isles of spice,
The subtle cargoes lie.

At least, 't is mutual risk,—
Some found it mutual gain;
Sweet debt of Life,—each night to owe,
Insolvent, every noon.

Emily Dickinson

919   *I dreaded that first robin so*

I dreaded that first robin so,
But he is mastered now,
And I'm accustomed to him grown,—
He hurts a little, though.

I thought if I could only live
Till that first shout got by,
Not all pianos in the woods
Had power to mangle me.

I dared not meet the daffodils,
For fear their yellow gown
Would pierce me with a fashion
So foreign to my own.

I wished the grass would hurry,
So when 't was time to see,
He'd be too tall, the tallest one
Could stretch to look at me,

I could not bear the bees should come,
I wished they'd stay away
In those dim countries where they go:
What word had they for me?

They're here, though; not a creature failed,
No blossom stayed away
In gentle deference to me,
The Queen of Calvary.

Each one salutes me as he goes,
And I my childish plumes
Lift, in bereaved acknowledgement
Of their unthinking drums.

Emily Dickinson

920   *I started early, took my dog*

I started early, took my dog,
And visited the sea;
The mermaids in the basement
Came out to look at me,

And frigates in the upper floor
Extended hempen hands,
Presuming me to be a mouse
Aground, upon the sands.

But no man moved me till the tide
Went past my simple shoe,
And past my apron and my belt,
And past my bodice too,

And made as he would eat me up
As wholly as a dew
Upon a dandelion's sleeve—
And then I started too.

And he—he followed close behind;
I felt his silver heel
Upon my ankle,—then my shoes
Would overflow with pearl.

Until we met the solid town,
No man he seemed to know;
And bowing with a mighty look
At me, the sea withdrew.

Emily Dickinson

921   *Essential oils are wrung*

Essential oils are wrung:
The attar from the rose
Is not expressed by suns alone,
It is the gift of screws.

The general rose decays;
But this, in lady's drawer,
Makes summer when the lady lies
In ceaseless rosemary.

Emily Dickinson

922   *It was not death*

It was not death, for I stood up,
And all the dead lie down;
It was not night, for all the bells
Put out their tongues, for noon.

It was not frost, for on my flesh
I felt siroccos crawl,—
Nor fire, for just my marble feet
Could keep a chancel cool.

And yet it tasted like them all;
The figures I have seen
Set orderly, for burial,
Reminded me of mine,

As if my life were shaven
And fitted to a frame,
And could not breathe without a key;
And 't was like midnight, some,

When everything that ticked has stopped,
And space stares, all around,
Or grisly frosts, first autumn morns,
Repeal the beating ground.

But most like chaos,—stopless, cool,—
Without a chance or spar,
Or even a report of land
To justify despair.

Emily Dickinson

923 *I cannot live with you*

I cannot live with you,
It would be life,
And life is over there
Behind the shelf

The sexton keeps the key to,
Putting up
Our life, his porcelain,
Like a cup

Discarded of the housewife,
Quaint or broken;
A newer Sèvres pleases,
Old ones crack.

I could not die with you,
For one must wait
To shut the other's gaze down,
You could not.

And I, could I stand by
And see you freeze,
Without my right of frost,
Death's privilege?

Nor could I rise with you,
Because your face
Would put out Jesus',
That new grace

Glow plain and foreign
On my homesick eye,
Except that you, than he
Shone closer by.

They'd judge us—how?
For you served Heaven, you know,
Or sought to;
I could not,

Because you saturated sight,
And I had no more eyes
For sordid excellence
As Paradise.

And were you lost, I would be,
Though my name
Rang loudest
On the heavenly fame.

And were you saved,
And I condemned to be
Where you were not,
That self were hell to me.

So we must meet apart,
You there, I here,
With just the door ajar
That oceans are,
And prayer,
And that pale sustenance,
Despair.

Emily Dickinson

924   *Safe in their alabaster chambers*

Safe in their alabaster chambers,
Untouched by morning and untouched by noon,
Sleep the meek members of the resurrection,
Rafter of satin and roof of stone.

Light laughs the breeze in her castle above them;
Babbles the bee in a stolid ear;
Pipe the sweet birds in ignorant cadence—
Ah, what sagacity perished here.

Emily Dickinson

925   *Jabberwocky*

'Twas brillig, and the slithy toves
    Did gyre and gimble in the wabe;
All mimsy were the borogoves,
    And the mome raths outgrabe.

'Beware the Jabberwock, my son!
    The jaws that bite, the claws that catch!
Beware the Jubjub bird, and shun
    The frumious Bandersnatch!'

He took his vorpal sword in hand:
    Long time the manxome foe he sought—
So rested he by the Tumtum tree,
    And stood awhile in thought.

And as in uffish thought he stood,
   The Jabberwock, with eyes of flame,
Came whiffling through the tulgey wood
   And burbled as it came!

One, two! One, two! And through and through
   The vorpal blade went snicker-snack!
He left it dead, and with its head
   He went galumphing back.

'And hast thou slain the Jabberwock?
   Come to my arms, my beamish boy!
A frabjous day! Callooh callay!'
   He shortled in his joy.

'Twas brillig, and the slithy toves
   Did gyre and gimble in the wabe;
All mimsy were the borogoves,
   And the mome raths outgrabe.

Lewis Carroll

926   *Song*

The feathers of the willow
Are half of them grown yellow
   Above the swelling stream;
And ragged are the bushes,
And rusty now the rushes,
   And wild the clouded gleam.

The thistle now is older,
His stalk begins to moulder,
   His head is white as snow;
The branches all are barer,
The linnet's song is rarer,
   The robin pipeth now.

Richard Watson Dixon

There was a lady lived in a hall,
Large in the eyes, and slim and tall;
And ever she sung from noon to noon,
Two red roses across the moon.

There was a knight came riding by
In early spring, when the roads were dry;
And he heard that lady sing at the noon,
Two red roses across the moon

Yet none the more he stopp'd at all,
But he rode a-gallop past the hall;
And left that lady singing at noon,
Two red roses across the moon.

Because, forsooth, the battle was set,
And the scarlet and blue had got to be met,
He rode on the spur till the next warm noon:—
Two red roses across the moon.

But the battle was scatter'd from hill to hill,
From the windmill to the watermill;
And he said to himself, as it near'd the noon,
Two red roses across the moon.

You scarce could see for the scarlet and blue,
A golden helm or a golden shoe;
So he cried, as the fight grew thick at the noon,
Two red roses across the moon!

Verily then the gold bore through
The huddled spears of the scarlet and blue;
And they cried, as they cut them down at the noon,
Two red roses across the moon!

I trow he stopp'd when he rode again
By the hall, though draggled sore with the rain;
And his lips were pinch'd to kiss at the noon
Two red roses across the moon.

Under the may she stoop'd to the crown,
All was gold, there was nothing of brown;
And the horns blew up in the hall at noon,
Two red roses across the moon.

William Morris

928 *In prison*

Wearily, drearily,
Half the day long,
Flap the great banners
High over the stone;
Strangely and eerily
Sounds the wind's song,
Bending the banner-poles.

While, all alone,
Watching the loophole's spark,
Lie I, with life all dark,
Feet tether'd, hands fetter'd
Fast to the stone,
The grim walls, square letter'd
With prison'd men's groan.

Still strain the banner-poles
Through the wind's song,
Westward the banner rolls
Over my wrong.

William Morris

929 *Near Avalon*

A ship with shields before the sun,
Six maidens round the mast,
A red-gold crown on everyone,
A green gown on the last.

The fluttering green banners there
Are wrought with ladies' heads most fair,
And a portraiture of Guenevere
The middle of each sail doth bear.

A ship which sailed before the wind,
And round the helm six knights,
Their heaumes are on whereby, half blind,
They pass by many sights.

The tattered scarlet banners there,
Right soon will leave the spear-heads bare.
Those six knights sorrowfully bear
In all their heaumes some yellow hair.

William Morris

930 *Summer dawn*

Pray but one prayer for me 'twixt thy closed lips;
    Think but one thought of me up in the stars.
The summer night waneth, the morning light slips,
    Faint and grey 'twixt the leaves of the aspen, betwixt
                                    the cloud-bars,
That are patiently waiting there for the dawn:
    Patient and colourless, though Heaven's gold
Waits to float through them along with the sun.
Far out in the meadows, above the young corn,
    The heavy elms wait, and restless and cold
The uneasy wind rises; the roses are dun;
They pray the long gloom through for daylight new
                                    born,
Round the lone house in the midst of the corn.
    Speak but one word to me over the corn,
    Over the tender, bowed locks of the corn.

William Morris

He came to the desert of London town
  Grey miles long;
He wander'd up and he wander'd down,
  Singing a quiet song.

He came to the desert of London town,
  Mirk miles broad;
He wander'd up and he wander'd down,
  Ever alone with God.

There were thousands and thousands of human kind
  In this desert of brick and stone:
But some were deaf and some were blind,
  And he was there alone.

At length the good hour came; he died
  As he had lived, alone:
He was not miss'd from the desert wide,—
  Perhaps he was found at the Throne.

James Thomson

932 *Music (after Sully Prudhomme)*

Kindly watcher by my bed, lift no voice in prayer,
Waste not any words on me when the hour is nigh,
Let a stream of melody but flow from some sweet
    player,
And meekly will I lay my head and fold my hands to die.

Sick am I of idle words, past all reconciling,
Words that weary and perplex and pander and conceal,
Wake the sounds that cannot lie, for all their sweet
    beguiling;
The language one need fathom not, but only hear and
    feel.

Let them roll once more to me, and ripple in my hear-
    ing,

Like waves upon a lonely beach where no craft anchor-
   eth:
That I may steep my soul therein, and craving naught,
   nor fearing,
Drift on through slumber to a dream, and through a
   dream to death.

George Du Maurier

933   *A psalm of Montreal*

Stowed away in a Montreal lumber room
The Discobolus standeth and turneth his face to the wall;
Dusty, cobweb-covered, maimed and set at naught,
Beauty lieth in an attic and no man regardeth:
      O God! O Montreal!

Beautiful by night and day, beautiful in summer and
   winter,
Whole or maimed, always and alike beautiful—
He preacheth gospel of grace to the skins of owls
And to one who seasoneth the skins of Canadian owls;
      O God! O Montreal!

When I saw him I was wroth and I said, 'O Discobolus!
Beautiful Discobolus, a Prince both among Gods and
   men,
What dost thou here, how camest thou hither, Disco-
   bolus,
Preaching gospel in vain to the skins of owls?'
      O God! O Montreal!

And I turned to the man of skins and said unto him, 'O
   thou man of skins,
Wherefore hast thou done thus to shame the beauty of
   the Discobolus?'
But the Lord had hardened the heart of the man of skins,
And he answered, 'My brother-in-law is haberdasher
   to Mr. Spurgeon.'
      O God! O Montreal!

'The Discobolus is put here because he is vulgar,
He has neither vest nor pants with which to cover his
  limbs;
I, Sir, am a person of most respectable connections—
My brother-in-law is haberdasher to Mr. Spurgeon.'
      O God! O Montreal!

Then I said, 'O brother-in-law to Mr. Spurgeon's
  haberdasher,
Who seasonest also the skins of Canadian owls,
Thou callest trousers "pants", whereas I call them
  "trousers",
Therefore, thou art in hell-fire, and may the Lord pity
  thee'
      O God! O Montreal!

'Preferrest thou the gospel of Montreal to the gospel of
  Hellas,
The gospel of thy connection with Mr. Spurgeon's
  haberdashery to the gospel of the Discobolus?'
Yet none the less blasphemed he beauty saying, 'The
  Discobolus hath no gospel,
But my brother-in-law is haberdasher to Mr. Spurgeon.'
      O God! O Montreal!

                                        Samuel Butler

934   *The ocean wood*

Grey woods within whose silent shade
   The ocean voice is dimly known:
Where undisturbed the violets fade,
   And roses perish overblown.

Calm rests the wave against the beach:
   Calm rocks the wave-bird on its tide,
And calmer in their heaven than each,
   The gleaming bands of sunset ride.

Soon will the ripple move again:
  Soon will the shorelark flute its song:
And in sweet emphasis of pain
  The rock-dove mourn the cliffs along.

Sweet shall resound the curlew's wail,
  New sails come sweeping up the sea.
But all the ships that ever sail
  Will bring no comfort home to me.

John Leicester Warren, Lord de Tabley

935   *What the bullet sang*

O joy of creation,
        To be!
O rapture, to fly
        And to be free!
Be the battle lost or won,
Though its smoke shall hide the sun,
I shall find my love—the one
        Born for me!

I shall know him where he stands
        All alone,
With the power in his hands
        Not o'erthrown;
I shall know him by his face,
By his godlike front and grace,
I shall hold him for a space
        All my own!

It is he—O my love!
        So bold!
It is I—all thy love
        Foretold!
It is I—O love, what bliss!
Dost thou answer to my kiss?
O sweetheart! what is this
        Lieth there so cold?

Bret Harte

Before the beginning of years
  There came to the making of man
Time, with a gift of tears;
  Grief, with a glass that ran;
Pleasure, with pain for leaven;
  Summer, with flowers that fell;
Remembrance fallen from heaven,
  And madness risen from hell;
Strength without hands to smite;
  Love that endures for a breath;
Night, the shadow of light,
  And life, the shadow of death.
And the high gods took in hand
  Fire, and the falling of tears,
And a measure of sliding sand
  From under the feet of the years;
And froth and drift of the sea;
  And dust of the labouring earth;
And bodies of things to be
  In the houses of death and of birth;
And wrought with weeping and laughter,
  And fashion'd with loathing and love,
With life before and after
  And death beneath and above,
For a day and a night and a morrow,
  That his strength might endure for a span
With travail and heavy sorrow,
  The holy spirit of man.

From the winds of the north and the south
  They gather'd as unto strife;
They breathed upon his mouth,
  They fill'd his body with life;
Eyesight and speech they wrought
  For the veils of the soul therein,
A time for labour and thought,
  A time to serve and to sin;

They gave him light in his ways,
  And love, and a space for delight,
And beauty and length of days,
  And night, and sleep in the night.
His speech is a burning fire;
  With his lips he travaileth;
In his heart is a blind desire,
  In his eyes foreknowledge of death;
He weaves, and is clothed with derision;
  Sows, and he shall not reap;
His life is a watch or a vision
  Between a sleep and a sleep.

Algernon Charles Swinburne

937 *A forsaken garden*

In a coign of the cliff between lowland and highland,
  At the sea-down's edge between windward and lee,
Wall'd round with rocks as an inland island,
  The ghost of a garden fronts the sea.
A girdle of brushwood and thorn encloses
  The steep square slope of the blossomless bed
Where the weeds that grew green from the graves of its
                                               roses
      Now lie dead.

The fields fall southward, abrupt and broken,
  To the low last edge of the long lone land.
If a step should sound or a word be spoken,
  Would a ghost not rise at the strange guests' hand?
So long have the grey bare walks lain guestless,
  Through branches and briars if a man make way,
He shall find no life but the sea-wind's, restless
      Night and day.

The dense hard passage is blind and stifled
  That crawls by a track none turn to climb
To the strait waste place that the years have rifled
  Of all but the thorns that are touch'd not of time.

The thorns he spares when the rose is taken;
  The rocks are left when he wastes the plain.
The wind that wanders, the weeds wind-shaken,
    These remain.

Not a flower to be press'd of the foot that falls not;
  As the heart of a dead man the seed-plots are dry;
From the thicket of thorns whence the nightingale calls
                        not,
  Could she call, there were never a rose to reply.
Over the meadows that blossom and wither
  Rings but the note of a sea-bird's song;
Only the sun and the rain come hither
    All year long.

The sun burns sere and the rain dishevels
  One gaunt bleak blossom of scentless breath.
Only the wind here hovers and revels
  In a round where life seems barren as death.
Here there was laughing of old, there was weeping,
  Haply, of lovers none ever will know,
Whose eyes went seaward a hundred sleeping
    Years ago.

Heart handfast in heart as they stood, 'Look thither,'
  Did he whisper? 'look forth from the flowers to the
                        sea;
For the foam-flowers endure when the rose-blossoms
                        wither,
  And men that love lightly may die—but we?'
And the same wind sang and the same waves whiten'd,
  And or ever the garden's last petals were shed,
In the lips that had whisper'd, the eyes that had lighten'd,
  Love was dead.

Or they loved their life through, and then went
                        whither?
  And were one to the end—but what end who knows?
Love deep as the sea as a rose must wither,
  As the rose-red seaweed that mocks the rose.

Shall the dead take thought for the dead to love them?
    What love was ever as deep as a grave?
They are loveless now as the grass above them
        Or the wave.

All are at one now, roses and lovers,
    Not known of the cliffs and the fields and the sea.
Not a breath of the time that has been hovers
    In the air now soft with a summer to be.
Not a breath shall there sweeten the seasons hereafter
    Of the flowers or the lovers that laugh now or weep,
When as they that are free now of weeping and laughter
        We shall sleep.

Here death may deal not again for ever;
    Here change may come not till all change end.
From the graves they have made they shall rise up never,
    Who have left nought living to ravage and rend.
Earth, stones, and thorns of the wild ground growing,
    While the sun and the rain live, these shall be;
Till a last wind's breath upon all these blowing
        Roll the sea.

Till the slow sea rise and the sheer cliff crumble,
    Till terrace and meadow the deep gulfs drink,
Till the strength of the waves of the high tides humble
    The fields that lessen, the rocks that shrink,
Here now in his triumph where all things falter,
    Stretch'd out on the spoils that his own hand spread,
As a god self-slain on his own strange altar,
        Death lies dead.

                                    Algernon Charles Swinburne

938   *Heredity*

    I am the family face;
    Flesh perishes, I live on,
    Projecting trait and trace
    Through time to times anon,

And leaping from place to place
Over oblivion.

The years-heired feature that can
In curve and voice and eye
Despise the human span
Of durance—that is I;
The eternal thing in man,
That heeds no call to die.

Thomas Hardy

939   *I look into my glass*

I look into my glass,
And view my wasting skin,
And say, 'Would God it came to pass
My heart had shrunk as thin!'

For then, I, undistrest
By hearts grown cold to me,
Could lonely wait my endless rest
With equanimity.

But Time, to make me grieve,
Part steals, lets part abide;
And shakes this fragile frame at eve
With throbbings of noontide.

Thomas Hardy

940   *A broken appointment*

You did not come,
And marching Time drew on, and wore me numb.—
Yet less for loss of your dear presence there
Than that I thus found lacking in your make

The high compassion which can overbear
Reluctance for pure loving kindness' sake
Grieved I, when, as the hope-hour stroked its sum,
    You did not come.

    You love not me,
And love alone can lend you loyalty;
—I know and knew it. But, unto the store
Of human deeds divine in all but name,
Was it not worth a little hour or more
To add yet this: Once you, a woman, came
To soothe a time-torn man; even though it be
    You love not me?

                                        Thomas Hardy

941 *Afterwards*

When the Present has latched its postern behind my
                                        tremulous stay,
    And the May month flaps its glad green leaves like
                                        wings,
Delicate-filmed as new-spun silk, will the neighbours
                                        say,
    'He was a man who used to notice such things'?

If it be in the dusk when, like an eyelid's soundless blink,
    The dewfall-hawk comes crossing the shades to alight
Upon the wind-warped upland thorn, a gazer may
                                        think,
    'To him this must have been a familiar sight.'

If I pass during some nocturnal blackness, mothy and
                                        warm,
    When the hedgehog travels furtively over the lawn,
One may say, 'He strove that such innocent creatures
                                        should come to no harm,
    But he could do little for them; and now he is gone.'

If, when hearing that I have been stilled at last, they
                                        stand at the door,
   Watching the full-starred heavens that winter sees,
Will this thought rise on those who will meet my face
                                        no more,
   'He was one who had an eye for such mysteries'?

And will any say when my bell of quittance is heard in
                                        the gloom,
   And a crossing breeze cuts a pause in its outrollings,
Till they rise again, as they were a new bell's boom,
   'He hears it not now, but used to notice such things'?

                                        Thomas Hardy

942   *The raven days*

   Our hearths are gone out, and our hearts are broken,
      And but the ghosts of homes to us remain,
   And ghostly eyes and hollow sighs give token
      From friend to friend of an unspoken pain.

   O, Raven Days, dark Raven Days of sorrow,
      Bring to us, in your whetted ivory beaks,
   Some sign out of the far land of To-morrow,
      Some strip of sea-green dawn, some orange streaks.

   Ye float in dusky files, forever croaking—
      Ye chill our manhood with your dreary shade.
   Pale, in the dark, not even God invoking,
      We lie in chains, too weak to be afraid.

   O Raven Days, dark Raven Days of sorrow,
      Will ever any warm light come again?
   Will ever the lit mountains of To-morrow
      Begin to gleam across the mournful plain?

                                        Sidney Lanier

943　*Struggle*

My Soul is like the oar that momently
　　Dies in a desperate stress beneath the wave,
Then glitters out again and sweeps the sea:
　　Each second I'm new-born from some new grave.

Sidney Lanier

944　*No worst, there in none*

No worst, there is none. Pitched past pitch of grief,
More pangs will, schooled at forepangs, wilder wring.
Comforter, where, where is your comforting?
Mary, mother of us, where is your relief?
My cries heave, herds-long; huddled in a main, a chief
Woe, world-sorrow; on an age-old anvil wince and
　　sing—
Then lull, then leave off. Fury had shrieked 'no linger-
　　ing! Let me be fell: force I must be brief'.

O the mind, mind has mountains; cliffs of fall
Frightful, sheer, no-man-fathomed. Hold them cheap
May who ne'er hung there. Nor does long our small
Durance deal with that steep or deep. Here! creep,
Wretch, under a comfort serves in a whirlwind: all
Life death does end and each day dies with sleep.

Gerard Manley Hopkins

945　*To R. B.*

The fine delight that fathers thought; the strong
Spur, live and lancing like the blowpipe flame,
Breathes once and, quenchèd faster than it came,
Leaves yet the mind a mother of immortal song.
Nine months she then, nay years, nine years she long
Within her wears, bears, cares and moulds the same:
The widow of an insight lost she lives, with aim
Now known and hand at work now never wrong.

Sweet fire the sire of muse, my soul needs this;
I want the one rapture of an inspiration.
O then if in my lagging lines you miss
The roll, the rise, the carol, the creation,
My winter world, that scarcely breathes that bliss
Now, yields you, with some sighs, our explanation.

Gerard Manley Hopkins

946   Hurrahing in harvest

Summer ends now; now, barbarous in beauty, the stooks
                                                    arise
    Around; up above, what wind-walks! what lovely
                                                behaviour
    Of silk-sack clouds! has wilder, wilful-wavier
Meal-drift moulded ever and melted across skies?

I walk, I lift up, I lift up heart, eyes,
    Down all that glory in the heavens to glean our
                                                Saviour;
    And, eyes, heart, what looks, what lips yet—gave you a
Rapturous love's greeting of realer, of rounder replies?

And the azurous hung hills are his world-wielding
                                                shoulder
    Majestic—as a stallion stalwart, very-violet-sweet!—
These things, these things were here and but the
                                                beholder
    Wanting: which two when they once meet,
The heart rears wings bold and bolder
    And hurls for him, O half hurls earth for him off
                                            under his feet.

Gerard Manley Hopkins

What, what, what,
What's the news from Swat?
  Sad news,
  Bad news,
Comes by the cable led
Through the indian ocean's bed,
Through the Persian Gulf, the Red
Sea and the Med-
Iterranean—he's dead.
The Ahkoond is dead!

For the Ahkoond I mourn.
  Who wouldn't?
He strove to disregard the message stern,
  But ahkoondn't.

Dead, dead, dead;
  Sorrow, Swat's!
Swats wha' hae wi' Ahkoond bled,
Swats whom he had often led
Onward to a gory bed,
  Or to victory,
  As the case might be.
Sorrow, Swats!
Tears shed,
  Shed tears like water,
Your great Ahkoond is dead!
  That Swat's the matter!

Mourn, city of Swat!
Your great Ahkoond is not,
But lain 'mid worms to rot:
His mortal part alone, his soul was caught
(Because he was a good Ahkoond)
Up to the bosom of Mahound.
Though earthly walls his frame surround
(For ever hallowed be the ground!)

And sceptics mock the lowly mound
And say, 'He's now of no Ahkound!'
(His soul is in the skies!)
The azure skies that bend above his loved
   Metropolis of Swat
He sees with larger, other eyes,
Athwart all earthly mysteries—
   He knows what's Swat.

Let Swat bury the great Ahkoond
   With a noise of mourning and of lamentation!
Let Swat bury the great Ahkoond
   With the noise of the mourning of the Swattish
                                    nation!
     Fallen is at length
     Its tower of strength,
Its sun had dimmed ere it had nooned:
Dead lies the great Ahkoond.
     The great Ahkoond of Swat
     Is not.

George T. Lanigan

948   *Margaritae Sorori*

A late lark twitters from the quiet skies
And from the west,
Where the sun, his day's work ended,
Lingers as in content,
There falls on the old, gray city
An influence luminous and serene,
A shining peace.

The smoke ascends
In a rosy-and-golden haze. The spires
Shine and are changed. In the valley
Shadows rise. The lark sings on. The sun,
Closing his benediction,

Sinks, and the darkening air
Thrills with a sense of the triumphing night—
Night with her train of stars
And her great gift of sleep.

So be my passing!
My task accomplish'd and the long day done,
My wages taken, and in my heart
Some late lark singing,
Let me be gather'd to the quiet west,
The sundown splendid and serene,
Death.

W. E. Henley

949   *Oh who is that young sinner?*

Oh who is that young sinner with handcuffs on his
     wrists?
And what has he been after that they groan and shake
     their fists?
And wherefore is he wearing such a conscience-stricken
     air?
Oh they're taking him to prison for the colour of his
     hair.

'Tis a shame to human nature, such a head of hair as his;
In the good old time 'twas hanging for the colour that
     it is;
Though hanging isn't bad enough and flaying would be
     fair
For the nameless and abominable colour of his hair.

Oh a deal of pains he's taken and a pretty price he's paid
To hide his poll or dye it of a mentionable shade;
But they've pulled the beggar's hat off for the world to
     see and stare,
And they're haling him to justice for the colour of his
     hair.

Now 'tis oakum and the treadmill for his feet
And the quarry-gang on Portland in the cold and in the
  heat,
And between his spells of labour in the time he has to
  spare
He can curse the God that made him for the colour of
  his hair.

A. E. Housman

950   *Tell me not here, it needs not saying*

Tell me not here, it needs not saying,
  What tune the enchantress plays
In aftermaths of soft September
  Or under blanching mays,
For she and I were long acquainted
  And I knew all her ways.

On russet floors, by waters idle,
  The pine lets fall its cone;
The cuckoo shouts all day at nothing
  In leafy dells alone;
And traveller's joy beguiles in autumn
  Hearts that have lost their own.

On acres of the seeded grasses
  The changing burnish heaves;
Or marshall'd under moons of harvest
  Stand still all night the sheaves;
Or beeches strip in storms for winter
  And stain the wind with leaves.

Possess, as I possessed a season,
  The countries I resign,
Where over elmy plains the highway
  Would mount the hills and shine,
And full of shade the pillared forest
  Would murmur and be mine.

For nature, heartless, witless nature,
　　Will neither care nor know
What stranger's feet may find the meadow
　　And trespass there and go,
Nor ask amid the dews of morning
　　If they are mine or no.

A. E. Housman

951　*Her strong enchantments failing*

Her strong enchantments failing,
　　Her towers of fear in wreck,
Her limbecks dried of poisons
　　And the knife at her neck,

The Queen of air and darkness,
　　Begins to shrill and cry,
'O young man, O my slayer,
　　To-morrow you shall die.'

O Queen of air and darkness,
　　I think 'tis truth you say,
And I shall die to-morrow;
　　But you will die to-day.

A. E. Housman

952　Veneta

Wind and waters ring the bells
　　That rang for them of high degree,
Trumpets are the sounding shells
　　In the city under the sea.

Where a queen was wont to hide
　　Her outwearied majesty,
Swim the fishes open-eyed
　　In the city under the sea.

Many a street lies broad and fair,
  Many a palace fair and free,
Neither a man nor woman there,
  In the city under the sea.

Mary Coleridge

953   *The other side of a mirror*

I sat before my glass one day,
  And conjured up a vision bare,
Unlike the aspects glad and gay,
  That erst were found reflected there—
The vision of a woman, wild
  With more than womanly despair.

Her hair stood back on either side
  A face bereft of loveliness.
It has no envy now to hide
  What once no man on earth could guess.
It formed the thorny aureole
  Of hard unsanctified distress.

Her lips were open—not a sound
  Came through the parted lines of red.
Whate'er it was, the hideous wound
  In silence and in secret bled.
No sigh relieved her speechless woe,
  She had no voice to speak her dread.

And in her lurid eyes there shone
  The dying flame of life's desire,
Made mad because its hope was gone,
  And kindled at the leaping fire
Of jealousy, and fierce revenge,
  And strength that could not change or tire.

Shade of a shadow in the glass,
   O set the crystal surface free!
Pass—as the fairer visions pass—
   Nor ever more return, to be
The ghost of a distracted hour,
   That heard me whisper, 'I am she!'

Mary Coleridge

954   *To memory*

Strange power, I know not what thou art,
Murderer or mistress of my heart.
I know I'd rather meet the blow
Of my most unrelenting foe
Than live—as I live now—to be
Slain twenty times a day by thee.

Yet, when I would command thee hence,
Thou mockest at the vain pretence,
Murmuring in my ear a song
Once loved, alas! forgotten long;
And on my brow I feel a kiss
That I would rather die than miss.

Mary Coleridge

955   *Solitude*

How still it is here in the woods. The trees
   Stand motionless, as if they do not dare
   To stir, lest it should break the spell. The air
Hangs quiet as spaces in a marble frieze.
Even this little brook, that runs at ease,
   Whispering and gurgling in its knotted bed,
   Seems but to deepen with its curling thread
Of sound the shadowy sun-pierced silences.

Sometimes a hawk screams or a woodpecker
   Startles the stillness from its fixèd mood
With his loud careless tap. Sometimes I hear
    The dreamy white-throat from some far-off tree
Pipe slowly on the listening solitude
   His five pure notes succeeding pensively.

Archibald Lampman

956   *Sailing to Byzantium*

I

That is no country for old men. The young
In one another's arms, birds in the trees,
—Those dying generations—at their song,
The salmon-falls, the mackerel-crowded seas,
Fish, flesh, or fowl, commend all summer long
Whatever is begotten, born, and dies.
Caught in that sensual music all neglect
Monuments of unaging intellect.

2

An aged man is but a paltry thing,
A tattered coat upon a stick, unless
Soul clap its hands and sing, and louder sing
For every tatter in its mortal dress,
Nor is there singing school but studying
Monuments of its own magnificence;
And therefore I have sailed the seas and come
To the holy city of Byzantium.

3

O sages standing in God's holy fire
And in the old mosaic of a wall,
Come from the holy fire, perne in a gyre,
And be the singing masters of my soul.

Consume my heart away; sick with desire
And fastened to a dying animal
It knows not what it is; and gather me
Into the artifice of eternity.

4

Once out of nature I shall never take
My bodily form from any natural thing,
But such a form as Grecian goldsmiths make
Of hammered gold and gold enamelling
To keep a drowsy emperor awake;
Or set upon a golden bough to sing
To lords and ladies of Byzantium
Of what is past, or passing, or to come.

W. B. Yeats

957   *Spleen*

I was not sorrowful, I could not weep,
And all my memories were put to sleep.

I watched the river grow more white and strange,
All day till evening I watched it change.

All day till evening I watched the rain
Beat wearily upon the window pane.

 was not sorrowful, but only tired
Of everything that ever I desired.

Her lips, her eyes, all day became to me
The shadow of a shadow utterly.

All day mine hunger for her heart became
Oblivion, until the evening came,

And left me sorrowful, inclined to weep,
With all my memories that could not sleep.

Ernest Dowson

Miniver Cheevy, child of scorn,
   Grew lean while he assailed the seasons;
He wept that he was ever born,
   And he had reasons.

Miniver loved the days of old
   When swords were bright and steeds were prancing;
The vision of a warrior bold
   Would set him dancing.

Miniver sighed for what was not,
   And dreamed, and rested from his labours;
He dreamed of Thebes and Camelot,
   And Priam's neighbours.

Miniver mourned the ripe renown
   That made so many a name so fragrant;
He mourned Romance, now on the town,
   And Art, a vagrant.

Miniver loved the Medici,
   Albeit he had never seen one;
He would have sinned incessantly
   Could he have been one.

Miniver cursed the commonplace
   And eyed a khaki suit with loathing;
He missed the mediæval grace
   Of iron clothing.

Miniver scorned the gold he sought,
   But sore annoyed was he without it;
Miniver thought, and thought, and thought,
   And thought about it.

Miniver Cheevey, born too late,
   Scratched his head and kept on thinking;
Miniver coughed, and called it fate,
   And kept on drinking.

Edward Arlington Robinson

We wait our turn, as still as mice,
For medicine free, and free advice:
Two mothers, and their little girls
So small—each one with flaxen curls—
And I myself, the last to come.
Now as I entered that bare room,
I was not seen or heard; for both
The mothers—one in finest cloth,
With velvet blouse and crocheted lace,
Lips painted red, and powdered face;
The other ragged, whose face took
Its own dull, white, and wormy look—
Exchanged a hard and bitter stare.
And both the children, sitting there,
Taking example from that sight,
Made ugly faces, full of spite.
This woman said, though not a word
From her red painted lips was heard—
'Why have I come to this, to be
In such a slattern's company?'
The ragged woman's look replied—
'If you can dress with so much pride,
Why are you here, so neat and nice,
For medicine free, and free advice?'
And I, who needed richer food,
Not medicine, to help my blood;
Who could have swallowed then a horse,
And chased its rider round the course,
Sat looking on, ashamed, perplexed,
Until a welcome voice cried—'Next!'

W. H. Davies

960   *I am the poet Davies, William*

I am the Poet Davies, William,
    I sin without a blush or blink:
I am a man that lives to eat;
    I am a man that lives to drink.

My face is large, my lips are thick,
   My skin is coarse and black almost;
But the ugliest feature is my verse,
   Which proves my soul is black and lost.

Thank heaven thou didst not marry me,
   A poet full of blackest evil;
For how to manage my damned soul
   Will puzzle many a flaming devil.

W. H. Davies

961   *The inquest*

I took my oath I would inquire,
   Without affection, hate or wrath,
Into the death of Ada Wright—
   So help me God! I took that oath.

When I went out to see the corpse,
   The four months' babe that died so young,
I judged it was seven pounds in weight,
   And little more than one foot long.

One eye, that had a yellow lid,
   Was shut—so was the mouth, that smiled;
The left eye open, shining bright—
   It seemed a knowing little child.

For as I looked at that one eye,
   It seemed to laugh, and say with glee:
'What caused my death you'll never know—
   Perhaps my mother murdered me.'

When I went into court again,
   To hear the mother's evidence—
It was a love-child, she explained.
   And smiled, for our intelligence.

'Now, Gentlemen of the Jury,' said
    The coroner—'this woman's child
By misadventure met its death.'
    'Aye, aye,' said we. The mother smiled.

And I could see that child's one eye
    Which seemed to laugh, and say with glee:
'What caused my death you'll never know—
    Perhaps my mother murdered me.'

W. H. Davies

962   *The railway junction*

From here through tunnelled gloom the track
Forks into two; and one of these
Wheels onward into darkening hills,
And one toward distant seas.

How still it is; the signal light
At set of sun shines palely green;
A thrush sings; other sound there's none,
Nor traveller to be seen—

Where late there was a throng. And now,
In peace awhile, I sit alone;
Though soon, at the appointed hour,
I shall myself be gone.

But not their way: the bow-legged groom,
The parson in black, the widow and son,
The sailor with his cage, the gaunt
Gamekeeper with his gun,

That fair one, who, discreetly veiled—
All, who so mutely came, and went,
Will reach those far nocturnal hills,
Or shores, ere night is spent.

I nothing know why thus we met—
Their thoughts, their longings, hopes, their fate:
And what shall I remember, except—
The evening growing late—

That here through tunnelled gloom the track
Forks into two; of these
One into darkening hills leads on,
And one toward distant seas?

Walter de la Mare

963   *The quartette*

Tom sang for joy and Ned sang for joy and old Sam
     sang for joy;
All we four boys piped up loud, just like one boy;
And the ladies that sate with the Squire—their cheeks
     were all wet,
For the noise of the voice of us boys, when we sang our
     Quartette.

Tom he piped low and Ned he piped low and old Sam
     he piped low;
Into a sorrowful fall did our music flow;
And the ladies that sate with the Squire vowed they'd
     never forget
How the eyes of them cried for delight, when we sang
     our Quartette.

Walter de la Mare

964   *The bead mat*

We had climbed the last steep flight of stairs;
     Alone were she and I:
'It's something I wanted to give to you,'
     She whispered with a sigh.

There, in her own small room she stood—
    Where the last beam of sun
Burned in the glass—and showed me what
    For me she had done:—

An oblong shining mat of beads,
    Yellow and white and green,
And where the dark-blue middle was
    A gold between.

I heard no far-off voice, no sound:
    Only her clear grey eyes
Drank in the thoughts that in my face
    Passed shadow-wise.

She clasped her hands, and turned her head,
    And in the watchful glass
She saw how many things had seen
    All that had passed.

She snatched her gift away: her cheek
    With scarlet was aflame:
'It isn't *anything*,' she said,
    'If *we*'re the same!'

Her eyes were like a stormy sea,
    Forlorn, and vast, and grey;
Wherein a little beaten ship
    Flew through the spray.

Walter de la Mare

965   *Dramatic fragment*

Sir, say no more.
Within me 't is as if
The green and climbing eyesight of a cat
Crawled near my mind's poor birds.

Trumbull Stickney

I went to turn the grass once after one
Who mowed it in the dew before the sun.

The dew was gone that made his blade so keen
Before I came to view the levelled scene.

I looked for him behind an isle of trees;
I listened for his whetstone on the breeze.

But he had gone his way, the grass all mown,
And I must be, as he had been,—alone.

'As all must be,' I said within my heart,
'Whether they work together or apart.'

But as I said it, swift there passed me by
On noiseless wing a bewildered butterfly.

Seeking with memories grown dim o'er night
Some resting flower of yesterday's delight.

And once I marked his flight go round and round,
As where some flower lay withering on the ground.

And then he flew as far as eye could see,
And then on tremulous wing came back to me.

I thought of questions that had no reply,
And would have turned to toss the grass to dry;

But he turned first, and led my eye to look
At a tall tuft of flowers beside a brook,

A leaping tongue of bloom the scythe had spared
Beside a reedy brook the scythe had bared.

The mower in the dew had loved them thus
By leaving them to flourish, not for us,

Nor yet to draw one thought of ours to him,
But from sheer morning gladness at the brim.

The butterfly and I had lit upon,
Nevertheless, a message from the dawn,

That made me hear the wakening birds around,
And hear his long scythe whispering to the ground,

And feel a spirit kindred to my own;
So that henceforth I worked no more alone;

But glad with him, I worked as with his aid,
And weary, sought at noon with him the shade;

And dreaming, as it were, held brotherly speech
With one whose thought I had not hoped to reach.

'Men work together,' I told him from the heart,
'Whether they work together or apart.'

Robert Frost

967   *Too anxious for rivers*

Look down the long valley and there stands a mountain
That someone has said is the end of the world.
Then what of this river that having arisen
Must find where to pour itself into and empty?
I never saw so much swift water run cloudless.
Oh, I have been often too anxious for rivers
To leave it to them to get out of their valleys.
The truth is the river flows into the canyon
Of Ceasing to Question What Doesn't Concern Us,
As sooner or later we have to cease somewhere.
No place to get lost like too far in the distance.
It may be a mercy the dark closes round us
So broodingly soon in every direction.
The world as we know is an elephant's howdah;

The elephant stands on the back of a turtle;
The turtle in turn on a rock in the ocean.
And how much longer a story has science
Before she must put out the light on the children
And tell them the rest of the story is dreaming?
'You children may dream it and tell it tomorrow.'
Time was we were molten, time was we were vapour.
What set us on fire and what set us revolving
Lucretius the Epicurean might tell us
'Twas something we knew all about to begin with
And needn't have fared into space like his master
To find 'twas the effort, the essay of love.

Robert Frost

968   *The bearer of evil tidings*

The bearer of evil tidings,
When he was half way there,
Remembered that evil tidings
Were a dangerous thing to bear.

So when he came to the parting
Where one road led to the throne
And one went off to the mountains
And into the wild unknown,

He took the one to the mountains.
He ran through the Vale of Cashmere,
He ran through the rhododendrons
Till he came to the land of Pamir.

And there in a precipice valley
A girl of his age he met
Took him home to her bower,
Or he might be running yet.

She taught him her tribe's religion:
How ages and ages since
A princess en route from China
To marry a Persian prince

Had been found with child; and her army
Had come to a troubled halt.
And though a god was the father
And nobody else at fault,

It had seemed discreet to remain there
And neither go on nor back.
So they stayed and declared a village
There in the land of the Yak.

And the child that came of the princess
Established a royal line,
And his mandates were given heed to
Because he was born divine.

And that was why there were people
On one Hymalayan shelf;
And the bearer of evil tidings
Decided to stay there himself.

At least he had this in common
With the race he chose to adopt:
They had both of them had their reasons
For stopping where they had stopped.

As for his evil tidings,
Belshazzar's overthrow,
Why hurry to tell Belshazzar
What soon enough he would know?

Robert Frost

969   *Tears*

It seems I have no tears left. They should have fallen—
Their ghosts, if tears have ghosts, did fall—that day
When twenty hounds streamed by me, not yet combed
    out
But still all equals in their rage of gladness

Upon the scent, made, one, like a great dragon
In Blooming Meadow that bends towards the sun
And once bore hops: and on that other day
When I stepped out from the double-shadowed Tower
Into an April morning, stirring and sweet
And warm. Strange solitude was there and silence.
A mightier charm than any in the Tower
Possessed the courtyard. They were changing guard,
Soldiers in line, young English countrymen,
Fair-haired and ruddy, in white tunics. Drums
And fifes were playing 'The British Grenadiers'.
Then men, the music piercing that solitude
And silence, told me truths I had not dreamed,
And have forgotten since their beauty passed.

Edward Thomas

970   *Tall nettles*

Tall nettles cover up, as they have done
These many springs, the rusty harrow, the plough
Long worn out, and the roller made of stone:
Only the elm butt tops the nettles now.

This corner of the farmyard I like most:
As well as any bloom upon a flower
I like the dust on the nettles, never lost
Except to prove the sweetness of a shower.

Edward Thomas

971   *Tea at the Palaz of Hoon*

Not less because in purple I descended
The western day through what you called
The loneliest air, not less was I myself.

What was the ointment sprinkled on my beard?
What were the hymns that buzzed beside my ears?
What was the sea whose tide swept through me there?

Out of my mind the golden ointment rained,
And my ears made the blowing hymns they heard.
I was myself the compass of that sea:

I was the world in which I walked, and what I saw
Or heard or felt came not but from myself;
And there I found myself more truly and more strange.

Wallace Stevens

972   *The Daniel jazz*

Darius the Mede was a king and a wonder.
His eye was proud, and his voice was thunder.
He kept bad lions in a monstrous den.
He fed up the lions on Christian men.

Daniel was the chief hired man of the land.
He stirred up the jazz in the palace band.
He whitewashed the cellar. He shovelled in the coal.
And Daniel kept a-praying: 'Lord, save my soul.'
Daniel kept a-praying: 'Lord, save my soul.'
Daniel kept a-praying: 'Lord, save my soul.'

Daniel was the butler, swagger and swell.
He ran upstairs. He answered the bell.
And *he* would let in whoever came a-calling:
Saints so holy, scamps so appalling.
'Old man Ahab leaves his card.
Elisha and the bears are a-waiting in the yard.
Here comes Pharoah and his snakes a-calling.
Here comes Cain and his wife a-calling.
Shadrach, Meshach and Abednego for tea.
Here comes Jonah and the whale,
And the *Sea*!

Here comes St Peter and his fishing-pole.
Here comes Judas and his silver a-calling.
Here comes old Beelzebub a-calling.'
And Daniel kept a-praying: 'Lord, save my soul.'
Daniel kept a-praying: 'Lord, save my soul.'
Daniel kept a-praying: 'Lord, save my soul.'

His sweetheart and his mother were Christian and meek.
They washed and ironed for Darius every week.
One Thursday he met them at the door:
Paid them as usual, but acted sore.
He said: 'Your Daniel is a dead little pigeon.
He's a good hard worker, but he talks religion.'
And he showed them Daniel in the lion's cage.
Daniel standing quietly, the lions in a rage.

His good old mother cried:—
'Lord, save him.'
And Daniel's tender sweetheart cried:—
'Lord, save him.'

And she was a golden lily in the dew.
And she was as sweet as an apple on the tree.
And she was as fine as a melon in the corn-field,
Gliding and lovely as a ship on the sea,
Gliding and lovely as a ship on the sea.
And she prayed to the Lord:—
'*Send* Gabriel. *Send* Gabriel.'

King Darius said to the lions:—
'Bite Daniel. Bite Daniel.
Bite him. Bite him. Bite him!'
Thus roared the lions:—
'We want Daniel, Daniel, Daniel,
We want Daniel, Daniel, Daniel.
Grrrrrrrrrrrrrrrrrrrrrrrrrrrrrrrr.
Grrrrrrrrrrrrrrrrrrrrrrrrrrrrrrrr.'
And Daniel did not frown,
Daniel did not cry.
He kept on looking at the sky.

And the Lord said to Gabriel:—
'Go chain the lions down,
Go chain the lions down.
Go chain the lions down.
Go chain the lions down.'
And *Gabriel* chained the lions,
And Gabriel chained the lions,
And *Gabriel* chained the lions,
And Daniel got out of the den,
And Daniel got out of the den,
And Daniel got out of the den.
And Darius said: 'You're a Christian child,'
Darius said: 'You're a Christian child,'
Darius said: 'You're a Christian child,'
And gave him his job again,
And gave him his job again,
And gave him his job again.

Vachel Lindsay

973   *A glass of beer*

The lanky hank of a she in the inn over there
Nearly killed me for asking the loan of a glass of beer;
May the devil grip the whey-faced slut by the hair,
And beat bad manners out of her skin for a year.

That parboiled ape, with the toughest jaw you will see
On virtue's path, and a voice that would rasp the dead,
Came roaring and raging the minute she looked at me,
And threw me out of the house on the back of my head!

If I asked her master he'd give me a cask a day;
But she, with the beer at hand, not a gill would arrange!
May she marry a ghost and bear him a kitten, and may
The High King of Glory permit her to get the mange.

James Stephens

Here in a distant place I hold my tongue;
I am O Rahilly!

When I was young,
Who now am young no more,
I did not eat things picked up from the shore:
The periwinkle and the tough dog-fish
At even-tide have got into my dish!

The great, where are they now! the great had said—
This is not seemly! Bring to him instead
That which serves his and serves our dignity—
And that was done.

I am O Rahilly!
Here in a distant place he holds his tongue,
Who once said all his say, when he was young!

James Stephens

975 *Tenebris interlucentem*

A linnet who had lost her way
Sang on a blackened bough in hell,
Till all the ghosts remembered well
The trees, the wind, the golden day.

At last they knew that they had died
When they heard music in that land,
And someone there stole forth a hand
To draw a brother to his side.

J. E. Flecker

976 A pact

I make a pact with you, Walt Whitman—
I have detested you long enough.
I come to you as a grown child
Who has had a pig-headed father;
I am old enough now to make friends.
It was you that broke the new wood,
Now is a time for carving.
We have one sap and one root—
Let there be commerce between us.

Ezra Pound

977 *Piano*

Softly in the dusk, a woman is singing to me;
Taking me back down the vista of years, till I see
A child sitting under the piano, in the boom of the
    tingling strings
And pressing the small, poised feet of a mother who
    smiles as she sings.

In spite of myself, the insidious mastery of song
Betrays me back, till the heart of me weeps to belong
To the old Sunday evenings at home, with winter out-
    side
And hymns in the cosy parlour, the tinkling piano our
    guide.

So now it is vain for the singer to burst into clamour
With the great black piano appassionato. The glamour
Of childish days is upon me, my manhood is cast
Down in the flood of remembrance, I weep like a child
    for the past.

D. H. Lawrence

Outside the house an ash-tree hung its terrible whips,
And at night when the wind rose, the lash of the tree
Shrieked and slashed the wind, as a ship's
Weird rigging in a storm shrieks hideously.

Within the house two voices arose, a slender lash
Whistling she-delirious rage, and the dreadful sound
Of a male thong booming and bruising, until it had
    drowned
The other voice in a silence of blood, 'neath the noise of
    the ash.

D. H. Lawrence

979 *Field-glasses*

Though buds still speak in hints
And frozen ground has set the flints
As fast as precious stones
And birds perch on the boughs, silent as cones,

Suddenly waked from sloth
Young trees put on a ten years' growth
And stones double their size,
Drawn nearer through field-glasses' greater eyes.

Why I borrow their sight
Is not to give small birds a fright
Creeping up close by inches;
I make the trees come, bringing tits and finches.

I lift a field itself
As lightly as I might a shelf,
And the rooks do not rage
Caught for a moment in my crystal cage.

And while I stand and look,
Their private lives an open book,
I feel so privileged
My shoulders prick, as though they were half-fledged.

Andrew Young

980 *A prehistoric camp*

It was the time of year
 Pale lambs leap with thick leggings on
Over small hills that are not there,
 That I climbed Eggardon.

The hedgerows still were bare,
 None ever knew so late a year;
Birds built their nests in the open air,
 Love conquering their fear.

But there on the hill-crest,
 Where only larks or stars look down,
Earthworks exposed a vaster nest,
 Its race of men long flown.

Andrew Young

981 *Concert-interpretation (Le sacre du printemps)*

The audience pricks an intellectual Ear . . .
Stravinsky . . . Quite the Concert of the Year!

Forgetting now that none-so-distant date
When they (or folk facsimilar in state
Of mind) first heard with hisses—hoots—guffaws—
The abstract Symphony (they booed because
Stravinsky jumped their Wagner palisade
With modes that seemed cacophonous and queer),
Forgetting now the hullabaloo they made,
The Audience pricks an intellectual ear.

Bassoons begin . . . Sonority envelops
Our auditory innocence; and brings
To Me, I must admit, some drift of things
Omnific, seminal, and adolescent.
Polyphony through dissonance develops
A serpent-conscious Eden, crude but pleasant;
While vibro-atmospheric copulations
With mezzo-forte mysteries of noise
Prelude Stravinsky's statement of the joys
That unify the monkeydom of nations.

This matter is most delicate indeed!
Yet one perceives no symptom of stampede.
The Stalls remain unruffled: craniums gleam:
Swept by a storm of pizzicato chords,
Elaborate ladies reassure their lords
With lifting brows that signify 'Supreme!'
While orchestrated gallantry of goats
Impugns the astigmatic programme-notes.

In the Grand Circle one observes no sign
Of riot: peace prevails along the line.
And in the Gallery, cargoed to capacity,
No tremor bodes eruptions and alarms.
They are listening to this not-quite-new audacity
As though it were by someone dead,—like Brahms.

But savagery pervades Me; I am frantic
With corybantic rupturing of Laws.
Come, dance, and seize this clamorous chance to func-
      tion
Creatively,—abandoning compunction
In anti-social rhapsodic applause!
Lynch the conductor! Jugulate the drums!
Butcher the brass! Ensanguinate the strings!
Throttle the flutes! . . . Stravinsky's April comes
With pitiless pomp and pain of sacred springs . ..
Incendiarize the Hall with resinous fires
Of sacrificial fiddles scotched and snapping! . . .

Meanwhile the music blazes and expires;
And the delighted Audience is clapping.

Siegfried Sassoon

982 *Sonnet*

I said I splendidly loved you; it's not true.
  Such long swift tides stir not a land-locked sea.
On gods or fools the high risk falls—on you—
  The clean clear bitter-sweet that's not for me.
Love soars from earth to ecstasies unwist.
  Love is flung Lucifer-like from heaven to hell.
But—there are wanderers in the middle mist,
  Who cry for shadows, clutch, and cannot tell
Whether they love at all, or, loving, whom:
  An old song's lady, a fool in fancy dress,
Or phantoms, or their own face on the gloom;
  For love of Love, or from heart's loneliness.
Pleasure's not theirs, nor pain. They doubt, and sigh,
And do not love at all. Of these am I.

Rupert Brooke

983 *Merlin*

O Merlin in your crystal cave
Deep in the diamond of the day,
Will there ever be a singer
Whose music will smooth away
The furrow drawn by Adam's finger
Across the meadow and the wave?
Or a runner who'll outrun
Man's long shadow driving on,
Break through the gate of memory
And hang the apple on the tree?
Will your magic ever show
The sleeping bride shut in her bower,

The day wreathed in its mound of snow
And Time locked in his tower?

984   *Piazza piece*

—I am a gentleman in a dustcoat trying
To make you hear. Your ears are soft and small
And listen to an old man not at all,
They want the young men's whispering and sighing.
But see the roses on your trellis dying
And hear the spectral singing of the moon;
For I must have my lovely lady soon,
I am a gentleman in a dustcoat trying.

—I am a lady young in beauty waiting
Until my truelove comes, and then we kiss.
But what grey man among the vines is this
Whose words are dry and faint as in a dream?
Back from my trellis, Sir, before I scream!
I am a lady young in beauty waiting.

John Crowe Ransom

985   *Winter remembered*

Two evils, monstrous either one apart,
Possessed me, and were long and loath at going:
A cry of Absence, absence, in the heart,
And in the wood the furious winter blowing.

Think not, when fire was bright upon my bricks,
And past the tight boards hardly a wind could enter,
I glowed like them, the simple burning sticks,
Far from my cause, my proper heat and centre.

Better to walk forth in the murderous air
And wash my wound in the snow; that would be
    healing;
Because my heart would throb less painful there,
Being caked with cold, and past the smart of feeling.

And where I went, the hugest winter blast
Would have this body bowed, these eyeballs streaming,
And though I think this heart's blood froze not fast
It ran too small to spare one drop for dreaming.

Dear love, these fingers that had known your touch,
And tied our separate forces first together,
Were ten poor idiot fingers not worth much,
Ten frozen parsnips hanging in the weather.

                                        John Crowe Ransom

986   *The love song of J. Alfred Prufrock*

> S'io credesse che mia risposta fosse
> A persona che mai tornasse al mondo,
> Questa fiamma staria senza piu scosse.
> Ma percioche giammai di questo fondo
> Non tornò vivo alcun, s'i'odo il vero,
> Senza tema d'infamia ti rispondo.

Let us go then, you and I,
When the evening is spread out against the sky
Like a patient etherised upon a table;
Let us go, through certain half-deserted streets,
The muttering retreats
Of restless nights in one-night cheap hotels
And sawdust restaurants with oyster-shells:
Streets that follow like a tedious argument
Of insidious intent
To lead you to an overwhelming question . . .
Oh, do not ask, 'What is it?'
Let us go and make our visit.

In the room the women come and go
Talking of Michelangelo.

The yellow fog that rubs its back upon the window-
    panes,
The yellow smoke that rubs its muzzle on the window-
    panes
Licked its tongue into the corners of the evening,
Lingered upon the pools that stand in drains,
Let fall upon its back the soot that falls from chimneys,
Slipped by the terrace, made a sudden leap,
And seeing that it was a soft October night,
Curled once about the house, and fell asleep.

And indeed there will be time
For the yellow smoke that slides along the street,
Rubbing its back upon the window-panes;
There will be time, there will be time
To prepare a face to meet the faces that you meet;
There will be time to murder and create,
And time for all the works and days of hands
That lift and drop a question on your plate;
Time for you and time for me,
And time yet for a hundred indecisions,
And for a hundred visions and revisions,
Before the taking of a toast and tea.

In the room the women come and go
Talking of Michelangelo.

And indeed there will be time
To wonder, 'Do I dare?' and 'Do I dare?'
Time to turn back and descend the stair,
With a bald spot in the middle of my hair—
(They will say: 'How his hair is growing thin!')
My morning coat, my collar mounting firmly to the
    chin,
My necktie rich and modest, but asserted by a simple
    pin—
(They will say: 'But how his arms and legs are thin!')

Do I dare
Disturb the universe?
In a minute there is time
For decisions and revisions which a minute will reverse.

For I have known them all already, known them all:
Have known the evenings, mornings, afternoons,
I have measured out my life with coffee spoons;
I know the voices dying with a dying fall
Beneath the music from a farther room.
    So how should I presume?
And I have known the eyes already, known them all—
The eyes that fix you in a formulated phrase,
And when I am formulated, sprawling on a pin,
When I am pinned and wriggling on the wall,
Then how should I begin
To spit out all the butt-ends of my days and ways?
    And how should I presume?

And I have known the arms already, known them all—
Arms that are braceleted and white and bare
(But in the lamplight, downed with light brown hair!)
Is it perfume from a dress
That makes me so digress?
Arms that lie along a table, or wrap about a shawl.
    And should I then presume?
    And how should I begin?

        .   .   .   .

Shall I say, I have gone at dusk through narrow streets
And watched the smoke that rises from the pipes
Of lonely men in shirt-sleeves, leaning out of win-
        dows? . . .
I should have been a pair of ragged claws
Scuttling across the floors of silent seas.

        .   .   .   .

And the afternoon, the evening sleeps so peacefully!
Smoothed by long fingers,
Asleep . . . tired . . . or it malingers,
Stretched on the floor, here beside you and me.

Should I, after tea and cakes and ices,
Have the strength to force the moment to its crisis?
But though I have wept and fasted, wept and prayed,
Though I have seen my head (grown slightly bald)
     brought in upon a platter,
I am no prophet—and here's no great matter;
I have seen the moment of my greatness flicker,
And I have seen the eternal Footman hold my coat, and
     snicker,
And, in short, I was afraid.

And would it have been worth it, after all
After the cups, the marmalade, the tea,
Among the porcelain, among some talk of you and me,
Would it have been worth while,
To have bitten off the matter with a smile,
To have squeezed the Universe into a ball,
To roll it towards some overwhelming question,
To say: 'I am Lazarus, come from the dead,
Come back to tell you all, I shall tell you all'—
If one, settling a pillow by her head,
     Should say: 'That is not what I meant at all;
     That is not it, at all.'

And would it have been worth it after all,
Would it have been worth while,
After the sunsets and the dooryards and the sprinkled
     streets,
After the novels, after the teacups, after the skirts that
     trail along the floor—
And this, and so much more?—
It is impossible to say just what I mean!
But as if a magic lantern threw the nerves in patterns on
     a screen:
Would it have been worth while
If one, settling a pillow or throwing off a shawl,
And turning toward the window, should say;
     'That is not it at all,
     That is not what I meant, at all.'

             .   .   .   .

No! I am not Prince Hamlet, nor was meant to be;
Am an attendant lord, one that will do
To swell a progress, start a scene or two,
Advise the prince; no doubt, an easy tool,
Deferential, glad to be of use,
Politic, cautious, and meticulous;
Full of high sentence, but a bit obtuse;
At times, indeed, almost ridiculous—
Almost, at times, the Fool.

I grow old . . . I grow old . . .
I shall wear the bottoms of my trousers rolled.

Shall I part my hair behind? Do I dare to eat a peach?
I shall wear white flannel trousers, and walk upon the
    beach.
I have heard the mermaids singing, each to each.

I do not think that they will sing to me.

I have seen them riding seaward on the waves
Combing the white hair of the waves blown back
When the wind blows the water white and black.

We have lingered in the chambers of the sea
By sea-girls wreathed with seaweed red and brown
Till human voices wake us, and we drown.

T. S. Eliot

987 *Madly singing in the mountains*

There is no one among men that has not a special failing:
And my failing consists in writing verses.
I have broken away from the thousand ties of life:
But this infirmity still remains behind.
Each time that I look at a fine landscape,
Each time that I meet a loved friend,
I raise my voice and recite a stanza of poetry
And am glad as though a God had crossed my path.

Ever since the day I was banished to Hsün-yang
Half my time I have lived among the hills.
And often, when I have finished a new poem,
Alone I climb the road to the Eastern Rock.
I lean my body on the banks of white stone:
I pull down with my hands a green cassia branch.
My mad singing startles the valleys and hills:
The apes and birds all come to peep.
Fearing to become a laughing-stock to the world,
I choose a place that is unfrequented by men.

Po Chü-i
Arthur Waley

988   Hospital barge at Cérisy

Budging the sluggard ripples of the Somme,
A barge round old Cérisy slowly slewed.
Softly her engines down the current screwed
And chuckled in her, with contented hum,
Till fairy tinklings struck their crooning dumb,
And waters rumpling at the stern subdued.
The lock-gate took her bulging amplitude.
Gently into the gurgling lock she swum.

One, reading by that sunset, raised his eyes
To watch her lessening westward quietly;
Till, as she neared the bend, her funnel screamed.
And that long lamentation made him wise
How unto Avalon in agony
Kings passed in the dark barge which Merlin dreamed.

Wilfred Owen

989   Futility

Move him into the sun—
Gently its touch awoke him once,
At home, whispering of fields unsown.
Always it woke him, even in France,

Until this morning and this snow.
If anything might rouse him now
The kind old sun will know.

Think how it wakes the seeds,—
Woke, once, the clays of a cold star.
Are limbs, so dear-achieved, are sides,
Full-nerved—still warm—too hard to stir?
Was it for this the clay grew tall?
—O what made fatuous sunbeams toil
To break earth's sleep at all?

Wilfred Owen

990   *Dulce et decorum est*

Bent double, like old beggars under sacks,
Knock-kneed, coughing like hags, we cursed through
    sludge,
Till on the haunting flares we turned our backs,
And towards our distant rest began to trudge.
Men marched asleep. Many had lost their boots,
But limped on, blood-shod. All went lame, all blind;
Drunk with fatigue; deaf even to the hoots
Of gas-shells dropping softly behind.

Gas! GAS! Quick, boys!—An ecstasy of fumbling,
Fitting the clumsy helmets just in time,
But someone still was yelling out and stumbling
And floundering like a man in fire or lime.—
Dim through the misty panes and thick green light,
As under a green sea, I saw him drowning.

In all my dreams before my helpless sight
He plunges at me, guttering, choking, drowning.

If in some smothering dreams, you too could pace
Behind the wagon that we flung him in,
And watch the white eyes writhing in his face,
His hanging face, like a devil's sick of sin;

If you could hear, at every jolt, the blood
Come gargling from the froth-corrupted lungs,
Bitter as the cud
Of vile, incurable sores on innocent tongues,—
My friend, you would not tell with such high zest
To children ardent for some desperate glory,
The old Lie: Dulce et decorum est
Pro patria mori.

Wilfred Owen

991　*The Cambridge ladies*

the Cambridge ladies who live in furnished souls
are unbeautiful and have comfortable minds
(also, with the church's protestant blessings
daughters, unscented shapeless spirited)
they believe in Christ and Longfellow, both dead,
are invariably interested in so many things—
at the present writing one still finds
delighted fingers knitting for the is it Poles?
perhaps. While permanent faces coyly bandy
scandal of Mrs. N and Professor D
. . . the Cambridge ladies do not care, above
Cambridge if sometimes in its box of
sky lavender and cornerless, the
moon rattles like a fragment of angry candy

E. E. Cummings

992　*Despite and still*

Have you not read
The words in my head,
And I made part
Of your own heart?
We have been such as draw
The losing straw—

You of your gentleness,
I of my rashness,
Both of despair—
Yet still might share
This happy will:
To love despite and still.
Never let us deny
The thing's necessity,
But, O, refuse
To choose
Where chance may seem to give
Loves in alternative.

Robert Graves

993   *The Devil's advice to story-tellers*

Lest men suspect your tale to be untrue,
Keep probability—some say—in view.
But my advice to story-tellers is:
Weigh out no gross of probabilities,
Nor yet make diligent transcriptions of
Known instances of virtue, crime or love.
To forge a picture that will pass for true,
Do conscientiously what liars do—
Born liars, not the lesser sort that raid
The mouths of others for their stock-in-trade:
Assemble, first, all casual bits and scraps
That may shake down into a world perhaps;
People this world, by chance created so,
With random persons whom you do not know—
The teaship sort, or travellers in a train
Seen once, guessed idly at, not seen again;
Let the erratic course they steer surprise
Their own and your own and your readers' eyes;
Sigh then, or frown, but leave (as in despair)
Motive and end and moral in the air;
Nice contradiction between fact and fact
Will make the whole read human and exact.

Robert Graves

On dwelling

Courtesies of good-morning and good-evening
From rustic lips fail as the town encroaches:
Soon nothing passes but the cold quick stare
Of eyes that see ghosts, yet too many for fear.

Here I too walk, silent myself in wonder
At a town not mine yet plainly co-extensive
With mine, even in days coincident:
In mine I dwell, in theirs like them I haunt.

And the green country, should I turn again there?
My bumpkin neighbours loom even ghostlier:
Like trees they murmur or like blackbirds sing
Courtesies of good-morning and good-evening.

Robert Graves

The recovery

From the dark mood's control
    I free this man; there's light still in the West.
The most virtuous, chaste, melodious soul
    Never was better blest.

Here medicine for the mind
    Lies in a gilded shade; this feather stirs
And my faith lives; the touch of this tree's rind,—
    And temperate sense recurs.

No longer the loud pursuit
    Of self-made clamours dulls the ear; here dwell
Twilight societies, twig, fungus, root,
    Soundless, and speaking well.

Beneath the accustomed dome
    Of this chance-planted, many-centuried tree
The snake-marked earthy multitudes are come
    To breathe their hour like me.

The leaf comes curling down
　　Another and another, gleam on gleam;
Above, celestial leafage glistens on,
　　Borne by time's blue stream.

The meadow-stream will serve
　　For my refreshment; that high glory yields
Imaginings that slay; the safe paths curve
　　Through unexalted fields

Like these, where now no more
　　My early angels walk and call and fly,
But the mouse stays his nibbling, to explore
　　My eye with his bright eye.

Edmund Blunden

996　*Report on experience*

I have been young, and now am not too old;
And I have seen the righteous forsaken,
His health, his honour and his quality taken.
　　This is not what we were formerly told.

I have seen a green country, useful to the race,
Knocked silly with guns and mines, its villages vanished,
Even the last rat and last kestrel banished—
　　God bless us all, this was peculiar grace.

I knew Seraphina; Nature gave her hue,
Glance, sympathy, note, like one from Eden.
I saw her smile warp, heard her lyric deaden;
　　She turned to harlotry;—this I took to be new.

Say what you will, our God sees how they run.
These disillusions are His curious proving
That He loves humanity and will go on loving;
　　Over there are faith, life, virtue in the sun.

Edmund Blunden

I saw the sunlit vale, and the pastoral fairy-tale;
The sweet and bitter scent of the may drifted by;
And never have I seen such a bright bewildering green,
   But it looked like a lie,
   Like a kindly meant lie.

When gods are in dispute, one a Sidney, one a brute,
It would seem that human sense might not know, might
                        not spy;
But though nature smile and feign where foul play has
                    stabbed and slain,
   There's a witness, an eye,
   Nor will charms blind that eye.

Nymph of the upland song and the sparkling leafage
                    young,
For your merciful desire with these charms to beguile,
For ever be adored; muses yield you rich reward;
   But you fail, though you smile—
   That other does not smile.

Edmund Blunden

998 *Black tambourine*

The interests of a black man in a cellar
Mark tardy judgment on the world's closed door.
Gnats toss in the shadow of a bottle,
And a roach spans a crevice in the floor.

Aesop, driven to pondering, found
Heaven with the tortoise and the hare;
Fox brush and sow ear topped his grave
And mingling incantations on the air.

The black man, forlorn in the cellar,
Wanders in some mid-kingdom, dark, that lies
Between his tambourine, stuck on the wall,
And, in Africa, a carcass quick with flies.

Hart Crane

999 *The winter house*

Out of the showering snow itself to build
Under the lintel that the eyebrows form
A winter house, whose phantom planks are filled
By old storm holding back against new storm,
By flakes too numerous for enmity
(No room to hate a multitude); and so
To shelter under a false canopy
And play at happy hutman in the snow
—This cannot last for long; a prickly threat
Assails me, of disaster overhead,
The ruinous working of that inward heat
That I had hoped would serve to warm my bed.
Now may the coward eyebrows try in vain
To re-assert the downward-pouring roof.
It honourably joins the snow again,
And comes to put my native fire to proof.

Norman Cameron

1000 *The compassionate fool*

My enemy had bidden me as guest.
His table all set out with wine and cake,
His ordered chairs, he to beguile me dressed
So neatly, moved my pity for his sake.

I knew it was an ambush, but could not
Leave him to eat his cake up by himself
And put his unused glasses on the shelf.
I made pretence of falling in his plot,

And trembled when in his anxiety
He bared it too absurdly to my view.
And even as he stabbed me through and through
I pitied him for his small strategy.

Norman Cameron

1001   *Jason and Medea*

The Night appeared to authorise it.
The snakes were curling in her tallow hair,
And he stood in the weak and fascinating
Parlour of singing sexes, debonair,
Knowing her hungry glance, her cool attraction,
The cheap and placid aroma of her smile.
Tomorrow was a carton of abstraction,
A little debt he always could defer.
And in a nest of snakes he courted her.

Alun Lewis

1002   *The force that through the green fuse drives the flower*

The force that through the green fuse drives the flower
Drives my green age; that blasts the roots of trees
Is my destroyer.
And I am dumb to tell the crooked rose
My youth is bent by the same wintry fever.

The force that drives the water through the rocks
Drives my red blood; that dries the mouthing streams
Turns mine to wax.
And I am dumb to mouth unto my veins
How at the mountain spring the same mouth sucks.

The hand that whirls the water in the pool
Stirs the quicksand; that ropes the flowing wind
Hauls my shroud sail.
And I am dumb to tell the hanging man
How of my clay is made the hangman's line.

The lips of time leech to the fountain-head;
Love drips and gathers, but the fallen blood
Shall calm her sores.
And I am dumb to tell a weather's wind
How time has ticked a heaven round the stars.

And I am dumb to tell the lovers' tomb
How at my sheet goes the same crooked worm.

Dylan Thomas

INDEX OF TITLES

INDEX OF POETS

INDEX OF FIRST LINES